W9-DAS-052

THE
NEW
AMERICAN
NATION
1775–1820

*A Twelve-Volume
Collection of Articles
on the Development
of the Early American
Republic*

Edited by

PETER S. ONUF
UNIVERSITY OF VIRGINIA

A GARLAND SERIES

NEW AMERICAN NATION
1775–1820

Volume
5

★

THE FEDERAL CONSTITUTION

Edited with an
Introduction by

PETER S. ONUF

GARLAND PUBLISHING, INC.
NEW YORK & LONDON
1991

Library of Congress Cataloging-in-Publication Data

The Federal Constitution / edited with an introduction by Peter S. Onuf.
   p.   cm. — (New American nation, 1776–1815 ; v. 5)
   Includes bibliographical references.
   ISBN 0-8153-0440-4 (alk. paper) : $49.99
   1. United States—Constitutional history. 2. United States—Politics
and government—Constitutional period, 1789–1809. I. Onuf, Peter S. II.
Series.
   E164.N45   1991 vol. 5
   [KF4541]
   973s—dc20
   [342.73'029]
   [973 s]
   [347.30229]   91-13164
             CIP

Printed on acid-free, 250-year-life paper.
Manufactured in the United States of America

THE NEW AMERICAN NATION, 1775–1820

EDITOR'S INTRODUCTION

This series includes a representative selection of the most interesting and influential journal articles on revolutionary and early national America. My goal is to introduce readers to the wide range of topics that now engage scholarly attention. The essays in these volumes show that the revolutionary era was an extraordinarily complex "moment" when the broad outlines of national history first emerged. Yet if the "common cause" brought Americans together, it also drove them apart: the Revolution, historians agree, was as much a civil war as a war of national liberation. And, given the distinctive colonial histories of the original members of the American Union, it is not surprising that the war had profoundly different effects in different parts of the country. This series has been designed to reveal the multiplicity of these experiences in a period of radical political and social change.

Most of the essays collected here were first published within the last twenty years. This series therefore does *not* recapitulate the development of the historiography of the Revolution. Many of the questions asked by earlier generations of scholars now seem misconceived and simplistic. Constitutional historians wanted to know if the Patriots had legitimate grounds to revolt: was the Revolution "legal"? Economic historians sought to assess the costs of the navigation system for American farmers and merchants and to identify the interest groups that promoted resistance. Comparative historians wondered how "revolutionary" the Revolution really was. By and large, the best recent work has ignored these classic questions. Contemporary scholarship instead draws its inspiration from other sources, most notable of which is the far-ranging reconception and reconstruction of prerevolutionary America by a brilliant generation of colonial historians.

Bernard Bailyn's *Ideological Origins of the American Revolution* (1967) was a landmark in the new historical writing on colonial politics. As his title suggests, Bailyn was less interested in constitutional and legal arguments as such than in the "ideology" or political language that shaped colonists' perception of and responses to British imperial policy. Bailyn's great contribution was to focus attention on colonial political culture; disciples and critics alike followed his lead as they explored the impact—and limits—of "republicanism" in specific colonial settings. Meanwhile, the social historians who had played a leading role in the transformation of colonial historiography were extending their work into the late colonial period and were increasingly interested in the questions of value, meaning, and behavior that were raised by the new political history. The resulting convergence points to some of the unifying themes in recent work on the revolutionary period presented in this series.

A thorough grounding in the new scholarship on colonial British America is the best introduction to the history and historiography of the Revolution. These volumes therefore can be seen as a complement and extension of Peter Charles Hoffer's eighteen-volume set, *Early American History*, published by Garland in 1987. Hoffer's collection includes numerous important essays essential for understanding developments in independent America. Indeed, only a generation ago—when the Revolution generally was defined in terms of its colonial origins—it would have been hard to justify a separate series on the "new American nation." But exciting recent work—for instance, on wartime mobilization and social change, or on the Americanization of republican ideology during the great era of state making and constitution writing—has opened up new vistas. Historians now generally agree that the revolutionary period saw far-reaching and profound changes, that is, a "great transformation," toward a more recognizably modern America. If the connections between this transformation and the actual unfolding of events often remain elusive, the historiographical quest for the larger meaning of the war and its aftermath has yielded impressive results.

To an important extent, the revitalization of scholarship on revolutionary and early national America is a tribute to the efforts and expertise of scholars working in other professional disciplines. Students of early American literature have made key contributions to the history of rhetoric, ideology, and culture; political scientists and legal scholars have brought new clarity and sophistication to the study of political and constitutional thought and practice in the founding period. Kermit L. Hall's superb Garland series, *United States Constitutional and Legal History* (20 volumes, 1985), is another fine resource for students and scholars interested in the founding. The sampling of recent work in various disciplines offered in these volumes gives a sense of the interpretative possibilities of a crucial period in American history that is now getting the kind of attention it has long deserved.

Peter S. Onuf

INTRODUCTION

The proceedings of the Constitutional Convention in Philadelphia during the summer of 1787 have long posed an interpretative puzzle for historians and legal commentators. James Madison provided the main source in his extensive notes on convention debates. The delegates held forth at great length on controversial issues, namely on how to apportion representation in the federal legislature, or on the proposed government's power to regulate trade. But, to the distress of later interpreters, delegates rarely specified their "original intent" in the drafting process. Proceeding in secret, they felt no need to justify themselves to a contemporaneous, much less to a future, audience. As a result, the meaning of the Constitution provoked controversy and confusion from its first publication. The result was the first "Great National Discussion," the vast, often brilliant outpouring of argument and invective accompanying the state ratifying conventions.

Historiographical disagreement over the federal Constitution centers on the goals of James Madison and his fellow reformers. Were they pragmatic politicians who sought to secure class and sectional interests by compromise and accommodation? Or did concessions to particular interests—most notoriously, to the slaveholders of South Carolina—reflect a principled commitment to union, independence, and republican government? A closer look at the historical context suggests that these questions are poorly framed: delegates did not see a clear, mutually exclusive distinction between principle and interest. They did share Madison's conviction that the union was at risk and with it all their interests and aspirations.

Recent work on Madison, including important essays and monographs by Lance Banning, Drew R. McCoy, and Jack N. Rakove, sheds new light on how on the "father of the Constitution" responded to the crisis of the Confederation. The failure of American diplomats to negotiate a commercial treaty with Great Britain and the inability of Congress and the state governments to respond effectively to British commercial discrimination convinced Madison that American independence depended on an "energetic" national government. At the same time, foreign secretary John Jay's offer to relinquish American rights to the navigation of the Mississippi in exchange for a commercial treaty with Spain provoked disunionist sentiment in the South and West. The possibilities of separate unions or of a continental monarchy that would impose union on recalcitrant states and sections were widely discussed in 1786–1787. But, despite his anxieties about foreign policy and domestic dissidence, Madison was *not* a thoroughgoing "consolidationist." How he and his coadjutors sought to craft a new federal balance that would sustain republican government in the states as well as national independence provides the narrative line of the convention proceedings.

Madison may have taken the lead at Philadelphia, but he suffered a series of setbacks, for instance, on his proposal to give Congress a veto power over state legislation and, most notably, on representation by population in the Senate. The federal Convention, as Banning argues, was a "learning experience" for delegates who explained to each other how a stronger central government would affect their states' vital interests. Several essays in this volume detail the process of constitutional construction, showing how a concessive spirit facilitated the continuing search for a more perfect balance among the branches of the proposed government and between federal and state governments.

The Federalist papers, written by Madison, Jay, and Alexander Hamilton, provided the first systematic commentary on the convention's work. Here, and with the ratification debates generally, the interpretative challenge is just the opposite from that presented by the convention itself. Generations of historians and political theorists have sought to draw coherent themes and fundamental principles from a powerfully argued and richly allusive but not always coherent text. Some of the best examples of modern writing on *The Federalist* are included in this volume. Interested readers should also consult extended commentaries by George W. Carey, David F. Epstein, and Albert Furtwangler.

The first essay reprinted here includes my own "Reflections" on recent writing about the drafting and ratification of the Constitution and is designed to serve as an extended introduction to the remainder of the volume. Numerous additional articles that shed important light on the themes developed in this and the next volume may be found in the series edited by Kermit Hall cited below.

Peter S. Onuf

ADDITIONAL READING

Terence Ball and J.G.A. Pocock. *Conceptual Change and the Constitution.* Lawrence: University Press of Kansas, 1988.

Richard Beeman, Stephen Botein, and Edward C. Carter II, eds. *Beyond Confederation: Origins of the Constitution and American National Identity.* Chapel Hill: University of North Carolina Press, 1987.

Herman Belz, Ronald Hoffman, and Peter J. Albert, eds. *To Form a More Perfect Union: The Critical Ideas of the Constitution.* Charlottesville: University Press of Virginia, 1991.

George W. Carey. *The Federalist: Design for a Constitutional Republic.* Urbana and Chicago: University of Illinois Press, 1989.

David F. Epstein. *The Political Theory of the Federalist.* Chicago: University of Chicago Press, 1984.

Max Farrand, ed. *The Records of the Federal Convention of 1787.* 4 vols. New Haven: Yale University Press, 1911–37. Supplement, ed. by James H. Hutson, 1987.

Albert Furtwangler. *The Authority of Publius.* Ithaca, NY: Cornell University Press, 1984.

Jack P. Greene. *Peripheries and Center: Constitutional Development in the Extended Polities of the British Empire and the United States, 1607–1788.* Athens: University of Georgia Press, 1986.

Kermit L. Hall. *United States Constitutional and Legal History.* 20 vols. New York: Garland, 1985.

Leonard Levy and Dennis J. Mahoney, eds. *The Framing and Ratification of the Constitution.* New York: Macmillan, 1987.

Michael Lienesch. *New Order of the Ages: Time, the Constitution and the Making of Modern American Political Thought.* Princeton, NJ: Princeton University Press, 1988.

Donald S. Lutz. *The Origins of American Constitutionalism.* Baton Rouge: Louisiana State University Press, 1988.

Forrest McDonald. *Novus Ordo Seclorum: The Intellectual Origins of the Constitution.* Lawrence: University Press of Kansas, 1985.

Frederick W. Marks III. *Independence on Trial: Foreign Affairs and the Making of the Constitution.* Baton Rouge: Louisiana State University Press, 1973.

Jack N. Rakove. *James Madison and the Creation of the American Republic.* Glenview, IL: Scott, Foresman, 1990.

CONTENTS

Volume 5—The Federal Constitution

Jack N. Rakove, "Solving a Constitutional Puzzle: The Treaty-making Clause as a Case Study," *Perspectives in American History*, 1984, 1 (New Series):233–281.

Isaac Kramnick, "The 'Great National Discussion': The Discourse of Politics in 1787," *William and Mary Quarterly*, 1988, 45(1)(Third Series): 3–32.

Richard C. Sinopoli, "Liberalism, Republicanism and the Constitution," *Polity*, 1987, 19(3):331–352.

Martin Diamond, "Democracy and *'The Federalist'*: A Reconsideration of the Framers' Intent," *American Political Science Review*, 1959, 53:52–68.

Robert J. Morgan, "Madison's Theory of Representation in the Tenth Federalist," *Journal of Politics*, 1974, 36(4):852–885.

Daniel W. Howe, "The Political Psychology of *'The Federalist,'*" *William and Mary Quarterly*, 1987, 44(3):485–509.

Jack N. Rakove, "The Madisonian Moment," *University of Chicago Law Review*, 1988, 55(2):473–505.

Stephen A. Conrad, "Metaphor and Imagination in James Wilson's Theory of Federal Union," *Law and Social Inquiry*, 1988, 13(1): 3–70.

ACKNOWLEDGMENTS

Volume 5—The Federal Constitution

Peter S. Onuf, "Reflections on the Founding: Constitutional Historiography in Bicentennial Perspective," *William and Mary Quarterly*, 1989, 46(2) (Third Series):341–375. Originally appeared in the *William and Mary Quarterly*. Courtesy of Yale University Sterling Memorial Library.

Cathy Matson and Peter S. Onuf, "Toward a Republican Empire: Interest and Ideology in Revolutionary America," *American Quarterly*, 1985, 37(4):496–531. Reprinted with the permission of the author, and the American Studies Association as publisher. Courtesy of Yale University Sterling Memorial Library.

E. James Ferguson, "Political Economy, Public Liberty, and the Formation of the Constitution," *William and Mary Quarterly*, 1983, 40(3) (Third Series): 389–412. Originally appeared in the *William and Mary Quarterly*. Courtesy of Yale University Sterling Memorial Library.

Stanley Elkins and Eric McKitrick, "The Founding Fathers: Young Men of the Revolution," *Political Science Quarterly*, 1961, 76(2):181–216. Reprinted with the permission of the American Political Science Association. Courtesy of Yale University Sterling Memorial Library.

Richard D. Brown, "The Founding Fathers of 1776 and 1787: A Collective View," *William and Mary Quarterly*, 1976, 33(3) (Third Series):465–480. Originally appeared in the *William and Mary Quarterly*. Courtesy of Yale University Sterling Memorial Library.

Calvin C. Jillson and Cecil L. Eubanks, "The Political Structure of Constitution Making: The Federal Convention of 1787," *American Journal of Political Science*, 1984, 28(3):435–458. Reprinted with the permission of the American Political Science Association. Courtesy of Yale University Social Science Library.

Michael P. Zuckert, "Federalism and the Founding: Toward a Reinterpretation of the Constitutional Convention," *Review of Politics*, 1986, 48(2):166–210. Reprinted with the permission of the University of Notre Dame. Courtesy of the *Review of Politics*.

Jack N. Rakove, "The Great Compromise: Ideas, Interests, and the Politics of Constitution Making," *William and Mary Quarterly*, 1987, 44(3) (Third Series):424–457. Originally appeared in the *William and Mary Quarterly*. Courtesy of Yale University Sterling Memorial Library.

Charles F. Hobson, "The Negative on State Laws: James Madison, The Constitution, and the Crisis of Republican Government," *William and Mary Quarterly*, 1979, 36(2) (Third Series):215–235. Originally appeared in the *William and Mary Quarterly*. Courtesy of Yale University Sterling Memorial Library.

Howard A. Ohline, "Republicanism and Slavery: Origins of the Three-Fifths Clause in the United States Constitution," *William and Mary Quarterly*, 1971, 28(4):563–584. Originally appeared in the *William and Mary Quarterly*. Courtesy of Yale University Sterling Memorial Library.

Shlomo Slonim, "The Electoral College at Philadelphia: The Evolution of an Ad Hoc Congress for the Selection of a President," *Journal of American History*, 1986, 73(1):35–58. Reprinted with the permission of the *Journal of American History*. Courtesy of Yale University Sterling Memorial Library.

Jack N. Rakove, "Solving a Constitutional Puzzle: The Treatymaking Clause as a Case Study," *Perspectives in American History*, 1984, 1 (New Series):233–281. Reprinted with the permission of the Cambridge University Press. Courtesy of Yale University Sterling Memorial Library.

Isaac Kramnick, "The 'Great National Discussion': The Discourse of Politics in 1787," *William and Mary Quarterly*, 1988, 45(1) (Third Series):3–32. Originally appeared in the *William and Mary Quarterly*. Courtesy of Yale University Sterling Memorial Library.

Richard C. Sinopoli, "Liberalism, Republicanism and Constitution," *Polity*, 1987, 19(3):331–352. Reprinted with the permission of the Northeastern Political Science Association. Courtesy of Yale University Sterling Memorial Library.

Martin Diamond, "Democracy and *The Federalist*: A Reconsideration of the Framers' Intent," *American Political Science Review*, 1959, 53:52–68. Reprinted with the permission of the American Political Science Association. Courtesy of Yale University Law Library.

Robert J. Morgan, "Madison's Theory of Representation in the Tenth Federalist," *Journal of Politics*, 1974, 36(4):852–885. Reprinted with the permission of the University of Notre Dame. Courtesy of Yale University Sterling Memorial Library.

Daniel W. Howe, "The Political Psychology of *The Federalist*,"*William and Mary Quarterly*, 1987, 44(3):485–509. Originally appeared in the *William and Mary Quarterly*. Courtesy of Yale University Sterling Memorial Library.

Jack N. Rakove, "The Madisonian Moment," *University of Chicago Law Review*, 1988, 55(2):473–505. Reprinted with the permission of the *University of Chicago Magazine*. Courtesy of Yale University Law School.

Stephen A. Conrad, "Metaphor and Imagination in James Wilson's Theory of Federal Union," *Law and Social Inquiry*, 1988, 13(1): 3–70. Reprinted with the permission of the American Bar Foundation. Courtesy of Yale University Law School.

Forum

Reflections on the Founding:
Constitutional Historiography in
Bicentennial Perspective

T HE general verdict is that the bicentennial has been an "intellectual bust."[1] The most highly regarded scholarly contributions, including works by Richard Morris, Forrest McDonald, Edmund S. Morgan, and Richard Bernstein and Kym Rice, succeeded in reaching a general audience without sacrificing rigorous professional standards, but do not advance bold new interpretations.[2] Meanwhile, the criticism

Mr. Onuf is a member of the Department of History, Southern Methodist University. He wishes to acknowledge the helpful criticism of Lance Banning, George A. Billias, Paul Finkelman, Ralph Lerner, Michael Lienesch, Cathy D. Matson, Jack N. Rakove, Herbert Sloan, Michael Vinson, David Weber, Gordon S. Wood, and Neil L. York. He also wishes to thank the many editors and authors who allowed him to read and comment on their forthcoming works.

[1] " 'Cerebral' celebration of the Constitution's bicentennial is derided as an 'intellectual bust'," *Chronicle of Higher Education*, XXXIII (Mar. 4, 1987), 6-8; Paul L. Murphy, "The Bicentennial's Scholarly Impact," *OAH Newsletter*, XVI (August 1988), 10-11. Murphy applauded contributions by Michael Kammen (cited in n. 3, below), Jack P. Greene (in n. 49), Richard B. Morris, Forrest McDonald, and Edmund S. Morgan (all in n. 2), but concluded that "full-scale revisionism was not a scholarly result of the Bicentennial." A similarly dim view was expressed by editor David Thelen in explaining why a special issue of the *Journal of American History* on "The Constitution and American Life" included nothing on the founding. "As we were deciding how to focus this issue," Thelen writes, "experts on the drafting and ratification of the Constitution suggested that there was little fresh thinking in their field and that specialists in it had not been much concerned with the long-range significance of constitutionalism" (*JAH* LXXIV [1987], 661). Much of the bicentennial scholarship justifies these negative assessments; it is also true that resources that could have supported serious work have been shamelessly squandered. For a scathing indictment of the U.S. Bicentennial Commission see Jamie Kitman and Ruth Yodaiken, "Bicentennial Bust: Celebrating (Yawn) the Constitution," *Nation*, CCXLVII (July 2/9, 1988), 1, 14-21.

[2] Richard B. Morris, *The Forging of the Union, 1781-1789* (New York, 1987), and *Witnesses at the Creation: Hamilton, Madison, Jay, and the Constitution* (New

1

continues, the plethora of fellowships and grants, conferences and publication opportunities has done little to rouse constitutional scholarship from its recent lethargy. In this essay I challenge these prematurely pessimistic assessments. Critics discount or overlook important new work because they do not see how the field itself is being redefined.

The bicentennial's alleged failure to stimulate good scholarship is usually attributed to the disparity between scholarly interests and the political and polemical distortions endemic to patriotic celebrations. As an episode in American cultural history, the recent celebration undoubtedly will be remembered as yet another display of vulgar commercialism and mindless patriotism. But readers of Michael Kammen's comprehensive cultural history of the Constitution, *A Machine That Would Go of Itself*, will recognize that such excesses are hardly unprecedented.[3] Certainly, the proceedings were not as objectionable as those marking the Revolutionary bicentennial in 1976. Historians then were not deterred from producing a remarkable body of work. They are doing so now, notwithstanding early reports to the contrary.

Historians have been slow to recognize the emergent scholarship for various reasons. In 1976 historians set the agenda for the scholarly bicentennial: new work on the Revolution developed and extended familiar themes in contemporary historiography. In 1987, however, historians found that they had to share a stage crowded with law professors and political scientists. As a result, many historians experienced the

---

York, 1985); Forrest McDonald, *Novus Ordo Seclorum: The Intellectual Origins of the Constitution* (Lawrence, Kan., 1985); Edmund S. Morgan, *Inventing the People: The Rise of Popular Sovereignty in England and America* (New York, 1988); Richard B. Bernstein with Kym S. Rice, *Are We to Be a Nation? The Making of the Constitution* (Cambridge, Mass., 1987). Other contributions of general interest by professional historians include Elizabeth P. McCaughey, *Government by Choice: Inventing the United States Constitution* (New York, 1987), and Christopher Collier and James Lincoln Collier, *Decision in Philadelphia: The Constitutional Convention of 1787* (New York, 1986). For a judicious assessment of these and other works see Richard B. Bernstein, "Charting the Bicentennial," *Columbia Law Review*, LXXXVII (1987), 1565-1624, esp. 1578-1597. Project '87's *This Constitution* deserves special praise: since it began publication in Sept. 1983, the magazine has succeeded admirably in presenting scholarship on the founding and American constitutionalism to a general audience. For good introductions to the historiography of the founding period see Jack P. Greene, ed., *The Reinterpretation of the American Revolution, 1763-1789* (New York, 1968), introduction; James H. Hutson, "Country, Court, and Constitution: Antifederalists and the Historians," *William and Mary Quarterly*, 3d Ser., XXXVIII (1981), 337-368, and "The Creation of the Constitution: Scholarship at a Standstill," *Reviews in American History*, XII (1984), 463-477; and Greene, *A Bicentennial Bookshelf: Historians Analyze the Constitutional Era* (Philadelphia, 1986).

[3] Michael Kammen, *A Machine That Would Go of Itself: The Constitution in American Culture* (New York, 1986).

bicentennial—at least I did—as a sustained exercise in defending "history" against alien disciplines.[4]

The most conspicuous assault came from proponents of "original intent" jurisprudence. As custodians of the documentary record, historians found themselves compelled to demonstrate that the founders' original intentions rarely could be definitively established, and certainly not on questions the founders did not even consider.[5] Political scientists presented a still more serious challenge. Encounters with political theorists influenced by the late Leo Strauss have been particularly bewildering: the Straussians condemn "historicism" and dismiss historians' efforts to contextualize key terms—like "equality"—in the political discourse of the founding era. Because these theorists so often invoke their own interpretations of fundamental "regime principles" to advance a conservative policy agenda, historians find them ideologically repellent and methodologically incomprehensible.[6]

Of course, good old-fashioned narrative history is a powerful antidote to antihistorical excesses in cognate disciplines. It is crucially important to get the record as straight as possible and, thanks to the great letterpress editions of the founding fathers (most of which are complete through the 1780s) and particularly to the estimable *Documentary History of the Ratification of the Constitution,* the primary source materials for a new history of the founding are now easily accessible.[7] It would be a mistake, however, to conclude that the publication of primary sources constitutes the historical community's only important contribution to the bicentennial or its most effective response to challenges from other disciplines.[8]

Emphasis on the incompatibility of history with original intent jurisprudence or Straussian political theory, although understandable in the contemporary political climate, is misleading. In fact, legal scholars and political scientists range across the ideological spectrum; even the so-

[4] Peter S. Onuf, "Historians and the Bicentennial," *OAH Newsletter,* XVI (May 1988), 4, 20.

[5] James H. Hutson, "The Creation of the Constitution: The Integrity of the Documentary Record," *Texas Law Review,* LXV (1986), 1-39; Jack N. Rakove, "Mr. Meese, Meet Mr. Madison," *Atlantic,* CCLVIII (Dec. 1986), 77-86.

[6] For a thoughtful discussion of the Straussians see Gordon S. Wood, "The Fundamentalists and the Constitution," *New York Review of Books,* XXXV (Feb. 18, 1988), 33-40.

[7] Merrill Jensen *et al.,* eds., *The Documentary History of the Ratification of the Constitution,* 16 vols. to date (Madison, Wis., 1976-   ). For a good survey of recent documentary editions see Bernstein, "Charting the Bicentennial," Columbia Law Rev., LXXXVII (1987), 1569-1577.

[8] In any case, historians deserve little credit for these projects. The prevailing sentiment, a function of waning interest in political and constitutional history, is that the money could be better spent. Politicians invest taxpayers' money in these projects in order to erect suitable monuments to prominent national leaders (with a few important exceptions), not to support historical research. As a result, historians tend to be as ambivalent about the papers projects as they are about bicentennial celebrations.

3

called Straussians resist and resent easy categorization. Many lawyers and
theorists are intelligent consumers—and in some cases, producers—of
historical scholarship. Their forays into the founding period have helped
push historical inquiry in interesting new directions. These advances will
remain obscure, however, until historians recognize that they are taking
part in a broad interdisciplinary "conversation."

In the following pages I will identify some of the interesting and
important themes that have emerged in recent constitutional scholarship.
Scholars from other disciplines have played a particularly conspicuous role
in the ongoing debate over the relative importance of different intellectual
traditions in the founding period. Although many questions remain
controversial, these exchanges have led to greater awareness of the
theoretical and rhetorical ambiguities and complexities of American
republican thought. The reassessment of republicanism has in turn
focused renewed attention on the specific contexts in which republican
ideas were deployed. An important consequence has been a revival of
interest in the "crisis of the union" and in the efforts of constitutional
reformers to construct—and conceptualize—a workable federal system.
Of course, as the ratification debates demonstrated, there was considerable confusion about what kind of regime the framers meant to establish—
and not only among critics of the proposed plan. Neither ratification nor
the adoption of the Bill of Rights put an end to this controversy. Instead,
as many scholars now recognize, the ratification debates represented only
the first episode in a continuing history of conflict over constitutional
interpretation.

I: IDEOLOGY AND EVENTS

The brilliant and influential analyses of republican ideology in the works
of Bernard Bailyn, J.G.A. Pocock, and, particularly, Gordon S. Wood
constitute the point of departure for important new work on the founding
period. Controversy over the assumptions and methods that should
govern the history of political thought has spurred scholars to reconsider
the meanings and uses of republican ideas in historical context. Yet, until
recently, the ideological interpretation has impeded scholarship. To many
readers, Wood's *Creation of the American Republic* seemed to offer the last
word on the transformation of political discourse in the Revolutionary
era.[9] Consensus on the importance of ideological change discouraged
scholars from pursuing more traditional, less analytical approaches to the
political and constitutional history of the period. As a result, historians lost
interest in the specific course of events that climaxed in the drafting and
ratification of the Constitution. But the bicentennial has helped renew
interest in the founding narrative and scholars are now beginning to
construct a new "story line" that connects ideology to events.

[9] Wood, *The Creation of the American Republic, 1776-1787* (Chapel Hill, N.C.,
1969); *"The Creation of the American Republic, 1776-1787:* A Symposium of Views
and Reviews," *WMQ*, 3d Ser., XLIV (1987), 549-640.

4

There is no logical reason why the study of political language should *not* be yoked to historical narrative. Indeed, it is precisely the efforts of students of ideology to contextualize ideas that distinguish them from traditional intellectual historians or from political theorists who focus on transcendent, immutable principles.[10] Difficulties arise instead from the kinds of stories ideological historians have chosen to tell, and the lessons they draw from the stories. Because they survey vast bodies of writing at extended "moments" of conceptual change, contingent outcomes and ambiguous intentions must be given short shrift. But problems of scope and scale do not adequately explain the shortcomings of constitutional scholarship. In this case the choice of story has been critical: too often, students of the founding have linked ideological changes to the broader and deeper transformation of American society and culture, *not* to the founding of the federal republic.

Efforts to uncover deeper structures of social life and underlying patterns of culture have enormously enriched our understanding as they have substantively redefined our discipline, with particularly striking results in colonial American history.[11] But the "new" history has not done some things very well—or at all—and this is particularly apparent in the case of the American founding. The question is whether the study of deep structures can be reconciled with the historians' commitment to historical narrative. In theory, a "deeper" study of eighteenth-century American society and culture should help explain how and why men thought and acted as they did at crucial moments. Until recently, however, the founders *as political actors* have been lost to view. From a structuralist perspective, the story of how and why constitutional reformers created a "more perfect union" simply does not seem very important.

Attacks on the "republican synthesis" from both within and without the historical discipline point toward a convergence of ideological and political history.[12] This does not mean that protagonists in the great debates over which ideological tradition was dominant at what point are about to lay down their cudgels—too much is at stake. But, at least to disinterested observers, these controversies underscore the importance of narrative.

[10] See J.G.A. Pocock, "Introduction: The State of the Art," in his *Virtue, Commerce, and History: Essays on Political Thought and History, Chiefly in the Eighteenth Century* (Cambridge, 1985), 1-34.

[11] Jack P. Greene and J. R. Pole, eds., *Colonial British America: Essays in the New History of the Early Modern Era* (Baltimore, 1984), esp. the editors' introduction, 1-17.

[12] On republican historiography see Robert E. Shalhope, "Toward a Republican Synthesis: The Emergence of an Understanding of Republicanism in American Historiography," *WMQ*, 3d Ser., XXIX (1972), 49-80, and "Republicanism and Early American Historiography," *ibid.*, XXXIX (1982), 334-356; Herbert Sloan and Peter Onuf, "Politics, Culture, and the Revolution in Virginia: A Review of Recent Work," *Virginia Magazine of History and Biography*, XCI (1983), 259-284, esp. 262-264; and Linda K. Kerber, "The Republican Ideology of the Revolutionary Generation," *American Quarterly*, XXXVII (1985), 474-495.

How can we determine the impact of "republicanism" or "liberalism"—or evangelical Protestantism or popular "moral economy"—without knowing what happened? And clearly we need to know what historical actors were talking about—how they defined their situation and what they hoped to accomplish—as well as what they "mean" as speakers of particular political languages. Recent work on the 1780s shows ideological historians to be increasingly responsive to these demands. They are beginning to work within a more modest but ultimately more illuminating narrative framework.

Of course, the revival of interest in "events" and in historical narrative is not confined to the study of the Constitution.[13] In fact, because of the peculiar circumstances of the bicentennial, this broader historiographical development has been welcomed more eagerly in other fields. The problem for constitutional specialists is that the story of the founding is so difficult to disentangle from patriotic mythology. One major advantage of an analytical, non-narrative approach has been that it has enabled historians to view the founding with a certain skeptical detachment and so avoid the more egregious distortions of the heroic story line that dominates popular history and is so often apparent in the work of political theorists and legal scholars. But the "return to narrative" does not require us to eschew the analytical approach or to forget that the founders were mere mortals acting within the political and rhetorical limitations of another time and place. Nor is a tedious recapitulation of the traditional founding narrative the desideratum. Instead, historians must recognize that the old story line is itself problematic and needs to be recast. No narrative is more important for the subsequent course of American history than the drafting and ratification of the federal Constitution and the successful inauguration of the new national government.

II: REPUBLICANS AND LIBERALS

The great achievement of republican historiography has been to redefine the American Revolution as an ideological transformation.[14] Bailyn and his students rejected the premises of consensus historians who emphasized the continuity of American social and political experience. By reconstructing the distinctive and radically changing political language of the Revolutionaries, the ideological historians made the Revolution seem

[13] On the return to narrative see esp. James A. Henretta, "Social History as Lived and Written," *American Historical Review*, LXXXIV (1979), 1293-1322. For suggestions that politics and public life should be central to the new narrative see William E. Leuchtenburg, "The Pertinence of Political History: Reflections on the Significance of the State in America," *JAH*, LXXIII (1986), 585-600; Thomas Bender, "Making History Whole Again," *New York Times Book Review*, Oct. 6, 1985, 1, 42-43; and Bender, "Wholes and Parts: The Need for Synthesis in American History," *JAH*, LXXIII (1986), 120-136.

[14] Bernard Bailyn, *The Ideological Origins of the American Revolution* (Cambridge, Mass., 1967).

revolutionary again. The "otherness" of the Revolutionary generation suddenly became apparent as its leading ideas—which, as heirs of the Revolution, we mistakenly think we know so well—were relocated in their original discursive contexts. Furthermore, these writers showed that ideas were not simply instrumental—enabling "aristocrats" to oppress the people—or merely representational of broadly shared assumptions and practices. Instead, these historians insisted that ideas were to some significant extent autonomous: the intentions of historical actors were shaped by what their language enabled them to conceive.

Critical commentators generally have acknowledged the ideological historians' great contributions to scholarship. But these critics also have identified—and, in their polemical heat, undoubtedly exaggerated—tendencies in "republican revisionism" that have deflected attention away from particular events and thus deemphasized and obscured the significance of the founding. First, the critics charged, the ideological historians have been so absorbed with reconstructing patterns of thought that they underestimated the agency and originality of individual thinkers. The republican revisionists portrayed the founders as "enmeshed in a net of meanings, intentions, and significations largely not of [their] making and largely beyond [their] control."[15] The revisionists' implicit assumption, Ralph Lerner writes, is that the founders could never *use* language to pronounce and enact principled commitments. The ideological approach minimized the importance of "individual thought and individual actors" and encouraged scholars to explicate the shared assumptions of speakers and their audiences in broadly inclusive "discursive communities."[16]

Other critics were less concerned with the revisionists' displacement of individual authorship and agency than with the assumption of an essentially homogeneous, middle-class patriot reading public.[17] The ideological interpretation, they concluded, was really nothing more than warmed-over consensus history. Insisting on a more fractured social landscape, these critics argued that nonelite audiences responded to alternative ideologies or, at least, *"mentalités."*[18] A more satisfyingly complex view of

[15] Ralph Lerner, "The Constitution of the Thinking Revolutionary," in Richard Beeman, Stephen Botein, and Edward C. Carter II, eds., *Beyond Confederation: Origins of the Constitution and American National Identity* (Chapel Hill, N.C., 1987), 36-68, quotation on p. 39. This essay has been republished, in slightly revised form, in Lerner, *The Thinking Revolutionary: Principle and Practice in the New Republic* (Ithaca, N.Y., 1987), 1-38.

[16] Lerner, "Thinking Revolutionary," in Beeman *et al.*, eds., *Beyond Confederation*, 44. Significantly, Bailyn began his *Ideological Origins* by stressing the importance of political pamphlets in creating such a "discursive community" in late provincial America (chap. 1, "The Literature of Revolution," 1-21).

[17] Joseph Ernst, " 'Ideology' and an Economic Interpretation of the Revolution," in Alfred F. Young, ed., *The American Revolution: Explorations in the History of American Radicalism* (Dekalb, Ill., 1976), 159-185.

[18] In addition to the essays collected in Young, ed., *American Revolution*, see James A. Henretta, "Families and Farms: *Mentalité in Pre-Industrial America,"*

7

the Revolutionary situation emerged as historians began to emphasize the social—and ideological—obstacles to mass mobilization.[19] Paradoxically, however, putative new connections between ideology (or ideologies) and society accelerated the historiographical movement *away* from political history. The study of political language—or of quasi- or prepolitical popular culture—enabled historians to go after bigger fish: by uncovering deeper collective patterns and structures, they could illuminate American society as a whole during a period of radical transformation.

In exploring the dimensions of this "real" American Revolution, republican revisionists and their critics—new left and liberal alike—have a common agenda. Current controversy centers on when and how Revolutionary republican ideology was supplanted or transformed by "liberalism" and modern America thereby came into being. The republican revisionists set the terms of this debate: in one of his more extravagant moments, J.G.A. Pocock proclaimed the Revolution "the last great act of the Renaissance"; with similar boldness, Gordon S. Wood asserted that the ratification of the Constitution marked "the end of classical politics in America."[20] John M. Murrin would push the "Great Transition" forward to accommodate the persistence of republicanism in postconstitutional political culture. By 1830, however, the configuration and therefore the meanings of key republican terms—virtue, corruption, the public good— had been radically altered. Charting these changes is a crucial historiographical challenge, Murrin suggests, for they may reveal when and how "North America experience[d] a transition from a premodern to a modern social order."[21] Labor historians, the chief legatees of new left historiography, find this general framework congenial,[22] but exponents of the neoliberal interpretation favor an earlier transformation. "Republican" thrusts into the early national period and "liberal" counterthrusts into the

---

WMQ, 3d Ser., XXXV (1978), 3-32. The "ideological project" proved to be compatible with parallel exercises in the new social history aimed at reconstructing family and community life. Though social historians disdained the elitist orientation of ideological history, they found high-level generalizations about ideology— particularly when "democratized" in the form of *mentalité*—indispensable in attempting to make sense of the structures they had uncovered.

[19] See, particularly, Robert A. Gross, *The Minutemen and Their World* (New York, 1976).

[20] Pocock, "Virtue and Commerce in the Eighteenth Century," *Journal of Interdisciplinary History*, III (1972), 119-134; Wood, *Creation of the American Republic*, 606.

[21] Murrin, "Self-Interest Conquers Patriotism: Republicans, Liberals, and Indians Reshape the Nation," in Jack P. Greene, ed., *The American Revolution: Its Character and Limits* (New York, 1987), 224-229, quotation on p. 225, and "Gordon S. Wood and the Search for Liberal America," *WMQ*, 3d Ser., XLIV (1987), 597-601.

[22] See, for example, Sean Wilentz, *Chants Democratic: New York City and the Rise of the American Working Class, 1788-1850* (New York, 1984), 61-103.

8

eighteenth century thus characterize a historiographical struggle for the "soul" of the new republic at the time of its founding.

The notion of a "Great Transition" is a beguiling one for students of American political thought; here—wherever and whenever it can be fixed—is an "event" of surpassing significance. But it is the kind of "event" that makes the conventional political narrative seem epiphenomenal and inconsequential. As a result, practitioners of this brand of intellectual history move from discourse—where change is manifest—to the analysis of underlying structures, *not* to the interpretation of political action. The real revolution in America—the transition to a modern social order—is not to be traced through the conventional military, political, and constitutional narratives. By the same logic, the real "founding" of the republic did not take place at Philadelphia but rather in this "modernization" of American life under the exigencies of war and postwar reconstruction.

Historians' lack of interest in the founding over the last generation reflects the ascendancy of the new social history and of a new history of ideas that seeks to give meanings to the structures uncovered by social historians. The assumption that "republicanism" explains everything—or that its supersession by "liberalism" is the decisive event in American political history—has made old-fashioned political narrative seem increasingly unimportant, except perhaps as it provides the occasion for polemical exchanges. As a result, recent historians generally have ignored the story of constitutional reform. Gordon Wood's *Creation of the American Republic,* the apparent exception, reveals the characteristic tendency of ideological history to dismiss the conventional narrative. For Wood, the Constitutional Convention is much less important than the ratification debates in which the Federalists, under intense pressure to justify the new regime, fashioned a "new science of politics." Wood viewed these debates as the crucible of the conceptual change that brought an end to "classical politics" in America. The delegates at Philadelphia, meeting in secret session, were *not* forced to think in new ways, no matter how hard-pressed they were to reconcile their different interests. Only when the Constitution was published did its defenders begin to explore its ideological implications. Their exchanges with Antifederalist critics took them far beyond the immediate political "crisis"—if there was one—to a struggle over the future of the American society. Wood thus posited a direct, if problematic, link between the two "foundings," political and ideological.[23] But his critics have questioned the neatness of the supposed break between "classical" and "modern" *at this time;* by doing so, they have accentuated the ideologists' tendency to extricate discursive "events" from a concrete narrative framework.[24] Consequently, challenges to

[23] Wood, *Creation of the American Republic,* esp. pt. 5, "The Federal Constitution."

[24] Gary J. Schmitt and Robert K. Webking, "Revolutionaries, Antifederalists, and Federalists: Comments on Gordon Wood's Understanding of the American Founding," *Political Science Reviewer,* IX (1979), 195-229, as well as the essays

9

Wood's interpretation have *not* rehabilitated the conventional founding narrative.

But Wood really wrote two books: a brilliant and compelling account of conceptual change in the context of state constitutional development is sandwiched between essays on republicanism and its putative demise. This interior narrative demonstrates that the study of political discourse need not strain toward metahistorical generalization but instead can illuminate concrete rhetorical and political situations. Furthermore, Wood shows that problematic ideas—like representation—could take on new meanings over the course of protracted struggles to draft and revise the state constitutions. These new understandings in turn facilitated and rationalized constitutional change. Much more modest in scope than *Creation's* introductory and concluding analyses of *national* ideological development, the book's central sections continue to command respect. Wood here shows how the history of political ideas can help us understand what actually happened and what it means; here the analysis of discourse illuminates the historical narrative.

III: BEYOND REPUBLICANISM

Recognition of the founders' individuality and agency has been made possible by the reconstruction of the diverse matrix of intellectual traditions available to them. Forced to counter criticism of their supposedly reductive and deterministic account of political language, students of republican ideology have increasingly emphasized its ambiguous tendencies and contradictory applications. As a result, the practical differences between the "republicans" and their "liberal" critics seem less consequential. The emerging picture of discursive pluralism, or what Isaac Kramnick calls the "profusion and confusion of political tongues among the founders," promises to reinstate agency and purposeful action in our accounts of the founding.[25]

Joyce Appleby, the most persistent critic of republican revisionism, suggests that the ideological historians have been misled by their uncritical borrowings from Clifford Geertz's cultural anthropology and Thomas Kuhn's influential conceptualization of the history of science. "Neither seventeenth-century England," where classical republicanism took shape, "nor eighteenth-century America" is comparable to the closed, cohesive communities studied by Geertz or Kuhn. "Both countries were intellec-

---

collected in the Wood symposium, cited in n. 9, above. For a spirited reply to his critics see Wood's "Ideology and the Origins of Liberal America," *WMQ*, 3d Ser., XLIV (1987), 628-640; for a restatement of his thesis see "The Political Ideology of the Founders," in Neil L. York, ed., *Toward a More Perfect Union: Six Essays on the Constitution* (Provo, Utah, 1988), 7-27.

25 Isaac Kramnick, "The 'Great National Discussion': The Discourse of Politics in 1787," *WMQ*, 3d Ser., XLV (1988), 3-32, quotation on p. 4.

tually as well as culturally pluralistic."[26] Competing discourses permitted original thought and autonomous agency. As John Patrick Diggins succinctly asserts, "Man does not obey ideas; he uses them."[27]

Defenders of the republican paradigm resent what they consider a caricature of their work in revisionist attacks: they never meant to deny individual agency. Pocock insists that the "history of discourse . . . is a history of utterance and response by relatively autonomous agents."[28] Republican discourse was not fixed inalterably in neo-Harringtonian civic humanism; indeed, the great virtue of Real Whig thought in America, as Bailyn showed in the *Ideological Origins,* was its capacity for synthesizing diverse discursive traditions. Liberal critics failed to acknowledge the complexity and ambivalence of the republican response to modernity delineated in *The Machiavellian Moment:* Pocock never "alleged that republican virtue was incompatible with trade and industry."[29] If reactionary oppositionists were "nostalgic" for an idealized agrarian order, others were enthusiastic proto-liberals; many displayed both attitudes at different times, or even the same time. After all, writes Lance Banning, "the analytical distinctions we detect" were not always "evident to those we study."[30] Banning concedes that he and his coadjutors may at first have overstated the significance of classical ideas. By now it should be clear, however, that "eighteenth-century opposition thought was always a complex blend of liberal and classical ideas. So was the thought of America's Revolutionary generation."[31]

Banning's reformulation of the republican position would seem compatible with the discursive pluralism described by Kramnick. At least for the founding period, if not for the 1790s, a cessation of hostilities may be in the offing. Liberals will concede that their discursive pluralism was not entirely incoherent and open-ended; republicans will grant that republicanism gave ample scope to contradictory impulses. This historiographical convergence is already apparent in various works that explore the

[26] Joyce Appleby, "Republicanism and Ideology," *Am. Qtly.*, XXXVII (1985), 461-473, quotation on p. 468. See also Isaac Kramnick, "Republican Revisionism Revisited," *AHR,* LXXXVII (1982), 629-664. For a fuller statement of Appleby's views see her *Capitalism and a New Social Order* (New York, 1984).

[27] Diggins, *The Lost Soul of American Politics: Virtue, Self-Interest, and the Foundations of Liberalism* (New York, 1984), 357.

[28] Pocock, "Introduction: The State of the Art," in his *Virtue, Commerce, and History,* 1-34, quotation on p. 34.

[29] Pocock, "The Varieties of Whiggism from Exclusion to Reform: A History of Ideology and Discourse," *ibid.,* 215-310, quotation on p. 272, and *The Machiavellian Moment: Florentine Political Thought and the Atlantic Republican Tradition* (Princeton, N.J., 1975).

[30] Lance Banning, "Jeffersonian Ideology Revisited: Liberal and Classical Ideas in the New American Republic," *WMQ,* 3d Ser., XLIII (1986), 3-19, quotation on p. 12; Wood, "Ideology and the Origins of Liberal America," *ibid.,* XLIV (1987), 634.

[31] Banning, "Jeffersonian Ideology Revisited," *WMQ,* 3d Ser., XLIII (1986), 12.

interpenetration of republican, liberal, and religious traditions in Revolutionary America.

Political theorists influenced by Leo Strauss have played an important role in reestablishing the ideological complexity of the founding era. Because of their hostility to "historicism" and their penchant for timeless truths, these theorists take umbrage at the ideological historians' contextualized, "relativistic" account of political language. Ironically, however, their efforts to rehabilitate the claims of Lockean liberalism or of Protestant Christianity have helped counter reductionist, ahistorical tendencies in republican historiography. Thus the theorists often have been more sensitive than historians to ideological ambiguities. Ralph Lerner, John T. Agresto, and Jean Yarbrough have explored the convergence of classical republican and liberal traditions in what Lerner calls "commercial republicanism." Thomas L. Pangle traces "modern republicanism" to Locke, arguing that classical precepts never figured prominently in the founders' theorizing. Certainly, these critics argue, Revolutionary ideology sanctioned individual enterprise as well as individual sacrifice; many progressive European and American thinkers were convinced that commercial activity was itself a source of general enlightenment and virtue.[32]

This ideological compound was highly unstable, as the history of Revolutionary and postwar politics demonstrated. The concept of "virtue," precisely because of its central place in the classical republican account, proved unusually volatile. According to Richard Vetterli and Gary Bryner, who devote an entire book to the concept, the founders "believed that republican virtue and liberal individualism—*self-interest, properly understood*—are compatible and interdependent." They conclude that popular religious beliefs helped mediate these apparently contradictory premises: Christianity was at the core of a "modern," distinctively American "concept of virtue."[33] Yarbrough posits a similar transvaluation:

[32] Lerner, "Commerce and Character," in his *Thinking Revolutionary*, 195-221; Agresto, "Liberty, Virtue, and Republicanism: 1776-1787," *Review of Politics*, XXXIX (1977), 473-504, esp. 492-496; Yarbrough, "The Constitution and Character: The Missing Critical Principle?" in Herman Belz, Ronald Hoffman, and Peter J. Albert, eds., *To Form a More Perfect Union: The Critical Ideas of the Constitution* (Charlottesville, Va., forthcoming). Pangle includes a sustained attack on the "republican synthesis" in *The Spirit of Modern Republicanism: The Moral Vision of the American Founders and the Philosophy of Locke* (Chicago, 1988), 28-39. Pangle's rehabilitation of liberal discourse in the Lockean tradition is one of the theorists' most important contributions to constitutional scholarship. On political economic thought generally see Drew R. McCoy, *The Elusive Republic: Political Economy in Jeffersonian America* (Chapel Hill, N.C., 1980), esp. chaps. 1-3; Cathy Matson and Peter Onuf, "Toward a Republican Empire: Interest and Ideology in Revolutionary America," *Am. Qtly.*, XXXVII (1985), 496-531; and Albert O. Hirschman, *The Passions and the Interests: Political Arguments for Capitalism before Its Triumph* (Princeton, N.J., 1977).

[33] Richard Vetterli and Gary Bryner, *In Search of the Republic: Public Virtue and the Roots of American Government* (Totowa, N.J., 1987), 8, 79, 249. Pangle

during the Revolutionary era the "self-denying virtues" of classical republicanism gave way to "virtues more compatible with a liberal democratic
republic."[34]

Critics of republican revisionism have performed a valuable service in
questioning the dominance of classical republican precepts in the founding
era. Recognition of discursive pluralism has forced ideological historians
to retreat from some of their bolder and less tenable generalizations about
the transformation of American society and culture; they have also
become more circumspect in specifying the salience of republican ideas
for particular political and rhetorical situations, as well as their distinctive
appeal to various social groups. But the debate over which was "the more
dominant tradition, republicanism or liberalism," has not been particularly
illuminating. "Not only is the question badly put," writes Wood, "but it
assumes a sharp dichotomy between two clearly identifiable traditions that
eighteenth-century reality will not support."[35] Perhaps, as James T.
Kloppenberg suggests, we should worry more about how these traditions—or, more accurately, their diverse constituencies—could work
together, and less about which one was dominant. "Because of the
ambiguities of the traditions from which [the Revolutionaries] drew," he
writes, "and because of the unsteadiness and the inconsistencies of the
arguments they advanced, they were able to join together behind a banner
of ideas stitched together from three different sources: religious, republican, and liberal."[36] The value of Kloppenberg's formulation is that it
draws attention to the ideological margins, or "ambiguities," and therefore
to the accommodation, under specific historical conditions, of apparently

---

discounts the importance of religion in the theorizing of the founders in his *Spirit
of Modern Republicanism*, 78-85.

[34] Yarbrough, "Constitution and Character," in Belz *et al.*, eds., *To Form a More
Perfect Union*. Richard C. Sinopoli develops a similar argument in "Liberalism,
Republicanism and the Constitution," *Polity*, XIX (1987), 331-352. "The modern
notion of civic virtue is a necessary concomitant of core liberal premises" (*ibid.*,
347). Lance Banning minimizes the conceptual transformation, suggesting that
"virtue" in the 18th-century oppositional tradition always implied "a jealous,
vigilant commitment to the public life," not self-abnegation or "a Spartan
uniformity of interests" ("Some Second Thoughts on Virtue and the Course of
Revolutionary Thinking," in Terence Ball and J.G.A. Pocock, eds., *Conceptual
Change and the Constitution* (Lawrence, Kan., 1988), 194-212, quotations on pp.
207, 206.

[35] Wood, "Ideology and the Origins of Liberal America," *WMQ*, 3d Ser., XLIV
(1987), 634.

[36] Kloppenberg, "The Virtues of Liberalism: Christianity, Republicanism, and
Ethics in Early American Political Discourse," *JAH*, LXXIV (1987), 9-33,
quotation on p. 20. For a provocative "dualist" reading of the Constitution that
stresses the interplay of a civic humanist tradition, "recalling the grandeur of the
Greek polis," and a privatistic "Christian suspicion of the claims of secular
community," see Bruce A. Ackerman, "The Storrs Lectures: Discovering the
Constitution," *Yale Law Journal*, XCIII (1984), 1013-1072, quotation on p. 1043.

contradictory ways of thinking. Such an approach emphasizes the importance of individual thinkers and actors in the processes of Revolutionary mobilization and constitutional politics.

A small group of "conceptual historians," including non-Straussian political theorists with a greater interest in context and a higher tolerance for "relativism," has begun to chart the interplay of discursive traditions—or tendencies—in the founding era. Drawing inspiration from Quentin Skinner's and Pocock's work on the history of political languages, these writers focus specifically on the conditions that facilitate "conceptual change."[37] Their premise, as set forth by political theorist Terence Ball and historian Pocock in their introduction to a new collection of conceptual histories, is that "political innovation and conceptual change went hand in hand." The struggle over the Constitution provides an extraordinary opportunity to explore the transformation of political language in specific contexts. "Profound political and conceptual changes can occur with almost unheard-of rapidity" when the outcome of a series of contests for such "obviously high stakes" so clearly depends on the "persuasive power" of the protagonists. "The upshot of this debate," Ball and Pocock conclude, "was that citizens of the fledgling republic ceased to speak a provincial variation of political English and began to speak in the terms of a political idiom that was distinctively and recognizably American."[38]

The notion of "idiom" is considerably more supple than "ideology." Republicanism, defined as a political idiom, becomes essentially problematic, not prescriptive. Ball suggests that "the search for 'the true nature of early American republican thought' is misguided . . . , because the true nature of republicanism was itself very much in dispute during the founding."[39] Ball thus shows "Publius" (Madison) locking horns with "Brutus" in a debate over basic definitions. Attempting to defend "the new Constitution's republican *bona fides*" against relentless Antifederalist attacks—and driven by a "growing sense of desperation"—Madison questioned the very premises of language itself in his remarkable *Federalist* No. 37.[40] This "linguistic turn" sanctioned the redefinition of familiar concepts in a way that facilitated—indeed, "constituted"—radical political changes.

---

[37] Skinner, *The Foundations of Modern Political Thought*, 2 vols. (Cambridge, 1978); J.G.A. Pocock, *Politics, Language, and Time: Essays on Political Thought and History* (New York, 1971), *Machiavellian Moment*, and *Virtue, Commerce, and History*.

[38] Ball and Pocock, eds., *Conceptual Change and the Constitution*, 1, 3, 4. For an elaboration of the premises and methodology of "conceptual change" see James Farr, "Conceptual Change and Constitutional Innovation," *ibid.*, 13-34, and the introduction to Terence Ball, *Transforming Political Discourse: Political Theory and Critical Conceptual History* (Oxford, 1988).

[39] Ball, " 'A Republic—If You Can Keep It'," in Ball and Pocock, eds., *Conceptual Change and the Constitution*, 137-164, quotation on p. 137.

[40] *Ibid.*, 155, 157.

"In revising the meaning of 'republic,' Publius had not merely changed the meaning of a word. He has constituted a world."[41]

Aside from Russell Hanson's analysis of the tension between American republicanism as it suddenly emerged in 1776 and the "democratic" tendencies unleashed by the Revolution, few other contributions in the Ball-Pocock volume fit the conceptual history mode.[42] In any case, political theorists usually do not know the history of the period well enough to contextualize political rhetoric convincingly. Perhaps it is fairer to say that historians have failed to provide a sufficiently detailed account of the period's political history to support sophisticated analyses of conceptual development. In the event, Gordon Wood's brilliant "conceptual histories" remain unsurpassed, and his *Creation of the American Republic* still provides the most comprehensive and compelling explanation for the emergence of a distinctively American "political idiom."

The elaboration of the conceptual history approach is nonetheless a welcome development. In effect, political theorists are asking historians to build on the pioneering efforts of the ideological school. For the conceptual history project to make significant progress, historians will have to show how political ideas were deployed and developed in specific rhetorical situations. The rewards such efforts may yield can be glimpsed in theorist Michael Lienesch's recently published *New Order of the Ages*. The debate over republicanism is Lienesch's point of departure: "American political thought was in transition, moving from classical republicanism to modern liberalism." The "hybrid mixture" of "republican and liberal themes" proved to be inherently unstable, writes Lienesch, particularly when Americans were divided over fundamental political and constitutional issues.[43] Drawing inspiration from Pocock's magisterial *Machiavellian Moment*, Lienesch explores a series of deeply problematic concepts— history, change, reform, development—in the political discourse of the founding era. The American "moment," he concludes, was marked by "a transformation in temporal thinking, in the way Americans thought about time."[44]

The debate over the Constitution, Lienesch argues, revolved around Federalist claims "that they had created a politics that would transcend time."[45] The new system, proponents of the new "political science" promised, would preserve republican government from the traditional pattern of corruption and decay. Not surprisingly, skeptical Antifederal-

[41] *Ibid.*, 160.

[42] Russell L. Hanson, " 'Commons' and 'Commonwealth' at the American Founding: Democratic Republicanism as the New American Hybrid," in Ball and Pocock, eds., *Conceptual Change and the Constitution*, 165-193. See also Hanson, *The Democratic Imagination in America: Conversations with Our Past* (Princeton, N.J., 1985), chap. 2.

[43] Lienesch, *New Order of the Ages: Time, the Constitution, and the Making of Modern American Political Thought* (Princeton, N.J., 1988), 7.

[44] *Ibid.*, 8.

[45] *Ibid.*, 136.

ists who tended "to think of politics in terms borrowed from classical political theory" had little faith in future "progress."[46] The resulting debates thus exposed a basic division among American republicans, with Federalists promoting a "liberal," progressive view of historical development and Antifederalists resisting dangerous innovations that jeopardized liberty.

Lienesch's contribution is to illuminate fundamental but generally neglected themes in constitutional discourse. He is less successful in relating his history of political thought to "contending ideological camps" as they formed and reformed from the early 1780s through the 1790s. The voices of the founders remain disembodied, just as the "persuasions"— ideologically identifiable clusters of thinkers"—remain ephemeral and elusive.[47] Precisely because Lienesch is so conscious of history—as concept *and* process—his failure to delineate specific contexts is much more conspicuous than it would be in a typical study of political thought.

IV: TOWARD FEDERALISM

Ideological or "conceptual" history in Lienesch's mode represents a significant move in the direction of narrative. But there are problems with the study of discourse, even when due attention is accorded to its actual historical context. These problems are particularly acute in the case of the American founding. First, and obviously, an ideological interpretation cannot proceed without "texts" that can be subjected to close reading. But what if historical actors had to deal with a set of "problems" that were not fully articulated and that continue to resist conceptualization?

Students of republicanism naturally emphasize issues—such as representation, or the dangers of corruption—that occupy a central place in the conventional, "classical" discourse. Wood thus focuses on the "crisis" of republican government in the states, as it was defined by Madison and other nationalist reformers. As a result, he tends to ignore the problems of interstate organization and international diplomacy that constituted the crisis of the *union*. Such a bias is understandable. As Jack N. Rakove shows, there was remarkably little discussion about the premises of the American union during the Confederation period.[48]

Recently, however, historians have begun to recognize the problematic character of the union—and the very real possibility of disunion—in the "critical period" before the convention met. The delicate and protracted negotiations at Philadelphia secured the union and determined the distinctive character of American federalism. From this perspective, an exclusive focus on the issues and ideas that marked the course of *state* constitutional development is fundamentally misleading. The founders

[46] *Ibid.*, 131.
[47] *Ibid.*, 12.
[48] Jack N. Rakove, *The Beginnings of National Politics: An Interpretive History of the Continental Congress* (New York, 1979), 183-191.

knew that they would have to overcome unprecedented practical and theoretical obstacles in order to construct a durable union. Jack P. Greene asserts that the enduring constitutional dilemma for American statesmen was to reconcile the claims of "center" and "periphery" in an extended imperial and then independent American polity.[49] The founders' great achievement was to create—if not fully to conceptualize—a workable federal regime.

The challenge for historians is to explain the relation between federalism and republicanism: when and why was the crisis of the union "republicanized"? It was Madison's genius, argues Rakove, to persuade his colleagues that the problems of the Confederation were rooted in the defects of republican government in the states. By reconceptualizing federalism in republican language, defenders of the new Constitution enjoyed the rhetorical advantage in the ratification fight. Focusing on the new regime's republican character, the Federalists diverted potentially dangerous discussion from the fragile intersectional accords and complicated federal machinery on which their hopes for the union were premised.[50]

Could it be that the proper "deconstruction" of the ratification debates leads back to federalism—and the problems of the union—and *not* into the deeper structure of American society? The founders "invented" federalism, John M. Murrin suggests, despite the *absence* of appropriate language and ideas in the political science of the day: the disjunction between this conventional wisdom and the exigencies of the union forced them to strike out in new directions.[51] As they designed a constitution for the extended republic, the founders could draw on a rich legacy of political argumentation in the states.[52] But there was no equivalent discourse on federalism. How then could the founders conceive solutions to the problems of the union? Perhaps, as I argued in *The Origins of the Federal Republic*, their thinking about the union was shaped by the experience of interstate

[49] Jack P. Greene, *Peripheries and Center: Constitutional Development in the Extended Polities of the British Empire and the United States, 1607-1788* (Athens, Ga., 1986). Greene acknowledges indebtedness to Andrew C. McLaughlin, *The Foundation of American Constitutionalism* (New York, 1932), and *A Constitutional History of the United States* (New York, 1935), and to Charles Howard McIlwain, *The American Revolution: A Constitutional Interpretation* (New York, 1923).

[50] Jack N. Rakove, "From One Agenda to Another: The Condition of American Federalism, 1783-1787," in Greene, ed., *American Revolution*, 80-103, esp. p. 98. See also Rakove, "The Road to Philadelphia, 1781-1787," in Leonard W. Levy and Dennis J. Mahoney, eds., *The Framing and Ratification of the Constitution* (New York, 1987), 98-111; and "Articles of Confederation," in Jack P. Greene, ed., *Encyclopedia of American Political History*, 3 vols. (New York, 1984), I, 83-91.

[51] Murrin, "1787: The Invention of American Federalism," in David E. Narrett and Joyce S. Goldberg, eds., *Essays on Liberty and Federalism: The Shaping of the U.S. Constitution* (College Station, Tex., 1988), 20-47.

[52] Wood, *Creation of the American Republic;* Willi Paul Adams, *The First American Constitutions: Republican Ideology and the Making of the State Constitutions in the Revolutionary Era,* trans. Rita and Robert Kimber (Chapel Hill, N.C., 1980).

conflict and the difficulties of defining congressional authority and promoting national interests under the Confederation. The dilemma of reconciling central authority and local autonomy may not have been a new one for Americans, but some sort of resolution was now seen as necessary to guarantee the new nation's political and constitutional stability and, therefore, its future prosperity and power. In the months before the Philadelphia Convention escalating intersectional tensions led many commentators to fear for the survival of the union, as did the new nation's rapidly deteriorating diplomatic situation.[53]

Why have historians typically neglected these problems and concerns? Frederick W. Marks III, author of *Independence on Trial* (1973), knows "of no other period in American history when foreign affairs has been so crucial for the future of the Republic yet so neglected by American historians."[54] The tendency to distinguish political from diplomatic history may be one explanation; this distinction has been reinforced by the assumption that the impulse for *national* constitutional reform came out of the *states*. From this perspective, the alleged problems of the union simply serve as a pretext for constitutional change: the real issue is how a stronger central government would affect relations among various classes and interest groups. Once headed in this direction, it is not surprising that historians have gone on to explore "underlying" conflicts in society and culture. But it may be more useful to move in the opposite direction: after all, with the union itself in jeopardy, no neat distinction between domestic and foreign politics could then or should now be drawn. Shays's Rebellion and other challenges to state authority, problems arising from the states' failure to comply with the Treaty of Paris, as well as efforts to create new states or establish separate sectional unions all threatened to Europeanize American politics, to make Americans foreigners to each other and leave them vulnerable to the interference of imperial powers. Concern over the future of the union may have been just that, and not merely a smokescreen for a "deeper" conflict over more fundamental issues.[55]

The founders were well aware of the range of possible outcomes. They did not take for granted the survival of the union or of the American nation—whatever that was. Perhaps there had been a continental patriotism in the early years of the war, but disillusionment and skepticism set

[53] Frederick W. Marks III, *Independence on Trial: Foreign Affairs and the Making of the Constitution* (Baton Rouge, La., 1973); Rakove, *Beginnings of National Politics*, 360-399; James H. Hutson, *John Adams and the Diplomacy of the American Revolution* (Lexington, Ky., 1980); Morris, *Forging of the Union*, 194-244; Peter S. Onuf, *The Origins of the Federal Republic: Jurisdictional Controversies in the United States, 1775-1787* (Philadelphia, 1983).
[54] Marks, "Power, Pride, and Purse: Diplomatic Origins of the Constitution," *Diplomatic History*, XI (1987), 303-319, quotation on p. 316.
[55] Onuf, *Origins of the Federal Republic*, 173-185; "State Sovereignty and the Making of the Constitution," in Ball and Pocock, eds., *Conceptual Change and the Constitution*, 79-98, and "Anarchy and the Crisis of the Union," in Belz et al., eds., *To Form a More Perfect Union.*

in soon.[56] Congress's "imbecility" was symptomatic of centrifugal tendencies that threatened to balkanize American politics. Drew R. McCoy
suggests that "the political history of the post-Revolutionary era is less a
story of ideological controversy . . . than it is a reflection of the daunting
challenge of fashioning political coherence from the recalcitrant materials
of a regionally differentiated colonial past."[57] Strains between the regions
were further complicated by conflicts over access to the undeveloped
West and by rising political demands from the new frontier settlements.[58]
The uproar over John Jay's proposal to barter away American navigation
rights on the Mississippi showed that the bonds of union—between North
and South, East and West—were indeed tenuous. Disagreements over
foreign policy, coupled with a growing awareness of distinct sectional
interests and of the practical impossibility of amending the Articles, led
anxious republicans to consider radical alternatives: some broached the
idea of an American monarchy; others looked toward the creation of new
regional confederations.[59] These were the desperate circumstances in
which a small band of constitutional reformers led by the studious young
Madison took the first tentative steps toward creating an "extended,"
continental republic.

The preconstitutional period seems more authentically "critical" in
recent writing, and with their greater sensitivity to the contingencies
historians are now better prepared to appreciate the contributions of key
actors to the founding story. An extraordinary outburst of interest in
Madison's career as constitutional theorist and reformer attests to the
growing recognition of individual agency and narrative complexity.[60]
Recent studies of other founders—notably James Wilson—have also
emphasized the wide range of intellectual traditions at work in the
Constitutional Convention.[61]

[56] Charles Royster, *A Revolutionary People at War: The Continental Army and
American Character, 1775-1783* (Chapel Hill, N.C., 1979).

[57] McCoy, "James Madison and Visions of American Nationality in the Confederation Period: A Regional Perspective," in Beeman *et al.*, eds., *Beyond
Confederation*, 226-258, quotation on p. 229.

[58] Onuf, *Origins of the Federal Republic*, 149-172; Thomas P. Slaughter, *The
Whiskey Rebellion: Frontier Epilogue to the American Revolution* (New York, 1986),
28-60; Onuf, *Statehood and Union: A History of the Northwest Ordinance* (Bloomington, Ind., 1987), 1-66.

[59] Onuf, "Constitutional Politics: States, Sections, and the National Interest," in
York, ed., *Toward a More Perfect Union*. See the informative discussions in Jensen
et al., eds., *Documentary History of Ratification*, XIII, 54-57 (disunion proposals),
and 168-172 (monarchical revival).

[60] The literature on Madison is voluminous: works centering on his "federalism"
are cited below. For a balanced account of his political theory and further citations
see Joseph F. Kobylka and Bradley Kent Carter, "Madison, *The Federalist*, and the
Constitutional Order: Human Nature and Institutional Structure," *Polity*, XX
(1987), 190-208.

[61] Stephen A. Conrad, "Polite Foundation: Citizenship and Common Sense in
James Wilson's Republican Theory," in Philip Kurland *et al.*, eds., *The Supreme*

The point of departure for most recent histories of the convention is the classic question of the relative importance of interest and principle for the delegates. The interpretative spectrum runs from James H. Hutson's contention that the convention was "devoted principally to harmonizing concrete interests" to "originalist" accounts that stress the founders' principled intentions.[62] Several recent writers seek to strike a balance by identifying the different kinds of issues that precipitated conflicts of interest or debates over principles. William E. Nelson argues that the delegates resolved conflicts of interest—over representation, slavery, and commerce—in a spirit of compromise, while reserving their most "lengthy and fiery debates" for "instrumental-reasoning disputes." Disagreement over the constitution of the executive, for example, did not revolve around "what each delegate desired for his own group in the present but what the delegates expected or feared for the nation as a whole in the future."[63] Although political scientist Calvin Jillson is less impressed than Nelson with the distinctive character of constitutional politics, he draws a similar distinction between "higher" level questions of constitutional design and "lower" level "distributive questions . . . directly affecting the political and economic interests of states and regions." But Jillson concludes that "distributive questions" generated the most controversy. "It was only at this 'lower' level of constitutional construction, where interests clashed so loudly and winners and losers were starkly clear, that the Convention was threatened with dissolution."[64]

Court Review—1984 (Chicago, 1985) 359-388, and "Federalism, Figuratively Speaking: Metaphor and Imagination in James Wilson's Theory of Federal Union," *Law and Social Inquiry*, XIII (1988), 3-70; Garry Wills, "James Wilson's New Meaning of Sovereignty," in Ball and Pocock, eds., *Conceptual Change and the Constitution*, 99-106. Forrest McDonald attempts to connect the various traditions with the deliberations of the convention in *Novus Ordo Seclorum.*

[62] Hutson, "Riddles of the Federal Constitutional Convention," *WMQ*, 3d Ser., XLIV (1987), 411-423, quotation on p. 423. Paul Finkelman argues for the primacy of slavery interests in his "Slavery and the Constitutional Convention: Making a Covenant with Death," in Beeman *et al.*, eds., *Beyond Confederation*, 188-225. "Originalist" scholarship is discussed below.

[63] Nelson, "Reason and Compromise in the Establishment of the Federal Constitution, 1787-1801," *WMQ*, 3d Ser., XLIV (1987), 458-484, quotations on pp. 466, 470. See also Ackerman, "Storrs Lectures," *Yale Law Jour.*, XCIII (1984), 1013-1072, and the discussion in Bernstein, "Charting the Bicentennial," *Columbia Law Rev.*, LXXXVII (1987), 1600-1602.

[64] Calvin C. Jillson, "Ideas in Conflict: Political Strategy and Intellectual Advantage in the Federal Convention," in Belz *et al.*, eds., *To Form a More Perfect Union.* For earlier accounts that focus on "coalition alignments" see Jillson, "Constitution-Making: Alignment and Realignment in the Federal Convention of 1787," *American Political Science Review*, LXXV (1981), 598-612, and Jillson and Cecil L. Eubanks, "The Political Structure of Constitution Making: The Federal Convention of 1787," *American Journal of Political Science*, XXVIII (1984), 435-458. For excellent discussions of specific problems in constitution making see

But if the founders sought the high ground, what specific "principles" inspired them? In this respect, the debate over Madison's conception of the extended republic and his role in the convention is illuminating. Rakove argues that Madison saw proportional representation as an essential republican principle. He and like-minded supporters of the Virginia Plan therefore sought to persuade small-state delegates, "who were merely defending the status quo," to give up the pernicious principle of equal state representation. But considerations of power and interest prevailed, particularly "once the specter of sectional conflict legitimated the small states' appeal to security." The so-called Great Compromise on representation was, in fact, a capitulation to small-state interest. "With it," Rakove concludes, "went not [Madison's] hopes for a better government but his confidence" that his original republican design "would provide the foundation upon which the entire system would rest."[65]

Banning views these same transactions in a much different light: *his* Madison is not the nationalist who appears in Rakove's account but is instead committed to a broadly federal division of powers. Even during the early weeks of the convention "Madison can be legitimately described as a determined 'nationalist' only in his quest for a structure and mode of operation that would make the general government effective and supreme *within its proper sphere,* which he consistently conceived as relatively small." Banning claims that setbacks on various representation questions and on his proposed veto on state laws represented a "learning experience" for Madison. If allowance for state agency compromised Madison's original conception of the new national government, he came to realize that the states also required security against possible encroachments. Throughout his career as constitutional reformer "Madison had been seeking 'the practicable sphere of a republic,' the 'middle ground' between excessive localism (and the tyranny of unrestrained majorities) and undue concentration of authority in distant, unresponsive rulers."[66] As he

---

Jack N. Rakove, "Solving a Constitutional Puzzle: The Treatymaking Clause as a Case Study," *Perspectives in American History,* N.S., I (1984), 233-281, and Shlomo Slonim, "The Electoral College at Philadelphia: The Evolution of an Ad Hoc Congress for the Selection of a President," *JAH,* LXXIII (1986), 35-58.

[65] Jack N. Rakove, "The Great Compromise: Ideas, Interests, and the Politics of Constitution Making," *WMQ,* 3d Ser., XLIV (1987), 424-457, quotations on pp. 427, 456. For a fuller statement of Rakove's views on Madison's political thought see his "The Madisonian Moment," *University of Chicago Law Review,* LV (1988), 473-505. George W. Carey agrees with Rakove that "from the early 1780's until shortly after the commencement of the system he helped to fashion, Madison was an energetic proponent of a strong national government," and that his " 'federalism' . . . can appropriately be characterized as 'pragmatic' " ("James Madison on Federalism: The Search for Abiding Principles," *Benchmark,* III [1987], 27-57, quotation on p. 33).

[66] Lance Banning, "The Practicable Sphere of a Republic: James Madison, the Constitutional Convention, and the Emergence of Revolutionary Federalism," in Beeman *et al.,* eds, *Beyond Confederation,* 162-187, quotations on pp. 169, 185. For

developed a keener appreciation of the requirements of American federalism, Madison withdrew from the nationalist positions he had assumed at the outset of the convention.

Was Madison a frustrated nationalist who, advocating the Constitution in the *Federalist* and at the Virginia Convention put the best face on a system he considered fundamentally flawed? Or was the strong national government he proposed in 1787 intended to redress a dangerous drift toward state sovereignty and thereby secure a durable federal balance? To a large extent, the answer to these questions hinges on how we think about federalism. From the nationalist perspective ably elaborated by Rakove, the irresistible conclusion is that federalism was the inadvertent product of political compromises and accommodations. Just as proponents of the New Jersey plan failed to make a reasoned case for equal state representation, Federalists could not offer any coherent theoretical rationale for the new system's federal features.

But why should the large-state position be privileged, simply because Madison theorized about it so brilliantly and has proven to be such a seminal thinker for succeeding generations of political scientists and historians? After all, Madison and his allies were not immune to political considerations as they sought to maximize the power of the large states in a reconstituted union. And even if the small states' defense of their corporate integrity was politically expedient, it still involved fundamental principles.[67] Ultimately, of course, it is probably impossible—and pointless—to distinguish motives so neatly: in practice, interest and principle cannot be disentangled at any level of argumentation. The question in this case is whether any of the delegates could have *intended* to construct a federal regime, thus seeking to develop the "middle ground" later staked out by Madison in *Federalist* No. 51.

According to Nelson, "issues of federalism could not be debated . . . as interest-group conflicts" because it could not be known "which groups

---

Banning's interpretation of Madison's earlier career and of his subsequent role in the Virginia convention see his "James Madison and the Nationalists, 1780-1783," *WMQ*, 3d Ser., XL (1983), 227-255; "Virginia: Nation, State, and Section," in Michael Gillespie and Michael Lienesch, eds., *Ratifying the Constitution* (Lawrence, Kan., forthcoming); and "1787 and 1776: Patrick Henry, James Madison, the Constitution, and the Revolution," in York, ed., *Toward a More Perfect Union*, 59-89. For compatible accounts of the convention see Banning, "The Constitutional Convention," in Levy and Mahoney, eds., *Framing and Ratification of the Constitution*, 112-131, and Melvin E. Bradford, "Such a Government as the People Will Approve: The Great Convention as Comic Action," *St. Louis University Public Law Review*, VI (1987), 215-228.

[67] Rosemarie Zagarri, *The Politics of Size: Representation in the United States, 1776-1850* (Ithaca, N.Y., 1987), 61-80. For a discussion of the importance of state size in constitutional politics see also Peter S. Onuf, "Maryland: The Small Republic in the New Nation," in Gillespie and Lienesch, eds., *Ratifying the Constitution*.

would control the federal and which groups would control the state governments."[68] But if future alignments of interest could not be predicted, most delegates agreed that there ought to be a division of authority between the states and the national government. As Greene argues in *Peripheries and Center*, Anglo-American constitutionalism had traditionally been conceptualized in spatial terms, with colonial corporate and individual rights offsetting and limiting the power of the metropolis. The challenge for constitutional reformers was to reconstitute the "center," "to work out a more precise allocation of authority between the national and state governments."[69]

Negotiating this "federal boundary" seems like an exercise in interest-group politics only if "nationalism" or "state sovereignty" are viewed as the only principled positions.[70] But recent work on the origins of American federalism suggests that most Americans rejected both of these extreme positions *on principled grounds*. Political theorist Michael Zuckert thus describes the range of proposals considered at Philadelphia as varieties of federalism, not as progressively diluted versions of Madison's original nationalist vision. John Dickinson believed that Madisonian federalism was fundamentally flawed: if, as Madison proposed, the states were denied any agency in the new general government, what security would they have against encroachments? A stable federal system depended on balancing national and federal elements *within* the central government as well as in the system as a whole. "From the point of view of Dickinson Federalism," it therefore follows that "the mode of constructing the Senate, adopted in the Connecticut Compromise, was not a . . . compromise. It was rather a proper and accurate way of expressing the compound they were aiming to create."[71]

Unlike the contemporaneous elaboration of republican ideology, the invention of American federalism proceeded in obscurity and confusion. But these conditions also were propitious for innovative thinking. "Americans needed a conceptual breakthrough," writes Murrin, if they were ever

---

[68] Nelson, "Reason and Compromise," *WMQ*, 3d Ser., XLIV (1987), 471.

[69] Greene, *Peripheries and Center*, 192.

[70] See Martin Diamond, "What the Framers Meant by Federalism," in Robert A. Goldwin, ed., *A Nation of States* (Chicago, 1963), 24-41, and William Jeffrey, Jr., "The Constitution: A Firm National Government," in Robert A. Goldwin and William A. Schambra, eds., *How Federal Is the Constitution?* (Washington, D.C., 1987), 16-37. For vigorous statements of the nationalist interpretation by an eminent historian see Richard B. Morris, "The Forging of the Union Reconsidered: A Historical Refutation of State Sovereignty over Seabeds," *Columbia Law Rev.*, LXXIV (1974), 1056-1093, and *Forging of the Union*, 52-79.

[71] Zuckert, "Federalism and the Founding: Toward a Reinterpretation of the Constitutional Convention," *Review of Politics*, XLVIII (1986), 166-210, quotation on p. 206. Also see Zuckert, "A System without Precedent: Federalism in the American Constitution," in Levy and Mahoney, eds., *Framing and Ratification of the Constitution*, 132-150.

to define "an acceptable boundary between central and local power."[72] The American federal system may not have been "so radical in form," Greene adds, "but it was fundamentally so in principle."[73] Both historians see the new conception of "popular sovereignty" that Wood explicated in *Creation of the American Republic* as the keystone of the new federalism: because it was distinguishable from governmental authority, popular sovereignty could justify a radical redistribution of power in the union.[74] In effect, Greene and Murrin suggest a conceptual reversal. Although federalism is conventionally seen as the means of implementing republicanism over an "extended sphere"—thereby securing the class interests of cosmopolitan elites across the continent—it seems equally plausible to assert the opposite: the designers of the federal union appropriated republican concepts in order to facilitate and rationalize federalism. The quest for an enduring federal system in turn provided the basic impulse toward rethinking republican premises. "The federalism of the Constitution," Murrin argues, "was conceptually impossible before the 1780s." But it may also be true that the redefinition and elaboration of republicanism in the ratification debates was inconceivable before the convention invented federalism, in what Murrin calls "the supreme moment of political invention or innovation" in American history.[75]

V: INTENTIONS AND INTERPRETATIONS

Federalist victories in the state conventions bring the story of the founding to its usual climax, with the adoption of the Bill of Rights serving as coda. But the ratification debates also represented the first great national effort to interpret the Constitution, and *this* story—as the contemporary controversy over "original intent" shows—has not yet been conclusively resolved.

Wary of the ways lawyers abuse history, historians naturally have been

[72] Murrin, "1787: The Invention of American Federalism," in Narrett and Goldberg, eds., *Essays on Liberty and Federalism*, 20-47, quotations on pp. 36, 21.

[73] Greene, *Peripheries and Center*, 205. On the conceptual development of key terms in the new federalism see the brilliant essay by J.G.A. Pocock, "States, Republics, and Empires: The American Founding in Early Modern Perspective," in Ball and Pocock, eds., *Conceptual Change and the Constitution*, 55-77; for the origins and implications of the "federal principle" see Vincent Ostrom, *The Political Theory of a Compound Republic: Designing the American Experiment*, 2d ed. (Lincoln, Neb., 1987), and Daniel J. Elazar, "Our Thoroughly Federal Constitution," Goldwin and Schambra, eds., *How Federal Is the Constitution*, 38-66.

[74] Wood, *Creation of the American Republic*, esp. 530-536. Edmund S. Morgan reaches similar conclusions, arguing that popular sovereignty was a "fiction" that enabled constitutional reformers to reorganize the union: "Madison was inventing a sovereign American people to overcome the sovereign states" (*Inventing the People*, 267). Morgan's book is most notable for its brilliant analysis of the political culture of representative government, particularly in chaps. 7-9.

[75] Murrin, "1787: The Invention of American Federalism," in Narrett and Goldberg, eds., *Essays on Liberty and Federalism*, 20-47, quotations on pp. 21, 22.

skeptical about the possibility of knowing the founders' intentions.[76] At the same time, skepticism about the historical record has not prevented historians from taking great interpretative leaps of their own. The differences separating originalist lawyers and theorists from historians are only incidentally methodological: the primary disagreement is over the proper subjects and objects of interpretation. Historians are drawn to the ratification controversy because the great outburst of polemics enables them to explore the American "mind" during a period of revolutionary transformation. They do not believe the ratification debates can tell us very much about the Constitution itself: at the very least, the text of the document is distorted by the protagonists' rhetorical excesses; more interestingly, this rhetoric is supposed to reveal deeper patterns of thought and motivation that the protagonists themselves did not fully grasp. These historiographical tendencies are reinforced by the fact that modern scholars know much more than did most of the delegates at the state ratifying conventions about the secret proceedings at Philadelphia. The result is that historians do not take the debates entirely seriously as constitutional commentary: they are more inclined to discuss what the delegates disclosed *unintentionally*—about themselves and about American political culture generally—than to consider their openly avowed *intentions*.

If lawyers and political theorists show lamentably little interest in contexts, historians—eager to get on with their story—tend to discount and disregard texts. This is conspicuously the case with the *Federalist*, which, historians are quick to note, did not reach a wide reading public outside of New York and probably had little impact on the ratification vote in that state. The very brilliance of Publius's arguments makes them anomalous, unreliable guides to the currents of contemporary discourse. But political scientists (of all persuasions) are not deterred by historians' caveats, and they have made the debate on the Constitution—this first great systematic effort to define the new constitutional regime—paradigmatic for commentaries up to the present. Thus, while historians emphasize the *Federalist*'s serial publication in the context of the New York ratification controversy, political and legal commentators treat the whole series as a single, more or less coherent text.[77]

The historians' approach has many advantages, particularly if the focus is on the ratification vote. If Hamilton's contributions to the *Federalist* or

---

[76] See the essays by Hutson and Rakove cited in n. 5, above.

[77] Notable recent additions to this literature include Garry Wills, *Explaining America: The Federalist* (Garden City, N.Y., 1981); David F. Epstein, *The Political Theory of* The Federalist (Chicago, 1984); Morton White, *Philosophy, The Federalist, and the Constitution* (New York, 1987); the essays collected in Charles R. Kesler, ed., *Saving the Revolution:* The Federalist Papers *and the American Founding* (New York, 1987); and Pangle, *Spirit of Modern Republicanism*. For an important recent contribution to the intellectual history of *The Federalist* see Daniel W. Howe, "The Political Psychology of *The Federalist*," *WMQ*, 3d Ser., XLIV (1987), 485-509.

his speeches at the state convention had any impact on wavering delegates, the impact was probably negative: in the end, moderate Antifederalists like Melancton Smith balked at the prospect of being excluded from the new union.[78] But this is only one, and perhaps not the most interesting, story line. The thrust of the ratification debates was not simply to gain votes but to explain and interpret the text and translate it into the language of popular constitutionalism. The history of constitutional interpretation thus begins with the document's first publication, if not with earlier speculation about the convention's proceedings.[79]

The *Federalist* naturally enjoys a privileged position in the history of constitutional commentary. For modern scholars "Publius" speaks with particular authority because Madison had played a leading role in drafting the Constitution. But, as literary historian Albert Furtwangler argues, the contemporaneous impact of the series depended on its persuasive, "candid" voice and its comprehensive rhetorical strategy: the *Federalist* "would embrace all other discussions in favor of the Constitution, and all opposing arguments would be ranged against it."[80] "Publius" did not *tell* his readers what the Constitution meant; in fact, he changed his mind, or at least his emphases, as the series progressed. The *Federalist* had to be responsive to the readers it hoped to persuade. According to Furtwangler, "the ratification process was in itself a great appeal to the sovereignty of the people through specially elected representatives. The *Federalist* goes one step further, and appeals for informed assent. . . . It reveals not only the voters but the framers in the act of deliberating. This, I believe, is the most enduring source of its authority. Its pages still hold the tension of arguments that are not conclusive."[81] The *Federalist* constituted an effort to make the Constitution meaningful by imputing plausible intentions to its authors; the framers' ultimate success depended on gaining the people's "informed assent."

Furtwangler's textual analysis of the *Federalist* raises questions about the status of the Constitution itself as the focus of hermeneutical controversy. To think about the Constitution as a "literary text" is to grant it both fixity of form and fluidity of meaning, thus creating a context for interpretation that would shape the subsequent history of American constitutionalism.

[78] David E. Narrett, "A Zeal for Liberty: The Anti-Federalist Case against the Constitution in New York," in Narrett and Goldberg, eds., *Essays on Liberty and Federalism*, 48-87; John P. Kaminski, "New York: The Reluctant Pillar," in Stephen L. Schechter, ed., *The Reluctant Pillar: New York and the Adoption of the Federal Constitution* (Troy, N.Y., 1985), 48-117, esp. 115-117; Robert H. Webking, "Melancton Smith and the *Letters from the Federal Farmer*," *WMQ*, 3d Ser., XLIV (1987), 510-528.

[79] The history of constitutional commentary can be most easily traced through the comprehensive, chronologically arranged *Documentary History of Ratification*, ed. Jensen *et al.*

[80] Furtwangler, *The Authority of Publius: A Reading of the Federalist Papers* (Ithaca, N.Y., 1984), 53.

[81] *Ibid.*, 87.

Americans were convinced that their rights as individuals would be secure only if they were defined in writing. Their *"liberal idea of a constitution"* emerged, Gerald Stourzh writes, as "the *protection of rights* became a central and not merely incidental part of the concept of constitution." The integrity and authority of the new state constitutions as written texts were clearly established through "the *dissociation* of legislative and sovereign power" and "the institutionalization of the constituent power of the people."[82]

By the time of the Constitutional Convention, the written constitution was a familiar genre. The genius of the founders, literary scholar Robert A. Ferguson suggests, was to draw on these earlier efforts: "a miracle of concision, . . . the Constitution confirms a familiar past. Every word belongs to the realm of common understanding," including many "taken directly from the constitutions of the states."[83] Federalists exploited these textual affinities as they pushed for ratification: the Constitution had the unmistakable form and language of a republican constitution. By these same standards, of course, the Articles of Confederation were radically defective, even unrepublican.

The founders' careful craftsmanship was crucial to the document's ultimately favorable reception, but it could not preempt controversy. Because the state constitutions provided conflicting models, the federal Constitution would not seem completely "familiar" anywhere. Furthermore, the state documents continued to spark controversy in many places, as partisans divided over the proper interpretation or implementation of specific constitutional provisions and in some cases pressed for comprehensive revisions. By appropriating state constitutional forms, the founders could make a plausible case for the new regime's essentially republican character. But they also opened the way for the "nationalization" of constitutional controversy, recognizing that their only hope lay in engaging the interest and attention of significant numbers of politically active Americans. The question was whether the new system would establish an adequate framework for national politics. Would the text of the Constitution foster the ongoing process of constitutional interpreta-

[82] Gerald Stourzh, *Fundamental Laws and Individual Rights in the 18th Century Constitution*, Bicentennial Essay No. 5 (Claremont, Calif., 1984), 17, 18. For the importance of explicit constitutional limitations in the founding era see Leslie Friedman Goldstein, "Popular Sovereignty, the Origins of Judicial Review, and the Revival of Unwritten Law," *Journal of Politics*, XLVIII (1986), 51-71; for a contrasting interpretation, emphasizing the importance of unenumerated fundamental laws, see Thomas C. Grey, "The Original Understanding and the Unwritten Constitution," in York, ed., *Toward a More Perfect Union*, 145-173.

[83] Ferguson, " 'We Do Ordain and Establish': The Constitution as Literary Text," *William and Mary Law Review*, XXIX (1987), 3-25, quotation on p. 9, and *Law and Letters in American Culture* (Cambridge, Mass., 1984), 59-84. But note the criticisms of Ferguson's reading by Michael Les Benedict, "Our 'Sacred' Constitution—Another View of the Constitution as Literary Text," *William and Mary Law Rev.*, XXIX (1987), 27-34.

27

tion that alone could make fundamental law a political reality? Although, of course, Federalists and Antifederalists answered this question differently, their disagreements—particularly when focused on the constitutional status of individual rights—provided the paradigmatic form for a national hermeneutic tradition.

The idea that the founding properly embraces both the drafting of the Constitution and the debates over its adoption suggests that the Antifederalists played a much more positive role than is customarily allowed. "Because they forced this debate and the creative achievements that followed from it," Wood writes, "the Antifederalists deserve to be numbered among the Founders."[84] The recent publication of Herbert Storing's collection of Antifederalist writings, his own extended essay on their political thought, and a spate of subsequent commentaries all indicate that the opponents of the Constitution are gaining new respect. The Antifederalists are now emerging as ardent defenders of republican liberty who had good reason to fear the dangerous tendencies of several constitutional provisions, not to mention the absence of a bill of rights.[85]

Historians and theorists continue to argue about whether the Antifederalists were really classical republicans or enterprising proto-liberals.[86] But our appreciation of the Antifederalists should not hinge on whether we find them looking backward or forward as they stand poised on the threshold of modernity. In any case, such simple characterizations cannot be applied to all Antifederalists. Important recent work by Saul Cornell on "Antifederalist populists" in backcountry Pennsylvania emphasizes the social and ideological diversity of the Constitution's opponents. Cornell argues that "we must abandon the idea that the Antifederalists were united

[84] Wood, "Political Ideology of the Founders," in York, ed., *Toward a More Perfect Union,* 7-27, quotation on p. 17.
[85] Herbert J. Storing, ed., *The Complete Anti-Federalist,* 7 vols. (Chicago, 1981); Storing's commentary, *What the Anti-Federalists Were For,* is vol. 1 of this set. Other recent commentaries include Michael Lienesch, "In Defence of the Antifederalists," *History of Political Thought,* IV (1983), 65-87; Walter Nicgorski, "The Anti-Federalists: Collected and Interpreted," *Review of Politics,* XLVI (1984), 113-125; Paul Finkelman, "Antifederalists: The Loyal Opposition and the American Constitution," *Cornell Law Review,* LXX (1984), 182-207; Murray Dry, "The Case against Ratification: Anti-Federalist Constitutional Thought," in Levy and Mahoney, eds., *Framing and Ratification of the Constitution,* 271-291; and Gary L. McDowell, "Federalism and Civic Virtue: The Antifederalists and the Constitution," in Goldwin and Schambra, eds., *How Federal Is the Constitution,* 122-144.
[86] On the Antifederalists' indebtedness to classical theory see Lienesch, *New Order of the Ages,* 131-133; for a quantitative comparison of Federalist and Antifederalist citations see Donald Lutz, "The Relative Influence of European Writers on Late Eighteenth-Century American Political Thought," *Am. Pol. Sci. Rev.,* LXXVII (1984), 189-197. Gordon S. Wood makes the provocative suggestion that "it was not the Federalists but the Antifederalists who were the real pluralists and the real prophets of the future of American politics" ("Interests and Disinterestedness in the Making of the Constitution," in Beeman *et al.,* eds., *Beyond Confederation,* 69-109, quotation on p. 102).

by a single homogenous political creed." Awareness of this diversity should not, however, obscure the homogenizing effects of the national debate over the merits of the Constitution. Some Americans, particularly in the backcountry, remained hostile toward the new regime long after ratification. But, as Cornell shows, the most significant effect of popular disorders like the Carlisle riot was to push "moderate" critics of the Constitution toward accommodation.[87]

Of course, the very existence of Antifederalists as a definable group was a function of the debate over the Constitution, and their arguments against it were primarily those of constitutionalists. They were troubled by the convention's lack of authority in proposing to abolish the Confederation;[88] they wanted to know whether the Constitution's "elastic" clauses would sanction a broad interpretation of national powers at the expense of the states and of individual citizens; as close readers and future strict constructionists, they wondered why the framers had omitted specific guarantees of individual rights. By raising these questions, the Antifederalists gained important concessions, both in the ultimate addition of a bill of rights and, perhaps equally important, in forcing defenders of the new system to eschew or at least conceal the consolidationist intentions many still privately entertained. Federalists were also constitutionalists, of course, and although they typically favored a somewhat looser construction of constitutional language than did their opponents, they still believed in the power of words. Their *own words* in defense of the proposed system—the texts they generated to explicate and, in a sense, complete the constitutional text—committed them to moderate federalist and libertarian positions.

Federalists had to show that the proposed Constitution was faithful to the standards of American constitutionalism and therefore truly "republican" in character. Thus they emphasized the document's similarity to the state constitutions, promising that traditional canons of construction would be applied to its provisions. These efforts were essential precisely because the new system would transform American politics so radically: the invention of American federalism could take place only within the broad constitutionalist consensus that emerged from the ratification debates. Formal and interpretative continuities helped make the "strange" seem familiar, enabling Americans to think of republican government in continental terms. According to the conventional wisdom, amply confirmed by American experience in the British empire, only a despotic

[87] Saul Cornell, "Aristocracy Assailed: Back-Country Opposition to the Constitution and the Problem of Antifederalist Ideology," *JAH* (forthcoming). On the persistence of backcountry hostility to national authority see Slaughter, *Whiskey Rebellion*. For a useful analysis of positions on the Constitution in Virginia, emphasizing the nationalizing tendencies of the debate, see Jon Kukla, "A Spectrum of Sentiments: Virginia's Federalists, Antifederalists, and 'Federalists Who Are For Amendments,' 1787-1788," *VMHB*, XCVI (1988), 277-296.

[88] The issue is considered at length in Richard S. Kay, "The Illegality of the Constitution," *Constitutional Commentary*. IV (1987), 57-80.

authority could govern a large territory. But both parties in the ratification debate assumed that the union *could* be preserved under a *republican* constitution. Controversy centered on how the text should be interpreted or amended in order to realize its ostensible objects: Antifederalists invoked Montesquieu, their authority on the dangers of size, as they pressed for adjustments in the proposed system that would guarantee its republican character. The question was whether the Constitution was sufficiently "constitutional" to counter the dangerous permutations of political authority so familiar to readers of ancient and modern history.

In establishing a "compound," "partly federal, partly national" regime, the Constitution had to meet three related tests: were its powers distributed and balanced in ways that would sustain limited, constitutional government? would the national government respect the "federal boundary" that defined the legitimate sphere of state authority? would individual rights be secure against federal encroachments? While insisting that these questions were all related, Antifederalists focused most of their attention on the dangerously ambiguous status of states and individual citizens under the proposed system. In response, defenders of the Constitution promised that the states had little to fear from a stronger union: on the contrary, the failure of constitutional reform—and the resulting collapse of the union—would jeopardize republican government in the states. But the issue, Antifederalists recognized as they warned against the horrors of national consolidation, ultimately came down to one of interpretation. Specific guarantees of *individual* rights would provide a corrective to potential abuses of national power within its own sphere, but because American federalism depended on the presence or agency of the national government in the states and of the states in the national government, the "line" between them was necessarily ambiguous and imprecise.

Given the "sweeping language of the Constitution," legal scholar H. Jefferson Powell writes, Antifederalists feared that the application of conventional techniques of statutory interpretation "would lead inexorably to the effective consolidation of the states into a single body politic with a single, omnipotent government." Preservation of the federal balance therefore required continuous vigilance and close adherence to the constitutional text. Although Powell suggests that "original intent" jurisprudence emerged only as an alternative to statutory construction in the late 1790s, when Jeffersonians began to argue that the Constitution was a compact among sovereign states whose "intentions" ought to control interpretation, this form of strict construction actually grew out of the Antifederalists' "anti-hermeneutic" textualism.[89] Antifederalists insisted that the Constitution *had* to be strictly construed in ways that would

[89] Powell, "The Original Understanding of Original Intent," *Harvard Law Review*, XCVIII (1985), 885-948, quotation on p. 905. The literature on "original intent" is enormous. For a good introduction see Bernstein, "Charting the Bicentennial," *Columbia Law Rev.*, LXXXVIII (1987), 1597-1607, and the citations to recent works at p. 1599n.

guarantee the continuing integrity of the states, whether or not the states were parties to a federal compact. Most opponents of the Constitution accepted ratification gracefully, embracing a mode of constitutional interpretation they hoped would secure states' rights within a more perfect union. Over the course of the debates some skeptics had already been persuaded that the Federalists did not harbor malevolent designs against the states or against individual liberties, and finally voted for the Constitution. The challenge then was to keep the founders true to their words. As Lance Banning concludes, "A leaning toward constitutional literalism, a tendency engendered by some of the strongest currents in Anglo-American thought and powerfully reinforced by Antifederalist prophecies of constitutional decay, prepared the way for constitutional apotheosis. It also does much to explain the appearance of an opposition party which would quickly elevate the Constitution as the palladium of American liberty."[90] This Constitution was, of course, a *federal* constitution. Whatever Madison and fellow "nationalists" originally intended, the convention had labored hard to fashion a workable federal balance. By promoting strict construction and exposing ambiguities in the text, Antifederalists and their Republican heirs sought to keep the new national government from destroying that balance. As a result, American republicanism was "federalized" and federalism—the great innovation of 1787—was "republicanized."

To a considerable extent, Federalist interpretations of the Constitution were shaped by Antifederalist criticism; the eventual adoption of the first ten amendments represented a still more direct response to their demands. The conventional image of these "men of little faith" thus seems fundamentally mistaken.[91] As they pressed defenders of the document to clarify their commitments to federalism, constitutionalism, and individual liberties, Antifederalists indicated their own willingness to join in the great experiment. By withdrawing demands for prior amendments, a crucial cohort of Antifederalists demonstrated remarkable faith in their opponents' good will and integrity.

When the new government was organized, Madison recognized that the demand for amendments constituted one of its first major tests. During the ratification campaign Federalists had portrayed the Constitution in the most favorable, least threatening light. But the credibility and authority of

[90] Lance Banning, "Republican Ideology and the Triumph of the Constitution, 1789-1793," *WMQ*, 3d Ser., XXXI (1974), 167-188, quotation on p. 179. Murray Dry writes that "the strict construction of congressional powers, and even more so, the states' rights view of the union, reflect a retention of the Anti-Federalist view of federalism" ("Case against Ratification," in Levy and Mahoney, eds., *Framing and Ratification of the Constitution,* 289). See also Richard E. Ellis, "The Persistence of Antifederalism after 1789," in Beeman *et al.,* eds., *Beyond Confederation,* 295-314.

[91] The characterization is from Cecelia M. Kenyon, "Men of Little Faith: The Anti-Federalists on the Nature of Representative Government," *WMQ,* 3d Ser., XII (1955), 3-43.

their interpretations could not be tested until the new system began to operate: would Federalists in power show the same solicitude for states' and individual rights? Expeditious action on the amendments proposed by the state ratifying conventions enabled the new Congress to answer this question in a most conspicuous way.

The adoption of the Bill of Rights was a critical episode in the history of constitutional legitimation. Of course, as many historians have noted, the substantive amendments focused on civil liberties, not on the inevitably more problematic and controversial questions concerning the "federal boundary."[92] But the distinction should not be overdrawn. For those who feared national consolidation, limits on federal power over states and individuals were inextricably connected: encroachments on individual liberties would mark the eclipse of the states as effective polities. The first ten amendments could not have resolved all interpretative ambiguities—and, at first, they played a minor role in constitutional history—but they did confirm a moderate, federalist consensus on the distribution of authority in the new system.

Charles Hobson suggests that the Tenth Amendment—"the powers not delegated to the United States by the Constitution, nor prohibited by it to the States, are reserved to the States respectively, or to the people"— simply elevated ambiguity to the status of fundamental law. Several state conventions had recommended the more precise wording—"expressly delegated"—that had appeared in Article II of the Confederation. By deleting "expressly," Madison hoped to bar any additional limits on federal power beyond those "he regarded as implied in the original Constitution." But, of course, Madison's understanding of what the Constitution "implied" was shaped by his experience of defending and explaining the document in the ratification controversy. Federalist efforts to parry Antifederalist attacks and to assuage popular anxieties "effectively foreclosed the possibility of a unitary national government for the United States." The Tenth Amendment may have been "superfluous . . . as a declaration of the 'federal' construction of the Constitution," Hobson concludes, "but only because its purpose had been accomplished in the clarification of terms by which the Constitution was presented and justified to the people before its enactment."[93]

Very little of the extensive historiography on the various amendments situates them in the context of *federal* constitutionalism. Strenuous debate over the interpretation of the establishment clause in the First Amendment is obviously driven by present-day concerns. Thomas J. Curry's

[92] Narrett, "Zeal for Liberty," in Narrett and Goldberg, eds., *Essays on Liberty and Federalism*, 48-87. But Nelson emphasizes "the Federalists' positive response to Antifederalist demands" and characterizes leaders of both groups as "disinterested statesmen working together in pursuit of the public good" ("Reason and Compromise," *WMQ*, 3d Ser., XLIV [1987], 482).

[93] Charles F. Hobson, "The Tenth Amendment and the New Federalism of 1789," in Jon Kukla, ed., *The Bill of Rights: A Lively Heritage* (Richmond, Va., 1987), 153-163, quotations on pp. 161, 162.

excellent book on church-state relations in America before the adoption of the amendment ought to—but probably will not—silence "nonpreferentialists" who advocate federal support of religion. Curry shows that Madison's language was understood to prevent the national government from recreating any one of the existing state "establishments" at the federal level; at the same time, however, the national government would not interfere with the states.[94] Stephen Botein wisely emphasizes the federal dimensions of the establishment issue: "the Constitution was a perfectly secular text" but "the constitutions of the separate states were anything but secular." The founders expected the states to play an important, distinctive role in American federalism, particularly in cultivating virtuous, intelligent, pious, and patriotic citizens. "Compared with the governments of the several states," Botein explains, the new national government was probably "too distant from the citizenry and too restricted in the scope of its responsibility to require an official religious dimension."[95]

Historians have also devoted considerable attention to the Second Amendment, guaranteeing "the right of the people to keep and bear arms." In this case, too, a squabble among historians coincides with contemporary constitutional controversy: were the framers of the amendment proceeding from classical republican premises in providing a "well-regulated militia" for communal defense, or were they libertarian republicans intent on securing individual liberties against the state?[96] David T. Hardy sensibly concludes that *both* intentions are present in the text: "the dual purpose of the second amendment was recognized by all early constitutional commentators; the assumption that the second amendment had but a single objective is in fact an innovation born of historical ignorance." Hardy's reconstruction of the amendment's textual history suggests how historians should approach the several amendments—also including the first, fourth, fifth, and sixth—which he says "were intended as a composite of constitutional provisions."[97] The effort to identify a

[94] Curry, *The First Freedoms: Church and State in America to the Passage of the First Amendment* (New York, 1986). Also see the sensible account in William Lee Miller, *The First Liberty: Religion and the American Republic* (New York, 1986), and Leonard W. Levy's broadside against the "nonpreferentialists" in *The Establishment Clause: Religion and the First Amendment* (New York, 1986).

[95] Stephen Botein, "Religious Dimensions of the Early American State," in Beeman *et al.*, eds., *Beyond Confederation*, 315-330, quotations on pp. 317-318, 322.

[96] Robert E. Shalhope, "The Ideological Origins of the Second Amendment," *JAH*, LXIX (1982), 599-614; Lawrence Delbert Cress, "An Armed Community: The Origins and Meaning of the Right to Bear Arms," *ibid.*, LXXI (1984), 22-42; Shalhope and Cress, "The Second Amendment and the Right to Bear Arms: An Exchange," *ibid.*, 587-593; Cress, "A Well-Regulated Militia: The Origins and Meaning of the Second Amendment," in Kukla, ed., *Bill of Rights*, 55-65.

[97] Hardy, "The Second Amendment and the Historiography of the Bill of Rights," *Journal of Law and Politics*, IV (1987), 1-62, quotations on pp. 60, 3.

single, controlling intention may fill a jurisprudential need, but, in these instances at least, it is fundamentally distorting.

Hardy's work on the Second Amendment brings us back to the political context. Congress had to juggle a variety of often contradictory proposals for amending the Constitution, but without jeopardizing the complicated balance of national and state powers worked out in Philadelphia and rationalized in the ratification debates. The adopted amendments would preclude expansive interpretations of federal power, but they would not prevent the new government from acting effectively in its own sphere. In the case of the Second Amendment, this meant that there would be no bar on "standing Armies, in time of Peace," as set forth in the Virginia Declaration of Rights, nor would the amendment interfere with Congress's constitutional authority (in Article I, Section 8) over the state militias. But the states retained considerable control over their own militias, most notably in naming their officers, and individual citizens retained the right to "keep and bear arms." The resulting complex of rights and duties makes sense only in the context of federal constitutionalism. For Madison, as he managed this and the other amendments through Congress, practical political considerations merged with a principled commitment to the new federalism. His overriding "intention" was to preserve that delicate federal balance—even at the risk of exposing the ideological "fault lines" modern commentators find so fascinating.[98]

VI: CONCLUSION

The adoption of the Bill of Rights is an integral part of the American founding. But how does it fit the broad story line suggested in this essay? What are the connections among the familiar episodes in the narrative—constitutional crisis, federal convention, ratification controversy, Bill of Rights? I suggest, first, that constitutional reformers were motivated by genuine anxieties about the survival of the union. The convention therefore plays a crucial role in my account: the framers had to overcome daunting political obstacles and construct a complicated system that would preserve and strengthen the union without destroying the states. As they groped toward federalism, questions of "interest" and of "principle" could not be neatly distinguished. But what did clearly emerge from Philadelphia was a commitment to the union and to the possibility of a continental constitutional republic.

Few Antifederalists were authentic disunionists or believed the Confederation an adequate foundation for enduring union. As a result, they participated in good faith, if with a healthy measure of skepticism, in a sustained discussion about the merits of the proposed system and the proper interpretation of the constitutional text. Defenders and critics of the document argued from shared republican and constitutionalist assumptions; they also proclaimed their fealty to federal principles. For most

[98] *Ibid.*, 4.

Americans, the range of constitutional and political possibilities had narrowed dramatically from the dark days preceding the convention. Federalists and Antifederalists argued each other into a moderate middle ground: proponents of the new system vehemently denied any intention of establishing a monarchical regime; opponents denied that they wanted to break the union up into separate confederacies.

But if the very fact of the ratification debates set the boundaries for a federal constitutionalist consensus, polemicists also inaugurated broadly divergent approaches to constitutional interpretation that have persisted to the present day. Debate centered on the federal character of the new regime: following Madison's lead, moderate Federalists insisted that the government of the union itself would be republican and therefore would not encroach on the states; Antifederalists demanded explicit constitutional guarantees of individual and state rights. From the perspective of liberal—and literal—constitutionalism, the omission of such guarantees was indeed troubling. The growing importance of the Bill of Rights in American constitutional jurisprudence in turn suggests that the Antifederalists who pressed for amendments were not benighted reactionaries but anticipated some of the constitutional dilemmas that would accompany the rise of the national state.

Notwithstanding pressures toward consensus and toward containing differences within the context of constitutional interpretation, Americans did not therefore speak with the same voice or pursue the same ends. Recognition of the complex federal structure that the founding generation created for itself and subsequent generations should enable us to understand better how Americans so long resisted tendencies toward ideological homogeneity and political centralization. The political culture of federalism remains a largely uncharted terrain, but we do know that Americans expected radically different things from government—and from themselves as citizens—at the local, state, and national levels.[99] This is the complicated constitutional context within which Americans encountered "modernity," however we may define that much-mooted term. The first task for historians of the founding, therefore, is not to tell how or why or when Americans became modern, but rather to show them constructing a political world for themselves that would shape their experience of, and responses to, subsequent changes.

[99] Yarbrough, "Constitution and Character," in Belz *et al.*, eds., *To Form a More Perfect Union;* Donald S. Lutz, *Popular Consent and Popular Control: Whig Political Theory in the Early State Constitutions* (Baton Rouge, La., 1980). For a good introduction to the historiography of federalism see Harold W. Hyman, "Federalism: Legal Fiction and Historical Artifact?" *Brigham Young University Law Review,* Vol. 1987, 905-925.

TOWARD A REPUBLICAN EMPIRE: INTEREST AND IDEOLOGY IN REVOLUTIONARY AMERICA

CATHY MATSON

University of Tennessee

PETER ONUF

Worcester Polytechnic Institute

CHANGING DEFINITIONS AND EVALUATIONS OF "INTEREST" OVER THE COURSE of the eighteenth century illuminate a great transformation in political ideology in post-Revolutionary America. When faced with the challenges of nation-making on a continental scale in the 1780s, Americans discovered that they could no longer rely on the ideas that had justified and sustained resistance to British power. The most important ideological challenge was to reconcile individual rights with the common good. Such a reconciliation required them to reformulate traditional republican premises so that the pursuit of private "interest" and the accumulation of wealth no longer seemed threatening to the health of the body politic. Indeed, it was only by conceiving of their new nation as a republican "empire of liberty," bound together by compatible private interests, that union itself was conceivable.

The Americanization of republican ideology is revealed in statements such as one which appeared in the *Pennsylvania Gazette* in 1784:

> To despise wealth, or to suppose it to be connected with principles unfavorable to the happiness of the state in its present commercial situation, is to depreciate the first of republican virtues, and to overturn the basis of freedom and empire in our country.[1]

That the writer should have endorsed commercial wealth is surprising enough. Republican ideologists traditionally linked its excessive accumulation with luxury and vice, the leading threats to good citizenship in their "Christian

---

[1] "Hear the Other Side of the Question," *Pennsylvania Gazette* (Philadelphia), 8 Sept. 1784.

Sparta." But the identification of private interest with "republican virtue" itself was a particularly bold stroke: this anonymous writer appropriated the language of self-denial, sacrifice, and disinterestedness to describe and legitimate the pursuit of self-interest.[2]

This essay offers a preliminary assessment of the sources and implications of this ideological transformation. Our premise is that Americans discovered new ways of thinking about the role of private interest in political life by drawing on traditions of economic thought that had emerged over the previous century and a half of Atlantic economic development. Americans' use of these ideas was to a large extent determined by the changing structure of the British imperial economy. As the dramatic expansion of international commerce undermined traditional conceptions of political and economic life, polemicists and policymakers on both sides of the Atlantic vigorously debated the implications of the new order. On one hand, "mercantilists" attempted to rationalize and regulate the circulation of commodities in order to promote national wealth and power. On the other, a smaller number of "free traders" wanted to exploit new opportunities and gain greater autonomy for commercial interests.[3]

---

[2]The literature on republicanism is enormous. Works that have particularly influenced our thinking include J.G.A. Pocock, *The Machiavellian Moment: Florentine Political Thought and the Atlantic Republican Tradition* (Princeton: Princeton Univ. Press, 1975), chs. 13 and 14; Isaac Kramnick, *Bolingbroke and His Circle: The Politics of Nostalgia in the Age of Walpole* (Cambridge: Harvard Univ. Press, 1968); John Murrin, "The Great Inversion, or Court versus Country: A Comparison of the Revolution Settlements in England (1688-1721) and America (1776-1816)," in J.G.A. Pocock, ed., *Three British Revolutions, 1641, 1688, 1776* (Princeton: Princeton Univ. Press, 1980), 368-453. On American republicanism see Bernard Bailyn, *The Ideological Origins of the American Revolution* (Cambridge: Harvard Univ. Press, 1967); Gary Nash, *The Urban Crucible: Social Change, Political Consciousness, and the Origins of the American Revolution* (Cambridge: Harvard Univ. Press, 1979), esp. ch. 13; and, for the best general account of republican political economy, Drew R. McCoy, *The Elusive Republic: Political Economy in Jeffersonian America* (Chapel Hill: Univ. of North Carolina Press, 1980), esp. ch. 1-3. For the use of Country ideas by Antifederalists, see James H. Hutson, "Country, Court, and Constitution: Antifederalism and the Historians," *William and Mary Quarterly* (hereafter *WMQ*), 3rd ser., 38 (1981), 337-68. On America as a "Christian Sparta," see Gordon S. Wood, *The Creation of the American Republic, 1776-1787* (Chapel Hill: Univ. of North Carolina Press, 1969), 114-18.

[3]Our discussion of economic thought in the early modern era draws heavily on Joyce Appleby, *Economic Thought and Ideology in Seventeenth Century England* (Princeton: Princeton Univ. Press, 1978). Her excellent study shows that a significant body of contemporary economic literature took issue with the post-Restoration policies commonly referred to as mercantile. We are arguing here not for the existence of a true "mercantile system," but instead that there was a continuing dialogue among various interests and the persistence of an important strain of economic behavior which contemporaries defined as "free trade." A good overview of recent work on mercantilism may be found in W. A. Speck, "The International and Imperial Context," in Jack P. Greene and J. R. Pole, eds., *Colonial British America: Essays in the New History of the Early Modern Era* (Baltimore: Johns Hopkins Univ. Press, 1984), 384-407. On the notion of "interest" see J. A. W. Gunn, *Politics and the Public Interest in the Seventeenth Century* (London: Routledge & Kegan Paul, 1969), esp. chs. 3, 5, 6; Albert O. Hirschman, *The Passions and the Interests: Political Arguments for Capitalism before its Triumph* (Princeton: Princeton Univ. Press, 1977); William Letwin, *The Origins of Scientific Economics* (Garden City, N.Y.: Doubleday, 1964); Ralph Lerner, "Commerce and Character: The Anglo-American as New-Model Man," *WMQ*, 36 (1979), 3-26. On the rise of commerce and banking and on debates over economic policy and theory see Charles Wilson,

Though, in theory, mercantilism and advocacy of free trade should have been diametrically opposed, they tended to converge in post-Revolutionary America. American merchants had long resisted the restraints of British mercantilism in their pursuit of new commercial opportunities; they did not need Adam Smith to tell them about the costs of state interference in the marketplace. But after Independence, when "free traders" sought access to hitherto forbidden markets, the latent political implications of agitation for commercial "freedom" became manifest. If free traders claimed that the needs of the new American empire were best served by promoting their private enterprises, they were also calculating realists who had become convinced by the 1780s that the protection and support of an effective national government were absolutely essential to their interests. Not surprisingly, then, post-Revolutionary Americans showed their indebtedness to mercantilist thought and practice when they began to reconstruct their state economies and attempted to create a "respectable" national government that could guarantee favorable terms of trade with the wider world. At the same time, however, Americans granted private interests a broad role in cementing the American union and promoting a more benign and peaceful world order. Their new republican synthesis thus incorporated a pronounced neo-mercantilist strain along with distinctively American commitments to "free trade" and personal "improvement."

The Traditional View of Interest

The traditional view of political economy articulated by republican theorists at the time of the American Revolution was founded upon the premise that political right and personal virtue flowed from the ownership of hereditary and transmissible land. In a virtuous republic, the majority of proprietors enjoyed a "happy mediocrity" through the ownership of modest freeholds. These landholdings guaranteed personal independence and autonomy, thus providing the material conditions for an orderly society governed by reason and self-restraint. Unencumbered title was a primary basis of social order as well as of individual rights; to lose title was to lose one's personal identity and political liberty.[4]

England's Apprenticeship, 1603-1763 (London: Longman, 1965), esp. chs. 6, 11; C. B. Macpherson, *The Political Theory of Possessive Individualism: Hobbes to Locke* (Oxford: Oxford Univ. Press, 1962); Charles M. Andrews, *The Colonial Period of American History*, 4 vols. (New Haven: Yale Univ. Press, 1928), vol. 4; P. G. M. Dickson, *The Financial Revolution in England: A Study in the Development of Public Credit* (London: Melbourne, 1967), chs. 1, 2. British free trade arguments are discussed in this essay; for American arguments see Victor L. Johnson, "Fair Traders and Smugglers in Philadelphia, 1754-1763," *Pennsylvania Magazine of History and Biography* (hereafter *PMHB*), 83 (1959), 125-49; John W. Tyler, "The First Revolution: Boston Merchants and the Acts of Trade, 1760-1774," Diss. Princeton Univ. 1980; and Cathy Matson, "Fair Trade, Free Trade: Economic Ideas and Opportunities in Eighteenth-Century New York City," Diss. Columbia Univ. 1985.
    [4]On the republican idealization of land ownership see Alan Macfarlane, *The Origins of English Individualism* (New York: Cambridge Univ. Press, 1979), esp. ch. 4.

Given these assumptions, republican theorists found the related implications of "interest" deeply disturbing. Interest was potentially dangerous to the health of a republic, whether it was the interest taken in loaning money or the private interest of individuals or groups. In the first sense, interest represented claims, rights, and bonds of obligation that could compromise personal independence and traditional authority. To meet this threat, republicans often favored rigorous restraints on usury and high-interest loans, as well as on more modern forms of "stockjobbing." In the second sense, interest suggested loyalties and commitments distinct from, and at least potentially opposed to, those of the larger community. This kind of interest could create an anticommunity of credit and debt or it could fragment existing communal bonds. In either case, excessive self-interest—the blatant disregard of social obligations—jeopardized social order.[5]

Republican ideology acquired new vitality in response to the efflorescence of interest and interest groups in the late seventeenth and eighteenth centuries. In the broadest sense, republicanism was a critique of the financial and administrative changes following the Glorious Revolution and an idealization of a traditional, static agricultural economy in which freeholders did not depend on credit at interest or risk their property in speculative enterprises. Merchants and manufacturers could not survive without borrowing: banks, annuities, war loans, flexible interest rates, and international networks of credit were the lifeblood of commerce. But traditionalists warned that as the Empire grew—and its "limbs rotted of interest"—there would be a corresponding weakening of the body politic.[6]

Debates over foreign policy exacerbated differences in the views of landed and commercial classes. Republicans identified the new commercial interests with Court Whigs who had supposedly fomented and financed the interimperial rivalries that had kept Britain involved in four long and costly wars over the eighteenth century. By Queen Anne's War (1702-13) critics of the new order became increasingly shrill. Although country gentlemen dominated Parliament, their influence over national policy diminished as they confronted new financial institutions, commercial interests, and political factions that extended to the farthest reaches of the Empire. With the return to peace in 1713, the government negotiated a controversial trade agreement with the traditional imperial rival, France—according to the opposition, a land of lace, brandy, and peasant poverty. Thereafter the Walpolean faction rose to consolidate the emerging

---

[5]For a classic statement of republican warnings against excessive self-interest see James Harrington, *The Commonwealth of Oceana* (London, 1656); rpt. *Oceana and Other Works*, ed. John Toland (London, 1771). See also Anthony Ashley Cooper, Third Earl of Shaftesbury, *Characteristicks of Men, Manners, Opinions, Times* (London, 1711); rpt., 2 vols. (Gloucester, Mass.: Peter Smith, 1963), 76, 183, 336.

[6]Edward Hatton, *The Merchant's Magazine: or, Tradesman's Treasury*, 9th ed. (London, 1734), 212. See also Dickson, *Financial Revolution*, chs. 1-2; Kramnick, *Bolingbroke and his Circle*, 39-47.

economic order. It was in this context that "interest" took on the invidious meanings that survived in oppositionist rhetoric until and beyond the American Revolution.

The landed classes were not uniformly hostile to the changes favoring commercial interests. Proponents of traditional political right and obligation rarely opposed commerce and manufacturing as such. Instead, they were troubled by the association between commerce and warfare—and higher land taxes—and by political factionalism and the corruption of the House of Commons through patronage. Similarly, while many oppositionists benefited from the expansion of credit, they warned against the dangers of a large, permanent public debt and of the risky speculative ventures long-term loans made possible.

From the republican perspective, the new potential for economic and political excess jeopardized public virtue. The web of market relations grew so complicated that unfamiliar buyers and sellers were encouraged to take every possible advantage of each other. Merchants gambled on the unpredictable values of goods; they were continually tempted to commit "fraud upon strangers."[7] Relations based on credit were irrational and fitful, and the merchant who followed an interest defined in such insubstantial terms could hardly be master of his own economic behavior. Rational as his daily choices might be, the dangers to which he exposed his character by relying on the vagaries of credit and the ploys and subterfuges of competitors seemed to preclude the emergence of a permanent, substantial commercial interest that could be made to support and advance the general welfare.

Many Americans agreed that the claims of reason, justice, and patriotism could be jeopardized by the pursuit of exotic goods in distant markets. As a New Yorker put it, the virtuous citizens should seek "the firm Bank that constantly secures us agoin' the impetuous Raging of that turbulent Sea of Passions which incessantly dash against the Frame of human Nature."[8] Certainly, another writer added,

---

[7]Since at least Aristotle observers typically distinguished between foreign trade in which "fraudulent" or "unnatural" means might be necessary and the domestic economy in which at least a modicum of economic justice was expected. Until the late seventeenth century, opponents of the new commercial interests worried about foreign practices invading the British-American economy. See, e.g., Aristotle, *Politics*, trans. and introd. Ernest Barker (Oxford: Oxford Univ. Press, 1958), 22-27; Francis Bacon, "Of Seditions and Troubles," in Sidney Warhaft, ed., *Francis Bacon: A Selection of His Works* (Indianapolis: The Odyssey Press, 1965), 79-86; Wilson, *England's Apprenticeship*, 57-65; and, in America, [Anon.], *A Satyre Upon the Times* (New York, 1702); [Lewis Morris], "Dialogue Concerning Trade: A Satirical View of New York in 1726," (New York, 1727); rpt. in *New York History*, 55 (1974), 199-229; [Robert Hunter], *Androboros* (New York, 1714); rpt. in *Bulletin of the New York Public Library*, 68 (1964), 153-90; "A Word in Season," *New-York Weekly Journal*, 5 Sept. 1737, and "Account of the Late Election," ibid., 19 Mar. 1739.

[8]"Philosophia," "On Wisdom," *New-York Weekly Journal*, 5 Oct. 1733.

there is such a bewitching Charm in Self-Interest, that the Mind, intoxicated by this delusive Syren, is generally impervious to Truth and Reason. ... A Man's personal Advantage gives so strange a Biass to his Reason, that he perceives not his own Injustice.[9]

Like their English counterparts, American critics of commerce attributed the dangers of excessive self-interest to a "thirst after luxury" imports. Following their own selfish impulses, American traders would divert staples to foreign nations in return for costly "superfluities," "artificialities" and "unnaturall" goods. Not only would such trade do little to satisfy the colonists' legitimate needs, it would also deprive British producers of valuable markets.[10] Said William Livingston, "that Luxury is the Harbinger of a dying State, is a Truth too obvious to require the Formality of Proof."[11] Unless colonists curbed their "habitual Tea-drinking," one form of luxury consumption which "so universally prevail[ed],"[12] there was a real danger that "we [might] Eat ourselves."[13] The extensive distribution of imported commodities amounted to a "prodigious increase of American luxury," such "an inseparable attendant on an increase of riches" that a merchant "must suit [his] cargo to the taste of customers; and not to old-fashioned notions of parsimony of former days."[14] In short, "Private Interest"—the gratification of an individual's appetites—was no more than a "dirty Shell" unless restrained by society.[15]

Republican warnings about the corrupting influence of commerce and the dangers of self-interest did not simply express the concerns of classes excluded from new sources of wealth and power. In fact, many spokesmen for the republican or Country position, in England and in America, were well situated

[9]"Remarks on a Petition," in William Livingston et al., *The Independent Reflector*, ed. Milton M. Klein (Cambridge: Harvard Univ. Press, 1963), 118-127; quotation, 118.

[10]Reverend John Miller, *A Description of the Province and City of New York* (New York, 1695), cited in Joseph Dorfman, *The Economic Mind of American Civilization*, 5 vols. (New York: Viking Press, 1948), 77-78. Also, *New York Mercury*, 1 Feb. 1764, 1 June 1768; Daniel Defoe, *The Complete English Tradesman*, 2 vols. (London, 1727), 1:89-90, 356; 2:121, 209, 211, 300, 332, 335; "John Trusty," *New-York Weekly Journal*, 22 Apr. 1734.

[11]William Livingston, "A Brief Consideration of New York," Special Collections, Columbia Univ. Library, New York; also; "Of the Extravagance of our Funerals," *Independent Reflector*, no. 29, 14 June 1753, rpt. in Klein, 257-62; quotation, 257.

[12]*New York Gazette*, 14 Nov. 1737; Esther Singleton, *Social New York Under the Georges*, 2 vols. (New York, 1902), 2:378-79. By the end of the colonial period, tea was the primary focus of concerns about luxury. See Peter Kalm, *Travels in North America, 1748-1751*, ed. Adolph Benson, 2 vols. (New York: Dover Publications, 1966), 1:361; *Essex Gazette* (Salem, Mass.), 4 Jan. 1774; *Pennsylvania Chronicle* (Philadelphia), 2 May 1768 and 28 Nov. 1768; *Pennsylvania Gazette* (Philadelphia), 17 Nov. 1773; *Newport Mercury*, 24 Jan. 1774 and 7 Feb. 1774; *New Hampshire Gazette* (Portsmouth), 22 July 1774; *Boston Evening Post*, 24 June 1775.

[13]"John Scheme," *New-York Weekly Journal*, 18 Mar. 1734.

[14]Robert Livingston, Jr. to William Alexander, 26 Mar. 1753, Alexander Papers, vol. 1, no. 25, New-York Historical Society.

[15]"Of Patriotism," *Independent Reflector*, no. 23, 3 May 1753, rpt. in Klein, 215-20; quotation, 216.

to reap the benefits of the new economic order. Their concern was with speculative bubbles, luxury consumption, political factionalism and corruption. But by invoking an idealized traditional political economy, oppositionists helped throw the new regime of commercial interests into bold relief. Their contribution was to clarify the equivocal character of these new interests and to force mercantilists to formulate new definitions of the national interest.[16]

Mercantilism: The New Structure of Interest

Mercantilist exponents of imperial expansion discarded many of the key assumptions of traditional political theory that continued to inform republican or Commonwealth critiques of the new commercial order. For them, society was not characterized by organic fixity; political space was not delimited by the estates of the landed classes. The boundaries of empire could be extended by the exercise of military power and successful commercial competition. Private trading ventures were particularly important because they provided new commercial connections which helped overcome scarcity, poverty, and unemployment.

In 1691 Dudley North set forth a basic mercantilist premise: "The whole World as to Trade, is but one Nation or People, and therein Nations are as Persons."[17] Commerce brought interested parties together on a world scale, making it possible to satisfy an ever greater range of needs. Obviously, wrote Carew Reynel, "riches are the convenience of the nation," and "people . . . [its] strength, pleasure and glory"; but he added, "trade preserves both."[18] Other writers pointed up the implications of this logic: "Trade and commerce are the pillars of prosperity and safety to England," according to one;[19] "its neglect," another concluded, "will be England's ruin and confusion."[20] But none matched Daniel Defoe's passion for trade,

---

[16]For oppositionists on trade as a helpmate of landed virtue see, e.g., Joseph Addison, "The Royal Exchange," 19 May 1711, in *Selections from the Tatler and the Spectator*, ed. Angus Ross (London: Penguin, 1982), 437-40; Richard Steele, "Sir Andrew Freeport defends Commerce," 19 Sept. 1711, ibid., 447-50; Jonathan Swift, *The History of the Four Last Years of the Queen*, ed. Herbert Davis (Oxford: Oxford Univ. Press, 1964). For an example of trade advocates' ambivalent attitudes toward agriculture see Sir Charles Whitworth, ed., *The Political and Commercial Works of that Celebrated writer Dr. Charles D'Avenant*, 5 vols. (London, 1771), 1:160, 4:240-42. See also Dickson, *Financial Revolution*, ch. 2.

[17][Dudley North], *Discourses upon Trade* (London, 1691), 13.

[18]Carew Reynel, *The True English Benefit or an Account of the Chief National Improvements* (London, 1674), 8-9.

[19]William de Britaine, *The Interest of England in the Present War with Holland* (London, 1672), 3-4. See also the 1674 mss. of John Locke cited in Macpherson, *Possessive Individualism*, 207; Joshua Gee, *The Trade and Navigation of Great Britain*, 3rd. ed., 2 vols. (London, 1731).

[20]James Whiston, *The Mismanagements in Trade Discover'd, And Adapt Methods to Preserve and Exceedingly Improve It* (London, 1704), 8.

42

the life of the nation, the soul of its felicity, the spring of its wealth, the support of its greatness. . . . ([I]f it should sink) the whole fabric must fall, the body politic would sicken and languish, its power decline, and the figure it makes in the world grow by degrees contemptibly mean.[21]

For these mercantilists "liberty" was defined not by an enduring relationship with the land but as the freedom to take risks and accumulate mobile wealth. The idea of "interest" was more and more frequently invoked by mercantilists to describe enlightened private behavior which produced beneficial results for the entire community.

American traders eagerly embraced the mercantilist justifications for the pursuit of self-interest. One merchant conceded that "every Man ought to promote the Prosperity of his Country, from a sublimer Motive than his private Advantage," but concluded that it was "extremely difficult, for the best of Men, to divest themselves of Self-Interest."[22] Another explained that sometimes interest "Connects People, who are intire Strangers," or "separates those who had the strongest natural Connections."[23] But most Americans recognized that, in some form, "Interest . . . governs all the world."[24]

According to the mercantilist account, the aggregate of personal fortunes and public treasure constituted the wealth of a nation. And no interest was so crucial to promoting national wealth and welfare as the "merchant interest." Merchants served the nation by venturing into a world that was usually at war and always infested by pirates, deceitful debtors, and ruthless competitors. As a result, the traditional conception of commercial enterprise as a means of "fraud upon strangers" began to give way to approval of the exchange of "refinements" which enriched and civilized the national community.

The merchant interest was the leading sector in advancing national wealth and power. As Richard Campbell explained, the "honest gain" of the merchant

[21]Daniel Defoe. *A Plan of the English Commerce* (New York: A.M. Kelley Publishers, 1967; orig. pub. London, 1728), 22.
[22]"Public Virtue to be Distinguished by public Honours," *The Independent Reflector*, no. 9, 25 Jan. 1753, rpt. in Klein, 111-17; quotation, 111. Also, Philip Livingston to Jacob Wendell, 23 July 1737, Livingston Mss., Museum of the City of New York.
[23]William Alexander to Peter Van Brugh Livingston, 1 Mar. 1756, Rutherford Collection, no. 93, New-York Historical Society.
[24]E. B. O'Callaghan, ed., *Documents Relative to the Colonial History of the State of New York* (hereafter cited *NYCD*), 15 vols. (Albany: Weed, Parsons, & Co., 1853-87) 5:8i. Also, "B.B.," "Modest Inquiry," *New York Gazette*, 2 June, 9 June, 16 June 1729. For classic statements on the universality of interest see, e.g., Francis Bacon, *The Advancement of Learning*, ed. W. A. Wright, 5th ed. (Oxford: Oxford Univ. Press, 1963; orig. pub. London, 1605); Thomas Hobbes, *Leviathan*, (London: Penguin, 1968; orig. pub., London, 1651), ch. 13; David Hume, *Essays, Moral, Political, and Literary*, ed. T. H. Green and T. H. Grose, 2 vols. (London: Longmans, Green, & Co., 1875; orig. pub., London, 1741-42), 1:176; Adam Smith, *The Wealth of Nations*, ed. Edwin Canaan (Chicago: Univ. of Chicago Press, 1976; orig. pub., London, 1776), 1:477.

"returns more than he carried out, adds so much to the National Riches and Capital Stock of the Kingdom." "Wealth and Plenty follow him . . . and Public Credit increases."[25] Even Commonwealth writers like Joseph Addison, with their well-known reservations about the impact of commerce on society, recognized the important role played by merchants: "there are not more useful Members in a Commonwealth than Merchants. They knit Mankind together in a mutual Intercourse of good Offices, [and] distribute the Gifts of Nature."[26] Moreover, the general prosperity which flowed from the rapid circulation of commercial wealth was the real basis for the "independence" and "virtue" to which landowners had previously made sole claim. "The lasting prosperity of the landed interest," said staunch mercantilist Malachy Postlethwayt, "depends upon foreign commerce" and the "well-grounded knowledge of political arithemetick" which secured a favorable balance of trade.[27]

Given the great contributions commercial interests made to the national welfare, mercantilists argued that it was crucial to direct regulatory policies not to the restraint of domestic commerce but to balancing international trade in England's favor. They concluded that exploiting the "exhorbitant Appetites" of foreign consumers for English goods represented the best means of promoting England's interest. Because there were global limits to the wealth for which trading nations competed, national treasure—and private fortunes—depended on a favorable ratio of exports over imports. Thus, as late as 1750, Joseph Harris believed that there was "but a certain proportion of trade," and "a limit to the vent and consumption of all sorts of commodities."[28] It followed, wrote Matthew Decker, that "if the Exports of Britain exceeded its Imports, Foreigners must pay the balance in Treasure and the Nations grow Rich." Such an advantageous balance would obtain only if foreigners developed a taste for British exports.[29] By the same logic, Britons should refrain—or be restrained—from excessive consumption of imports.

The mercantilists' conception of commercial "liberty" privileged new forms and uses of property while reorienting state policy toward exploiting new and unpredictable opportunities abroad. In promoting "balance," mercantilist writers emphasized the need for state support of commercial interests. Securing interest through a system of "artificial legislashun" was not new to the early modern world, but it gained momentum—and more elaborate theoretical justification—over the eighteenth century. When commercial policies failed to

[25]Richard Campbell, *The London Tradesman* (London, 1747), 284-86.
[26]Addison, "Royal Exchange," 439.
[27]Malachy Postlethwayt, *The Universal Dictionary of Trade and Commerce, translated from the French of the celebrated Monsieur Savary*, 2 vols. (London, 1766), 2:107-08.
[28]Joseph Harris, *An Essay upon Money and Coins* (London, 1757), 28, 101; Thomas Mun, *England's Treasure by Forraign Trade* (Oxford: Oxford Univ. Press, 1928; orig. pub., London, 1664). See the discussion in Appleby, *Economic Thought and Ideology*, ch. 2.
[29]Matthew Decker, *Essay on the Causes of the Decline of the Foreign Trade* (London, 1744; written 1739), 14.

maintain a favorable balance of trade or to permit merchants to advance their private interests, it was easy to blame political factionalism rather than economic causes beyond state control. The regime of interest flourished as private enterprises and state power converged.[30]

By the early eighteenth century Britain's growing prosperity and power enabled economists to turn their attention to domestic material consumption and to consider the advantages of exchanges within the empire.[31] In its basic sense, consumption referred to the satisfaction of material needs and desires. The passion to consume could stimulate socially useful activity, commentators asserted, as long as it did not distort or displace individual reason and responsibility. Even in the seventeenth century, economists suggested that "the exhorbitant Appetites of Men" were "the main spur to Trade . . . Industry and Ingenuity" "when nothing else will incline them."[32] As Nicholas Barbon explained, "it is not Necessity that causeth the Consumption. Nature may be Satisfied with little; but it is the wants of the Mind, Fashion and the desire of Novelties and Things Scarce that causeth Trade."[33] These accounts reflected changing attitudes toward luxury consumption. "Trade," wrote Charles Davenant in 1692, "brings in that wealth which introduces luxury," a presumably pernicious result. But, considering "the posture and condition of other countries . . . it is become with us a necessary evil."[34] Yet, if for mercantilists the necessity of luxury consumption was becoming clearer, its "evil" was rapidly attenuating.

The successes of self-interested merchants in the international economy and the resulting array of goods available to consumers showed that commerce could give shape and purpose to the "perpetual restless ambition" of the great mass of the people "to raise themselves." Because of commerce consumers gained access to "more of life's necessitous goods," not to mention the less "necessitous arts and manufactures" that satisfied "fashion" and "mere opinion."[35] Indeed, many items once considered luxuries were now thought to be necessities. By acting as a "salve upon our great appetites," luxury imports

---

[30]Daniel Defoe asked, "What has trade to do with your political quarrels, and what business have party men with the commerce of the nation?" Defoe, *Some Thoughts on the Subject of Commerce* (London, 1713), 8. On the role of the state see Andrews, *Colonial Period*, vol. 4, ch. 11; Gunn, *Politics and Public Interest*, ch. 5. See also Gee, *Trade and Navigation of Great Britain*; Richard Gouldsmith, *Some Considerations on Trade and Manufactures* (London, 1725); Erasmus Philips, *The State of the Nation in respect to her Commerce, Debts, and Money* (London, 1725), esp. 1-8; William Wood, *Survey of Trade*, 2 vols. (London, 1718), esp. 1:130-36, 152-54.

[31]On consumption, in addition to the works cited in n. 3, see Neil McKendrick, "Commercialization and the Economy," in Neil McKendrick, John Brewer, and J. H. Plumb, *The Birth of a Consumer Society* (Bloomington: Univ. of Indiana Press, 1982), esp. 9-194.

[32][North], *Discourses upon Trade*, 27.

[33]Nicholas Barbon, *A Discourse of Trade* (London, 1690), 72-73.

[34]Davenant, *On the Plantation Trade*, in Whitworth, *Works of D'Avenant*, 2:75.

[35]Ibid. Also, [Anon.], *An Account of the French Usurpation upon the Trade of England* (London, 1679); [Anon.], *Considerations on the Present State of the Nation* (London, 1720).

could elevate and civilize English consumers while satisfying their baser
impulses. Properly directed, foreign trade could introduce "refinements,"
"arts" and "politeness."[36]

The growth of consumer demand and new definitions of individual "needs"
were the keys to a prosperous modern economy. Even Joseph Addison endorsed
the expanding scope of consumption: "Nature indeed furnishes us with the bare
Necessities of Life, but Traffick gives us a great Variety of what is Useful . . .
Convenient and Ornamental." Commerce, while not essential for sustaining life
itself, was requisite for civilized comfort.[37] John Trenchard and Thomas
Gordon, who, like Addison, scorned stockjobbers and the "monied interest,"
shared his opinion that commerce brought "civilized virtues" and
"politeness."[38]

Mercantilist writers agreed that the growing wealth and power of the empire
were fueled by the rapid circulation and consumption of goods. Regulations and
prohibitions could guarantee an orderly system of trade while curbing excesses
and imbalances in consumption patterns. Within this regulated framework, the
reciprocal interests of merchants and their customers converged with the
national interest. Coincidentally, by regulating the flow of imports, the
mercantilist system could check the deleterious effects of luxury consumption on
private character.

Anglo-American readers could trace the emerging rationale for interest and
consumption through the works of eminent philosophers as well as those of
polemical writers. Acknowledging the dangers of unbounded acquisitiveness for
political and social order, John Locke in his "Second Treatise" argued that the
most pernicious effects of competitive self-interest could be controlled by a
voluntary compact among free individuals to form a commonwealth. Political
authority would coordinate and secure the multiplicity of interests while self-
regarding individuals would restrain themselves in order to protect their
property. Thus, Locke liberated "ceaseless, perpetual motion" only to seek its
proper limits. It was his confidence in the ability of interested individuals to

---

[36] On the benefits of luxury see John Houghton, *A Collection of Letters for the Improvement of
Husbandry and Trade* (London, 1681), 60; Defoe, *The Complete English Tradesman*, 2:226,
231-33; Joseph Massie, "The Natural Rate of Interest," (London, 1750), rpt. in Jacob Hollander,
ed., *Reprints of Economic Tracts* (Baltimore: n.p., n.d.), 20, 53; David Hume, "Of the Balance of
Trade" and "Of Commerce," in Eugene Rotwein, ed., *David Hume: Writings on Economics*
(Madison: Univ. of Wisconsin Press, 1955), 66-77, 3-18. See also Kramnick, *Bolingbroke and His
Circle*, 201-04; John Sekora, *Luxury: The Concept in Western Thought, Eden to Smollett* (Baltimore:
Johns Hopkins Univ. Press, 1977), ch. 2.
[37] Addison, "Royal Exchange," 439.
[38] John Trenchard, with Thomas Gordon, *Cato's Letters*, 3rd. ed., 4 vols. in 2 (London, 1733;
orig. pub. London, 1720-23; facs. rpt. New York: Russell & Russell, 1969), 1:11, 134-35; 2:51-54,
71-74, 272-77; 3:24, 27-28.

control and coordinate their appetites and interests that set him apart from less optimistic critics of the new order.[39]

David Hume's 1752 essays represent a further, important step in the legitimation of interest. He justified the "love of gain" and consumption of the world's bounty, while downplaying resulting political factionalism and cyclical economic crises. Although mild forms of mercantile regulation might be necessary to protect and encourage "infant interests," they should not be allowed to restrain individual initiative. Hume's attempt to establish lawful patterns in economic phenomena brought him to the verge of a conception of a self-correcting economy. He thought that if there were a "general agreement" about the "benefits of luxury," the community should be prepared for alternating periods of high prices and interest rates, scarcities and gluts. It was in the long-term general interest to ride out these temporary disturbances.[40] More than most of his contemporaries, Hume emphasized the connection of interest to personal agency rather than institutional restraint. A ruler's responsibility "aims only at possibilities" rather than constant intervention. Hume's economic analysis led him to one of the most far-reaching and authoritative endorsements of modest luxury consumption before the American Revolution.

Hume's cautious endorsement of interest and consumption paled next to the polemical productions—and actual behavior—of merchants who chafed at what they considered excessive regulation. "Freedom" in trade was never far below the surface of their rhetoric. Even in the seventeenth century, groups of merchants throughout the empire appealed for relief from commercial duties or exemption from regulation on the grounds that restriction was harmful to the national welfare as well as to their personal interests. The continuing influence of "free trade" among the Dutch provided one influential model for commercial success. Particularly after 1713, when the focus of British mercantile rivalry shifted from the Dutch to the French and Spanish, commercial propagandists repeatedly extolled the benefits of the "hollander free trade."[41] Many American traders found these arguments attractive.

---

[39]John Locke, "The Second Treatise," in *Two Treatises of Government*, ed. and introd. Peter Laslett (New York: Mentor, 1965; orig. pub. London, 1689), pars. 22, 123, 127.

[40]David Hume, "Of Commerce," "Of Interest," "Of the Balance of Trade," in Rotwein, *Economic Writings*, 3-32, 47-59, 60-77.

[41]The Dutch example of free ports and open trade with foreigners was prominent in Carew Reynel, Dalby Thomas, John Pollexfen, William Petty, Charles Davenant, and, to a lesser degree, Daniel Defoe. See the suggestive comments in Andrews, *Colonial Period*, 4:131-37, 346n. On the shift after 1713 see Charles Wilson, *Profit and Power: A Study of England and the Dutch Wars* (London: Longmans, 1957), ch. 7; [Anon.], *A Discourse consisting of Motives for the Enlargment of Freedom of Trade* (London, 1645); Sir William Temple, "Observations on the United Provinces," in *The Works of Sir William Temple*, 2 vols. (London, 1720), 1:1-36.

Free Trade

The leading premise of mercantilist colonial policy was that national greatness depended on encouraging vigorous trade—and consumption—throughout the empire. Spokesmen for colonial commercial interests recognized the advantages of this trade for their clients, endorsing the mercantilist axiom that "We are all linked in a Chain of Dependence on each other, & when properly regulated, by the most prudential Laws, form a beautiful Whole, having within ourselves the rich Sources of an active Commerce & diffusive Happiness throughout."[42]

American merchants had a vested interest in imperial prosperity and power. But the success of the mercantile system could not completely disguise the subordinate, dependent status of the colonies. When mercantilist writers considered the colonial relation, it became clear that there would be no "balance" of power and plenty within the empire. "The very nature of colonies," Postlethwayt explained, was "that they ought to have no culture or arts, wherein to rival the arts and culture of their parent country." Nor could colonies "in justice consume foreign commodities, with an equivalent for which their mother country consents to supply them," or "sell to foreigners, such of their commodities as their mother country consents to receive."[43] Throughout the colonial period mercantilists asserted their right to enjoy a "monopoly" of colonial consumption.[44]

Though the full implications of these claims were felt only late in the colonial period, local conditions earlier led many Americans to question mercantilist premises. A number of particular cases strongly suggested that "to sett Trade Free" was the "wisest course." "Liberalitye with respect to duties and the items of our traffick" would present new opportunities to trade in southern Europe and the foreign West Indies.[45] Finding the goods and markets which brought the best prices was not always compatible with trade regulations dictated by distant authorities; bounties to promote production of new staples might be useful, but prohibitions on other exports could pose considerable hardships. It was "the Interest of the City and Country to Lay no Duties," as one New York pamphleteer put it.[46] Regulations, another said, were a mere "Solecism in

[42]*New York Mercury*, 24 Jan. 1764.

[43]Postlethwayt, *Universal Dictionary*, 2:107-08.

[44]Lord Sheffield, *Observations on the Commerce of the American States*, 6th ed. (London, 1784), 162.

[45]For early proposals to free American trade from duties and prohibitions, see, e.g., *NYCD*, 3:46, 51-54; *Calendar of State Papers, Colonial Series, America and the West Indies*, ed. W. Noel Sainsbury and J. W. Fortescue (London: Her Majesty's Stationery Office, 1880-1969), vol. 1677-80, 41; ibid., vol. 1675-76, 871, 898-99.

[46]Cadwallader Colden, *The Interest of the City and Country to Lay No Duties* (New York, 1726), 1-23; "The Interest of the City and Country," *New York Journal*, 5 Sept. 1757; *NYCD*, 3:289; *Journal of the Votes and Proceedings of the Assembly of New York*, 2 vols. (New York, 1764-66), 1:548, 551-52, 638, 641, 645.

Trade, and the Bane of Industry." The best encouragement, as "Self-Interest is the grand Principle of all Human Actions," was "Liberty" in commerce.[47]

Local commercial interests faced great difficulties in securing dependable markets during the early decades of colonial history. Regulations that attempted to promote specific patterns of production and exchange throughout the empire could be disastrous locally. For instance, one writer claimed, it would be a great mistake to promote production of hemp, potash, iron, and other "manufactures": "the main bent of our farmers is to produce grain." Tinkering with the natural "bent" of colonial economies would divert capital from commerce while requiring producers to wait patiently for uncertain profits.[48]

By the 1750s, free trade advocates moved beyond such prudential—and narrowly self-interested—concerns to argue for the expansive potential of unregulated trade. The Seven Years' War provided diverse chances to enter commerce or enhance existing connections. Colonial economies were now relatively mature and diversified: paper money experiments had proved useful in circulating domestic commodities and easing debts; urban centers drew a wide range of necessities from their expanding hinterlands, and accumulated capital and skills even permitted the founding of a few, pioneering manufacturing enterprises. Yet in the depression which followed the war, Americans portrayed themselves as victims of misguided policies. "Why is the trade of the colonies more circumscribed than the trade of Britain?" a Boston writer asked: "Can any one tell me why trade, commerce, arts, sciences, & manufactures, should not be as free for an American as for a European?"[49] From this perspective, "freedom" was coming to mean not only the absence of political interference, but also to suggest the positive value of seeking "a free and open trade with all the powers of Europe."[50]

Free trade arguments became increasingly popular in the late colonial period. Even more than mercantilists who, by definition, were committed to regulation and restraint, free traders celebrated the beneficent effects of interest and consumption. Growing awareness of this possibility of acquiring and using an

[47]*New York Mercury*, 3 Oct. 1754; Archibald Kennedy, *Observations on the Importance of the Northern Colonies under Proper Regulations* (New York, 1750), 6-9, 16; *New York Gazette*, 4 Apr. 1765.

[48]Gov. Hunter to Board of Trade, 12 Nov. 1715, Cadwallader Colden, on New York's trade, 1723, Gov. Cosby to Board of Trade, 18 Dec. 1732, *NYCD*, 1:713-14, 714-21; *New York Gazette*, 21 Jan., 28 Jan., 4 Feb. 1735.

[49]"John Hampden," *Boston Gazette*, 9 Dec. 1765; also, ibid., 16 Dec., 23 Dec. 1765. On the Seven Years' War see Stanley Pargellis, ed., *Military Affairs in North America, 1748-1765* (New York: D. Appleton-Century Co., 1936); Fred Anderson, *A People's Army: Massachusetts Soldiers and Society in the Seven Years' War* (Chapel Hill: Univ. of North Carolina Press, 1984); Theodore Thayer, "The Army Contractors for the Niagara Campaign, 1755-1756," *WMQ*, 14 (1957), 31-46; quotation, 32. On the scale of economic opportunities by the time of the war see Joyce Appleby, "The Social Origins of American Revolutionary Ideology," *Journal of American History*, 64 (1978), 935-58.

expanding share of the commodities circulating worldwide made many Americans impatient with all restraints on commerce. Paternal political authority—now manifested in the "fickel opinions" of mercantilist policy-makers—stifled the rage for new items of consumption. The free traders offered a powerful critique of imperial politics as well as an appealing alternative to commercial restraint: merchants, not politicians, were true public servants, because they alone could satisfy the diverse needs and desires of the consuming public. "Former rarities" and the "infinite number of other curiosities" they had brought to America were the free traders' proud contribution to the welfare of their countrymen.[51]

According the free trade logic, elimination of artificial political obstructions between the original production and ultimate acquisition and consumption of the world's wealth would create a truly "natural economy." Some free traders even anticipated Adam Smith's argument for the inevitable social redistribution of wealth. A New Yorker thus dismissed the threat of a dynamic economy to social order:

> The private interests and passions of men naturally lead them to divide and distribute the stock of society, among all the different employments . . . as nearly as possible in the proportion which is most agreeable to the interest of the whole society.[52]

In effect, the public interest would be defined through the uninhibited play of private interests in the marketplace.

While such arguments gained considerable public sympathy for the free trade position, they were obviously intended to justify blatantly self-interest behavior. Smugglers, the most colorful and conspicuous exponents of free trade in practice, did not scruple to defy imperial law in order to provide luxuries to avid colonial consumers. To advance their illicit interests they "made the mode" for such goods as lemons, spices, fine apparel, and snuff into "necessity," thereby earning broad popular support for their "insubordination."[53]

---

[50]Robert M. Weir, ed., "Two Letters by Christopher Gadsden," *South Carolina Historical Magazine*, 75 (1974), 169-76; quotation, 175.

[51]See, e.g., Roger Coke, *A Discourse of Trade* (London 1670; written 1668), 24-41; and Sir Matthew Decker, *Essay on the Causes of the Decline of Foreign Trade* (London, 1744), 1-6.

[52][Anon.], "The Commercial Conduct of the Province of New York," (1767), Special Collections, Columbia University. Also, Smith, *Wealth of Nations*, 1:291-93; 2:145.

[53]On the connection between smuggling and luxury consumption see Cal Winslow, "Sussex Smugglers," in E. P. Thompson et al., *Albion's Fatal Tree: Crime and Society in Eighteenth-Century England* (New York: Pantheon, 1975), 119-66, esp. 148-49; James B. Hedges, *The Browns of Providence Plantation: The Colonial Years* (Cambridge: Harvard Univ. Press, 1952); Tyler, "The First Revolution"; Johnson, "Fair Traders"; Matson, "Fair Trade, Free, Trade," ch. 6. Merchant letters offer considerable evidence; see those of Philip Cuyler, John Ludlow, and Peter R. Livingston (New-York Historical Society, New York City), and Thomas Riche and Thomas Wharton (Historical Society of Pennsylvania, Philadelphia).

Even before there was a higher cause around which to rally—the constitutional liberty and national interest of the American people—smugglers, privateers, and international traders taught Americans how to defend their new habits of consumption. The right to consume suggested, in turn, an emerging idea of the public interest fundamentally at odds with mercantilist imperialism. The aggregate of individual interest was not merely the "public welfare," but "America's interest"; the foreigner was not only French and Spanish, but British as well. Such was the meaning of the merchants' outcry in 1774 when the Tea Act gave an undue "monopoly interest" to the British East India Company, making American smugglers and foreign traders feel that "we should soon have found our trade in the hands of foreigners"—that is, British merchants.[54] Moreover, unrestrained pursuit of forbidden commodities in foreign markets was elevated to a private right: "every man has a natural right to exchange his property with whom he pleases and where he can make the most advantage of it." Therefore, recent British policy jeopardized private rights at the same time that it demonstrated the common disadvantages faced by American interests in the imperial economy.[55]

Free traders could claim to serve the public by providing access to the world's circulating goods at low prices and without artificial limitations. They helped push Americans one more step away from the traditional conception of political economy idealized by republican theorists. But the free traders' facile identification of private and public interest was hard to defend during wartime, when interimperial rivalries fractured world markets and when sacrifices (of private interests) were obviously necessary. By definition free traders were hostile to legislative restraint; they sought access to market opportunities regardless of state policy. Thus they responded to the exigencies of war and attempts to enforce mercantile regulation with undeviating determination to serve their own interests, even if this meant trading with the enemy or ignoring customary price levels. To their critics—including may of their erstwhile customers—free traders were excessively passionate in the pursuit of self-interest and represented the very antithesis of the virtuous, self-denying patriotism that war demanded.

Close observers in Britain had not failed to register alarm that the opportunities of the Seven Years' War and postwar period had "given rise to A NEW SYSTEM OF INTERESTS" which "opened a new channel of business; and brought into operation a new Concatenation of powers" antithetical to an orderly mercantile economy.[56] Officials in America generally agreed that

[54]Hezekiah Niles, *Principles and Acts of the Revolution in America* (Baltimore: n.p., 1822), 16.

[55]Lt. Gov. Colden to Earl of Dartmouth, 2 Nov. 1774, *NYCD*, 8:511; "Virginia Instructions for the Deputies," *New York Gazette*, 6 June and 26 Sept. 1765; *Rivington's New York Gazetteer*, 25 Aug. 1774.

[56]Thomas Pownall, *The Administration of the British Colonies*, 4th ed. (London, 1768), 1. Also, Malachy Postlethwayt, *Great Britain's Commercial Interest Explained and Improved*, 2 vols. (London, 1757), 1:482-83.

merchants, especially in the "Illicit Trade," "abhor every limitation of Trade and Duty on it, and therefore gladly go into every measure whereby they hope to have Trade free."[57]

By the eve of the Revolution, London merchants who formerly allied their interests with American traders were far less inclined to exert pressure on Parliament to remove distasteful legislation. The Londoners felt "America's free trade parties" would not be satisfied with reform and would "never rest till they have obtained a free trade with all the world."[58] This skepticism seemed justified as large numbers of American merchants withdrew from their own nonimportation agreements with the claim that they were "starving on the slender Meals of Patriotism."[59]

Virtue and Liberty

If free trade arguments were self-serving—and obviously inappropriate during a period of political crisis—Americans found mercantilist ideas equally problematic. Two severe depressions after the Seven Years' War challenged colonial merchants' continuing faith in regulations decreed by metropolitan authority. When Parliament responded to the "new system of interests" in America with a spate of reform measures there was still further reason to question mercantilist precepts. Some American merchants began to associate mercantilism more with oppression than opportunity.[60] In the words of one noted merchant leader, mercantilism was no more than a "glaring monument" to "the all-grasping nature of unlimited power," not the model of power and plenty in a system of orchestrated interests. The antithesis of virtue and liberty, the empire was designed to serve the narrow "interest of a selfish European island."[61] Even William Pitt, Lord Shelburne, and Edmund Burke doubted the wisdom of restraining the colonists who "naturally seek the vent of goods which satisfied private interest."[62] Perhaps, as the London *Public Advertiser* noted, Britain wrongfully asked for "a pitiful Pittance in the Form of a Tax," when it could "with a Good-Will, obtain Millions by fair Commerce."[63]

[57]Cadwallader Colden, *The Letters and Papers of Cadwallader Colden, Collections of New-York Historical Society*, 9 vols. (New York, 1917-35), 6:62-66, 136-40, 161-63, 166-73.

[58]*Public Advertiser* (London), 3 Jan., 28 Feb., 4 May 1775.

[59]*NYCD*, 8:217, 219; "Answer . . . by Six Merchants," *New York Gazette and Weekly Mercury*, 2 July 1770; "Philo-Veritas," ibid., 23 July 1770.

[60]Marc Egnal, "The Economic Development of the Thirteen Continental Colonies, 1720 to 1775," *WMQ*, 32 (1975), 191-222. See the citations in n. 65 below.

[61]"Address by John Hancock to the People of Boston," 5 March 1774; Niles, *Principles and Acts*, 63.

[62]Edmund Burke to Richard Champion, 10 Jan. 1775; to Rockingham, 23 Aug., 14 Sept., 1775, in *The Correspondence of Edmund Burke*, ed. Charles William, 4 vols. (London: F. and J. Rivington, 1844), 2:2-3, 55-56, 62; William Pitt to General Monckton, 8 Oct. 1759, in *The Correspondence of William Pitt*, ed. G. S. Kimball, 2 vols. (New York: Macmillan Co., 1906), 2:320-21; William Cobbett, ed., *Parliamentary History of England*, 36 vols. (London: T. C. Hansard, 1806-20), 17:1179, 18:648.

[63]*Public Advertiser*, 15 Jan. 1770.

Americans were too firmly convinced of the advantages of commercial prosperity to embrace fully the traditional republican alternative to mercantilism. True enough, the colonial merchants' opposition to imperial reform converged—up to a point—with the patriotic call for the sacrifice of private interest to the public good. The nonimportation movements required colonists to forego levels of consumption to which they had been accustomed. But this was the sort of "sacrifice" that many merchants, eager for relief from overpurchasing and swollen inventories, welcomed. When nonimportation was transformed into the Continental Association, with its ban on "every species of extravagance and dissipation,"[64] patriot leaders may have demanded, as John Murrin suggests, "an extraordinary excess of virtue."[65] Price controls and local enforcement committees were part of the new machinery of public virtue, as were a new series of prohibitions on trade to the lucrative West Indies markets. Merchants, concerned about their own dwindling opportunities, warned that these new regulations could become so excessive that they would impoverish the new nation and undercut the war effort.

When the Revolution began, patriot leaders had to reconcile their calls for virtuous self-sacrifice with the imperatives of financing and managing the war effort. In 1775 John Jay proposed to modify the Association Agreement so that well-placed smugglers could acquire ammunition and salt for the army in West Indian and Dutch markets; later that year he noted that "we have more to expect from the enterprise, activity, and industry of private adventurers, than from the lukewarmness of assemblies."[66] Many Americans were forced to agree, however reluctantly, that "trade flourishes best, when it is free."[67] Within months of setting up the commissary and paymaster departments, Congress was inundated with proposals from former merchants whose businesses (they claimed) were now all but defunct because of the Association and whose "thirst after interest" steered them toward the prospects of business in the interior. "Projectors" came forward with plans to start ironworks, construct barracks, hire wagons, requisition supplies, raise sheep for wool and salted meat rations, and distill substitutes for rum. When Congress turned reluctantly to the private

---

[64]Worthington C. Ford, ed., *Journals of the Continental Congress* (hereafter *JCC*), 34 vols. (Washington, D.C.: GPO, 1904-37), 1:75-80.

[65]Murrin, "Great Inversion," 396. On the difficulties of balancing private opportunity and public-spirited sacrifice during nonimportation, see also, e.g., Ronald Hoffman, *A Spirit of Dissension: Economics, Politics, and the Revolution in Maryland* (Baltimore: Johns Hopkins Univ. Press, 1973), ch. 2; Edward Papenfuse, *In Pursuit of Profit: The Annapolis Merchants in the Era of the American Revolution* (Baltimore: Johns Hopkins Univ. Press, 1975); Edmund Morgan, "The Puritan Ethic and the Coming of the American Revolution," *WMQ*, 24 (1967), 3-18. For analyses of the economic situation, see Paul G. E. Clemens, *The Atlantic Economy and Maryland's Eastern Shore: From Tobacco to Grain* (Ithaca: Cornell Univ. Press, 1980), esp. ch. 6; Joseph Ernst and Marc Egnal, "An Economic Interpretation of the American Revolution," *WMQ*, 29 (1972), 3-36; Nash, *Urban Crucible*, ch. 13.

[66]*JCC*, 3:476-77.

[67]Thomas Paine, *The Crisis* (Albany, 1792; rpt. Garden City, N.Y.: Doubleday, 1973), 178; also, 100-01, 120-21, 170-71, 174-75.

contract system in 1779 almost all the recipients were former successful wholesale merchants from northern cities.[68]

Yet if the economic imperatives of war saved Americans from an excess of virtuous self-denial, they also clarified the limits of free trade. While free trade had given Americans a "taste for refinements" and images of a bountiful future, a Smithian congeries of interested individuals competing in the marketplace could not adequately articulate or implement revolutionary goals. Certainly the problems of raising and provisioning an army, currency inflation, and flagging spirits in both civilian and military sectors after the first year of formal warfare all called into question whether or not Americans had enough virtue to eradicate—or at least control—corruption, venality, and luxury. Too much "freedom" seemed to jeopardize the success of the Revolution.[69]

A wide range of critics—including conservative Whigs as well as radical republicans—thus challenged enterprising Americans to sharpen their justifications of interest and consumption. The demands of the war deflected merchants from their traditional role of promoting transatlantic trade and prosperity. Though merchants still had a vital role to play in securing political liberty, they would have to subordinate their activities to the common cause. Southern congressmen like John Rutledge, Richard Henry Lee, and Samuel Chase well understood that military victory and political independence were necessary preconditions for the development of the American economy: they could not be achieved without a widespread willingness to sacrifice immediate and particular interests. Revolutionary leaders persuasively argued in the years from 1775 to 1777 that unbridled self-interest would subvert military mobilization and civilian morale.

Yet patriotic appeals for public sacrifice enjoyed mixed success at best. The wartime stimulus to key sectors of the economy illuminated the growing gap

---

[68]E. Wayne Carp, *To Starve the Army at Pleasure: Continental Army Administration and American Political Culture, 1775-1783* (Chapel Hill: Univ. of North Carolina Press, 1984), chs. 2-3; Richard D. Brown, *Revolutionary Politics in Massachusetts: The Boston Committee of Correspondence and the Towns, 1772-1774* (Cambridge: Harvard Univ. Press, 1970), 190; Victor L. Johnson, *The American Commissariat During the Revolutionary War* (Philadelphia: Univ. of Pennsylvania Press, 1941), 37-47, 51-53; Eric Foner, *Tom Paine and Revolutionary America* (New York: Oxford Univ. Press, 1976), 145-82; Clarence Ver Steeg, *Robert Morris, Revolutionary Financier* (New York: Octagon Books, 1972), 10-20; Robert A. East, *Business Enterprise in the American Revolutionary Era* (Gloucester, Mass: Peter Smith, 1964), 30-48, 195-96; Richard Buel, "Time: Friend or Foe of the Revolution?" in Don Higginbotham, ed., *Reconsiderations on the Revolutionary War* (Westport, Conn.: Greenwood Press, 1978), 124-43.

[69]See, e.g., Benjamin Rush, "On the Defects of the Confederation," in Dagobert D. Runes, ed., *The Selected Writings of Benjamin Rush* (New York: Philosophical Library, 1947), 28-31; George Washington to James Warren, 31 Mar. 1779, in John C. Fitzpatrick, ed., *The Writings of George Washington*, 39 vols. (Washington, D.C.: GPO, 1931-44), 14:312; John Adams to Mercy Otis Warren, 8 Jan. 1776, *Warren-Adams Letters, Collections of the Massachusetts Historical Society*, 2 vols. (Boston, 1917-25), 2:202; Benjamin Rush to James Searle, 21 Jan. 1778, *PMHB*, 3 (1879), 233. In general see Carp, *To Starve the Army*, and Charles Royster, *A Revolutionary People at War: The Continental Army and American Character, 1775-1783* (Chapel Hill: Univ. of North Carolina Press, 1979), 186-89, 192-94, 200-07.

between the rhetoric of self-restraint and the reality of economic opportunity.[70] Neo-mercantilist price controls and trade regulations failed conspicuously to restrain enterprising Americans from exploiting unprecedented opportunities to produce and supply needed goods. The dilemma was clear to all who would confront it: enforce a regime of virtue to sustain the war effort, at the risk of destroying the material foundations of the nascent republic; or permit commercial interests the freedom they had sought from mercantilist regulation, while jeopardizing a public spirit of self-sacrifice—and disinterestedness. These questions were never far below the surface during the Revolutionary era, even when attention focused on political and constitutional issues.

The ideological resolution of this dilemma was to suggest that by being virtuous now Americans could be prosperous in the future. Temporary restraints on consumption were made more palatable by being linked to the idea of an emergent American interest: nonimportation offered the prospect of American self-sufficiency outside of the British empire. If patriotism called for denial and sacrifice, it also called forth ringing affirmations of the possibilities of material development. Ambitious plans for American expansion took shape in proposals by "enlightened societies" for the promotion of "useful arts and manufactures" for mining, spinning and many other "industrious endeavors." New manufactures together with the westward expansion of settlement and trade promised unprecedented abundance. In such visions, American justified their privations and anticipated just rewards for their virtue.[71]

The combined force of wartime emergency and republican ideology led to an Americanization of political economic thinking. The great task for revolutionary political economists was to realign interests—the conventional triad of agriculture, manufacturing, and commerce—so that they reinforced each other and sustained the new political order. As a result, and notwithstanding the wisdom of the free traders, commerce was subjected to neo-mercantilist restraints: Americans demonstrated a willingness to employ state power to promote integrated and balanced economic development. At the same time, economists emphasized the commercial character of agriculture, recognizing the leading importance of primary agricultural production for domestic and international markets in sustaining American prosperity. Their identification and equalization of interests (agriculture was described as a form of manufacturing) prompted a shift in emphasis from consumption to production in thinking about

---

[70]"Notes of Debates," 4 Oct., 20 Oct., 21 Oct. 1775, *JCC*, 3:479, 498-99, 501; Richard Morris, *Government and Labor in Early America* (New York: Columbia Univ. Press, 1946), 92-135; Wood, *Creation of the Republic*, 419-40.

[71]"A Fair Trader," writing in *Pennsylvania Packet*, 3 Dec. 1778, said that although "private vices" did not create "public benefits," the private enterprises of Americans laid the foundation for future expansion. See also Pelatiah Webster, "An Essay on Free Trade and Finance," in Webster, *Political Essays on the Nature and Operations of Money, Public Finances and Other Subjects* (Philadelphia, 1791), 25-28; East, *Business Enterprise*, ch. 9; Wood, *Creation of the Republic*, 606-12.

the new nation's economic prospects. While consumption, at least luxury consumption, had always been problematic for republicans, the focus on production helped reconcile a dynamic economy with republican values. The pursuit of interest when conceived as productive activity could be assimilated to hard work and other "Puritan" virtues. The broader conception of related, productive interests also tended to reintegrate economy and polity: unlike the colonial merchant interest, these interests were clearly located *within* the new republics, not on their peripheries.

American Revolutionaries groped toward a new conception of political economy. Colonial writers had frequently emphasized the continent's tremendous potential for economic development: "Nature has furnished us with every Thing for our Advantage, and we only want Frugality and Industry to make us Opulent."[72] By 1775 some commentators felt that America's natural endowments were sufficient to "bid defiance to the whole world."[73] America could become "a whole empire" "and it may be extended farther and farther to the utmost ends of the earth, and yet continue firmly compacted."[74] During the Revolutionary era even more Americans embraced this optimistic vision of their collective destiny.

Economy and Polity

A more positive assessment of the role of interests in American politics was possible when key assumptions about economy were recast. Most important was the shift in emphasis from consumption to production in accounts of the new nation's economic prospects. This shift implied that the pursuit of interest was no longer merely the appropriation of natural resources for private use or simply the circulation of existing wealth. Instead, production suggested the creation of new values in which the larger community ultimately shared. Wealth was both the just reward of productive enterprise and, functioning as capital, the means of creating new wealth. The new emphasis on production suggested that individual enterprise did more than satiate consumers' appetites: it could increase the wealth of America and the world. The traditional critique of luxury, embedded in an economy of consumption, made little sense from this new perspective.

Visions of the new nation's productive potential figured significantly in the political and constitutional debates of the 1780s. The problems of demobilization, interstate jealousies, and the disruption of traditional trading patterns presented formidable obstacles to economic recovery after the war. But the ebullient celebration of their country's future prosperity inspired hopeful

[72]"John Trusty," *New-York Weekly Journal,* 22 Apr. 1734.
[73]"A Speech Delivered in Carpenter's Hall," 16 Mar. 1775, *Pennsylvania Evening Post,* 13 Apr. 1775.
[74]"Crispin," *Essex Gazette,* 14 Jan. 1772; "A Plan to perpetuate the union," *Virginia Gazette* (Purdie & Dixon), 29 Apr. 1773.

Americans to look beyond these temporary troubles. A growing number of commentators insisted that there was little to fear form the vicissitudes of commercial enterprise, for it returned the wealth that made civilized society possible. As William Barton wrote in 1786, "A CIVILIZED nation, without commerce, is a solecism in politics."[75] Such logic anticipated the Utilitarian calculus: commercial prosperity produced a "happy people," capable of satisfying civilized wants.[76] With commerce defined in this way it was easier to conceive of a productive domestic economy of imperial proportions.

Proponents of commercial development recognized that their view of wealth and interest defied conventional republican wisdom, and they responded to misgivings about selfishness and luxury by attacking the fundamental premises of the republican model. Virtue, defined as the negation of self-interest in behalf of the public good, may have been essential to the survival of primitive agricultural communities before the dawning age of reason and commerce. But, Barton explained, "the wants, fears, nay the very nature of man, necessarily constitute him a social animal"; the development of commerce was an expression of this social nature. Political economists like Barton proposed to substitute a scheme of progressive historical development for the republicans' cycles of growth and decay. Thus, while republican theorists privileged past over present by idealizing a golden age when material conditions best supported a virtuous—and static—citizenry, the new economists looked forward to an increasingly bountiful future premised on the pursuit of private interests.

Americans could only fulfill their national destiny, David Daggett insisted in a debate at Yale College on sumptuary legislation, by "acting in that character in which the God of nature had placed us" and "divesting ourselves of our contracted ideas in politics." Because of the new nation's advanced stage of development, "we must be a . . . luxurious people":

> And as soon as you can cause us to exchange our refinement for barbarity, our learning for ignorance, and our liberty for servitude, then may we see parsimony take the place of luxury, and I may add too misery and wretchedness triumphing over happiness.[77]

Commercial enterprise was directly linked with historical progress. Conversely, servitude and poverty were associated with the absence of "wants" in a

---

[75]"An American" [William Barton], *The True Interest of the United States, and Particularly of Pennsylvania* (Philadelphia, 1786), 1.

[76]Item dated Worcester, 17 Nov. 1785, *New-Jersey Gazette* (Trenton), 28 Nov. 1785. See the discussion in J. R. Pole, *The Gift of Government* (Athens: Univ. of Georgia Press, 1983), 32-40, 146-48.

[77]David Daggett, Debate over Sumptuary Laws by M. A. Candidates at Yale, 13 Sept. 1786, *New-Haven Gazette and Connecticut Magazine*, 12 Oct. 1786. See the discussions in Michael Lienesch, "Development: The Economics of Expansion," a chapter in his forthcoming book, and Ronald Meek, *Social Science and the Ignoble Savage* (Cambridge, Eng. Cambridge Univ. Press, 1976).

primitive, precommercial economy. Daggett thus discovered a progressive historical role—and a moral rationale—for consumption patterns that republican moralists had identified with corruption and decay and earlier commercial theorists had connected with particular interests, narrowly conceived.

The political economists began their historical accounts with a dark age of natural barbarism, not the golden age favored by republican theorists. Though the earliest men were unrestrained by society, they did not enjoy true "liberty." Lacking objects toward which to direct and develop their will, "savages" were left enslaved by their animal natures. "Industry results from our wants," "Spectator" wrote in the *New-Haven Gazette*: "the savages will inform us that their indolence and poverty are the consequence of their having no other wants but the want of taste and a knowledge of the comforts and conveniences of civil society." But in a higher stage, "taste, refinement & extravagance" produced the "many elegant improvements" which made civilized Americans "so happy" and "so wealthy" and "distinguish[ed] us from savages."[78]

A century earlier, observers noted that "exhorbitant Appetites" were a source of trade which introduced new articles of consumption and, in turn, advanced the national economic welfare. By the 1780s "luxury" or "elegance" had become the attributes of a civilized society, the palpable evidence of progressive movement toward a higher stage of historical development. Liberty was as much the product of civilized society as the "wants" it created and satisfied; it was not the legacy of a more virtuous, bygone age. William Vans Murray argued in the *American Museum* that the real meaning of liberty only became clear with the rise of commercial civilization. "The rights and characteristics, which develope with cultivation, are possibly to be enjoyed in that state only of social maturity, from which a sense of them springs." Early modern theorists had generalized from primitive, precommercial conditions. But, wrote Murray, it was a "romantic . . . fiction" to believe that luxury and liberty were incompatible: "luxury, in a correspondent stage of his improvement" was as "natural" to civilized men "as that rudeness or simplicity, supposed concomitant with virtue, from which he emerges."[79]

The argument for luxury justified the continuing revolution in taste and consumption in America. The economists' idea of historical progress made luxury safe for republican society by dissociating it from the indolence and sloth they said were characteristic of primitive societies. Instead, "taste" and "refinement" spurred industry and improvement: a society of civilized consumers was necessarily a society of industrious producers.

---

[78]"Spectator," *New-Haven Gazette*, 3 Mar. 1785.
[79]William Vans Murray, "Political sketches," dated Middle Temple, Apr. 1787 (written 1784-85), *American Museum*, 2 (Sept. 1787), 237, 234, 233. For a striking contrast see John Locke's separation of a "golden age" from an era of "ambition" and "fancy" (and money), "Second Treatise," pars. 110-11.

The inequalities in wealth that would surely result from all this enterprise posed a more serious dilemma for proponents of commercial expansion. Republican theorists insisted that a broadly equal distribution of property was essential to the survival of republican institutions: a free, virtuous citizenry had to enjoy a substantial degree of economic independence. One solution was simply to deny that there was any connection between economic interests and political power "in a genuine republic": "Americanus" claimed that "all good men in private stations, are on an equality, whatever may be the disparity in their fortunes."[80] Constitutional developments in revolutionary America gave such arguments a certain plausibility: the gradual erosion of property tests for voting and office-holding promised to extricate private and public realms from their corrupting embrace. Noah Webster took the argument a further, crucial step, suggesting that the nature of property in a free society precluded the oppression of the propertyless. He conceded that unequal landholding in a regime where titles were secured to specific families or classes was incompatible with republicanism. But this was not true of "the very great inequality of property" created by commerce; because "this inequality is *revolving from person to person* and entitles the possessor to no pre-eminence in legislation, it is not dangerous to the liberties of the rest of the state."[81]

The movement to liberate politics from property-holding—one of the great achievements of American constitutionalists—made republican warnings about the dangers of economic inequality seem less compelling. Under competitive market conditions, and without the artificial support of government power, the pursuit of interest by private individuals or groups by definition would be either rational, and therefore beneficial to the larger community, or self-defeating. Further, the mobility of property and property-holders meant that interests were not fixed so long as there were no obstacles to the free circulation of wealth throughout the community. Finally, the economists argued, the social utility of property freely and productively deployed made traditional anxieties about the self-perpetuating power of the propertied classes obsolete.

Yet if the political economists depended on a "spirit of enterprize" to promote the rising glory of America, it did not follow that government had no role to play.[82] After all, the point of the economists' various, related efforts was to persuade the states and particularly Congress to formulate effective policy

---

[80]"Americanus" [William Barton?], "On American Manufactures," *Columbian Magazine*, 1 (Sept. 1786), 28.

[81]Noah Webster, Jr., *Sketches of American Policy* (Hartford, 1785), 18, our emphasis. For an earlier argument that the pursuit of commercial interests would tend to redistribute wealth, which in turn would have a salutary effect on political participation, see Sir James Steuart, *Inquiry into the Principles of Political Economy*, ed. A. S. Skinner, 2 vols. (Chicago: Univ. of Chicago Press, 1966; orig. pub., London, 1767), 1:215-17, 278-79.

[82]Introductory remarks to [David Humphreys], "The Happiness of America," *Columbian Magazine*, 1 (Oct. 1786), 67.

responses to the postwar depression. Merchants, manufacturers, and commercial farmers saw their problems in roughly similar terms. Promoters of American commerce, for instance, bemoaned the absence of a coherent national policy, predicting that the new nation would be drawn back into Britain's orbit. "While we have no national system of commerce," "Common Sense" wrote in 1783, "the British will govern our trade by their own laws and proclamations as they please."[83] American trade could not prosper until American traders met their counterparts on equal terms. As the merchants of Philadelphia complained:

> we are at this time under the effects of European systems, which, abridging us of the most beneficial parts of the commerce we had with them, ungenerously invite us to those only, which have a tendency to impoverish and weaken our country.[84]

Manufacturers also argued that British neo-colonialism jeopardized not only their interests but the new nation's "independence" as well. "If we are 'too young' for manufactures, we are too young for our independence," a New York writer insisted.[85] American independence was also vulnerable in the West where Britain and Spain stood ready to exploit Congress's failure to develop the national domain in an orderly and systematic fashion.

The reformers' prescriptions for these and other problems were neo-mercantilist: enterprise could cement the union and redeem nature's promise of boundless prosperity *if* interests were properly protected, promoted, and harmonized.[86] "Independence" implied an interdependence of interests throughout the union as well as national "respectability" and power at home and abroad. Some reformers promoted integrated, intersectional economic development so that Americans could avoid corrupting connections with Europe and "make a world within themselves."[87] Others wanted to strengthen the

---

[83]"Common Sense," dated New York, 2 Dec. 1783, *Virginia Gazette* (Richmond), 3 Jan. 1784. This essay was a response to Lord Sheffield's contemptuous treatment of congressional policy in his *Observations on Commerce*.

[84]"Memorial of Committee of Merchants and Traders of Philadelphia to the Pennsylvania Assembly," 6 Apr. 1785, *Virginia Journal* (Alexandria), 16 June 1785.

[85]Item dated New-York, 4 Nov. 1785, *Virginia Journal*, 17 Nov. 1785. See also "Observator," no. III, *New-Haven Gazette*, 27 Oct. 1785.

[86]See the discussion in Nicholas G. Onuf and Peter S. Onuf, "American Constitutionalism and a Liberal World Order," paper delivered at Organization of American Historians, Minneapolis, Minnesota, April 1985. On American foreign policy in the founding era see James H. Hutson, *John Adams and the Diplomacy of the American Revolution* (Lexington: Univ. of Kentucky Press, 1980), and Gerald Stourzh, *Benjamin Franklin and American Foreign Policy*, 2nd ed. (Chicago: Univ. of Chicago Press, 1969).

[87]Richard Price, *Observations on the Importance of the American Revolution*, 2nd ed. (London, 1785), rpt. in Bernard Peach, ed., *Richard Price and the Ethical Foundations of the American Revolution* (Durham, N.C.: Duke Univ. Press, 1979), 210. See also item dated Philadelphia, 18 Aug. 1787, *Virginia Gazette and Winchester Advertiser*, 29 Aug. 1787, describing "foreign commerce" as "the avenue of foreign vices": but trade among the states "will destroy neither the lives nor morals of our citizens, nor check population. It will moreover help to bind the States together."

national economy so that American merchants could establish advantageous trade links abroad. But the differences between isolationists and internationalists were more apparent than real. Whether America became independent of the world or a part of a "system" of world trade "founded in justice and reciprocity of interest," the new nation had to exploit its productive potential.[88]

The bounties of nature, which the pseudonymous "Cato" called "the basis of the glorious edifice," suggested a new conception of "union." Simply, America was the arena for unprecedented economic development. While images of this potential emphasized the "internal riches" to be drawn from the undeveloped West and the advantages of "an immensely rich and extensive continent," the idea of "natural" union, grounded in reciprocal interest, was broadly appealing.[89] "Lycurgus" celebrated the "grandeur and magnificence" of the continent; "the empire of the United States" was situated in the "most fertile and flourishing" region, affording "a prospect of wealth and commerce which future ages alone can realize."[90] Enterprising settlers from all parts of the union would move into the inland empire where "the invigorating breath of industry" would "animate . . . all the regenerating powers of nature."[91] The great wealth thus produced would flow back through long-settled regions, promoting both domestic commerce and manufactures and a favorable balance of trade abroad.[92]

According to reformers, America's economic problems lay not in a conflict of interests but in the failure of policies to secure interests. Development theorists had begun to overcome the widespread perception that the interests of different classes and sections were inevitably opposed, an old view which the political struggles of the postwar period amply supported. Reversing its prewar tendency to promote a narrower conception of interest, the New York Chamber of Commerce complained in 1785 that "landholder and merchant" had been "seduced into a false idea that their real interests are different."[93] Self-serving as such appeals might have been—especially in these years of state and sectional jealousy—their rhetoric pointed toward new conceptions of union. The old dichotomy between merchants and the landed interests was beginning to give way to an awareness that an array of domestic producers in myriad economic pursuits contributed to the well-being of the community. The vast, anticipated

[88]Ezra Stiles, *The United States Elevated to Glory and Honour*, 2nd ed. (Worcester, 1785), 49-50.

[89]"Candidus," *London Evening Post*, n.d. given, rpt. in *Pennsylvania Gazette*, 21 July 1784; "COLLECTIVE OBSERVATIONS" (on the United States) dated New York, 1 June 1786, *Connecticut Courant* (Hartford), 5 June 1786. For further discussion of the development theme see Peter S. Onuf, "Liberty, Union, and Development: Visions of the West in the 1780s," *WMQ*, 43 (forthcoming). On the importance of "nature" and "natural rights" arguments for American expansionism see Albert K. Weinberg, *Manifest Destiny: A Study of Nationalist Expansionism in American History* (Baltimore: Johns Hopkins Univ. Press, 1935), esp. ch. 1.

[90]"Lycurgus," no. 1, *New-Haven Gazette and Connecticut Magazine*, 16 Feb. 1786; rpt. in *Connecticut Courant*, 27 Feb. 1786, and *Maryland Gazette*, 24 Mar. 1786.

[91]Item dated New-York, 20 July 1786, *Freeman's Journal*, 26 July 1786.

[92]Item dated Worcester, Mass., 17 Nov. 1785, *New-Jersey Gazette*, 28 Nov. 1785.

[93]New York Chamber of Commerce, Circular to the States, 30 Sept. 1785; ibid., 21 Nov. 1785.

expansion of productive activity and wealth was depicted as a grand cooperative enterprise. Because all producers needed markets for their goods, they had an "interest" in the wealth and welfare of potential customers. Promoters of development saw that interests were varied and interdependent. In their view, the union was a continental marketplace, a natural regime of free exchange which should not be obstructed by artificial state distinctions.

Even before the Revolution many Americans recognized the potential for productive enterprise in such areas as mining, refining, and textiles. The failure to establish profitable manufactures was most often attributed not to capital shortages or high labor costs, but to arbitrary British prohibitions. Now that Americans controlled their own destiny, formulation of coherent national economic policy promised to unlock the vast natural resources of the continent. Thus, economic developers who came forward in the early 1780s shared the common premise that there was a gap between America's natural endowments and the actual, disappointing performance of the economy. One day, a New Jersey writer predicted, Americans will look back "with astonishment at the trivial causes which have impeded their progress."[94] A Marylander added, "no country perhaps abounds with raw materials of every kind, proper for manufactures, more than America; but from various causes, her inhabitants have hitherto neglected to improve the bounties of a benign Providence."[95] The Americans' failure to "improve their advantages" was unnatural, "Observator" explained in a series of essays in the *New-Haven Gazette*. The defective structure of American politics under the Articles of Confederation fractured a natural harmony of interests and prevented the systematic exploitation of nature:

> Circumstanced, as we at present are, with respect to government, it would be as impracticable to confine the views of the different states, or unite them in any one consistent plan of measures, as it would to unite all the streams of water on the continent, and confine them in one channel. The consequence of this is, our public, political interests, and with them individual interests (for they will stand or fall together) cannot be promoted, but must be neglected, and in the end inevitably ruined.[96]

Significantly, "Observator" aligned "nature" with the interests of individuals and of the American people generally against artifical state distinctions that precluded "consistent" (continental) measures. Interest was natural, and those who followed its lead were true patriots: according to "Cato," another contributor to the *Gazette*, "In a people so enlightened as ours, advantages

---

[94]Item dated Trenton, ibid. 24 July 1786.
[95]Item in *Maryland Gazette*, 17 Apr. 1787
[96]"Observator," no. I, *New-Haven Gazette*, 25 Aug. 1785.

should seem to call forcibly for improvement, and to inspire a generous ambition." Unfortunately, America's natural advantages remained "unoperative, since we refuse to enjoy or direct them to their true and capital purposes." Americans were too influenced by "partial and incomplete notions of civil and political liberty," and were thus unwilling to accord necessary powers to the national government.[97]

A committee of Boston traders and manufacturers articulated the developers' conception of union in a letter to their counterparts in New Haven:

> The States are so extensive in their boundary, so various in their climate, and so connected in their national interest, that if a plan could be adopted throughout the confederaton for the exchange of the produce and manufactures of each state, we conceive it would serve to cement a general union, and prove a means to promote the interest of the whole.[98]

Defects in the organization of national politics and an exaggerated solicitude for state sovereignty thwarted both private interests and the public good. To the extent that states pursued interests of their own, thus directing the interests of their citizens toward competition and conflict with neighboring states, "the dissolution of all continental connections" was sure to follow. The necessary tendency of states' interest, Noah Webster wrote, was "to enlarge their own bounds, and augment their wealth and respectability at each other's expence." The result was the "jealousy, ill-will and reproaches" characteristic of competing consumers, not the laudable ambition for both private and public wealth and glory that the natural bounties of the continent should have called forth.[99]

Proponents of national constitutional reform juxtaposed the "real" interests of individual Americans and the natural destiny of the continent for economic development with the partial and artificial interests of state governments squabbling over relative advantage. In 1785 a writer in the *Pennsylvania Gazette* exulted (somewhat prematurely) in what he saw as an emerging consensus for investing Congress with extensive commercial powers, the necessary, "radical cure" for the nation's "distresses." "Every man in America," he wrote, "either from motives of self-interest, or the more exalted motives of patriotism and philanthropy, feels himself affected in the situation of these rising republics."[100] The suggestion that patriotism and self-interest were convergent, at least when confronting the problem of union, became a staple in nationalist rhetoric.

---

[97]"Cato," "To the Public," *New-Haven Gazette and Connecticut Magazine*, 25 Jan. 1787.
[98]John Gray et al., "To the Tradesmen and Manufacturers of Newhaven," dated Boston, 20 Aug. 1785, *New-Haven Gazette*, 29 Sept. 1785.
[99]Webster, *Sketches of American Policy*, 45.
[100]Item in *Pennsylvania Gazette*, 29 June 1785.

How could nationalists be so confident that the pursuit of interest would advance the common good? First they insisted on the ultimately harmonious character of private interests. As Tench Coxe put it, "agriculture appears to be the spring of our commerce, and the parent of our manufactures." This interrelatedness meant that advances in one sector would promote the fortunes of the others: the growth of manufactures "will improve our agriculture . . . accelerate the improvement of our internal navigation, and bring into action the dormant powers of nature and the elements."[101] Conversely, setbacks in one sector would reverberate throughout the economy. "Annihilate commerce," a New Jersey writer warned, "and you effectually ruin the landed interest by sinking the value of lands."[102]

The circulation of goods created new wealth for enterprising individuals who exploited commercial opportunities at home and abroad. The pursuit of profit dissolved conventional distinctions among interests. In development rhetoric, the effort to establish the identity of interests was reflected in references to land as "our great staple" and to agriculture as "our principal manufacture": the business of all enterprising Americans was essentially the same.[103] The crucial distinction was rather between the world of the marketplace—where interests converged—and the savage, barbarian world beyond. "All the world is becoming commercial," Thomas Jefferson concluded. Not only were "Our citizens" busily pursuing profitable opportunities, but they "have had too full a taste of the comforts by the arts and manufactures to be debarred the use of them."[104]

Visions of the continent's great productive potential best captured the sense that private enterprises served the public good. If the American people were the advance guard of commercial civilization, the American continent invited them to "industry, application, and improvement." Richard Henry Lee wrote that the new nation "abound[ed] with all those primary and essential materials for human industry to work upon, in order to produce the comfort and happiness of

---

[101]T[ench] C[oxe], "An Enquiry into the Principles on which a Commercial System for the United States should be founded," *American Museum*, 1 (June 1787), 499, and idem, "An address to an assembly of the friends of American manufactures," Philadelphia, 9 Aug. 1787, ibid., 2 (September 1787), 255. See also New York [City] Chamber of Commerce, *Gentlemen, The interest of the landholder. . . .* (Broadside, New York, 1785) on the importance of "the union of the farmer, the merchant and mechanic."

[102]"One of the People," *New-Jersey Gazette*, 20 Sept. 1784. The same point was made by "Farmer," "To the Inhabitants of Maryland," 12 Feb. 1786, *Maryland Journal*, 17 Feb. 1786.

[103][Barton], *The True Interest of the United States, and Particularly of Pennsylvania* (Philadelphia, 1786), 11; "Americanus" [Barton?], "On American Manufactures," *Columbian Magazine*, 1 (Sept. 1786), 27-28.

[104]Jefferson to Washington, 15 Mar. 1784, in Julian P. Boyd, ed., *The Papers of Thomas Jefferson*, 21 vols. to date (Princeton: Princeton Univ. Press, 1950-), 7:26. A western North Carolinian agreed: "We have lived in maritime countries, and have tasted the benefits of commerce." Extract of a letter from Davidson Co., North Carolina, 20 Oct. 1786, *Virginia Journal*, 15 Feb. 1787.

mankind.''[105] Nature also provided access to its bounty. "Farmer," a proponent of efforts to extend the navigability of the Potomac, asserted that the United States was "accomodated by nature in a most extraordinary manner for an easy, general and intimate communication." It was incumbent on an enterprising people to use—and improve—these natural highways.[106] One "modern writer" was convinced that "No country under the sun" was "better calculated for commerce than America."[107]

In 1785, Independence Day orator John Gardiner described the continent's promise—and Americans' responsibility to it:

> If we make a right use of our natural advantages we soon must be a truly great and happy people. When we consider the vastness of our country, the variety of her soil and climate, the immense extent of her sea-coast, and of the inland navigation by the lakes and rivers, we find a *world within ourselves*, sufficient to produce whatever can contribute to the necessities and even the superfluities of life.[108]

Gardiner's "if" was crucial: "right use" required both the liberation of individuals to pursue their interests as producers and consumers and the creation of a national constitutional regime that would bring all these interests to "one focus."

Others noted the "imbecilities" of state and national governments which impeded development of America's productive potential. Federalists argued that union was "natural" and that the interests of individuals, classes, and sections would be harmonious—if only artificial, political obstacles were removed. A New York writer best captured this benign conception of interest, as the guarantor of America's future prosperity and power. "It will be evident" to the delegates to the Annapolis Convention, if they lay "aside all local attachments, and every private sinister view"

> that the natural produce and situation of each state is such, that if they can bring them, as it were, to one focus, where they may unite and act together, it must give great energy to the commerce of these states. No part of Europe has so many resources within themselves, or so calculated to answer every kind of commerce, as the United States of America.[109]

In these images of a productive landscape conventional distinctions among

[105]Richard Henry Lee to John Adams, 28 May 1785, in Edmund Cody Burnett, ed., *Letters of the Members of the Continental Congress*, 8 vols. (Washington, D.C.: The Carnegie Institute of Washington, 1921-36), 8:128.

[106]"Farmer," "To the Inhabitants of Potomomack River," dated 10 Aug. 1784, *Virginia Journal*, 18 Aug. 1784.

[107]Item dated New-York, 20 July 1786, *Freeman's Journal*, 26 July 1786.

[108]Gardiner, *An Oration, Delivered July 4, 1785*. . . . [in Boston] (Boston, 1785), 35.

[109]Item dated New York, 29 Aug. 1786, *New-Jersey Gazette*, 11 Sept. 1786.

"interests" gave way to an inclusive notion of enterprise. Conflicts over commerce and territory among the states could lead to the brutal anarchy of a "state of nature" in the new world. Rather than man mastering nature, according to the developers' plans, nature would then master man—surely a reversal of the "natural" order of things. Enterprise meant industrious activity directed toward *future* rewards. Looking west, then, Americans could conceive of forward progress in time, as well as space. Economic development in turn provided the key to both expansion and consolidation: a growing union would be drawn closer together through the quickening pace of market exchange and the spread of internal improvements. Yet everything hinged on strengthening the union, *"the basis of our grandeur and power."*[110] Only then, "Examiner" wrote in the *Virginia Journal*, would "the honest citizen be relieved and protected; industry . . . be encouraged and commerce . . . flourish."[111]

A Union of Interests

The insubstantiality of the union was a favorite theme of writers who promoted the new political economy. "In time of war we were bound together by fear," a New Yorker wrote. But now "the breath of jealousy has blown the cobweb of our confederacy asunder."[112] In the *Connecticut Magazine* "Lycurgus" made great fun of

> that supposed union which seems to be contained in our Articles of Confederation. It is not a union of sentiment;—it is not a union of interest;—it is not a union to be seen—or felt—or in any manner perceived.

Instead, he concluded, "it is a *Political* union," meaning, by his definition, "imperceptible or invisible."[113]

The structure of national politics under the Confederation encouraged state leaders to see membership in the union as instrumental and contingent.

---

[110]New York Chamber of Commerce, "Circular to the States," 30 Sept. 1785, *New-Jersey Gazette*, 21 Nov. 1785. Drew McCoy emphasizes the extent to which Jeffersonians believed that expansion across space could suspend the effects of historical development. McCoy, *The Elusive Republic*, passim. For another view, see Andrew R.L. Cayton, "Planning the Republic: The Federalists and Internal Improvements on the Old Northwest," paper delivered at Organization of American Historians, Minneapolis, Minnesota, April 1985, and Onuf, *Liberty, Union, and Development*."

[111]"Examiner," no. 1, *Virginia Journal*, 8 Feb. 1787.

[112]Item dated New York, 23 Apr. 1787, rpt. from *Massachusetts Sentinel* (Boston) in *Carlisle Gazette* (Pennsylvania), 9 May 1787.

[113]"Lycurgus," no. 2, *New-Haven Gazette and Connecticut Magazine*, 23 Feb. 1786. On the politics of the Confederation period see Jack N. Rakove, *The Beginnings of National Politics: An Interpretive History of the Continental Congress* (New York: Alfred A. Knopf, Inc., 1979), and Peter S. Onuf, *The Origins of the Federal Republic: Jurisdictional Controversies in the United States, 1775-1787* (Philadelphia: Univ. of Pennsylvania Press, 1983).

Federalists pointed out that sanctions all flowed one way. The states held Congress on leading strings: they could and did ignore congressional calls for money; they pursued their own land and commercial policies regardless of the other states. State governments obstructed and distorted the natural harmony of interests and the Confederation Congress was ill-equipped to promote national economic development. The Articles perpetuated the provisional, "imbecilic" character of American national politics by preserving residual powers in the states and by giving each state an equal vote in Congress. Any one state had the right to veto important, constitutional changes in the Confederation. Finally, by keeping Congress at one remove from the people—Congressmen were elected by state legislatures—the Confederation government could neither claim popular allegiance nor offer effective protection and support to national interests. Though never invoked, the states' ultimate sanction was well understood: they could withdraw from the union altogether. In light of such threats, Congress might easily be pressured into favoring a particular state's or section's interests. Under the Articles, the United States was not a true polity.

If the weakness of Congress encouraged state leaders to define and pursue their own interests, these centrifugal forces also helped define the agenda for national politics under a more durable union. Out of the postwar conflict of interests Federalists articulated a conception of enlightened private interest which became the necessary precondition for union. Their arguments made two things clear. First, many interests transcended the partiality and selfishness of states: they were regional or even continental in scope. Even strictly local interest groups found themselves exposed to threats that could not be dealt with on the state level. Second, the existing union was woefully inadequate for either promoting or protecting particular interests—including those of the states themselves.

The Federalists failed to persuade many Americans that everyone would benefit under their new constitutional regime. But recent experience did suggest that the expansion of federal powers and the promotion of specific interests *could* be linked. In this way, at least some Americans worked toward a new conception of union. A more perfect union would permit and promote the expansive pursuit of "natural ambition" and through the celebration of interests guarantee the future wealth and power of the new empire of liberty.[114]

The crucial connection between interest and union that became the hallmark of agitation for national constitutional reform was anticipated in postwar programs for regional economic development. Virginians anxious to promote trade links with the rapidly expanding western settlements argued that the scope of commerce had to be coextensive with the expanding republican empire. According to a Virginia newspaper,

[114]Jacob E. Cooke, ed., *The Federalist Papers* (Middletown, Conn.: Wesleyan Univ. Press, 1961), nos. 84, 37, 39, 40, 48, 49, passim.

The opening of the Navigation of Potowmack is, perhaps, a Work of more political than commercial Consequence, as it will be one of the grandest Chains for preserving the federal Union[:] the Western World will have free Access to us, and we shall be one and the same People, whatever System of European Politics may be adopted.[115]

The developers' premise was that a durable union finally depended on shared interests. All other claims on westerners' loyalties were airy and insubstantial.

Pessimists, of course, could pursue the same logic to another conclusion: the impossibility of harmonizing the interests of East and West—or North and South—meant that disunion was inevitable. Yet even as intersectional controversy—for instance, over the navigation of the Mississippi—drove nationalists like James Madison to despair, sectional alignments pointed toward a more durable union. Cooperation between Virginia and Maryland in the Potomac project—both states provided subsidies—is a good case in point. These states had been the leading antagonists in the western lands controversy in which "big" states squared off against "little" states. The struggle for control of the West was a classic test of early American ideas of state sovereignty and equality, reinforcing throughout its protracted life the conventional idea that one state's gain was another's loss. But the development of the Potomac promised to enrich both states, strengthening bonds between them even while cementing the union of East and West.

Proponents of regional development saw that interests were not adequately defined or represented by existing jurisdictions. A few visionaries therefore called for a general renegotiation of state boundaries. "Yankee Doodle" wanted Connecticut to become a part of New York, and thereby "reap every advantage of the [state] impost and waste lands." "There can be no odds" against such a consolidation "but in name, and who would risk a quarrel of such magnitude"—a war of conquest against New York, the only alternative for Connecticut and other areas dependent on the port of New York—"for a name?"[116] By Yankee Doodle's reckoning, statehood was insubstantial—only a "name"—while a union of states sharing common interests would be of real, substantial value. In this way, the traditional view of states and union was turned on its head: in "Lycurgus's" terms, the union was perceptible and visible. This was a crucial step toward the new constitutional regime.

Few Americans seriously advocated an end to the states—though many would have been happy to see Rhode Island wiped off the map. But pleas for stronger ties between particular states were increasingly common. Calls for the creation of regional confederations in the months before the Philadelphia convention reflected this concern. Despairing of establishing an effective national

[115]Item dated Alexandria, *Virginia Journal and Alexandria Advertiser*, 25 Nov. 1784.
[116]"Yankee Doodle," "To the Inhabitants of Connecticut," *Connecticut Courant* (Hartford), 6 Mar. 1786.

government, proponents of stronger union looked for the next best thing in distinct sectional governments. The New England states, according to one of the best known proposals, might withdraw from the existing union and institute " a new Congress, as the Representative of the nation of New-England, and leave the rest of the Continent to pursue their own imbecile and disjointed plans."[117] Another writer—this time a southerner—proceeded to divide the United States into four republics: New England; the Middle States, beginning with New York; the South, including Virginia; and the new western states.

> This division seems to be pointed out by climate, whose effect no positive law ever can surpass.—The religion, manners, customs, exports, imports, and general interest of each being then the same, no opposition, arising from difference in these (as at present) would any longer divide their councils—unanimity would render us secure at home, and respected abroad, and promote agriculture, manufactures, and commerce.[118]

The writer's appeal to "nature"—in this case, meaning the climate—was typical in contemporary discourse. Further, proponents of separate confederacies had a clear vision of the purposes a stronger union should serve, even if they remained skeptical about the chances of establishing one for the entire continent. Perhaps, they reasoned, the good example of one more perfect, though partial union would inspire the other states to "join a confederation that may rescue them from destruction."[119]

The talk of separate confederations represented the culmination of a long-term process of defining and attempting to promote interests along sectional lines. Those who most seriously flirted with disunion had been promoters of consolidation—or "union"—on a regional scale: they were primed to throw their support behind a new constitution that promised to satisfy their demand for a "new and stronger union," on a grander scale.[120] These sectionalists-cum-nationalists provided the impulse for constitutional reform. The now-famous compromises securing their respective interests would be the great work of the Philadelphia convention.[121]

[117]Letter in *Independent Chronicle* (Boston), 15 Feb. 1787. The letter was reprinted in *Maryland Gazette*, 6 Mar. 1787.
[118]"A Hint' from the southern papers", *Independent Chronicle*, 19 Apr. 1787.
[119]Letter, ibid. 15 Feb. 1787.
[120]Ironically, sectional division came to be used as a rhetorical club to beat opponents of the Federal Constitution—and a stronger union—over the head. Madison claimed that "The opposition with some has disunion assuredly for its object; and with all for its real tendency." Patrick Henry, for instance, was said to favor a southern confederation. Though Anti-Federalists certainly did have doubts about the future of a continental republic, these accusations were vastly exaggerated. Madison to Edmund Pendleton, 21 Feb. 1788, Robert A. Rutland et al., eds., *The Papers of James Madison*, 14 vols. to date (Chicago: Univ. of Chicago Press and Charlottesville: Univ. of Virginia Press, 1962-), 10:532-33.
[121]Nathan Dane warned, "whether the plans of the Southern, Eastern, or Middle states succeed, never, in my opinion, ought to be known." Dane to Rufus King, Max Farrand, ed., *The Records of the Federal Convention of 1787*, 4 vols. (New Haven: Yale Univ. Press, 1911-37), 3:48-49.

But the new constitution was not simply the product of sectional compromises. There were positive advantages of union, some of which were suggested by the very writers who emphasized sectional distinctiveness. Thus, as a South Carolina writer urged, America's future greatness depended on intersectional harmony. A national navigation act protecting American shipping—a northern interest—would also benefit the South:

> the numbers and industry of the northern States would give security, strength and splendour to the south; and the wealth of the south . . . would then enrich ourselves, and reward the laborious inhabitants of the north, and thus would the resources of each part contribute to add to the strength and glory of the whole empire.[122]

Promoters of manufactures emphasized not only sectional interdependence but also the mutual reliance of agricultural, commercial, and manufacturing sectors. The attainment and preservation of true American independence meant integrated—intersectional—economic development. Disunion would destroy the possibility of integrated economic development on a continental scale. It would mean, wrote Edward Carrington of Virginia, that "the prospects of America will be at an end as to any degree of National importance, let her fate be what it may as to freedom or Vassalage."[123]

The alternatives—on one hand, union and national economic development; on the other, disunion and underdevelopment—were clearest when Americans looked west. Preachers, poets, and polemicists agreed that the West would be the great arena for the future glory and wealth of the entire nation. The goal of congressional western policy therefore was to create optimum conditions for the rapid development of commercial agriculture. Planners hoped to attract—and mix—settlers from all parts of the country and from all over the world. Yet the success of this policy depended on a vigorous national government that could police the national domain, protect whites and Indians from each other, and percent neighboring imperial powers from extending their influence. The price of weakness would be endemic frontier violence, foreign adventurism, retarded development and the rupture of the union.

The value of union became clearer and more substantial as it became identified with real interests—with the needs of existing interest groups seeking to shape national policy, and with a vision—or dream—of harmonizing interests and intersectional reconciliation through economic growth. The key element in the reconception of union was an assessment of the costs of disunion. Through this

---

[122]Item dated Charlestown, Mass. ("a writer of South Carolina says . . ."), 21 Feb. 1786, *Maryland Gazette*, 17 Mar. 1786.

[123]Carrington to Madison, 13 June 1787, Rutland, *Madison Papers*, 10:52-53: "An attempt to confederate upon terms materially opposed to the particular Interests would in all probability occasion a dismemberment . . ."

accounting, the purposes that union should serve were defined. Of course, union meant different things to different people. But Federalists were able to exploit rising expectations—and frustrations—in the years leading up to the Philadelphia Convention. Local and sectional interests demanded more effective central—or at least regional—government. At the same time, reformers could speak to the aspirations of individual Americans, and their dreams of self-improvement and national greatness.

Though many Americans remained skeptical during the ratification controversy, the union, so reconceived, was broadly appealing. It legitimated the private pursuit of happiness in a new world of rising expectations and apparently boundless opportunity, while addressing more traditional concerns about preserving republicanism and securing American independence. Economic development was the precondition of true independence; republican government guaranteed development.

The new idea of union was not simply clever Federalist rhetoric. It was instead the product of a protracted, often painful, process of defining what Americans hoped to get from their Revolution. This process of definition clarified the limits of existing arrangements and the costs of failing to reform them. It gave new meanings to an insubstantial idea. A union defined by interest became more specific and concrete; defined by dreams of individual and collective prosperity and happiness, it reentered the realm of the mythic, revivifying the old language of America's manifest destiny.[124*]

[124]See the interesting discussion in Mason L. Lowance, Jr., *The Language of Canaan: Metaphor and Symbol in New England from the Puritans to the Transcendentalists* (Cambridge: Harvard Univ. Press, 1980), 208-46.

*The authors wish to acknowledge the helpful comments of Michael Bellesiles of the University of California, Irvine and John Zomchick of the University of Tennessee.

Political Economy, Public Liberty, and the Formation of the Constitution

E. James Ferguson

URING the presidential campaign of 1800, the Philadelphia merchant Charles Pettit wrote a pamphlet entitled *An Impartial Review of the Rise and Progress of the Controversy between the Parties Known by the Names of the Federalists, and Republicans.* His thesis was that the current political arguments repeated those of the past and that the basic issues dividing Americans had always been the same, namely, a difference of opinion as to the legitimate limits of governmental power. He traced this issue from the resistance to Britain through the Revolution, the adoption of the Constitution, and the party battles of the 1790s. The *principles,* he said, were rooted in the British past—in struggles between Country and Court parties, between low and high church, between Whigs and Tories. No need to explain these terms, he said: "They have borne so conspicuous a part in history, especially in that of England, that you cannot mistake their Common meaning."[1]

The meaning may have been evident to Pettit's readers, but until very recently its implications would have escaped American historians, except in the realm of political ideas. There the continuities between British and American experience have always been recognized, and the current restatement of the whig interpretation of the American Revolution continues to expand and deepen that relationship. Political ideas alone, however, do not define such major events in early American history as the adoption of the Constitution and the rise of national political parties. The formation of the national government was a complex act, involving a broad constituency, and it was significant on a number of levels. Its distinctive character, in fact, was to a large extent shaped by a heavy infusion of economic factors. An analogous political-economic process affected British development, and in this context nation building in both countries followed similar lines. Recent studies have exposed some of the cardinal

Mr. Ferguson is a member of the Department of History at Queens College, City University of New York and Editor Emeritus of the Papers of Robert Morris. He is preparing a book on themes presented in this article.

[1] [Pettit], *An Impartial Review* . . . (Philadelphia, 1800), 18.

affinities,[2] but the linkages of America with the British past are more direct than has yet been supposed. The relationships display a fuller view than we have had of the total historical circumstances attending the formation of the national government of the United States.

The circumstances that concern us emerged at the end of the seventeenth century, when Britain faced problems whose solution entailed far-reaching changes in the country's institutions. One problem the government had to deal with concerned the general economy: there was a need for adequate business credit and a more abundant medium of exchange. More pressing, however, were the debts contracted during King William's War, which were so large that they could not be coped with in the ordinary way. Numerous proposals were considered as different groups advanced their interests. Land was the chief form of wealth and politically the strongest force in the kingdom; hence many schemes would have made land the basis of public and private credit. Nevertheless, Parliament in 1694 chartered the Bank of England, which was oriented toward mercantile and banking interests.[3] Two years later a "National Land Bank of Parliament" was chartered, although opposition from the ministry and the Bank of England kept it from going into operation.[4] In other respects public finance registered two innovative choices. The first was to borrow money without commitment to repay it. The outstanding feature of the British "funded debt," which distinguished it from previous debts, was that no pledge was given ever to repay the principal. The second decision was to form a partnership between government and large corporations, starting with the Bank of England but extending later to the

[2] Drew R. McCoy, *The Elusive Republic: Political Economy in Jeffersonian America* (Chapel Hill, N.C., 1980); Joyce Appleby, "The Social Origins of American Revolutionary Ideology," *Journal of American History*, LXIV (1978), 935-958; James H. Hutson, "Country, Court, and Constitution: Antifederalism and the Historians," *William and Mary Quarterly*, 3d Ser., XXXVIII (1981), 337-368.

[3] On the landed interest see G. E. Mingay, *English Landed Society in the Eighteenth Century* (London, 1963), 4-5, 11-12. On the financial precedents and the various proposals see J. Keith Horsefield, *British Monetary Experiments, 1650-1710* (Cambridge, Mass., 1960), 93-124. On the origin and growth of the funding system see E. L. Hargreaves, *The National Debt* (New York, 1966 [orig. publ. London, 1930]), 1-113; P.G.M. Dickson, *The Financial Revolution in England: A Study in the Development of Public Credit, 1688-1756* (New York, 1967), 36-50; and J.E.D. Binney, *British Public Finance and Administration, 1774-92* (Oxford, 1958), 104-106.

[4] Dennis Rubini, "Politics and the Battle for the Banks, 1688-1697," *English Historical Review*, LXXXV (1970), 693-714. In 1693 a parliamentary committee endorsed a proposal for a land bank. Horsefield, *British Monetary Experiments,* 156-179; Middleton Walker, *A Proposal for Relieving the Present Exigencies of the Nation by a Land Credit* (London, 1721), i-iii. Contemporary pamphlets cited in this article may be found in the Goldsmith's Library, University of London; the Henry E. Huntington Library, San Marino, Calif.; and the Kress Library, Harvard University, Cambridge, Mass. The pamphlets often lack pagination.

South Sea Company and the East India Company, which became the financial agents of the government. Loans were floated through these corporations, and they also took responsibility for servicing the debt, that is, for paying the interest in return for the commitment to them of specific tax revenues.[5] Meanwhile, the Bank of England contributed to the solution of general economic problems. It was the chief depository of government funds; it lent money to private business; and its notes provided a medium of exchange.

Britain's funded debt became the marvel of the age, a "standing miracle in politics, which at once astonishes and over-awes the states of Europe."[6] The ability to borrow, limited only by having to pay interest, was the crucial factor in Britain's victories in eighteenth-century wars. Funding also contributed to internal political stability: an economic interest of citizens in the "funds" generated loyalty to the regime established by the Revolution of 1689.[7] These benefits, however, came at a high price. The debt rose from £12,700,000 in 1702 to over £132,000,000 in 1763,[8] and taxes were heavy. According to a recent estimate, per capita taxes in Britain, stated in constant values, were twice those in contemporary France and consumed a larger proportion of the value of total commodity output.[9]

Although unevenly assessed in different areas, land taxes hit agriculture hard. Consumption and therefore the prices of farm products were held down until the 1740s by the stability of the British population. Advanced methods raised productivity but required greater investment and more operating capital. The land tax therefore contributed to the decline of the yeomanry and lesser gentry during the first half of the century. By 1800, three-fourths of England's farms were tilled by tenants, the yeoman farmer was virtually extinct, and the lesser gentry had become a depressed class

[5] Some loans were floated in the 1740s and 1750s independently of the three companies (Hargreaves, *National Debt*, 53, 58-59).

[6] Quoted from a pamphlet by Thomas Mortimer (1769) in Dickson, *Financial Revolution*, 16.

[7] *Ibid.*, 9-11, 16-19. On the creation of economic interest see Isaac Kramnick, *Bolingbroke and His Circle: The Politics of Nostalgia in the Age of Walpole* (Cambridge, Mass., 1968), 40, and Bolingbroke's comment in "A Dissertation on Parties," in David Mallett, ed., *The Works of the Late Right Honorable Henry St. John, Lord Viscount Bolingbroke* (London, 1777), II, 273-274. On the importance of funding a war see Dickson, *Financial Revolution*, 9-10, and Binney, *British Public Finance*, 106. On the interaction between war and economic development see Charles Wilson, *England's Apprenticeship, 1603-1763* (New York, 1965), 313.

[8] Hargreaves, *National Debt*, 65, 91. Annual interest rose in the same period from £1,200,000 to £5,000,000. See Binney, *British Public Finance*, 106, and Dickson, *Financial Revolution*, 16.

[9] The estimate is given by Peter Matthias and Patrick O'Brien, "The Social and Economic Burden of Tax Revenue Collected for the Central Government, Britain and France, 1715-1785" (unpubl. paper, Istituto Internazionale di Storia Economica "Francesco Datini," Prato, Italy, 1976).

whose social positions and political and administrative responsibilities exceeded their incomes.[10] Mercantile and financial elements, on the other hand, escaped heavy taxation and benefited from Britain's economic progress. They were exempted from taxation on their holdings of the government debt. It appears that the funding system stimulated commerce and played a fundamental role in a "financial revolution" that set the stage for the Industrial Revolution. The mass of negotiable securities created by the debt provided a huge, secure, liquid, and profitable field for long- and short-term investment of capital that would otherwise have been idle or forced into competitive investment in land. Funding, as David Hume observed, gave merchants a kind of money that constantly increased in their hands by interest accumulation, enabling them to trade upon a smaller margin of profit and with a greater volume of business. The securities themselves were a national medium of exchange and in addition backed the note issues of the Bank of England and of a host of private banks. An organized stock market sprang into existence.[11]

Many Britons regarded these developments not as a cause for rejoicing but as evidence of national decline.[12] Such an attitude was rooted in the social theory of the Enlightenment that tied together economics and internalized morality. Social organization was perceived to have progressed from primitive hunting to pasturage to agriculture and ultimately to commerce and manufactures, with each stage attended by appropriate personal and social behavior. The unhampered movement of society into the later stages produced advantages otherwise unobtainable but also risked the abasement of many human values. Criticism of the funding system therefore emanated from people of different social ranks and political affiliations, including Whigs, Tories, landed noblemen, country gentlemen, small farmers, and London merchants. The attack was pressed on many levels.[13] It was charged that funding diverted investment from

[10] Mingay, *English Landed Society*, 15, 84. See also *ibid.*, 50-52, 80-89, 94-97, and Kramnick, *Bolingbroke*, 56-60. On the land tax and its incidence see W. R. Ward, *The English Land Tax in the Eighteenth Century* (London, 1953), 2-4, 6-10, 17-23.

[11] David Hume, *Writings on Economics*, ed. Eugene Rotwein (Madison, Wis., 1955), 93-94. See also Dickson, *Financial Revolution*, 11-13; Kramnick, *Bolingbroke*, 39-55; and A. L. Morton, *A People's History of England* (London, 1938), 290.

[12] The fullest exposition of this point is McCoy, *Elusive Republic*, 5-61. See also Hutson, "Country, Court, and Constitution," *WMQ*, 3d Ser., XXXVIII (1981), 357-368.

[13] Bernard Bailyn enlarges on the breadth and variety of this criticism, but in the context of British politics and constitutional disputes (*The Ideological Origins of the American Revolution* [Cambridge, Mass., 1967], 32-43). Kramnick devotes a chapter to examining the scope of the opposition. Commenting on the "ambivalence" of the Commonwealthmen, he writes: "In the thought of these Commonwealthmen or 'honest Whigs,' much of what appears to be opposed to the prevailing thought and mores of the period is really a substantial social and political nostalgia. A great deal of the thought of the Commonwealthmen is tied to gentry discontent and reflects a longing for a return to pre-Revolutionary England"

production into speculation, burdened industry with taxation, and elevated domestic prices to the point where Britain could not compete in international trade. Allegedly, the rentiers who held most of the debt were mere consumers; hence a large part of national income flowed into nonproductive uses, encouraging luxury and extravagance. Foreign investment in the debt drew money out of the country in interest payments. The government was less able to deal with emergencies because its tax resources were previously allocated.[14]

Defenders of the system countered by praising the effects and extenuating the evils of social and economic change. The funded debt was a national blessing. It afforded productive employment for private capital. Public securities and bank notes supplied the circulating medium indispensable to an advanced economy, and the availability of credit stimulated economic growth. Admittedly money was not real wealth, but the "trite maxim, that money makes money," was nevertheless literally true. Finally, the "magic of public credit" was a pillar of strength in war, and in domestic affairs an advantage to the nation.[15]

The social consequences of the financial system aroused more emotion. Speculation in securities was not a new phenomenon, but its institutionalization spawned a class of professional dealers whose activities offended

---

(*Bolingbroke*, 236-261, quotation on p. 236). See also H. Trevor Colbourn, *The Lamp of Experience: Whig History and the Intellectual Origins of the American Revolution* (Chapel Hill, N.C., 1965), 50-51.

[14] These themes will be examined below, but see Dickson, *Financial Revolution*, 18-34; Hargreaves, *National Debt*, 76-77, 81; and John Carswell, *From Revolution to Revolution: England 1688-1776* (London, 1973), 3. A contemporary pamphlet that covers most of the arguments is *Essays. I. On the Public Debt. II. On Paper Money, Banking & C. III. On Frugality* (London, 1755). Numerous pamphlets, especially those of Sir Humphrey Mackworth, show that efforts were made before 1721 in Parliament to introduce methods like those in the colonies by issuing paper money and establishing land banks. The efforts obviously had no success. See his *A Proposal for Paying Off the Publick Debts by the Appropriated Funds, without Raising any Taxes upon Land, Malt, or Other Things* ... (London, 1720). See also [Anonymous], *An Essay for Establishing a New Parliament Money* ... (London, 1720).

[15] The quotations are from [P. Murray], *Thoughts on Money Circulation, and Paper Currency* (Edinburgh, 1758), and a contemporary pamphlet cited in Hargreaves, *National Debt*, 83-85. Among contemporary writings that range over these points are *Some Consideration on Publick Credit and the Nature of Its Circulation in the Funds. Occasioned by a Bill Now Depending in the House to Prevent the Pernicious Practice of Stock Jobbing* (London, 1733), and *An Essay on the Sinking Fund*, 2d ed. (London, 1737). For a middle position, critical of political corruption and financial mismanagement but positive toward the funding program, see [William Pulteney], *Some Considerations on the National Debts, the Sinking Fund, and the State of Public Credit* ... (London, 1729), and *An Enquiry into the Conduct of Our Domestick Affairs from the Year 1721 to the Present Time* (London, 1734). See also Kramnick, *Bolingbroke*, 52-53, and Hargreaves, *National Debt*, 58-59, 73-74, 79-81, 83-85, 88-90.

common morality. A few writers dared to extenuate the evils of stockjob-bing,[16] but the "infamous Practice" was generally execrated "as a Business founded upon nothing that is solid, rational, or honest, but merely upon Artifice, Trick, and Catch." Stock dealers were denounced as vicious cheats who spread false rumors and ensnared the innocent. They symbol-ized what was widely believed to be the abasement of human values to money and the displacement of honest labor by fraud. "The more Methods there are in a State for acquiring Riches without Industry or Merit," one writer charged, "the less there will be of either in that state." It was considered self-evident that getting rich by "sudden and extraordi-nary methods" rather than by honest industry must be ruinous to the public. Twice, in 1697 and 1734, Parliament enacted legislation to limit the numbers and curb the activities of stockjobbers. The rapid accumula-tion of wealth by speculative means was widely believed to have corrupted general morality and raised up a rootless paper aristocracy in place of the natural leaders of the society.[17]

Involved in the lamented alterations of class status were the property losses of the small landed gentry. Although their misfortunes were sometimes imputed to their own extravagance, it was widely asserted that the yeomanry and lesser gentlemen of the countryside were being driven to the wall by taxation.[18] In a pamphlet published in 1755 one writer said that over the preceding sixty years nine-tenths of the land of England had changed hands as owners were forced to sell. When the art of funding was introduced, he continued, the common talk was that the people would be undone by it. The outcome proved the accuracy of that prediction: the people were being sacrificed to the pecuniary interest of 20,000 stock-holders. Let no one believe, he said, that they would stand for this forever.[19]

[16] Even preachers were said to have turned to speculating, a fact exemplifying a change of manners. *A Letter to a Conscientious Man; Concerning the Use and Abuse of Riches; and the Right and Wrong Ways of Acquiring Them* . . . (London, 1720). See *Some Considerations on Publick Credit and the Nature of Its Circulation.*

[17] The quotations are from *Letter to a Conscientious Man,* 22, and "An Essay towards Preventing the Ruine of Great Britain" (1721), in George Berkeley, *A Miscellany, Containing Several Tracts on Various Subjects* (Dublin, 1752). The Tory Daniel Defoe vehemently denounced speculators (see his *The Anatomy of Ex-change-Alley: Or, a System of Stock-Jobbing* . . . [London, 1719]). So did Thomas Gordon and John Trenchard (see *Cato's Letters; or, Essays on Liberty, Civil and Religious, and Other Important Subjects,* 3d ed. rev. [London, 1733], I, 7-19, 42-50, IV, 12-23). On efforts to curb stockjobbers see *Truth: A Letter to the Gentlemen of Exchange Alley: Occasioned by the Bill Now Depending in the House to Prevent the Pernicious Practice of Stock Jobbing* (London, 1733), and [James Milner], *A Letter to a Friend Concerning the Proposals for the Payment of the Nation's Debts* (London, 1720). See also Kramnick, *Bolingbroke,* 46-48, and Dickson, *Financial Revolution,* 20, 32-34.

[18] Mingay, *English Landed Society,* 47-48, 59; Kramnick, *Bolingbroke,* 56-61; Ward, *English Land Tax,* 2-3, 6-10, 17-22.

[19] *Essays. I. On the Public Debt,* 14-15, 17. Mingay writes that high taxes during war brought numerous estates on the market (*English Landed Society,* 38).

The Bank of England came in for its share of obloquy. It was denounced as a monopoly that favored certain individuals at others' expense and discriminated against country gentlemen. It was accused of having taken advantage of the government's necessities. One critic observed that abuses of this sort could be expected: "It is not in the Nature of such a Corporation to have any Consideration to the Publick Good, while they could venture to ruin the whole for the gratifying their Revenge, or suppressing a Rival." The main objection to the Bank, however, was its supposed influence, actual or potential; it was considered likely to "grow upon" the government and control it.[20]

As the public debt increased, there was less possibility of getting rid of it without a repudiation. The burden was sustained by reducing interest from 6 percent early in the century to 2 percent. Continuous application of a sinking fund might have reduced the principal, and this was always fondly thought of, but repeated wars put it out of the question. When wars stopped, taxes were greatly reduced and chance of debt payment diminished. Hence the funding system tended to grow beyond the reach of its adversaries.[21] Political storms continued to hover over it, however, because it raised constitutional issues. Anti-administration spokesmen saw in it the chief source of executive influence, arguing that the barriers against monarchical power raised by the Revolution of 1689 were eroded by vast flows of money in and out of the treasury; patronage at the

[20] The quotations are from *A Short View of the Apparent Dangers and Mischiefs from the Bank of England* (London, 1707), 7-9, and *Remarks upon the Bank of England* . . . (London, 1705). See also [John Broughton], *The Vindication and Advancement of Our National Constitution and Credit* . . . (London, 1710), and *A Letter to a Person of Quality Relative to the Bank of England and Credit of the Nation* ([London], 1710).

[21] Schemes for dealing with the debt varied in credibility. Some resembled what was done in America. Several writers advocated paying off part or all of the debt with some kind of paper instrument issued by the government, which was to circulate as currency and be sunk by taxation. More than one writer put forth the idea, common in America, that government was a better sponsor of a circulating medium than any set of private bankers (see n. 14). See Dickson, *Financial Revolution*, 20-21, and among contemporary pamphlets John Broughton, *An Essay upon the National Credit of England: Introductory to a Proposal Prepared for Establishing the Public Credit* . . . (London, 1706), and *Vindication and Advancement of Our National Constitution and Credit;* [John] Asgill, *An Abstract of the Publick Funds Granted and Continued to the Crown since 1 Wm & M and Still Existing* (London, 1715); William Leigh, *An Essay upon Credit, Being a Proposal for the Immediate and Entire Payment of the Publick Debts* . . . (London, 1715), *Considerations on the Present State of the Nation, as to Publick Credit, Stocks, the Landed and Trading Interests* (London, 1720), and *An Essay on Paper Circulation: And a Scheme Proposed for Supplying the Government with Twenty Millions, without any Loan or New Tax* (London, 1764); [John Perceval], *A Proposal for Selling Part of the Forest Lands and Chaces, and Disposing of the Produce towards the Discharge of That Part of the National Debt, Due to the Bank of England; and for the Establishment of a National Bank & C.* (London, 1763); and Walker, *Proposal for Relieving the Present Exigencies.*

command of the king and his supporters had overwhelmed all constitutional restraints.[22]

These intellectual positions betray an agrarian bias and a hostility
toward social change that was considered destructive of established values
and class relationships. They also have a Country flavor suggestive of the
attitudes of persons outside the administration and deprived of its favors,
and sometimes, as well, of the attitudes of persons imbued with "an
instinctive hatred of courts and a rooted distrust of Government."[23] Yet in
spite of ulterior motives, it seems unquestionable that the denunciation of
the funding system and its consequences was too widespread to be
ascribed to mere party. Such views expressed internalized values that
transcended political affiliation. The Tory radical Henry St. John, Viscount Bolingbroke articulated the whole range of opposition arguments
and spent much of his life crusading against the funding system. A
nobleman who cherished the hierarchical institutions of the past, he
attributed the decline of liberty since the Revolution of 1689 less to the
power lust of his archrival, Robert Walpole, than to the government's
fiscal policies.[24] Another critic, who subscribed to a quite different
political catechism, was John Trenchard, a Real Whig widely read by
partisans of liberty in America. He characterized Britain as "staggering
under the Weight and Oppression of its Debts, eaten up with usury, and
exhausted with Payments." He suggested that acts of graft or bribery that
involved members of Parliament be made felonies punished by death.[25]

[22] Dickson, *Financial Revolution*, 20; Kramnick, *Bolingbroke*, 28.
[23] The quotation is from Archibald S. Foord, *His Majesty's Opposition, 1714-
1830* (Oxford, 1964), 25.
[24] Bolingbroke embraced the Whig version of the Revolution of 1689, regarding it as a reaffirmation of ancient Saxon liberties. It had been undermined, in his
view, by the government's fiscal policies. The large perpetual debt conferred upon
the executive mechanisms of patronage of an entirely new order of magnitude.
Not the prerogative, as in the 17th century, but the power of money had become
the chief menace to liberty. It also had degraded morals, enslaved the many to the
few, and elevated lower-class men without family or intrinsic merit, subverting the
ancient order of society. Among his political writings, along with issues of his
magazine, the *Craftsman*, are "Remarks on the History of England," "A Dissertation on Parties," and "Some Reflections on the Present State of the Nation . . . ,"
published in Mallett, ed., *Works of Bolingbroke*, I, 313-521, II, 1-259, III, 145-179.
Bolingbroke's attitudes and philosophy are examined at length in Kramnick,
Bolingbroke, esp. 18-28, 73-79.
[25] Trenchard wished that politicians would not spend all their time in the Alley
carousing over champagne and burgundy, but condescend to drink a cup of ale
with the poor, despised, and mortgaged country gentlemen, from whom they
would hear another language—about bribery and bargains made between former
ministers and stockjobbers as well as other vicious and fraudulent practices relative
to public finance. The politicians might then discover that the "Rusticks" were
uneasy at the spectacle of those who, a few years ago, would have doffed their hats
to them, now riding about in coaches-and-six with pompous liveries and atten-
dants, while they themselves walked on foot, and all this while their "Country-

Another Real Whig, Richard Price, writing a generation later, remarked that "not only the preservation of our Trade and Liberties, but the very Being of the State depends at present on a reduction of our debts." He held the funding system mainly responsible for the growth of executive influence. To put an end to it, he wanted to reinvigorate the sinking fund and make it a felony to divert the fund to other purposes on the ground that such an act was no less treasonous than killing the king.[26]

The eminent jurist William Blackstone, by any criterion a member of the establishment and reputedly a sound interpreter of majority opinion, denounced the funding system in his *Commentaries*. Admitting that a certain amount of debt might be "highly useful" to a commercial nation, he held that Britain's debt had without question increased beyond any justification or utility to commerce and that taxes injured trade and manufactures, caused price inflation, drained money from the productive classes into the hands of the idle, depleted natural resources by drawing away payments to foreigners, and impaired the power of the state by anticipating its revenues. Like Bolingbroke, he thought the financial system responsible for defeating the ancestral efforts of Englishmen to curb the growth of executive power.

> Our national debts and taxes . . . have . . . in their natural conse-
> quences thrown such a weight of power into the executive scale of
> government, as we cannot think was intended by our patriot ances-
> tors. . . . The entire collection and management of so vast a revenue,
> being placed in the hands of the crown, have given rise to such a
> multitude of new officers, created by and removable at the royal
> pleasure, that they have extended the influence of the government to
> every corner of the nation. . . . Upon the whole I think it is clear that,
> whatever the *nominal*, the real power of the crown has not been
> weakened by any transaction in the last century.[27]

David Hume was a believer in the expediency of ruling men through their vices, but he did not approve of the funding system. What should we

---

Understandings" could not discover the least merit, virtue, or public service done by those "shining Gallants" to warrant such distinction. Although the attitude he had described might be attributed to envy, it was nevertheless one held by responsible people (*Some Considerations upon the State of Our Publick Debts in General, and of the Civil List in Particular*, 2d ed. [London, 1720], 4-7.

[26] Price wrote that excessive taxation had forced landowners to sell their property and forced people to emigrate from the country. Taxes had doubled the market price of common necessities, discouraging marriage and the raising of families. It was axiomatic, he said, that such heavy taxes would cause any country to decline (*An Appeal to the Public on the Subject of the National Debt* [London, 1772], 44-60, quotation on pp. 46-47).

[27] Blackstone, *Commentaries on the Laws of England* (Philadelphia, 1771 [orig. publ. Oxford, 1765-1769]), I, 327, 333, 335-336.

say, he asked, of the new doctrine that a public debt is an advantage in itself and that, without any necessity for doing so, a state should create unlimited funds, debts, and taxes in order to promote economic development? He traced this process to its prospective extreme, when taxes would transfer the whole income of the society to the government's creditors. Then, he said, "adieu to all ideas of nobility, gentry, and family." Social cohesion and tradition would vanish, loyalties evaporate, and no means would be available for countering tyranny. Public elections would be determined only by bribery and corruption, and the middle power in society between king and commoner would be destroyed.[28]

Britain at mid-century led the nations of Europe in wealth and power, and the fiscal policies of the government had contributed heavily to this result. Astonishingly, however, there was a sense of national decline, in which those very policies, and the political and economic changes associated with them, occupied a central position. What was interpreted to be pervasive corruption in government and society, the losses inflicted upon broad classes of the population, and the violation of traditional ethical norms had evoked such widespread criticism as to impair the credibility of the regime, at least among the literate and articulate persons whose views constituted public opinion. Certainly, the endless recital of the venality of British political and social institutions had undermined the loyalty of Americans and in no small degree rationalized their separation from the empire. As one scholar has noted, "the revolt against England went far beyond a repudiation of monarchical government; it entailed a passionate rejection of the British form of political economy."[29]

About the time England funded its debt and chartered its bank, the colonies established a different set of financial institutions. Their problems were somewhat similar; they, too, needed sources of private credit and a more adequate medium of exchange. Their governments had experienced difficulty in borrowing money. In other respects, however, their circumstances were unlike those of England. Their economy was relatively backward, confined more largely to agriculture and household processes, more oriented toward subsistence production, and deficient in capital. Commerce and manufactures were on a much smaller scale. It may, in fact, have been the weakness of the private sector that induced colonies to employ government agencies rather than private enterprises in matters of public finance. In any case, the means used, unlike those in Britain, operated directly on the people, without private interpositions and profits.

To pay expenses all the colonial governments eventually employed

---

[28] Hume, *Writings on Economics*, ed. Rotwein, 92, 98-99, 100-105, quotation on p. 98. Since no future ministry could be expected to avoid war or in time of peace reduce the debt, Hume thought Britain would probably go bankrupt. Having said this, he added that the government would always be able to restore its credit somehow and repeat the process.

[29] McCoy, *Elusive Republic*, 48-49, 61.

"currency finance." Under this system, governments borrowed money, not by procuring loans at interest from individuals or institutions, but simply by printing paper money or certificates, issuing them to pay debts, and redeeming them in receipt of taxes and other payments to the government. Another way of issuing paper money was through land banks. To provide private credit and a general medium of exchange, the colonies capitalized the value of land, their principal form of wealth, which was "melted down . . . and made to circulate in paper."[30] Every colony except Virginia set up loan offices that lent paper money to borrowers on the security of real property. As borrowers repaid loans over a period of years, the money was canceled and withdrawn. Like the bills issued directly by the government, those from the loan office circulated as a medium of exchange and were accepted for taxes and other payments to the government. The nearly universal opinion was that land banks aided the economy, especially in times of economic depression.

Under the circumstances prevailing in the colonies, currency finance had singular advantages. It avoided any use of hard money, which was always in short supply, and it freed the available coin for overseas payments to finance imports.[31] The system was cheap for the government. Since money issued in payment of expenses usually bore little or no interest, the government obtained credit for nearly nothing. The interest charge inherent in delayed payment was forfeited by the people. The system also tended to prevent the accumulation of large public debts. Whenever debts were increasing, the currency of which they consisted was abundant and widely distributed. Nearly always a war was going on, business was good, and heavy taxes could be levied to pull money out of circulation. If the money had depreciated because too much had been issued, it could be withdrawn all the more easily at its depreciated value.

[30] The term is derived from E. James Ferguson, "Currency Finance: An Interpretation of Colonial Monetary Practices," *WMQ*, 3d Ser., X (1953), 153-180, which describes the system in general terms and contains an extensive bibliography. On the introduction of the system in Massachusetts see Andrew McFarland Davis, ed., *Colonial Currency Reprints, 1682-1751* (New York, 1964 [orig. publ. Boston, 1911]), 2-47, and on contemporary thought on the subject, E.A.J. Johnson, *American Economic Thought in the Seventeenth Century* (London, 1932), 192-200. The phrase, frequently repeated in writings of the period, was probably derived from Sir James Steuart, *An Inquiry into the Principles of Political Oeconomy*, ed. Andrew S. Skinner (Chicago, 1966 [orig. publ. London, 1767]), II, 444.

[31] See Jack P. Greene and Richard M. Jellison, "The Currency Act of 1764 in Imperial-Colonial Relations, 1764-1766," *WMQ*, 3d Ser., XVIII (1961), 516; Johnson, *American Economic Thought*, 153-154; and Burnham Putnam Beckwith, *Contemporary English and American Theories Concerning the Effect of Commercial Banking on the Supply of Physical Capital* (Los Angeles, 1935), 8. The release of coin for foreign payments was recognized in Sir Humphrey Mackworth, *An Answer to Several Queries Relating to the Proposal for Payment of the Publick Debts . . .* (London, 1720), 7-8.

Again, the losses fell on people in their private capacity, not on the government.[32]

The system did not enrich individuals. Even if money or certificates bore interest, the rate was usually too low to attract private investment, and therefore public finance did not create a rentier class. No bankers or financial institutions tapped the flow of public revenue and debt repayment; the government dealt directly with the people. The same was true of land bank loans; the interest went to the government, not to bankers, and in several colonies it was an important public revenue.[33]

It is evident that public finance did little to promote the institutional development of business enterprise. In the 1750s Massachusetts began paying the interest and principal on most of its paper issues in specie, and moneyed men were reported to be eager to invest. In Maryland certain paper emissions were redeemable in sterling bills of exchange on advantageous terms, and as the redemption date approached, speculators hoarded the notes. With these exceptions—and they were of limited scope—public finance did not, as in Britain, produce a body of securities to serve the needs and foster the growth of business enterprise. The opposite, in fact, is probably closer to the truth: the functions assumed by government in providing private credit and a medium of exchange may have forestalled the development of private financial institutions in the colonies.[34]

Finally, the system of currency finance was conducive to public virtue as it was defined in America, for it meant cheap government, low taxes,

[32] Richard Price was among those who commented on the facility of debt redemption in America (*Additional Observations on the Nature and Value of Civil Liberty and the War with America . . .* [London, 1777], 65n).

[33] John Taylor is worth quoting on this point. Commenting on the differences between Pennsylvania's colonial land bank and the state's banking institutions after the Revolution, he wrote: "Then the tax was paid by individuals to the publick; now it is paid by the publick to individuals. Then it was paid to assist industry, and defray publick expenses; now to enrich idleness, and supply the means of luxury to a separate interest. Then the publick required a knowledge of the amount paid, from its own representatives; now it pays an amount unknown, to corporations in which it is not represented. Then the publick received five or six per centum of individuals for paper currency; now it pays ten or twelve per centum to individuals for the same currency. That species of paper currency could not corrupt legislatures or nurture aristocracy; this must do both" (*An Inquiry into the Principles and Policy of the Government of the United States* [Fredericksburg, Va., 1814], 305-306).

[34] This may answer the point raised by Roger W. Weiss, who argues that there was enough hard money in the colonies to support specie payment generally if it had been properly expanded by banks ("The Issue of Paper Money in the American Colonies, 1720-1774," *Journal of Economic History*, XXX [1970], 770-784). On Massachusetts and Maryland respectively, see Andrew McFarland Davis, *Currency and Banking in the Province of the Massachusetts-Bay* (New York, 1900), I, 233-252, and Joseph Albert Ernst, *Money and Politics in America, 1755-1775: A Study in the Currency Act of 1764 and the Political Economy of Revolution* (Chapel Hill, N.C., 1973), 146-153.

minimal state power, and the separation of government from private interest. Land banks leaned toward the agricultural interest, it is true, but appropriately, since most of the people were farmers; in any case, the system was not inimical to the mercantile interest and was fairly neutral in its social effects. The arrangements were appropriate to America's agrarian circumstances, and they lacked the political and social by-products of the fiscal system in Britain. Before the Revolution, Britain did not try to force an alternative upon the colonists, who therefore had no occasion to reflect upon the connection between currency finance and their conceptions of liberty.[35]

The alternative was posed for the first time by the rise of the Nationalist movement in the closing years of the Revolution. The populist impulse that had led to war and Independence was by this time blunted by military and financial reverses, and political initiative had passed to conservatives who stood for social discipline, taxation, sound money, and laissez-faire. An effort was being made to strengthen the powers of Congress, in which enterprise the guiding spirit was the prominent Philadelphia merchant and politician Robert Morris, whom Congress appointed superintendent of finance in 1781. Rich and addicted to big projects, Morris set for himself the task of transforming the nation's institutional structure from the Office of Finance. In the course of his administration from 1781 to 1784, he drafted a blueprint for change that Congress adopted as official policy.[36]

Like a page in double-entry bookkeeping, the blueprint had two columns. One added up to political centralization. The financial collapse of Congress had proved what was always evident in theory, that the basic source of Congress's weakness under the Articles of Confederation was lack of the power to tax. From 1781 on, Morris and his supporters labored to persuade the states to sanction an amendment to the Articles giving Congress the power to collect a duty on imports. If the states had done so, Morris was ready with a portfolio of taxes sufficient to found and maintain the sovereignty of Congress. At first the impost (as the duty on imports was known) was urged as a war measure, but as the fighting ended, the only justification for federal taxes the nation would fully accept was payment of the Revolutionary debt; hence constitutional reform became linked with payment of the debt. This relationship was more than a marriage of convenience; it was one of natural affinity, for a well-managed debt would help cement the union by creating, as it had in England, an economic interest in supporting the government.

The other column in the Nationalist blueprint listed the economic

[35] A proposal for a colonies-wide land bank was raised and abandoned after 1763. See Joseph Albert Ernst, "The Currency Act Repeal Movement: A Study in Imperial Politics and Revolutionary Crisis, 1764-1767," *WMQ*, 3d Ser., XXV (1968), 177-211.

[36] The analysis of the political-economic content of the Nationalist program given here follows E. James Ferguson, "The Nationalists of 1781-1783 and the Economic Interpretation of the Constitution," *JAH*, LVI (1969), 241-261.

reforms that were integrated with debt payment. Morris perceived in the debt a means of creating investment capital for economic development. He proposed to fund the debt in the English manner by committing taxes to pay the interest without obligation to discharge the principal, except possibly by a sinking fund. Merely paying interest regularly, however, could be expected to raise the depreciated market value of securities (ten to fifteen cents on the dollar after 1782) and thereby create capital in the hands of the moneyed men who held securities.[37] Morris was alert to the potential uses of this newly available capital in banking operations. He once said he had planned to establish a bank before the Revolution;[38] in any case, one of his early acts as superintendent of finance was to found the Bank of North America, the country's first commercial bank. It was also a national bank, chartered by Congress and a depository of federal funds. James Madison, notifying Edmund Randolph of the opening of the bank, remarked that "it is pretty analogous in its principles to the bank of England."[39] Morris understood that the negotiable federal securities created by funding would serve as bank capital and that this capital could be multiplied at least two or three times in the process of issuing bank notes. As bank notes became available, he intended to do away with state paper money. Propertied men had lost confidence in it, but the country needed some kind of paper medium. The immediate answer to the problem was bank notes backed by public securities.[40] In sum, Morris and the Nationalists associated constitutional revisions with mercantile-capitalist reform of the country's economic institutions.

The Enlightenment instructed men in the uniformity of nature: similar causes produced similar effects. Such Nationalists as Morris and Alexander Hamilton openly admired the public credit of Britain, its wealth and industrial prowess, and the discipline that enabled the government to levy high taxes and induced the people to pay them. They had similar goals for the United States, which Morris conceived of as rising to "Power, Consequence, and Grandeur."[41] Like their associates, Morris and Hamil-

[37] The fullest exposition of Morris's economic philosophy is his report to Congress, dated July 29, 1782. Funding, he said, would put "property into those hands that could render it most productive" (Francis Wharton, ed., *The Revolutionary Diplomatic Correspondence of the United States* [Washington, D.C., 1889], V, 619-634, quotation on p. 625).

[38] Mathew Carey, ed., *Debates and Proceedings of the General Assembly of Pennsylvania, on the Memorials Praying a Repeal or Suspension of the Law Annulling the Charter of the Bank* (Philadelphia, 1786), 37.

[39] Madison to Randolph, Jan. 8, 1782, Edmund C. Burnett, ed., *Letters of the Members of the Continental Congress* (Washington, D.C., 1921-1936), VI, 289-290.

[40] For other contemporary reflections on banking see James Wilson, "Considerations on the Bank of North America," in Robert Green McCloskey, ed., *The Works of James Wilson* (Cambridge, Mass., 1967), II, 824-840, and Thomas FitzSimons's remarks in Carey, ed., *Debates in Pa. Assembly*, 104-106.

[41] "Circular to the Governors of the States," July 25, 1781, in E. James Ferguson and John Catanzariti, eds., *The Papers of Robert Morris, 1781-1784*, I (Pittsburgh, Pa., 1973-   ), 380-384, quotation on p. 381.

ton expressed disdain for popular government, its disorderliness and disregard of what they considered basic principles. Their version of Enlightenment ideas centered on powerful government, general and uniform laws, social discipline under elite guidance, and economic institutions oriented toward commercial and financial progress. They stood opposed on a broad front to the common American attachment to local rights, the institutional framework of the existing economy, a Country party bias in politics, and popular elements always pushing toward political and social democracy.[42]

From the Nationalist standpoint, the solution lay at hand: the British system, with its proven results, must be established in the United States. Morris was soon referring to Congress's unpaid obligations as "the funded debt," even though there were no taxes to pay it, and at least once he referred to unpaid obligations due to one of his correspondents as money "in the funds," as though it were something valuable.[43] Shortly after the Revolution, even though federal taxes were still not to be had, Morris demonstrated the consistency of his thought by proposing to the Pennsylvania legislature that the Bank of North America take over the payment of interest on the federal debt owed to citizens of the state in return for the commitment of state taxes to the bank.[44]

By the summer of 1782 every state except Rhode Island had ratified the impost amendment,[45] and within that state debate on the subject became intense. The published opposition, which centered in the *Providence Gazette*, showed that Rhode Islanders had not forgotten the lessons of history. In addition to objections based on various grounds of expediency and economic interest, the debate brought forth the standard arguments used in Britain, refurbished and adapted to local conditions. Centralism, rather than the king, represented despotism: in place of the royal executive was Congress, whose powers, it was said, would swell with revenues and engulf local liberties. Funding would enrich speculators, steal the rewards of productive labor, encourage the idle and profligate, generate swarms of bureaucrats, give rise to a standing army, and burden the country with perpetual debt. A variant on the British debate was the greater importance attached to a permanent commitment of revenues to Congress; Americans seem to have been more alert to the danger of surrendering legislative control over money grants. They also appear to have been more apprehensive of "insensible," indirect taxes, such as the

---

[42] On the broad division of ideology in early American politics see Jackson Turner Main, *Political Parties before the Constitution* (Chapel Hill, N.C., 1973); McCoy, *Elusive Republic*, in which it is a central topic; and Hutson, "Country, Court, and Constitution," *WMQ*, 3d Ser., XXXVIII (1981), 361-363.

[43] Diary, June 28, 1782, Robert Morris Papers, Library of Congress. See Morris to Nathaniel Appleton, Apr. 16, 1782, in Wharton, ed., *Diplomatic Correspondence*, V, 311-312.

[44] Carey, ed., *Debates in Pa. Assembly*, 41-42.

[45] Georgia never ratified the impost, but the fact was ignored.

impost, which were held to foster tyranny by taking money from the people without their knowing it.[46]

Newspaper writers referred to Britain's experience with funding as a matter of common knowledge. The system would most certainly have the same effect in America "which a similar measure had in Great Britain," said "Freeholder"—"that is, systematically establishing a debt never to be paid, and to keep the country in perpetual slavery."[47] "I have no more hopes from the virtue of Americans vested with revenue and uncontrollable power," wrote "Cato," "than I have of the Britons."[48] "A Bagman" thoroughly agreed: "Human nature is the same on both sides of the Atlantic, and the period may come when American Assemblies may be bought no less than a British Parliament."[49] "What in the name of common sense," exclaimed "Thought on the Five per Cent," "have we to do with the financing of the trans-atlantic world? What is it to us, by what methods the powers of Europe, Asia, and Africa draw resources from their forlorn, distressed and enslaved subjects? The science of modern financiering will suit a land of slaves, but America I hope in God, will never consent to a scheme that opens the door for unperceptible draughts of money from their pockets."[50]

Such arguments were somewhat extraneous to the issue, which was the state's economic interest in the impost. In any case, Rhode Island rejected the impost, the measure failed, and the war ended. The Nationalists were for a time in eclipse. Nevertheless, they had succeeded in committing Congress and in some degree the country to policies predicated upon strengthening the central government. The Nationalist movement stayed alive, and within a few years a new scene opened with the adoption of the Constitution. It remained then for Secretary of the Treasury Alexander Hamilton to execute the Nationalist economic program. His accomplishment may seem less noteworthy because part of his program was already in the public domain and not original with him. If the setting is properly understood, however, what he achieved should appear more impressive, for his program was intended to overthrow a full-fledged and viable system of currency finance, which had operated for nearly a century and was integrated with the country's political and economic stage of develop-

[46] Among articles reciting these themes, all in the *Providence Gazette* (Rhode Island), see "S. A.," Apr. 20, "Argus," Aug. 3, 10, "A Citizen," Aug. 17, "A Countryman," Sept. 21, Oct. 26, "A Freeholder," Oct. 26, "Candid," Dec. 28, 1782, unsigned, Feb. 23, and "Democritus," Apr. 5, 1783 (reprinted from *Freeman's Journal* [Philadelphia]). Several of these writers were published in both the *Independent Chronicle. And the Universal Advertiser* (Boston) and the *Providence Gaz.* See also "A Farmer," *Independent Chronicle,* July 25, 1782, and "A Lover of Liberty," *Pennsylvania Gazette* (Philadelphia), Jan. 25, 1783.

[47] *Providence Gaz.*, Nov. 9, 1782.

[48] *Ibid.*, Jan. 30, 1783, reprinted from *Continental Journal, and Weekly Advertiser* (Boston).

[49] *Providence Gaz.*, Aug. 24, 1783.

[50] Supplement to *ibid.*, Oct. 19, 1782.

ment. In audacity and scale Hamiltonian funding resembles the political revolution accomplished by the Constitution, for it, too, was a rational construction that exceeded the necessity calling it forth and was adapted to historical conditions that had, as yet, only a prospective existence.

The parental relation of British to Hamiltonian funding needs no emphasis. Beyond the connections already explored, one may cite Hamilton's report to Congress that frequently refers to the British experience. What is less apparent, because it is unspoken in his report, is his repudiation of the traditional modes of currency finance. To propose, as he did, the redemption at face value in specie of depreciated securities that had been sold by their owners to speculators at extreme discounts was a radical departure from the American past.[51] The great bulk of the debts of the Revolution had been sunk by government at depreciated market values. There were at hand customary methods for doing this, such as receiving securities for taxes or in payment for western lands. Hamilton mentioned in his report another method, which he referred to as discrimination: to give original holders of securities the full value but only the market price to secondary holders.[52] This method, if adopted, would have cut the total public debt nearly in half. The general disinclination to make full payment also figured in the opposition to federal assumption of state debts. If the states paid rather than Congress, it was certain that most of them would do it at market rather than face value.[53]

[51] Following similar tactics employed in Britain, Hamilton forced creditors to accept a reduction of interest from 6% to about 4½%. This enabled the government to assume the expense of taking on state debts and did not impair the market value of federal securities.

[52] E. James Ferguson, *The Power of the Purse: A History of American Public Finance, 1776-1790* (Chapel Hill, N.C., 1961), 296; Harold C. Syrett *et al.*, eds., *The Papers of Alexander Hamilton* (New York, 1961-1979), VI, 73-75.

[53] Ferguson, *Power of the Purse*, 311-312. The preamble to an act of the Pennsylvania assembly is candid and exceptionally lucid on this point: "And whereas the prospect of an appreciation, unless regulated on just and equitable principles, might likewise be followed by a train of evils as pernicious as those we have experienced, and not only encourage, but enable persons as have obtained large sums for small value, to derive an undue advantage. . . . And whereas the evils and inconveniences hitherto attending the depreciation of the [Continental] currency . . . have in a great measure been balanced by a real reduction and discharge of a very great part of the national debt, in so much, that it would now be a manifest public injustice, as well as a burthen intolerable to be borne, to tax the good people of this State, or of the United States, to pay that part of the public debt over again, which by a kind of common consent has been discharged by the said depreciation." The legislature endorsed Congress's act of Mar. 18, 1780, which repudiated 39/40ths of the value of Continental currency. *Laws Enacted in the Third Sitting of the Fourth General Assembly of the Commonwealth of Pennsylvania* (n.p., n.d.), chap. 177, dated June 1, 1780.

Examples of proposals to reduce the debt put forth in the newspapers are: by a discrimination, "Public Credit," quoted from the *Maryland Journal* (Baltimore) in the *Daily Advertiser* (New York), Feb. 23, 1790; by accepting securities in the sale

Nevertheless, Nationalist arguments as to the benefits of funding were commonly understood. The creditors' memorial to Congress in 1789 that elicited Hamilton's report on public credit declared that

> a certain amount of funded debt . . . is a national benefit. The creation of a new species of money by this means, naturally increases the circulation of cash, and extensively promotes every kind of useful undertaking and enterprise in agriculture, commerce, and mechanics. . . . It has been well maintained that, after the revolution in England, a funding system was there encouraged as the best means of attaching the great and powerful body of stockholders to the Government. The policy is infinitely more forcible when applied to the case of the United States. . . . In short, a debt originating in the patriotism that achieved the independence, may thus be converted into a cement that shall strengthen and perpetuate the Union of America.[54]

Hamilton included these points in his report, adding economic detail somewhat appropriate to agricultural interests. Funding would not only promote national unity and strength in foreign affairs but would have economic advantages for every class in the community. Public creditors would gain wealth from the rise in security values. Securities would function as money in all kinds of transactions and increase the supply of investment capital. Merchants would operate on a larger scale and at lower profit margins, drawing compensatory income from capital still resident in liquid securities. Such factors would expand foreign trade, benefit manufactures and agriculture, and, as in Britain, raise American land values, which had depreciated heavily since the Revolution.[55]

Hamilton's system had two general factors in its favor. The first was the firmness with which he was supported by the nation's elite. In the minds of most of the nation's leaders the general political situation in 1790 ruled out anything much less than full payment, at least of the federal debt. The political consequences of doing otherwise were risky. Reversion to currency finance would have sacrificed the main ends of the adoption of the Constitution, diminishing the government's credit at home and

---

of western lands, "Verax," *New-York Daily Gazette,* Mar. 3, 1790; by discriminating against secondary holders and sinking securities by taxation, "A Private Citizen," quoted from the *Connecticut Courant and Weekly Intelligencer* (Hartford) in the *Pa. Gaz.,* Mar. 10, 1790. Other procedures included simple repudiation, conversion of the entire debt into paper money and sinking it by taxation, distribution of the debt among the states, and distribution of the debt down to the level of private individuals, assessing each man his share (Ferguson, *Power of the Purse,* 302).

[54] "Memorial of the Public Creditors of Philadelphia," in Joseph Gales, comp., *The Debates and Proceedings in the Congress of the United States . . . [Annals of Congress]* (Washington, D. C., 1834), I, 792-795, 904.

[55] Syrett *et al.,* eds., *Hamilton Papers,* VI, 70-89.

abroad, alienating the most ardent supporters of the regime, and alarming men of property who had endured one round of private and public debt repudiation during the Revolution and now wanted a government that would put a stop to that sort of thing. In the House debates on funding, only three or four members dared confront the secretary's program head-on by proposing currency finance methods or a revaluation of the debt. To advocate such policies in this company was tantamount to coming out for mob rule and the abolition of debts.

The second reason for Hamilton's success was the discrediting of traditional methods of public finance during the Revolution. Total depreciation had so soured human relations and caused such moral revulsion as to weaken the legitimacy of paper money. David Ramsay's denunciation was not merely an elitist opinion:

That the helpless part of the community were legislatively deprived of their property, was among the lesser evils, which resulted from the legal tender of the depreciated bills of credit. The iniquity of the laws estranged the minds of many of the citizens from the habits and love of justice. The mounts which government had erected, to secure the observance of honesty in the commercial intercourse of man with man, were broken down. Truth, honor, and justice were swept away by the overflowing deluge of legal iniquity.[56]

From the fact that during the postwar economic depression seven states established land banks and issued paper money one might infer that currency finance was still held in favor by the general run of people. In these and other states a few men stood up in the legislature and extolled the benefits of land banks and paper money; no other way was known of coping with economic depression. However, the tentativeness of public acceptance was unmistakably revealed by the debates in the conventions held to act upon the Constitution. The issue of state paper money was then squarely on the line because the Constitution expressly prohibited it, to all appearances permanently depriving states of a resource they had long relied upon. It is significant that in all the published debates there is not a single defense of paper money in principle. The issue was sometimes indirectly approached, as in North Carolina, where the delegates expressed apprehension that the federal government might impoverish the people by redeeming Continental money and other depreciated debts at face value. Otherwise, there was no forthright defense of the old system. It appears that the opponents of the Hamiltonian program were placed in a contradictory position. Without much question, a general desire to scale down debts existed, but the once-acceptable methods of doing so were currently in disrepute.

[56] David Ramsay, *The History of the American Revolution* (Dublin, 1793 [orig. publ. Philadelphia, 1789]), I, 441.

Hamilton's program was modeled on British lines. It called for issuing new federal stock in exchange for the full value of Revolutionary state and federal debt certificates. Interest on stock was to be about 4½ percent, reduced from the original 6 percent. The principal, like that of the English debt, was to be redeemable only by a federal sinking fund. This plan, passing through Congress, was challenged only by James Madison's motion to discriminate in favor of original as opposed to secondary holders of the old debt. Madison proposed to restore 6 percent interest but to issue new stock only up to the market value of old securities held by secondary holders and to give the balance up to face value to original holders.

Madison's scheme might have helped to sidetrack the opposition to federal proposals or at least blunt the issue. Not much compassion existed in the country at large for original holders, although the idea of compensating them had sentimental appeal and conformed to the highest standards of public virtue. Compared with Hamilton's program, however, Madison's scheme meant a heavier load of debt and less promotion of wealth and capitalist interest. It was therefore not a proposition that could mobilize widespread popular opposition to Hamilton's proposals. It was, in fact, a false issue that understandably aroused the ire of Senator William Maclay, who urged Madison to go for 3 percent interest and redemption of the principal only by sale of western lands. These terms would have kept the debt at market value and allowed it to be redeemed more easily, according to tested and customary methods. When Madison refused without explaining his reasons, Maclay growled in his diary: "The obstinacy of this man has ruined the opposition."[57]

Madison's motion was applauded outside Congress but chiefly, it would appear, as a means of discrediting the claims of secondary holders preparatory to scaling them down.[58] In the *Connecticut Courant* a major theme was enunciated by "Private Citizen," who had his doubts about the public credit so cherished by the speculators: "The people of Europe are bowing down, like asses, beneath the burden imposed by this *cursed credit*." Instead of European systems of finance that would saddle the people with perpetual debts, "Private Citizen" wanted to levy direct taxes payable in securities and thereby dispose of the debt quickly "*without any burden to the people*."[59] Dispose of it at market value, he might have added; that was the American way.

Hamilton's opponents in the press ranged through the traditional

[57] Ferguson, *Power of the Purse*, 300-301.

[58] Hamilton wrote in 1795: "It may justly be doubted whether any of those who professed to advocate compensation to the original holders were even sincere in the proposition." He also said, "There never was a doubt that if the idea of the discrimination had obtained it would have resulted in a fraud on alienees without benefit to the alienors" (Syrett *et al.*, eds., *Hamilton Papers*, XIX, 3, 73). In 1790 a writer expressed contempt for those who advocated discrimination merely to justify reducing the debt ("Honestus," *New York Daily Advertiser*, Feb. 3, 1790).

[59] "A Private Citizen," reprinted in *Pa. Gaz.*, Mar. 10, 1790.

arguments. Funding would spawn roving bands of predatory officeholders; it would aggrandize the executive branch and unbalance the Constitution. It would promote endless war. It would not, as Hamilton said, create capital for investment but instead penalize productive enterprise. As the British experience demonstrated, taxes would raise production costs to the point where exports could not compete abroad. Interest on securities held by foreigners would drain money out of the country. Speculation would create a "nation of stockjobbers," raise luxury and indolence above toil and frugality, and enable drones to feed on the labor of industrious bees. Adam Smith, David Hume, and Richard Price were cited to disprove Hamilton's contention that the inflationary effects of funding would raise the current low price of land.[60] One writer, like several in the past, was prepared to estimate the physical dimensions of Britain's debt measured in coin. Calculated in gold guineas, the debt would weigh five million pounds troy weight, and the writer doubted whether there was enough gold in the whole world to pay it.[61]

Intellectually as well as numerically, the opposition was rather feeble in 1790, and even the congressional debate the next year over the Bank of the United States got scant attention in the press. The charter of the BUS allowed three-fourths of the stock to be subscribed in federal securities, which thus came to rest in their foredestined home. The bank acted as a government depository, and its notes (all the more necessary, along with those of other banks, after the constitutional prohibition of state paper money) provided a general medium of exchange. The bank conducted private business, extending credit to merchants. Although overtly modeled upon the Bank of England, the BUS was far more the creature of government patronage than its prototype. It had no function in servicing the public debt. On the other hand, the government furnished a good deal of the specie required for its initial operations by subscribing for a fifth of the bank's stock and paying for this in specie over a period of ten years. In contrast with the exactions usually made upon government banks in Europe, the BUS paid no bounty or gratuity to the government, receiving its privileges for nothing.

As the institutional structures of the Nationalists rose into place during these years, the predictable results followed. The market value of federal and assumed state securities advanced by perhaps $38,000,000 from 1786

[60] See "Publicola," Feb. 22, 1790, and "Fair Play," Mar. 16, 1790, *Daily Advertiser* (New York); "An Independent Observer," *N.-Y. Daily Gaz.*, Mar. 1, 1790; "Plain Argument," reprinted from the *Virginia Chronicle* (Norfolk) in the *Daily Advertiser*, Mar. 26, 27, 1790; and "Equity," "A Farmer," and "A Pennsylvanian," in the *Pa. Gaz.*, Feb. 3, 10, Apr. 21, 1790.
[61] "National Debt of England," *Federal Gazette and Philadelphia Daily Advertiser*, Apr. 17, 1790. Another writer had calculated that at the rate of 12 hours a day the debt would require over 142 years to count, that it would weigh over 61 million troy pounds, and, if laid side-by-side, the coins would reach twice around the globe (*Independent Chronicle*, Aug. 22, 1782).

to 1792,[62] and the consequent redistribution of national wealth generated capital for business. How much of it was actually applied to that purpose is uncertain, but within seven months after August 1791 seventeen corporations were started, and by 1793, before the effect of the European war could be registered, twelve banks, including the BUS, were added to the four in existence, raising total bank capital from $2,500,000 to $18,000,000.[63] These and other financial institutions created a mass of liquid securities that facilitated capital investment. Bank notes gradually replaced state paper money as a circulating medium. A stock market sprang up, along with a mania for speculation that, according to its critics, infected people of all social ranks. A financial panic occurred in 1792. Foreigners entered the picture; by 1789 they owned five or six million dollars in federal securities, and by 1803 some $32,000,000 out of a total of $70,000,000. The United States was still far short of matching the achievements of Great Britain, but a start had been made, and in the same direction.[64]

In a country so predominantly agricultural and Country-minded, it is not surprising that opposition to Hamiltonian measures should have eventually materialized on a broad scale. Americans had not forgotten their British past. "The political reputation of their principal [Alexander Hamilton]," wrote "Caius," in the *National Gazette*, "is built on the basis of humble and servile imitation of British systems of finance." Striking a pose typical of every phase of a debate that had gone on for nearly a hundred years in Britain, "Brutus" warned "the Secretary and his cohorts" to "beware how far they push their schemes." "Let them remember that altho' the republican jealousy of the people may sleep for a time, that it is not extinct, and that when the people begin to feel the pressure of oppressive and perpetual taxes, and the numerous impositions that attend them, that they may, by one exertion, overturn that complicated fabric the funding system, the cause of all these evils, and bury the enormous fortunes which have been made under it in its ruins."[65] By 1792 exertion

---

[62] Ferguson, "Nationalists of 1781-1783," *JAH*, LVI (1969), 278-279. Curtis P. Nettels estimated the appreciation at $30,000,000 (*The Emergence of a National Economy: 1775-1815* [New York, 1962], 121).

[63] Nettels, *Emergence of a National Economy*, 122; [Samuel Blodget, Jr.], *Economica: A Statistical Manual for the United States* (Washington, D.C., 1806), 60, 99, 159.

[64] The estimates for 1789 are Hamilton's. Hamilton to George Washington, Aug. 18, 1792, Syrett *et al.*, eds. *Hamilton Papers*, XII, 243. On the other estimates see Nettels, *Emergence of a National Economy*, 125, 236; Ralph W. Hidy, *The House of Baring in American Trade and Finance: English Merchant Bankers at Work, 1763-1861* (Cambridge, Mass., 1949), 34-35; and [Blodget], *Economica*, 99, 128. Investment in western lands, another field of foreign enterprise, was shortly cut off by the war in Europe.

[65] *National Gazette* (Philadelphia), Feb. 6, Apr. 5, 1792. The newspaper was by this time loaded with Republican arguments and repeated those in newspapers elsewhere.

had begun in earnest, as the quarrel between Jefferson and Hamilton came into the open, dissent became coherent, and many newspapers moved into the opposition. Hammering away in every issue, the press revived all the arguments of the British debate and hurled them at the administration in an assault that would ultimately bring down the Federalist regime.

Many years later Jefferson wrote that the "object was to preserve the legislature pure and independent of the Executive, to restrain the administration to republican forms and principles, and not permit the constitution to be construed into a monarchy, and to be warped in practice into all the principles and pollutions of their favorite English model."[66] John Taylor of Caroline put it more succinctly. "Is it not time," he asked in 1794, "to enquire, whether the constitution was designed to beget a government, or only a British system of finance?"[67]

The British funding system was instrumental to that country's rise to national greatness in the eighteenth century. It vastly increased the power of government in both domestic affairs and foreign wars. It was essential to the economic growth that raised Britain to world eminence in commerce, finance, and industrial development. Progress, of course, had adverse side effects. The entire political process was invaded and corrupted by new forms of wealth and influence. Economic change uplifted certain classes of the population but depressed others, especially the smaller landed gentry and the yeomanry. Human relations at every level were commercialized beyond previous norms, and a society distrustful of the benefits of change became critical of the erosion of values associated with a stabler, more agrarian way of life. Criticism of the government's policies and the trend of events was broadly based and intense.

As colonial America was less hampered by feudal survivals, so was it less disturbed than Britain by the emergence of higher forms of capitalist development. Its public institutions were adapted to parochial agrarian conditions. Currency finance did nothing to elevate governmental power or promote the evolution of business enterprise, and it gave political corruption little sustenance. While supportive of agriculture, it did not discriminate against other social interests. Since it tended to keep governmental apparatus, public debts, and taxes at minimal levels, it corresponded with American political ideals and concepts of public liberty.

In the closing years of the Revolution, the Nationalists under the aegis of such leaders as Robert Morris, Gouverneur Morris, and Alexander Hamilton started a secondary revolution directed against the political-economic establishment of the American states. Admirers of the British system, they wished to introduce its salient elements into the United States; that is, they wanted to build up the power of the central

[66] Thomas Jefferson, *The Anas*, in Paul Leicester Ford, ed., *The Works of Thomas Jefferson*, I (New York, 1904), 171-178.
[67] John Taylor of Caroline, *A Definition of Parties* ... (Philadelphia, 1794), 7.

government both at home and in foreign affairs, and to promote economic growth on a scale and along lines analogous to what had taken place in Britain. British history afforded ample precepts for their efforts and even a methodology, for British financial institutions had originally been contrived in part to support the regime set up by the Revolution of 1689. In America the Nationalists combined a funding system modeled upon Britain's with a constitutional amendment giving Congress the power of taxation, always considered the basis of sovereignty, and they linked it all with payment of the Revolutionary debt. The political results were certain to be a stronger national government, and the economic consequences would be similar to those produced by funding in Britain. A mercantile-capitalist reform of economic institutions was tied to political centralization. The program represented a conscious effort to introduce the British system into the United States.

Although they failed at the close of the Revolution, the Nationalists triumphed a few years later with the adoption of the Constitution, which conferred ample powers on Congress. As far as he could—that is, as far as the affairs of the central government were concerned—Hamilton rejected traditional modes of currency finance and funded the debt in what was sometimes termed the European manner. With the formation of the Bank of the United States the next year, the economic phases of the Nationalist program were completed. The expected results began to materialize.

The Nationalists were not alone in knowing the lessons of history, and from the beginning they were countered by opponents equally conversant with the political, social, and economic effects of the British financial system. For the same reasons the Nationalists admired it, their opponents hated it, and they had recourse to all the arguments employed by their counterparts in the long debate that had taken place in Britain. The opposition in America lacked effective leadership in 1790 and, above all, the support of the country's elite. But as the full outlines of the British system materialized in Hamilton's policies and the new government became more secure, the opposition intensified, especially after Jefferson broke with the administration. The struggle that followed, terminating in the victory of the "Country party," was the continuation of an interplay begun in Britain nearly a century earlier. If Charles Pettit had put events in a wider context, he would have given us a full-dimensional history of the establishment of the national government.

THE FOUNDING FATHERS

YOUNG MEN OF THE REVOLUTION

THE intelligent American of today may know a great deal about his history, but the chances are that he feels none too secure about the Founding Fathers and the framing and ratification of the Federal Constitution. He is no longer certain what the "enlightened" version of that story is, or even whether there is one. This is because, in the century and three quarters since the Constitution was written, our best thinking on that subject has gone through two dramatically different phases and is at this moment about to enter a third.

Americans in the nineteenth century, whenever they reviewed the events of the founding, made reference to an Olympian gathering of wise and virtuous men who stood splendidly above all faction, ignored petty self-interest, and concerned themselves only with the freedom and well-being of their fellow-countrymen. This attitude toward the Fathers has actually never died out; it still tends to prevail in American history curricula right up through most of the secondary schools. But bright young people arriving at college have been regularly discovering, for nearly the last fifty years, that in the innermost circle this was regarded as an old-fashioned, immensely oversimplified, and rather dewy-eyed view of the Founding Fathers and their work. Ever since J. Allen Smith and Charles Beard wrote in the early years of the twentieth century, the "educated" picture of the Fathers has been that of a group not of disinterested patriots but of hard-fisted conservatives who were looking out for their own interests and those of their class. According to this worldlier view, the document which they wrote—and in which they embodied these interests—was hardly intended as a thrust toward popular and democratic government. On the contrary, its centralizing tendencies all reflected the Fathers' distrust of the local and popular rule which had been too little restrained under the Articles of Confederation. The authors of the Constitution represented the privileged part of society. Naturally, then, their desire for a strong central government was, among other things, an effort to achieve solid national guarantees for the rights of property— rights not adequately protected under the Articles—and to obtain for the propertied class (their own) a favored position under the new government.

181

This "revisionist" point of view—that of the Founding Fathers as self-interested conservatives—has had immeasurable influence in the upper reaches of American historical thought. Much of what at first seemed audacious to the point of lèse majesté came ultimately to be taken as commonplace. The Tory-like, almost backward-turning quality which this approach has imparted to the picture of constitution-making even renders it plausible to think of the Philadelphia Convention of 1787 as a counter-revolutionary conspiracy, which is just the way a number of writers have actually described it. That is, since the Articles of Confederation were the product of the Revolution, to overthrow the Articles was—at least symbolically—to repudiate the Revolution. The Declaration of Independence and the Constitution represented two very different, and in some ways opposing, sets of aspirations; and (so the reasoning goes) the Philadelphia Convention was thus a significant turning-away from, rather than an adherence to, the spirit of the Declaration.

In very recent years, however, a whole new cycle of writing and thinking and research has been under way; the revisionists of the previous generation are themselves being revised. The economic ideas of the late Professor Beard, which dominated this field for so long, have been partially if not wholly discredited. And yet many of the old impressions, intermingled with still older ones, persist. Much of the new work, moreover, though excellent and systematic, is still in progress. Consequently the entire subject of the Constitution and its creation has become a little murky; new notions having the clarity and assuredness of the old have not as yet fully emerged; and meanwhile one is not altogether certain what to think.

Before the significance of all this new work can be justly assessed, and before consistent themes in it may be identified with any assurance, an effort should be made to retrace somewhat the psychology of previous conceptions. At the same time, it should be recognized that any amount of fresh writing on this subject will continue to lack something until it can present us with a clear new symbolic image of the Fathers themselves. The importance of this point lies in the function that symbols have for organizing the historical imagination, and the old ones are a little tired. The "father" image is well and good, and so also in certain respects is the "conservative" one. But we may suppose that these men saw themselves at the time as playing other rôles too, rôles that did not partake so much of retrospection, age, and restraint as those which would come to be assigned to them in after years. The Republic is now very old, as republics go, yet it *was* young once, and so were its founders. With youth goes energy, and the "energy" principle may be more suggestive now, in reviewing the experience of the founding, than the principle of paternal conservatism.

I

Charles A. Beard, who in 1913 published *An Economic Interpretation of the Constitution of the United States*, did more than any single figure to make of the Constitution something other than a topic for ceremonial praise. By calling it a product of economic forces, Beard established an alternative position and enabled the entire subject to become one for serious historical debate. He thus created the first real dialectic on the Constitution and Founding Fathers, and for that reason Beard's work must still be taken as the point of departure for any historical treatment of that subject.

For Beard, the reality behind the movement for a constitution in the 1780's was economic interest. The animating surge came from holders of depreciated Continental securities who were demanding that their bonds be paid at par, and from conservative elements throughout the Confederation who wanted a national bulwark against agrarian-debtor radicalism. Beard thus identified the Federalists as those who wanted protection for property, especially personal property. The Anti-Federalists, on the other hand, were the great mass of agrarian debtors agitating for schemes of confiscation and paper money inflation in the state legislatures. Their hard-earned taxes would go to support any new bonds that a stronger United States government might issue; conversely, further fiscal experimentation on their part would be checked by national power. The Anti-Federalists, those who opposed a new constitution, were therefore the radicals; the Federalists, who favored it, were the conservatives.

Beard's argument was immediately challenged and kept on being challenged, which helped it to retain the fresh attractiveness of an avant-garde position for many years. But the man's influence grew, and his work played a vital part in historical thinking until well after the Second World War. Historical thinking, however, has its own historical setting. Why should such a statement as Beard's not have been made until the twentieth century, more than 125 years after the event?

In the nineteenth century the American Constitution had operated as the central myth of an entire political culture. While that culture was still in the tentative stages of its growth, still subject to all manner of unforeseen menaces, and with very little that was nationally sacred, there reigned everywhere the tacit understanding that here was the one unifying abstraction, the one symbol that might command all loyalties and survive all strife. The Constitution thus served multiple functions for a society that lacked tradition, folk-memory, a sovereign, and a body of legend. The need to keep the symbol inviolate seems to have been felt more instinctively during its earlier history than later on. Public controversy of the bitterest kind might occur over the charter's true meaning; enemies might accuse each other of misconstruing the document; but one did not challenge the myth itself. Americans even fought a civil war with both sides claiming to be the true upholders of the Constitution. Thus it was natural that when the historians of the nineteenth century—Bancroft, Hildreth, Frothingham, Fiske, McMaster—came to describe the origins of the Constitution, they should reach for the non-controversial idiom and imagery of a Golden Age. The Supreme Law had been fashioned and given to the people by a race of classic heroes.[1]

America's veneration for its Constitution became steadily more intense in the years that followed the Civil War. Now it was the symbol not only of the Union, for which that generation had made such heavy sacrifices, but also of the unfettered capitalism which was turning the United States into one of the richest and most powerful nations in the world. The new material order—wasteful, disorderly, already acquainted with

---

[1] Richard B. Morris has pointed out that in Henry Dawson there was at least one exception to this universal veneration for the Constitution. Dawson in 1871 published an article wherein he deplored the ancestor-worship which already wreathed the Fathers and their work. See Morris, "The Confederation and the American Historian," *William and Mary Quarterly*, XIII, 3rd ser. (April 1956), pp. 139-56; Dawson, "The Motley Letter," *Historical Magazine*, IX, 2nd ser. (March 1871), pp. 157 *et seq.*

labor disturbances, yet immensely productive—was watched over by the benevolent and solicitous eye of the Constitution.

In 1888, in a setting darkened by portents of industrial warfare, John Fiske published *The Critical Period of American History,* an account of the events leading to the Philadelphia Convention of 1787. It was an instant success; the notion of the Confederation interlude as a "critical period" was dramatically perfect. A time of trouble, political drift, threatening disunity, and irresponsible agitation provided the occasion at Philadelphia for a supreme act of disinterested statesmanship. There, an intrepid conclave of Old Romans rose above personal and local concerns and presented their countrymen with an instrument of vigorous and effective government.

By the opening of the twentieth century, the state of mind in which men could uncritically ascribe a sort of immaculateness to their political and legal arrangements had altered sharply. By then a profound economic and social crisis had been met and overcome, but with remnants of psychological crisis left unresolved in its wake. The ending of the depression and hard times of the 1890's, the defeat of Populism and Bryanism, the election of McKinley and return of Republican rule—these things were not enough to restore the old complacent innocence. The American public, now full of guilty misgivings, had begun to ask itself searching questions about the evils of the existing order and about the price it had allowed itself to pay for material progress. The answer which was hit upon by publicists and civic spokesmen was *vested interest.* The formula was not exactly new, but after the experience of the 1890's, when public rhetoric had abounded in sinister allusions to "Wall Street" and "the monopolies," it was no more than natural that the "vested interest" concept should have taken on an immensely new and widened range of application. The "interests" were the shadowy powers that manipulated things and made them run the way they did. Thus vested interest came to be seen in the Progressive Era—those years roughly from the turn of the century through the First World War—as the ultimate reality behind the life of affairs.

It was in that era, moreover, that "reality" itself first came to be a synonym for all the equivocal, seamy, and downright evil facts of life from which innocent and respectable people are normally sheltered. Few periods in American history have been so strikingly noted for civic awareness and the reforming spirit—and reform meant getting to the bottom of things. The most efficacious step in exorcising an evil was exposing it. Thus the literature of exposure, which claimed an enormous amount of journalistic and literary energy, did much to whet and sustain that generation's relish for reform. "Muckraking" meant dredging up heaps of grubby "reality" for all to behold. "Reality," as Richard Hofstadter has said,

> was the bribe, the rebate, the bought franchise, the sale of adulterated food. It was what one found in *The Jungle, The Octopus, Wealth against Commonwealth,* or *The Shame of the Cities.* . . . Reality was a series of unspeakable plots, personal iniquities, moral failures, which, in their totality, had come to govern American society. . . .

The sheer excitement of discovery tended to leave people's perceptions of appearance and reality somewhat unbalanced. It is perhaps too much to say that anything hidden was taken as bad (though there were certainly strong presumptions); yet one of the great unspoken dogmas of American thought, implanted in this period, was that the "facts of life" had to be hidden in order to qualify as "real."

In academic precincts, meanwhile, such thinkers as Roscoe Pound, John Dewey, Thorstein Veblen, Arthur Bentley, and J. Allen Smith had begun to challenge the older static and formalist theories of law, philosophy, economics, and government. They were no longer so interested in the formal outlines which enclosed, say, government or the law; they were much more concerned to locate the dynamic forces inside these realms—to identify the powers that made them really work. Thus "economic interest" as a kind of *élan vital*, a basic prime mover, came to be given greater and greater emphasis. "Wherever we turn, wrote E. R. A. Seligman as early as 1902, ". . . we are confronted by the overwhelming importance attached by the younger and abler scholars to the economic factor in political and social progress." Here was "reality" being given an intellectual and scholarly sanction.

In view of this mounting preoccupation with "interests," one might be led to conclude that significant numbers of intelligent people were approaching a "class" theory of society not unlike that of Marx—a theory in which classes and class interests contended more or less frankly with each other for advantage. Yet by and large this did not happen; these were not the terms in which most people thought about society. For one reason, there was very little evidence to support such a theory. But a more important reason was that, to a people saturated in democratic prejudices, "class" habits of thought were fantastically difficult to understand, let alone imitate. To the Progressive mind, the way vested interest worked was not so much through class as through *conspiracy*.

Vested interest and conspiracy were concepts so closely related that they were almost synonymous. The interests worked in secret; their power rested on stealthy understandings and was exercised through the pulling of invisible strings. Hidden from view, they might freely circumvent the law and gain their ends by corrupting and manipulating the agencies of government. The Marxian view that a man openly and automatically reflected the interests of his class, doing this even in the name of ideals and justice, was incomprehensible to most Americans. The mediating term between economic interest and political action had to be something both simpler and more disreputable, and the techniques such as could not bear daylight. One important source of this attitude was the Progressive faith in the essential honesty of the people. Only the few, acting in secret, would set their interests against those of the nation. They achieved their aims not by consulting the majority will but by thwarting and evading it. Thus when writers of the Progressive period tried to weigh the importance of economic factors in any political development, the imagery they slipped into was almost invariably that of a conspiracy against the people. Such a mode of conceiving reality would even be brought to bear upon the origins of the United States Constitution.

Two of Charles Beard's immediate precursors in that realm were J. Allen Smith and Algie Simons. They were, for their own purposes, innovators; yet in a broader sense their minds followed a typical Progressive pattern. In J. Allen Smith's *Spirit of American Government, A Study of the Constitution* (1907), the myth of the Philadelphia convention as a forum of distinterested statesmen came under sharp attack. Claiming that "it was the property-owning class that framed and secured the adoption of the Constitution," Smith seemed to be feeling his way toward an economic interpretation based on class. But this tentative theme was quickly overshadowed by the central idea, that of a conspiracy against democratic rule:

Democracy . . . was not the object which the framers of the American Constitution had in view, but the very thing they wished to avoid. . . . Accordingly the efforts of the Constitutional Convention were directed to the task of devising a system of government which was just popular enough not to excite popular opposition and which at the same time gave the people as little as possible of the substance of political power.

Algie Simons, who was a convinced socialist and should therefore have hewed more consistently to the doctrine of class interest, fell into much the same sort of reasoning. In *Social Forces in American History* (1912), Simons' words seemed at first full of cool detachment when he said that it was not necessarily bad for the Constitutional Convention to have been virtually a committee of the propertied class, because that class "represented progress." But the lures of "conspiracy" in the end proved too much for him. Simons' closing rhetoric almost sweats with rural superstition as he tells his readers that

the organic law of this nation was formulated in secret session by a body called into existence through a conspiratory trick, and was forced upon a disfranchised people by means of dishonest apportionment in order that the interests of a small body of wealthy rulers might be served.

But it was Charles A. Beard, taking up the "class interest" formula in his famous *Economic Interpretation* the following year, who succeeded to all intents and purposes in making it stick. Whereas neither Smith nor Simons had made any secret of their reforming passions (they denied that the Constitution was a sacred document, so their fellow-citizens should feel free to change it if they wished), Beard disclaimed any intention of writing a political tract. He would simply be the observer of historical events, impassively examining the facts. All he wanted to do was discover whether in fact economic forces had played a significant part in the drafting and ratification of the Constitution. Early in his book Beard insisted that it was not his purpose "to show that the Constitution was made for the personal benefit of the members of the Convention," but merely to determine whether the Fathers represented "distinct groups whose economic interests they understood and felt in concrete, definite form, through their own personal experience with identical property rights. . . ." Then, setting in motion an impressive system of scholarly apparatus, he proceeded to answer his own questions.

Beard's ostensible argument—that the Fathers were pursuing class rather than personal interests and that there was a real distinction between them—had a certain Marxian subtlety, but he would not have made his case with very many Progressive readers if he had actually stuck to it. Instead, in the course of his book that side of the case, the "class" side, slipped entirely out of sight while the personal side, the one that really engaged Beard's mind, just grew and grew. The distinction was impossible to maintain; even to him it was probably not very serious. At any rate, the reason he was able to create his sensation was that the things he showed the Fathers doing were of exactly the sort that the muckraking magazines had, in other connections, made all too familiar.

Beard's basic research materials were a batch of old Treasury records which had never previously been opened ("reality"), and in them he found the names of a number of the Federalist leaders, members of the Philadelphia Convention as well as delegates to ratifying conventions in the various states. These men held substantial amounts of Continental securities which—Beard reasoned from later developments—would rise sharply in value with the establishment of a strong central government. This seemed to explain the energy with which they worked to bring such a government into being, and this was just the sort of evidence that impressed Beard's contemporaries most. Beard himself, for all his disclaimers, sums up his argument in language whose dominant theme is *direct personal interest*. Here, three of his thirteen conclusions are quite explicit:

(1) The first firm steps toward the formation of the Constitution were taken by a small and active group of men immediately interested through their personal possessions in the outcome of their labors.

(2) The members of the Philadelphia Convention who drafted the Constitution were, with a few exceptions, immediately, directly, and personally interested in, and derived economic advantages from, the establishment of the new system.

(3) The leaders who supported the Constitution in the ratifying conventions represented the same economic groups as the members of the Philadelphia Convention; and in a large number of instances they were also directly and personally interested in the outcome of their efforts.

Accompanying the principal theme of personal interest were several sub-themes:

(1) The Constitution was essentially an economic document based upon the concept that the fundamental private rights of property are anterior to government and morally beyond the reach of popular majorities.

(2) [The entire process, from the calling of the Philadelphia Convention to the ratifying of the Constitution, was unrepresentative and undemocratic; there was no popular vote on calling the convention; a large propertyless (and therefore disfranchised) mass was not represented at Philadelphia; and only a small minority in each state voted for delegates to the ratifying conventions.][2]

(3) [Where battles did occur over ratification], the line of cleavage . . . was between substantial personalty interests on the one hand and the small farmers and debtor interests on the other.

Beard thus managed in the end to have it both ways; he charged the Fathers, as members of a class, with things of which he had said he was not going to accuse them as individuals. But the distinction was too fine to matter a great deal; the response to the book, both favorable and hostile, was based on the secrets Beard had unearthed about the Fathers as individuals. Few of his readers had paid much attention to the subtle relationship which he had tried to establish between class interest and political ideology, so few could have noticed when the relationship began to dissolve. Actually, few had had any real quarrel with capitalism in the first place; the Progressive mentality was simply frightened by *big* capitalism—that is, by the vested interests. Beard himself was nothing if not a Progressive, fully immersed in his times. It was the interests and their inside doings that caught the Progressive imagination; it was this that the Progressives longed to befool and discomfit by public exposure. If Beard was to show that the Federal Constitution was not a product of abstract political theory but of concrete economic drives, there was no happier way of doing it than to paint the Founding Fathers in the familiar image of the vested interests—the small group of wealthy conspirators hostile to, even contemptuous of, the majority will, and acting for clear, "practical" reasons such as rigging the value of public securities.

Despite the bursts of pained protests which *An Economic Inter-*

---

[2] Not a direct quotation but a summary of four of the thirteen conclusions.

pretation initially drew from many older academics (who either thought that Beard could comprehend no motives other than base ones, or else concluded that he must be a socialist), it also drew plenty of praise from academic as well as non-academic quarters. Not only did the book do well for a scholarly monograph, it did better and better as time went on. In the 1920's the reforming side of Progressivism had lost its popularity, but this was not true of the debunking side. Meanwhile the success of Vernon L. Parrington's *Main Currents in American Thought* (which owed much to Beardian influences), as well as of Beard's own *Rise of American Civilization*, served to keep Beard's views before the public.

The *Economic Interpretation* came fully into its own in the New Deal era. The times by then required a conception of the Constitution that would stress the flexible, rather than the rigid and immutable aspects of the document. Former President Hoover, and even the Supreme Court, were apparently insisting in the face of all enlightened opinion that social and economic experimentation of any kind was ruled out by the spirit of the Constitution. Yet it would be reasonable enough to expect that the Constitution should respond to the economic needs of the present, if there were convincing historical proof that its very birth had been in response to the economic needs of its framers. American intellectuals, moreover, had by this time become a good deal more accustomed to ideas of class conflict than formerly. To significant numbers of them the image of class struggle was now appealing enough that they had begun applying it in a spirit of experimentation to a great variety of problems. Business groups of every sort had fallen into bad odor. This was the setting in which prophetic insights came to be ascribed to the writings of Charles A. Beard. Those writings by the late 1930's had become voluminous, and the Master had acquired a legion of followers.

And the Master himself could still have it both ways. Marxist and quasi-Marxist interpretations of society could, and did for a season, draw much historical sanction from his pages. At the same time Beard had bequeathed to American historical method something far more pervasive, a technique of explanation which could take "class" interpretations or leave them alone. This was the "reality" technique, which assumes that the most significant aspects of any event are those concealed from the eye.

Men's true intentions are to be judged neither from the words we hear them speak nor the deeds we see them do, and the "real" forces behind historical change will turn out, more often than not, to be those of conspiracy.

II

In 1940 certain new and interesting corollaries were added to the mode of approach which, due so largely to Beard's example, had come to influence historical thinking on the formation of the Constitution. In that year Merrill Jensen published *The Articles of Confederation: An Interpretation of the Social-Constitutional History of the American Revolution, 1774-1781.* Jensen's own approach was consistent with most of the general principles which had been laid down by Beard. But whereas Beard's primary interest had been with the Federalists—the men who led and supported the campaign for a new constitution— Jensen turned his attention to the Anti-Federalists, those who had opposed the constitutional movement. What, he asked, was the nature of the political system which the Constitution displaced, and what were the aims and intentions of the men who had created that system?

In the face of most prior opinion to the contrary, Jensen found in the Confederation just the sort of loose arrangement most favorable to democratic self-rule on the local and state level, inasmuch as the primary authority was located in the state legislatures. It was for achieving exactly this object, he thought, that the Confederation's strongest supporters—such leaders as Samuel Adams, Patrick Henry, Thomas Burke, and Richard Henry Lee—had pushed the Colonies into the Revolution in the first place. Conversely, those who opposed the Confederation were the men who had at first been reluctant to support the Revolution. They had feared the consequences of a break with England because that would remove the one central power strong enough to restrain the forces of local democracy. These men did, to be sure, join the Patriot forces after the break had become inevitable. Yet almost at once they began working for a continental government which might supply the stabilizing and conservative force previously maintained by the Crown. Their eventual triumph would come, of course, at Philadelphia in 1787.

In a second book, *The New Nation* (1950), Jensen considered the accomplishments of the Confederation, together with the social and economic conditions of the period from 1781 to 1789. He concluded that the "critical period" was really not so critical after all. American ships were not excluded from many foreign ports; tariff wars between states were the exception rather than the rule; the Confederation government had solved the problem of western lands and was well on the way to settling the outstanding boundary disputes. By 1786 the economic depression which had struck the country in 1784 was coming to an end. Even the problem of national credit was not so serious as the Federalists wanted people to believe, since a number of the states had assumed responsibility for portions of the Continental debt held by their own citizens. Had the states been brought to accept a national impost—a tariff duty on incoming foreign goods levied solely and exclusively by Congress, the revenue of which would be reserved for the support of the government— the Confederation would have been fully capable of surviving and functioning as a true federal establishment.

The collapse of the Confederation, Jensen argued, was not the logical outcome of weakness or inefficiency. It was the result of a determined effort by a small but tightly-organized group of nationalists to impose a centralized government upon the entire country despite the contrary desires of great majorities everywhere:

> Most of these men were by temperament or economic interest believers in executive and judicial rather than legislative control of state and central governments, in the rigorous collection of taxes, and, as creditors, in strict payment of public and private debts. . . . They deplored the fact that there was no check upon the actions of majorities in state legislatures; that there was no central government to which minorities could appeal from the decisions of such majorities, as they had done before the Revolution.

These were the men who conspired to overthrow the Confederation and who masterminded the triumph of the Constitution.

There were points at which Jensen had not seen eye to eye with Beard. He was more impressed, for instance, by the Fathers' general outlook and ideology than by their property holdings; unlike Beard, moreover, he denied that the Confederation era was a time of serious economic difficulty. Yet he had actually strengthened the Beardian logic at more than one point, and the differences were minor in the light of the convictions which united the two in spirit and intention. The work of Merrill Jensen, like that of Beard and Parrington and J. Allen Smith before him, still balanced on the assumption that the energy behind the American Constitution was conspiratorial energy, and that the Constitution came into being by means of a coup d'état—through the plotting of a well-disciplined Toryish few against the interests of an unvigilant democratic majority.

Indeed, Merrill Jensen's *The New Nation*—published two years after the death of Charles Beard—was the last major piece of Constitution scholarship to be done in the Progressive tradition, and represented the end of an era. By that time, 1950, Beard's own notions had begun to arouse not the admiration, but the suspicion, of a new generation of postwar intellectuals.

III

A few modest little articles, case studies of ratifying conventions held in individual states in 1788, had begun appearing here and there in the regional quarterlies. In 1947 there was one by Philip Crowl on Maryland, another on North Carolina by William Pool in 1950, still another on Virginia by Robert Thomas in 1953. Such fragments, of course, could not be expected to cause much immediate stir. But these studies carried implications, similar in each case, that would prove in the long run profoundly damaging to the whole structure of Beardian scholarship and Beardian reasoning.

A major item in that reasoning had been Beard's assumption that the principle which differentiated Federalists from Anti-Federalists was the principle of class and property interests—that the Federalists as a group were upholding one kind of class interest and defending one form of property while the Anti-Federalists, presumably, represented something else, something basically opposed. For some reason, Beard had never taken the trouble to check the Anti-Federalist side of his equation. Thomas, in his study of the delegates to the Virginia ratifying convention (where the fight had been unusually bitter), discovered that the members of both sides held property of essentially the same kind, in approximately the same amounts, and represented the same social class—the planting gentry. The other studies showed a similar pattern. In short, the conflict over ratification was apparently fought out not between classes, but between cliques of the same ruling class within these states, and whatever the conflict's "real" basis, it was not a struggle over property rights as such. Beard's "class" and "property" formula was simply indeterminate; the story had to be found elsewhere.

By 1956, Beard's *Economic Interpretation* had been set up for the *coup de grâce*. The executioner was Robert E. Brown, a professor at Michigan State who had been at work for some time implacably compiling a catalogue of the Master's offenses. In his *Charles Beard and the Constitution*, published that year, Brown tracked Beard through every page of the latter's masterpiece and laid the ax to virtually every statement of importance that Beard had made in it. There was absolutely no correlation between the Philadelphia delegates' property holdings and the way they behaved on the question of a constitution. It was not true that large numbers of adult males were disfranchised; the suffrage was remarkably liberal everywhere. Farmers as a class were by no means chronically debtors; many were creditors and many others were both. The supporters of Shays' Rebellion (the debtors' uprising in western Massachusetts which occurred during the fall and winter of 1786-1787) were certainly not united against the Constitution; if they had been, it could never have been ratified, since the Shaysites had a clear majority at the time of the Massachusetts convention. Nor did the Philadelphia delegates know that the Continental debt would be funded at par. If they had, the banker Robert Morris, for one, would never have speculated in western lands with the thought of paying for them in depreciated Continental paper.

Not only was Beard's evidence inconclusive at all points, Brown insisted, but there were even occasions when the Master had not been above doctoring it. He edited Madison's Federalist No. 10 to eliminate all but its economic emphasis; he quoted only those passages of the Philadelphia debates that made the Fathers look least democratic; he arranged his treatment of the ratification process in an order that violated chronology, centered unjustified attention on states where hard struggles did occur, overlooked the ease with which ratification was achieved in other states, and thus created a wildly exaggerated picture of the opposition at large.

Brown's book was respectfully received; there was little inclination to dispute his arguments; no champions arose to do serious battle for the departed Beard. Some of the reviewers were a little dismayed at Brown's tone; they thought it need not have been quite so ferocious. And the book did seem to bear out the principle that any work of destruction in the realm of discourse, however necessary, must be executed within restrictions that make for a certain stultification. Richard Hofstadter remarked in this connection that Brown was "locked in such intimate embrace with his adversary that his categories are entirely dictated by Beard's assertions." Even Brown, in his way, had toyed with the "reality" theme. He had exonerated the Fathers of conspiratorial intentions but convicted Charles Beard in their place: Beard had cooked the evidence, had conspired to hide the truth.

The first effort in recent years to view the Constitution all over again in a major way, shaking off the Beardian categories and starting as it were from scratch, has been undertaken by Forrest McDonald. *We The People,* published in 1958, was the first of a planned trilogy whose design was to survey anew the entire story of how the Constitution was brought into existence. Although McDonald, like Brown, felt it necessary to show the inadequacy of Beard's conclusions, his strategy was quite different from Brown's; it was undertaken less to discredit Beard than to clear the way for his own projected treatment of the great subject. In the *Economic Interpretation,* Beard had made a number of proposals for research which he himself had not performed—and never did perform—but which would, Beard felt, further corroborate his own "frankly fragmentary" work. McDonald began by undertaking the very research which Beard had suggested, and its results convinced him that Beard had simply asked all the wrong questions.

One of the things McDonald investigated in *We The People* was an assumption upon which Beard had put a great deal of stress, the notion of a fundamental antagonism between "personalty" and "realty" interests at the time of the Philadelphia Convention. ("Personalty" was wealth based on securities, money, commerce, or manufacturing; "realty" was landed property whose owners' outlook tended to be primarily agrarian.) He found that there was no such split in the Convention. The seven men who either walked out of the Convention or else refused to sign the completed document were among the heaviest·

security-holders there, and represented "an all-star team of personalty interests." In state after state, moreover, there was no appreciable difference between the property holdings of Federalists and Anti-Federalists. Finally, the three states that ratified the Constitution unanimously—Delaware, New Jersey, and Georgia—were overwhelmingly dominated by agrarian interests.

Unlike Brown, McDonald was quite unwilling to write off the possibility of an economic analysis (his book's subtitle was *The Economic Origins of the Constitution*); it was just that Beard's particular economic categories led nowhere. Beard's sweeping "personalty" and "realty" classifications were meaningless, and he had deceived himself profoundly in supposing that the Federalists' property interests "knew no state boundaries" but were "truly national in scope." On these two points of difference McDonald set up an entirely new and original research scheme, and in so doing effected a really impressive conceptual maneuver. He was quite ready, in the first place, to find "economic forces" behind the movement for a constitution, but these must be sought not in "classes" or in broad categories of property but rather in the specific business interests of specific groups in specific places. The other organizing category would be the individual states themselves. The political framework within which any group had to operate was still that imposed by the state; the states were, after all, still sovereign units, and the precise relationship between economic forces and political action depended almost entirely on the special conditions within those states, conditions which varied from one to the other.

By abandoning Beard's "national" framework and recasting the entire problem on a state-by-state basis, McDonald made it possible to see with a sudden clarity things which ought to have been obvious all along. The states where ratification was achieved most readily were those that were convinced, for one reason or another, that they could not survive and prosper as independent entities; those holding out the longest were the ones most convinced that they could go it alone. The reasons for supporting ratification might vary considerably from state to state. For Georgia, an impending Indian war and the need for military protection could transcend any possible economic issue; New York, at one time imagining for itself an independent political and economic future, would finally ratify for fear of

113

being isolated from a system which already included ten states and which might soon be joined by a seceded New York City.

The single problem of the Continental debt took different forms in different states. New Jersey, Massachusetts, and New York had each assumed portions of the debt held by their own citizens, but New Jersey and Massachusetts found their obligations intolerably burdensome while New York did not. Massachusetts had put an excessively heavy load on its direct property and poll-tax system; thus any possibility of the debt's being funded by a new Federal government should have found both the Boston security-holder and the Shaysite debtor more than willing to support such a government—and this, it appears, is about what happened. In New York and New Jersey an additional key to the debt issue was the question of a national tariff. New York had a state tariff, which was part of a financial system worked out to service the debt, and for that reason the state had been reluctant to accept a national impost in 1786. New Jersey, on the other hand, with no ocean trade of any account and having to receive most of its imports through New York, had no such revenue, was hard pressed to maintain interest payments on its debt, and thus had everything to gain from both a national impost and a national funding system. New Jersey was one of the first to ratify, and did so unanimously.

Recognizing the importance of specific location made it also easier and more natural to appreciate the way in which particular interests in particular places might be affected by the question of a stronger national government. Boston shipping interests, for example, seem to have been less concerned in the 1780's over class ideology or general economic philosophy than over those conditions of the times which were especially bad for business. The British would not let them into the West Indies, the French were excluding their fish, and their large vessels were no longer profitable. A strong national government could create a navy whose very existence would reduce high insurance rates; it could guarantee an orderly tariff system that would remove all pressure for higher and higher state tariffs; and it could counter British and French discrimination by means of an effective navigation act. Manufacturing interests would also tend to favor the Constitution, though not necessarily on principle; the vigor of their support would depend on the size of their establishments and the extent to which they competed with England.

Support from Pennsylvania iron and Connecticut textiles would be particularly energetic. So also with the wheat and tobacco farmers of the Connecticut Valley, though not for the same reason. They had to pay import taxes to New York for the goods they bought ,(their crops were sold there); they were heavily taxed, at the same time, to support a state-funded debt which they would be only too glad to see removed by a central government. Farmers in the Kentucky area, on the other hand, could be very suspicious of a Constitution under which northeastern shipping interests might influence the government to surrender free navigation on the Mississippi in return for a favorable trade treaty with Spain.

Forrest McDonald's work, according to him, has only just begun; years of it still lie ahead. But already a remarkable precision of detail has been brought to the subject, together with a degree of sophistication which makes the older economic approach—"tough-minded" as it once imagined itself—seem now a little wan and misty. The special internal conditions of the several states now seem fully valid as clues to the ratification policies of those states, each in its separate turn. And there is a credibility about the immediate needs and aspirations of particular groups, and the way they varied from place to place, that Beard's "interests" never quite possessed—or if they did, they had long since lost their hold on the modern mind.

And yet there are overtones in McDonald's work—for all its precise excellence, perhaps partly because of it—that have already succeeded in creating a new kind of "reality" spell. McDonald is very open-minded about all the manifold and complex and contradictory forces that converged upon the movement for a constitution. But somehow the ones he takes most seriously— the "real" forces behind the movement—were specific, particular, circumscribed, hard, and immediate. They were to be looked for mostly on the local level, because that is where one really finds things. A state—the largest permissible "reality" unit— was an agglomeration of specific, particular, immediate localities. There were interests to be served, political or economic, and they were *hard*. They were pursued rationally and without sentimentality; men came down where they did because their hard, immediate, specific interests brought them there. But are we prepared to say that the final result was just the sum—or extension—of these interests?

115

No doubt large enough numbers of people were convinced of the economic advantages they would gain under a new federal government that we may, thanks to Professor McDonald, account for a considerable measure of the support which the Constitution received. In places where there was a balance to tip, we have a much better idea of just how it happened. Still, Merrill Jensen pointed out some time ago that the economic situation was already somewhat on the mend by 1786. There were, moreover, certain powerful states such as Virginia and New York that might very well have thrived either as independent units or in coalitions with their immediate neighbors. And conditions in general could not have been so desperate that a national government was absolutely required for solving economic problems, let alone for staving off economic collapse. The steps actually taken were not the only ones possible; there were certainly alternatives, and it is hard to believe that they would all have led to disaster.

The new approach is extremely enlightening and useful. But has it yet taken on life? When will it fully engage the question of initiative and energy? How do we account for the dedication, the force and éclat, of Federalist leadership? When all is said and done, we do not exactly refer to the "interests" of a James Madison. We wonder, instead, about the terms in which he conceives of personal fulfillment, which is not at all the same. What animates him? The nationalist movement *did* have a mystique that somehow transfigured a substantial number of its leaders. What was it like, what were its origins?

IV

The work of Merrill Jensen, done in the 1930's and 1940's, has suffered somewhat in reputation due to the sweep and vehemence of the anti-Beardian reaction. Yet that work contains perceptions which ought not to be written off in the general shuffle. They derive not so much from the over-all Beardian traditions and influences amid which Jensen wrote, as from that particular sector of the subject which he marked off and preëmpted for his own. Simply by committing himself—alone among Beardians and non-Beardians—to presenting the Confederation era as a legitimate phase of American history, entitled to be taken seriously like any other and having a positive side as well as a negative one, he has forced upon us a peculiar point of view which, by the same token, yields its own special budget of insights. For example, Jensen has been profoundly impressed by the sheer force, determination, and drive of such nationalist leaders as Hamilton, Madison, Jay, Knox, and the Morrises. This energy, he feels, created the central problem of the Confederation and was the major cause of its collapse. He deplores this, seeing in the Confederation "democratic" virtues which it probably never had, finding in the Federalists an "aristocratic" character which in actual fact was as much or more to be found in the Anti-Federalists, smelling plots everywhere, and in general shaping his nomenclature to fit his own values and preferences. But if Professor Jensen seems to have called everything by the wrong name, it is well to remember that nomenclature is not everything. The important thing—what does ring true—is that this driving "nationalist" energy was, in all probability, central to the movement that gave the United States a new government.

The other side of the picture, which does not seem to have engaged Jensen's mind half so much, was the peculiar sloth and inertia of the Anti-Federalists. Cecelia Kenyon, in a brilliant essay on these men,[3] has shown them as an amazingly reactionary lot. They were transfixed by the specter of power. It was not the power of the aristocracy that they feared, but power of any kind, democratic or otherwise, that they could not control for themselves. Their chief concern was to keep governments as limited and as closely tied to local interests as possible. Their minds could not embrace the concept of a national interest which they themselves might share and which could transcend their own parochial concerns. Republican government that went beyond the compass of state boundaries was something they could not imagine. Thus the chief difference between Federalists and Anti-Federalists had little to do with "democracy" (George Clinton and Patrick Henry were no more willing than Gouverneur Morris to trust the innate virtue of the people), but rather in the Federalists' conviction that there was such a thing as national interest and that a government could be established to care for it which was fully in keeping with republican principles.

[3] "Men of Little Faith: The Anti-Federalists on the Nature of Representative Government," *William and Mary Quarterly*, XII, 3rd ser. (January 1955), pp. 3-43.

To the Federalists this was not only possible but absolutely necessary, if the nation was to avoid a future of political impotence, internal discord, and in the end foreign intervention. So far so good. But still, exactly how did such convictions get themselves generated?

Merrill Jensen has argued that the Federalists, by and large, were reluctant revolutionaries who had feared the consequences of a break with England and had joined the Revolution only when it was clear that independence was inevitable. The argument is plausible; few of the men most prominent later on as Federalists had been quite so hot for revolution in the very beginning as Patrick Henry and Samuel Adams. But this may not be altogether fair; Adams and Henry were already veteran political campaigners at the outbreak of hostilities, while the most vigorous of the future Federalists were still mere youngsters. The argument, indeed, could be turned entirely around: the source of Federalist, or nationalist, energy was not any "distaste" for the Revolution on these men's part, but rather their profound and growing involvement in it.

Much depends here on the way one pictures the Revolution. In the beginning it simply consisted of a number of state revolts loosely directed by the Continental Congress; and for many men, absorbed in their effort to preserve the independence of their own states, it never progressed much beyond that stage even in the face of invasion. But the Revolution had another aspect, one which developed with time and left a deep imprint on those connected with it, and this was its character as a continental war effort. If there is any one feature that most unites the future leading supporters of the Constitution, it was their close engagement with this continental aspect of the Revolution. A remarkably large number of these someday Federalists were in the Continental Army, served as diplomats or key administrative officers of the Confederation government, or, as members of Congress, played leading rôles on those committees primarily responsible for the conduct of the war.

Merrill Jensen has compiled two lists, with nine names in each, of the men whom he considers to have been the leading spirits of the Federalists and Anti-Federalists respectively. It would be well to have a good look at this sample. The Federalists— Jensen calls them "nationalists"—were Robert Morris, John Jay, James Wilson, Alexander Hamilton, Henry Knox, James Duane,

George Washington, James Madison, and Gouverneur Morris. Washington, Knox, and Hamilton were deeply involved in Continental military affairs; Robert Morris was Superintendent of Finance; Jay was president of the Continental Congress and minister plenipotentiary to Spain (he would later be appointed Secretary for Foreign Affairs); Wilson, Duane, and Gouverneur Morris were members of Congress, all three being active members of the war committees. The Anti-Federalist group presents a very different picture. It consisted of Samuel Adams, Patrick Henry, Richard Henry Lee, George Clinton, James Warren, Samuel Bryan, George Bryan, George Mason, and Elbridge Gerry. Only three of these—Gerry, Lee, and Adams—served in Congress, and the latter two fought consistently against any effort to give Congress executive powers. Their constant preoccupation was state sovereignty rather than national efficiency. Henry and Clinton were active war governors, concerned primarily with state rather than national problems, while Warren, Mason, and the two Bryans were essentially state politicians.

The age difference between these two groups is especially striking. The Federalists were on the average ten to twelve years younger than the Anti-Federalists. At the outbreak of the Revolution George Washington, at 44, was the oldest of the lot; six were under 35 and four were in their twenties. Of the Anti-Federalists, only three were under 40 in 1776, and one of these, Samuel Bryan, the son of George Bryan, was a boy of 16.

This age differential takes on a special significance when it is related to the career profiles of the men concerned. Nearly half of the Federalist group—Gouverneur Morris, Madison, Hamilton, and Knox—quite literally saw their careers launched in the Revolution. The remaining five—Washington, Jay, Duane, Wilson, and Robert Morris—though established in public affairs beforehand, became nationally known after 1776 and the wide public recognition which they subsequently achieved came first and foremost through their identification with the continental war effort. All of them had been united in an experience, and had formed commitments, which dissolved provincial boundaries; they had come to full public maturity in a setting which enabled ambition, public service, leadership, and self-fulfillment to be conceived, for each in his way, with a grandeur of scope unknown to any previous generation. The careers of the Anti-Federalists, on the other hand, were not only state-centered but—aside from those of Clinton, Gerry, and the young Bryan—rested heavily on events that preceded rather than followed 1776.

As exemplars of nationalist energy, two names in Professor Jensen's sample that come most readily to mind are those of Madison and Hamilton. The story of each shows a wonderfully pure line of consistency. James Madison, of an influential Virginia family but with no apparent career plans prior to 1774, assumed his first public rôle as a member of the Orange County Revolutionary Committee, of which his father was chairman. As a delegate from Orange County he went to the Virginia convention in 1776 and served on the committee that drafted Virginia's new constitution and bill of rights. He served in the Virginia Assembly in 1776 and 1777 but failed of re-election partly because he refused to treat his constituents to whisky. (He obviously did not have the right talents for a state politician.) In recognition of Madison's services, however, the Assembly elected him to the Governor's Council, where he served from 1778 to 1780. Patrick Henry was then Governor; the two men did not get on well and in time became bitter political enemies. At this period Madison's primary concern was with supplying and equipping the Continental Army, a concern not shared to his satisfaction by enough of his colleagues. It was then, too, that he had his first experience with finance and the problems of paper money. He was elected to the Continental Congress in 1780, and as a member of the Southern Committee was constantly preoccupied with the military operations of Nathanael Greene. The inefficiency and impotence of Congress pained him unbearably. The Virginia Assembly took a strong stand against federal taxation which Madison ignored, joining Hamilton in the unsuccessful effort to persuade the states to accept the impost of 1783. From the day he entered politics up to that time, the energies of James Madison were involved in continental rather than state problems—problems of supply, enlistment, and finance—and at every point his chief difficulties came from state parochialism, selfishness, and lack of imagination. His nationalism was hardly accidental.

The career line of Alexander Hamilton, *mutatis mutandis*, is functionally interchangeable with that of James Madison. Ambitious, full of ability, but a young man of no family and no money, Hamilton arrived in New York from the provinces at the age of 17 and in only two years would be catapulted into a brilliant career by the Revolution. At 19 he became a highly effective pamphleteer while still a student at King's College, was captain of an artillery company at 21, serving with distinction in the New York and New Jersey campaigns, and in 1777 was invited to join Washington's staff as a lieutenant-colonel. He was quickly accepted by as brilliant and aristocratic a set of youths as could be found in the country. As a staff officer he became all too familiar with the endless difficulties of keeping the Continental Army in the field from 1777 to 1780. With his marriage to Elizabeth Schuyler in 1780 he was delightedly welcomed into one of New York's leading families, and his sage advice to his father-in-law and Robert Morris on matters of finance and paper money won him the reputation of a financial expert with men who knew an expert when they saw one. He had an independent command at Yorktown. He became Treasury representative in New York in 1781, was elected to Congress in 1782, and worked closely with Madison in the fruitless and discouraging effort to create a national revenue in the face of state particularism. In the summer of 1783 he quit in despair and went back to New York. Never once throughout all this period had Alexander Hamilton been involved in purely state affairs. His career had been a continental one, and as long as the state-centered George Clinton remained a power in New York, it was clear that this was the only kind that could have any real meaning for him. As with James Madison, Hamilton's nationalism was fully consistent with all the experience he had ever had in public life, experience whose sole meaning had been derived from the Revolution. The experience of the others—for instance that of John Jay and Henry Knox—had had much the same quality; Knox had moved from his bookstore to the command of Washington's artillery in little more than a year, while Jay's public career began with the agitation just prior to the Revolution and was a story of steady advancement in continental affairs from that time forward.

The logic of these careers, then, was in large measure tied to a chronology which did not apply in the same way to all the men in public life during the two decades of the 1770's and 1780's. A significant proportion of relative newcomers, with prospects initially modest, happened to have their careers opened up at a particular time and in such a way that their very public personalities came to be staked upon the national quality of the experience which had formed them. In a number of outstanding cases energy, initiative, talent, and ambition had combined with a conception of affairs which had grown immense in scope and promise by the close of the Revolution. There is every reason to think that a contraction of this scope, in the years that immediately followed, operated as a powerful challenge.

V

The stages through which the constitutional movement proceeded in the 1780's add up to a fascinating story in political management, marked by no little élan and dash. That movement, viewed in the light of the Federalist leaders' commitment to the Revolution, raises some nice points as to who were the "conservatives" and who were the "radicals." The spirit of unity generated by the struggle for independence had, in the eyes of those most closely involved in coördinating the effort, lapsed; provincial factions were reverting to the old provincial ways. The impulse to arrest disorder and to revive the flame of revolutionary unity may be pictured in "conservative" terms, but this becomes quite awkward when we look for terms with which to picture the other impulse, so different in nature: the urge to rest, to drift, to turn back the clock.

Various writers have said that the activities of the Federalists during this period had in them a clear element of the conspiratorial. Insofar as this refers to a strong line of political strategy, it correctly locates a key element in the movement. Yet without a growing base of popular dissatisfaction with the status quo, the Federalists could have skulked and plotted forever without accomplishing anything. We now know, thanks to recent scholarship, that numerous elements of the public were only too ripe for change. But the work of organizing such a sentiment was quite another matter; it took an immense effort of will just to get it off the ground. Though it would be wrong to think of the Constitution as something that had to be carried in the face of deep and basic popular opposition, it certainly required a series of brilliant maneuvers to escape the deadening clutch of particularism and inertia. An Anti-Federalist "no" could register on exactly the same plane as a Federalist "yes" while requiring a fraction of the energy. It was for this reason that the Federalists, even though they cannot be said to have circumvented the popular will, did have to use techniques which in their sustained drive, tactical mobility, and risk-taking smacked more than a little of the revolutionary.

By 1781, nearly five years of intimate experience with the war effort had already convinced such men as Washington, Madison, Hamilton, Duane, and Wilson that something had to be done to strengthen the Continental government, at least to the point of providing it with an independent income. The ratification of the Articles of Confederation early in the year (before Yorktown) seemed to offer a new chance, and several promising steps were taken at that time. Congress organized executive departments of war, foreign affairs, and finance to replace unwieldy and inefficient committees; Robert Morris was appointed Superintendent of Finance; and a 5 per cent impost was passed which Congress urged the states to accept.

By the fall of 1782, however, the surge for increased efficiency had lost the greater part of its momentum. Virginia had changed its mind about accepting the impost, Rhode Island having been flatly opposed all along, and it became apparent that as soon as the treaty with England (then being completed) was ratified, the sense of common purpose which the war had created would be drained of its urgency. At this point Hamilton and the Morrises, desperate for a solution, would have been quite willing to use the discontent of an unpaid army as a threat to coerce the states out of their obstructionism, had not Washington refused to lend himself to any such scheme. Madison and Hamilton thereupon joined forces in Congress to work out a revenue bill whose subsidiary benefits would be sufficiently diffuse to gain it general support among the states. But in the end the best that could be managed was a new plan for a 5 per cent impost, the revenues of which would be collected by state-appointed officials. Once more an appeal, drafted by Madison, was sent to the states urging them to accept the new impost, and Washington wrote a circular in support of it. The effort was in vain. The army, given one month's pay in cash and three in certificates, reluctantly dispersed, and the Confederation government, with no sanctions of coercion and no assured revenues, now reached a new level of impotence. In June, 1783, Alexander Hamilton, preparing to leave Congress to go back to private life, wrote in discouragement and humiliation to Nathanael Greene:

There is so little disposition either in or out of Congress to give solidity to our national system that there is no motive to a man to lose his time in the public service, who has no other view than to promote its welfare. Experience must convince us that our present establishments are Utopian before we shall be ready to part with them for better.

Whether or not the years between 1783 and 1786 should be viewed as a "critical period" depends very much on whose angle they are viewed from. Although it was a time of economic depression, the depressed conditions were not felt in all areas of economic life with the same force, nor were they nearly as damaging in some localities as in others; the interdependence of economic enterprise was not then what it would become later on, and a depression in Massachusetts did not necessarily imply one in Virginia, or even in New York. Moreover, there were definite signs of improvement by 1786. Nor can it necessarily be said that government on the state level lacked vitality. Most of the states were addressing their problems with energy and decision. There were problems everywhere, of course, many of them very grave, and in some cases (those of New Jersey and Connecticut in particular) solutions seemed almost beyond the individual state's resources. Yet it would be wrong, as Merrill Jensen points out, to assume that no solutions were possible within the framework which then existed. It is especially important to remember that when most people thought of "the government" they were not thinking of Congress at all, but of their own state legislature. For them, therefore, it was by no means self-evident that the period through which they were living was one of drift and governmental impotence.

But through the eyes of men who had come to view the states collectively as a "country" and to think in continental terms, things looked altogether different. From their viewpoint the Confederation was fast approaching the point of ruin. Fewer and fewer states were meeting their requisition payments, and Congress could not even pay its bills. The states refused to accept any impost which they themselves could not control, and even if all the rest accepted, the continued refusal of New York (which was not likely to change) would render any impost all but valueless. Local fears and jealousies blocked all efforts to establish uniform regulation of commerce, even though some such regulation seemed indispensable. A number of the states,

New York in particular, openly ignored the peace treaty with England and passed discriminatory legislation against former Loyalists; consequently England, using as a pretext Congress' inability to enforce the treaty, refused to surrender the northwest posts. Morale in Congress was very low as members complained that lack of a quorum prevented them most of the time from transacting any business; even when a quorum was present, a few negative votes could block important legislation indefinitely. Any significant change, or any substantial increase in the power of Congress, required unanimous approval by the states, and as things then stood this had become very remote. Finally, major states such as New York and Virginia were simply paying less and less attention to Congress. The danger was not so much that of a split with the Confederation—Congress lacked the strength that would make any such "split" seem very urgent—but rather a policy of neglect that would just allow Congress to wither away from inactivity.

These were the conditions that set the stage for a fresh effort—the Annapolis Convention of 1786—to strengthen the continental government. The year before, Madison had arranged a conference between Maryland and Virginia for the regulation of commerce on the Potomac, and its success had led John Tyler and Madison to propose a measure in the Virginia Assembly that would give Congress power to regulate commerce throughout the Confederation. Though nothing came of it, a plan was devised in its place whereby the several states would be invited to take part in a convention to be held at Annapolis in September, 1786, for the purpose of discussing commercial problems. The snapping-point came when delegates from only five states appeared. The rest either distrusted one another's intentions (the northeastern states doubted the southerners' interest in commerce) or else suspected a trick to strengthen the Confederation government at their expense. It was apparent that no serious action could be taken at that time. But the dozen delegates who did come (Hamilton and Madison being in their forefront) were by definition those most concerned over the state of the national government, and they soon concluded that their only hope of saving it lay in some audacious plenary gesture. It was at this meeting, amid the mortification of still another failure, that they planned the Philadelphia Convention.

The revolutionary character of this move—though some writers have correctly perceived it—has been obscured both by the stateliness of historical retrospection and by certain legal peculiarities which allowed the proceeding to appear a good deal less subversive than it actually was. The "report" of the Annapolis meeting was actually a call, drafted by Hamilton and carefully edited by Madison, for delegates of all the states to meet in convention at Philadelphia the following May for the purpose of revising the Articles of Confederation. Congress itself transmitted the call, and in so doing was in effect being brought to by-pass its own constituted limits. On the one hand, any effort to change the government within the rules laid down by the Articles would have required a unanimous approval which could never be obtained. But on the other hand, the very helplessness which the several states had imposed upon the central government meant in practice that the states were sovereign and could do anything they pleased with it. It was precisely this that the nationalists now prepared to exploit: this legal paradox had hitherto prevented the growth of strong loyalty to the existing Confederation and could presently allow that same Confederation, through the action of the states, to be undermined in the deceptive odor of legitimacy. Thus the Beardian school of constitutional thought, for all its errors of economic analysis and its transposing of ideological semantics, has called attention to one element—the element of subversion—that is actually entitled to some consideration.

But if the movement had its plotters, balance requires us to add that the "plot" now had a considerable measure of potential support, and that the authority against which the plot was aimed had become little more than a husk. Up to this time every nationalist move, including the Annapolis Convention, had been easily blocked. But things were now happening in such a way as to tip the balance and to offer the nationalists for the first time a better-than-even chance of success. There had been a marked improvement in business, but shippers in Boston, New York, and Philadelphia were still in serious trouble. Retaliatory measures against Great Britain through state legislation had proved ineffective and useless; there was danger, at the same time, that local manufacturing interests might be successful in pushing through high state tariffs. In the second place, New York's refusal to reconsider a national impost, except on terms that would have removed its effectiveness, cut the ground from under the moderates who had argued that, given only a little time, everything could be worked out. This did not leave much alternative to a major revision of the national government. Then there were Rhode Island's difficulties with inflationary paper money. Although that state's financial schemes actually made a certain amount of sense, they provided the nationalists with wonderful propaganda and helped to create an image of parochial irresponsibility.

The most decisive event of all was Shays' Rebellion in the fall and winter of 1786-1787. It was this uprising of hard-pressed rural debtors in western Massachusetts that frightened moderate people everywhere and convinced them of the need for drastic remedies against what looked like anarchy. The important thing was not so much the facts of the case as the impression which it created outside Massachusetts. The Shaysites had no intention of destroying legitimate government or of redistributing property, but the fact that large numbers of people could very well imagine them doing such things added a note of crisis which was all to the Federalists' advantage. Even the level-headed Washington was disturbed, and his apprehensions were played upon quite knowingly by Madison, Hamilton, and Knox in persuading him to attend the Philadelphia Convention. Actually the Federalists and the Shaysites had been driven to action by much the same conditions; in Massachusetts their concern with the depressed state of trade and the tax burden placed them for all practical purposes on the same side, and there they remained from first to last.

Once the balance had been tipped in enough states, to the point of a working consensus on the desirability of change, a second principle came into effect. Unless a state were absolutely opposed—as in the extreme case of Rhode Island—to any change in the Articles of Confederation, it was difficult to ignore the approaching Philadelphia Convention as had been done with the Annapolis Convention: the occasion was taking on too much importance. There was thus the danger, for such a state, of seeing significant decisions made without having its interests consulted. New York, with strong Anti-Federalist biases but also with a strong nationalist undercurrent, was not quite willing to boycott the convention. Governor Clinton's solution was to send as delegates two rigid state particularists, John Yates and

Robert Lansing, along with the nationalist Hamilton, to make sure that Hamilton would not accomplish anything.

We have already seen that nineteenth century habits of thought created a ponderous array of stereotypes around the historic Philadelphia conclave of 1787. Twentieth century thought and scholarship, on the other hand, had the task of breaking free from them, and to have done so is a noteworthy achievement. And yet one must return to the point that stereotypes themselves require some form of explanation. The legend of a transcendent effort of statesmanship, issuing forth in a miraculously perfect instrument of government, emerges again and again despite all efforts either to conjure it out of existence or to give it some sort of rational linkage with mortal affairs. Why should the legend be so extraordinarily durable, and was there anything so special about the circumstances that set it on its way so unerringly and so soon?

The circumstances *were*, in fact, special; given a set of delegates of well over average ability, the Philadelphia meeting provides a really classic study in the sociology of intellect. Divine accident, though in some measure present in men's doings always, is not required as a part of this particular equation. The key conditions were all present in a pattern that virtually guaranteed for the meeting an optimum of effectiveness. A sufficient number of states were represented so that the delegates could, without strain, realistically picture themselves as thinking, acting, and making decisions in the name of the entire nation. They themselves, moreover, represented interests throughout the country that were diverse enough, and they had enough personal prestige at home, that they could act in the assurance of having their decisions treated at least with respectful attention. There had also been at work a remarkably effective process of self-selection, as to both men and states. Rhode Island ignored the convention, and as a result its position was not even considered there. There were leading state particularists such as Patrick Henry and Richard Henry Lee who were elected as delegates but refused to serve. The Anti-Federalist position, indeed, was hardly represented at all, and the few men who did represent it had surprisingly little to say. Yates and Lansing simply left before the convention was over. Thus a group already predisposed in a national direction could proceed unhampered by the friction of basic opposition in its midst.

This made it possible for the delegates to "try on" various alternatives without having to remain accountable for everything they said. At the same time, being relieved from all outside pressures meant that the only way a man could expect to make a real difference in the convention's deliberations was to reach, through main persuasion, other men of considerable ability and experience. Participants and audience were therefore one, and this in itself imposed standards of debate which were quite exacting. In such a setting the best minds in the convention were accorded an authority which they would not have had in political debates aimed at an indiscriminate public.

Thus the elements of secrecy, the general inclination for a national government, and the process whereby the delegates came to terms with their colleagues—appreciating their requirements and adjusting to their interests—all combined to produce a growing esprit de corps. As initial agreements were worked out, it became exceedingly difficult for the Philadelphia delegates not to grow more and more committed to the product of their joint efforts. Indeed, this was in all likelihood the key mechanism, more important than any other in explaining not only the peculiar genius of the main compromises but also the general fitness of the document as a whole. That is, a group of two or more intelligent men who are subject to no cross-pressures and whose principal commitment is to the success of an idea, are perfectly capable—as in our scientific communities of today—of performing what appear to be prodigies of intellect. Moving, as it were, in the same direction with a specific purpose, they can function at maximum efficiency. It was this that the historians of the nineteenth century did in their way see, and celebrated with sweeping rhetorical flourishes, when they took for granted that if an occasion of this sort could not call forth the highest level of statesmanship available, then it was impossible to imagine another that could.

Once the Philadelphia Convention had been allowed to meet and the delegates had managed, after more than three months of work, to hammer out a document that the great majority of them could sign, the political position of the Federalists changed dramatically. Despite the major battles still impending, for practical purposes they now had the initiative. The principal weapon of the Anti-Federalists—inertia—had greatly declined in effectiveness, for with the new program in motion it was no longer enough simply to argue that a new federal government was unnecessary. They would have to take positive steps in blocking it; they would have to arouse the people and convince them that the Constitution represented a positive danger.

Moreover, the Federalists had set the terms of ratification in such a way as to give the maximum advantage to energy and purpose; the key choices, this time, had been so arranged that they would fall right. Only nine states had to ratify before the Constitution would go into effect. Not only would this rule out the possibility of one or two states holding up the entire effort, but it meant that the Confederation would be automatically destroyed as an alternative before the difficult battles in New York and Virginia had to be faced. (By then, Patrick Henry in Virginia would have nothing but a vague alliance with North Carolina to offer as a counter-choice.) Besides, there was good reason to believe that at least four or five states, and possibly as many as seven, could be counted as safe, which meant that serious fighting in the first phase would be limited to two or three states. And finally, conditions were so set that the "snowball" principle would at each successive point favor the Federalists.

As for the actual process of acceptance, ratification would be done through state conventions elected for the purpose. Not only would this circumvent the vested interests of the legislatures and the ruling coteries that frequented the state capitals, but it gave the Federalists two separate chances to make their case—once to the people and once to the conventions. If the elected delegates were not initially disposed to do the desired thing, there was still a chance, after the convention met, of persuading them. Due partly to the hampering factor of transportation and distance, delegates had to have considerable leeway of choice and what amounted to quasi-plenipotentiary powers. Thus there could be no such thing as a fully "instructed" delegation, and members might meanwhile remain susceptible to argument and conversion. The convention device, moreover, enabled the Federalists to run as delegates men who would not normally take part in state politics.

The revolutionary verve and ardor of the Federalists, their resources of will and energy, their willingness to scheme tirelessly, campaign everywhere, and sweat and agonize over every vote meant in effect that despite all the hairbreadth squeezes and rigors of the struggle, the Anti-Federalists would lose every crucial test. There was, to be sure, an Anti-Federalist effort. But with no program, no really viable commitments, and little purposeful organization, the Anti-Federalists somehow always managed to move too late and with too little. They would sit and watch their great stronghold, New York, being snatched away from them despite a two-to-one Anti-Federalists majority in a convention presided over by their own chief, George Clinton. To them, the New York Federalists must have seemed possessed of the devil. The Federalists' convention men included Alexander Hamilton, James Duane, John Jay, and Robert Livingston —who knew, as did everyone else, that the new government was doomed unless Virginia and New York joined it. They insisted on debating the Constitution section by section instead of as a whole, which meant that they could out-argue the Anti-Federalists on every substantive issue and meanwhile delay the vote until New Hampshire and Virginia had had a chance to ratify. (Madison and Hamilton had a horse relay system in readiness to rush the Virginia news northward as quickly as possible.) By the time the New York convention was ready to act, ten others had ratified, and at the final moment Hamilton and his allies spread the chilling rumor that New York City was about to secede from the state. The Anti-Federalists, who had had enough, directed a chosen number of their delegates to cross over, and solemnly capitulated.

In the end, of course, everyone "crossed over." The speed with which this occurred once the continental revolutionists had made their point, and the ease with which the Constitution so soon became an object of universal veneration, still stands as one of the minor marvels of American history. But the document did contain certain implications, of a quasi-philosophical nature, that make the reasons for this ready consensus not so very difficult to find. It established a national government whose basic outlines were sufficiently congenial to the underlying commitments of the whole culture—republicanism and capitalism—that the likelihood of its being the subject of a true ideological clash was never very real. That the Constitution should mount guard over the rights of property—"realty," "personalty," or any other kind—was questioned by nobody. There had certainly been a struggle, a long and exhausting one, but we should not be deceived as to its nature. It was not fought on economic

131

grounds: it was not a matter of ideology: it was not. in the fullest and most fundamental sense, even a struggle between nationalism and localism. The key struggle was between inertia and energy; with inertia overcome, everything changed.

There were, of course, lingering objections and misgivings; many of the problems involved had been genuinely puzzling and difficult; and there remained doubters who had to be converted. But then the perfect bridge whereby all could become Federalists within a year was the addition of a Bill of Rights. After the French Revolution, anti-constitutionalism in France would be a burning issue for generations; in America, an anti-constitutional party was undreamed of after 1789. With the Bill of Rights, the remaining opponents of the new system could say that, ever watchful of tyranny, they had now got what they wanted. Moreover, the Young Men of the Revolution might at last imagine, after a dozen years of anxiety, that *their* Revolution had been a success.

STANLEY ELKINS

SMITH COLLEGE

ERIC MCKITRICK

COLUMBIA UNIVERSITY

Notes and Documents

The Founding Fathers of 1776 and 1787:
A Collective View

Richard D. Brown

In many ways the signers of the Declaration of Independence and the members of the Constitutional Convention are the best known, most intensively studied people in early American history. Biographies, analyses of their. social and economic status, and explorations of their political ideas and activities abound. Their eyes look out at us from the currency, and our cities and streets carry their names. Yet while we know much about the Founding Fathers as individuals, we have no systematic investigation of them as a demographic group, perhaps because they are too few in number and too distinctively elite to furnish data for large-scale generalizations about the nature of society in the Revolutionary era. Yet these ninety-nine men (listed in Table I) are an intrinsically significant subject for collective treatment because of their key historical roles. Selected by their peers, they composed the uppermost layer of the Revolutionary leadership. Collective analysis enables us to elucidate political and status relationships, to chart the degree of social distance between the Founding Fathers and ordinary citizens, and to clarify the extent to which the Founding Fathers were a socially homogeneous group. In light of recent analyses of broader categories of the political elite,[1] such an approach can improve our understanding of society and politics during the creation of the national government.[2]

Mr. Brown is chairman of the Department of History, University of Connecticut. He thanks George A. Waller and Clark Strickland, University of Connecticut graduate students, for their assistance in compiling and processing the data. The study was supported by a grant from the University of Connecticut Research Foundation.

[1] James Kirby Martin, *Men in Rebellion: High Governmental Leaders and the Coming of the American Revolution* (New Brunswick, N.J., 1973); P. M. G. Harris, "The Social Origins of American Leaders: The Demographic Foundations," *Perspectives in American History* III (1969), 159-344; Jackson Turner Main, *The Upper House in Revolutionary America, 1763-1788* (Madison, Wis., 1967); Sidney H. Aronson, *Status and Kinship in the Highest Civil Service: Standards of Selection in the Administrations of John Adams, Thomas Jefferson, and Andrew Jackson* (Cambridge, Mass., 1964).

[2] Data have been gathered chiefly from printed sources, biographical dictionaries, biographies, and genealogies. In several instances, state historical societies and

133

Who were the Founding Fathers, and where were they born? The immediate answer is that they were mostly (86 percent) native Americans. (See Table II.) Fourteen percent were immigrants. Nearly two-thirds (64 percent) were descended from families that had been resident in the colonies before 1700, and one-quarter (26 percent) came from families that arrived before 1640, in the first phase of settlement. (See Table III.) Among the signers of the Declaration, the proportion descended from the pre-1640 settlers was one-third (35 percent), much higher than among the members of the Constitutional Convention, of whom only 14 percent shared such early colonial backgrounds. On the basis of such data one is tempted to conclude that in the most direct, personal terms the Revolutionary leadership of 1776 included men who were defending their existing American identity, not simply those who were in the process of establishing one.[3]

In their family origins the Founding Fathers were so similar to the broader elite of Revolutionary executive officeholders as to be indistinguishable from them. They were also much like the executive elite of the John Adams administration, although by the late 1790s the proportion of immigrants among this elite was less than 5 percent. Taken together, these data suggest a gradual "Americanization" of the political upper crust stretching from the 1760s to 1800 and accelerated by the departure of the loyalist elite, the one group within the late colonial and early national political elite that was dominated by immigrants and first-generation natives (54 percent).[4]

Yet when one considers the Founding Fathers' origins according to region, it is evident that the overall data conceal some significant differences. New England, especially, and the South were led by indigenous elites. More than 95 percent of the New England delegates were natives of the region; there was only one immigrant among them (Matthew Thornton, a Scots-Irish New Hampshire signer of the Declaration). Three-quarters of the Southern delegates were natives of that region, and 90 percent were native Americans.[5] In contrast, barely one-half of the delegates from the Middle States were natives of the area (53 percent), and fully 25 percent were

---

archives provided additional data. Yet notwithstanding the prominence of the Founding Fathers, the single fact that can be ascertained positively for every one of them is the death date. At the time of their births and marriages, and the births of their children, they were not always prominent, nor was the quality of record keeping so high as to allow total recovery of the information. Data on wives and children are often so inaccessible as to preclude their inclusion in the analysis. The amplitude of the data varies according to region, with information for New England more complete than for either the Middle States or the South. In the generalizations that follow, I attempt to allow for such regional discrepancies.

[3] Jack P. Greene, "Search for Identity: An Interpretation of the Meaning of Selected Patterns of Social Response in Eighteenth-Century America," *Journal of Social History*, III (1969-1970), 189-220.

[4] Martin, *Men in Rebellion*, 102; Aronson, *Status and Kinship*, III, 113.

[5] The non-southern native Americans who represented the South included three born in New England and four born in the Middle Atlantic region.

immigrants.[6] Considering their family descent, the coherence of the New England and Southern elites in meeting British challenges seems more than accidental. In these regions imperial reforms challenged deeply rooted native elites.[7]

Regional differences are also illustrated through an occupational analysis of the Founding Fathers.[8] For even though the law was the most numerous single occupation for all three regions, lawyers were in a majority only among the Middle Atlantic delegates. (See Table IV.) New England was distinct in that there were no farmers in its group. It stood in sharp contrast to the Southern delegates, nearly one-third of whom were planters. These figures are not especially surprising in light of what historians have long known about the economies of the regions. They further establish regional differences within the Revolutionary elite.

What is perhaps less expected is that lawyers did not compose majorities in either the Declaration of Independence or Constitutional Convention groups, although at 40 percent (N=19) and 49 percent (N=23), respectively, theirs was the most numerous occupation. The prominence of lawyers in both gatherings has long been recognized, but in the case of the Continental Congress, particularly, it may have been overemphasized. Farmer-planters and merchants were also numerous. At the signing of the Declaration of Independence, they together (43 percent, N=20) outnumbered the lawyers.[9] At the Constitutional Convention, however, the lawyers were far more

[6] The non-Middle Atlantic native Americans representing the Middle Atlantic region included three born in New England and five born in the South.

[7] See Thad W. Tate, "The Coming of the Revolution in Virginia: Britain's Challenge to Virginia's Ruling Class, 1763-1776," *William and Mary Quarterly*, 3d Ser., XIX (1962), 323-343.

[8] Classifying the Founding Fathers by occupation entails subjective judgments in several cases. In all cases, assignments of occupations are based on overall career up to 1776 or 1787. For some, such as John Adams, the lawyer, George Clymer, the merchant, and George Washington, the planter, the assignment is clear-cut. There are six men, however, who practiced two distinct occupations simultaneously; William Ellery and Roger Sherman, for example, were both lawyers and merchants. These six have been excluded from occupational analyses. Two occupations, ironmaster and printer, were unique and are also excluded. In addition, there are a few, such as Samuel Adams and Alexander Hamilton, who seem to have been most clearly identified as politicians and have therefore been classified as such. For purposes of the discussion that follows, those who earned their livings directly from agriculture, both farmers and planters, are grouped together in a "Farmer-Planter" category. A separate classification is used for those "Landowners" who chiefly dealt in real estate and lived off rents and speculative transactions. Although some would question a few of the assignments, such as Benjamin Franklin as "printer" (thus excluded) rather than "politician," more than 80% of the assignments are straightforward and certain. Yet it is worth noting that the clear, specialized occupational categories of 20th-century analysis are slightly anachronistic when applied to unspecialized, wide-ranging "gentlemen" of the 18th century. John Adams, the lawyer, also operated a farm, and George Washington, the planter, was also a major real estate speculator.

[9] Among the signers were 10 farmer-planters, 10 merchants, and 19 lawyers.

numerous than merchants and farmer-planters, who together mustered only 28 percent (N=13). When one considers that lawyers were losing ground in the state assemblies between 1776 and 1787, such figures suggest that the Constitutional Convention was seen as an enterprise particularly suited to lawyers. Indeed, the subsequent records of the Adams and Jefferson administrations, in which nearly 75 percent of high appointees were lawyers, suggest that training in law was becoming a prime requisite for the national officeholding elite from 1787 onward.[10]

One reason for this exceptional role is apparent in patterns of geographic mobility that substantially differentiated lawyers, politicians, and professional men from merchants, farmer-planters, and large landowners. Half the lawyers, politicians, and professionals were not natives of the colonies or states they represented. From the standpoint of geographic mobility the law was the most national, cosmopolitan occupation. Among the merchants, farmer-planters, and landowners, however, such mobility was unusual; two out of three were natives of the colony or state that sent them to the Congress or the Convention. (See Table IV.) That the farmer-planters were more deeply rooted than lawyers in their particular states comes as no surprise. But the similarity between merchants and farmer-planters, setting merchants apart from lawyers and professionals, is somewhat unexpected. Merchants possessed portable assets and traded across regions; like most lawyers they were urban, but like the farmer-planters they generally possessed long-standing connections with the people of their states.

In all occupations the paternal ethnic backgrounds of the Founding Fathers were overwhelmingly British (97 percent, N=62). (See Table V.) The non-British delegates were descended from early seventeenth-century Dutch and Swedish families, and had been assimilated into British political culture.[11] Aside from blacks, the one major ethnic group not represented was that of the German-Americans, who were more numerous in the general population than the Dutch and Swedes combined. In contrast to the ease with which the Irish were incorporated into the elite group, the absence of the Germans suggests that eighteenth-century America was primarily a British melting-pot. Scots, Irish, Welsh, Scots-Irish, and other eighteenth-century immigrants joined with the English, but the Germans remained apart.[12]

---

[10] Jackson Turner Main, *The Social Structure of Revolutionary America* (Princeton, N.J., 1965), 211-212; Aronson, *Status and Kinship*, 89. Martin, *Men in Rebellion*, 68-69, finds that only 30% of the high government elite were lawyers in the 1770s. David J. Rothman, *Politics and Power: The United States Senate, 1869-1901* (Cambridge, Mass., 1966), 115, finds that 73% of the U.S. Senators in the 1870s were lawyers, a figure that dropped to 57% in the 1890s.

[11] Henry Laurens and James Bowdoin, prominent leaders of Huguenot descent, were not signers of the Declaration or members of the Convention of 1787. Still, it appears that by the late 18th century the small Huguenot group had been assimilated into the elite. See Table V.

[12] As late as the Jackson period, Germans, perhaps because of their pietist heritage, were generally absent from the national elite. Aronson, *Status and Kinship*, 113.

Ethnically, as well as politically, the Revolution was a conflict between British peoples.

The lives of the Founding Fathers ranged across the eighteenth century. All were born after 1700, two before 1710 and one after 1760. (See Table VI.) The average birth year for signers of the Declaration was 1731; that of the members of the Constitutional Convention was 1743.[13] The majority of the entire group (76 percent) were born between 1720 and 1750. The fact that the average age of the Founding Fathers at both events was virtually identical (43), and the preponderance of the 1730s and 1740s cohort at each gathering, provide an indication of what contemporaries viewed as the age of leadership. Few men in their twenties were participants in the highest political councils. More seasoning was wanted. The choice of thirty-five years as the minimum age for the president under the Constitution was a direct outgrowth of such general expectations and practices.[14]

The degree to which the Founding Fathers were distinct from the general American population may be inferred from their marriage and family patterns. (See Table I.) Although they married with much the same frequency as the rest of the population (more than 90 percent), the ages at which they married and the sizes of their families more closely followed the norms of the British peerage than those of ordinary Americans.

The age at first marriage for the Founding Fathers was 29.4.[15] Such an advanced marriage age appears to be a direct correlate of social standing. Among American colonists, only seventeenth-century university men, mostly clerics, delayed their marriages at a similar rate. In the eighteenth century most American men, whether Salem merchants or mariners, whether Pennsylvania Quakers or New England farmers, married between the ages of 23 and 26.[16] Even in England, where marriage was somewhat more delayed

[13] The combined group average birth year was 1737.

[14] The mean age of signers was 43.8 years (N = 48). The mean age of members of the Constitutional Convention was 43.5 (N = 41). In New England, selectmen and other high officials were seldom under age 40 at first election. See Robert S. Gross, *The Minutemen and Their World* (New York, 1976), 13, 62-63, 70-71, and Michael Zuckerman, *Peaceable Kingdoms: New England Towns in the Eighteenth Century* (New York, 1970), chap. 6. The cohort median age of U.S. Congressmen at first election between 1789 and 1800 was 40-44; it dropped to 35-39 in the decade 1841-1850, and rose again to 40-44 during 1891-1900. Allan G. Bogue and Jerome M. Clubb, "American Congressmen and the Processes of Modernization," Preliminary Report for Brockport Conference (1974), Table VIII. A revised version is forthcoming in the *Journal of American History*.

[15] It was highest among merchants (31.0 years), lowest among farmer-planters (27.5 years). Lawyers, at 29.5 years, were close to the norm. See Table IV.

[16] Bernard Farber, *Guardians of Virtue: Salem Families in 1800* (New York, 1972), 38, 41; Robert V. Wells, "Quaker Marriage Patterns in a Colonial Perspective," *WMQ*, 3d Ser., XXIX (1972), 418; John Demos, *A Little Commonwealth: Family Life in Plymouth Colony* (New York, 1970), 193, Table IV; Philip J. Greven, Jr., *Four Generations: Population, Land, and Family in Colonial Andover, Massachusetts* (Ithaca, N.Y., 1970), 35, 206, 208; Daniel Scott Smith, "The Demographic History of Colonial New England," *Journal of Economic History*,

than in America, the mean age was between 25 and 27.[17] During the same period, men in British ducal families married at the average age of 28.6, a figure similar to that of the Founding Fathers and about two years later than the average Englishman.[18] Presumably, ambitious young men in the American elite postponed marriage until their careers were suitably launched.

The marriage partners of the Founding Fathers also distinguished them from most Americans. In the population at large, the overwhelming majority of marriages were between natives of the same town or county. Nearly all were between natives of the same state.[19] But among the Founding Fathers fully 46 percent married natives of other states.[20] This cosmopolitanism sets them apart dramatically. Taken in conjunction with their delay of marriage, the social distance between the Founding Fathers and their constituencies appears substantial.

The number of their children sets them apart in a similar way. During the period 1750 to 1800, when most of their children were born, the average size of completed American families was between six and seven children.[21] Among the Founding Fathers the average was significantly lower—4.8.[22] (See Table VII.) The reasons for this smaller number of children seem to be the later marriage age and perhaps the practice of family limitation.[23] For the

XXXII (1972), 177, Table III; Kenneth A. Lockridge, "The Population of Dedham, Massachusetts, 1636-1736," *Economic History Review*, XIX (1966), 330.

[17] E. A. Wrigley, "Family Limitation in Pre-Industrial England," in Michael Drake, ed., *Population in Industrialization* (London, 1969), 157-194, esp. 164.

[18] T. H. Hollingsworth, "A Demographic Study of the British Ducal Families," in Drake, ed., *Pop. in Industrialization*, 73-102, esp. 87.

[19] This is the universal presumption, not yet sustained empirically, although several studies point this way. Susan L. Norton, "Marital Migration in Essex County, Massachusetts, in the Colonial and Early Federal Periods," *Journal of Marriage and the Family*, XXXV (1973), 406-418; Douglas Lamar Jones, "Geographic Mobility and Society in Eighteenth-Century Essex County, Massachusetts" (Ph.D diss., Brandeis University, 1975); Gross, *Minutemen*, 175, n. 8.

[20] Thirty-seven (54%) of the Founding Fathers married women born in the same state as themselves, while 31 (46%) married natives of other states.

[21] Smith, "Demographic History," *Jour. Econ. Hist.*, XXXII (1972), 406; Wells, "Quaker Marriage Patterns," *WMQ*, 3d Ser., XXXIX (1972), 441; Robert V. Wells, "Family Size and Fertility Control in Eighteenth-Century America: A Study of Quaker Families," *Population Studies*, XXIV (1970), 74; Ansley J. Coale and Melvin Zelnik, *New Estimates of Fertility and Population in the United States* (Princeton, N.J., 1963), 36. See Table VII.

[22] The range was considerable—from Roger Sherman's 15 children to George Washington's none.

[23] Wells, "Family Size," *Pop. Studies*, XXIV (1970), 78-80; Wrigley, "Family Limitation," in Drake, ed., *Pop. in Industrialization*, 164. It may also be noted that Founding Fathers were more frequently separated from their wives by public business than were ordinary people and for that reason may have experienced lower fertility rates. Farmer-planters, the earliest marriers, had the largest families, 5.4 children; merchants, the latest to marry, had fewer than average, 4.8. Lawyers, who married at about the average age, had the average number of children, 5.0.

birth-spacing patterns in their families are much like those of English families reported by E. A. Wrigley and Quaker families reported by Robert V. Wells, where the mean intervals between the births of first, second, and third children ranged from 24 to 30 months, and where spacing patterns suggest that family limitation was practiced deliberately.[24] As with age at marriage, the number of children born to the Founding Fathers is close to that of eighteenth-century British ducal families (4.5).[25] It is not, however, entirely outside the range of behavior among other American sub-groups. By 1800 the Salem maritime population had even smaller families, averaging between four and five children; and in the period 1800-1830 Quaker families averaged only 5.02 children.[26] Taking a longer perspective, it appears that with respect to family size, the Founding Fathers anticipated by a generation or two the nineteenth-century trend among white Americans toward fewer children.[27]

In contrast to the distinctive marriage and parenthood record of the Founding Fathers, their longevity does not clearly distinguish them from the general white population.[28] Their mean age at death was 66.5 years. (See Table IV.) This figure is very close to that of men in British ducal families, but whether it sets the Founding Fathers off from the white American population is not clear. Certainly they lived longer than men who followed especially high-risk occupations, such as mariners and ship captains, but when compared to merchants, artisans, and farmers, their life expectancy of 26.5 more years at age 40 does not appear unusual.[29] Indeed, longevity

[24] Wrigley, "Family Limitation," in Drake, ed., *Pop. in Industrialization*, 171; Wells, "Family Size," *Pop. Studies*, XXIV (1970), 78-80; Wells, "Quaker Marriage Patterns," *WMQ*, 3d Ser., XXIX (1972), 440. Although "early births" of infants less than 9 months after marriage were relatively infrequent, I have data on seven, six of whose fathers were New Englanders. Thomas Jefferson, whose first child was born eight months after his marriage, is the only non-New Englander in my data. The others are Benjamin Franklin (Boston native), Pa., four months; Nathaniel Gorham, N.H., one month; Stephen Hopkins, R.I., four months; William Samuel Johnson, Conn., eight months; Robert Treat Paine, Mass., two months; and Roger Sherman, Conn., eight months.

[25] Hollingsworth, "British Ducal Families," in Drake, ed., *Pop. in Industrialization*, 93.

[26] Farber, *Guardians of Virtue*, 45; Wells, "Family Size," *Pop. Studies*, XXIV (1970), 74.

[27] Coale and Zelnik, *New Estimates*, 36. The entire United States population reached the level of the Founding Fathers in 1861-1862.

[28] Compare the expectancy of 25.2 years for Massachusetts males at age 40 in 1790. Richard B. Morris, ed., *Encylopedia of American History*, rev. ed. (New York, 1961), 468.

[29] Farber, *Guardians of Virtue*, 45; Michael Drake, *Population and Society in Norway, 1735-1865* (London, 1969), 47; Conrad Taeuber and Irene B. Taeuber, *The Changing Population of the United States* (New York, 1958), 273; Hollingsworth, "British Ducal Families," in Drake, ed., *Pop. in Industrialization*, 82.

among the Founding Fathers appears to have varied by occupation, with merchants enjoying the longest lives.[30]

Judging from the seasonal distribution of deaths among the Founding Fathers it seems possible that elite status, and the greater geographic mobility it entailed, may have shortened their lives. (See Table VIII.) Deaths were most frequent during the period from May through November, months when travel and communication were at their height. It was during these months that legislatures met and the bulk of trade was conducted. The communication of disease peaked during these months, and elite political figures, traveling to courts, legislatures, and markets, were more exposed than artisans and farmers who stayed put in their localities. Yet in the absence of reliable data on causes of deaths one can only speculate on the hazards involved in such travel.

The influence of warmer weather, which favored bacteria as well as communication, is especially evident in the death pattern of the New Englanders, who were four times as likely to die in the seven months from May through November than in the five months December through April. Rather than costing the lives of adults, the hard New England winter preserved them. It froze diseases into inactivity. To the south the same pattern prevailed, although less intensely. From New York to Georgia the incidence of deaths during the warmer months was twice as great as during the colder ones. It is uncertain whether this difference from New England should be attributed to higher levels of microbial activity or to more communication (or both) during the colder months.

The deaths of the Founding Fathers occurred over a forty-year period, roughly from 1790 to 1830. (See Table IX.) When Thomas Jefferson was elected president in 1800, over half of the Founding Fathers were still alive. Thereafter they died at the rate of 16 to 19 per decade. By 1829, when Andrew Jackson took office as president, there were only three survivors. By this time their direct political influence, which for twenty-eight years between 1789 and 1817 had kept the presidency exclusively in their hands, had vanished.

Yet the demise of the Founding Fathers did not signal any dramatic change in the social backgrounds of the national elite. In their ethnic origins and length of family settlement in America, the executive elite under Jackson would differ only slightly from the Founding Fathers. The national elite was becoming less English but not less British in its origins; and while it included fewer men who traced their descent from seventeenth-century settlers, it also included many fewer who were themselves immigrants.[31] From the standpoint of occupations the key change—the emergence of lawyers as the preponderant group—had occurred years before. Among the signers of the Declaration the lawyers had been a rising minority, but at the Constitutional

[30] Merchants, 67.9 years; lawyers, 65.7 years; farmer-planters, 65.0 years. See Table IV.

[31] Aronson, *Status and Kinship*, 111, 113.

Convention they were already preponderant. Under the national government their role increased through the early decades of the nineteenth century.[32]

Whether the social distance between the national elite and the population as a whole was stable after 1787 is not certain. When one considers the differences in the patterns of marriage and family-rearing between the Founding Fathers and the general population, it is apparent that by the period 1776-1787 national leaders were already a group set apart. Since lawyers generally married later and farther afield, and were more mobile than merchants and farmer-planters, this kind of social distance was increasing in the early national period as the percentage of lawyers grew.

It is also likely that the national elite was growing more homogeneous in the early nineteenth century, becoming predominantly native lawyers of long-settled British lineage.[33] Here the diversity of the Founding Fathers is particularly significant. For if New England and Southern leaders were alike in being descended chiefly from seventeenth-century British settlers, they were quite different in their occupations, and only a minority among them were lawyers. Moreover, the leaders of the Middle States, who were mostly lawyers, were frequently not natives of the states they led, and one-quarter of them were immigrants to America. In their social backgrounds the members of the national elite of the Revolutionary era were, as befitted the variety of polities and economies they represented, a heterogeneous group. From this perspective their performance in achieving national unity through repeated compromises is especially striking. Collective analysis suggests that the shared British political culture of the Founding Fathers was more important than economic interest, occupation, or provincial origin in shaping American unity.

[32] Ibid., 89.
[33] Ibid., 89, 111, 113.

TABLE I

LIST OF SUBJECTS AND SELECTED DATA

Name	Signer/ Convention	Colony or State Represented	Birthplace	Lifespan	Occupation	Date Family in America	Family Origin	No. of Marriages	Age at First Marriage	No. of Children
John Adams	1	MA	MA	1735-1826	lawyer	1636	Eng	1	29.0	5
Samuel Adams	1	MA	MA	1722-1803	politician	1636	Eng	2	27.1	6
Abraham Baldwin	2	GA	CT	1754-1807	minister			0	None	0
Josiah Bartlett	1	NH	MA	1729-1795	physician			1	24.2	0
Richard Bassett	2	DE	MD	1745-1815	lawyer			2	29.7	3
Gunning Bedford, Jr.	2	DE	PA	1747-1812	lawyer			1		4
John Blair	2	VA	VA	1732-1800	lawyer			1		4
William Blount	2	NC	NC	1749-1800	politician	1670	Eng	1	28.9	5
Carter Braxton	1	VA	VA	1736-1797	planter			2	18.8	7
David Brearly	2	NJ	NJ	1745-1790	lawyer	1680	Eng	2		1
Pierce Butler	2	SC	Ire	1744-1822	politician		Ire	1	26.5	5
Charles Carroll	1	MD	MD	1737-1832	planter		Ire	1	30.7	2
Daniel Carroll	2	MD	MD	1730-1796	planter		Ire	1		10
Samuel Chase	1	MD	MD	1741-1811	*	1730	Eng	2	21.1	8
Abraham Clark	1	NJ	NJ	1726-1794	lawyer			1	26.0	5
George Clymer	3	PA	PA	1739-1813	merchant		Eng	1	25.8	
William Richardson Davie	2	NC	Eng	1756-1820	lawyer	1763	Eng	1		2
Jonathan Dayton	2	NJ	NJ	1760-1824	lawyer			2	37.7	
John Dickinson	2	DE	MD	1732-1808	lawyer			2	22.8	9
William Ellery	1	RI	RI	1727-1820	**	1690	Eng	1	27.7	1
Oliver Ellsworth	2	CT	CT	1745-1807	lawyer	1645	Eng	2	40.1	5
William Few	2	GA	MD	1748-1828	+	1682	Ire	1		4
Thomas Fitzsimmons	2	PA	Ire	1741-1811	merchant			2	25.7	10
William Floyd	1	NY	NY	1734-1821	landowner		Wales	1		0
Benjamin Franklin	3	PA	MA	1706-1790	printer+	1682	Eng	3		9
Elbridge Gerry	3	MA	MA	1744-1814	merchant	1730	Eng	1	41.5	3
Nicholas Gilman	2	NH	NH	1755-1814	politician	1638	Eng	0	None	0
Nathaniel Gorman	2	MA	MA	1738-1796	merchant	1643	Eng	1	25.3	9
Button Gwinnett	1	GA	Eng	1735-1777	*	1765	Wales	1	22.0	3
Lyman Hall	1	GA	CT	1724-1790	minister	1633		2	28.1	
Alexander Hamilton	2	NY	BWI	1757-1804	politician		Scot	1	23.9	
John Hancock	1	MA	MA	1737-1793	merchant			1	38.6	0
Benjamin Harrison	1	VA	VA	1726-1791	planter			1		
John Hart	1	NJ	CT	1711-1779	farmer	1634	Eng	1		12
Joseph Hewes	1	NC	NJ	1730-1779	merchant	1635		0	None	0

Name		Born	Rep	Dates	Occupation	Anc. Yr	Origin		Age	
Thomas Heyward, Jr.	1	SC	SC	1746-1809	lawyer	1737	Scot	2	26.7	3
William Hooper	1	NC	MA	1742-1790	lawyer	1638	Eng	1	25.2	7
Stephen Hopkins	1	RI	RI	1709-1785	merchant	1731	Eng	2	19.6	4
Francis Hopkinson	1	NJ	PA	1737-1791	lawyer			1	30.9	0
William Churchill Houston	2	NJ	NC	1746-1788	+			1		3
Samuel Huntington	1	CT	CT	1731-1796	lawyer	1633		1	29.7	6
Jared Ingersoll, Jr.	2	PA	PA	1749-1822	lawyer			1	32.2	0
Thomas Jefferson	1	VA	VA	1743-1826	***		Eng	1	28.7	7
Daniel of St. Thomas Jenifer	2	PA	MD	1723-1790	farmer			0	None	7
William Samuel Johnson	2	CT	CT	1727-1819	lawyer		Eng	2	22.1	7
Rufus King	2	MA	MA	1755-1827	lawyer	1680	Eng	1	31.0	10
John Langdon	2	NH	NH	1741-1819	merchant	1660	Neth	1	35.7	9
John Lansing	2	NY	NY	1754-1829	lawyer	1640	Eng	1	27.3	4
Francis Lightfoot Lee	1	VA	VA	1734-1797	planter	1641	Eng	1		9
Richard Henry Lee	1	VA	VA	1732-1794	planter	1641	Wales	2	25.9	13
Francis Lewis	1	NY	BWI	1713-1802	merchant	1738	Scot	1	32.3	2
Philip Livingston	1	NY	NY	1716-1778	merchant	1763	Scot	1	24.3	5
William Livingston	1	NJ	NY	1723-1790	lawyer	1673	Ire	1		11
Thomas Lynch, Jr.	1	SC	SC	1749-1779	lawyer	1700		1		
James McClurg	2	VA	VA	1746-1823	physician	1771	Ire	1	30.2	0
James McHenry	1	MD	Ire	1753-1816	physician	1725	Scot	2	29.3	5
Thomas McKean	1	DE	PA	1734-1817	lawyer			2	43.5	12
James Madison	2	VA	VA	1751-1836	planter			1	None	5
Alexander Martin	2	NC	NJ	1748-1807	politician			0		3
Luther Martin	2	MD	MD	1748-1826	lawyer			2	25.7	4
George Mason	2	VA	VA	1725-1792	planter	1655	Eng	1	22.2	1
John Francis Mercer	1	SC	SC	1759-1821	politician	1720	Eng	1	23.2	10
Arthur Middleton	2	PA	SC	1742-1787	planter			1	57.9	7
Thomas Mifflin	1	PA	PA	1744-1800	merchant	1680	Eng	1	23.4	9
Gouverneur Morris	1	NY	NY	1752-1816	landowner	1670	Eng	1	35.2	1
Lewis Morris	3	PA	NY	1726-1798	merchant			1		1
Robert Morris	1	PA	PA	1734-1806	farmer	1740	Eng	1		8
John Morton	1	PA	DE	1724-1777	*	1654	Swed	2	23.6	2
Thomas Nelson, Jr.	1	VA	VA	1738-1789	lawyer	1700	Scot	1	22.6	
William Paca	1	MD	MD	1740-1799	lawyer			1	39.0	3
Robert Treat Paine	1	MA	MA	1731-1814	lawyer	1639		1	33.2	3
William Paterson	2	NJ	Ire	1745-1806	lawyer		Ire	1	23.2	4
John Penn	2	NC	VA	1740-1788	merchant			1		
William Leigh Pierce	2	GA		1740-1789	lawyer			1		
Charles Pinckney	2	SC	SC	1757-1824	lawyer			2	30.5	
Charles Cotesworth Pinckney	2	SC	SC	1746-1825	lawyer			2	27.6	
Edmund Randolph	2	VA	VA	1753-1813	lawyer			1	23.0	

143

Name	Signer/Convention	Colony or State Represented	Birthplace	Lifespan	Occupation	Date Family in America	Family Origin	No. of Marriages	Age at First Marriage	No. of Children
George Reed	3	DE	MD	1733-1798	lawyer	1720	Ire	1	29.3	5
Caesar Rodney	1	DE	DE	1728-1784	farmer	1681	Eng	0	None	0
George Ross	1	PA	DE	1730-1779	lawyer	1703	Scot	1	21.3	3
Benjamin Rush	1	PA	PA	1745-1813	physician	1683	Eng	1	30.0	2
Edward Rutledge	1	SC	SC	1749-1800	planter			2	24.3	
John Rutledge	2	SC	SC	1739-1800	lawyer			1	23.7	
Roger Sherman	3	CT	MA	1721-1793	**	1636	Eng	2	28.6	15
James Smith	1	PA	Ire	1719-1806	lawyer	1729	Ire	1		3
Richard Dobbs Spaight	2	NC	NC	1758-1802	politician	1740	Ire	1		2
Richard Stockton	1	NJ	NJ	1730-1781	lawyer	1656		1		3
Thomas Stone	1	MD	MD	1743-1787	lawyer	1628	Eng	1		3
Caleb Strong	2	MA	MA	1745-1819	lawyer	1630	Eng	1	32.8	9
George Taylor	1	PA	Ire	1716-1781	ironmaster+	1736	Ire	2		2
Matthew Thornton	1	NH	Ire	1714-1803	physician	1718	Ire	1		5
George Walton	2	GA	VA	1741-1804	lawyer	1682	Eng	1		
George Washington	2	VA	VA	1732-1799	planter	1657	Eng	1	26.9	0
William Whipple	1	NH	MA	1730-1785	merchant	1638	Eng	1		1
William Williams	1	CT	CT	1731-1811	merchant	1637	Eng	1	39.8	3
Hugh Williamson	2	NC	PA	1735-1819	physician	1730	Scot	1	53.1	
James Wilson	3	PA	Scot	1742-1798	lawyer	1765	Scot	2	29.2	7
John Witherspoon	1	NJ	Scot	1723-1794	minister	1768	Scot	2	25.6	
Oliver Wolcott	1	CT	CT	1726-1797	lawyer	1636	Eng	1	28.2	5

Notes: *Signer/Convention:* The number 1 indicates signer of Declaration of Independence; 2 indicates member of Constitutional Convention; 3 indicates participation in both. *Occupation* was assigned based on the overall career up to 1776 or 1787 and includes a subjective assessment.

* Merchant-Planter, not included in tabulations relating to occupation.

** Lawyer-Merchant, not included in tabulations relating to occupation.

*** Lawyer-Planter, not included in tabulations relating to occupation.

+ None of these has been included in tabulations relating to occupation.

TABLE II

REGION OF BIRTH AND REGIONS REPRESENTED

Region of Birth   Region Represented

	N. E.		Middle		South		Totals	
	N	%	N	%	N	%	N	%
New England	20	95	3	8	3	7	26	27
Middle	0	0	19	53	4	10	23	24
South	0	0	5	14	29	73	34	35
America	20	95	27	75	36	90	83	86
Europe	1	5	9	25	4	10	14	14
Totals	21	100	36	100	40	100	97	100

TABLE III

SETTLEMENT LONGEVITY

Activity   Date of Family Arrival in America

	1600-1639		1640-1699		1700-1779		Totals	
	N	%	N	%	N	%	N	%
DI	12	35	9	26	13	39	34	100
CC	3	14	13	62	5	24	21	100
Both	1	17	1	17	4	66	6	100
Totals	16	26	23	38	22	36	61	100

TABLE IV

COMPARISON BY OCCUPATIONS

Occupation	Activity						Region						Colony of Birth and State Represented		Age at First Marriage		Age at Death	
	DI		CC		Both		New England		Middle		South		Different	Same				
	N	%	N	%	N	%	N	%	N	%	N	%	N	N	N	Yrs.	N	Yrs.
Merchant	7	17	5	12	3	60	7	37	6	18	2	5	5	9	11	31.0	13	67.9
Lawyer	17	40	21	50	2	40	8	42	18	55	14	38	19	22	28	29.5	35	65.7
Politician	1	2	7	17	0	0	2	11	1	3	5	14	4	4	5	26.4	7	60.4
Minister	2	5	1	2	0	0	0	0	1	3	2	5	3	0	2	26.8	3	63.5
Physician	3	7	3	7	0	0	2	10	1	3	3	8	4	2	4	34.4	4	69.8
Farmer-Planter	10	24	5	12	0	0	0	0	4	12	11	30	3	11	7	27.5	10	65.0
Landowner	2	5	0	0	0	0	0	0	2	6	0	0	0	2	2	24.5	2	79.2
Totals	42	100	42	100	5	100	19	100	33	100	37	100	37	50	59	29.4	74	66.0

TABLE V

ETHNIC BACKGROUND

Origin of Family	%	N
England	57	37
Scotland	16	10
Ireland*	19	12
Wales	5	3
Netherlands	2	1
Sweden	2	1
Totals	100	64

* This category includes Irish, Anglo-Irish, Scots-Irish.

TABLE VI

COHORT GROUPS

Activity	Births of Founding Fathers by Decade													
	1700-09		1710-19		1720-29		1730-39		1740-49		1750-59		1760-69	
	N	%	N	%	N	%	N	%	N	%	N	%	N	%
DI	2	4	6	11	12	22	21	38	14	25	0	0	0	0
CC	1	2	0	0	5	9	10	19	21	41	14	27	1	2
Combined	2	2	6	6	16	16	28	28	33	32	13	13	1	1

TABLE VII

FAMILY SIZE

No. of Children	N (Mean: 4.8)	No. of Children	N (Mean: 4.8)
0	8	8	2
1	7	9	6
2	8	10	5
3	12	11	1
4	7	12	2
5	11	13	1
6	2	14	0
7	7	15	1

TABLE VIII

DISTRIBUTION OF DEATHS BY REGION AND MONTH

Region	J	F	M	A	M	J	J	A	S	O	N	D
N. Eng.	2	1	0	1	3	2	3	1	1	2	5	0
Middle	3	3	1	2	3	3	4	6	4	2	3	2
South	5	2	3	1	4	2	5	3	3	7	5	3
Totals	10	6	4	4	10	7	12	10	8	11	12	5

TABLE IX

DEATHS BY FIVE-YEAR PERIODS

Period	N	Period	N	Period	N	Period	N
1775-1779	7	1795-1799	12	1815-1819	8	1835-1839	1
1780-1784	3	1800-1804	11	1820-1824	9		
1785-1789	8	1805-1809	8	1825-1829	7		
1790-1794	14	1810-1814	10	1830-1834	1		

The Political Structure of Constitution Making: The Federal Convention of 1787*

Calvin C. Jillson, *Louisiana State University*
Cecil L. Eubanks, *Louisiana State University*

The authors contend that our understanding of the Federal Convention and of the Constitution that it produced has been substantially and unnecessarily clouded by an ancient dispute between the adherents of two very broad traditions of political analysis. A "rationalist" line of interpretation has consistently argued for the centrality of ideas and political principles to the outcome of the Convention's debates, while a "materialist" tradition has consistently stressed the importance of practical politics and economic interests. The authors integrate these alternative traditions of analysis and explanation by demonstrating that a dynamic relationship of mutual interdependence existed between philosophical *and* material influences in the Convention. The authors demonstrate, through both empirical and interpretive means, that, although questions of both philosophical and material content and import were before the Convention throughout, questions of each general type dominated the Convention's attention during particular phases of its work. Therefore, the focus of debate and decision, as well as the voting coalitions that confronted one another over the issues under discussion, were organized around shared principles at some stages, while at other times they were organized around conflicting material interests.

Ever since men began reflecting on politics they have oscillated between two diametrically opposed interpretations. According to one, politics is conflict. . . . According to the other . . . , politics is an effort to bring about the rule of order and justice.

—*Maurice Duverger (1966, p. xii)*

Introduction

This study contends that our understanding of the Federal Convention and of the Constitution that it produced has been substantially and unnecessarily clouded by an ancient dispute between the adherents of two very broad traditions of political analysis. Robert Dahl located the epistemological source of this intellectual dispute by identifying "two fundamentally different types" of explanation for the relationship between political institutions and the broader socioeconomic and cultural contexts within which they rise. Dahl (1963) has argued that "a *Rationalist* explanation . . . gives primacy to the way men think about politics. . . . But

*Earlier versions of this paper were presented before the LSU Political Science Department's colloquium on "The Study of Politics in the Social Sciences" and at the 1982 Southern Political Science Association meetings. We are very grateful to the many friends and colleagues who contributed various forms of support, counsel, and encouragement during its development. Special thanks go to Thornton Anderson, Larry Dodd, Leroy Rieselbach, Vincent Ostrom, William Riker, Eric Uslaner, Chris Wolfe, Jim Bolner, Robert Becker, Van Crabb, Lance Brouthers, and Rick Wilson.

149

since men do not have equal power, it is the philosophical beliefs of the rulers that are [treated as] particularly critical. . . . A *Materialist* explanation . . . holds that . . . the way people think about politics is a rationalization or defense of the political, social, and economic institutions that they think will maximize their own material interests" (pp. 107–8). Because rationalist and materialist explanations of politics and political behavior are based in radically different epistemological traditions, they have frequently been viewed as mutually exclusive by devotees who adhere to them with ideological fervor.

We argue that the impact of this dispute on studies of the Federal Convention has been both clear and almost wholly unfortunate. One line of interpretation has consistently argued for the centrality of ideas and political principles to the outcome of the Convention's debates, while the other has stressed the importance of practical politics and economic interests.

In this study we attempt to integrate these alternative traditions of explanation and analysis by demonstrating that a dynamic relationship of mutual interdependence existed between philosophical *and* material influences in the Convention. Our thesis is that principles guided action on distinguishable types of questions, while on other sets of questions personal, state, and regional interests encroached upon, and in some cases overwhelmed and subordinated, the independent impact of ideas. More importantly, we demonstrate that questions of each general type dominated the Convention's attention during particular phases of its work, so that at some stages, the dominant voting coalitions were organized around shared principles, while at other times the dominant coalitions were organized around conflicting material interests.

Conflicting Interpretations: Principle versus Interest

Americans entered the twentieth century convinced that British Prime Minister William Gladstone had captured the special character of the American Constitution in describing it as "the most wonderful work ever struck off at a given time by the brain and purpose of man" (Smith, 1980, p. 94). Yet, less than a decade into the new century, J. Allen Smith (1907) set the tone for an explicitly materialist interpretation of the Convention's work by arguing that "the American scheme of government was planned and set up to perpetuate the ascendancy of the property-holding class" (p. 298). Charles A. Beard (1913) elaborated this "economic interpretation" of the motives of the Framers and the outcome of their deliberations. He concluded that "the members of the Philadelphia Convention which drafted the Constitution were, with a few exceptions, immediately, directly, and personally interested in, and derived economic advantages from, the establishment of the new system" (1913, p. 324).

By mid-century, the charges against the Founders had become less personal, but no less materialist in character. John P. Roche (1961) applied the assumptions of democratic pluralism to his analysis of the Convention and concluded that the Constitution was no more than a particularly impressive example of "political improvisation" (p. 810). It was "a patchwork sewn together under the pressure of both time and events by a group of extremely talented democratic politicians'' (p. 815). Though Roche did not intend his reading to "suggest that the Constitution rested on a foundation of impure or base motives" (p. 801) many analysts feared that the cumulative impact of his and other materialist interpretations of the Founding had diminished the nation's sense of direction and purpose. Walter Lippmann (1955) concluded that "the public philosophy [that guided the nation's early development] is in large measure intellectually discredited among contemporary men. . . . The signs and seals of legitimacy, or rightness and of truth, have been taken over by men who reject . . . the doctrine of constitutional democracy" (pp. 136–37).

The recovery of a sound and effective "public philosophy" did not come quickly. Fully twenty years after Lippmann wrote, Martin Diamond (1976) was forced to conclude that "the old root American ideas have been challenged on nearly every front and cast into doubt by the most powerful contemporary intellectual currents" (p. 3). In defense of the Founders and the political system that they created, Diamond adopted and promoted a view that clearly, even combatively, emphasized the impact of ideas and political principles over material interests in the Convention. He argued that "the Convention supplies a remarkable example of . . . how theoretical matters govern the disposition of practical matters" (Diamond, 1981, p. 30). In Diamond's view, "the debate over the Constitution was a climactic encounter between two rival political theories of how the ends of democratic consent, liberty and competent government can best be obtained" (1981, p. 54). Despite the profound impact of Diamond's work on many students of American political ideas and institutions, others have continued to embrace the predominately materialist view that we have identified with Smith, Beard, and Roche.

Despite the persistence of this long-standing dispute within the tradition of constitutional studies, we take the view of Maurice Duverger that politics is "always and at all times both the instrument by which certain groups dominate others . . . and also a means . . . of achieving some integration of the individual into the collectivity for the general good" (1966, p. xiii). Therefore, we seek to demonstrate that debate moved between two levels of constitutional construction and that these levels represented significant shifts in the relative importance of political principles and material interests in the Convention.

This reading of the Convention's work has been given impressive theoretical support by two important analytical distinctions concerning the logical structure of constitutional choice made some twenty years ago by James Buchanan and Gordon Tullock and elaborated more recently by Vincent Ostrom. Buchanan and Tullock (1962) began their attempt to develop a "positive" or "economic theory of constitutions" by distinguishing between the "operational" level of practical politics and the "ultimate constitutional level of decision-making" (p. 6). Ostrom (1979) has expanded on this distinction by explaining that choice at "the *constitutional level* focuses upon alternative sets of rules or institutional arrangements . . . that apply to the taking of future operational decisions" (p. 2). At the

Calvin C. Jillson and Cecil L. Eubanks

operational level, on the other hand, "one is concerned with who gets what, when, and how," and at this level, "the primary preoccupation of inquiry is with the play of the political game within a given set of rules" (ibid., p. 1).

When concern focuses exclusively upon choice and decision at the constitutional level, Buchanan and Tullock (1962) suggest that the constitution-maker must address two related but analytically distinct sets of issues or questions. "Individuals choose, first of all, the fundamental organization of activity. Secondly, they choose the decision-making rules" (Buchanan and Tullock, 1962, p. 210). This distinction highlights the fact that the first order of business during constitutional construction is to address what, in this essay, we will call "higher" level questions of regime type and of the basic options for institutional design. Only when these decisions have been made does choice pass to what we will refer to as a "lower" level of constitutional design, where the decision rules that will regulate and order behavior within the regime's primary institutions are selected. These "lower" level choices specify the ways in which later operational decisions will be made, by whom, and over what range of issues.

At the "higher" level, the constitution-maker wrestles with general questions concerning the scope, scale, and form appropriate to government. Will the regime be an aristocratic, democratic, or mixed republic? Will the government have a legislative or an executive focus? Will its legislature be bicameral or unicameral? Will its executive be one man or several? These questions are less likely to be decided with reference to the economic status, social role, or material characteristics of the constitution-maker than with reference to his philosophical assumptions concerning the interplay among human nature, political institutions, and the good society.

As the general institutional design and the relationships that will pertain among its component parts become clear, the individual constitution-maker moves closer to the realm of practical politics. The questions that dominate this "lower" level of constitutional design concern the regulation of political behavior through rules governing such specific matters as citizenship, suffrage and voting, eligibility to office, and representation. The choices made concerning these matters determine the context of day-to-day politics at the operational or practical level. Therefore, questions at this level are much more likely to be decided with direct reference to the political, economic, and social characteristics of the chooser, his state, or his region than with reference to his philosophical principles.

Our intention in this essay is to suggest that the division of scholarly analysis into rationalist versus materialist or principle versus interest interpretations of the Convention's work derives from a tendency of scholars to focus on one level of constitutional choice or the other. Those who posit the dominance of ideas in the Convention have concentrated their attention almost exclusively on the "higher" level of constitutional choice, where the group is choosing among regime types (as in extended versus small republic forms). Those analysts who posit the dominance of interests in the Convention have focused on questions at the "lower" level of constitutional choice, where debate over specific decision rules (as in proportional versus equal representation in the legislature) tends to bear much more the interest-laced character of practical politics.

Further, we show that when the Convention concentrated on "higher" level questions of constitutional design, coalitions formed along lines of intellectual cleavage. During these phases of the Convention's work, the delegates from the more nationally oriented Middle Atlantic states opposed the more locally oriented delegates representing the northern and southern periphery. When the focus shifted to "lower" level choices among specific decision rules, each of which represented an alternative distribution of authority within and over the institutions of government, the states split along lines defined by economic and geographic interest, state size (large versus small), and region (North versus South).

The Extended Republic versus Traditional Republicanism: Power and Principle

The Convention's first two weeks of substantive debate, 29 May to 9 June, saw a fundamentally important clash of ideas at the "higher" level of constitutional choice (Jensen, 1964, p. 43; Smith, 1965, pp. 36–41). In broad outlines very similar to those sketched by Martin Diamond, Douglass Adair (1957) has argued that the American Constitution was born in a clash between a new science of republican politics, spawned by the Scottish Enlightenment, and traditional republicanism. In addition, Adair contended that "the most creative and philosophical disciple of the Scottish school of science and politics in the Philadelphia Convention was James Madison," and "his most amazing political prophecy . . . was that the size of the United States and its variety of interests could be made a guarantee of stability and justice under a new constitution" (1957, p. 346). Madison's theory of the "extended republic" sought to offer a positive new approach to providing "a republican remedy for the diseases most incident to republican government" (Earle, 1937, p. 62).

Nonetheless, Madison's "new science" met substantial opposition from delegates who clung to the traditional republicanism that had informed the Revolution, the early state constitutions, and the Articles of Confederation. As Martin Diamond (1972) correctly noted: "The main thrust of the opposition resulted from the more general argument that only the state governments (small republics), not some huge central government, could be made effectively free and republican" (p. 635).

These alternative visions of the appropriate scope and scale for republican government did not stand on equal terms as the Convention opened. After a decade of upheaval and turbulence at the state level and impotence at the level of the Confederation, traditional republican solutions had come to be questioned by nearly everyone and rejected by many. Whereas Madison arrived in Philadelphia with a new understanding of the governing potential inherent in the republican form, the traditional republicans arrived clinging to old nostrums whose credibility seemed clearly to be on the wane. Cecilia Kenyon (1955) has captured the predicament of these dispirited republicans by describing them as "men of little faith" (p. 3). Perhaps more to the point, they were "men of shaken faith," men whose political principles many now thought more appropriate to spawning a revolution than to providing the proper basis for just and stable republican government (Wood, 1969, pp. 396–413).

James Madison and those members of the Convention who sought to enhance dramatically the authority and independence of the national government moved decisively and successfully to capture the Convention's agenda and therewith to set the tone of its deliberations. The adoption, on 29 May, of Madison's Virginia Plan gave the "extended republic" men an initial edge because their general principles obviously underlay its specific provisions. On 30 May, they sought to solidify this potential advantage by putting the Convention on record in favor of radical change. Therefore, Edmund Randolph moved "that a *national* Government [ought to be established] consisting of a *supreme* Legislative, Executive and Judiciary" (Farrand, 1911, vol. 1, p. 33).

Many delegates sympathized with this root and branch approach, but others were wary, preferring the incremental approach to the Convention's business enunciated by John Dickinson of Delaware. Dickinson simply thought that wholesale change was unnecessary. "We may resolve therefore, . . . that the confederation is defective; and then proceed to the definition of such powers as may be thought adequate to the objects for which it was instituted. . . . The enquiry should be—

1. What are the legislative powers which we should vest in Congress.

2. What judiciary powers.

3. What executive powers" (Farrand, 1911, vol. 1, p. 42).

Table 1 highlights the dramatic division within the Convention over how to proceed and over the purposes and intentions that underlay the alternative approaches. The extended republic men (factor 1) sought to undertake immediately the radical changes necessary to institute a truly national government, while the small republic men (factor 2) favored incremental changes in the existing Confederation. The fact that nearly two-thirds (64.3 percent) of the variance in the roll-call voting over the Convention's first two weeks is captured by this two-factor solution indicates that this cleavage was both deep and stable.

The extended republic men from the Middle Atlantic region, led by Virginia's Madison and by Pennsylvania's James Wilson and Robert Morris, obviously held the early initiative. This largely reflected the fact that the small republic men had yet to formulate an acceptable balance between national and state authority that could be offered as a coherent alternative to Madison's Virginia Plan. As a consequence, their opposition lacked the conviction and cohesion that characterized the support for Madison's extended republic. This uncertainty was evident in the fact that two of the small republic delegations, Massachusetts and North Carolina, gave substantial support to the extended republic cause. These two states split their support almost evenly between the two factors, while no state on the first factor provided even modest support for the incremental approach favored by the small republic men.

TABLE 1

Extended Republic versus Small Republic: Power and Principle—Two-Factor
Solution for Roll-Call Votes 1–36, 29 May–9 June, Varimax Rotation (Ortho)

	1 Extended Republic	2 Small Republic	h^2
New Hampshire	absent	absent	absent
Massachusetts	(.60)	(.67)	.81
Connecticut	−.21	(.63)	.44
New York	(.76)	.29	.66
New Jersey	absent	absent	absent
Pennsylvania	(.82)	−.10	.68
Delaware	(.70)	.08	.49
Maryland	(.77)	−.12	.60
Virginia	(.66)	.32	.54
North Carolina	(.51)	(.68)	.73
South Carolina	−.04	(.86)	.74
Georgia	.27	(.81)	.73
Sum of squares	3.50	2.93	6.43
Percentage of variance explained	35.00	29.30	64.30

NOTE: The following definitions may help those who are not familiar with factor analysis to interpret the table above and those which follow. The columns headed by numbers and titles contain factor loadings. "The loadings . . . measure which variables (state voting delegations) are involved in what factor (coalition of state voting delegations) and to what degree. They are correlation coefficients between variables and factors" (Rummel, 1970, p. 137). "The column headed h^2 displays . . . the portion of a variable's (state's) total variance that is accounted for by the factors and is the sum of the squared loadings for a variable" (Rummel, 1970, p. 142). Parentheses identify the states that achieve full coalition membership, defined as factor loadings of .50 or higher. See the methodological appendix for a brief discussion of the factor model employed in this study.

Madison's vision of a great commercial republic, ruled by a powerful national government that would regulate with competence and justice the activities of the several states, was directly challenged by John Dickinson on 2 June. In Dickinson's view, the critical problem posed by government in a free society was the danger that authority might concentrate and become tyrannical (Bailyn, 1969, pp. 55–93). To minimize this constant danger, Dickinson argued, the national government should remain weak and "the Legislative, Executive, & Judiciary departments ought to be made as independent [separate] as possible" (Farrand, 1911, vol. 1, p. 86).

On 4 June, Madison set about dismantling Dickinson's argument that the defense of republican liberty required a strict separation of responsibilities between the departments of a modestly empowered national government. In this important speech, Madison carefully presented and explained the theoretical underpinnings of his "extended republic." William Pierce of Georgia recorded that "Mr. Madison in a very able and ingenious Speech . . . proved that the only way to make a Government answer all the end of its institution was to collect the wisdom of its several parts in aid of each other [by blurring a pure separation of powers] whenever it was necessary" (Farrand, 1911, vol. 1, pp. 110). By stressing the principle of "checks and balances" as a supplement and buttress to a strict "separation of powers," the extended republic men sought to create a governmental structure in which each department was fully capable of and motivated to self-defense. If the integrity of the structure and its ability to forestall tyranny by maintaining separate centers of power could be depended upon, then great power could be given to the national government in the knowledge that one branch would check potential abuses of the other.

As the full implications of Madison's program became clearer to the small republic men, they struggled with increasing determination against the idea that substantial authority at the national level could be either necessary or safe. On 6 June, Roger Sherman contended that great power could not be well used because "the objects of the Union . . . were few" (Farrand, 1911, vol. 1, p. 133). Moreover, great power should not be housed at the national level because most "matters civil & criminal would be much better in the hands of the States" (ibid.). Therefore, Sherman concluded, "the Genl. Government [should] be a sort of collateral Government which shall secure the States in particular difficulties. . . . I am against a Genl. Government and in favor of the independence and confederation of the States" (ibid., pp. 142–43).

Madison met Sherman's opposition to a "Genl. Government" by challenging his assumption that the responsibilities of the national government would be few. In addition to those objects noted by Sherman (defense, commerce, and disputes between the states), Madison "combined with them the necessity, of providing more effectually for the security of private rights, and the steady dispensation of Justice" (Farrand, 1911, vol. 1, p. 134). Most of the delegates agreed when Madison argued that interested local majorities had been "the source of these unjust laws complained of among ourselves" (p. 135). Madison proposed a solution to the problem of majority tyranny that few others understood and that many saw as dangerously speculative. "The only remedy is to enlarge the sphere . . . as far as the nature of Government would admit. . . . This [is] the only defense against the inconveniences of democracy consistent with the democratic form of Government" (p. 136).

Madison's opponents knew that additional powers would have to be granted to a central government, but the idea of a truly national government clashed directly with the philosophical assumptions with which they (and most Americans with them) had been operating since before the revolution. Yet, bereft of viable alternatives, these "men of shaken faith" could oppose only half-heartedly when Madison contended that "it was incumbent on [them] to try this [extended republic] remedy, and . . . to frame a republican system on such a scale & in such a form as will control all the evils which have been experienced" (Farrand, 1911, vol. 1, p. 136). While the conflict remained at this "higher" level of constitutional choice, the small republic men cast about for alternatives to Madison's frighteningly radical approach. None came readily to hand (Diamond, 1981, p. 27).

Large States versus Small States: Power and Interest

On 7 June the tenor of the questions before the Convention began to drift from the high plane of theory to the rough and tumble of practical, interest-driven power politics. Dickinson opened the discussion on 7 June by restating the modest commitment of the small republic men to "the preservation of the States in a certain degree of agency" (Farrand, 1911, vol. 1, p. 153). James Wilson, on behalf of the supporters of the Virginia Plan, observed that the "doubts and difficulties" surrounding the place of the state governments in the proposed system derived from the threat that they seemed to pose to the independence and effectiveness of the national government; "he wished to keep them from devouring the national Government" (ibid.).

Those delegates who followed the logic of Madison's extended republic expected any initiative left with the state governments to be misused. Their theoretical principles told them that small republics had always been violent and short-lived because interested local majorities, possessed of the means, invariably acted unjustly. Therefore, Charles Pinckney proposed "that the National Legislature should have authority to negative all [State] Laws which they should judge to be improper" (Farrand, 1911, vol. 1, p. 164). Madison seconded the Pinckney motion, saying that he "could not but regard an indefinite power [Pinckney had called it a "universality of power"] to negative legislative acts of the States as absolutely necessary to a perfect system" (ibid.).

Elbridge Gerry, Gunning Bedford, and William Paterson sprang to the defense of the states. Gerry scornfully rejected the idea of "an indefinite power to negative legislative acts of the States" as the work of "speculative projector(s)" whose theory had overwhelmed their experience and their judgment (Farrand, 1911, vol. 1, pp. 164–65). Bedford reminded his small state colleagues of the dangers inherent in such a plan. Paterson reinforced Bedford's remarks by holding up "Virginia, Massachusetts, and Pennsylvania as the three large States, and the other ten as small ones" (p. 178). He concluded that "the small States will have everything to fear. . . . New Jersey will never confederate on the plan before the Committee. She would be swallowed up" (ibid., pp. 178–79). James Wilson responded in kind for the large states. He said that "if the small States [would] not confederate on this plan, Pennsylvania and [he presumed] some other States, would not confederate on any other" (ibid., p. 180). This exchange indicates how quickly and decisively the Convention's focus shifted from general theories about the nature of republican government to the impact of various modes of representation on particular states and regions. It also highlights the interest-laced character (who gets what, when, and how) of discussion at the "lower" level of constitutional choice.

Table 2 shows how dramatically the voting alignments changed when the Convention's attention shifted from "higher" to "lower" level questions of constitutional choice. During the Convention's first two weeks, the states of the Deep South (the Carolinas and Georgia) had been wary of Madison's plan to place great power at the national level. Nonetheless, the extended republic men had successfully overcome the objections of the delegates from the Northeast and the Deep South to establish firmly the principle of a strong national government. Now the question was who would wield this great power? Under these new circumstances, the rapidly growing states of the Deep South joined Massachusetts, Pennsylvania, and Virginia (factor 1 of Table 2) to pursue proportional representation in both houses of the national legislature. The large states were opposed by five smaller states from the Middle Atlantic region (factor 2 of Table 2) demanding equal representation in at least one branch of the proposed legislature. The opposition voting pattern in Table 2 accounts for over one-half (50.7 percent) of the variance in the voting of all the states present between 11 June and 17 July.

The confrontation intensified on 11 June when Roger Sherman of Connecticut suggested that seats in the House of Representatives be allocated to the states in proportion to the number of free inhabitants, with each state to have one vote

TABLE 2

Large States versus Small States: Power and Interest—Two-Factor Solution for Roll-Call Votes 37–156, 11 June–16 July, Varimax Rotation (Ortho)

	1 Large States	2 Small States	h^2
New Hampshire	absent	absent	absent
Massachusetts	(.80)	.13	.66
Connecticut	.13	(.59)	.37
New York	−.02	(.52)	.27
New Jersey	−.13	(.75)	.58
Pennsylvania	(.65)	.09	.43
Delaware	−.08	(.74)	.56
Maryland	.25	(.78)	.68
Virginia	(.73)	.08	.54
North Carolina	(.79)	.12	.64
South Carolina	(.55)	−.22	.36
Georgia	(.69)	−.10	.49
Sum of squares	3.13	2.45	5.58
Percentage of variance explained	28.45	22.25	50.70

in the Senate. The large state men still demanded proportional representation in both houses. Rufus King of Massachusetts and Wilson of Pennsylvania countered with a motion proposing "that the right of suffrage in . . . [the House of Representatives] ought not to be according to the rule established in the Articles of Confederation [equality], but according to some equitable ratio of representation," which after some discussion passed seven to three with one abstention (Farrand, 1911, vol. 1, p. 196). The large state coalition unanimously voted yes and was joined by Connecticut in pursuance of Sherman's suggested compromise. New York, New Jersey, and Delaware opposed the measure, while the Maryland delegates were divided. Wilson then sought to reinforce the allegiance of the southerners to the large state coalition by awarding them a three-fifths representation for their slaves. Only New Jersey and Delaware opposed (ibid., p. 201). Pressing the large state advantage, Wilson and Alexander Hamilton moved that "the right of suffrage in the 2nd branch [the Senate] ought to be according to the same rule as in the 1st branch" (ibid., p. 202). They were successful by the same six-to-five alignment that appears in Table 2. Thus, proportional representation in both houses, for a time, had been achieved by the triumph of the large states.

The opposing coalitions held firm through 29 June, when Connecticut's Oliver Ellsworth again declared the need for a compromise settlement. Wilson, arguing against any compromise by the large states on this crucial issue, adamantly rejected the idea, saying, "If a separation must take place, it could never happen on better grounds" (Farrand, 1911, vol. 1, p. 482). Gunning Bedford of Delaware answered for the small states, "I do not, gentlemen, trust you. If you possess the power, the abuse of it could not be checked; and what then would prevent you from exercising it to our destruction?" (ibid., p. 500).

With the proceedings obviously at a dangerous impasse, a compromise committee was chosen on 2 July that not only failed to include Wilson and Madison but also omitted every one of the strong spokesmen for the large state interest in proportional representation. Elbridge Gerry, who some weeks earlier had called Madison a "speculative projector," was elected committee chairman. According to Gerry, the small states held "a separate meeting . . . of most of the delegates of those five States [factor 2 of Table 2], the result of which was, a firm determination on their part not to relinquish the right of equal representation in the Senate" (Farrand, 1911, vol. 3, p. 264). With the small states still unyielding, no course was left but to compromise. On 5 July, Gerry delivered the report of his committee to the Convention. It proposed: "That in the first branch of the Legislature each of the States now in the Union be allowed one Member for every forty thousand inhabitants. . . . That in the second Branch of the Legislature each State shall have an equal Vote" (Farrand, 1911, vol. 1, p. 524). Between 5 July and 16 July when the Connecticut Compromise was finally adopted, the North and the South battled over the apportionment of seats in the House of Representatives through two additional compromise committees and interminable floor debates to insure that the regions of the new nation would be institutionally positioned to defend their paramount interests (Jillson, 1981, pp. 36–41).

Executive Power and Citizen Participation: Principle and Interest

The coalitions that had aligned behind conflicting views of republican government during the Convention's first two weeks resurfaced immediately following the Connecticut Compromise as the Convention's focus turned again to questions at the "higher" level of constitutional choice. These familiar coalitions, still divided by philosophical differences concerning the nature of republican government, controlled the Convention's business for the next five weeks, well into late August. The small republic men (factor 1 of Table 3) sought to control the potential for abuse of governmental power by means of a strict separation of departments, a modest empowerment, and the use of explicit constitutional prohibitions and restraints where danger still seemed to lurk. Madison repeatedly enunciated the counterargument in favor of "checks and balances" as a supplement to a pure "separation of powers" that the extended republic men considered definitive and to which they frequently referred during debate over questions at the "higher" level of constitutional choice. He argued that

> if a Constitutional discrimination of the departments on paper were a sufficient security to each against encroachments of the other, all further provisions would indeed be superfluous. But experience had taught us a distrust of that security; and that it is necessary to introduce such a balance of powers and interests, as will guarantee the provisions on paper. Instead therefore of contenting ourselves with laying down the Theory in the Constitution that each department ought to be separate and distinct, it was proposed to add a defensive power to each which should maintain the Theory in practice. In so doing we did not blend the departments together. We erected effectual barriers to keep them separate. (Farrand, 1911, vol. 2, p. 77; see also *The Federalist*, nos. 47, 48, and 51)

An initial glance at Table 3 would seem to indicate that the six-member coalition of large and small Middle Atlantic states, ranging from Connecticut to Virginia, would again outnumber the five-member coalition of peripheral states, made up of New Hampshire and Massachusetts in the North with the Carolinas and Georgia in the Deep South. But on closer analysis, the match begins to look more even, perhaps even positively skewed in favor of the peripheral group.

The factor loadings for the peripheral states on factor 1 are not only quite strong, but all five are closely clustered between .70 and .79. Obviously, the very divisive battles of the several weeks past had cost the small republic coalition almost nothing in terms of support among its core members. Within the coalition of Middle Atlantic states, the situation was quite different. The small states had become much more wary of their large state colleagues. This is clearly indicated by the modest commitments of Connecticut, New Jersey, and Delaware to the coalition of Middle Atlantic states. Therefore, in close votes on critical issues, the likelihood was that the coalition of Middle Atlantic states would be weakened by the relatively frequent defection of its smaller members.

On 17 July, the day immediately following the resolution of the struggle between the large and small states over political control of the legislative branch, the question of the general form appropriate to the executive establishment was

TABLE 3

Small Republic Localists versus Extended Republic Cosmopolitans—
Two-Factor Solution for Roll-Call Votes 157–399, 17 July –29 August,
Varimax Rotation (Ortho)

	1 Small Republic	2 Extended Republic	h^2
New Hampshire	(.75)	.14	.58
Massachusetts	(.70)	.12	.51
Connecticut	.24	(.52)	.33
New York	absent	absent	absent
New Jersey	.08	(.58)	.35
Pennsylvania	.16	(.71)	.53
Delaware	.19	(.55)	.34
Maryland	−.04	(.66)	.43
Virginia	.19	(.63)	.43
North Carolina	(.71)	.21	.55
South Carolina	(.79)	.06	.63
Georgia	(.70)	.19	.52
Sum of squares	2.84	2.36	5.20
Percentage of variance explained	25.82	21.45	47.27

taken up. Early in the Convention Roger Sherman had expressed the doctrine of
executive power to which the small republic men (on factor 1 of Table 3) adhered
when he said that he "considered the Executive magistracy as nothing more than
an institution for carrying the will of the Legislature into effect" (Farrand, 1911,
vol. 1, p. 65). Sherman's views were immediately challenged by the extended
republic men (on factor 2 of Table 3), who held that power need not be severely
limited if its undue concentration in any single branch of government was avoided.
Seen in this light, a powerful and independent executive could be used to restrain
a volatile and potentially dangerous legislature (Bailyn, 1967, pp. 55–93; Wood,
1969, pp. 18–28, 352–59, 430–38).

The Convention quickly translated these two perspectives on executive power
into three major structural elements: mode of appointment (by the legislature or
by specially chosen electors); length of term (tenure); and reeligibility (Jillson,
1979, p. 388). It was apparent to the delegates that these elements were themselves interrelated and that they all revolved around the question of the relationship
of the executive branch to the legislature. Charles Warren (1928) has noted that
"the views of most of the delegates as to length of term and as to re-election were
dependent on the *mode* of election" (p. 365).

The battle over executive selection was rejoined on 17 July over the clause
"To be chosen by the National Legislature," which, after two challenging pro-

posals for popular election and selection by electors were soundly rejected, won unanimous approval. To counter the peripheral states' (factor 1 of Table 3) achievement of selection by the national legislature, the Middle Atlantic states (factor 2 of Table 3), behind Gouverneur Morris of Pennsylvania, successfully moved to strike out "to be ineligible a second time," arguing that to do otherwise would be to institutionalize inexperience at the helm of the national government. When a motion was defeated to strike out the seven-year term as well, the Convention was left with legislative selection and a long term of seven years, but with reeligibility permitted; thus, virtually assuring, in Madison's words, that "the Executive could not be independent of the Legislature, if dependent on the pleasure of that branch for a re-appointment" (Farrand, 1911, vol. 2, p. 34). Even the advocates of a broadly empowered national executive hesitated at the prospect of an unrestricted eligibility to successive long terms of office.

The question of executive selection reappeared on 19 July, allowing Ellsworth of Connecticut to reintroduce the idea of electors. The six Middle Atlantic states, ranging in a solid phalanx from Connecticut to Virginia, voted in favor of electors, while the three states of the Deep South opposed electors and Massachusetts divided on the issue (Farrand, 1911, vol. 2, p. 58). Both reeligibility and a six-year term were also quickly approved. Though the principle of electoral selection now seemed to enjoy majority support in the Convention, the practical question of distributing power among the states as they participated in that process continued to defy resolution (Thach, 1923, p. 102).

This problem in "lower" level constitutional design, the allocation of presidential electors among the states, was directly confronted on 20 July when Oliver Ellsworth, speaking for the small Middle Atlantic states, proposed "the following ratio: towit—one for each State not exceeding 200,000 inhabitants, two for each above that number and not exceeding 300,000 inhabitants, and, three for each state exceeding 300,000" (Farrand, 1911, vol. 2, p. 57). James Madison, always the advocate and defender of proportional representation, observed "that this would make in time all or nearly all the States equal. Since there were few that would not in time contain the number of inhabitants entitling them to 3 Electors" (ibid., p. 63). With this proportional representation view again dominating the large state delegations, New Jersey and Delaware abandoned their large state colleagues to join the five members of the peripheral coalition in reinstituting legislative selection, a long term, and an ineligibility. Soon thereafter, the Convention adjourned for ten days to give the Committee of Detail "time to prepare and report the Constitution" (ibid, p. 128).

The critical questions facing the Convention over the three weeks immediately following the delivery of the Committee of Detail report on 6 August concerned the stance that the new republic would take toward its citizens, particularly those citizens who might hold office in the new government. On the one hand, the cosmopolitan delegates from the Middle Atlantic states, generally supporting Madison's "extended republic," held a cautious but optimistically positive view of the ordinary citizen's ability to participate in a well-constructed national government broadly empowered to govern freely as changing times and an indeterminate future might dictate. On the other hand, the localist delegates of the peripheral coalition, generally fearful of concentrated power and supporting the "small republic" view, took a much less optimistic view of the quality of popular participation and of the feasibility of constructing adequate "checks and balances" in any government awarded great discretion. The small republic men still thought it both wise and expedient to depart as little as possible from a pure theory of "separation of powers."

The debates that occurred during the week of 9 to 15 August on residency qualifications for the House and the Senate provide an example of the middle states' openness and the peripheral states' skepticism toward the nation's citizens. On 9 August, Gouverneur Morris proposed a 14-year residency requirement for Senators, "urging the danger of admitting strangers into our public Councils" (Farrand, 1911, vol. 2, p. 235). Charles Pinckney agreed when George Mason indicated that "he should be for restraining the eligibility into the Senate, to natives," were it not for the fact that many foreigners had served nobly in the Revolution (ibid.). Pierce Butler of South Carolina supported Mason and Morris, observing that foreigners bring with them "ideas of Government so distinct from ours that in every point of view they are dangerous" (ibid., p. 236).

Madison and his nationalistic supporters from the middle states thought this approach unnecessary, illiberal, and unbecoming to the nation. Madison indicated that "he thought any restriction in the Constitution . . . improper: because it [would] give a tincture of illiberality to the Constitution" to bar new citizens from the Senate for fully 14 years, let alone to restrict that high privilege to natives. Benjamin Franklin rose to Madison's support, also dwelling on the "illiberality," as well as the adverse impact on European opinion, of such an idea permanently ensconced in the Constitution. Wilson joined Madison and Franklin in pointing to "the illiberal complexion which the motion would give to the System" (Farrand, 1911, vol. 2, p. 237).

The vote on Morris's motion for a 14-year residency requirement, then one for 13 years, and, finally, another for 10 years were all defeated by a Middle Atlantic bloc of states stretching from Massachusetts to North Carolina. Finally, nine years was proposed and narrowly approved. Wilson sought to turn this modest victory into positive momentum for the middle state nationalists by moving to reconsider the citizenship requirement for the House in order to reduce it from seven years to three. Though this motion was defeated by a united Periphery, a futher attempt was made to attach "a proviso that the limitation [of seven years] should not affect [the rights of] any person now a Citizen" (Farrand, 1911, vol. 2, p. 270). In response, a familiar chorus of voices from the Periphery argued that even this presumption in favor of immigrants who had attained citizenship under state laws would constitute a danger. John Rutledge observed that "the policy of precaution was as great with regard to foreigners now Citizens; as to those who are to be naturalized in [the] future." Sherman supported Rutledge with the very remarkable statement that "the U. States have not invited foreigners nor pledged their faith that they should enjoy equal privileges with native Citizens" (ibid.). Madison, Morris, and Wilson presented counterarguments, but when the votes were recorded a familiar pattern was evident. Once again, a united coalition of the Periphery had successfully exploited the divisions within the more diffuse coalition of Middle Atlantic states to transform its conservative preferences into constitutional provisions.

With these fundamental questions of executive selection and citizen participation at least temporarily resolved, both coalitions sought to exert their influence on collateral issues. The peripheral group did so always for the general purposes of limiting power and maintaining the cherished doctrine of "separation of powers." The middle state coalition sought to provide each department, or combinations thereof, with the ability to defend itself. Once the integrity of the structure was guaranteed, the extended republic men took care to avoid minute restrictions on the assumption that future governments, confronting new and unforeseen problems, would need to draw on an unrestricted range of options.

Slavery, Commerce, Executive Selection and the West: State and Regional Interest

As the Convention moved into late August, several critical issues at the "lower" level of constitutional choice, including some provision for the critical regional issues of slavery and commercial regulation, for executive selection, and for control of the western lands, stood unresolved. Initially, it seemed that the dominant coalition of peripheral states would resolve each of these issues in its own favor against the increasingly desultory opposition of the Middle Atlantic states. As the middle state coalition tottered toward collapse, the more cohesive peripheral coalition seemed to gather new strength as its northern and southern wings quickly and smoothly came to an accommodation on the dangerous and divisive regional issues of the slave trade and commercial regulation.

When debate on the slave trade opened on the morning of 22 August, General Charles Cotesworth Pinckney went directly to the regional economics of the conflict between the states of the Upper South (Maryland and Virginia of the middle state coalition) and the states of the Lower South (the Carolinas and Georgia of the peripheral coalition) on this volatile issue. General Pinckney said, "South Carolina & Georgia cannot do without slaves. As to Virginia she will gain by stopping the importations. Her slaves will rise in value, & she has more than she wants" (Farrand, 1911, vol. 2, p. 371). For the shipping interests so dear to the northern wing of the peripheral coalition Pinckney held out the prospect that "the more slaves, the more produce to employ the carrying trade; The more consumption also, and the more of this, the more revenue for the common treasury" (ibid.).

Though Dickinson and others from the middle Atlantic argued that further importations were "inadmissible on every principle of honor and safety," King spoke for the dominant peripheral coalition when he remarked that "the subject should be considered in a political light only" (Farrand, 1911, vol. 2, p. 372).

Viewed from this practical perspective, King feared that "the exemption of slaves from duty whilst every other import was subjected to it, [was] an inequality that could not fail to strike the commercial sagacity of the Northn & middle States" (ibid., p. 373). General Pinckney agreed that allowance for a modest duty would "remove one difficulty," and G. Morris quickly moved to broaden the ground for compromise to include the sensitive regional concerns of slavery and commercial regulation, saying, "these things may form a bargain among the Northern & Southern States" (ibid., p. 374). A compromise committee of one member from each state was quickly appointed.

Luther Martin, Maryland's representative on the committee, later reported that the substance of the committee's report involved an interregional quid pro quo between the northern and southern wings of the peripheral coalition. "The eastern States, notwithstanding their aversion to slavery, were very willing to indulge the southern States, at least with a temporary liberty to prosecute the slave-trade, provided the southern States would, in their turn, gratify them, by laying no restrictions on navigation acts" (Farrand, 1911, vol. 3, p. 210–11). The Deep South would be allowed to continue importing slaves until at least 1800, while the northern states would be allowed to set commercial policy by simple majority vote of the national legislature.

The Commerce and Slave Trade Compromise was reported to the floor on 24 August but was not debated until 25 August. In the interim, the Convention returned to the complex issue of executive selection. Again, the Middle Atlantic states were powerless against a united coalition of peripheral states. The precise question before the Convention was whether the Periphery's preference for legislative selection would be exercised by separate ballots in the House and Senate, or, as Rutledge now suggested, in the hope of driving a wedge between Pennsylvania and Virginia and their small state allies, by "joint ballot" of both houses voting together. Sherman immediately objected that the "joint ballot" would deprive the smaller states "represented in the Senate of the negative intended them in that house." When the vote was taken, New Hampshire, Massachusetts, and the Carolinas were supported by the largest of the Middle Atlantic states, Pennsylvania, Maryland, and Virginia, in approving the measure seven to four. Delegates from the smaller states quickly sought to reestablish their influence in the presidential selection process by proposing that each state delegation should have one vote even if the polling was done by "joint ballot." The motion was lost by a single vote, five to six, when Pennsylvania and Virginia again joined the peripheral states to turn back their former allies. The remnants of the Middle Atlantic state coalition successfully avoided final defeat by postponing the issue.

When debate on the provisions of the Commerce and Slave Trade Compromise opened on the morning of 25 August, General Pinckney moved to extend the period during which free importation of slaves would be allowed from 1800 to 1808. On this amendment, and on the entire clause as amended, the commercial northeast, New Hampshire, Massachusetts, and Connecticut, anticipating northern control over commercial regulation in direct exchange for their support on this matter of the slave trade, joined the Deep South to defeat the Middle Atlantic states of New Jersey, Pennsylvania, Delaware, and Virginia. With the southern half of the compromise thus easily confirmed, the northern sections dealing with commercial regulation were postponed and did not reappear until 29 August.

In the interim, the delegates from South Carolina maneuvered to gain additional security for their property in slaves, while many other southerners grew increasingly apprehensive that they had given up too much in agreeing to commercial regulation by simple majority. When the northern half of the compromise did come before the Convention, Charles Pinckney moved to strike out the section allowing simple majority decision on commercial questions. Fearing that the entire Commerce and Slave Trade Compromise (particularly the right to continue importations) might come unhinged, the older Pinckney argued that the "liberal conduct toward the views of South Carolina" shown by the northern states had convinced him that "no fetters should be imposed on the power of making commercial regulations" (Farrand, 1911, vol. 2, pp. 449–50).

Despite the assurances offered by General Pinckney, opinion in the southern delegations ran strongly to the view that commercial regulation by simple majority was an invitation to southern destruction. Mason argued strenuously that "the *Majority* will be governed by their interests. The Southern States are the *minority* in both Houses. Is it to be expected that they will deliver themselves bound hand & foot to the Eastern States?" (Farrand, 1911, vol. 2, p. 451). Randolph was finally driven to declare that "there were features so odious in the Constitution as it now stands, that he doubted whether he should be able to agree to it" (ibid., p. 452). Putting the interests of the southern states in commercial regulation at the disposal of the northern states "would compleat the deformity of the system" (ibid.). Despite this deeply rooted southern opposition, a solid bloc of six northern states, ranging from New Hampshire to Delaware, joined only by South Carolina, defeated Maryland, Virginia, North Carolina, and Georgia on the question.

South Carolina's service to the northern states was quickly rewarded by an additional increment of security for her property in slaves. The Convention approved Butler's proposal that "any person bound to service . . . [escaping] into another State . . . shall be delivered up to the person justly claiming their service or labor" (Farrand, 1911, vol. 2, p. 454). But, the cost to larger southern interests, in which South Carolina obviously shared, was high. South Carolina's blind pursuit of security for her property in slaves broke the South as an effective force in the Convention.

With the peripheral coalition broken by the shattering of its southern wing and the coalition of Middle Atlantic states disrupted by a renewed tension between its large and small members, the tone of the Convention's final days was unmistakably set by the debates that began on 30 August over control of the unsettled western lands. Daniel Carroll of Maryland opened this confrontation by moving to strike out a provision requiring "the consent of the State to [lands under its jurisdiction] being divided" (Farrand, 1911, vol. 2, p. 461). Carroll argued that this was an absolutely fundamental point with those states that did not hold claims to vast tracts of the western territory (Jensen, 1966, p. 150; Rakove, 1979, p. 352).

Pennsylvania's James Wilson opposed Carroll's motion, arguing that "he knew nothing that would give greater or juster alarm than the doctrine, that a political society is to be torne asunder without its own consent" (Farrand, 1911, vol. 2, p. 462). This argument struck the delegates from the smaller states as yet another brazen rejection of principle in favor of interest. Luther Martin said that "he wished Mr. Wilson had thought a little sooner of the value of *political* bodies. In the beginning, when the rights of the small States were in question, they were phantoms, ideal beings. Now when the Great States were to be affected, political Societies were of a sacred nature" (ibid., p. 464). When the votes were counted, New Jersey, Delaware, and Maryland stood alone.

It was eminently clear to the delegates from the smaller states that the Convention was once again slipping out of control and that dangerous consequences could result. If the larger states effectively dominated the executive selection process and the vast resources represented by the unsettled lands in the West, their stature in the new system could only be enhanced, while that of the smaller states would just as certainly decline. With these concerns foremost in the minds of the delegates from the smaller states, a committee of one member from each state was appointed on 31 August to resolve matters that still remained undecided. The Brearley Committee on postponed and undecided parts reported briefly on 1 September, but it was not until 4 and 5 September that it delivered the main components of its complex and controversial compromise report to the full Convention.

Table 4 highlights both the impact of the issues that broke the dominant coalitions in late August and the nature of the new alignments that emerged from the Brearley Committee to dominate the Convention's final days. The large states were effectively isolated (see factor 2 of Table 4), while the five southern states, their influence in the Convention largely spent, were scattered harmlessly across all three factors in Table 4. The small states, on the other hand, emerged from the Brearley Committee determined to defend a report that was designed to enhance dramatically their potential for influence in the new government (Warren, 1928, p. 664).

Most of the members of the new majority of small and northern states had long preferred executive selection by specially chosen electors to legislative selection. The Brearley Committee report envisioned a return to electoral selection, but perhaps more importantly, the failure of any candidate to receive a majority of the electoral votes would result in the reference of the five leading candidates to the Senate (where the small states had an equal vote with the large states) for final selection. Madison, Morris, and Mason feared that the Senate would ultimately decide "nineteen times in twenty" (Farrand, 1911, vol. 2, p. 500). Further, treaties, as well as ambassadorial, Supreme Court, and other major administrative appointments were to be made by the President only "with the Advice and Consent of the Senate" (ibid., pp. 498–99). And finally, although

TABLE 4

A New Northern Majority Defends the Role of the Small States—
Three-Factor Solution for Roll-Call Votes 441–569, 4–17 September,
Varimax Rotation (Ortho)

	1	2	3	
	Northern Majority	Large State Minority	Southern Minority	h^2
New Hampshire	(.72)	.44	.25	.77
Massachusetts	(.62)	(.55)	-.18	.73
Connecticut	(.78)	.22	.03	.63
New York	absent	absent	absent	absent
New Jersey	(.81)	.04	.18	.69
Pennsylvania	.16	(.80)	.03	.66
Delaware	(.74)	.04	.18	.59
Maryland	.45	.23	(.59)	.61
Virginia	-.07	(.76)	.38	.73
North Carolina	.04	.05	(.81)	.65
South Carolina	.38	(.55)	.11	.45
Georgia	.45	.37	.45	.53
Sum of squares	3.29	2.26	1.51	7.06
Percentage of variance explained	29.90	20.50	13.90	64.30

the House would charge the President in impeachable offenses, the final disposition of these charges would occur in the Senate. These provisions gave the smaller states what many of the delegates thought would be fearfully direct control over the appointment, conduct in office, and removal of the President. Both the larger states (factor 2 of Table 4) and the Deep South (dispersed across factors 1, 2, and 3 of Table 4) opposed these dramatic enhancements of senatorial authority. Yet, as the Convention entered its final days, neither the large states nor the southern states were in a position to oppose effectively the Brearley Committee report and the determined phalanx of small Middle Atlantic and northeastern states that stood behind it.

The great fear of many delegates was that the powers added to the Senate to enhance the role of the small states in the new government had set the stage for aristocracy. Much of 5 September was taken up by the expression of such fears and by the search for ways to alleviate them without reducing the influence of the smaller states over the process of executive selection. Mason feared that, "considering the powers of the President & . . . the Senate, if a coalition should be established between these two branches, they will be able to subvert the Constitution (Farrand, 1911, vol. 2, p. 512). Randolph's comments "dwelt on the tendency of such an influence in the Senate over the election of the President in addition to its other powers, to convert that body into a real & dangerous Aristocracy" (ibid., p. 513).

In light of these fears, felt by small state men as well as large, it is not surprising that the response was immediate and overwhelmingly positive when Connecticut's Roger Sherman, speaking for the dominant majority of small northern states, proposed that recourse in the event that no candidate had a majority of the electoral votes for president should not be to the Senate, but to "the House of Representatives . . . each State having one vote" (Farrand, 1911, vol. 2, p. 527). Mason quickly responded that he "liked the latter mode best as lessening the aristocratic influence on the Senate" (ibid.). Nearly everyone agreed, as the vote on Sherman's motion was approved ten to one, with Delaware alone still adamant about retaining this authority in the Senate (ibid.). This solution allowed the small states to retain their dominant position in the executive selection process, while simultaneously alleviating the fear that the Senate had come to be a dangerously powerful body. With this last and most difficult question finally resolved, the Convention hurried toward adjournment.

Conclusion

We began this essay with an argument about the nature of political reality, namely, that it is characterized by the interaction of alternative visions of the community's general interest or common good with the partial and exclusive interests of the individuals, groups, classes, states, and regions that comprise the community. Throughout this essay, we have sought to show that the debates and decisions of the Federal Convention bear the distinctive marks of that grudging accommodation between principles and interests that is characteristic of democratic politics.

General principles, such as republicanism, federalism, separation of powers, checks and balances, and bicameralism, define the structure of government only in vague outlines. Therefore, discussion of general principles serves merely to identify the broad paths along which the general interests and the common good of the community can be pursued. Other considerations, primarily deriving from diverse political, economic, and geographic interests, suggest and often virtually determine the modifications, adjustments, and allowances that principled consistency must make to political expediency. James Madison made precisely this point in a letter that accompanied a copy of the new Constitution sent to Jefferson in Paris in late October 1787. Madison explained that "the nature of the subject, the diversity of human opinion, . . . the collision of local interests, and the pretensions of the large & small States will . . . account . . . for the irregularities which will be discovered in [the new government's] structure and form" (Farrand, 1911, vol. 3, p. 136). Similarly, Alexander Hamilton felt constrained to warn his readers in the first number of *The Federalist* that though "our choice should be directed by a judicious estimate of our true interests, unperplexed and unbiased by considerations not connected with the public good, . . . the plan . . . affects too many particular interests, not to involve in its discussion a variety of objects foreign to its merits" (Earle, 1937, p. 3).

In our attempt to illustrate and explain the interaction between principles and interests in the Federal Convention, we used three interpretive devices. The first was a theoretical distinction between a "higher" level of constitutional choice, where we expected and found the influence of principle to guide action, and a "lower" level of constitutional choice, where we expected and found the influence of political and economic interests to be decisive. The second device, factor analysis, was used to analyze the roll-call voting record left by the Convention. Through this means, we identified the voting coalitions that formed among the states at the various stages of the Convention's business. Finally, we engaged in a close examination of the Convention's debates in order to link the contending voting coalitions to the conflicting patterns of political principle at the "higher" level and to opposing patterns of political, economic, and geographic interests at the "lower" level of constitutional choice.

We conclude that the Federal Convention of 1787, from its opening day on 25 May until its final adjournment on 17 September, confronted two distinct, but intimately related, aspects of constitutional design. The first was general. What kind of republican government should be constructed? As the delegates considered and discussed alternative visions of the relationship between human nature, the institutions of government, and the quality of the resulting social order, the temper and tone of their deliberations was quiet and philosophical. Some measure of detachment was possible at the "higher" level of constitutional choice because the debates over general principles provided little indication of precisely how the choice of one set of principles over another would affect the specific interests of particular individuals, states, or regions.

While the delegates considered questions of basic constitutional design, they seemed almost oblivious to the conflicts of interest that inevitably arose as they moved to the "lower" level of constitutional choice, where their theories and principles would be shaped and molded into practical arrangements for governing. When distributional questions came to the fore, debate intensified, tempers flared, and conflict predominated. Questions touching upon the allocation of representatives and presidential electors, the status of slavery, and regulation of the nation's commerce and its western lands directly affected the political, economic, and social interests of distinct classes, states, and regions. Indeed, it was only at this "lower" level of constitutional construction, where interests clashed so loudly, that the Convention was threatened with dissolution.

Manuscript submitted 21 September 1983
Final manuscript received 5 January 1984

APPENDIX

Methodological Note

In this study, we employ factor analysis primarily in its role as a "confirmatory" or "hypothesis-testing" device. As Harman (1976) explains, "Confirmatory factor analysis may be used to check or test . . . a given hypothesis about the structure of the data" (p. 6). The introduction to this paper offers a hypothesis designed to explain the complex interactions that characterized the Federal Convention's business. Others have offered alternative explanations. Factor analysis will aid in showing which of these explanations comports most easily with the empirical "structure of the data."

This study employs a principal component Q-factor analysis throughout (Rummel, 1970, pp. 112–13). We group states (variables in the matrix columns) on the basis of their responses to the 569 roll-call votes (cases in the matrix rows) taken during the Convention. The 12 states that attended the Convention comprise the variables in this study. They are New Hampshire, Massachusetts, Connecticut, New York, New Jersey, Pennsylvania, Delaware, Maryland, Virginia, North Carolina, South Carolina, and Georgia. As indicated above, the cases are the 569 roll-call votes taken during the Convention as recorded in Farrand's *The Records of the Federal Convention of 1787* (1911). Votes were coded for analysis as follows: 1—yes, 2—no, 3—absent, 4—divided. Each factor analysis in this study begins from a correlation matrix (Nie, 1970). Since voting in the Convention was by state delegation, rather than by individual delegate, deletion of absences and divided votes allows each cell of each correlation matrix to define the degree of association between two states in yes and no voting.

REFERENCES

Adair, Douglass. 1957. That politics may be reduced to a science: David Hume, James Madison and the Tenth Federalist. *Huntington Library Quarterly*, 20 (August):343–60.

Bailyn, Bernard. 1969. *The ideological origins of the American Revolution*. Cambridge: Harvard University Press.

Beard, Charles A. 1913. *An economic interpretation of the Constitution of the United States*. New York: Macmillan.

Buchanan, James M., and Gordon Tullock. 1962. *The calculus of consent: Logical foundations of constitutional democracy*. Ann Arbor: University of Michigan Press.

Dahl, Robert. 1963. *Modern political analysis*. New York: Prentice-Hall.

Diamond, Martin. 1972. The Federalist. In Leo Strauss and Joseph Cropsey, eds., *History of political philosophy*, 2d ed. Chicago: Rand McNally: pp. 631–51.

———. 1975. The Declaration and the Constitution: Liberty, democracy and the founders. *The Public Interest*, 41 (Fall):39–55.

———. 1976. The American idea of man: The view from the founding. In Irving Kristol and Paul Weaver, eds., *The Americans: 1976*. Lexington, Mass.: Lexington Books: pp. 1–23.

———. 1981. *The founding of the democratic republic*. Itasca, Ill.: Peacock.

Duverger, Maurice. 1966. *The idea of politics*. London: Methuen.

Earle, Edward Mead, ed. 1937. *Federalist papers*. New York: Modern Library.

Farrand, Max. 1911. *The records of the Federal Convention of 1787*. 4 vols. New Haven: Yale University Press.

Harman, Harry H. 1976. *Modern factor analysis*. Chicago: University of Chicago Press.

Jensen, Merrill. 1964. *The Articles of Confederation: An interpretation of the social-consitutional history of the American Revolution 1774–1781*. Madison: University of Wisconsin Press.

———. 1966. *The making of the American Constitution*. New York: Van Nostrand Reinhold.

Jillson, Calvin. 1979. The executive in republican government: The case of the American founding. *Presidential Studies Quarterly*, 9 (Fall):386–402.

———. 1981. The representation question in the Federal Convention of 1787: Madison's Virginia plan and its opponents. *Congressional Studies*, 8 (1):21–41.

Kenyon, Cecilia. 1955. Men of little faith: The Anti-Federalists on the nature of representative government. *William and Mary Quarterly*, 12:3–43.

Lippmann, Walter. 1955. *The public philosophy*. New York: Mentor.

Nie, Norman. 1970. *Statistical program for the social sciences*. New York: McGraw-Hill.

Ostrom, Vincent. 1979. Constitutional level of analysis: Problems and prospects. Convention paper delivered at the meetings of the Western Political Science Association in Portland, Ore., 22–24 March 1979.

Rakove, Jack N. 1979 *The beginnings of national politics: An interpretive history of the Continental Congress.* New York: Knopf.

Roche, John P. 1961. The founding fathers: A reform caucus in action. *American Political Science Review,* 55 (December);799–816.

Rummel, Rudolph J. 1970. *Applied factor analysis.* Evanston: Northwestern University Press.

Smith, David G. 1965. *The Convention and the Constitution.* New York: St. Martin's.

Smith, J. Allen. 1907. *The spirit of American government.* Reprint ed. Cambridge: Belknap Press, 1965.

Smith, Page. 1980. *The shaping of America: A people's history of the young republic.* Vol. 3. New York: McGraw-Hill.

Thach, Charles C. 1923. *The creation of the presidency 1775–1789.* Baltimore: Johns Hopkins Press.

Warren, Charles. 1928. *The making of the Constitution.* Reprint ed. New York: Barnes & Noble, 1967.

Wood, Gordon. 1969. *The creation of the American republic 1776–1787.* New York: Norton.

Federalism and the Founding: Toward a Reinterpretation of the Constitutional Convention

Michael P. Zuckert

The issue of federalism at the Constitutional Convention was considerably more complex than it is normally taken to have been, and most of·the prevailing understandings of the settlement of the federalism issue in the Constitution suffer from failing to appreciate that complexity. There were at least six rather distinct versions of federalism "on the table" in Philadelphia; most found embodiment in one or another of the major plans before the Convention, although two of the schemas that are especially important for understanding the final Constitution have gone almost entirely unrecognized because they were not incorporated in separate comprehensive plans. Neither the older view that the Constitution's federalism is a "bundle of compromises" nor the currently popular view that it is essentially a nationalist document with some few federal reservations holds up when examined in the light of the "federalisms" at the Convention.

In an essay he apparently intended to stand as preface to his notes on the Convention debates, James Madison singled out the Constitution's solution to the problem of federalism as its most singular and remarkable feature. The Americans established

> a system without a precedent ancient or modern, a system founded on popular rights, and so combining a federal form with the forms of individual Republics, as may enable each to supply the defects of the other and obtain the advantages of both.[1]

That unprecedented combination the Americans brought forth did not spring from the soil without great effort or all at once. Not only did they make major false starts in their search for a union, but the form upon which they finally settled in the Constitution emerged only after a difficult winnowing of six distinct alternative models of union taken up in the Constitutional Convention. The nature of the federal union finally proposed can be properly understood only in the context of the varieties of federalism it competed against for the support of the delegates. Since six distinct models were competing, the issue of federalism is necessarily more complex than the currently most sophisticated accounts, which focus on two models only, federal or confederal and national or unitary, take it to be.[2] I shall discuss the models for the most part in the chronological order in which they were relevant to the Convention since that is the only order in which they all can be intelli-

166

gible. Nonetheless, it may help the reader to have the following chart, identifying the models and arranging them from most federal in nature to most unitary, in advance.

Name	Embodiment
Traditional Federalism, or Federal System	Articles of Confederation
Reformed Federalism, or Federal Government	New Jersey Plan
Dickenson Federalism, or Federal Compound	No comprehensive plan
	Connecticut Compromise
Randolph Federalism, or Compound System	Virginia Plan
Madison Federalism, or National Compound	Virginia Plan plus Madison's proposed negative
Hamilton Federalism, or Consolidating Compound	Hamilton Plan

PURELY FEDERAL FORMS: FEDERAL SYSTEM AND FEDERAL GOVERNMENT

The Convention met in order to revise the federal system within which the states then existed; none of the delegates and few even of the later Anti-Federalists were willing to defend the Articles of Confederation without important changes. Nonetheless, the Articles were the reigning legality when the Convention met and the principles of federalism they embodied served as the point of departure for the delegates' thinking about the problems and possibilities of federal union.

The Articles of Confederation conform in every way to the confederal principle of union as a union of the member states, for purposes of the states as such, and only indirectly for purposes of the human beings who compose the member states.[3] If we measure the Articles against Madison's list of the relevant variables in *Federalist*, No. 39, we can easily see how "federal" the Articles were. Their legal source was not just the states, but the state legislatures. The state legislatures, too, were the source of the ordinary power of the confederal government in that they appointed, and

could recall at will, the delegates to the Congress. The Confederacy's powers operated on the states and not on individuals. While
rather extensive, the powers granted the Articles government were
clearly of the federal sort; it had custody of foreign affairs concerns and a few other common interests of the states. It lacked all
powers to deal with matters internal to its member states, even
powers which proved relevant and indeed essential for carrying
out the objects assigned to it, such as a revenue power and a
power to regulate commerce. Finally, the power to make changes
in the system was entirely in the hands of the state legislatures,
and proceeded according to the principle of unanimous consent
implicit in the idea that the states were the real entities of the union and the consent of all was necessary for the terms of the union
to be changed. While hardly necessary, the Articles made explicit
what was implicit in the whole:

> Each state retains its sovereignty, freedom, and independence, and
> every Power, Jurisdiction and Right, which is not by this confedera-
> tion expressly delegated to the United States, in Congress assembled
> (Article II).[4]

The Articles' failures were well known. Lacking any enforcement powers, the confederal government proved unable to carry
out confederal policy. Lacking a revenue power, the Articles government was constantly on the verge of bankruptcy. Lacking the
power to regulate commerce, the Articles government stood by
while some of the states waged commercial warfare against others.
Efforts to amend the Articles began early and persisted up until
the Convention itself. But the difficult amending mechanism and
the differential advantages a few states could extract under existing arrangements combined to frustrate reform. Even most Anti-
Federalists sought reform of the Articles. Herbert Storing concludes, on the basis of his comprehensive survey of Anti-Federalist
writings: "the Anti-Federalists nevertheless agreed that a Union
was wanted, that it required an efficient government, and that the
Articles of Confederation did not provide such a government."[5]
Jackson Turner Main, much more inclined than Storing to accept
the revisionist view of the Confederation period, finds that

> while the Anti-Federalists denied that the Articles of Confederation
> had completely failed, they nonetheless admitted the need for re-
> form. . . . No one could deny that the changes were required.[6]

But the nature of the change required did not command the same unanimity. Most support probably existed for a reform of the Articles which would preserve their purely federal character, while making them more effective. This federal alternative can be called, following Madison, a *Federal Government,* as contradistinguished from the *Federal System* embodied in the Articles. The Articles, Madison argued, did not establish a government at all.

> A sanction is essential to the idea of law, as coercion is to that of Government. The federal system [under the Articles] being destitute of both, wants the great vital principles of a Political Constitution. Under the form of such a constitution, it is in fact nothing more than a treaty of amity and of alliance, between independent and Sovereign states.[7]

The most obvious way to supply the want of coercion and thus to transform the "alliance" of the Articles into a real government, or "political constitution," is to arm the general government with coercive powers. But so long as the general government operates only on its member states, it remains a purely federal union in the sense of a state of states. Such a change could occur within the basic framework of the Articles of Confederation. Thus, Congress authorized the Convention at Philadelphia "for the sole and express purpose of revising the Articles of Confederation" so as to "render the federal constitution adequate to the exigencies of Government and the preservation of the Union."

In addition to recognizing the need for some enforcement power in the general government, broad consensus also existed for granting some additional powers to the general government. There was widespread agreement that Congress ought to be given some sort of power over commerce, and some revenue authorities in addition to the requisitions which had worked so badly in the confederation period.[8] These additional powers had been regularly proposed, and even nearly adopted during the 1780's. But neither these powers nor the coercive power was understood to qualify the properly federal character of the union.

This reformed version of the purely federal Articles, this *Federal Government,* formally became part of the Convention's agenda when the New Jersey delegation submitted a plan embodying its principles. Three key features characterized the New Jersey Plan. It was explicitly a "revision, correction, and enlargement" of the Articles of Confederation; the Articles remain the skeleton of the new system. Accordingly, the composition of the chief institution of government remained exactly as it had been — the New Jersey Plan proposed no change whatever in the source or mode of operation of the Articles Congress. However, the Congress would receive substantial new powers under the New Jersey Plan, precisely the powers experience had shown were badly needed. Congress could raise an independent, but importantly limited revenue. It could levy what had been called in the years before the Revolution, external taxes, *i.e.*, taxes on imports, as well as a certain very limited class of "internal taxes," in the form of stamp taxes on certain specified items. The New Jersey Plan then grants to the general government at least some of the powers the American colonists had earlier refused to concede to the Empire. Requisitions would supply revenues beyond those collected under Congress' powers of direct taxation, just as in the Articles, but the New Jersey Plan provided further that "if such requisitions be not complied with," Congress would have the power "to direct the collection thereof in the non-complying States and for that purpose to devise and pass acts directing and authorizing the same." The New Jersey Plan also authorized a commerce power "to pass Acts for the regulation of trade and commerce as well with foreign nations as with each other," again a power claimed by the English before the Revolution. The powers granted to the general government in the New Jersey Plan seem to have been those in the Articles plus those claimed by the British which experience had shown were indispensable to an effective union.

The third feature of the New Jersey Plan made quite explicit the transformation from a Federal System into a Federal Government: "if any State shall oppose or prevent the carrying into execution such acts or treaties, the federal Executive shall be authorized to call for the power of the Confederated States, or so much thereof as may be necessary to enforce and compel an obedience to such Acts, or an observance of such Treaties." While one might well find this "provision for military coercion [to be] an amazing grant of power," yet one ought not to characterize this or its other features as "daring to go far in a simply national direction."[9] The provision for coercion drastically strengthened the *federal* union created by the Articles, even, as Madison saw it, created a government where there was none before, but it remains a federal feature. "Federal" and "weak," "national" and "strong" are not pairs of synonyms. Paterson and the other sponsors of the New Jersey

Plan saw the provision of coercion, in some ways so desperate a feature of their plan, as a means of preserving the federal character of the union, and of saving it from incorporating the national elements in the leading alternative plan. The New Jersey Plan increased the powers of the general government, but underlined their federal character; it surely did not, as has been suggested, "move far beyond the Articles in the ends . . . it proposed for the Union." It merely sought means which might effectuate those ends without departing from the federal principle. Jackson Turner Main testifies to the essentially federal character of the New Jersey Plan when he concludes that "all the evidence suggests that the changes in the Articles which the Antifederalists themselves would have wrought are precisely those of the Paterson, or New Jersey Plan, which represented not merely the ideas of the small state delegates but those of the Antifederalists."[10]

That the New Jersey Plan contemplated a rudimentary executive and judiciary for the general government does not qualify these conclusions. While the independent revenue and the ultimate coercive authority gave the general government some actual governing tasks, requiring an executive of some sort, the main thrust of the New Jersey Plan was to keep enforcement in the hands of the states and to keep the general government out of enforcement inside the states in every circumstance except the last resort. The grant of the commerce power, for example, specified that "all punishments, fines, forfeitures and penalties to be incurred for contravening such acts, rules and regulations shall be adjudged by the Common Law Judiciaries of the State." The judiciary of the United States, indeed, is to have a power of review over such judgments in order to correct errors, an important but limited breach of the principle that the agencies of the general government do not operate inside the states. Likewise, the judiciary of the United States would have appellate jurisdiction over cases involving ambassadors, various matters occurring on the high seas (not even original jurisdiction here!), cases where a foreigner has an interest in the construction of any treaty (not treaties in general), and cases involving the regulation of trade or collection of revenues.

The general government's judicial as well as its executive powers are thus for the most part supervisory over the states in the relatively few matters where the general government was legitimately concerned; the states, not the general government, re-

179

mained the body which, for the most part, administered federal law in the United States. While this supervisory power was an innovation which might increase the likelihood of compliance with the policies of the general government, it remains a fundamentally federal feature of the plan, for once again it involves the general government relying on, in the first instance, and operating on in the second, its member states.

Both supporters and opponents of the New Jersey Plan concurred in designating it a "purely federal" plan. So Paterson called it on 14 June (I Farrand, 240); and so Lansing considered it (I Farrand, 249-50). Madison referred to it as a plan which did not "depart from the principle of the Confederation" and Randolph declared it "the federal plan" (I Farrand, 242). Hamilton found that it left the states in possession of their sovereignty (I Farrand, 283). In fact, no one at the Convention denied that the New Jersey Plan remained a federal plan even with its innovations over the Articles; and, as Jackson Turner Main concludes, during the ratification debates, the Anti-Federalists, committed to a "purely federal" union, were generally willing to accept reforms of the sort embodied in the New Jersey Plan, including the provisions for coercing recalcitrant states.[11] The New Jersey Plan did not represent a movement toward a national system, but a movement away from the *Federal System* lacking all enforcement powers, all coercion, of the Articles to a *Federal Government,* a real government with real enforcement powers, but powers which operate in the federal manner. Given the experience the Americans had had with the Articles, that transformation was the most obvious and least radical change that might preserve the federal form and yet "render the federal constitution adequate to the exigencies of government and the preservation of the union."

Randolph Federalism: The Compound System

While country and Convention expected something close to the New Jersey Plan, the efforts of James Madison produced a decisively different beginning point for the Convention which in turn produced a decisively different end-product. In the years before the Convention, Madison had probably devoted more sustained time and effort to the problem of federal union than any other man in North America. His thinking too followed the natural trace from *Federal System* to *Federal Government,* but his thinking went much farther as well. Merely adding powers to the general government, even the radical enforcement power, would not, Madison saw, provide effective, safe government. Much more drastic changes in internal structure, mode of operation, and source of authority were required. A month before the scheduled opening of the Convention Madison wrote to Governor Randolph that his "ideas of a reform strike so deeply at the old confederation, and lead to such a systematic change, they scarcely admit to the expedient" of being "engrafted" onto the Articles.[12] Madison's efforts to sway his fellow delegates from Virginia must have been extremely effective, for, to mention one example, they converted Governor Randolph from his earlier view "that the alterations should be grafted on the old confederation" to the more drastic reform proposal associated with his name.[13] Winning the Virginia delegation to his view was obviously a great victory for Madison, although, as we shall see, he proved unable to win the delegation's support for his full plan but could carry them only partway.

A common view of the Convention as a whole and of the Virginia Plan within it, has something of a Hegelian cast: a nationalist (consolidationist) Virginia Plan meets a purely federal New Jersey Plan or Articles of Confederation, and from their synthesis derives the peculiar compound of national and federal via the Connecticut Compromise that we call federalism.[14] Most of the best students of the Convention now affirm the major premise of that Hegelian scenario. "In short," says Martin Diamond, "the original intention of the leading Framers, all of whom supported the Virginia Plan, was to establish a fully national government." And, according to another, the adoption of the Connecticut Compromise is what "made the government partly national, partly federal."[15]

That Hegelian scheme, however, runs counter to Madison's own understanding of the Virginia Plan and of the final Constitution. While he accepted the description of the Constitution as "partly national, partly federal," he did not trace acquisition of that character to the Convention but to the original Virginia Plan itself. Madison insists in his two most important pre-Convention writings that he seeks a "middle ground" between a consolidation and a purely federal system.[16] And the plan which Madison characterized as a "middle ground" was itself more nationalist than the Virginia Plan.

The most authoritative account of the Virginia Plan is Ran-

dolph's speech introducing it. It is meant to provide, he emphasizes, more adequate means to the ends already sought in the federal system. Randolph's list of the defects of the Confederation
consisted of its failures to achieve the ends for which it was instituted, not its failure to seek ends beyond these. "The Confederation fulfilled none of the objects for which it was formed" (29
May; I Farrand, 24).

A glance at the ends Randolph lists reveals their federal character:

> The character of such a government ought to secure 1. against for-
> eign invasion: 2. against dissentions between members of the Union,
> or seditions in particular states: 3. to procure to the several states
> various blessings of which an isolated situation was incapable: 4. to
> be able to defend itself against encroachment: and 5. to be para-
> mount to the state constitutions. (29 May; I Farrand,18.)

The ends mentioned, with the possible exception of the last, to
which we shall turn in a moment, are ends of the states as such,
not of individuals. They are ends which with perfect justice could
be attributed to the Union under the Articles. This list surely does
not include what Martin Diamond identifies as "the most important matters—e.g., 'security of private rights and the steady dispensation of justice.' "[17] If the Virginia Plan intended to give positive custody of those further ends to the general government, then
we might be justified in denominating it a national or consolidationist scheme; but it stays far from embracing these ends. Indeed, Randolph's statement of ends is much closer to the view of
the ends of the union put forward later in the Convention by
"Sherman of Connecticut, one of the intelligent defenders of the
federal principle," than it is to the nationalist ends identified by
Diamond.[18] According to Sherman:

> The objects of Union . . . were few. 1. defence against foreign dan-
> ger. 2. against internal disputes and a resort to force. 3. Treaties with
> foreign nations. 4. regulating foreign commerce, and drawing reve-
> nue from it. Those and perhaps a few lesser objects alone rendered a
> confederation of the States necessary. (6 June; I Farrand, 133.)

Sherman summarized his position in a way that could be applied
to Randolph's statement:

> In short, let the General Government be a sort of collateral Govern-
> ment which shall secure the States in particular difficulties such as

foreign war, or a war between two or more States. (6 June; I Farrand, 142-43.)

Two of Randolph's items appear to go beyond any on Sherman's list. As his third "object," Randolph mentioned that the general government ought "to produce to the several states various blessings, of which an isolated situation was incapable." That he did not mean by this that the general government was "to deal with the vast bulk of political matters" is perfectly clear from his explanation of the sorts of "blessings" he had in mind:[19] "That there are many advantages, which the U.S. might acquire, which were not attainable under the confederation — such as a productive impost — counteraction of the commercial regulation of other nations — pushing a commerce *ad libitum* — etc. etc." (I Farrand, 19).[20]

Randolph's fifth object — "to be paramount to the state constitutions" — signifies no general supremacy, but only the paramountcy implicit in the notion of a general government.

> It [the Confederation government] was not even paramount to the state constitutions, ratified as it was in many of the States. . . . State Constitutions formed at an early period of the war, and by persons elected by the people for that purpose. . . . The confederation . . . had its ratification not by any special appointment from the people, but from the several assemblies. No judge will say that the confederation is paramount to a state constitution. (I Farrand, 19, 26.)

Randolph's paramountcy, then, is the superior legal authority of the general government in its proper sphere of action, and not a general supremacy of a national government over the states. The means to achieve this end is not a grant of general legislative power, which the Virginia Plan does not contain, but the legal derivation of the general government from the people via popular ratification of its Constitution, which the Virginia Plan does contain.

While the ends were federal and could already be ascribed to the Union, Randolph Federalism incorporated two important innovations with respect to means. The first principle of Randolph Federalism was the need to grant powers commensurate to the objects of the general government. The idea of a delegation of particular powers to the general government was an old and familiar feature of federal systems and one with which the Americans were familiar from their experience both within the British Empire and within the Confederacy. In delegating certain objects and the powers to effect them to the general government, the Virginia Plan remained squarely within the bounds of traditional federalism. But the powers, if not the objects, destined for the general government surely went beyond those granted in the Articles. To each of the objects or ends Randolph listed coresponds a power or powers; like the objects, the powers retain a distinctly federal character.

As we have seen, the paramountcy of the general government was to be secured theoretically via popular ratification of the new Constitution; that paramountcy was to be secured more practically via the grant of a new power to the national legislation: "to call forth the force of the Union against any member of the Union failing to fulfill its duty under the articles thereof" (Resolution 6). Another new power would also help secure that paramountcy as well as defend against encroachment by the states, *viz.*, the power "to negative all laws passed by the several States, contravening in the opinion of the National Legislature the articles of Union" (Resolution 6). That negative, together with the power "to legislate in all cases . . . in which the harmony of the United States may be interrupted by the exercise of individual Legislation," would meet Randolph's second object of "securing against dissentions between members of the Union."

Randolph Federalism would "procure to the several States various blessings, of which an isolated situation was incapable" through the grant of power "to legislate in all cases to which the separate States are incompetent." The regulation of foreign and interstate commerce and the drawing of revenue therefrom seems to be, on the evidence of Randolph's previously quoted explanation of this object, the chief content of this vaguely defined power. Finally, the first object of the Confederacy, "security against foreign invasion," would be met through the carry-over grant of "the Legislative Right vested in Congress by the Confederation," and the new powers already mentioned which would make those old powers more effective. There is, thus, a close correlation between the objects specified by Randolph for the Union and the powers to be granted by the Virginia Plan. The following schema captures the relationships between powers and objects in a useful, if somewhat simplified way.

Object	Power
1. To secure against foreign invasion	1. Legislative Rights

vested in Congress by the Confederation (as invigorated by other powers).

2. To secure against dissentions between members of the union

2. To legislate in all cases in which the harmony of the United States may be interrupted by the exercise of individual Legislation.

3. To procure to the several States various blessings . . .

3. To legislate in all cases to which the separate States are incompetent.

4. To be able to defend itself against encroachments from the States

4. To negative all state laws contravening the articles of Union

5. To be paramount to the state constitutions

5. To call forth the force of the Union against any member of failing to fulfill its duty under the articles thereof.

Popular Ratification of Constitution

The federal character of the powers to be conveyed in the Virginia Plan shows forth not merely in the powers' close connection to the essentially federal objects, but in their clear character as supplementary to the states. Broad and important as the general government's powers would have been under the Virginia Plan, they were clearly meant to supplement state legislation which was, as a matter of course, assumed to continue being the primary kind of legislation. Only when foreign powers are involved, or when the individual states were incompetent, that is, in matters concerning the states as a collectivity and to which therefore the individual states were necessarily incompetent, or where the individual states threatened the harmony of the union through encroaching on each other or the general government would the general government be empowered to act.[21]

Most students of the Convention have been less inclined to see the supplementary, that is, federal, character of the powers in the Virginia Plan, than to be impressed by the very general, even vague, and sweeping character of those powers, especially in contrast with the far more precise enumeration which ultimately prevailed in the Constitution. Now it is rather difficult to give an authoritative interpretation of the intended scope and contents of the Virginia Plan's proposed powers, because they were hardly discussed at the Convention before being replaced by an enumeration.

Many years later, Madison maintained that the strongly nationalist interpretation of his delegation's proposals was unjustified, and suggested that the shift to an enumeration accorded with the intention of the Virginia Plan's drafters. In 1833 he insisted that

> It cannot be supposed that these descriptive phrases [respecting powers] were to be left in their indefinite extent to Legislative discretion. A selection and definition of the cases embraced by them was to be the task of the Convention.[22]

Indeed, said Madison, the whole of the Virginia Plan was "a mere sketch in which omitted details were to be supplied in the general terms and phrases to be reduced to their proper details"; and so the convention understood and treated it.[23]

Irving Brant, a partisan of the nationalist reading of the Virginia Plan, has impugned Madison's testimony from the 1830's as an effort to preserve his reputation against the charges of inconsistency which were sometimes leveled against him. The records of the debates on 31 May do not, Brant holds, support Madison's claim that he always looked to the Convention "to select and define the cases embraced by" the general language of the Virginia Plan. Several of the delegates, concerned about "the vagueness of the term 'incompetent' " requested "an exact enumeration" of what this might include. Madison replied in a way Brant claims belies his later claims:

> Mr. Madison said that he brought with him into the Convention a strong bias in favor of an enumeration and definition of the powers necessary to be exercised by the national Legislature; but had also brought ["grave" — in the unedited version, according to Brant; "some" — in Pierce's notes of the same speech] doubts concerning its practicability. His wishes remained unaltered; but his doubts had become stronger. What his opinion might ultimately be he could not yet tell. (31 May; I Farrand, 53.)

His "ultimate opinion" decidedly favored enumeration. Madison and the Virginia delegation supported a motion favoring an enu-

meration on 16 July, and thereafter supported every effort to secure an enumeration.[24] If Madison ever was attached to the vague
and general language of Resolution 6 as inherently preferable to
an enumeration on any ground, much less on the ground of a
covert commitment to granting plenary legislative powers to the
general government, he surely hid that commitment by word and
deed in every way. However, the events of 6 May, as reported by
William Pierce of Georgia, support Madison's 1833 description of
the Convention's understanding of the Virginia Plan. When Sherman objected to Resolution 6 as "too indefinitely expressed," Madison replied, according to Pierce, that "it was necessary to adopt
some general principles on which we should act"; the Virginia
proposals were "general principles" to guide and be filled in by the
Convention. George Wythe, another delegate from Virginia, emphasized the temporary and guiding character of the general language; he "observed that it would be right to establish general
principles before we go into details," a thought endorsed immediately by Rufus King, who "was of the opinion that the principles
ought first to be established before we proceed to the framing of
the Act." Randolph also "was of opinion it would be impossible to
define the powers and the length to which the federal Legislature
ought to extend just at this time" (31 May; I Farrand, 60). On 16
July, after the Connecticut Compromise, the Convention returned
to Resolution 6, and once again a member questioned its vagueness. Even at that late moment, Nathaniel Gorham of Massachusetts replied:

> The vagueness of the terms constitutes the propriety of them. We are
> establishing general principles, to be exended hereafter into details
> which will be precise and explicit. (II Farrand, 17.)

In the first discussion of the issue, on 31 May,

> Mr Butler repeated his fears that we were running into an extreme
> in taking away the powers of the States, and called on Mr. Randolph
> for the extent of his meaning.
>   Mr. Randolph disclaimed any intention to give indefinite powers
> to the national Legislature, declaring that he was entirely opposed to
> such an inroad on the State jurisdictions, and that he did not think
> any consideration whatever could ever change his determination.
> His opinion was fixed on this point. (I Farrand, 53.)

Indeed it was, for he found even the enumeration of the final

Constitution to give too "indefinite and dangerous power . . . to Congress" (15 September; II Farrand, 631), an objection he repeated in his letter to the speaker of the Virginia House of Delegates, explaining his reason for failing to sign the Constitution.[25]

The first great principle of the Virginia Plan then is power adequate to the objects of the general government, with both objects and powers still understood essentially in the traditional federal manner.[26] The second great principle of the Virginia Plan represents a far greater innovation in the form and principle of federalism: the general government is to be derived and to operate as independently and separately of its member states as possible. While the general government would remain essentially federal in objects and powers, it would partake of the characteristics of an ordinary national government in its structure and mode of operation. The Virgina Plan itself then is properly designated a "compound," partly national, partly federal.

Randolph Federalism adopts national means to federal ends. Madison's first great theoretical discovery was that the federal ends the Americans sought could not be adequately achieved via federal means—certainly not the federal means of the *Federal System* embodied in the Articles. But not the federal means of a *Federal Government* of the type embodied in the New Jersey Plan either. Although *Federal Government*, in theory at least, remedies the decisive lack of the *Federal System*—want of coercive power—it retains a defect almost as debilitating—the intervention of the state legislatures in the constitution and operation of the system. That defect negates the grant of coercive power and in practice returns *Federal Government* to the principles of voluntary operation which proved fatal to *Federal Systems*.

Governments exist to secure the interests and protect the rights of those they govern. In a properly constructed government such a congruity between the policy of the government and the interests of the governed might be thought to lead to a system that could essentially be voluntary. Madison was one of the earliest to challenge this conclusion as fallacious and to reconsider the issue of federal organization in the light of that challenge. Government may pursue the interest of the governed and yet still require coercion. On occasion, men are mistaken about where their interest lies; passion or short-run interest may blind them. More importantly, without a coercive authority to enforce the common interest, the individual interest of men may well lead them to actions adverse to the interests and rights of others. A fair and equal tax burden, for example, may be in the interest of each citizen, or of each member state of a confederacy, but it is even more to the interest of each to avoid paying the tax at all, or to pay less, especially if the benefits the taxes support continue. Even if the benefits may not continue, it is frequently the interest of each individual not to pay, for if he pays he may bear the burdens and not derive the benefits unless the others contribute their share, which the individual as such cannot guarantee. Only "mutual coercion, mutually agreed to" can make actual the common interest which exists in principle.

In a confederacy the barriers to voluntary compliance are even greater. Men in collectivities are even less likely to be restrained in their pursuit of advantage than individuals since they are less restrained by concern for their reputation. Moreover, the state governments embody not only the separate and partial interests of their states as individual entities within the system, but have other separate and special interests as governments. The governors of the states have a personal stake in their governments, in their own power and position, which makes them the natural enemy of the general government. "Experience," Madison said, "had evinced a constant tendency in the States to encroach on the federal authority; to violate national Treaties, to infringe the rights and interests of each other" (8 June; I Farrand, 164). Wilson claimed that "examination" would show that "the opposition of States to federal measures had proceeded much more from the Officers of the States, than from the people at large," an opposition he traced to the fact that "the state officers were to be the losers of power" (31 May, 6 June; I Farrand, 49, 133).

To enforce the laws on the states via the states themselves is equivalent to seeking voluntary compliance which will not be forthcoming. To enforce the laws via applying coercion against the states is no better. George Mason of Virginia, for one, early in the Convention, "argued very cogently that punishment could not in the nature of things be executed on the States collectively." Randolph expanded on the point: "Coercion he pronounced to be impracticable, expensive, cruel to individuals. It tended also to habituate the instruments of it to shed the blood and riot in the spoils of their fellow citizens, and consequently trained them up for the service of ambition" (16 June; I Farrand, 256). The broad and important conclusion which Madison first and the others after him drew was that a properly constructed federal system must omit the agency of the states as such everywhere practicable.

The primary insight is the *negative* one that the agency of the states must be avoided; the consequence is the great positive innovation for which American federalism is best known. While the Union is a union of states, that is, federal, to be successful it must operate not on states, but on individuals. Secondly, the general government must derive its institutions entirely separately from the states as well, for every place where the states as such have a say in the selection or behavior of the officers of the general government is a place filled by a potential enemy.

The main institutional features of the Virginia Plan reflect this formative principle of Randolph Federalism. The general government requires its own agencies of action, and so must possess executive and judicial establishments as well as a legislature. All these institutions must draw their officers in a way that avoids the states. Thus, the people are to elect the lower house of the legislature, which in turn is to elect the upper house and the executive.

The structural innovations also demanded a shift in the basis of representation. Under the Confederacy, Madison pointed out, "the acts of Congress depended so much for their efficacy on the cooperation of the States, that these had a weight both within and without Congress, nearly in proportion to their extent and importance." Under the conditions the equality of representation was not so disturbing or unjust as it would be under a system which operates "without the intervention of the State Legislatures," such as the Virginia Plan proposed. Under these latter conditions the "weight" of the states must receive proportional representation in the legislature because it would not find expression in the administration.

Why we have called *Randolph Federalism* a *Compound System,* or might have called it an *Uncompounded Compound,* should now be clear. The system is a compound, a mix of the federal and the national, but each level of government is unmixed or uncompounded. The general government, in its structure and operation, has no federal elements; the states, with a few exceptions to be discussed in a moment, are also autonomous of the general government, neither operating nor operated on by it. Not the general government but the system as a whole is partly national, partly federal via the division of objects and authorities between the two levels of the system.

In this novel kind of federal system the major issue concerns the line of division between the powers of the different governments. Again it was Madison's genius to see that some provision had to be made for drawing the lines. Within the Virginia Plan, that provision is the power in the legislature of the general government to negative laws of the States contrary to the Constitution and to the constitutional laws and treaties of the general government. This negative was one of three places in the Virginia Plan where the federal mode of operation—one level of government acting on another—was retained. The other two were the provision for use of coercion against recalcitrant states and the continued reliance on the requisition for revenue. In the course of its deliberations the Convention came to see all three as anomalies and acted to purify the Constitution by adopting substitutes more in accord with its national means of action. The presence of these "federal" features in the Virginia Plan testifies to the degree to which its authors conceived themselves to be creating a *federal* system, albeit an exceedingly novel one.

Understanding the Virginia Plan in terms of *Randolph Federalism* or the *Compound System* clarifies the much-misunderstood resolutions Randolph brought forward on 30 May in an attempt to characterize the plan he had introduced the day before. "That a union of the states, merely federal, will not accomplish the objects proposed by the Articles of the Confederation . . . " went the text of the first new resolution. It is clear from our discussion that the Virginia Plan does not propose a union "merely federal"; it is worth noting, however, that Randolph's language suggests a federal union but one that is not "merely federal." Moreover, he reaffirms quite explicitly here that the objects sought in his plan are the same as those sought by the Articles of Confederation.

The third resolution raises a closely related issue. "Resolved, that a national government ought to be established, consisting of a supreme judicial, legislative and executive" (30 May; I Farrand, 33). Note that Randolph does not say the *Union* is to be national; rather its government is to be so, as indeed it is, because it operates on individuals as national governments do. While the government is national, the objects of union are federal and the union itself is to be not *"merely federal."* Randolph clarified the meaning of "supreme" as used in his third new resolution. As Yates reports the discussion,

The term "supreme" required explanation—It was asked whether it was intended to annihilate state governments? It was answered, only so far as the powers intended to be granted to the new government should clash with the states, when the latter was to yield. (30 May; I Farrand, 39.)

Neither the plan itself nor the language of Randolph's third resolution justifies the conclusion so many contemporary scholars draw about the character of the plan.

The Virginia Plan [says one of them] proposed the creation of a powerful government which it throughout described by the shocking term "national." . . . When the Convention opened, there was no thought of the mixed form we now call federal. . . . Accordingly, the delegates thought only of two mutually exclusive alternatives: confederal or federal association versus national government.

That same scholar concludes, therefore, that when the Convention adopted

Randolph's third resolution it "was pointed to a simply national government, and not the 'composition' which finally resulted."[27]

But Madison himself rejected this sort of interpretation of the Virginia Plan:

Will you pardon me for pointing out an error of fact into which you have fallen, as others have done, by supposing that the term, "national" applied to the contemplated Government, in the early stage of the Convention, particularly in the propositions of Mr. Randolph, was equivalent to "unlimited" or consolidated. This was not the case. The term was used, not in contradistinction to a limited, but to a "federal" Government. As the latter operated within the extent of its authority thro' requisitions on the confederated States, and rested on the sanction of State Legislatures, the Government to take its place, was to operate *within the extent of its powers* directly and coercively on individuals, and to receive the higher sanction of the people of the States. And there being no technical or approporate denomination applicable to the new and unique system, the term national was used.[28]

Most contemporary scholars ignore those explanations by Madison, or like Irving Brant, brush them aside as Madison's attempt to salvage his reputation for consistency. But Madison's later comments accord perfectly with all the evidence of the debates, as well as with Randolph's own gloss on wherein lay the national character of his proposals at the Convention. "The true question," Randolph said after. the New Jersey Plan was put forward, "is whether we shall adhere to the federal plan, or introduce the national plan." And how does Randolph distinguish federal from national in this context — "according to the mode by which the end of a general government can be attained." The federal mode of the Paterson plan proceeds via "coercion" of the member states, a mode, we have seen, of which Randolph despaired. The national alternative is to employ the mode of "real legislation" as in his own plan. "We must resort therefore to a National *Legislation over individuals*" (16 June; I Farrand, 255-56). Randolph's contemporary exposition of the term "national" is, therefore, identical to Madison's later exposition.

If we deny the Virginia Plan to have been nationalist in the sense of the current interpretations of it, are we thereby committed to the opposite view, the state sovereignty view of the Constitution? Randolph's second resolution of 30 May speaks directly to this question. "Resolved that no treaty or treaties among the whole or part of the States as sovereignties, would be sufficient." In part, this resolution merely affirms that a real "political constitution," complete with coercive authorities, rather than a voluntary system of alliances, is required for an effective union. But it also suggests that the states can no longer be considered as "individual sovereignties" if there is to be a sufficient union. The issue of the locus of sovereignty in the American federal system was actually much less prominent at the Convention than its later importance would suggest.

There were some — notably Luther Martin on the federal side, Hamilton and perhaps Gouverneur Morris on the national side — who clung to the view that sovereignty must reside somewhere, in one government or the other. These few delegates insisted that one or the other must be sovereign, but the main thrust of the delegates' thought was away from such a drastic either/or. Madison, both at the Convention and later, felt that too much was made of the abstract issue of sovereignty. "There was a gradation, he observed, from the smallest corporation, with the most limited powers, to the largest empire with the most perfect sovereignty" (29 June; I Farrand, 463-64). While one finds this "most perfect sovereignty" in some political societies, it is by no means a universal phenomenon; "a compleat supremacy somewhere is not necessary in every society." Very late in his life, reflecting on the nullification thesis, Madison reiterated the very same attitude toward the abstraction of sovereignty he expressed in 1787: "those who deny the possibility of a political system, with a divided sovereignty like that of the U.S. must choose between a government purely consolidated, and an association of governments purely federal."[29] Neither alternative, in Madison's view, was as good as the compound, divided system the Constitution provided. If, Madison seems to think, the compound republic of the United States is incompatible with the abstract doctrine of sovereignty, then so much the worse for the doctrine of sovereignty.

The Americans of the Founding generation dealt with the problem of sovereignty by drawing a novel distinction between the sovereign and the government. The Americans saw that the people were sovereign and retained their sovereignty, delegating only so much as they chose to their government or dividing it between different governments. Neither government is sovereign; both, as James Wilson said, "were derived from the people — both meant for the people" (25 June; I Farrand, 405-06). Both governments are subordinate to the sovereign authority, the people, but deriving equally from the sovereign are equal to each other. No constitutional right of nullification or secession remains in the states; but no claim to general supremacy inheres in the Union.

Let us conclude this long discussion of the Virginia Plan by restating the main principles of Randolph Federalism.

(1) The whole system to be instituted is a composite, a mix of the federal and national principles.

(2) The general government, however, is not to be compounded itself. It is to be structured and is to operate entirely according to the national principle, with no agency of the states in it or on it and as little of it on the states as possible. The core is separateness. As James Wilson put it, "all interference between the general and local governments should be obviated as much as possible" (31 May; I Farrand, 49). Checks and other provisions for the proper and safe operation of the general government are to be entirely internal to it, with no dependence on the states in this respect.

(3) While the general government's powers are to remain essentially federal in character, they are to be adequate to the federal objects entrusted to it.

The Two National Compounds: Madison Federalism and Hamilton Federalism

Contrary to almost everybody's expectations, the Convention tentatively committed itself right at the outset to Randolph Federalism. In the course of further deliberations a variety of other forms of federalism, some more, some less distant from Randolph Federalism, were brought forward to vie for the Convention's favor. James Madison, chief author of Randolph Federalism, also sponsored one of the main alternatives to the Virginia Plan. This fact is less paradoxical than it may seem at first, for the Virginia Plan embodied only part of what Madison wanted and indeed failed to incorporate some features he considered most important of all.

While there were several differences between the Virginia Plan and the proposals Madison prepared prior to the Convention or indicated he preferred during the convention, only one need concern us here. Among the legislative powers of the general government in the Virginia Plan, it will be recalled, was the power "to negative all laws passed by the several States, contravening in the opinion of the National Legislature the articles of Union." But in his letters to Randolph and Washington, Madison had proposed a far more radical power: "over and above the positive [legislative] power, a negative *in all cases whatsoever* on the legislative acts of the States."[30] This extraordinary power was "not some theoretical will-o'-the-wisp for Madison" either, for several times during the Convention he attempted, unsuccessfully, to secure its adoption. And after the Convention Madison wrote Jefferson a letter strongly regretful over his inability to prevail on this head. As the editors of Madison's papers put it, the letter reveals Madison to have been profoundly disappointed with the results of

> the convention. [He] doubted the workability of the plan agreed upon at Philadelphia because it lacked the one ingredient that in his view was essential: . . . a power vested in the national legislature to negative, or veto [all] state laws.[31]

On one occasion Madison and his ally on this issue, Charles Pinckney, provoked a vote in the Convention which explains why the universal veto did not appear in the Virginia Plan. While Virginia lined up as one of only three states supporting the universal negative, its victory there was exceedingly narrow, Blair, Mc-

Clung, and Madison himself in favor, but Randolph and Mason against (8 June; I Farrand, 168). Madison apparently could not bring these two important members of his delegation so far as to support his universal negative.

The important difference between Randolph Federalism and Madison Federalism inheres in the difference between Randolph's partial negative and Madison's preferred universal negative. This difference is in part a matter of different means to a common end, and in part a matter of different ends. On 8 June when he moved for the universal negative, Charles Pinckney stated the common end Randolph Federalism and Madison Federalism sought from the negative:

> that the States must be kept in due subordination to the nation: that if the States were left to act for themselves in any case, it would be impossible to defend the national prerogatives, however extensive they might be on paper; that this universal negative was in fact the corner-stone of an efficient national government. (I Farrand, 164.)

According to this understanding of the negative, its purpose was essentially defensive and federal in character, to protect against state encroachments on the proper prerogatives and acts of the general government.[32] Every successful federal system requires some means of controlling encroachments by the members states on each other and on the general government. The negative substitutes for the most obvious such method; it would "render the use of force unnecessary" (6 June; I Farrand, 165).

Given the defensive federal end of protecting against encroachments, the delegates pressed the sensible objection that the means proposed, the universal negative, went well beyond the evil. Jefferson captured the delegates' concerns when he wrote Madison that his universal negative "fails in an essential character, that the hole and the patch should be commensurate." The patch was much greater than the hole, Jefferson wrote, because

> Not more than 1 out of 100 state-acts concern the Confederacy. This proposition then, in order to give them 1 degree of power which they ought to have, gives them 99 more which they ought not to have, upon a presumption that they will not exercise the 99.[33]

The common end the two versions of the negative share is obviously compatible with the general character of Randolph Federalism; while that model takes as its chief path the division of realms of action between the different levels of government, general and local, and the separate derivation and operation of each within its own realm, it recognizes the need to find an alternative to coercion for keeping each of the levels from encroaching on the other. Since, as Madison says, "the necessity of a general Government proceeds from the propensity of the States to pursue their particular interests in opposition to the general interest," the great need implicit in the very enterprise of establishing a federal constitution is to guard above all against state encroachments.

Yet Madison's device was, *ceteris paribus,* more at odds with the overall character of Randolph Federalism than Randolph's favored partial negative. The operative idea of Randolph Federalism was, after all, the division of the spheres and the separate operation of each government within its sphere, or, to put it differently, the minimization of the places at which either level of government had an agency of any sort in the operation of the other. Both versions of the negative violated that principle. But Madison's did so to a far greater extent, and in a way that, to most of the delegates, threatened the basic idea of the separation of the spheres by providing too strong an instrument for maintaining the separation. One can hardly help but think that if the defensive purpose had been Madison's only purpose for the universal negative that he would have favored instead Randolph's narrower version.

Even Randolph's version was seen by the delegates as too contrary to the basic principle of Randolph Federalism. On 17 July the Convention decisively opted for a judicial protection against state encroachments rather than legislative protection via the negative. The negative, in whatever form, interfered too much with the states, had too many technical problems (*e.g.,* what does a state do while it awaits approval of its laws? Could Congress review the legislation of thirteen states?) and involved too much interaction between governments as such, rather than between governments and individuals on which the Virginia Plan on the whole relied (17 July; II Farrand, 27-28; also cf. discussions on 23 and 28 August).

Safeguarding against encroachments, this eminently federal end was not the only, or even the chief end for which Madison sought the universal negative, however. But the true role Madison contemplated for the negative fails to emerge at all clearly from the records of the Convention. In a word, Madison saw the negative as the device, and the only device in the American context, for solving the hitherto insoluble problem of republicanism in a wholly republican manner. The unsolved problem was the problem of majority faction; the solution, we all know, was the extended republic. What is not so well-known, however, was that the constitutional means by which Madison meant to embody that solution was the negative.[34] When Madison wrote complainingly to Jefferson on 24 October 1787 he was saying that the Convention had failed "to secure individuals against encroachments on their rights" when it failed to accept the universal negative. The Constitution at most provided a partial protection of rights.[35]

On 6 June, Roger Sherman cited the fewness of the "objects of union" in defense of his view that the state legislatures should continue selecting delegates to the federal legislative assembly; Sherman's list of objects, we have already seen, nearly coincided with the list Randolph himself presented along with the Virginia proposals. Sherman's speech prompted Madison, however, to counter with a speech Brant calls "the most significant of the convention."[36] Madison

> differed from the member from Connecticut in thinking the objects mentioned to be all the principal ones that required a National Government. Those were certainly important and necessary objects; but he combined with them the necessity, of providing more effectually for the security of private rights, and the steady dispensation of justice. (6 June; I Farrand, 134.)

Madison goes well beyond Sherman and Randolph in the ends he sought from the general government; his further ends, "the security of private rights, and the steady dispensation of justice," are properly national ends as opposed to federal ends. He proposes to make the general government responsible for the most fundamental concerns of individual citizens. Madison Federalism is decidedly more nationalist in aspiration than the Virginia Plan's embodiment of Randolph Federalism.

At this point Madison's position becomes subject to numerous misunderstandings. The source of the misunderstanding, I think, is this: at the time Madison made his speech on the ends of the general government, no proposal before the Convention in fact embodied that end. The Virginia Plan embodied only the narrower federal ends of Randolph Federalism. Madison, however, had in mind the universal negative as the provision which would achieve the further national ends. The failure to recognize the connection between the two respects in which Madison Federalism goes beyond Randolph Federalism — the further nationalist ends and the universal negative — is responsible for the most common misunderstandings of Madison's position at the Convention. The most common inaccuracy attempts to stretch the Virginia Plan to fit the nationalist ends of Madison Federalism. Martin Diamond is the most sophisticated adherent of this view and the strains thus show up most tellingly in his rendition. Diamond takes the following statement by Madison: "Those were certainly important and necessary objects; but he combined with them the necessity of providing more effectually for the security of private rights, and the steady dispensation of justice"; and translates it thus: "Madison would place the most important matters — e.g., security of private rights and the steady dispensation of justice — under a national government." But Madison had not said that these "most important matters" should be "placed under a national government." Nowhere in the Virginia Plan, nowhere in the Convention, nowhere in his pre-Convention writings had Madison ever faintly suggested that these concerns should be placed under the general government. He even more surely never said what Diamond next transforms Madison's 6 June speech into: "Republicanism [according to Madison] not only permits but requires taking away from the states responsibility for the security of private rights, and the steady dispensation of justice, else rights and justice will perish under the state governments." [37] Diamond, moreover, strongly overstates the effect of Madison's speech, when he suggests that with it Madison brought the small state "pure federalist — small republicans" to see they might "have their cake and eat it too"; that is, to see that an extended republic, and thus a nationalist solution to the problem of union, was not a threat but a salvation to republicanism. The evidence from the Convention suggests the extended republic argument had very little impact. For that day, four sets of notes besides Madison's own survive. Three of the four take no notice of that part of Madison's speech at all; the fourth, by Hamilton, states it only to refute it (I Farrand,140-47).

The lack of impact on the other delegates explains, I think, one of the most curious features of Madison's behavior at the Convention. We know, from the letters to Washington and Randolph before, and Jefferson afterwards that Madison always defended his universal negative primarily in terms of the extended republic-nationalists ends of union argument he deployed on 6 June. But on

8 June, when the universal negative, a feature he cared for passionately, was on the floor, Madison spoke only of its federal, defensive role of checking encroachments, and not of its national role of preventing injustice. Why did Madison keep silent on all this when it was needed, when the delegates were about to vote down the universal negative as too large a patch for the hole? Only the argument for the negative as serving the national ends might save it, if anything could. Madison did not employ that argument, I would suggest, because his trial balloon presentation on 6 June, no doubt a warm-up for the soon to come effort to extend the negative, did not get off the ground with the delegates, just as it did not get off the ground with his own delegation, just as it did not get off the ground with Jefferson. Madison's extended republic argument, far from transforming the Convention and winning the others over, met with such a resounding silence that Madison himself hesitated to employ it when it was needed.

One important consequence of the failure of the extended republic argument is that Madison nowhere at the Convention gave an adequate account of the relationship between the extended republic and the negative. For that we must look to the important pre- and post-Convention letters to his fellow Virginians. Now Madison's extended republic analysis is so well-known, and has been so well-presented, especially by Diamond, that it hardly needs repetition here. I want only to bring out certain features of Madison's argument which show its intimate ties to the negative.

Madison saw the extended republic argument as presenting not only a solution to the problem of republicanism, but to the problem of government more generally. The problem of political construction requires combining two features which do not easily cohere. "The great desideratum in Government is, so to modify the sovereignty as that it may be sufficiently neutral between different parts of the Society to control one part from invading the rights of another, and at the same time sufficiently controlled itself, from setting up an interest adverse to that of the entire Society." More briefly put, the need is to combine a sufficient independence from society (neutrality) with a sufficient dependence on society (control). Each half of this need can be met by a pure form of government well-known to history and theory. "In absolute monarchies, the Prince may be tolerably neutral towards different classes of his subjects," and may therefore achieve the requisite independence from elements of society. However, the absolute monarch "may sacrifice the happiness of all to his personal ambition or avarice," because he lacked sufficient dependence on society. The very feature of the monarch's position which provides neutrality and independence also is responsible for the dangerous depredations he can make against society as a whole.

The traditional small republic on the other hand provides a solution to the problem the monarch does not solve. "In small republics, the sovereign will is controlled from such a sacrifice of the entire society, but is not sufficiently neutral towards the parts composing it." Republican theorists, Jefferson included, failed to see the way in which republicanism itself failed to supply a complete solution to the problem of government.

> They found their reasoning on the idea, that the people composing the Society, enjoy not only an equality of political rights; but that they have all precisely the same interests, and the same feelings in every respect. Were this in reality the case, their reasoning would be conclusive. The interest of the majority would be that of the minority also; . . . We know however that no Society ever did or can consist of so homogenous a mass of citizens.

Since society consists of differentiated and conflicting interests, republican government's dependence on society, the very feature which protects society from the private interests of the ruler, almost guarantees that government will be captured by any interest in society which can command a majority.[38]

Neither a republic nor a monarchy then can by itself solve the political problem. But a combination of the two can do better than either alone. "As a limited Monarchy tempers the evils of an absolute one; so an extensive Republic ameliorates the administration of a small Republic."[39] Madison's expression here is so concise that it requires some explication. The first solution, the limited monarchy, differs from the absolute not by supplanting the monarch, who after all supplies the required neutrality, but supplements him with a limiting and controlling republican element in the form of a popular assembly. The combination of the monarchic and the republican provides the desired combination of qualities in the limited monarchy.

Madison is even clearer that this is so with respect to the large republic: "an extensive republic meliorates the administration of a small Republic." [40] The large does not replace the small republic, but the combination of the large republic and the small republic produces the same effects as the limited monarchy's combination. In the "wholly republican" solution Madison projects for the United States, the extensive republic plays the role of the monarchical element in the mixed solution of the English constitution. As Madison writes to Washington, the extended republic is to possess "a negative in all cases whatsoever on the legislative acts of the States, *as heretofore exercised by the kingly prerogative.*"[41]

The vehicle for the operation of the large republic in the large-small republic combination is the same, then, as the vehicle for the operation of the monarchical in the monarchic-republican combination of the limited monarchy. The solution lies no more in arming the government of the large republic with positive legislative powers to supplant the small republics in providing security of rights and the administration of justice than it would in granting the monarch parliament's legislative powers. Should the general government begin to exercise legislative authorities reserved to the small republics, one might well say that the "monarchic element" of the combination was overswollen.

Madison projects a constitutional embodiment for the extended republic far different from the nationalist or consolidated unitary system contemporary interpreters see in him.[42] While he did not look to a consolidationist solution there is a good reason for the prevalent contemporary misunderstanding that he did so. The extended republic argument in itself, as Madison presents it, would seem able to support positive as well as negative powers. One must wonder why Madison did not himself follow out what seems the logic of his own argument. While Madison in 1787 never devoted extensive space to this issue he did provide enough of his reasoning so that his position can be reconstructed.

Madison preferred the negative embodiment of the extended republic, or the combination of the extended and small republics, because the negative could secure the "great desideratum of government" at least as well as the simple extended republic could. Through the negative the general government could intervene to prevent the injustice and instability of law that Madison saw as the greatest defects of the state small republics. The transfer of care for rights and ordinary concerns of justice was not necessary to achieve the salutary effects Madison sought. In the American context of preexisting states and fear of a consolidated union, it made good sense to aim at that form of the extended republic which fit most easily with that context, especially if it were as effective as the politically unacceptable alternative. Madison's inability to procure even this version of Madison Federalism shows how foolish it would have been for him to have aimed at the simply nationalist version of the extended republic.

According to Madison, the small-extended republic combination was even more effective at securing the "great desideratum" than the extended republic alone. More than once at the Convention, Madison emphasized that the United States were too extensive and too various to be subjected to one uniform legislative power. Responding to some of the small state delegates, for example, Madison argued:

> The expedient proposed by them was that all the States should be thrown into one mass and a new partition be made into 13 equal parts. Would such a scheme be practicable? The dissimilarities existing in the rules of property, as well as in the manners, habits, and prejudices of the different states, amounted to a prohibition of the attempt. (19 June; I Farrand, 321.)

Obviously, that variety "amounted to a prohibition of the attempt" to consolidate the union also. On another occasion Madison indicated his essential agreement with the strong feelings favoring retention of the states. "I mean however to preserve the State rights with the same care, as I would trials by jury" (30 June; I Farrand, 499-500; cf. I Farrand, 490).[43] And why is Madison so strong on "state rights"?

> The great objection made against an abolition of the State Governments was that the General Government could not extend its care to all the minute objects which fall under the cognizance of the local jurisdictions. The objection as stated lay not against the probable abuse of the general power, but against the imperfect use that could be made of it throughout so great a variety of objects. (21 June; I Farrand, 3567.)

James Wilson, one of the so-called arch-nationalists, echoed the same thought: "our country is too extensive for a single government, no despot ever did govern a country so extensive" (19 June; I Farrand, 330).

While the extended republic is republican and through its electoral controls supplies some of that dependence on society that is needed to provide safety against government oppression, Madison

had serious reservations about the efficacy of republican safeguards in the very large republic.

> It must be observed however [he wrote to Jefferson] that this doc-
> trine can only hold within a sphere of a mean extent. As in too small
> a sphere oppressive combinations may be too easily formed against
> the weaker party; so in too extensive a one, a defensive concert may
> be rendered too difficult against the oppression of those entrusted
> with the administration.[44]

A federal rather than a unitary extended republic is Madison's
hedge against the uncertain safety devices in the very large area.
Madison responded to some of the worries about the dangers of
largeness in *Federalist*, No. 14, by reassuring his readers that

> the general government is not to be charged with the whole power of
> making and administering laws: its jurisdiction is limited to certain
> enumerated objects, which concern all the members of the republic,
> but which are not to be attained by the separate provisions of any
> . . . Were it proposed by the plan of the convention, to abolish the
> governments of the particular States, its adversaries would have
> some ground for their objection.

In full-fledged Madison Federalism, which goes considerably
beyond the Constitution in this respect, the hedge against the potential failure of republican safety features in the extended sphere
is precisely the negative. As Madison wrote to Washington before
the Convention, "Might not the national prerogative here suggested [*i.e.*, the negative] be found sufficiently disinterested for the
decision of local questions of policy, whilst it would itself be sufficiently restrained from the pursuit of interests adverse to those of
the whole society."[45] Madison emphasizes it is the prerogative, that
is, the power, that is restrained so as to secure the requisite safety.
Arming the general government with a negative power to help secure rights and the steady dispensation of justice within the
States, rather than with positive power to provide those things directly itself, helps to prevent the "due independence" which the extent of the extended republic supplies from turning into a source
of danger.

A negative power also secures the desired neutrality more effectively than a positive legislative power would. Would not the negative, he asks Washington, "be found sufficiently disinterested for
the decision of local questions of policy" so as to supply the great

desideratum of "neutrality between contending interests"? The general government's disinterest is grounded largely on the localism of those local questions of policy, on the absence of a direct stake of the general government in the issues or their outcome. That distance, and therefore that disinterest, would be overcome if the general government had another sort of prerogative, a positive legislative authority, which transformed a series of unconnected local issues of policy into questions of national policy. So long as the legislature of the general government exercises a negative, and does so in the context of a review of decisions essentially taken elsewhere, the questions retain their distinctly local character.

Madison Federalism, in sum, is Randolph Federalism plus Madison's universal negative. The negative was intended to embody Madison's theoretical insight into the way in which a combination of the small republic with an extended republic could cure the diseases of republican government the small republic itself could not cure. The combination could provide more adequately for the security of rights and the steady dispensation of justice through providing the difficult combination of dependence and independence from society that was necessary. While Randolph Federalism embodied the great innovation of employing nationalist means to federal ends, Madison Federalism added to that a way to use a largely federal means, the negative, to secure clearly nationalist ends, security of rights. Madison Federalism is properly seen as the National Compound, because it violates the leading principle of Randolph Federalism — the separate constitutions and operation of each level of government. Under Madison Federalism the states continue to be excluded from agency in the general government, but the general government is given a most important agency in the operation of the state governments. Madison proved unable to move the delegates to accept his brand of federalism, but he did not fail altogether. Some of the more obvious evils in the states — paper money, impairments of contract, bills of attainder — were directly forbidden in the text of the Constitution. Madison considered this an unsatisfactory and pale version of his negative, but it went at least partway towards serving the ends peculiar to his vision of union.

Hamilton's plan of union had even less support among the delegates and influence on the Constitution which they wrote. His version of federalism is most useful for providing contrast to Ran-

dolph and Madison Federalism and helps bring out the true character of the other two. Hamilton was never one of those who mistook the Virginia Plan for a simply national system. The plan
from Virginia, as much as that from New Jersey, was federal in
character. Because they were federal, among other reasons, "he
was obliged . . . to declare himself unfriendly to both plans." What
was needed instead was a truly "national one" (I Farrand, 283-84).
The evils that follow in the train of federal systems are so great
that they can "be avoided only by such a compleat sovereignty in
the General Government as will turn all the strong principles and
passions . . . necessary for the support of Government . . . on its
side" (I Farrand, 285-86). A division of sovereignty, such as both
plans attempt, never works. "Two Sovereignties can not coexist
within the same limits." A "compound" is inherently unstable; one
or the other government must swallow up the other.[46]

The best solution, it would appear, would be "to extinguish the
State Governments."

> He did not mean however to shock the public opinion by proposing
> such a measure. On the other hand he saw no *other* necessity for de
> clining it. (I Farrand, 287.)

The only kind of federal system which he believed might succeed went well beyond the principles of both Randolph Federalism
and Madison Federalism, although in its basic features it built on
Madison's innovations. A division of legislative authority, a restriction of the general government to certain specified objects (or
worse, powers) was an impossible provision, even in Hamilton's
federal model. The legislature in Hamilton Federalism must possess "power to pass all laws whatsoever." The plenary positive legislative power does not suffice either. "The Governour or President
of each State shall be appointed by the General Government"—
apparently by the Governour (President) with approval by the
Senate—"and shall have a negative upon the laws about to be
passed in the State of which he is Governour or President." This is
obviously a much stronger negative than Randolph Federalism
contemplates, and stronger too than even Madison's negative.
Since each state will have a separate Governour to wield the negative it will surely be more extensively used than under Madison's
plan wherein one body must exercise the negative for all the
states.

Just as in Randolph Federalism, the states are to have no agency in the selection or operation of the general government's officers; but unlike Randolph Federalism the general government is to have extensive agency, via the governours, the negative, and the national legislature's plenary legislative powers, in the constitution and operation of the states' governments. In this respect Hamilton Federalism goes well beyond Madison Federalism's gestures towards national agency in state government. If the end result of Hamilton Federalism looked to be genuine consolidation, that was probably not foreign to Hamilton's intention. His plan could have shown the delegates—it surely should show us—how great a distance there is between a truly national-aspiring version of federal union and the versions of Randolph and Madison.

DICKENSON FEDERALISM, OR THE FEDERAL COMPOUND

Dickenson Federalism, like Madison Federalism, stands on the base of Randolph Federalism, but intentionally violated the Compound System's principle of no agency of either government in the other. Dickenson Federalism is a Federal Compound, however, because it moves in the opposite direction from Madison Federalism and builds state agency into the general government. Unlike the other models there was no single plan at the Convention essentially embodying the Federal Compound. During the course of the Convention many features of a Dickenson Compound sort were considered and a few were accepted, the chief of which were the provisions concerning the Senate. The chief gain provided by a recognition of Dickenson Federalism as a separate model of union will lie in a revision of the standard views of the Great Compromise.

John Dickenson in his Fabius Letters of 1788, expressed the main point I wish to propound in this section:

> There is another improvement equally deserving regard, and that is, the varied representation of sovereignties and people in the constitution now proposed. It has been said, that this representation was a mere compromise. It was not a mere compromise. *The equal representation of each state in one branch of the legislature,* was an original substantive proposition, made in convention, very soon after the draft offered by Virginia.[47]

The outlines of the position emerged very early in the Conven-

207

tion, under the sponsorship of Richard Spaight and Pierce Butler of the Carolinas. The issue even then was the Senate although not the principle of representation but the mode of selection. The Virginia Plan contemplated that the lower house select the upper house. Butler defended Spaight's motion that the state legislatures rather than the lower house select the Senate, by observing "That the taking of so many powers out of the hands of the States as was proposed, tended to destroy all the balance and security of interests among the States which it was necessary to preserve" (31 May; I Farrand, 51).

And not long afterwards we find quite unambiguous evidence of the emerging attractiveness of the Federal Compound to many of the delegates. The occasion was the first set of deliberations on the executive. As has been frequently observed, the executive gave the delegates a particularly difficult time; Dickenson captured the difficulty all felt to a greater or lesser degree:

> He went into a discourse of some length, the sum of which was, that Legislative, Executive, and Judiciary departments ought to be made as independent as possible; but that such an Executive as some seemed to have in contemplation was not consistent with a republic; that a firm Executive could only exist in a limited monarch. (2 June; I Farrand, 86.)

A "firm" executive conflicts with the commitment to republicanism, for it requires certain kinds of emotional attachments to the person or family of the monarch which could not exist in a republic. It required a certain elevation of one man above the whole, which runs counter to the republican ethos. "The spirit of the times — the state of our affairs, forbade the experiment, if it were desirable" (I Farrand, 86, 87). Nontheless Dickenson and many of the others saw that the great virtues of firmness and stability a strong and independent executive could bring were also important to the republican structure of the new government. According to Dickenson, America had to seek substitutes for the monarchic attachments which made the English executive work well.

> In place of these attachments we must look out for something else. One source of stability is the double branch of the Legislature. The division of the Country into distinct States formed the other principal source of stability. This division ought to be maintained, and considerable powers left to the States. This was the ground of his consolation for the future fate of his Country. Without this, and in

case of a consolidation of the States into one great Republic we might read its fate in the history of smaller ones. (2 June; I Farrand, 86.)

Dickenson's analysis and prescription nearly mirrors Madison's. The melancholy fate of republics, that sorry story of turbulence and folly, follows from the lack of those "attachments" which develop in monarchies, provide a focus for loyalty, a damper on conflict, and produce a modicum of stability. That kind of attachment and loyalty, and resulting stability, in America comes from the division into states. Just as for Madison the extended republic should be given an agency in the states to allow the extended republic "to meliorate" the evils of the small republic, so for Dickenson, the states should be given an agency in the general government so they can be guaranteed their role in providing the requisite stability to America's republican institutions. The inability to develop a really proper executive on republican grounds suggested to Dickenson then that the aspiration of the Virginia Plan to construct a proper structure wholly internal to the general government was unrealizable. He sought therefore to build state agency into the general government. Dickenson Federalism differs from the "purely federal" solutions of the Federal System or Federal Government, however, by virtue of accepting the national features of the Virginia Plan. Dickenson Federalism differs from the Randolph and Madison versions in that it would make the states part of the checks and balances operative in the general government where the Virginians would not.

Exactly what agency ought to be given to the states was uncertain. Dickenson delivered his speech on 2 June in defense of a motion to make the "executive removable by the legislature at the request of a majority of State legislatures," which was defeated. In the same speech, it should be noted, Dickenson proposed the measure that the Convention ultimately adopted as the Connecticut Compromise: "He hoped that each State would retain an equal voice at least in one branch of the National legislature" (2 June; I Farrand, 87).

During the first phase of the Convention, from its opening through 5 June, when the delegates made a first sweep through the Virginia Plan, no features of Dickenson Federalism were adopted or even strongly put forward. The main thrust of the first sweep was an acceptance of the principle of Randolph Federalism, if not of every detail of the Virginia Plan. However, after 6 June, features of both Madison and Dickenson versions were pressed in an effort to adjust what looked to be the basic floor plan of Randolph Federalism in one direction or the other. At this time, Madison Federalism was shut out cold, but Dickenson Federalism won a few victories. On 7 June, Dickenson moved and the Convention adopted unanimously that the state legislatures select the representatives to the upper house. On the following day Gerry moved that the national executive be selected by the executives of the several states. And so it went with similar skirmishes over the judiciary and composition of the legislature. In general, the delegates showed themselves more open to Dickenson Federalism than to Madison Federalism, but unwilling to compromise the basic principle of Randolph Federalism with many admixtures of state agency in the general government.

As the deliberations went on, especially after the introduction of the New Jersey Plan, the rationale for Dickenson's Federal Compound broadened somewhat from the earliest versions. Just as Madison Federalism contained a feature designed to keep the separate levels of government operating within their own sphere, so the partisans of Dickenson Federalism sought such a device. Election of representatives to the national government by the states was the favorite device. "If it were in view to abolish the State Governments," said Sherman, "the elections ought to be by the people. If the State Governments are to be continued, it is necessary in order to preserve harmony between the National and State Governments that the elections to the former should be made by the latter." While Sherman believed the two governments "ought to have separate and distinct jurisdictions," they also "ought to have a mutual principle interest in supporting each other" (6, 7 June; I Farrand, 133, 150). That is, the principle of separateness required some mixing of agency in order to be effective.

The states might also contribute to the system of checks and balances if they were given some agency in the general government.

> The preservation of the States in a certain degree of agency is indispensable. It will produce that collision between the different authorities which should be wished for in order to check each other. . . . If the state governments were excluded from all agency in the national one, and all power drawn from the people at large, the consequence would be that the national Government would move in the same di-

rection as the State Governments now do, and would run into all the same mischiefs. (7 June; I Farrand, 152-53.)

The advocates of Dickenson Federalism, therefore, saw it as making a positive contribution to the operation of the federal government, making the states in effect integral parts of the internal operation of the national government. But more narrowly defensive concerns arose also. Mason voiced one of these when he observed that "whatever power may be necessary for the National Government a certain portion must necessarily be left in the States."

> The State legislatures also ought to have some means of defending themselves aginst encroachments of the National Government. . . . And what better means can we provide than the giving them some share in, or rather to make them a constituent part of the national establishment. There is danger on both sides no doubt; but we have only seen the evils arising on the side of the State governments. Those on the other side remain to be displayed. (7 June; I Farrand, 155-56.)

The Dickenson Federalists differed from Randolph and Madison Federalists in their more balanced appraisal of the problem of "encroachments." For the most part they accepted the analysis which showed the need for some guard in the general government against encroachments by the states: most supported the partial negative at first, and later the judicial remedy which replaced it. Some, like Dickenson himself, even supported the universal negative, further evidence that the universal negative was not perceived as a consolidationist feature. But the Randolph and Madison Federalists hesitated to accept parallel checks against encroachments "on the other side." On this they proved unable to carry a majority of the delegates, unable to counteract what must have seemed the sober good sense of a man like Connecticut's Dr. Johnson:

> They [the die-hard Randolph and Madison Federalists] wished to leave the States in possession of a considerable, tho subordinate jurisdiction. . . . He wished it therefore to be well considered whether in case the States, as was proposed, should retain some portion of sovereignty at least, this position could be preserved, without allowing them to participate effectually in the General Government, without giving them each a distinct and equal vote for the purpose of de-

fending themselves in the general Councils. (21 June; I Farrand, 355.)

Madison and Wilson, the two strongest opponents of Dickenson Federalism, remained unmoved by the argument for defense, not because they did not share the concern for preventing encroachment "on the other side" but because they felt certain that encroachments from that side were so much less likely than state encroachment on the general government. "All the examples of other confederacies prove the greater tendency in such systems to anarchy than to tyranny; to a disobedience of the members than to usurpations of the federal head" (21 June ; I Farrand, 356). The internal principles of operation of the general government will prevent its encroaching on the states, but the reverse did not hold. Even if, Madison suggests, the states were "reduced to corporations dependent on the general Legislature," the attachment of the people to their states would make itself felt in the general government. The converse, however, is not true. The states, as corporate bodies, have a stake in evading the mandates of the general government. Every place where the states as such have an agency in the general government provides an ingress for their evasive and anarchic tendencies.

To the concerns for the positive contributions the states could make toward the proper operation of the general government, and for the defensive needs to protect the states as such against encroachments by the general government, was added a third ground for Dickenson Federalism. This too was essentially a defensive concern, but not for the states as such so much as for some of the states against others of the states. Here finally the small state-large state controversy becomes relevant as part of the story of Dickenson Federalism. While the Convention might well have broken up had no satisfactory resolution of this issue been possible, nonetheless it has generally been overrated in importance. Certainly one ought not to see the main features of the first half of the Convention in terms of this conflict.

The two defensive concerns of Dickenson Federalism are precisely analogous to Madison's analysis of the different types of dangers government posed. On the one hand, acording to Madison, government can pose a threat to society as a whole, when the interests of the rulers as such conflict with the interests of the ruled as such. On the other hand, one segment of society can pose a threat to other segments of society through capturing government. Likewise, the general government can threaten the states as such with encroachments, or some of the states may capture the general government and threaten others of the states. The most likely danger of the latter sort that the delegates foresaw under the principles of the Virginia Plan was to the small states from the large.

> Mr. Paterson considered the proposition for a proportional representation as striking at the existence of the lesser States. . . . Give the large States an influence in proportion to their magnitude, and what will be the consequence? Their ambition will be proportionately increased, and the small States will have everything to fear. (9 June; I Farrand, 177-78.)

While the small state delegates insisted on an equality of representation in at least one branch of the legislature as a safeguard for their interests, the opponents of Dickenson Federalism pronounced their fears "chimerical."

> That it is not necessary to secure the small states against the large ones [Madison] conceived to be . . . obvious. Was a combination of the large ones dreaded? This must arise from some interest common to Virginia, Massachusetts, and Pennsylvania, and distinguishing them from the other States or from the mere circumstance of similarity of size.

But, no such common interest existed. Madison willingly conceded the general point that "wherever there is danger of attack there ought to be given a constitutional power of defence." But he strenuously denied there was any "danger of attack" by the large against the small states, just as he had earlier denied there was any real danger to the states as such from the general government (cf. I Farrand, 447-48).

Not only was there no need for defenses of this sort, the defense of state equality in the legislature was especially pernicious. Equal representation of the states opens the system to the most unjust possibility of minority rule. "The majority of the states might still injure the majority of the people" (30 June; I Farrand, 486). The principle, "which was confessedly unjust, . . . must infuse mortality into a Constitution which we wished to last forever" (29 June; I Farrand, 465).

As the debate proceeded the partisans of Dickenson Federalism

213

came to a quite precise and sophisticated understanding of the character of the Constitution they sought. The Constitution was to be a compound, "partly national; partly federal" as Ellsworth put it. The "government is to be formed for . . . the States as political Societies, . . . as well as for the individuals composing them." "As in some respects the States are to be considered in their political capacity," argued Dr. Johnson, "and in others as districts of individual citizens, the two ideas embraced on different sides, instead of being opposed to each other, ought to be combined; that in one branch the people ought to be represented; in the other the States" (29 June; I Farrand, 461-62; 468). The mode of constructing the Senate, adopted in the Connecticut Compromise, was not, then, from the point of view of Dickenson Federalism, a compromise. It was rather a proper and accurate way of expressing the compound they were aiming to create.

The Randolph and Madison Federalists, however, believed the Dickenson Federalists were mistaken in their understanding of the nature of the compound. James Wilson gave probably the best expression of the alternative view.

> Both Governments were derived from the people—both meant for the people—both therefore ought to be regulated on the same principles. . . . In forming the [general government], we ought to proceed, by abstracting as much as possible from the idea of State Governments. With respect to the province and objects of the general government they should be considered as having no existence. . . . The general government is not an assemblage of states, but of individuals for certain political purposes—it is not meant for the States, but for the individuals composing them; the individuals therefore not the States ought to be represented in it. (25 June; I Farrand, 405-406.)

That alternate view, it should be clear, is pure Randolph Federalism: the compound resides in the whole, not in either of the parts. From the point of view of Wilson or Madison, the Great Compromise was indeed a compromise because it introduced a federal feature, a foreign feature from another type of system, into the structure of the general government, whereas the federal features belonged only in the system as a whole, not in the general government.

The Dickenson Federalists responded that so long as the states did in fact exist and were desired to continue existing, they would and should have an effect on the operation of the general government. Whether state agency was explicitly built into the Constitution or not, there would be state agency and, the Dickenson Federalists feared, overwhelming state agency by the larger states. As they saw it, Randolph Federalism was neither altogether desirable nor altogether possible.

Who was right, who wrong in this conflict over state agency? Which interpretation of the implications of the peculiar compound being constructed was best? No decisive answer can be given to these questions. That fact, I think, paved the way for the prominence of interest as a basis for the settlement of the dispute. The delegates chose their stand on the answer pretty much as it affected their state's interest as they understood that. The outcome was as it was partly because the Convention voted according to those rules which allowed a majority of the states to rule a majority of the people; it also came out as it did, however, because the small state delegates favoring Dickenson Federalism feared they might lose a great deal if they lost this issue, and the others, less certain than Madison and Wilson of the simple supremacy of the Randolph Federalism interpretation of the union, decided not only to accommodate their colleagues, but to embody some elements inspired by caution in the radically innovative Constitution they were preparing.

The great conflict at the Convention, which was resolved by the so-called Great Compromise, was broader and more principled, or at least fit into a more principled context, than the usual picture of a small state vs. large state conflict. It was also much less broad and much less principled than the "pure Federalist-New Jersey Plan" partisans versus the "simple nationalist-Virginia Plan" partisans of many other of the usual accounts. The core conflict was between Randolph Federalists and Madison Federalists (identical to the Randolph variety on this issue) on the one side, and Dickenson Federalists, allied with the thoroughly defeated partisans of Reform Federalism or Federal Government, on the other. While the Dickenson Federalists won this particular battle, the war on the whole went to the other side. Or rather, since Dickenson Federalism accepted the basics of Randolph Federalism, the final Constitution qualified the pure Compound System only slightly, relative to the large doses of state agency a more thoroughgoing Dickenson Federalism might have produced.

We are now in a position to characterize the Constitution in terms of the variety of federalisms that clashed in Philadelphia in 1787. It is unmistakably Randolph Federalist at its core, in some ways more so even than the original Virginia Plan. However, elements both of Madison Federalism, in some of the constitutional limits placed on the states, and of Dickenson Federalism in some of the state agency built into the general government, in the Senate and to a lesser extent in the electoral college, also make part of the constitutional order.

NOTES

The author wishes to dedicate this article to the memory of Herbert Storing.

¹ James Madison, "Preface to debates in the Convention of 1787" in *The Records of the Federal Convention of 1787*, ed. Max Farrand (New Haven: Yale University Press, 1966), III: 539. (Hereafter III Farrand, 539.)

² Martin Diamond, "What the Framers Meant by Federalism," in *A Nation of States*, ed. Robert A. Goldwin (Chicago: Rand McNally Publishing Co., 1963), pp. 26-28. See also Diamond's, "The *Federalists'* View of Federalism" in *Essays on Federalism* (Clarmont, 1962).

³ Cf. Montesquieu, *De L'Esprit des Lois*, bk. 9; *Federalist*, No. 9.

⁴ This paper is not the place to pursue the issue, but it should be clear that I disagree with the view pressed by many that the version of the Articles finally adopted was substantially more confederal than the earlier, allegedly nationalistic Dickenson draft. The chief locus for the claim of a real difference is Merrill Jensen, *The Articles of Confederation* (Madison: University of Wisconsin Press, 1948), chap. 6. Cf. Winton U. Solberg, *The Federal Convention and the Formation of the Union of the American States* (Indianapolis: Bobbs-Merrill, 1958), p. lxxi, William P. Murphy, *The Triumph of Nationalism: State Sovereignty, the Founding Fathers, and the Making of the Constitution* (Chicago: Quadrangle Books, 1967), chap. 1; and Forrest McDonald, *E Pluribus Unum* (Indianapolis: Liberty Press, 1979), pp. 38-39. More accurate is Gordon S. Wood, "Democracy and the Constitution" in *How Democratic Is the Constitution*, ed. Robert A. Godwin and William A. Schambra (Washington, D.C.: American Enterprise Institute, 1979), pp. 6-7.

⁵ Herbert Storing, *What the Anti-Federalists Were For* (Chicago: University of Chicago Press, 1982), p. 49; cf. pp. 2, 14, 42, 44-49. Cf. James Madison, "Notes on Debates, Feb. 21, 1787" in *Papers of J. Madison*, 9: 291.

⁶ Jackson Turner Main, *The Antifederalists: Critics of the Constitution* (Chicago: 1964), p. 180. The classic source for the "revisionist" view of the Confederation period is Merrill Jensen, *The New Nation* (New York: Knopf, 1950). A sensible review of the whole issue, giving weight to both sides, is Clinton Rossiter's *1787: The Grand Convention* (New York: 1966), chaps. 1-2: and Ralph Ketcham, *From Colony to Country* (New York: Macmillan, 1974).

⁷ James Madison, "Vices of the Political System of the United States," April 1781, *Papers*, 9: 357.

⁸ Cf. Main, *Antifederalists*, pp. 181-84; and Max Farrand, *The Framing of the Constitution of the United States* (New Haven: Yale University Press, 1913), chaps. 3, 6.

⁹ Diamond, "What the Framers Meant by Federalism," p. 38. The clearest judgment on the issue is in Andrew C. McLaughlin, *A Constitutional History of the United States* (New York: Appleton-Century Co., 1935), p. 116.

¹⁰ Diamond, "What the Framers Meant by Federalism," p. 38; Main, *The Antifederalists*, p. 285; cf. Gordon S. Wood, *The Creation of the American Republic* (Williamsburg: University of North Carolina Press, 1969), p. 547.

¹¹ Main, *Antifederalists*, p. 181. Cf. Farrand, *Framing of the Constitution*, p. 89; David J. Smith, *The Convention and the Constitution* (New York: St. Martin's Press, 1965), p. 37; Charles Warren, *The Making of the Constitution* (Boston: Little, Brown and Co., 1929), p. 221; Gordon Wood, "Democracy and the Constitution," p. 9. All references to Convention debates will be left in the text, identified by date, and volume and page numbers in the Farrand edition.

¹² Madison to Randolph, 8 April 1787, *Papers*, 9: 369. For a more detailed discussion of Madison's thinking before the convention see M. Zuckert, "Madison's 'Middle Ground' "; Irving Brant, *James Madison: Father of the Constitution*. (Indianapolis: Bobbs-Merrill, 1950), pp. 13-14, and Charles F. Hobson, "The Negative on State Laws: James Madison, the Constitution, and the Crisis of Republican Government," *William and Mary Quarterly*, 3rd series; 36: 220-21.

¹³ Randolph to Madison, 27 March 1787, *Papers*, 9: 369. Madison seems to have succeeded very well with Washington also, who "appears to have supported Madison's views in particular" during the Convention: McLaughlin, *A Constitutional History of the United States*, p. 149.

¹⁴ Rossiter, *1787*, pp. 191-94. The basic Hegelian plot also runs through Alfred H. Kelly and Winfred A. Harbison, *The American Constitution*, 5th ed. (New York: Norton, 1976), chap. 5, esp. pp. 115-16; John P. Roche, "The Founding Fathers: A Reform Caucus in Action," *American Political Science Review*, 55 (1961), 28-29; Broadus Mitchell and Louise Pearson Mitchell, A *Biography of the Constitution of the United States*, 2nd ed. (New York: Oxford University Press, 1975), pp. 54-56; Hobson, "The Negative on State Laws," pp. 218, 226, 228, 230-32; Murphy, *The Triumph of Nationalism*, pp. 145-56; Brant, *James Madison*, chaps. 1-6; Alpheus T. Mason, *The States Right Debate*, 2nd ed. (Englewood, New Jersey: Prentice-Hall, 1964), pp. 30-60.

¹⁵ Martin Diamond *et al., The Democratic Republic*, 2nd ed. (Chicago: Rand McNally, 1968), p. 54. Brant, *James Madison*, p. 87. The tendency to understand the Convention in this manner seems especially characteristic of post-New Deal studies. Earlier students, such as Farrand, Warren, and McLaughlin, are much more cautious in their assessment of the Virginia Plan. Just as the Civil War generation read the Convention notes with their particular set of concerns in mind, so does the post-New Deal generation find in the intentions of the Framers justification for the nationalist exercise of powers by the federal government in our time. Wood, *Creation of the American Republic*, p. 472-73, 525-32.

¹⁶ Madison to Randolph, 8 April 1787, *Papers*, 9: 369; Madison to Washington, 16 April 1787, *Papers*, 9: 383.

¹⁷ Diamond, "What the Framers Meant by Federalism," p. 35. The honor of inventing the phrase "partly national, partly federal" seems to belong to Oliver Ellsworth (29 June).

¹⁸ *Ibid.*, p. 33

¹⁹ *Ibid.*, p. 31.

²⁰ Cf. McHenry's somewhat broader version of this point (I Farrand, 26) with the later discussion of enumerated powers (II Farrand, 615-16).

²¹ Cf. Abraham Baldwin's account of the consensus on powers at the Convention (Stiles, *Diary*, III Farrand, 168-69).

²² Madison to John Tyler, III Farrand, 526-28. Cf. Madison's essentially similar explanation in a letter dating from 1831: "The extent of the powers to be vested, also tho' expressed in loose terms, evidently had reference to limitations and definitions, to be made in the progress of the work, distinguishing it from a plenary and Consolidated Government" (Madison to N. P. Trist, December 1831, III Farrand, 517).

²³ Madison to Taylor, III Farrand, 529.

[24] Brant, *James Madison,* pp. 35, 101; cf. II Farrand, 17.

[25] Edmund Randolph to the Speaker of the Virginia House of Delegates, 10 October 1787 (III Farrand, 126-27). For further evidence on Madison's view, see his discussion of the powers of the general government in his letter to Jefferson, 24 October 1787, *Papers,* 9: 212-14.

[26] The degree to which the Virginia Plan remains federal in character can be seen from its continued heavy reliance on a requisition power for revenue. Cf. Randolph on 21 May (I Farrand, 19, 25), Sherman on 6 June (I Farrand, 133; cf. 143); and especially the debate on 11 June (I Farrand, 207), and Paterson on 16 June (I Farrand, 259). Cf. Madison to Washington, *Papers,* 9: 383; to Jefferson, 24 October 1787, *Papers,* 9: 208; Wilson on 11 June (I Farrand, 205-208) on additional sources of revenue. And consider Madison's comments on 28 June (I Farrand, 447) with his comments on the general welfare clause (III Farrand, 483; IV Farrand, 85)

[27] Diamond, "What the Framers Meant by Federalism," pp. 31, 32, 33; *Democratic Republic,* p. 54.

[28] Madison to Andrew Stevenson, 25 March 1826, III Farrand, 473 (emphasis added). Cf. Madison to N. P. Trist, December 1831, III Farrand, 516-18. Madison to John Tyler, III Farrand, 524-31.

[29] Madison to Jefferson, 24 October 1787, *Papers* 9: 208. Madison, "Notes on Nullification, '1835-1836.' " in *Writings,* ed. Hurst, 9: 606-607.

[30] Madison to Washington, 16 April 1787, *Papers,* 9: 383.

[31] *Papers,* 9: 205. Cf. also Madison's letter to Jefferson on 6 September 1787, Papers, 9: 162-64. Also Wood, "Democracy and the Constitution," p. 16; Hobson, "The Negative on State Laws," p. 216, 230-31, 233.

[32] Consider also Madison's discussion of the British imperial constitution in his letter to Jefferson of 24 October 1787, *Papers,* 10: 211.

[33] Jefferson to Madison, 20 June 1787, *Papers,* 10: 64. Cf. Madison to Jefferson, 19 March 1787, *Papers,* 9: 318; Hobson, "The Negative on State Laws," p. 216. Consider the comments of Gerry and Williamson in the floor debate on the negative.

[34] The only place where this is at all properly recognized is Hobson, "The Negative on State Laws." Also cf. Christopher Wolfe, "On Understanding the Constitutional Convention of 1787," *Journal of Politics,* 39 (1977), 73-118.

[35] Madison to Jefferson, 24 October 1787, *Papers,* 10: 212-14.

[36] Brant, *James Madison,* p. 43.

[37] Diamond, "What the Framers Meant by Federalism," pp. 35, 38.

[38] All quotations are from the letter to Jefferson of 24 October 1787, but similar statements appear in letters to Washington, Randolph, etc.

[39] "Vices of the Political System of the United States," *Papers,* 9: 357.

[40] *Ibid.*

[41] Madison to Washington, 16 April 1787, *Papers,* 9: 383.

[42] An important witness to Madison's not seeking the nationalist route to the extended republic is Mason's testimony in the Virginia ratifying convention (III Farrand, 330-31).

[43] Cf. however Brant's thoroughly implausible attempt to discount this statement (*James Madison,* pp. 88-89).

[44] Madison to Jefferson, 24 October 1787, *Papers,* 10: 214.

[45] Madison to Washington, 16 April 1787, *Papers,* 10: 214.

[46] Cf. Diamond's judgment that the compound is inherently unstable in "*The Federalists'* View of Federalism" especially. Diamond follows Hamilton in this judgment, but Madison seems to have been far more hopeful of the potential stability of a well-constructed compound.

[47] III Farrand, 304.

The Great Compromise:
Ideas, Interests, and the
Politics of Constitution Making

Jack N. Rakove

OF all the questions that may be asked about the intentions of the framers of the Constitution, seemingly the least puzzling involve explaining the decision to give the states an equal vote in the Senate. On no other subject are the records of debate so explicit or the alignments so apparent. Nor did any other question evoke the same conspicuous range of responses that came into play during the debates leading up to the Great Compromise of July 16, 1787: everything from heavy-handed threats and poker-faced bluffs to heartfelt pleas for accommodation, from candid avowals of interest to abstract appeals for justice. The speeches and vignettes that most vividly reveal the mood of the Federal Convention—its tension and even passion—also centered on this decision. Yet for all this, the conflict is readily reducible to a single issue: whether the states would retain an equal vote in one house of the national legislature, or whether schemes of proportional representation would be devised for both upper and lower chambers. And the outcome of the controversy can be explained with equal elegance. When the small-state leaders proved unyielding after seven weeks of struggle, their opponents accepted defeat and began the process of pragmatic accommodation that would characterize the remaining two months of deliberation.

That this one question so long preoccupied the convention is nevertheless a cause for some regret. Modern constitutional commentary would have been better served had the framers devoted even a day or two more to such issues as the scope of judicial review or the nature of executive power. Yet in one fundamental sense the apparent clarity of the politics of the Great Compromise nicely reflects the prevailing image of the convention as a cumulative process of bargaining and compromise in which a rigid

Mr. Rakove is a member of the Department of History at Stanford University. This article was written with the generous support of Project '87 and of a Constitutional Fellowship from the National Endowment for the Humanities. A version was presented in February 1985 at a conference on "A Meeting among Friends: Delegates to the Constitutional Convention," sponsored by the Friends of Independence National Historical Park. The author wishes to express his gratitude to Richard R. Beeman and Peter S. Onuf for their comments on that occasion, and to Alison Gilbert Olson for thoughtful criticism delivered since.

adherence to principle was subordinated to the pragmatic tests of reaching agreement and building consensus.

Such an emphasis has one obvious advantage. It enables scholars to cast the deliberations of 1787 within the familiar frameworks that we ordinarily use to analyze legislative politics. Historians and political scientists have thus tended to interpret the results of the convention in more or less equivalent terms: as the pragmatic work of "a reform caucus in action," or as reflections of changing alignments among delegations that can be charted by identifying either key bargains or shifts in voting blocs.[1] Such approaches assume that the Federal Convention, however exceptional or unprecedented it seemed at the time, was ultimately an assembly not so different from other deliberative bodies whose actions reflect the play of competing interests espoused by representatives sharing a well-defined set of fundamental values. Thus if disagreement as to which explanatory model works best accounts for the "disarray" that James H. Hutson has found in current interpretations of the convention, its final results still go far to support his conclusion that "considering the convention as a gathering devoted principally to harmonizing concrete interests will simplify efforts to understand it."[2] For in the end, concessions were made to every interest that manifested itself at the convention, and as the weeks wore on, these were often described, quite self-consciously, as gestures of conciliation.

Were the politics of the Federal Convention really quite so conventional? The major scholarly dissenters from this view have been political theorists who are concerned to recover both the deep convictions upon which the framers acted and the principles that the Constitution itself incorporated. Only rarely, however, does this reverential view of "the founding" help to unravel the nuances of political *behavior* within the convention. Too often the search for these ruling ideas either blurs the distinction between the concerns that prevailed among the framers and the arguments that would soon be made "out-of-doors" in support of the

[1] John P. Roche, "The Founding Fathers: A Reform Caucus in Action," *American Political Science Review*, LV (1961), 799-816; Calvin C. Jillson, "Constitution-Making: Alignment and Realignment in the Federal Convention of 1787," *ibid.*, LXXV (1981), 598-612; William H. Riker, "The Heresthetics of Constitution-Making: The Presidency in 1787, with Comments on Determinism and Rational Choice," *ibid.*, LXXVIII (1984), 1-16.

[2] Hutson, "The Creation of the Constitution: Scholarship at a Standstill," *Reviews in American History*, XII (1984), 463-477, and "Riddles of the Federal Constitutional Convention," *William and Mary Quarterly*, 3d Ser., XLIV (1987), 423. Professor Olson has suggested to me that this equation of the convention with "normal" deliberative politics errs in implying that conflicting values and appeals to theory do not enter into the ordinary business of legislation. While I would certainly agree that they do, Hutson is still probably correct to argue that historians prefer to treat the convention's success as a tribute to the framers' talents, if not for logrolling, then at least for pragmatic accommodation.

Constitution,[3] or else it exaggerates the relative influence that earlier authorities or texts (Locke, Montesquieu, the Declaration of Independence) exerted on the thinking of the framers.

At first glance, these disparate emphases on interests and ideas—to evoke the classic antinomies of historiography—do not sit well with one another. Either the framers appear, as Elbridge Gerry lamented a month into the debates, merely as "political negociators" intent on protecting particular interests, or else they are cast as visionary statesmen whose "reason," in Martin Diamond's formulation, "constructs the system within which the passions of the men who come after may be relied upon" to operate safely.[4] But at bottom these approaches are more complementary than exclusive. Just as the historian can take for granted the framers' deeper commitments and go on to examine how they actually reached decisions, so, too, the political theorist can pay quick homage to their genius for compromise and proceed with the quest for higher principles.

Accepting that ideas and interests separately deserve credit does not, however, enable us to assess the elusive interplay between them within the actual context of the convention's deliberations.[5] If current scholarship on the convention is indeed in disarray, part of the reason may lie in the difficulty of determining just what role appeals to theory and principle played in the debates. The task (as James Madison might say) is to find "a middle ground" somewhere between the clouded heights of great principles and the familiar terrain of specific interests. Some of the arguments the framers advanced were doubtless designed simply to legitimate positions rooted in interest. Others carried deeper conviction on their merits, however, and deserve to be examined with the same seriousness with which they were originally proposed.

Two sets of considerations justify assessing how appeals to theory affected the unconventional politics of constitution making. First, the key decision of July 16 cannot be construed simply as a triumph for pragmatism. Had bargaining and compromise actually set the tone for the convention, it is difficult to see why their appeal took so long to unfold. Leading spokesmen for the small states presented their ultimatum within the first week of debate, and an assembly composed of ten or eleven delegations, most of whose basic positions were evident from the outset, left little room for

[3] Thus historians are justified in objecting to the uncritical presumption implicit in the title of an influential essay by Martin Diamond, "Democracy and *The Federalist:* A Reconsideration of the Framers' Intent," *Am. Pol. Sci. Rev.*, LIII (1959), 52-68.

[4] Max Farrand, ed., *The Records of the Federal Convention of 1787*, rev. ed. (New Haven, Conn., 1937), I, 467; Diamond, "Democracy and *The Federalist*," *Am. Pol. Sci. Rev.*, LIII (1959), 67-68.

[5] On this same point see Calvin C. Jillson and Cecil L. Eubanks, "The Political Structure of Constitution Making: The Federal Convention of 1787," *American Journal of Political Science*, XXVIII (1984), 435-458, which begins with many of the assumptions that inform this essay and pursues several of the same issues, though reaching somewhat different conclusions.

maneuvering in the interest of building a dominant coalition. In the end, the Great Compromise was a compromise in name only. The small states carried their position by the narrowest margin possible: five states to four, with Massachusetts, by all rights a member of the large-states bloc, divided by the votes of Gerry and Caleb Strong. The victors naturally called this decision a compromise. But the losers rightly saw it as a defeat and continued to deny that the nominal concession extended to them—the power of the House over money bills—was consequential.

Second, although the vote of July 16 was a breakthrough, it was so long in the making precisely because the preceding seven weeks of debate were dominated not by efforts to find common ground but by a campaign designed to break the resistance of the small states by persuasion, rational argument, and appeals to principle. During these weeks, the large-state delegates were indeed involved in something more than an interested effort to gain the maximum legislative influence for their constituents. Their arguments marked an attempt to formulate a theory of representation superior to that which had prevailed at the outset of the Revolution, to reconceive the basis upon which individuals and interests alike could be most appropriately represented in government. In place of the received view that imagined a polity composed of the rulers and ruled, of the few and the many, or (more to the point) of fictive corporate units, they were struggling to fashion a more realistic—or modern—image of society.[6] Unlike the spokesmen for the small states, who were merely defending the status quo, the large-state leaders needed to devise arguments that their antagonists could simply not rebut. In the end, of course, reason did not prevail against will. But to explain why it did not may illuminate the complex interplay between ideas and interests that shaped the special nature of constitutional politics. And more than that, a careful reconstruction of this struggle demonstrates that James Madison's theory of the extended republic was very much at the center of debate throughout these opening weeks.

No one could have been surprised that the issue of representation became the great sticking point of the convention. It had been, after all, the first question of substance raised at the First Continental Congress of 1774. Rather than bog down in controversy over this issue, Congress had agreed to give each colony one vote. This precedent held up over the next few years, when Congress haltingly went about the task of framing confederation. Against the withering arguments of a succession of large-state delegates—first Patrick Henry and John Adams, later James Wilson—members from the small states clung to the principle of equal state

[6] These themes have been treated with great insight and nuance in J. R. Pole, *Political Representation in England and the Origins of the American Republic* (London, 1966), which locates the proceedings of 1787 in a context extending from late 17th-century English thought to the development of 19th-century political democracy.

voting.[7] As Adams himself confessed in 1774, serious practical difficulties militated against any scheme of proportional representation. Even could Congress have agreed upon a principle for apportionment, it lacked the information it needed to determine how many votes each colony should receive. Moreover, the political situation that confronted Congress in the mid-1770s further undercut the arguments that the spokesmen for the large states were making. The critical decisions Congress had to take ultimately called not so much for bare majorities as for consensus and even unanimity, and this in turn made fair apportionment seem less urgent.

Rooted as it was in Revolutionary expediency, the victory that the small states gained in drafting the Articles never carried great intellectual conviction, but its theoretical implications gathered importance as criticism of the Articles mounted in the 1780s. Because the principle of an equal state vote was naturally conducive to an image of a federation of sovereign states joined for specific purposes, it sharply limited the range of additional *powers* that would-be reformers of the Articles could seriously consider bestowing on the union. The principle worked best in areas where it was still possible to perceive a broad national interest to which the states could generally accede—most conspicuously in the realm of foreign affairs. If the exercise of a particular power would have a discriminatory impact upon individual states or regions, however, or upon the particular *interests* they contained, a scheme of voting based on equal corporate units quickly became more problematic. If Congress received authority to regulate commerce or levy taxes, property would become the direct object of national legislation, in which case it seemed inherently unfair for Delaware to cast a vote of equal weight with Pennsylvania.

In practice, the requirement of unanimous state approval made the adoption of any amendment to the Confederation improbable and a change in the principle of representation inconceivable. Rather than propose a wholesale revision, reformers such as James Madison and Charles Thomson favored the adoption of modest amendments whose gradual benefits would make Americans less suspicious of national government. Only after they abandoned the tactics of piecemeal reform in the waning months of 1786 did it become not only possible but necessary to restore the issue of representation to the central place it had occupied in the original debates over confederation. "The first step to be taken is I think a change in the principle of representation," Madison wrote Edmund Randolph in early April 1787, and on the other side of the question, small-state delegates such as George Read and John Dickinson of Delaware quickly foresaw the challenge they would confront.[8]

---

[7] For the debate of Sept. 5, 1774, see the notes kept by John Adams and James Duane, in Paul H. Smith, ed., *Letters of Delegates to Congress, 1774-1789* (Washington, D.C., 1976-   ), I, 27-31. See also the discussions in Pole, *Political Representation*, 344-348, and Jack N. Rakove, *The Beginnings of National Politics: An Interpretive History of the Continental Congress* (New York, 1979), 140-141.

[8] The discussion of Madison's ideas that begins here and continues through the

Because of the central role that Madison played at Philadelphia and the commanding position his ideas now occupy in all interpretations of "the founding," one must ask why he insisted upon making a shift to some scheme of proportional representation the "ground-work" upon which all other changes would rest. The current canon of interpretation holds that when Madison considered the problem of representation, his principal concern was to establish "such a process of elections as will most certainly extract from the mass of the Society the purest and noblest characters which it contains."[9] In point of fact, however, Madison's commitment to proportional representation preceded in time and exceeded in clarity the development of his ideas about the electoral mechanisms that would bring the right men into office. When he first outlined his plans for the Constitutional Convention to Thomas Jefferson in mid-March 1787, he already contemplated a system in which the vote of a congressman from Delaware would count the same as that of one from Massachusetts or Virginia. Yet when he drafted a similar letter to George Washington four weeks later, he was still uncertain whether the lower house of the national legislature should be elected "by the people at large, or by the legislatures"—hardly a trivial point.[10] And while it is likely that Madison privately preferred that members of the lower house be popularly chosen by secret ballot in electoral districts, he never sought to engraft such regulations on the Constitution. His most explicit remarks on the subject conceded that the states would retain the right to determine how congressmen were to be selected. As late as October 1788, when the laws regulating the first federal elections were being framed, he observed that "it is perhaps to be desired that various modes should be tried, as by that means only the best mode can be ascertained." In 1787 Madison was prepared to accept whatever electoral systems the states adopted so long as principles of equitable apportionment were vindicated.[11]

---

remainder of this section is based primarily on his letters to Thomas Jefferson, Mar. 19, 1787, Edmund Randolph, Apr. 8, 1787, and George Washington, Apr. 16, 1787, in William T. Hutchinson et al., eds., *The Papers of James Madison* (Chicago and Charlottesville, Va., 1962-   ), IX, 317-322, 368-371, 382-387, and on his memorandum on the "Vices of the Political system of the U. States" [April 1787], *ibid.*, 345-357. The three letters are particularly valuable for the light they shed not only on Madison's strategy but also on the meaning of key passages of his memorandum. For the concerns of the Delaware delegates see Read to Dickinson, Jan. 6, 1787, R. R. Logan Collection, box 4, Historical Society of Pennsylvania, Philadelphia, and Read's further letters of Jan. 17 and May 21, in William T. Read, *Life and Correspondence of George Read* ... (Philadelphia, 1870), 438-439, 443-444.

9 "Vices of the Political system," in Hutchinson et al., eds., *Madison Papers*, IX, 357.

10 Madison to Washington, Apr. 16, 1787, *ibid.*, 384.

11 The clearest statement of Madison's ideas about elections is found in his letter to Caleb Wallace, Aug. 23, 1785, discussing a constitution for Kentucky, *ibid.*, VIII, 353-354. See also his remarks in the convention, Aug. 9, 1787, in Farrand, ed., *Records*, II, 240-241, and Madison to Jefferson, Oct. 4, 1788, in Hutchinson et

To suggest that Madison's thoughts about elections remained somewhat inchoate is not to imply that they were less important than his forthright commitment to proportional representation. The true difficulty is to set this preliminary devotion to a change in voting within the larger cluster of ideas with which he had armed himself during his preparations for Philadelphia. So much has been written about the theory of the extended republic that one hesitates to add another commentary to the existing midrash. Yet most recent analyses have been directed not toward explaining the actual deliberations at Philadelphia but rather toward reconstructing the general reasoning that allowed Madison to reconcile the American commitment to republicanism with the idea of a national government. If we are to understand the strategy he pursued at Philadelphia—and more particularly his reasons for making proportional representation in both houses of the national legislature the sine qua non of reform—it is necessary to link Madison's analysis of the failings of the federal and state regimes with the expedient political calculations upon which he acted in the spring of 1787.[12]

Madison addressed the issue of proportional representation most

---

al., eds., Madison Papers, XI, 276. Commenting later on Jefferson's draft of a new constitution for Virginia, Madison preferred the idea of statewide voting for senators, who would, however, represent particular districts (Madison to Jefferson, Oct. 15, 1788, ibid., 286). Georgia and Maryland used the same scheme to elect representatives to the First Congress. The question whether the framers, and Madison in particular, thought they had established mechanisms for the "filtration of talent" is also examined in Jack N. Rakove, "The Structure of Politics at the Accession of George Washington," in Richard Beeman, Stephen Botein, and Edward C. Carter II, eds., Beyond Confederation: Origins of the Constitution and American National Identity (Chapel Hill, N.C., 1987), 261-294.

[12] A useful introduction to Madison's ideas is Robert J. Morgan, "Madison's Theory of Representation in the Tenth Federalist," Journal of Politics, XXXVI (1974), 852-885, which, despite its title, does not focus exclusively on the final version of the theory presented in that seminal essay. More important for considering the entire range of his motives and concerns are Charles F. Hobson, "The Negative on State Laws: James Madison, the Constitution, and the Crisis of Republican Government," WMQ, 3d Ser., XXXVI (1979), 215-235, and three essays by Lance Banning: "James Madison and the Nationalists, 1780-1783," ibid., XL (1983), 227-255; "The Hamiltonian Madison: A Reconsideration," Virginia Magazine of History and Biography, XCII (1984), 3-28; and "The Practicable Sphere of a Republic: James Madison, the Constitutional Convention, and the Emergence of Revolutionary Federalism," in Beeman, Botein, and Carter, eds., Beyond Confederation, 162-187, all of which attempt to mute the nationalist excesses in Irving Brant's portrait of the young statesman. Finally, no scholar should overlook Douglass Adair's two seminal essays, "The Tenth Federalist Revisited" and "'That Politics May Be Reduced to a Science': David Hume, James Madison, and the Tenth Federalist," in Trevor Colbourn, ed., Fame and the Founding Fathers: Essays by Douglass Adair (Chapel Hill, N.C., 1974), 75-106, to which Garry Wills, Explaining America: The Federalist (Garden City, N.Y., 1981), adds excessive nuance.

explicitly in his preconvention letters to Jefferson, Randolph, and Washington. He conceded that, under the Articles, the larger states exercised "more weight and influence" than the smaller, and he further noted that the "equality of suffrage if not just towards the larger members" of the union was "at least safe to them," since the states retained the power to determine how and even whether to comply with acts of Congress. "Under a system which would operate in many essential points without the intervention of the State legislatures," however, "the case would be materially altered." Clearly, the starting point of this analysis was the inefficacy of a federal system that made Congress so dependent on the states. As Madison observed in his concurrent memorandum on the vices of the political system, an administration resting on the "voluntary compliance" of the states "will never fail to render federal measures abortive." Madison accordingly concluded that the new government had to be empowered to act not indirectly through the states but directly upon their populations. Stripping the states of what might be called their federal functions would undermine their major claim to a right of equal representation.[13]

Madison had never doubted the justice of such a change; what was new was his belief that it had now become both "practicable" and necessary. The smallest states would oppose any change, but Madison assumed that, in *regional* terms, apportionment would appeal to both the North, because of "the actual superiority of their populousness," and to the South, because of "their expected superiority." (Like others, he expected population movements to carry emigrants southwest toward the Gulf of Mexico rather than northwest toward the Great Lakes.) "And if a majority of the larger States concur," he concluded, "the fewer and smaller States must finally bend to them." There was thus no question whose account had to be credited when the fears of the small states came to be balanced against the claims of the larger: "the lesser States must in every event yield to the predominant will." For the deeper challenge the convention faced, Madison believed, would involve overcoming not the arguments of the small states but the reservations of the large states. "The consideration which particularly urges a change in the representation," he wrote Washington, "is that it will obviate the principal objections of the larger States to the necessary concessions of power."[14] Without that, the large states would never grant even the minimal additional powers the union required, and the small states would have to acquiesce because they, too, understood the manifest failings of the Confederation.

Perhaps federal concerns alone provided sufficient justification for proportional representation. But Madison, of course, no longer believed in limiting the agenda of the convention to the inadequacy of the Confederation. The great achievement of his preconvention studies had been to forge a comprehensive framework within which the hitherto

[13] Hutchinson *et al.*, eds., *Madison Papers*, IX, 369, 383, 352.
[14] *Ibid.*, 318-319, 383.

distinct issues of the "imbecility" of the union and the debilities of republican government within the states could be considered together. The time had come not only to rescue Congress from the states, but to save the states from themselves. In fashioning his theory of the extended republic, then, Madison had two preeminent goals in mind. In the first place, he was certainly intent on refuting the received wisdom that held that stable republican governments could be established only in small, relatively homogeneous societies. He had to demonstrate that a national republic could avoid the "vices" that had produced the "multiplicity," "mutability," and finally the "injustice" of state legislation. Scholarly debate will long continue as to which of two key elements of this theory would matter more at the *national* level of politics: the obstacles the extended republic would place to the formation of factious majorities in the body politic or the legislature, or the encouragement it would give to the recruitment of a talented and conscientious class of legislators.[15] But both prongs of this argument bent to the same point: to prove that national lawmaking would escape the vicious pressures that prevailed in the state assemblies.

This would cure only half the evil. For in the second place, Madison was also convinced that the injustice of state lawmaking required vesting the national legislature with "a negative *in all cases whatsoever* on the legislative acts of the States, as heretofore exercised by the Kingly prerogative." Such a power, he told Randolph, was "the least possible abridgement of the State Soveriegnties [*sic*]" that could be made. Without it the national government could still avoid the evils of faction, but the vices that were already operating within the states would go untreated. Nothing better measures the depth of Madison's attachment to this proposal than his willingness to associate it with both the Declaratory Act of 1766 and the long-resented exercise of a royal veto over colonial legislation. And to obviate the objection that national review of state laws would delay the timely execution of necessary acts, he was even prepared to establish some sort of federal proconsular authority, empowered "to give a temporary sanction to laws of immediate necessity."[16]

Madison's attachment to this proposal had important implications for his ideas about representation. Beyond all the other arguments in favor of both proportional representation and popular election, the need to preserve the device that he had hailed as the solution to "the great desideratum" of republican government reinforced his unwillingness to compromise on the issue of apportionment.[17] Foreseeing that a bicameral

[15] *Ibid.*, 353-354. See also especially Banning, "Hamiltonian Madison," *VMHB*, XCII (1984), 12-14, disputing the emphasis placed on the "filtration of talent" in Wills, *Explaining America, passim,* and Gordon S. Wood, *The Creation of the American Republic, 1776-1787* (Chapel Hill, N.C., 1969), 502-506.

[16] Hutchinson *et al.*, eds., *Madison Papers,* IX, 318, 370, 383; Hobson, "Negative on State Laws," *WMQ,* 3d Ser., XXXVI (1979), 215-235.

[17] The absolute centrality of the negative on state laws to Madison's thinking is confirmed not only by the "immoderate digression" justifying its importance in his

veto would prove unwieldy, he early decided that "the negative on the laws might be most conveniently exercised" by the upper chamber of the national legislature. Two conclusions followed from this. First, the large states could never accept the national veto if it were vested in a senate constituted along the same lines as the existing Congress. Second, the negative would prove ineffective if the members of the upper house were elected by the state legislatures and were thus dependent on their will.[18] These considerations helped Madison to concentrate his thinking about both apportionment *and* election, making him realize (perhaps belatedly) the importance of denying the legislatures any direct electoral role in the national government. Allowing the legislatures to exercise such power would reinforce the claim to equal representation of corporate units, while impairing the ability of the national legislature to exercise the powers Madison hoped it would soon acquire. Finally, because Madison viewed the upper house as the single most important institution of government, the question of its composition became even more sensitive.[19]

But what other than a credulous confidence in the good intentions of the large states could lead the small states to entrust either the veto or any other substantial powers to a body in which they would no longer enjoy an

---

famous letter to Jefferson of Oct. 24, 1787, but also by a close comparison of his memorandum on the vices of the political system with his letter to Washington of Apr. 16. Such a comparison clearly demonstrates that Madison linked the somewhat murky language of the penultimate paragraph of the memorandum, with its call for "such a modification of the Sovereignty as will render it sufficiently neutral between the different interests and factions," to the justification of the veto and his concern with the problem of factious majorities within the states. Madison's faith in the capacity of the extended republic to permit the election of better representatives was thus "an auxilliary desideratum" to the pet scheme of a national veto in the sense that it would bring to office men capable of exercising so sensitive an authority. Hutchinson *et al.*, eds., *Madison Papers*, IX, 357, 383-384, X, 214.

[18] Madison to Washington, Apr. 16, 1787, *ibid.*, IX, 385. One should note, however, that the Virginia Plan also divided the exercise of the negative on state laws between Congress and the proposed Council of Revision, which would be composed jointly of the national executive and a select number of the federal judiciary (presumably the Supreme Court). Congress (or the Senate) would have authority to override the council's action, but Madison may also have hoped that the legislators would ordinarily defer to its judgment. On the other hand, because Madison also doubted whether executive and judicial authority, taken together or separately, could ever match the political influence or strength of local elected officials, he may also have felt that a veto on state laws, to be effective, would require the endorsement of one or both houses of Congress.

[19] See Madison's convention speech of June 26, in which the defense of a nine-year term for senators rests on the assumption that, over time, the upper chamber would have a special role in preventing a putative future majority of those who "will labour under all the hardships of life, & secretly sigh for a more equal distribution of its blessings," from making "agrarian attempts" against the rights of a propertied minority (Farrand, ed., *Records*, I, 422-423).

equal vote? Their great professed fear was that the relative reduction of their representation would expose them to the rapacious impulses of a putative coalition of the large states. As Gunning Bedford of Delaware noted on June 8, when a motion for the congressional negative was before the convention, "it seems as if Pa. & Va. by the conduct of their deputies wished to provide a system in which they would have an enormous & monstrous influence."[20]

It was in part to overcome this objection that the most familiar element of Madison's theory was addressed: the recognition that "all civilized societies are divided into different interests and factions, as they happen to be creditors or debtors—Rich or poor—husbandmen, merchants or manufacturers—members of different religious sects—followers of different political leaders—inhabitants of different districts—owners of different kinds of property &c &c." Ordinarily this passage (or the more polished variation in the tenth *Federalist*) is cited in the context of Madison's refutation of the orthodox notion that the stability of a republic rested upon the virtue of its citizens and the similarity of their interests. But in two major respects his realistic image of the actual sources of faction was also directly relevant to the issue of proportional representation. For if, in the first place, Madison could indeed prove that the extension of the republic would work to protect *all* interests against factious majorities, the claims of the small states to equal representation for purposes of security would be sharply undercut. The small states would no longer need an equal vote because the process of national legislation would operate to prevent any majority from trampling upon the rights of any minority. The obstacles erected against the coalescence of factious majorities would keep the legislature from adopting measures inimical to their interests, while the prospect that congressmen would be drawn from distinguished and enlightened ranks of leadership would assure that the policies eventually adopted would be framed, as Madison later explained in *Federalist* No. 10, by those "whose wisdom may best discern the true interest of their country."[21]

This part of the argument explained why the small states did not *need* equal representation, but Madison further sought to demonstrate why they did not *deserve* it. To make their case conclusive, spokesmen for the large states had to refute the claim that the states deserved representation as corporate units, as the sovereign constituencies of which the union was originally and immutably composed. This was precisely what the modern image of society that forms the very heart of Madison's theory enabled them to do. Implicit in its logic lay the recognition that states themselves were not real interests deserving representation. As political entities they were mere units of convenience that ultimately embodied only the fictitious legal personality of all corporations. States possessed interests, but these interests were rooted in the attributes of individuals: in property, occupation, religion, opinion. Moreover, since congeries of

[20] *Ibid.*, 167-168.
[21] Hutchinson *et al.*, eds., *Madison Papers*, IX, 355, X, 268.

interests could be found within any state, however small—witness Rhode Island—the principle of unitary corporate representation was further suspect. And, of course, the larger a state was, the more varied and complex the interests it contained would be. Nor, finally, was size itself an interest capable of manifesting itself in any situation *other than a constitutional convention*, where the rules of voting would first have to be determined. As Madison and his allies repeatedly argued, the only consideration that ever seemed likely to unite such disparate aggregates of interests as Pennsylvania, Virginia, and Massachusetts was the constitutional claim for proportional representation.

The connection between the specific claim for proportional representation and the ostensibly more general concerns expressed in Madison's preconvention memorandum on the vices of the political system was thus intimate. Convinced both that the desired reforms could be attained only if the large states received justice on the issue of apportionment *and* that the extended republic would operate as he predicted, Madison intended to put his theory to more effective use than the mere rebuttal of trite objections lifted from dog-eared copies of Montesquieu. What he carried to Philadelphia was not a set of discrete proposals but a comprehensive analysis of the problems of federalism and republicanism. Nor was he inclined to rank the components of his theory in order of importance, discriminating those that were essential from those that were merely desirable. Within this argument there was no room for the "compromise" that would eventually prevail. And his resistance to concessions had roots that ran deeper than logic. For Madison went to the convention in the grip of a great intellectual passion. The quiet but powerful sense of discovery that suffuses the concluding section of his memorandum had been converted into self-confidence and conviction.[22]

Yet comprehensive and even integrated as this theory was, it had critical weaknesses. The most obvious, of course, was the pet scheme of the negative on state laws, which was found vulnerable to a wide range of objections. But at Philadelphia two other problems proved even more threatening. One was the difficulty of devising a satisfactory procedure for electing the upper house, one that could safely deprive the state legislatures of a claim to representation. Here the indefinite character of Madison's ideas served him poorly, especially since his desire to render the Senate independent of both the legislatures and the people made it difficult to specify just what social entities it was representing.

The other problem that Madison had not thought through had more ominous overtones. How well would his favorite image of a society "broken into a greater variety of interests, of pursuits, of passions"[23] work

---

[22] As Hobson, echoing Adair, has aptly noted, "Madison embarked on his mission to Philadelphia with the confidence of one who had discovered the proper cure for the disease that afflicted the American political system" ("Negative on State Laws," *WMQ*, 3d Ser., XXXVI [1979], 225).

[23] Hutchinson *et al.*, eds., *Madison Papers*, IX, 357.

when the convention confronted certain stark conflicts, rooted in specific interests, that cut across state lines? No one entered the convention more keenly aware of the danger of sectional divisions than Madison.[24] Yet here, too, it is by no means clear how well he had reconciled his general theory of the multiple sources of faction with the dangers both to minority rights and to the permanent interest of the union that sectional differences evoked.

Madison was the best prepared of the delegates who gathered in Philadelphia in May 1787, but he was not he only one who had pondered just how the deliberations were to be structured. Among his colleagues, the nearest potential competitor may have been John Dickinson of Delaware, who had taken the leading role in preparing the first official draft of the Articles of Confederation eleven years earlier. Perhaps it was memories of that experience that led Dickinson, on May 30, to urge the convention to pursue "a more simple mode" of action than the one implicit in the Virginia Plan that had been presented just the day before. Rather than seek agreement on broad principles, he argued, the convention need only agree "that the confederation is defective; and then proceed to the definition of such powers as may be thought adequate to the objects for which it was instituted." Inclined by temperament and principle alike to pursue conciliation, Dickinson sensed that the convention would greatly improve its chances for success if it postponed taking on the question of representation until consensus had been built on other, more tractable issues.[25]

On many other points Dickinson and Madison were in agreement. But in the event it was Madison's notion of the course the deliberations should take that prevailed. Chance as much as foresight made this possible: only the tardy arrival of other delegations enabled the Virginians to draft the plan that Randolph presented on May 29.[26] But Madison knew an opportunity when he saw one, especially when it involved setting the agenda upon which others would act. Where Dickinson and Roger Sherman, among others, would have postponed considering changes in

[24] Rakove, *Beginnings of National Politics*, 349-350, 368-380.
[25] Farrand, ed., *Records*, I, 42 (as recorded by James McHenry; Madison did not cite this speech, though his notes and McHenry's correspond in other respects). It was probably also with Dickinson's encouragement that the Delaware assembly had formally instructed its delegates to oppose any alteration in the existing rule of voting. In 1775, when leading the opposition to Independence within Congress, Dickinson had arranged for the Pennsylvania assembly to issue appropriate instructions to its delegates. On Dickinson's role in 1787 see James H. Hutson, "John Dickinson at the Federal Constitutional Convention," *WMQ*, 3d Ser., XL (1983), 256-282.
[26] Madison, Washington, George Wythe, and John Blair were all present in Philadelphia by May 14; Mason, Randolph, and James McClurg arrived within the next few days. Only then did the Virginia delegation begin to caucus.

the formal organization of the national government until its additional powers had been precisely enumerated, the Virginia Plan thrust in a different direction.

The plan had a preemptive intent. It presupposed that the powers of the new central government would be substantial but sought to defer discussion of their precise nature and scope until basic agreement had been reached on the structure and composition of its several branches. Rather than detail the specific functions the government would discharge, Article 6 of the plan merely offered a general statement of the principal powers to be accorded to the legislature. These powers were formidable, extending as they did to "the Legislative Rights vested in Congress by the Confederation," to "all cases to which the separate States are incompetent, or in which the harmony of the United States may be interrupted by the exercise of individual [state] legislation," to a national veto over state laws "contravening . . . the articles of Union," and to the right "to call forth the force of the Union agst. any member . . . failing to fulfill its duty." The contrast between this open-ended language and the carefully delimited amendments to the Articles proposed hitherto could not have been more striking. Finally, on the critical issue of representation the Virginia Plan called for "suffrage . . . to be proportioned to the Quotas of contribution, or to the number of free inhabitants, as the one or the other rule may seem best in different cases." The sole concession extended to the states as such was to permit their assemblies to nominate the candidates from whom the members of the upper house would be chosen by the lower house, which itself would be popularly elected.[27]

As Madison and his colleagues sought to define the issues, then, the problem of representation had to be resolved first. Because the national government was to be so powerful, justice demanded that its political will—vested in the legislature—embody the real constituent interests of the society, not the artificial claims of the states. Only after this principle was accepted would the convention be free to determine the powers of the national government as a whole and to allocate them among its branches.

Insistence on this rule of action guided the conduct of the large-state delegates throughout the opening weeks of debate. They had privately considered how to attain their goal even before the Virginia Plan was presented. At some point before the committee on rules delivered its report on May 28, Gouverneur Morris and Robert Morris argued "that the large States should unite in firmly refusing to the small States an equal vote" in the convention. The Virginians, fearing that an early clash "might beget fatal altercations," disagreed, replying that "it would be easier to prevail" on the small states "in the course of the deliberations" than to require them to "throw themselves on the mercy of the large States" at the outset.[28] This logic set the strategy the large-state coalition pursued. From

---

[27] Farrand, ed., *Records*, I, 20-21.
[28] *Ibid.*, 11 (May 28). Madison is ambiguous as to when this decision was taken; he notes only that the issue became "a subject of conversation" at some point

May 28, Madison and his principal allies—James Wilson, Alexander Hamilton, Rufus King—acted on the belief that superior arguments would ultimately prove persuasive. Only when the convention seemed poised near deadlock in late June did they begin to contemplate even modest compromise, but what is more remarkable is the consistency of the positions, both theoretical and tactical, that they held down to the last summative debate of July 14.

Issues other than representation were, of course, discussed during this period, but no more than tentative progress could be made on any of them until the question of apportionment was resolved. In this sense, at least, the entire span of seven weeks can be treated as one sustained debate. Yet to understand the particular purposes to which arguments were put, as well as their respective strengths and weaknesses, it is useful to reconstruct the three major stages into which the proceedings leading to the decision of July 16 can be divided. The first of these began with the reading of the Virginia Plan on May 29 and ended when the committee of the whole agreed to a revised version of its resolutions on June 13. The introduction of the New Jersey Plan on June 15 ushered in a second phase that lasted until July 2, when a motion to give each state an equal vote in the Senate narrowly failed, with five states on either side and Georgia divided. This vote immediately gave rise to the election of a committee "to devise & report some compromise."[29] Its report, delivered on July 5, provided the basis for the remaining discussions preceding the key decision of July 16.

The initial debate on the Virginia Plan followed the lines Madison desired—and not because his opponents were stunned by the scope of the changes envisioned. Some of the deceptive ease with which the committee of the whole raced through the Virginia Plan reflected the "shyness" of which Benjamin Franklin and John Rutledge complained on June 1.[30] But leading spokesmen for the small-state position immediately recognized where the logic of the Virginia Plan led. Dickinson revealed as much in calling for "a more simple mode" of proceeding on May 30 and again three days later when he observed that the conflict over representation "must probably end in mutual concession," in which "each State would retain an equal voice at least in one branch of the National Legislature." Sherman similarly grasped the central issue on June 6, when he argued that the state legislatures should elect the lower house because "the objects of the union . . . were few," and again on June 11, when he echoed Dickinson by declaring that "the smaller States would never agree to the plan on any other principle" than an equal vote in the Senate. The strongest evidence of the resentment that Madison's tactics provoked can be found in an encounter that took place immediately after the reading of the New Jersey

---

"previous to the arrival of a majority of the States," which could refer either to the period before May 25 or to the morning of the 28th (*ibid.*, 10).

[29] *Ibid.*, 511.
[30] *Ibid.*, 65.

Plan on June 15, when an angry Dickinson took Madison aside to make sure the message was clear. "You see the consequence of pushing things too far," he asserted. "Some of the members from the small States . . . are friends to a good National Government; but we would sooner submit to a foreign power, than submit to be deprived of an equality of suffrage, in both branches of the legislature."[31]

This anger was far from unjustified, for from the outset Madison and his allies evinced a candid determination to reject the claim for an equal state vote. "[W]hatever reason might have existed for the equality of suffrage when the Union was a federal one among sovereign States," Madison observed on May 30, "it must cease when a national Governt. should be put into the place."[32] More important, the arguments they adduced to support this position were fundamentally consistent if not identical with the comprehensive theory that Madison had forged before the convention, and they were arrayed in essentially the same interlocking configuration. Thus on May 31, when the South Carolina delegates objected to "the vagueness" of the clause authorizing national legislation "in all cases to which the State Legislatures were individually incompetent," a chorus of large-state delegates spoke in favor of the idea of proceeding with an adoption of general principles, with Randolph, Wilson, and Madison all concluding that "it would be impossible to enumerate the powers which the federal Legislature ought to have." Charles Pinckney, Wilson, and Madison voiced similar sentiments on June 8 in support of the national negative of state laws.[33] When Elbridge Gerry and Sherman spoke against *direct* popular election of the lower house, Wilson and George Mason replied that "there is no danger of improper elections if made by *large* districts."[34]

Even more notable was the speech that followed by Madison, who seized upon Sherman's statement that "the objects of the Union" would not extend beyond foreign affairs and the prevention of interstate disputes to deliver his first presentation of the problem of faction and his argument for the extended republic. If Madison's account of his speech of June 6 is to be trusted, his performance must have been impressive yet perplexing. For in his eagerness to prove that the proper objects of the union would go well beyond those of the Confederation, he ranged far more widely than he needed to do before finally concluding that popular elections "may safely be made by the People if you enlarge the Sphere of Election."[35]

---

[31] *Ibid.*, 42, 87, 133, 201, 242.

[32] *Ibid.*, 37.

[33] *Ibid.*, 53-54, 59-60, 164-168.

[34] *Ibid.*, 132-134. Since Connecticut (like Rhode Island) already used at-large popular elections to select its delegates to Congress, it could be argued that Sherman was simply attempting to stake a claim for legislative election to the upper house. Cf. John Lansing's remark on June 20 that "Delegates [to Congress] however chosen, did not represent the people merely as so many individuals; but as forming a sovereign State" (*ibid.*, 336).

[35] *Ibid.*, 132-136, 143 (as quoted by King). It is troubling that the notes of

Strictly speaking, he did not have to discuss the danger of factious majorities or the history of conflicts between debtors and creditors in Greece and Rome in order to justify popular election of one house of the legislature—which is precisely what makes his eagerness to do so the more revealing. The most plausible explanation of this speech is that Madison was anxious to seize the first opportunity that offered to present the new teaching he had carried to Philadelphia.

In only two respects did this effort to use the opening fortnight of debate to seize the higher ground fall short of the objectives Madison had set. One reverse initially occurred within the Virginia delegation itself, when Randolph and Mason insisted on limiting the proposed negative to potential conflicts between state law and national interest, rather than extend it to "all cases whatsoever" in order to protect private rights within the states. In this form, however, the veto still received the approval of the committee of the whole (which, however, rejected Pinckney's amendment to extend it to all cases).[36] Potentially more damaging was the decision of June 7 to have the state legislatures elect the Senate. Wilson and Madison opposed this idea vigorously, denying that it would produce the benefits its supporters foretold. How, they asked, could legislative election work to bring "characters, distinguished for their rank in life and weight of property" into the Senate, as Dickinson suggested, or to enable it to "provide some check in favor of the commercial interest agst. the landed," as Gerry intimated? These objections elicited weak responses. But one additional argument had been made in favor of the motion, and even some of the large-state delegates conceded its force. As Mason put it, "the State Legislatures also ought to have some means of defending themselves agst. encroachments of the Natl. Govt." It was probably this consideration that led the ten states on the floor to vote unanimously to accept legislative election.[37]

Yet the implications of this decision were ambiguous. On the one hand, legislative election implied that the Senate would in some sense represent the states as states, and this in turn could be used to reinforce their claim for an equal vote. On the other, if the essential purpose of legislative

Madison's speech by Robert Yates, King, and Hamilton do not record the full argument that appears in Madison's own version.
[36] Ibid., 164-168.
[37] Ibid., 150-157. In defense of the proposition that the state legislatures would be attentive to the "commercial & monied interest" in their election of senators, Gerry did argue that "the people are for paper money when the Legislatures are agst. it." But when the issue of the national negative was discussed the next day, "a negative to paper money and similar measures" provided the only class of cases in which he was prepared to support Madison's pet proposal. And when on June 26 Madison described the role the Senate must eventually play in protecting the rights of property, Gerry agreed "that he did not deny the position of [Madison] that the majority will generally violate justice when they have an interest in so doing; But [he] did not think there was any such temptation in this Country." Ibid., 165, 173, 425.

election was to enable the states as a class to protect themselves against federal encroachment, all senators would presumably be sensitive to the rights of their constituents, regardless of the rules of suffrage. The consensus in favor of legislative election thus did not extend to the issue of voting in the Senate, and so on June 11 the committee of the whole voted, six states to five, to base suffrage in the Senate on the same proportional rule established for the lower house.[38]

What had been largely absent from the debate thus far was any sustained effort to explain exactly how the specific rights and interests of the small states would be either injured or protected should proportional representation be instituted in both houses.[39] The second phase of debate that began with William Paterson's reading of the New Jersey Plan on June 15 brought this issue to the fore. In appearance the New Jersey Plan offered a genuinely confederal alternative to the nationalistic thrust of the Virginia Plan. In the substance of the powers it would have conferred on the union, it resembled the proposals for amending the Confederation that had been discussed during the 1780s. And while it followed the Virginia Plan in recommending three independent branches of government, its key provision was to retain a unicameral legislature in which each state would have one vote. Since it was generally believed that such an assembly could not be safely vested with broad legislative authority, the New Jersey Plan could not pretend to grant the union anything like the sweeping authority envisioned in its counterpart.[40]

This was so conspicuously its major weakness that one has to ask whether the New Jersey Plan was meant to be taken seriously on its merits. Some delegates professed to be skeptical from the start. Charles Pinckney put the point directly when he dismissed the entire scheme as little more than a ruse: "the whole comes to this," Pinckney scoffed; "Give N[ew] Jersey an equal vote, and she will dismiss her scruples, and concur in the Nati[ona]l system."[41] Pinckney was a touch too sarcastic, but his analysis was not far from the mark. For the New Jersey Plan was not equivalent to the Virginia Plan; though it would have empowered the union to use force to compel delinquent states to perform their duty—a drastic remedy whose impracticality was easily exposed—it simply would not have given the federal government the authority that most delegates believed necessary. This its supporters tacitly conceded when they barely bothered to defend the plan's actual provisions. Instead, their central line of argument ran against the legitimacy, not the merits, of the Virginia Plan. The convention, they declared, had no right to consider any change in the

[38] *Ibid.*, 193.

[39] The two noteworthy exceptions to this were Gunning Bedford's speech opposing the congressional veto on June 8 and David Brearley's remarks of June 9 seconding William Paterson's motion to resume discussion of the rule of suffrage (*ibid.*, 167, 177).

[40] See especially the comments of James Wilson on this point, *ibid.*, 254.

[41] *Ibid.*, 255.

basic principle of the existing confederation—the representation of states as corporate units—and even if it did, there was little chance that so sweeping a revision could ever be adopted.[42]

From Madison's perspective, however, the manifest shortcomings of the New Jersey Plan provided the same convenient foil that Sherman had offered on June 6. When Madison rose on June 19 to deliver a final indictment of the plan's inadequacies, he used the occasion to present a second and more complete statement of his theory of the extended republic. The New Jersey Plan, he argued, would not "provide a Governmt. that will remedy the evils felt by the States both in their united and individual capacities." After again reviewing, item by item, his memorandum on the vices of the political system, Madison was careful to return to the central issue of proportional representation. "The great difficulty lies in the affair of Representation," he concluded, "and if this could be adjusted, all others would be surmountable." And again, he rested his case on an appeal to justice, now reinforced by a final reminder that the admission of new states endowed with "an equal vote" would enable "a more objectionable minority than ever [to] give law to the whole."[43]

On its merits, then, the New Jersey Plan had little to commend it, and immediately after Madison spoke, the committee of the whole rejected Paterson's resolutions by a decisive margin of seven states to three, with one divided. A revealing interlude followed. The task and opportunity that now awaited the large-state leaders was to convert this commanding majority into a durable coalition in favor of proportional representation in both houses. The campaign began immediately. One after another, Wilson, Hamilton, and King took the floor. In part their remarks were conciliatory. Wilson began by dissociating himself from Hamilton, whose famous speech of the day before had implied that the state governments should be "swallow[ed] up"—whereupon Hamilton complained that he had been misunderstood and that "he admitted the necessity of leaving in them, subordinate jurisdictions." But the three speakers also broadened the intellectual foundation upon which proportional representation in both houses could be vindicated. At the high level of theory King explained why the states did not "possess the peculiar features of sovereignty," while Hamilton more pointedly reminded the small states that "all the peculiarities which distinguish the interests of one State from those of another" would operate to prevent combinations among Pennsylvania, Virginia, and Massachusetts.[44]

Only a brief rejoinder from Luther Martin interrupted this stream of argument. But the silence of the New Jersey Plan's advocates is mislead-

[42] These were the two principal reasons cited by both John Lansing and Paterson in their speeches of June 16, which apparently constituted the only remarks made in support of the New Jersey Plan (*ibid.*, 249-250).

[43] *Ibid.*, 314-322.

[44] *Ibid.*, 287, 322-325.

ing, for they had already achieved their point. Their basic purpose was not to move the convention to pursue a more prudent agenda of reform. It was rather to convince the large states that the scope of change envisioned in the Virginia Plan could never be adopted unless the small states were accorded an equal vote in one house. Should the large states persist in *their* ultimatum, the small states would respond in kind and accept nothing that went much beyond the modest amendments discussed in the mid-1780s. The real debate over the thrust of the New Jersey Plan thus began only *after* its rejection. Indeed, the most significant discussions of the next week and a half nominally addressed issues that, as Mason put it, one "did not expect . . . would have been reagitated."[45]

But in point of fact it was during the final third of June that the great issues between the two contending sides were most clearly drawn and the strengths and weaknesses of the large-state position also became evident. The critical exchanges of this period occurred over three motions introduced by opponents of bicameral proportional representation. The first of these, proposed on June 20 by John Lansing of New York, was to vest additional powers not in a new legislature but in the existing Congress. The second, introduced by Lansing on the 28th, was to base representation in the *first* house "according to the rule established by the Confederation."[46] This was rejected on Friday the 29th, whereupon Oliver Ellsworth immediately moved that each state should be accorded an equal vote in the Senate. After a day and a half of debate, the convention reassembled on Monday, July 2, to reject Ellsworth's motion on a tie vote. But the narrowness of its defeat revealed that the effort to translate the majority against the New Jersey Plan into a coalition in favor of proportional representation in both houses had failed. This vote led immediately to the election of a committee to propose a compromise and thus to the final phase of debate preceding the decision of July 16.

What form did the debates of June 20-30 take? In one sense, the specter of deadlock led partisan advocates on both sides to offer comparable threats and insinuations on behalf of the interests of their constituents. But in a more fundamental respect the opposing positions of the large and small states were asymmetrical. The character and substance of the arguments presented on either side of the question were not equivalent, nor did the advocates use ideas in quite the same way. The central challenge confronting the small states was simply to find additional bases for legitimating the existing principle of corporate representation. In this endeavor consistency was useful but not always necessary. For the small states' inherent interest in preserving some vestige of the precedent

---

[45] *Ibid.*, 338.
[46] *Ibid.*, 336-338, 445. On the 16th Ellsworth had offered a similar motion to the effect "that the Legislative power of the U.S. should remain in Congs." This had gone unseconded, although Madison privately noted that "it seemed better calculated for the purpose" than the introductory motion of the New Jersey Plan. *Ibid.*, 255.

of 1774 was so strong that they were prepared to use whatever arguments came readily to hand.

In practice, the defense of the equal state vote was deployed along three parallel lines, any two of which could be abandoned as circumstances dictated. The first and most conspicuous held that the interests of the small states would be entirely ignored or overwhelmed should proportional representation prevail in both houses. A second position asserted that the continued existence of the state governments could not be assured "without allowing them to participate effectually in the Genl. Govt.," and that this in turn required "giving them each a distinct and equal vote for the purpose of defending themselves in the general Councils." Finally, the same logic could be extended to imply that the existence of the states "as political societies"—that is, as self-governing communities—similarly depended on the principle of equal representation in the upper house.[47]

The flaws in each of these positions were easy to detect, and leading speakers from the large states hammered away at them relentlessly. On the whole, it is difficult to resist concluding that the small-state delegates knew they had the weaker arguments. Time and again they were battered in debate. Again, as during the interlude over the New Jersey Plan, Madison, Wilson, and King were content to take the opposing claims at face value and refute them on their merits; only rarely, if at all, did they evoke counterarguments that posed genuine difficulties.

On what basis "was a combination of the large [states] dreaded?" Madison asked on June 28, shortly after Luther Martin had finally concluded his rambling defense of state sovereignty. What "common interest" did Virginia, Massachusetts, and Pennsylvania share that would enable them to coalesce against the other states? His answer amounted, in effect, to a restatement of his theory of faction. "In point of situation they could not have been more effectually separated from each other by the most jealous citizen of the most jealous state," Madison declared. "In point of manners, Religion and the other circumstances, which sometimes beget affection between different communities, they were not more

[47] *Ibid.*, 355, 461-462. In both cases the speaker was William Samuel Johnson, who did not clearly distinguish between the idea of representing either the state governments as such or the integral communal interests they were somehow presumed to embody. But cf. the remarks of Sherman during the final debate of July 14: "Mr. Sherman urged the equality of votes not so much as a security for the small States; as for the State Govts. which could not be preserved unless they were represented & had a negative in the Gen[era]l Government." But if this was meant to affirm that the states were to be represented in a corporate capacity, one is hard-pressed to see how Sherman could logically then add that "he had no objection to the members in the 2d b[ranch] voting per capita," since a divided delegation would testify to the existence of disparate interests within a state. *Ibid.*, II, 5. The entire question of the nature of statehood in the Revolutionary era needs to be reconsidered in the light of Peter S. Onuf's conceptually brillant study of *The Origins of the Federal Republic: Jurisdictional Controversies in the United States, 1775-1787* (Philadelphia, 1983).

assimilated than the other States." Nor, of course, did they have common economic interests. Hamilton echoed the same point the next day, and Wilson came back to it again on the 30th, noting in passing that "no answer has yet been given to the observations of [Madison] on this subject." This at last goaded Ellsworth to object that "the danger of combinations among" the large states was "not imaginary." This response did not seem to carry great conviction: Ellsworth immediately added that "altho' no particular abuses could be foreseen by him, the possibility of them would be sufficient to alarm him."[48] The closest the small states could come to identifying the danger they faced was to suggest that the very prospect of · dominance would lead the large states to discover suitable objects for mutual self-aggrandizement.

As a means of describing the general range of interests that the union already embraced, then, Madison's theory of the extended republic provided a credible answer to the objections of the small states—and it was so used. But his conception of faction could also be invoked, though less easily, against the claim that the states were themselves interests deserving equal representation as sovereign corporate units. Here the ambiguity of the argument advanced especially by the Connecticut delegates demanded a more complex response. Their most clearly developed claim asserted that the state *governments* would be unable to protect themselves if they were deprived of a voice in the national legislature. Alternatively, they argued that the participation of the states ought to be encouraged because "without their co-operation it would be impossible to support a Republican Govt. over so great an extent of Country."[49] But while these claims were certainly compatible with the idea of legislative election, they did not logically require an equal state vote. They were further vulnerable to exactly the range of criticisms of the Articles of Confederation that Madison had compiled during his researches of 1786-1787 and that he and others repeatedly raised throughout the debates. "All the examples of other confederacies prove the greater tendency in such systems . . . to a disobedience of the members than to usurpations of the federal head," Madison reminded the convention on June 21. "Our own experience had fully illustrated this tendency." To allow jealous state assemblies to appoint senators, King warned, would result in their "constantly choos[ing] men subservient to their own views as contrasted to the general interest."[50] And in a way that many members intuitively understood but never fully articulated, combining legislative election with the idea of an equal vote reinforced this fear of a parochial and potentially indecisive upper house precisely because it evoked the

---

[48] Farrand, ed., *Records,* I, 447-448, 466, 483-485. Ellsworth did go on to suggest two possible bases of "combination": a commercial treaty in which only "three or four free ports & no more were to be established" and "concert . . . in the appointment of the great officers."

[49] Oliver Ellsworth, speech of June 25, *ibid.,* 406.

[50] *Ibid.,* 356-357, 359.

prevailing image of the existing Congress. "A reform would be nugatory & nominal only," King complained, "if we should make another Congress of the proposed Senate."[51]

Madison and Wilson might have opposed legislative election less strongly had they been confident that their opponents would be willing to stop there. But believing, with reason, that the case for protecting the state governments was meant to justify the claim for an equal vote, they had to contest the idea that states deserved representation on any basis, whether as sovereign members of the union, coordinate governments, or simply communities.[52] Here, again, the arguments advanced by Wilson, Hamilton, and King were consistent with Madison's general theory, which traced the origin and persistence of faction to the attributes of individuals. Benjamin Franklin put the point plainly on June 11 when he noted that "the Interest of a State is made up of the interests of its individual members. If they are not injured, the State is not injured."[53] The logical extension of this point was not only to deny that state governments were legitimate interests in themselves, but also to suggest, as Wilson noted on June 20 and again the next day, that within the sphere of national politics the interests of state legislators and their constituents were not identical. "A private citizen of a State is indifferent whether power be exercised by the Genl. or State Legislatures, provided it be exercised most for his happiness," Wilson argued. "His representative has an interest in its being exercised by the body to which he belongs."[54] The large-state leaders conceded that the less populous states would lose influence. But they heatedly argued that the citizens of the small states would be no less free than any others, and no less capable of reaping the benefits of a reinvigorated union.[55] And it was on this basis—rather than on its impact on the power of the state governments—that the new government would ultimately be judged.

What is most striking about the response of the small-state spokesmen

[51] *Ibid.*, 489. See also the similar remarks of William Davie, *ibid.*, 488, delivered, however, while attempting to stake out a middle ground.

[52] *Ibid.*, 417. See also the comment that Madison added (probably much later) to his notes for the debate of June 25 over the election of the Senate: "It must be kept in view that the largest States particularly Pennsylvania & Virginia always considered the choice of the 2d. Branch by the State Legislatures as opposed to a proportional Representation to which they were attached as a fundamental principle of just Government" (*ibid.*, 408). Their ability to maintain this position, however, was weakened by the conspicuous support that the mode of legislative election received from Mason and Gerry. Had the large states been able to prevail on the major question of the equal vote, Madison would almost certainly have attempted to secure some other form of election. In his view, again, the question of election was subordinate to the issue of apportionment. See his comment of June 25, *ibid.*, 407.

[53] *Ibid.*, 199.

[54] *Ibid.*, 343-344, 359.

[55] Hamilton, speech of June 29, *ibid.*, 466.

to this argument is that they avoided meeting it seriously on its own terms. They did not seek to demonstrate that the states—or at least their states— did indeed constitute cohesive communities of interest. Only at the close of the debate of June 30 did Ellsworth assert that "domestic happiness" could never be attained by acts of a national government but depended on the preservation of the rights of the states. The defense of an equal vote rested instead on claims of original sovereignty, on the need to secure both the rights of state governments and the interests of small states, and on candid avowals that the small states could not be expected to act from "pure disinterestedness" when the call for proportional voting itself proved that the large states were "evidently seeking to aggrandize themselves at the expense of the small."[56]

Yet the overall weakness of their theoretical arguments did little to impair the political position of the small states. For these arguments, and the motions that occasioned them, were directed not toward a strategy of persuasion but toward two more immediate purposes. In the first place, the three motions introduced by Lansing and Ellsworth after June 20, by providing continuing tests of the relative strength of the two parties, demonstrated that the large states could not translate the alignment of June 19 into a new coalition. Second, and more important, they provided the small states with leverage for the "compromise" that Ellsworth, Sherman, and Dickinson had indicated would prove both acceptable and necessary all along. Each narrow defeat their coalition suffered strengthened the claim for compromise. This was why questions that the convention had seemingly settled were "reagitated" after June 20. Ellsworth disclosed the logic of this gambit immediately after Lansing's second motion was rejected on June 29. "He was not sorry on the whole" about the result of "the vote just passed," he declared, for "he hoped it would become a ground of compromise with regard to the 2d. branch." He thereupon moved to give the states an equal vote in the upper house.[57]

Ellsworth justified this proposal in part with the famous image of a union that was "partly national; partly federal"; but the argument he pressed more vigorously was the familiar one of security: "the power of self-defence was essential to the small States." An equal vote in the second house would accord them the same protection the large states enjoyed in the first. "If security be all that the great States wish for," he argued the next day, "the 1st. branch secures them." But security was not in fact what the large states desired, Wilson and Madison replied, nor was it to be equated with justice. The true issue was not protection but legislation— that is, the ability of the national government to act, consistent with the will and interests of whatever majority would be represented in Congress.

[56] *Ibid.*, 491-492; the second speaker quoted is Gunning Bedford. A negative proof of the lack of reliance placed on the image of the states as social communities is that Madison felt no need to reiterate the evidence for the pervasive impact of faction within the states.

[57] *Ibid.*, 468-469.

Even if a popular majority were adequately protected in the first house, Madison replied, a majority of states could still injure their "wishes and interests" by blocking the measures they desired, by extracting "repugnant" concessions in exchange for their passage, or by using the "great powers" that would presumably be exercised by the Senate alone—most notably, the negative on state laws—to "*impose* measures adverse" to their concerns.[58]

It was at this point that Madison injected a new argument, touching upon an issue that he had not explicitly addressed in his preconvention writings or previous debates. The concluding passage of his speech of June 30 is well known for its frank invocation of the danger of sectionalism. Madison agreed

> that every peculiar interest whether in any class of citizens, or any description of States, ought to be secured as far as possible. . . . But he contended that the States were divided into different interests not by their difference of size, but by other circumstances; the most material of which resulted partly from climate, but principally from ⟨the effects of⟩ their having or not having slaves. These two causes concurred in forming the great division of interests in the U. States. It did not lie between the large & small States: it lay between the Northern & Southern. [A]nd if any defensive power were necessary, it ought to be mutually given to these two interests. He was so strongly impressed with this important truth that he had been casting about in his mind for some expedient that would answer the purpose.

One solution to this problem, Madison hinted, would be to apportion representation in one house to free inhabitants only, and to total population in the other. But "he had been restrained from proposing this expedient by two considerations," he concluded; "one was his unwillingness to urge any diversity of interests on an occasion when it is but too apt to arise of itself—the other was the inequality of powers that must be vested" in the two houses.[59]

---

[58] *Ibid.*, 468-469, 482-487, 496-497, 504. The reference to the negative on state laws is found not in Madison's own notes for this speech but in those kept by Yates and Paterson.

[59] *Ibid.*, 486-487. Since the force of the observations in the following pages hinges in part on the accuracy of Madison's own account of this speech, one should note that Yates's and Paterson's notes on this speech do not contain anything that corresponds to these concluding remarks (although Yates does attribute comparable sentiments to Madison on June 29; *ibid.*, 476). Both suggest that Madison instead ended his speech by reminding the convention that the large states would not accept the desired negative on state laws if it were exercised by an improperly constituted senate. That point, by itself, is consistent with the general argument of this essay, since it demonstrates that Madison's commitment to proportional representation was still integrally bound to his general theory of the extended republic. But it is not beyond the realm of possibility that when Madison later

Madison had not discovered the danger of sectionalism only in the course of the convention. He was, after all, the principal author of the original version of the three-fifths clause, as it had first appeared in the congressional revenue plan of April 18, 1783,[60] and one of the major concerns that had led him in the fall of 1786 to accept the necessity of a general constitutional convention was his fear that the sectional rift within Congress over the navigation of the Mississippi portended the imminent devolution of the union into two or three regional confederacies.[61] Moreover, notwithstanding his professed reluctance to identify any further "diversity of interests" within the convention, it is noteworthy that Madison broached his hint *before* the application of the three-fifths clause to the issue of representation in the lower house had become controversial. If he was now willing to risk all the difficulties that the interjection of the sectional issue raised, it could only have been because he sensed that the tide of debate was turning against his position. For the invocation of sectional conflict could cut in two quite different directions. On the one hand, it could certainly be used to show that the immediate conflict between small and large states was not the major danger the union faced; on the other, by calling attention to fundamental differences not simply between states but between entire regions, it also encouraged every delegation to ask how its constituents might be protected should the balance of power within Congress swing against their particular interests.

If these were the assumptions upon which Madison rested his concluding remarks of the 30th, his expectations were well founded. The vote of July 2 revealed that deadlock itself could provide a sufficient rationale for compromise, regardless of the merits of the arguments on either side. Immediately after Ellsworth's motion was rejected, the convention elected a committee to frame a compromise, and its very composition revealed how strong the sentiment for accommodation had become. For while the large states were represented by those delegates whose previous state-

---

prepared the transcript of his notes, he could have found reasons both personal and political to suggest that he had been quick to perceive the dangers of sectionalism and to attempt to propose, however tentatively, more explicit means of using the Constitution to accommodate the differences between the two major regions. This suspicion would take on greater weight if one believes, as this author does, that from the Missouri crisis on, Madison hoped that one great service the posthumous publication of his notes could provide would be to demonstrate to later generations how accommodation in the interest of union had become the dominant motif of the convention.

[60] See Madison's notes on debates in Congress for Mar. 28, 1783, in Hutchinson *et al.*, eds., *Madison Papers*, VI, 407-408.

[61] This concern further reinforced his commitment to proportional representation. For while the retention of a scheme of state voting, even if it applied only to the Senate, threatened to leave the South in the minority position in which it had been placed in Congress in 1786, the belief that population movements were tending south and west promised to bring southern interests into closer parity with those of the North.

ments augured best for conciliation—Gerry, Franklin, and Mason—the members elected from the small states included its leading partisans: Paterson, Ellsworth, Martin, and Gunning Bedford. Moreover, Madison must have sensed that the opportunity for rational persuasion was evaporating. On the central issue of voting there was little left to say. Of the nine days of debate that followed the committee's report on July 5, only two were devoted to the key issue of voting in the upper house.[62] Controversy centered instead on the precise apportionment of representation within the lower house, and as Madison must have expected, this in turn forced each delegation to assess the question of sectional balance.

The debate over apportionment had both geographical and chronological dimensions. It pitted the northern states not only against the southern states but conceivably also against the future states of the West, whose interest in opening the Mississippi to American navigation might lead them into a natural alliance with the South. And it required determining not only how seats would originally be allocated but also how later decisions about reapportionment would be made: by a legislature that was either free to act on its own discretion—which could enable the section holding the opening advantage to prolong its power—or was obliged to follow a constitutional rule. The central consideration that drove the convention to give constitutional sanction to both the three-fifths clause and periodic reapportionment was the need to assure the southern states that their current inferiority would be eased or even reversed by the anticipated movement of population to the west and south. The net result of this debate was supported by every state but Delaware (whose delegation was divided) and may plausibly be described as a compromise that, ironically, rested on the mistaken assumption that the southern states would soon control the lower house while the northern states would enjoy at least an initial advantage in the Senate.

Within the context of the larger debate over representation in two houses the sociology of sectionalism had one obvious intellectual advantage. It described objective interests and differences that everyone understood were fated to endure well beyond the adjournment of the convention and that reflected in the most profound terms the underlying characteristics of individuals, states, and entire regions. The same could not be said about the mere size of a state, which in Madison's view could be a source of division only within the convention. If congressmen from Connecticut and New Jersey later found themselves opposed to their colleagues from Virginia, were their differences more likely to arise from disparities in the size of their states or in their economic and social systems? In this sense, the reference to slavery, divisive as it was on other grounds, buttressed the case against equal state representation, simply because it provided a far superior model of the actual competing interests that any national government would continually need to reconcile. In a

---

[62] The subject was debated on Friday, July 6, and again from Monday the 9th through Friday the 13th.

telling exchange on July 9 Madison even caught Paterson in an embarrassing contradiction, when the New Jersey delegate opposed counting
slaves for purposes of apportionment on the ground that "the true
principle of representation" was to provide "an expedient by which an
assembly of certain individls. chosen by the people is substituted in place
of the inconvenient meeting of the people themselves." Madison must
have fairly leaped to his feet to remind Paterson that such a "doctrine of
Representation which was in its principle the genuine one, must for ever
silence the pretensions of the small States to an equality of votes with the
large ones."[63]

Yet the marginal gains to be reaped in this way did not outweigh the
costs. The more carefully the question of apportionment in the lower
house was examined, the more difficult it became for any delegate to
ignore considerations of *regional* security. Rather than treat sectional
differences as an alternative and superior way of describing the real
interests at play in national politics, the delegates saw them instead as an
additional conflict that also had to be accommodated if an enduring union
was to be established. In this sense, the apportionment issue reinforced
the position that the small states had clung to all along. For it called
attention not to the way in which all interests could be protected in an
extended and extending republic, but rather to the need to safeguard the
most conspicuous interests of North and South. This defensive orientation in turn enabled even some large-state delegates to see virtue as well
as necessity in the call for an equal state vote. If the security of a limited
number of interests was to be the first object of the new government, a
Senate in which each state voted equally afforded a promising basis of
reassurance. No one could predict with any accuracy how the shifting tides
of migration and population would affect the long-term composition of the
House of Representatives. Calculations of influence based simply on
numbers of states were far less daunting. And if the admission of new
states was to be regulated by a legislature in which each major region could
hope to have especial influence in one house, it was possible to foresee
how some balance between (or among) the sections might be maintained
over time.

Gouverneur Morris put the point with typical candor (as well as
inconsistency) on Friday, July 13. The week before, he had rejected the
argument that an equal vote in the Senate was needed "to keep the
majority of the people from injuring particular States" with as sharp a
riposte as was imaginable. "But particular States ought to be injured for
the sake of a majority of the people," he insisted, "in case their conduct

[63] Farrand, ed., *Records*, I, 561-562. Madison quoted Paterson again in his final
speech of July 14 (*ibid.*, II, 8). On July 12 William Samuel Johnson similarly noted
"that wealth and population were the true, equitable rule of representation,"
though here he proposed to include "blacks *equally* with the *whites*," perhaps
because the link between taxation and representation had now been forged (*ibid.*,
I, 593).

should deserve it." Since then, however, Morris had taken the lead in opposing fixed constitutional rules for apportionment—especially rules prescribing the inclusion of slaves and the extension of equal rights to the new settlements; he had staked his case not on his earlier invocation of "the dignity and splendor of the American Empire" but on avowals of regional interest so transparent that Madison complained that Morris "determined the human character by the points of the compass." Still, inconsistency and insight are not always mutually exclusive. Even while lamenting on the 13th that "there can be no end of demands for security if every particular interest is to be entitled to it," Morris revealed where this concern could readily lead. "The consequence of such a transfer of power from the maritime to the interior & landed interest," he declared, "will . . . be such an oppression of commerce, that he shall be obliged to vote for the vicious principle of equality in the 2d. branch in order to provide some defence for the N. States agst. it."[64]

For lawyerly sophism Morris had few peers. In their own final defenses of proportional representation Madison, Wilson, and King opted for consistency. Almost everything that was said during the few days that were given to the main points of the ostensible compromise recapitulated not only arguments made earlier but the basic asymmetry of the two positions. With compromise itself the issue now before the convention, the small states no longer had to defend their position in theoretical terms, while the large-state spokesmen, left with correspondingly little room for maneuver, could only make a final appeal along the lines they had already established. Thus when Gerry suggested that it might be better "to proceed to enumerate & define the powers to be vested in the Genl. Govt." before deciding the rule of voting, Madison continued to insist that such determinations could be made only after the issue of representation was resolved. Again, the arguments against the equal state vote do not appear to have been effectively rebutted. When delegates from the large states dismissed as inconsequential the ostensible concession that would restrain the Senate from initiating or amending appropriations bills, their comments elicited only weak responses from the proponents of a compromise. Paterson even declined to say whether it was "a valuable consideration or not."[65] Only on July 14 did the large-state delegates belatedly suggest a tepid compromise of their own whereby no state would have more than five senators. But their final speeches restated the major principles they had adhered to all along. King asserted that no credible threat to either the small states or the state governments had ever been identified; Wilson argued that the legislative election of senators would afford adequate security for the states; and Madison rejected Ellsworth's image of a union "partly federal" by denying that there would be "a single

[64] *Ibid.*, 551-553, 584, 604.
[65] *Ibid.*, 551.

instance in which the Genl. Govt. was not to operate on the people individually."[66]

In his final comments, Madison echoed his conclusions of June 30. An equal state vote would not merely give the small states the security they craved; in practice it would also enable them to thwart the majority will. But he then cited one last "serious consideration" that he felt should be opposed to the claim for an equal state vote—and he did so in a way that implicitly called into question much of what he had argued hitherto. "It seemed now to be pretty well understood that the real difference of interests lay, not between the large & small but between the N. & Southn. States," Madison reminded his colleagues, alluding, of course, to the previous days of debate over the apportionment of representation in the lower house. "The institution of slavery & its consequences formed the line of discrimination," with the five states from Maryland south arrayed against the eight from Delaware north. The disparity would remain even should a scheme of proportional representation be adopted for both houses, "but not in the same degree [as] at this time; and every day would tend towards an equilibrium" of sectional power.[67]

Did "equilibrium" as Madison used it here mean anything different from the "security" that Ellsworth had sought for the small states? The debate over apportionment had exposed the central tension—or even contradiction—that lay at the core of the general theory that Madison labored so hard to develop. For the recognition that there was one overriding issue that threatened to establish a great "division of interests" between slave and free states could not be easily rendered compatible with the pluralist imagery of the diverse sources of faction. In both instances, it is true, Madison expressed concern for the protection of minority rights, by which he meant, principally but not exclusively, rights of property.[68] Yet radically different inferences could be drawn from these two attempts to trace the origins of faction.

The theory that Madison had formulated on the eve of the convention,

[66] Ibid., II, 6-11, quotation on p. 9. Sherman, in the very last speech recorded for July 14, did respond to Madison by "signif[ying] that his expectation was that the Genl. Legislature would in some cases act on the federal principle of requiring quotas."

[67] Ibid., 9-10.

[68] It is noteworthy that in his memorandum on the vices of the political system, and again in his speech of June 19, Madison cited the existence of slavery within a state as one of three examples of ways in which "a minority may in an appeal to force, be an overmatch for the majority." One would like to think that by arguing that "where slavery exists the republican Theory becomes still more fallacious," Madison was condemning slavery as a system based on brute coercion. But since the context in which this point was cited concerns the inability of the existing Congress to intervene to protect the laws and constitutions of the states "against internal violence," the more likely reference is to the danger of slave rebellions. Hutchinson et al., eds., Madison Papers, IX, 350-351; see also Farrand, ed., Records, I, 318.

with its emphasis on the multiple and mutable sources of interested behavior, promised to assure an array of minorities that their rights and concerns would be treated justly in a national legislature that they could never hope to control.[69] But this conception of the sources of faction purported to describe "all civilized Societies" and was thus, in a sense, abstract and even disembodied. The same could not be said of the portrait of the United States that Madison had first etched in his speech of June 30 and to which he returned in his exchange with Paterson on July 9 and again in his closing remarks of July 14. But what did one see when the new republic was described in these gross terms: a society embracing "so great a number of interests & parties" or a nation divisible into two great and potentially antagonistic factions, either of which could readily imagine how future changes in regional population and influence might threaten its prosperity, institutions, and values alike? And what notion of legislation was more compatible with this image: one that would allow majorities to govern while promising protection to all interests, defined principally in terms of the attributes of *individuals;* or one that implied, as the small states continually insisted, that the first task in the construction of a national legislature was to provide specific constitutional guarantees for certain broad groupings of *states,* whether large or small, northern or southern? And which political goal had become more important: over-coming the objections of all the populous states to granting additional powers to a government founded (as King put it) on the "viccious [*sic*] constitution of Congs. with regard to representation & suffrage,"[70] or convincing the southern states in particular that their interests would not be endangered in a government in which they could not initially hope to command a majority?

In the end, as the remarks of both Madison and Morris suggest, the framers could not avoid reverting to the idea that states somehow were the essential constituent elements of the polity and that simple residence in the same state would establish the first and most natural bond of individual political loyalty. Even Madison found it hard to convert his brilliant conception of faction into a more detailed map of the diverse interests that actually existed both among and within the states. It is striking that in all

[69] In this respect it is important to recall the discussion of the nature of legislation that provides the transition in the tenth *Federalist* between Madison's account of "the latent causes of faction" and his argument about "the means of controlling its *effects.*" "The principal task of modern legislation," Madison argued, is "the regulation of these various and interfering interests" that arise from "the various and unequal distribution of property." The examples he then provided of regulation—notably the encouragement of "domestic manufactures"—indicate that Madison understood the creative or positive character of legislation. "Yet what are many of the most important acts of legislation," he also asked, "but so many judicial determinations . . . concerning the rights of large bodies of citizens?" [Alexander Hamilton, James Madison, and John Jay], *The Federalist,* ed. Benjamin Fletcher Wright (Cambridge, Mass., 1961), 131-132.

[70] Farrand, ed., *Records,* I, 135, 136, II, 7.

their efforts to demonstrate that no objective interest could work to unite Virginia, Pennsylvania, and Massachusetts in the exercise of a federal condominium, the spokesmen for the large states never thought to cite the existing diversity of interests within their own states to disprove the conspiracy theories of their antagonists. None of them ever suggested that representatives elected by small farmers in Pennsylvania and Maryland might have more in common with each other than they would with merchant congressmen from Philadelphia or Baltimore. "If Va. should have 16 votes & Delre. with several other States together 16," reasoned Nathaniel Gorham of Massachusetts, "those from Virga. would be more likely to unite than the others, and would therefore have an undue influence."[71] Nor for that matter did delegates from the small states attempt to argue that their constituents were no more likely to coalesce for obstructive purposes than were the large states in pursuit of domination.

There was, moreover, another reason why the arguments for proportional representation in both houses fell short of being persuasive. In his speech of July 14 King suggested that "the idea of securing the State Govts." logically required the creation of a tricameral legislature. For if the first house was designed to represent the people directly, the second "was admitted to be necessary, and was actually meant, to check the 1st. branch, to give more wisdom, system, & stability to the Govt."; after that was assured, the third could operate for the "purpose of . . . representing the States as such and guarding by equal votes their rights & dignities."[72] Awkward and even frivolous as such a scheme would be, King's rationale illustrated one crucial point. In his conception as in Madison's, whatever representative character the Senate might enjoy was essentially incidental to the major substantive functions it was meant to fulfill as well as to the attributes its members were expected to possess. Hamilton's notion of a Senate composed of members serving for life was more than any true republican could accept; but the independence he hoped this tenure would secure did not at bottom differ from what Madison had in mind when he argued for a nine-year term that "should not commence till such a period of life as would render a perpetual disqualification . . . inconvenient."[73] It was the Senate that would serve as the great guardian of national interests, charged, as almost all of the framers originally expected it would be, with responsibility for war and foreign affairs, as well as with the negative on state laws.[74] Within this framework the proportional vote was no more designed to enable the Senate to reflect the actual distribution of interests within society than the aversion to legislative election was

---

[71] *Ibid.*, 404-405. Gorham was speaking of the idea of using a less than strictly proportional scale in the apportionment of the Senate, but the assumptions underlying this remark are applicable to both houses.

[72] *Ibid.*, II, 6-7.

[73] *Ibid.*, I, 289-292, 421-423.

[74] See Jack N. Rakove, "Solving a Constitutional Puzzle: The Treatymaking Clause as a Case Study," *Perspectives in American History*, N.S., I (1984), 233-281.

intended to make it more dependent on the popular will. The former was required merely to persuade the large states to approve the desired augmentation of national power, the latter to prevent the Senate from becoming "another edition of Congs."[75] through an improper solicitude for provincial concerns.

The great flaw in this conception was that it risked ceasing to be a scheme of representation. The relation between senators and their constituents required nothing more of the former than that they possess some knowledge of local circumstances—without which they were hardly likely to be chosen in the first place. Yet Madison never developed a clear or persuasive conception of how the selection process would actually operate. His failure is the more striking because the central place that the Senate occupied in his constitutional theory suggests that it, far more than the lower house, was meant to be the destination of those whom he hoped would emerge from "such a process of elections as will most certainly extract from the mass of the Society the purest and noblest characters which it contains." He knew better what he wanted to avoid than what he hoped to institute. "If an election by the people, or thro' any other channel than the State Legislatures promised as uncorrupt & impartial a preference of merit, there could surely be no necessity for an appointment by those Legislatures," he observed on June 7.[76] But the vote of that date revealed that legislative election of senators, for all its faults, was preferred by a decisive majority of the convention. From that point on, Madison found himself having to hope either that the damage could be limited without jeopardizing the cause of proportional representation or that an eventual victory on apportionment could be used to reverse the decision on election. But once the specter of sectional conflict legitimated the small states' appeal to security, that opportunity was lost. With it went not his hopes for a better government but his confidence that the analysis he had framed in the spring would provide the foundation upon which the entire system would rest.

To examine the role that particular arguments played within the overall structure of the debates of 1787 does not require us to conclude that the Federal Convention took the form of a seminar in political theory or of sustained intellectual combat between Madison and the ghost of Montesquieu. But the opening weeks of debate were nevertheless very much concerned with testing the appeal and the merits of the original formulation of the theory of the extended republic that James Madison brought to Philadelphia. All of the major components of his thought figured prominently in the debates leading up to the decision of July 16. That result and the consequences that followed from it cannot be described simply as a referendum on Madison's theory. But neither can

[75] Farrand, ed., *Records*, I, 490.
[76] "Vices of the Political system," in Hutchinson *et al.*, eds., *Madison Papers*, IX, 357; Farrand, ed., *Records*, I, 154.

the making of the Constitution be adequately explained unless careful attention is paid both to the range of uses to which Madison and his allies put his ideas and to the difficulties they encountered in defending the broad theory. Perhaps all the reasoning in the world could not have dislodged the likes of Roger Sherman and William Paterson from the position in which they entrenched themselves from the start. But until that became evident, the deliberations of 1787 involved an unconventional and complex interplay of ideas and interests, which goes far toward explaining why the nuances of constitutional politics retain their inherent fascination two centuries later.

The Negative on State Laws: James Madison, the Constitution, and the Crisis of Republican Government

Charles F. Hobson

T HE name of James Madison is inseparably linked with the United States Constitution of 1787. The chief spokesman at the Federal Convention for a radically new plan of government, Madison subsequently championed the Constitution as "Publius" in *The Federalist* and as a delegate to the Virginia ratifying convention; in 1789 he brought the process of constitution-making to a successful close by guiding through the First Congress the amendments that became the Bill of Rights. For these achievements and for his lifelong role as a constitutional expositor, he has been justly acclaimed "Father of the Constitution."

The familiar image of Madison as "Father" and as the philosopher of American federalism, although not inaccurate, has contributed to a misunderstanding of his intentions and accomplishments at the Philadelphia Convention. There is a tendency to consider his thoughts and actions during and after the Convention all of a piece, to assume an identity between Madison the Convention deputy and Madison the author of the "Publius" essays. Historians and biographers see him as the dominant personality of the Convention, the mastermind of that historic assembly who overcame the obstacles of state particularism and sectional jealousy to fashion a new government that accorded with his principal ideas for a constitution.[1] Often

Mr. Hobson is an editor of the Papers of James Madison at the University of Virginia. He wishes to thank Robert A. Rutland and William W. Abbot for suggestions and comments.

[1] Phrases such as "master-builder of the constitution," "leading spirit," "mastery of the Convention," "richly deserved to be called the 'Father of the Constitution,'" have been routinely employed to describe Madison's performance. See, for example, Max Farrand, *The Framing of the Constitution of the United States* (New Haven, Conn., 1913), 196-197; Charles Warren, *The Making of the Constitution* (Cambridge, Mass., 1928), 57; Irving Brant, *James Madison: Father of the Constitution, 1787-1800* (Indianapolis, 1950), 154-157; Clinton Rossiter, *1787: The Grand Convention* (New York, 1966), 247; Ralph Ketcham, *James Madison: A Biography* (New York, 1971), 229; and Adrienne Koch's introduction to *Notes of Debates in the Federal Convention of 1787 Reported by James Madison* (Athens, Ohio, 1966), xi, xvii-xviii.

overlooked, however, are Madison's two crucial defeats at Philadelphia—
losses which meant that instead of regarding the Constitution as a great
personal triumph, he was in fact disappointed with the Convention's final
draft. On successive days in mid-July he lost the battle for proportional
representation in both houses of the legislature and suffered the rejection of
his proposal to give the national legislature a "negative," or veto, over the
laws of the states.

Although his dogged pursuit of proportional representation in the national legislature is well known, Madison's espousal of a legislative negative
on state laws is veiled in relative obscurity. In his quest for a genuinely
national government, however, the Virginia reformer was no less determined
to arm the national legislature with this veto power than he was to obtain
proportional representation in both legislative branches. Indeed, after the
compromise on representation was adopted on July 16, Madison refrained
from further protest on that issue; but the July 17 vote against the negative
did not deter him from pushing for its reinstatement late in the Convention.
Thus the negative was not some theoretical will-o'-the-wisp that Madison the
practical politician quickly abandoned; rather, it occupied a central place in
his plan for extending the sphere of republican government. He consequently
relinquished the idea with the utmost reluctance, while privately doubting
the efficacy of the finished Constitution because it lacked this vital feature.

Since it did not become a part of the Constitution, the negative on state
laws has received only cursory treatment in histories of the Federal Convention. These accounts emphasize such themes as the contest between the large
and small states, the protracted battle over representation, and the origins of
American "federalism." If discussed at all, the negative is likely to be
dismissed as an unrealistic expedient, a curious aberration from the Convention's true course: the creation of a viable federal system.[2]

Madison scholars also have not given proper emphasis to his proposal for
the negative on state laws, perhaps because his advocacy of it does not square
with his later career. The problem of reconciling the high-flown nationalist
of 1787 with the subsequent exponent of a balanced "partly federal, and
partly national" government may never be satisfactorily resolved. The usual
approach, particularly in studies of Madison's political thought, has been to
fit the early Madison into the mold of what he later became, thereby missing

[2] The negative is virtually ignored in Farrand, *Framing of the Constitution;*
Rossiter, *Grand Convention;* and Broadus Mitchell and Louise Pearson Mitchell, *A
Biography of the Constitution of the United States: Its Origin, Formation, Adoption,
Interpretation* (New York, 1964). The most thorough summary of the debate over
the negative is in Warren, *Making of the Constitution,* 164-171, 316-324. See also
William P. Murphy, *The Triumph of Nationalism: State Sovereignty, the Founding
Fathers, and the Making of the Constitution* (Chicago, 1967), 214-219.

the full intensity of his nationalism.[3] In what is still the only book-length work on the statesman's political philosophy, Edward M. Burns, arguing that Madison's early nationalism was more apparent than real, tries to explain away the negative, while making Madison an advocate of "dual sovereignty" from the very beginning. No scholar was more familiar with Madison's writings and the sources of his ideas than the late Douglass Adair, yet in his essays on Madison he never mentions the negative. In tracing the origins of *The Federalist* No. 10, Adair necessarily turns to Madison's letters, memoranda, and speeches of the spring and summer of 1787; but in using these sources he highlights only those passages that reappeared in that famous paper. The Madison of the Federal Convention is always in the process of becoming "Publius," and the effect is to obscure the important differences between the two.[4] To read Madison's pre-Convention writings and Convention speeches as early drafts of the polished essays of "Publius," or to focus only on those ideas of Madison's that won acceptance at Philadelphia, is to fail to appreciate the comprehensiveness of his program for remedying the ills of the American political system. Exclusive attention to *The Federalist* will not provide such an understanding, for those essays were an improvised, ad hoc performance, in which the author served up his nationalism in a diluted form. The Constitution Madison expounded and defended as "Publius" was a pale version of the plan he had carefully worked out before the Philadelphia meeting.

Madison regarded the crisis of the Confederation in the 1780s as foremost a crisis of republican government. The question at stake for him was whether a government that derived its authority from the people and was administered by persons appointed directly or indirectly by the people would

[3] An exception is Irving Brant, who best captures the significance of the negative in Madison's reform plans, though he does not attempt to place it in the framework of the statesman's republican political theory (*Madison*, 12-13, 36-38, 104-105, 127-129).

[4] Edward McNall Burns, *James Madison: Philosopher of the Constitution* (New Brunswick, N.J., 1938), 10-11, 98-102; Douglass Adair, "The Authorship of the Disputed Federalist Papers," " 'That Politics May be Reduced to a Science': David Hume, James Madison, and the Tenth Federalist," and "James Madison," in Trevor Colbourn, ed., *Fame and the Founding Fathers: Essays by Douglass Adair* (Chapel Hill, N.C., 1974), 27-74, 93-106, 124-140; Adair, "The Intellectual Origins of Jeffersonian Democracy" (Ph.D. diss., Yale University, 1943), chap. 6. Other studies that pay scant attention to the negative include Adrienne Koch, *Jefferson and Madison: The Great Collaboration* (New York, 1950), 34-39; Neal Riemer, "The Republicanism of James Madison," *Political Science Quarterly*, LXIX (1954), 45-64; Riemer, "James Madison's Theory of the Self-Destructive Features of Republican Government," *Ethics*, LXV (1954), 34-43; and Marvin Meyers, ed., *The Mind of the Founder: Sources of the Political Thought of James Madison* (Indianapolis, 1973), xvii-xlviii.

prove to be more than a vain hope or merely theoretical ideal. On the eve of the Federal Convention he sensed a widespread disillusionment with republicanism among Americans, but at the same time he saw a unique opportunity for introducing a new theory that would place republican government on a more secure and lasting foundation. Of the reforms he offered at the Convention to accomplish this end, none in Madison's view was more important than the one to vest the national legislature with the power to negative state laws. That he contemplated so radical a device is proof enough that in 1787 he leaned more toward "consolidation" than he later cared to admit. His statement that he would seek a "middle ground" between the "individual independence of the States" and "a consolidation of the whole into one simple republic" did not mean that he had in mind something fundamentally the same as the federal system of the completed Constitution.[5]

Madison's "middle ground" was in fact a good deal closer to consolidation than to the existing confederate system and much farther from the midpoint between these two extremes than was the plan the Convention ultimately approved. He wished the states to be retained only where they would "be subordinately useful," that is, reduced to a status similar to that of counties. "In a word; the two extremes before us are a perfect separation and a perfect incorporation, of the 13 States. In the first case they would be independent nations subject to no law, but the law of nations. In the last, they would be mere counties of one entire republic, subject to one common law. In the first case the smaller States would have every thing to fear from the larger. In the last they would have nothing to fear. The true policy of the small States therefore lies in promoting those principles and that form of Gov[ernmen]t which will most approximate the States to the condition of counties."[6] Though he opposed the creation of one simple republic as inexpedient and unattainable, his proposal for a negative on state laws was the means of uniting the advantages of a single enlarged republic to the existing American state system. In 1787, Madison was thus scarcely less a consolidationist than Alexander Hamilton; the real difference between the two was that Hamilton unblushingly preferred a monarchy on the British model while Madison sought to establish a national government on republican principles.

[5] Madison to Washington, Apr. 16, 1787, in William T. Hutchinson *et al.*, eds., *The Papers of James Madison* (Chicago and Charlottesville, Va., 1962-   ), IX, 383, hereafter cited as *Papers of Madison*. Taking their cue from Brant, scholars in recent years have begun to emphasize the uncompromising nationalism of Madison's so-called middle ground. See John P. Roche, "The Founding Fathers: A Reform Caucus in Action," *American Political Science Review*, LV (1961), 799-816, and especially Alpheus T. Mason, ed., *The States Rights Debate: Antifederalism and the Constitution*, 2d ed. (New York, 1972), 30-60.
[6] Speech of June 28, 1787, in *Papers of Madison*, X, 81-82.

Madison introduced his scheme for the negative in letters to Thomas Jefferson, Edmund Randolph, and George Washington in the spring of 1787. The idea was suggested to him by the prerogative of the British crown to review acts of the colonial legislatures and to disallow those deemed to be injurious to the general interests of the empire. The utility of a negative, he remarked at the Convention, was "sufficiently displayed in the British system. Nothing could maintain the harmony and subordination of the various parts of the empire, but the prerogative by which the Crown, stifles in the birth every Act of every part tending to discord or encroachment." Madison conceded that the royal prerogative had often gone against the American interest during the colonial period, but he insisted that the same would not be true of a negative on state laws exercised by an elective, responsible, and informed legislative body. Madison's negative was to be a previous veto *"in all cases whatsoever,"* rather than a subsequent disallowance or repeal. In effect, Madison proposed nothing less than an organic union of the general and state governments: the general legislature was to be "an essential branch of the State Legislatures." "The States c[oul]d of themselves then pass no operative act, any more than one branch of a Legislature where there are two branches, can proceed without the other."[7]

Far from considering a general negative extreme, Madison was convinced that it was "absolutely necessary, and . . . the least possible encroachment on the State jurisdictions." If the central government lacked this "defensive power," its positive powers would prove ineffectual and the states would continue to overstep their proper bounds. "Another happy effect of this prerogative," he added, "would be its controul on the internal vicis[s]itudes of State policy; and the aggressions of interested majorities on the rights of minorities and of individuals."[8] He had arrived at this conclusion after a period of intensive study of history and reflection on his own experience as a statesman. Madison fully embraced the Enlightenment's faith in the utility of history. To study the past was to look in a mirror, or even a crystal ball, for throughout all time and in all places human nature had remained constant and the same events had proceeded from the same causes in an ever-recurring cycle. History yielded important lessons, especially of a "monitory" kind, and therefore prescribed a course of action.[9] When the American Confederation

[7] Madison to Jefferson, Mar. 19, 1787, in *Papers of Madison*, IX, 317-322; Madison to Randolph, Apr. 8, 1787, *ibid.*, 368-371; Madison to Washington, Apr. 16, 1787, *ibid.*, 382-387; speeches of June 8, 28, and July 17, 1787, *ibid.*, X, 39-42, 79-83, 102-103.

[8] Madison to Washington, Apr. 16, 1787, *ibid.*, IX, 383-384.

[9] On the use of history by the Founding Fathers see Douglass Adair, " 'Experience Must Be Our Only Guide': History, Democratic Theory, and the United States Constitution," in Colbourn, ed., *Fame and the Founding Fathers*, 107-123. See Adair, "Authorship of the Disputed Federalist Papers," *ibid.*, 71n, for Madison's frequent use of the word "monitory."

seemed to be heading for a crisis in the 1780s, it was only natural for Madison to turn to history for instruction.

In 1786 he undertook a systematic investigation of ancient and modern confederacies and drew up a long memorandum on the subject. This was no academic exercise in comparative history but a highly selective digest of facts and commentary on the federal form which he later put to good use. Citing his sources with scholarly care, he organized his information according to the constitutions, "federal authority," and "vices" of these confederacies—the Amphyctionic and Achaean of ancient Greece, and the Helvetic (Switzerland), Belgic (Netherlands), and Germanic (Holy Roman Empire) of modern Europe. The investigation showed that however the institutions of these confederacies differed, their histories followed a similar pattern of internal strife, civil war, anarchy, and foreign invasion. Confederacies—unions or leagues of states whose members retained their essential sovereignty and had equal representation in the federal councils—were at best fragile creations, always tending toward impotence or dissolution. The individual members constantly evaded, defied, or encroached on the central authority. Madison discerned these same fatal tendencies in the short life of the American confederation. The warning seemed clear: in order to avoid the fate of other confederacies, the United States must eliminate the flaws of the federal form, perhaps to the extent of abandoning it altogether.[10]

In the spring of 1787, Madison prepared another memorandum, "Vices of the Political System of the United States," the logical complement to that on ancient and modern confederacies. Here his source was the immediate one of personal experience rather than the intermediate one of books, but the two were mutually reinforcing. As a member of both the Continental Congress and the Virginia House of Delegates during the 1780s, he was a daily witness to the "vices" he now spelled out, such as the refusal of the states to comply with their requisition quotas, the encroachments by the states on the federal authority and on one another's rights, the lack of uniformity in matters of trade and taxation, and in general the lack of coercive power in the central government.[11] Madison had long been concerned with the problem of maintaining and enforcing the federal authority. As early as 1781, shortly after entering Congress, he proposed an amendment to the Articles of Confederation authorizing Congress "to employ the force of the United States as well by sea as by land to compel the States to fulfill their federal

[10] "Notes on Ancient and Modern Confederacies," Apr.-June [?], 1786, in Papers of Madison, IX, 3-24. Madison used this memorandum in his speech of June 19, 1787, and in The Federalist Nos. 18, 19, and 20. Ibid., X, 57, 299-304, 305-309, 320-324.

[11] "Vices of the Political System of the United States," Apr. 1787, ibid., IX, 345-358. Madison repeated the substance of this memorandum in his speeches of June 6 and June 19, 1787. Ibid., X, 32-34, 55-63.

engagements." As long as the United States remained a confederation of quasi-sovereign states, Madison believed that the federal government needed this coercive power. When drawing up his reform measures in the spring of 1787, he again recommended that "the right of coercion should be expressly declared," though he was troubled by "the difficulty and awkwardness of operating by force on the collective will of a State." A union based on the principle of coercion, he admitted, "seemed to provide for its own destruction. The use of force ag[ain]st a State, would look more like a declaration of war, than an infliction of punishment." By the time the Convention met, he was ready to drop this provision. To establish the central authority on a firm foundation he now had a better plan: a national government that would operate directly on individuals and have the power to negative state laws. [12]

The negative would eliminate the subordination of the general government to the states which was the curse of the Confederation. If the authority of the federal government in a confederate system could be maintained only by a self-defeating resort to coercion, the negative power in a national system founded on proportional rather than equal representation would "create such a mutuality of dependence" between the general and state governments as to preclude the necessity of force. In a burst of Newtonian imagery Madison likened the negative to gravity: it was "the great pervading principle that must controul the centrifugal tendency of the States; which without it, will continually fly out of their proper orbits and destroy the order and harmony of the political System." He invariably described this prerogative as a "defensive" power, one that would enable the central government to resist aggressive encroachments by the states. From his perspective in 1787 this problem far outweighed that of controlling the general authority, though his vision of an extended republican government embraced a solution to that problem as well. [13]

As a defensive weapon, the negative would not only help preserve the supremacy of the central government but would have even more beneficial effects in controlling the internal affairs of the states. It was the state governments, Madison believed, that exhibited the most alarming symptoms of the disease besetting the American confederacy. The dominant theme of "Vices of the Political System" was not the weaknesses of the Confederation government, serious as these were, but the "multiplicity," the "mutability," and above all the "injustice" of state laws. A dozen years of independence, Madison contended, had brought luxuriant growth of confusing, con-

[12] "Proposed Amendment of Articles of Confederation," Mar. 12, 1781, *ibid.*, III, 17-19; Madison to Jefferson, Oct. 3, 1785, *ibid.*, VIII, 374; Madison to Washington, Apr. 16, 1787, *ibid.*, IX, 385; speech of May 31, 1787, *ibid.*, X, 21.
[13] Madison to Washington, Apr. 16, 1787, *ibid.*, IX, 385; speech of June 8, 1787, *ibid.*, X, 41.

tradictory, and often unnecessary laws that disrupted the economic and commercial life of the states and gave an unfair advantage to persons who could exploit the situation. "Every new regulation concerning commerce or revenue, or in any manner affecting the value of the different species of property," Madison later wrote in *The Federalist*, "presents a new harvest to those who watch the change and can trace its consequences; a harvest reared not by themselves but by the toils and cares of the great body of their fellow-citizens." But the most serious consequence of this legislative instability was that it undermined the people's confidence in their government. Madison devoted the longest section of his memorandum to the injustice of state laws, a subject that led him to reflect on the doctrine of majority rule, the fundamental principle of republican government. The state governments, he noted, provided little security for the personal rights of individuals and minorities, a circumstance especially troubling because violations of these rights seemed to arise from the very nature of republicanism. In republics the majority made the laws, but too often these laws, rather than reflecting the public good or general interest of the whole society, ratified the selfish interests of a dominant faction in that society—whether debtors, creditors, planters, merchants, manufacturers, members of a certain religious sect, inhabitants of a particular region, or some other political, economic, or cultural group. Whenever the opportunity presented itself, there was nothing to restrain a majority faction from seizing control of the government and imposing its designs on the minority.[14]

Madison found evidence all about him to confirm this observation, as state legislatures under the sway of popular leaders enacted paper money, legal tender, debt installment, and stay laws that trampled on property rights and corrupted public morals. Paper money was in his view the most common form of injustice perpetrated by the state governments. Wherever it was issued, this "fictitious" money inevitably depreciated. If made a legal tender, it enabled debtors to defraud their creditors; if not a tender, it hurt debtors by driving out specie. It rewarded extravagance and speculation while upsetting the balance of trade and discouraging frugality. It served, in short, "to disgrace Republican Gov[ernmen]ts in the eyes of mankind." Even as he was attending the Philadelphia Convention, Madison witnessed a stoppage of paper money in the city, evidently the result of a conspiracy by speculators who hoped to buy up the paper at a cheaper rate and then sell it to citizens for payment of taxes. "Nothing but evil springs from this imaginary money wherever it is tried," he remarked, "and yet the appetite for it where it has

---

[14] "Vices of the Political System of the United States," Apr. 1787, *ibid.*, IX, 353-357; *The Federalist* No. 62, *ibid.*, X, 539-540. Madison's analysis of factions in this section of his memorandum was later incorporated into *The Federalist* No. 10. *Ibid.*, 263-270.

not been tried, continues to be felt." Although Virginia had so far resisted the contagion, he continued to worry that the legislature would enact a paper emission under the sponsorship of Patrick Henry.[15]

If state legislatures by paper money and other measures undermined the rights of property, they also posed a serious threat to the still more sacred rights of conscience. Such a threat had recently appeared in Virginia in the form of the "General Assessment" bill, which proposed a tax for the support of "Teachers of the Christian Religion." The bill seemed to Madison a clear violation of the Virginia Declaration of Rights, but a large majority favored it at the 1784 session of the state assembly. Although a bare majority was able to postpone consideration of the bill until the next session, and during the interval Madison led a successful campaign against the religious assessment, the experience was a sobering reminder of the precariousness of so-called unalienable rights in a society and government operating under the rule of a majority. "True it is," he wrote in his broadside "Memorial and Remonstrance" against the bill, "that no other rule exists, by which any question which may divide a Society, can be ultimately determined, but the will of the majority; but it is also true that the majority may trespass on the rights of the minority." After grappling with this dilemma during the next two years, Madison came up with a solution that provided "a republican remedy for the diseases most incident to republican government."[16]

The real crisis in America, Madison emphasized, had its origins in the turbulent majorities who ruled the state legislatures. Their repeated violations of private rights did more, he thought, to create the climate of reform that produced the Federal Convention than did the obvious weaknesses of the central government.[17] Although as a delegate to Congress from 1780 to 1783 he had consistently supported greater powers for the Confederation, Madison significantly did not come to see the need for a completely new constitution for the United States until after his service in the Virginia assembly from 1784 to 1787. During his four sessions in the House of Delegates he became increasingly disillusioned and finally disgusted with the proceedings of that

[15] Madison to Jefferson, Aug. 12, 1786, *ibid.*, IX, 94-95; "Notes for Speech Opposing Paper Money," ca. Nov. 1, 1786, *ibid.*, 158-159; Madison to Pendleton, Apr. 22, 1787, *ibid.*, 396; Madison to Jefferson, July 18, 1787, *ibid.*, X, 105-106.
[16] "Notes for Debates on the General Assessment Bill," Dec. 23-24, 1784, *ibid.*, VIII, 195-199; Madison to Monroe, Dec. 24, 1784, *ibid.*, 200; Madison to Jefferson, Jan. 9, 1785, *ibid.*, 229; "Memorial and Remonstrance Against Religious Assessments," ca. June 20, 1785, *The Federalist* No. 10, *ibid.*, 299; *ibid.*, X, 269-270.
[17] Speech of June 6, 1787, *ibid.*, X, 32; Madison to Jefferson, Oct. 24, 1787, *ibid.*, 212. That the framers of the Constitution, and Madison in particular, were chiefly concerned with the shortcomings of the state governments is the theme of Edward S. Corwin's suggestive essay, "The Progress of Constitutional Theory between the Declaration of Independence and the Meeting of the Philadelphia Convention," *American Historical Review*, XXX (1925), 511-536.

body. A typical assembly, he soon discovered, enacted scores of laws, of which a few had genuine merit but the rest were either inconsequential or positively harmful. Following the path of least resistance, the legislators postponed consideration of the most important bills to the waning days of the session, when they were eager to return home, and then generally preferred stopgap measures over long-term solutions. The result was often carelessly drawn legislation that soon had to be revised or repealed. Each successive assembly consumed a greater proportion of its time undoing the mischief produced by its predecessors. After one year in the House, Madison had already become so concerned with "fluctuating and indegested [sic] laws" that he considered proposing a special committee of "a few select and skilful individuals" to prepare all the bills to be taken up at each session.[18]

The instability and confusion resulting from poorly written, vague, or redundant laws was bad enough, but even more alarming was the postwar decline in the quality of the members of the legislature. The wrong kinds of men—those who lacked a sense of the public good or desired to promote some selfish object—were increasingly attracted to legislative service, transforming the assembly into an arena for an unseemly scramble for private advantage. Madison alluded to this ominous development when he remarked to Washington that publication of a bill to reorganize the courts would, "instead of calling forth the sanction of the wise and virtuous, be a signal to interested men to redouble their efforts to get into the Legislature," meaning the county court lawyers who resisted this change. Land speculators who acquired property on credit and sought legislative protection from their creditors were another "interested" group. According to Madison, "the unjust laws of the States had proceeded more from this class of men, than any others." Lacking enough colleagues who had similarly elevated views of public policy, Madison was continually frustrated in his attempts to uphold the honor of the state in such matters as the payment of British debts and contributions to the federal treasury. Equally unsuccessful were his efforts to stir the legislature to devise a coherent revenue system, complete the revisal of the laws, reform the state constitution, and reorganize the court system.[19]

[18] For Madison's experience in the Virginia legislature see, for example, Madison to Jefferson, July 3, 1784, Jan. 9, 1785, Jan. 22, 1786, in Papers of Madison, VIII, 92-95, 222-232, 472-481, and Dec. 4, 1786, Feb. 15, 1787, ibid., IX, 189-192, 267-269; Madison to Monroe, Dec. 30, 1785, Jan. 22, 1786, ibid., VIII, 465-466, 482-484, and May 13, 1786, ibid., IX, 55; Madison to Caleb Wallace, Aug. 23, 1785, ibid., VIII, 351-352; Madison to Washington, Dec. 7, 1786, ibid., IX, 199-200; Madison to James Madison, Sr., Dec. 12, 1786, ibid., 205-206; Madison to Washington, Dec. 24, 1786, ibid., 224-225; and Madison to Edmund Pendleton, Jan. 9, 1787, ibid., 243-245.
[19] Madison to Washington, Dec. 24, 1786, ibid., IX, 243-245. The comment on land speculators is from Madison's speech of July 26, 1787. Ibid., X, 117.

This unhappy experience in the Virginia legislature demonstrated to Madison that local efforts by the "wise and virtuous" to make state government responsible were bound to fail. Indeed, the unruliness that characterized all the state legislatures raised serious doubts about the future of republican government in America. The crisis of republicanism in the states coincided with the crisis of the union during the winter of 1787, and Madison boldly took upon himself the task of solving both by means of fundamental constitutional reform. While others ominously predicted that the United States must either become a monarchy or dissolve into several hostile confederacies, the Virginian rejected these gloomy alternatives. Spurred by the urgency of his mission, he set about ways of "rendering the Republican form competent to its purposes."[20]

To revive republicanism and strengthen the union, cherished objects that he regarded as complementary, Madison formulated (with an assist from David Hume) a new theory of republican government. Close observation of the state governments had supplied him with abundant evidence that belied the dictum that republics were suited only to a small geographical area. Indeed, he now perceived that their perennial instability was directly related to the very narrowness of their limits, Rhode Island being a prime example. The smaller the jurisdiction, the more easily a faction could become a majority and oppress the minority. To correct this structural flaw Madison stood the traditional theory on its head: he proposed to extend the sphere of republican government, stretching its boundaries to take in a greater number of parties, groups, and factions so that it would be less likely to fall into the hands of a majority dominated by a single interest or passion.[21] The good news Madison carried to Philadelphia was that there was nothing intrinsically wrong with republican government; a republic could achieve stability by expanding to its proper geographical limits.

Madison embarked on his mission to Philadelphia with the confidence of one who had discovered the proper cure for the disease that afflicted the American political system. He brought with him a plan to "perpetuate the Union, and redeem the honor of the Republican name," one designed to make it the interest of republicans to be nationalist and that of nationalists to be republicans.[22] He offered a means of strengthening the central government without resorting to monarchy while showing that a strong union provided a setting in which republicanism would not only survive but flourish. In his

[20] Madison to Washington, Feb. 21, 1787, ibid., IX, 286; "Notes on Debates in Congress," Feb. 21, 1787, ibid., 291-292; Madison to Pendleton, Feb. 24, 1787. ibid., 295; Madison to Randolph, Feb. 25, Apr. 8, 1787, ibid., 299, 371.

[21] "Vices of the Political System," Apr. 1787, ibid., 354-357. For Hume's influence on Madison see Adair, " 'That Politics May Be Reduced to a Science,' " in Colbourn, ed., Fame and the Founding Fathers, 93-106.

[22] Madison to Pendleton, Feb. 24, 1787, in Papers of Madison, IX, 295.

proposed national republic the legislative negative on state laws was the vital power that would transform thirteen semi-independent republics into one extended republic. It would establish the supremacy of the national government and prevent violations of private rights. This prerogative was not only the specific remedy for the "vices" of the existing Confederation but, more generally, the means of redeeming republican government from the opprobrium it had lately suffered, making it respectable before the world. Madison's belief in the negative as a republican panacea explains his outspoken and persistent advocacy of this power at the Federal Convention.

Though he had no illusions about the difficulty of the task before him, Madison hoped that the Convention would be receptive to his ideas and reject all "temporising expedients." The prospects for a fundamental reform along the lines he suggested came closest to realization during the first two weeks of the Convention. The delegates in committee of the whole readily agreed to discard the Articles of Confederation and accepted the substance of Madison's proposals as embodied in the Virginia Plan. In one important particular this plan did not go as far as he wished: instead of a negative *"in all cases whatsoever,"* it provided that the power of the national legislature to veto state laws should be restricted to unconstitutional acts, a concession probably necessary to win the support of the entire Virginia delegation. The committee approved this limited veto without a murmur of dissent on May 31.[23]

On June 8, Charles Pinckney, perhaps after consulting with Madison, moved to broaden the negative power to include "improper" acts of the states. Madison seconded the motion, declaring that "an indefinite power to negative legislative acts of the States [was] absolutely necessary to a perfect system," and urged its adoption in two speeches. After a spirited day-long debate, the motion was voted down, but the qualified negative remained in the report submitted by the committee of the whole on June 13. During the six weeks that followed, the delegates formally considered this report, with the discussion centering on the vexing question of representation. Much to Madison's chagrin, the Convention on July 17 reversed the committee's earlier unanimous approval and rejected the qualified negative by a vote of seven to three, a defeat all the more painful to Madison because he had just lost the fight for proportional representation in the Senate. Late in August, Pinckney, supported by Madison, revived the negative in modified form, but in a close vote the Convention refused to consider this proposition.[24]

[23] Madison to Pendleton, May 27, 1787, *ibid.*, X, 11-12; Max Farrand, ed., *The Records of the Federal Convention of 1787* (New Haven, Conn., 1937), I, 21, 54.

[24] Farrand, ed., *Records*, I, 164-168, 229, II, 27-28, 390-392. As indicated by the vote of June 8, Edmund Randolph and George Mason were probably responsible for the milder version of the negative contained in the sixth resolution of the Virginia Plan.

Despite the attempted revival in August, the vote of July 17 marked the Convention's decisive rejection of the negative on state laws. By this date even the limited veto, which had passed so easily six weeks earlier, appeared under closer scrutiny to have insuperable disadvantages. Critics repeatedly warned that the people would never accept a plan that reduced their state legislatures to nullities. Small-state delegates in particular suspected that the negative would be the specific instrument of the large states to "crush the small ones." After the adoption of the compromise that gave the states equal representation in the Senate, moreover, large-state delegates became less enthusiastic about such a power.[25] There were also doubts about the general legislature's fitness to exercise this power—about the competence of a Georgian, for example, to decide on the expediency of a law that was to operate in New Hampshire—but the most telling objection to the negative was its apparent impracticability: Congress would have to sit constantly merely to review state laws and would therefore have no time for other business. "Is it conceivable," asked John Lansing, "that there will be leisure for such a task? [T]here will on the most moderate calculation, be as many Acts sent up from the States as there are days in the year." Others wondered whether all state laws, including those urgently needed, were to be suspended until approved by the national legislature.[26]

Madison had anticipated some of the practical objections to the negative, but he was more effective in defending its theoretical virtues than in explaining how it would actually work. To avoid keeping the entire Congress in continuous session, and perhaps also to conciliate the small-state critics, he suggested that the negative power should reside exclusively in the Senate. As for laws of immediate necessity, he vaguely hinted that an "emanation" of this power should "be vested in some set of men within the several States" who would give a temporary sanction to such laws. What he meant by this "emanation" is unclear. As one delegate observed, however, the only alternative to sending all state laws up to the national legislature was to have the national government appoint the state governors, who would have a veto over state legislation. Alexander Hamilton and Charles Pinckney openly proposed this modification, and Madison may also have considered it. But the proposition smacked too much of the old hated royal government and could only have made the negative appear even more objectionable.[27]

Under increasing criticism as both politically inexpedient and practically unworkable, the negative by mid-July was no longer compatible with the

[25] *Ibid.*, I, 165-167, 250, 438, II, 27-28. In the July 17 vote Virginia could muster support only from Massachusetts and North Carolina, Pennsylvania being a notable defection.

[26] *Ibid.*, I, 167-168, 337, II, 27, 390.

[27] Madison to Jefferson, Mar. 19, 1787, in *Papers of Madison*, IX, 318; Madison to Randolph, Apr. 8, 1787, *ibid.*, 370; speeches of June 8 and July 17, 1787, *ibid.*, X, 42, 102-103; Farrand, ed., *Records*, I, 293, II, 391; Brant, *Madison*, 105.

theory of the Convention. Its doom had become certain with the adoption of the compromise on representation of July 16. The decision to retain equal representation of the states in the Senate ended Madison's hope of seeing a purely national government established. Henceforth the government contemplated by the Convention was to have a mixed character—"*partly federal and partly national,*" said Oliver Ellsworth, an interpretation that Madison outspokenly resisted at the time, though he later borrowed the phrase and put it to good use in *The Federalist* No. 39. The negative power, the mechanism for transforming a confederate system into a national one, would be an anomaly in a government that retained a modified federal structure.[28]

Though not persuaded of the merits of the negative, the framers of the Constitution nevertheless shared Madison's concern to bring about a due subordination of the states and to establish some measure of central control over their internal affairs. Unlike the Virginian, however, who wished to make the general legislature an integral part of the state legislatures, the majority had come to believe that the task of controlling the states more properly belonged to the judiciary. Indeed, the decision to discard the negative was made easier because a judicial means of achieving the same ends had emerged during the deliberations. Thomas Jefferson, then in Paris as the American minister, had already strikingly anticipated such an alternative in a letter to Madison of June 1787 that was highly critical of the proposed negative: "Would not an appeal from the state judicatures to a federal court, in all cases where the act of Confederation controuled the question, be as effectual a remedy, and exactly commensurate to the defect[?]" At the Convention Roger Sherman was the first to suggest that the negative power was unnecessary because the state courts would consider invalid "any law contravening the authority of the Union."[29] This reasoning led to the formulation of the "supreme law" clause of Article VI of the Constitution, which not coincidentally was introduced immediately following the rejection of the negative on July 17. In its final form this clause declared the Constitution, laws, and treaties of the United States to be the "supreme law of the land" and specifically made the enforcement of this supremacy an obligation of the state judges, who thereby became the first line of defense against the unconstitutional acts of the states. That the Supreme Court would be the ultimate line of defense was implicit in the jurisdiction of the federal judiciary as defined in Article III and was made explicit by the twenty-fifth section of the Judiciary Act of 1789, providing for appeals from state tribunals

[28] In supporting his motion of June 29, 1787, to give each state an equal vote in the Senate, Ellsworth admitted "that the effect of this motion is, to make the general government *partly federal and partly national*" (Farrand, ed., *Records*, I, 474). Madison denied this distinction in his speech of July 14 (*Papers of Madison*, X, 101).

[29] Jefferson to Madison, June 20, 1787, in *Papers of Madison*, X, 64. For Sherman's remarks see Farrand, ed., *Records*, II, 27.

to the Supreme Court.[30] As an additional precaution the framers wrote into the Constitution specific prohibitions and restraints on the states, including an absolute ban on coinage and paper money. Together, the supremacy clause, the judiciary article, and the restrictions on the states constituted the judicial substitute for the legislative negative on state laws.

By transferring to the judiciary the task of upholding the national interest and protecting individual rights, the framers laid the groundwork for the unique career of the Supreme Court that became one of the distinguishing features of the federal government of the United States after 1789. This significant step toward the realization of American federalism was one that Madison, the later exponent and celebrant of that system, could lay no claim to have supported at the Federal Convention. Indeed, he remained far from satisfied that the judicial remedy would be an adequate substitute for the negative on state laws. Only the national legislature, he maintained, could effectively and peacefully enforce the national supremacy while serving as an impartial arbitrator of conflicts among interests within the states. That the judiciary would one day command the respect and deference which would enable it to perform this role was a development that he could not have foreseen in 1787.[31]

To Madison, the most serious defect of the judicial remedy was that, unlike the legislative veto, it could not operate until after the injury had occurred. The procedure was too cumbersome and costly, and would therefore fail to provide an immediate and full measure of justice. It would be "more convenient to prevent the passage of a law, than to declare it void after it is passed," he noted, especially where an individual might not be able to afford the expense of the appellate process. He also doubted whether a state would peacefully obey a judicial decree against it, and a resort to force was the rock on which other confederacies had foundered. The ability of the judiciary to protect private rights within the states, moreover, was limited to

[30] Farrand, ed., *Records*, II, 28-29; Andrew C. McLaughlin, *A Constitutional History of the United States* (New York, 1935), 182-185, 235-237, 395-396.

[31] In time, to be sure, Madison came to accept federal judicial review of state legislation as a substitute for the congressional negative. This is the only sense in which he consistently upheld the doctrine of judicial review. He remained unfriendly to that doctrine in the other sense, namely, the power of the judiciary to review the acts of its own legislature. Indeed, one reason for his advocacy of a congressional veto of state laws was his belief that the state judges "must give the state laws their operation, although the law abridges the rights of the national government" (Yates's report of Madison's speech of June 8, 1787, in *Papers of Madison*, X, 41-42n). Moreover, his proposal at the Convention to give the executive and judiciary a joint "revisionary" power over legislative bills was designed to preclude "the question of a Judiciary annulment of Legislative *Acts*." Speeches of June 6 and July 21, 1787, *ibid.*, 35-36, 109-110; Madison to Monroe, Dec. 27, 1817, in Gaillard Hunt, ed., *The Writings of James Madison*, VIII (New York, 1908), 406-407.

certain specific objects. The restrictions on the states did not go far enough: "Injustice may be effected by such an infinitude of legislative expedients, that where the disposition exists it can only be controuled by some provision which reaches all cases whatsoever. The partial provision made, supposes the disposition which will evade it."[32] When these restrictions were under discussion late in the Convention, Madison could not resist bringing up the negative again, though he did not make a formal motion. But the prevailing opinion, even of such an otherwise thoroughgoing nationalist as Gouverneur Morris, who had consistently denounced the negative, was that within the states "a majority must rule, whatever may be the mischief done among themselves."[33] This was precisely the "mischief" that Madison believed to be among the worst vices of the American political system and one that he hoped the Convention would remedy by adopting the negative on state laws. With a keen sense of disappointment he confided to Jefferson, shortly before the Convention adjourned, his opinion that the Constitution would "neither effectually *answer* its *national object* nor prevent the local *mischiefs* which every where *excite disgusts* ag[ain]st the *state governments.*"[34]

In his next letter Madison amply fulfilled a promise to Jefferson to explain his disappointment with the Constitution. On the surface, this remarkable communication, dated October 24, 1787, is a straightforward report of the proceedings at Philadelphia. Embodied in the account, however, is a carefully reasoned defense of the negative on state laws—in effect a separate essay. Scholars have either ignored this "immoderate digression" (as Madison called it) or missed its main point, although it is the most comprehensive statement of his political thought at the time of the Federal Convention. Burns, for example, admits that the letter expressed "what appeared to be a nationalist bias," but concludes that its author "was not so ardent a champion of concentrated government as [this letter] might indicate." Adrienne Koch selects quotations from the passage in point which exclude all mention of the negative and make it appear that Madison was expounding the theory of the Constitution rather than delivering a sharp critique of it. Adair cites the letter as an explanation of the "theory of the new constitution" and as a stage in the development of *The Federalist* No. 10. Ralph Ketcham, apparently confusing the legislative veto of state acts with the power to coerce the states, quotes the letter to show that Madison had abandoned the idea of the negative. The two were not the same, however; Madison had given up coercion as inappropriate in a national government, but not the negative. Indeed, he discarded coercion in the belief that the negative would obviate a resort to force.[35]

---

[32] Madison to Jefferson, Oct. 24, 1787, *Papers of Madison,* X, 211-212.
[33] Farrand, ed., *Records,* II, 439-440.
[34] Madison to Jefferson, Sept. 6, 1787, in *Papers of Madison,* X, 163-164. Italics indicate words written in code.
[35] Burns, *Madison: Philosopher of the Constitution,* 98-103; Koch, *Jefferson and*

The purpose of Madison's digression on the negative was to demonstrate the impotence of the proposed government without this prerogative and especially to answer Jefferson's pointed criticism of it in his letter of the preceding June. The negative "fails in an essential character, that the hole and the patch should be commensurate," Jefferson had written. "But this proposes to mend a small hole by covering the whole garment."[36] In his reply Madison restated the ideas he had put forward in memoranda, letters, and speeches during the preceding seven months. Although he said nothing new, he cast this letter in a form that revealed for the first time the full scope and interrelatedness of those ideas. On different occasions during the spring of 1787 he had sketched his theory of the extended republic and introduced his scheme for the veto of state laws. Not until he wrote Jefferson after the Convention, however, did he discuss both together in a way that suggested how the negative was to have been the means of giving full effect to his republican theory.[37]

Madison organized his argument around the two purposes which the negative was designed to effect: "1. to prevent encroachments on the General authority. 2. to prevent instability and injustice in the legislation of the States." Under the first he summarized the history of ancient and modern confederacies and the American experience under the Articles of Confederation—a distressing tale of constant struggle between head and members that always ended with the predominance of the latter. Despite its "material" difference from the existing system, the Constitution offered only a slight improvement over the Articles of Confederation; the union was now "a feudal system of republics," which was hardly better than a "Confederacy of independent States." And the melancholy history of the feudal constitutions was evidence enough to predict a similar pattern of struggle for domination between the federal and state governments.[38]

The crux of Madison's argument was his discussion of the second of the two purposes, preventing injustice in the states. Until now Madison had not explained why the central government, armed with the power to disallow state laws, would act as a "disinterested and dispassionate umpire in disputes between different passions and interests in the State" without becoming an

---

Madison, 36-39; Adair, "Authorship of the Disputed Federalist Papers," and " 'That Politics May Be Reduced to a Science,' " in Colbourn, ed., *Fame and the Founding Fathers*, 61, 102; Adair, "Intellectual Origins of Jeffersonian Democracy," 237 and 237n; Ketcham, *Madison*, 302. A recent anthology of Madison's writings omits the Oct. 24, 1787, letter. Had the editor included it, he might have avoided a misstatement about the negative in his introduction (Meyers, ed., *Mind of the Founder*, xxxvii).

[36] Jefferson to Madison, June 20, 1787, in *Papers of Madison*, X, 64.
[37] Madison to Jefferson, Oct. 24, 1787, *ibid.*, 206-219 (209-214 for the defense of the negative).
[38] *Ibid.*, 209-210.

engine of tyranny.[39] Why would private rights be more secure under the protection of the general government than those of the states, he asked, since both operate under the republican principle of majority rule? Madison answered this question with a full exposition of his theory of the extended republic, which he had not previously communicated to Jefferson. He repeated almost verbatim the analysis in "Vices of the Political System," showing that factions were endemic to republics and that majority factions could not be restrained from committing injustice by an appeal to higher motives. The only solution was to enlarge the republic to embrace a multitude of diverse interests so that it would have a built-in protection against domination by a single party. The majorities that formed in the government of this extended republic would tend to be disinterested majorities, strongly disposed to seek the general good of the society. It followed that this government, immune from the virus of majority tyranny, could be safely entrusted with the power to veto state laws and thereby prevent an outbreak of that virus where it was most likely to appear.[40]

Although it remained implicit in Madison's analysis, the complementary relationship between the negative power and the theory of the extended republic was clear from the juxtaposition of the two in this letter. To Madison, the negative was the instrument for making his republican theory work in the special case of the United States. In a single consolidated republic such a prerogative was unnecessary. The American state governments, for example, did not need this power to control the counties within their borders because the latter were by definition creatures of the states and subordinate to them. But the United States was an enlarged republic containing a set of state republics. In this compound system a negative on state laws would give effect to Madison's theory within these smaller republics as well as within the national republic and would eliminate "the evil of imperia in imperio." The relationship between the general and state governments would then be analogous to that between the state and county governments. At the same time, the general government, because of its extended sphere, would exercise the negative power with moderation, restraint, and regard for the public good. Madison concluded his digression on the negative with an observation that has been frequently misinterpreted as a statement of the theory of the new Constitution:

> The great desideratum in Government is, so to modify the sovereignty as that it may be sufficiently neutral between different parts of the Society to controul one part from invading the rights of another, and at the same time sufficiently controuled itself, from setting up an interest adverse to that of the entire Society. In absolute monarchies, the Prince

[39] Madison to Washington, Apr. 16, 1787, ibid., IX, 384.
[40] Madison to Jefferson, Oct. 24, 1787, ibid., X, 212-214.

may be tolerably neutral towards different classes of his subjects, but may sacrifice the happiness of all to his personal ambition or avarice. In small republics, the sovereign will is controuled from such a sacrifice of the entire Society, but is not sufficiently neutral towards the parts composing it. In the extended Republic of the United States, The General Government would hold a pretty even balance between the parties of particular States, and be at the same time sufficiently restrained by its dependence on the community, from betraying its general interests.

It is clear, however, that Madison did not believe that the proposed Constitution fulfilled "the great desideratum in Government," for it only partly answered the purposes of his ideal extended republic.[41]

The message Madison conveyed to Jefferson was that the Constitution was only a partial reform and for that reason likely to fail. It was not enough that the new plan embodied his theory of the extended republic, for without the negative the effects of faction could be controlled only at the federal level. Without a strong barrier to the acts of interested majorities in the states, the Constitution lacked the essential ingredient for securing justice, the true end of republican government. "A reform . . . which does not make provision for private rights," he warned, "must be materially defective."[42] Thus on the very eve of his debut in The Federalist, Madison was highly dissatisfied with, not to say contemptuous of, the proposed government. The October 1787 letter was a strong dose of nationalism that contrasted sharply with "Publius's" celebration of the Constitution and indeed with all of Madison's subsequent writings. After this full and candid critique he ceased his advocacy of the negative on state laws and never again spoke ill of the Constitution. Beginning with The Federalist, he devoted his career to the service of a governmental charter that he originally believed to be inadequate to preserve the union or to secure private and minority rights.

In deciding to don the mask of "Publius," Madison made the practical statesman's choice of the lesser evil, sacrificing "theoretical propriety to the force of extraneous considerations."[43] Given the alternatives, he preferred the risk of the Constitution, defective as it was, to the anarchy he was certain would result from continuing under the Articles of Confederation. Having carefully constructed a theoretical framework to support a plan the Convention had rejected, Madison in The Federalist brilliantly improvised and salvaged as much as he could of that framework to support the modified federal system of the Constitution. Though privately he believed that the Constitution embodied "the evil of imperia in imperio"—that it was a crazy-

[41] Ibid., 209, 214.
[42] Ibid., 212.
[43] The Federalist No. 37, ibid., 363.

quilt "feudal system of republics"[44] whose distribution of powers was dangerously tilted in favor of the states—as "Publius" he skillfully shifted the emphasis, turning apparent defects into virtues. The great latitude left to the states, for example, rather than being a threat to the central government and ultimately its ruin, became the means of arresting the career of an aggressive federal engine (Nos. 45 and 46). The "feudal system of republics" became the judiciously mixed government, "partly federal, and partly national" (No. 39). Rather than dwell on the continuing danger of unjust acts by majorities in the states, "Publius" confined himself to showing how the enlarged federal republic would avoid the turbulence and violence of faction (Nos. 10 and 51). As presented to the world in *The Federalist*, the theory of the extended republic was thus considerably reduced in scope, being no longer connected with the defense of the negative on state laws.

As "Publius" Madison suppressed his own views in order to make the best case for a plan which he believed to be flawed. How long he retained his private misgivings about the Constitution can only be conjectured. The last hint of dissatisfaction came in the summer of 1789 while he served as patron of the amendments that became the Bill of Rights. At that time he was still seeking to place additional curbs on the states. Of the amendments he proposed, the one he considered to be the most valuable would have prohibited the states from violating the rights of conscience, the freedom of the press, and the trial by jury in criminal cases. The Senate rejected the amendment, however, and Madison, sensing that the reaction to the excesses of the state governments had run its course, made no further attempt to perfect the Constitution. An opponent of his amendment echoed the prevailing sentiment when he admonished Congress "to leave the State Governments to themselves, and not interfere with them more than we already do."[45]

The problem of controlling the effects of faction in the states, which had loomed so large in his mind during the 1780s, ceased to be Madison's major concern after 1789. Though the solution agreed to at Philadelphia fell short of his hopes, the Constitution improved the situation enough to make this issue politically moribund. During the next decade Madison continued to be preoccupied with faction, but events forced him to shift his focus to the federal government. Despite its extended sphere, that government proved more susceptible to faction than he had foreseen in 1787. The threat of oppression, moreover, came not from a *majority* faction (whose dangers his

[44] Madison to Jefferson, Oct. 24, 1787, *ibid.*, 209-210.
[45] Joseph Gales, comp., *The Debates and Proceedings in the Congress of the United States* . . . , I (Washington, D.C., 1834), 448-459, 783-784. Not until the Fourteenth Amendment was adopted after the Civil War were further constitutional restrictions imposed on the states.

previous warnings had dwelled on almost exclusively) but from a highly organized and influential "moneyed interest" that had somehow seized the reins of power and was adroitly maintaining its control through "corruption."[46] To combat the Hamiltonian system of funded debts, banks, and encouragements for manufactures, Madison adopted a strategy of opposition that necessarily forced him to retreat from his high nationalism of 1787 (even to the point of flirting with the doctrine of "state interposition" in 1799). In responding to the unexpected developments of the 1790s, the erstwhile skeptic became a firm believer in the Constitution; he came to appreciate the balance between the federal and national features of the government, a balance that he had celebrated in *The Federalist*, but without inner conviction.

[46] See Richard Hofstadter, *The Idea of a Party System: The Rise of Legitimate Opposition in the United States, 1780-1840* (Berkeley, Calif., 1969), 68-69, 83-84.

Republicanism and Slavery: Origins of the Three-Fifths Clause in the United States Constitution

Howard A. Ohline[*]

AMERICAN historians have become increasingly aware of how the institution of slavery and the problems of race created tension in Western culture.[1] During the Revolutionary crisis of the eighteenth century when new constitutional principles and structures emerged in North America, slavery inevitably created friction in politics. Some historians have argued that the three-fifths clause in the United States Constitution was a product of significant conflict over the issue of slavery in the Convention of 1787. Others attach little importance to the clause. It is the purpose of this essay to analyze these arguments and to introduce a new interpretation of the discord that led to the inclusion of the three-fifths clause in the Constitution.

The clause ordained that three-fifths of the number of slaves in a state would be added to the number of free citizens, including bond servants but excluding Indians not taxed, to determine how many congressmen the state would send to the House of Representatives. The same formula specified the amount of direct taxes the state would pay to the national government.[2] The usual interpretation of the political conflict behind the establishment of this procedure in the Constitution is as follows: northerners wanted to count slaves in determining

[*] Mr. Ohline is a member of the Department of History, Temple University.
[1] David Brion Davis, *The Problem of Slavery in Western Culture* (Ithaca, N. Y., 1966); Winthrop D. Jordan, *White Over Black: American Attitudes Toward the Negro, 1550-1812* (Chapel Hill, N. C., 1968); Staughton Lynd, *Class Conflict, Slavery, and the United States Constitution: Ten Essays* (Indianapolis, 1967).
[2] Article I, Section 2. The three-fifths clause also affected the selection of presidential electors because the number from each state equaled the total of its representatives and senators. Article II, Section 1. The electoral college was agreed to in the Convention after the three-fifths principle was approved. Once it was decided that the president would not be elected by the national legislature, some southerners preferred a system of electors instead of the direct election of the president in order to enhance the influence of southern states whose slave populations could not vote. Max Farrand, ed., *The Records of the Federal Convention of 1787* (New Haven, Conn., 1937), II, 31-32.

each state's share of direct taxes but not representation; southerners, in determining representation but not taxes; thus, the three-fifths clause represented a compromise that reconciled North-South sectional differences.[3] This interpretation, however, is not supported by the history of the Convention. First, the idea that the three-fifths formula originated in the Convention is historically inaccurate. The ratio of three slaves to five free citizens had been worked out five years before when the Confederation Congress sought a new base for national taxes.[4] Second, virtually no southerner in the Philadelphia Convention opposed the direct taxation of slaves, although some feared a poll tax that applied only to slaves.[5] Finally, few northerners in the Convention opposed the principle of counting slaves for purposes of representation.

Historians who have argued that the conflict over the three-fifths clause was a major chapter of the Convention's proceedings fall into two groups. One is primarily southern. It was influenced by Frank L. Owsley, who taught at Vanderbilt University during the 1930s and 1940s, and who argued that the South insisted upon the three-fifths clause as a "sine qua non" for joining the Union in 1787. Thus, Albert F. Simpson, one of Owsley's students, believed that "the issue of slave representation was born in an atmosphere of sectionalism, in the midst of the first great North-South fight for the balance of power in the national government." The compromise over representation and taxation was minor. "The major bargain was a 'trade' between the North and the South . . . in order to maintain a political balance between the

[3] John A. Garraty, *The American Nation: A History of the United States* (New York, 1966), 148; T. Harry Williams et al., *A History of the United States* (New York, 1959), 176; Richard Hofstadter et al., *The American Republic*, I (Englewood Cliffs, N. J., 1959), 241; Charles A. and Mary R. Beard, *The Rise of American Civilization* (New York, 1927), 319.

[4] Under the Articles of Confederation representation was based on state equality and taxation was based on the value of land. Thus, the issue of slavery in connection with either representation or taxation had been avoided during the Revolutionary period. In 1783, however, Congress recommended an amendment making population the basis for apportionment of taxes among the states. In this amendment, which failed of approval, Congress worked out the three-fifths formula for the purposes of taxation. Edmund Cody Burnett, *The Continental Congress* (New York, 1941), 221-222, 226; Merrill Jensen, *The New Nation: A History of the United States During the Confederation 1781-1789* (New York, 1950), 73, 75; Clinton Rossiter, *1787: The Grand Convention* (New York, 1966), 173n.

[5] Farrand, ed., *Records*, II, 143; III, 360.

two sections."[6] This thesis held that from the beginning in 1787 sectional conflict focused on the institution of slavery and that then and later northern antislavery sentiment was motivated primarily by political instead of humanitarian or ideological motives.[7]

These southern historians, however, were not the first to single out the three-fifths clause as a major issue in the Constitutional Convention. During the post-Civil War decades, northern historians as well as politicians condemned it as one of several clauses in the Constitution that sanctioned the institution of slavery.[8] Sometimes referred to as "abolitionist historians," these writers held as did Owsley and his followers later that the three-fifths clause was a major political issue between the North and South. The major difference, of course, was that the "abolitionist" school condemned the clause as an immoral concession and denied that it was the outgrowth of legitimate political compromise. Rather, they viewed it as the product of a counterrevolution or conspiracy machinated by a southern minority. Unfortunately, their stress on conspiratorial themes led more to condemnation than to explication of the origins of the clause in the Convention.

Contradicting these views was the interpretation of Progressive historians who denied that the clause was ever an important issue in the Convention. In 1913 the foremost collector of documents on the Constitution, Max Farrand, rejected the moral indignation of the abolitionists and concluded that the "three-fifths rule was a mere incident in

[6] Albert F. Simpson, "The Political Significance of Slave Representation, 1787-1821," *Journal of Southern History*, VII (1941), 315, 318. Owsley taught that the Civil War was caused, in part, "by destroying the sectional balance of power which . . . had been established by the three-fifths ratio clause in the Federal constitution." Frank L. Owsley, "The Fundamental Cause of the Civil War: Egocentric Sectionalism," *ibid.*, VII (1941), 9, 3-18.

[7] Glover Moore, *The Missouri Controversy, 1819-1821* (Lexington, Ky., 1953), 7-8, *passim*. Moore's book was also a product of Owsley's influence and was the logical conclusion of the southern argument that the issue of slavery was essentially an issue of sectional political power.

[8] Horace Greeley, *The American Conflict: A History of the Great Rebellion in the United States of America,* . . . I (Hartford, Conn., 1864), 43-46; Henry Wilson, *History of the Rise and Fall of the Slave Power in America,* I (Boston, 1872), 42-44; Hermann von Holst, *The Constitutional and Political History of the United States: 1750-1833. State Sovereignty and Slavery,* trans. John J. Lalor and Alfred B. Mason, I (Chicago, 1877), 289; James Schouler, *History of the United States of America, under the Constitution,* I (New York, 1880), 45-46. A 20th-century history of the same genre is Dwight Lowell Dumond, *Antislavery: The Crusade for Freedom in America* (New York, 1961), 37.

that part of the great compromise which declared that 'representation ought to be proportioned according to direct Taxation.'" Farrand saw no reason to explain how or why the clause appeared in the Constitution. He merely accepted its wording as evidence as to the real conflict underlying its acceptance. Progressive indifference to the issue of slavery was subsequently challenged by the historians from Vanderbilt, and more recently from a neo-abolitionist point of view.[9]

In the last decade Staughton Lynd has led a sophisticated attempt to reassess the origins of the three-fifths principle.[10] Essentially, Lynd has combined the moralistic abolitionist interpretation with a southern frame of reference. Using the conspiracy model to impugn the clause as, "if not a covenant with death and an agreement with hell, . . . at least a dramatic instance of . . . pragmatic conservatism," he has also employed a North-South sectional model to explain the conflict that led to its adoption. But unlike earlier historians, Lynd found the conspiracy to have taken place between the Constitutional Convention in Philadelphia and the Confederation Congress in New York City. He argued, with good but circumstantial evidence, that the three-fifths clause was part of a sectional swap for the provision in the Northwest Ordinance of 1787 prohibiting slavery north of the Ohio River, which was adopted by Congress at virtually the same time. Thus, northerners and southerners were fighting over the same issue in 1787 that they fought over in the Missouri Compromise of 1820 and the Compromise of 1850. Slavery, according to Lynd, was a major question from the beginning, which is precisely what the Vanderbilt historians had been saying since the late 1930s. Unlike them, however, Lynd's moralism was abolitionist in sentiment: the clause "sanctioned slavery more decidedly than any previous action at a national level" and was achieved because the members of the Convention "were ready to compromise the concept that all men are equal."[11]

Lynd correctly pointed out that some southerners supported the pro-

[9] Max Farrand, *The Framing of the Constitution of the United States* (New Haven, Conn., 1913), 108; Frederick Jackson Turner, *The Significance of Sections in American History* (New York, 1932), 26-27. The best account of the indifference of Progressive historians to the issue of slavery is Staughton Lynd, "On Turner, Beard and Slavery," *Journal of Negro History*, XLVIII (1963), 235-250.

[10] Staughton Lynd, "The Compromise of 1787," *Political Science Quarterly*, LXXXI (1966), 225-250. Reprinted in Lynd, *Class Conflict*, 185-213. See also Jay A. Sigler, "The Rise and Fall of the Three-Fifths Clause," *Mid-America*, XLVIII (1966), 271-277.

[11] Lynd, *Class Conflict*, 186, 185, 213.

portional representation of population because they believed that population in the South would increase and because they were confident of controlling the West in the future.[12] But if the dispute over the three-fifths clause was only a sectional compromise between the North and South, Lynd's hypothesis does not explain convincingly what the North received in exchange. His attempt to build a hypothetical case about the Northwest Ordinance fits his North-South sectional model, but ignores the complexity of the problem within the Convention.

Whatever the three-fifths clause meant to Americans after 1787, in the Philadelphia Convention it was not primarily the product of a sectional struggle for political power or a rejection of Revolutionary ideals. Convention politics were fraught with sectionalism, but the maneuvering over the issue of representation and slavery was too complex to be fully understood in a simple North-South frame of reference. The clause was an essential part of an effort to weaken the principle of state sovereignty and establish the republican ideal that the people were sovereign, and was instrumental in bringing about a national union in which representation was related to the changing distribution of population. The key to political reform sought by many eighteenth-century English radicals had been the destruction of the rotten borough system and the adoption of a political structure in which representation in Parliament was based directly on population.[13] The radical principle of equal representation became part of American Revolutionary ideology, because it largely conformed with the structure of colonial institutions. By the time of the Revolution the concept that a legislative assembly should be a mirror of society was the heart of republican ideology.[14] Any legislature that was based on less would destroy republicanism.[15] But the paradox in the eighteenth century was that a national legislature accurately reflecting

[12] *Ibid.*, 185-213. Another recent account of the origins of the three-fifths clause also suggests that southerners "had the most to gain from the switch to proportional representation." Donald L. Robinson, *Slavery in the Structure of American Politics, 1765-1820* (New York, 1971), 179, *passim.*

[13] Bernard Bailyn, *The Ideological Origins of the American Revolution* (Cambridge, Mass., 1967), 47, 250.

[14] John Adams, *Thoughts on Government: Applicable to the Present State of the American Colonies* (1776), in Charles Francis Adams, ed., *The Works of John Adams, . . .* IV (Boston, 1851), 195.

[15] Gordon S. Wood, *The Creation of the American Republic, 1776-1787* (Chapel Hill, N. C., 1969), 56, 119, 186.

eighteenth-century American society would also have to reflect the institution of slavery.

The dispute over the three-fifths clause in the Convention was related to the problem of *how* society would be mirrored in the national legislature. One group of delegates, primarily from Virginia and Pennsylvania, supported a constitutional census in which the three-fifths rule would be explicit because they wanted the legislature to be in the image of a dynamic expanding society. Another group largely from New England, but with support at times from South Carolina, wanted the legislature to protect and emulate a static differentiated society by permitting the legislature itself to control the ratio of representation. Both groups contained northerners and southerners, and both supported the principle of counting slaves for the purpose of determining representation, but disagreed over how it should be done. While the rhetoric of the debate was sometimes sectional in character, the actual struggle was between two types of republicanism.[16] The major assumption of the first group was that the people were sovereign and constitutional control of representation should limit legislative power, while the assumption of the latter was that the legislature was sovereign and its control of representation would protect private property from popular whim. Paradoxically, it was the issue of how to count the slaves that became the means of assuring that representation would be regulated by a census beyond the control of the national legislature, because southerners came to fear, as the debate developed, that if Congress fixed representation it might not use slaves to determine ratios in the future.

The idea of counting slaves in computing representation was brought to Philadelphia by Charles Pinckney of South Carolina. An enterprising planter and lawyer who owned 111 slaves,[17] Pinckney was probably the only delegate to arrive with a prepared plan of government for a new union. He circulated the plan, which advocated a three-fifths formula rather than counting all the slaves, before serious debate began in the

[16] Robinson has also concluded that the conflict over the three-fifths clause was between two types of republicanism, but my thesis about the nature of the republicanism of each group differs substantially from his. *Slavery in American Politics,* 184-185.

[17] The slaveholdings of each delegate have been conveniently collected by Forrest McDonald. His statistics have been used in this essay, although they are based on the 1790 census and the exact number of slaves owned undoubtedly changed between 1787 and 1790. *We the People: The Economic Origins of the Constitution* (Chicago, 1958), 81.

Convention. Although no copy of the plan survives, its main points have been reconstructed.[18] George Read, a lawyer from New Castle, Delaware, saw it on May 21 and reported to a fellow delegate that it had a design for a bicameral legislature in which the first house was to be elected by the state legislatures "in proportion to [the] number of white inhabitants and three-fifths of all others."[19] James Wilson, a Philadelphia lawyer and constitutional theorist, also examined Pinckney's plan, though when is not known. Wilson noted that the lower House of Delegates was to be elected by the state legislatures, and was "To consist of one Member for every [blank] thousand Inhabitants ⅗ of Blacks included."[20] And if Read knew of the three-fifths proposal, James Madison and Edmund Randolph, the major architects of the Virginia plan of union, which was favored by the larger states, were also aware of it before the debates began, because all three were fellow boarders with Pinckney at Mrs. House's in Philadelphia.[21]

Pinckney was unable to convince Madison and Randolph that the three-fifths formula should become an explicit part of their Virginia or large state plan. The two, who owned twenty-three slaves between them, believed in the republican principle of proportional representation, but could not decide whether it should be based on property or population. Consequently, the Virginia plan avoided defining the exact basis of representation by recommending that the makeup of both houses of the legislature be proportional to "Quotas of contribution, or to the number of free inhabitants."[22] The exact meaning of these alternatives was not made clear to the delegates,[23] and during the ensuing discussions over the plan

[18] J. Franklin Jameson, *Studies in the History of the Federal Convention of 1787* (American Historical Association *Annual Report,* I [Washington, 1902]), 117-120.

[19] George Read to John Dickinson, Philadelphia, May 21, 1787, William T. Read, ed., *Life and Correspondence of George Read, a Signer of the Declaration of Independence* . . . (Philadelphia, 1870), 443-444.

[20] James Wilson Manuscripts, II, 26-37, Historical Society of Pennsylvania, Philadelphia.

[21] Charles Warren, *The Making of the Constitution* (Boston, 1928), 116.

[22] Farrand, ed., *Records,* I, 20.

[23] Irving Brant interpreted the phrase "Quotas of contribution" to mean the 1783 formula, i.e., "proportionate to free inhabitants plus three fifths of the slaves." *James Madison: Father of the Constitution, 1787-1800* (Indianapolis, 1950), 32. This is highly improbable, for the choice presented by the Virginia plan would then have been between counting three-fifths of the slaves or none. Brant offered no evidence that this was the case. Brant merely accepted Madison's own later definition

Madison revealed that he himself was dissatisfied with the alternatives presented. He feared that the second, which based representation solely on the number of free inhabitants, would lead to southern objections. On the other hand, he agreed with Rufus King, a lawyer from Newburyport, Massachusetts, that quotas would not work if, as Madison wanted, revenue was to be based on direct taxes and tariffs instead of state requisitions. Quotas would perpetuate the political structure of the Confederation.[24]

During the first weeks of the Convention, disagreement about representation was between the large and small states. William Paterson of New Jersey opposed any proposal that would destroy the concept of state equality. John Dickinson, the famous Philadelphia lawyer and pamphleteer who represented Delaware, combined the idea of proportional representation in one house according to the "sums paid within each State" to the new government with state equality in the second house. David Brearley, the chief justice of the New Jersey Supreme Court, believed that, in order to preserve state sovereignty and resolve the friction between large and small states, existing boundaries should be redrawn to form thirteen equal states. Roger Sherman, the mayor of New Haven, Connecticut, advocated proportional representation of "free inhabitants" in the first house and equal representation of states in the second.[25]

Unable to decide how representation should be determined, the delegates could proceed no farther than to agree on June 11, two weeks after the reading of the Virginia plan, to reject the principle of state equality in the lower house of the legislature. Immediately John Rutledge, the leader of a major political faction in South Carolina, who owned 243 slaves, and Pierce Butler, a rice planter who owned 143, proposed that representation be based on "quotas of contribution."[26] But many southerners who favored proportional representation of population, although certainly preferring Rutledge's and Butler's formula over the

---

of the phrase "Quotas of contribution," for if such was the actual alternative at the time, why did the Virginians not use Pinckney's more specific wording? Moreover, most delegates interpreted the alternatives presented by the Virginia plan to be between the representation of property and population. William Paterson, for instance, understood the alternatives to be "Quantum of Property or Number of Souls." Farrand, ed., *Records*, I, 27.
[24] *Ibid.*, 36.
[25] *Ibid.*, 87, 91, 175, 176-179.
[26] McDonald, *We the People*, 79, 82.

alternate "free inhabitants," were swayed by James Wilson's counter-suggestion that representation be based on "the whole number of white and other free Citizens and inhabitants of every age sex and condition including those bound to servitude for a term of years and three fifths of all other persons."[27] Thus, the issue of the three-fifths formula was never primarily at stake, for the Convention well might have followed the precedent of 1783 if the final decision had been to base representation on quotas. Wilson, a Pennsylvanian, considered by his biographer to have been one of the most democratic members of the Convention, placed the three-fifths principle before the delegates in the hope of restoring representation by population instead of property and eliminating the requisition system that had kept the Confederation bankrupt during the 1780s.[28] Whatever collusion there was between him and Madison on the matter was directed toward using the three-fifths rule to gain southern support for basing representation on population instead of quotas. The three-fifths principle became the rationale that permitted southerners to accept a revolutionary change in representation in the national government, paradoxically helping to weaken the financial control of the states and establish the republican ideal that the people were sovereign.[29] At this point in the Convention, too, Wilson was not attempting to establish a North-South compromise over taxation and representation. Nothing in his motion on June 11 related to the question of national revenue.

There was virtual unanimity for the principle of counting slaves. One oft quoted objection was that of Elbridge Gerry, a Marblehead merchant who represented Massachusetts, and who opposed incorporating the principle in a rule basing representation on population, but on the grounds that he did not understand how slaves could be considered other than as property. Otherwise, Wilson's proposal brought together a coalition of all the large states, including Gerry's Massachusetts, and all the states with large numbers of slaves, and thereby isolated the small state interest. After two weeks of confusion, there was general agreement among the delegates to transform the 1783 rule of taxation into a rule of representation. The vote on Wilson's motion in the committee of the whole was nine in favor with the two small states of New Jersey and

[27] Farrand, ed., *Records*, I, 196, 200-201.
[28] Charles P. Smith, *James Wilson, Founding Father, 1742-1798* (Chapel Hill, N. C., 1956), 218, 230.
[29] Warren, *Making of the Constitution*, 209.

Delaware opposed.[30] In fact, the near unanimity achieved by Wilson's rule of representation for the lower house encouraged him to recommend that it be applied to the upper as well. The vote on this proposal was six ayes and five nays, reflecting the strength of the commitment to preserve some element of state sovereignty in any new system of representation. Massachusetts, Pennsylvania, Virginia, North Carolina, South Carolina, and Georgia voted for, and Connecticut, New York, New Jersey, Delaware, and Maryland voted against, using population and the three-fifths rule as the basis for representation in the second house of the legislature.[31] Gerry, who opposed using the three-fifths rule in the lower house, favored it for the other chamber, again suggesting that he had not opposed it earlier on moral grounds.[32] By June 13, the delegates in the committee of the whole had approved the three-fifths principle for purposes of representation in both houses of the national legislature by a vote that did not divide along sectional lines.

Thereafter Madison, Wilson, and Alexander Hamilton resisted any attempt to alter the plan agreed to in the committee of the whole and successfully persuaded the delegates to dismiss the small state or New Jersey plan. While this would not have established the three-fifths principle with regard to representation, because it continued the system of state equality existing under the Articles of Confederation, it would have established it for taxation by changing the basis of requisitions from the value of land to "the whole number of white and other free citizens and inhabitants of every age sex and condition . . . and three fifths of all other persons." This was not a northern but a small state proposal that would have perpetuated the requisition system. Nor was it antisouthern, because basing quotás on population would not have been more burdensome than basing quotas on land in the South.[33]

The delegates then turned to the report of the committee of the whole and took up Wilson's proposal on June 27. Again the plan was attacked by the protectors of state sovereignty. Oliver Ellsworth, a Hartford lawyer and financial speculator representing Connecticut, moved that representa-

[30] Farrand, ed., *Records*, I, 201. The cross-sectional character of this vote is often overlooked.
[31] *Ibid.*, 202.
[32] Elbridge Gerry to the vice president of the Convention of Massachusetts, Cambridge, Jan. 2, 1788, *ibid.*, III, 264.
[33] *Ibid.*, I, 243.

tion in the Senate be based on state equality. William Samuel Johnson, the newly appointed president of Columbia College, who also represented Connecticut, argued that if the states were to continue to exist they must have some power of self-defense.[34] In this context, rather than in an attack on the three-fifths clause, Madison finally resorted to the arguments of southern sectionalism. If the new government was to have a "defensive power," that is, power on one level of government to protect itself from another, Madison suggested that the Constitution should institutionalize a North-South division based on slavery. Real political interest, he asserted, "resulted partly from climate, but principally from [the effects of] . . . having or not having slaves."[35]

The context in which Madison spoke is important because his statement is often cited to show that the three-fifths clause was primarily a sectional issue in the Convention.[36] At the time, however, no one was disputing the three-fifths clause for the House; Madison obviously was attempting primarily to prevent the reestablishment of state equality in the Senate. As a tactical maneuver, he observed that sectional groups were a more realistic alternative upon which to base representation in a national legislature. It could be achieved, he said, by constructing a bicameral legislature in which population would "be represented in one branch according to the number of free inhabitants only; and in the other according to the whole no. counting the slaves as free."[37] The South would have the advantage in one house, leaving the North the advantage in the other. But the sincerity of Madison's ideas may be judged by the fact that he never supported them seriously.[38] In the context of the debate his argument was

[34] Ibid., 461, 468-469.
[35] Ibid., 486; James Madison to Thomas Jefferson, New York, Mar. 19, 1787, Julian P. Boyd, ed., The Papers of Thomas Jefferson, XI (Princeton, N. J., 1955), 220.
[36] Lynd, Class Conflict, 201; Simpson, "Slave Representation," Journal Southern Hist., VII (1941), 316.
[37] Farrand, ed., Records, I, 486-487.
[38] This recommendation was not pushed by Madison primarily because it conflicted with his view of legislative powers. He hoped that the two houses would have different functions. The Senate, for instance, would have the power to negate state laws; the House would have primary control over appropriations. If each branch had different powers, the representation of sections in each house as he suggested would result, not in sectional equilibrium, but in an imbalance between the North and South. Madison could not support his own proposal because the "inequality of powers that must be vested in the two branches, . . . would destroy the equilibrium of interests." Ibid., 487, 497.

a feint in defense of the proposal to use persons instead of states as the basis of representation; Madison introduced sectionalism in an ironical way only to protect the plan already endorsed by the Convention. While his resort to this strategy reflected the fact that many members of the Convention did view national politics in terms of sectional interests, his doing so is no evidence that the three-fifths clause originated in sectionalism. It had been accepted before that issue was raised.

The vote on Ellsworth's proposal resulted in a tie, five states for and five against.[39] After this vote on July 2, the Convention formed a special "grand committee" of one representative from each state to resolve the impasse over representation. Three days later, Gerry, the chairman, returned with the recommendation that each state have one member for each forty thousand inhabitants, including three-fifths of the slaves, in the lower house. Each state would have an equal vote in the upper house.[40] This report, plus the return to the Convention of Gouverneur Morris, a tactless but sophisticated member of the New York landed aristocracy who represented Pennsylvania, created new alternatives over representation. The committee's support of state equality in the Senate forced the South Carolinians to counter again with a proposal to use quotas for the Senate if it did not represent population.[41] Morris concurred, arguing that "property was the main object of Society . . . [and] it ought to be one measure of the influence due to those who were to be affected by the Government." Morris spoke for a small group that wished to establish a Senate that would represent property and exhibit an "aristocratic Spirit."[42] Morris wanted to perpetuate the classic mixed or balanced constitution that distinguished between the holders of wealth and the mass of people in the branches of its legislature.[43]

Morris's group also were afraid that representation based on popula-

---

[39] The tie was due to a changed vote in the Georgia delegation. Abraham Baldwin split his delegation by swinging in favor of state equality in the Senate, which he likely would not have done if the issue were the three-fifths clause itself. Warren, *Making of the Constitution*, 462.

[40] Luther Martin, *Genuine Information, Delivered to the Legislature of the State of Maryland, . . .* (1787); Elbridge Gerry to the vice president of the Convention of Massachusetts, Jan. 21, 1788, both in Farrand, ed., *Records*, III, 188, 265-266.

[41] *Ibid.*, I, 529.

[42] *Ibid.*, 533.

[43] Max M. Mintz, *Gouverneur Morris and the American Revolution* (Norman, Okla., 1970), vii-viii, 185-187.

tion instead of property in the lower house would "enable the poor but numerous Inhabitants of the western Country to destroy the Atlantic States."[44] They seized the opportunity to broaden the debate and attacked proportional representation of population in the lower chamber on the grounds that population was an unstable rule and an improper index of political ability. At Morris's suggestion the delegates appointed a new committee, including himself, Nathaniel Gorham, Edmund Randolph, John Rutledge, and Rufus King, to restudy the Gerry report. Morris then proposed that the Convention determine the representation in the lower house of the first Congress and that the federal legislature exercise this power thereafter.[45]

Morris's committee, however, did not dismiss the principle of including slaves in fixing representation. Its report divided fifty-six representatives in the lower house among the states "upon the principles of their wealth and number of inhabitants." When questioned what the committee meant by the rule of "wealth and number of inhabitants," Nathanial Gorham of Massachusetts explained that they had taken into consideration "the number of blacks and whites with some regard to supposed wealth" as their guide,[46] but the specific formula was not detailed in the report. The most important aspect of the Morris report was the power to determine future representation it gave to the national Congress, guided only by the vague rule of "wealth and number of inhabitants." Legislative control over the formula of representation would permit established states to fix the representation of new.

Significantly, the sponsors of both the New Jersey and Virginia plans opposed the Morris report. William Paterson disliked including slaves in any calculation of representation, although ironically, his most outspoken opposition to the idea was directed at Morris's report, which did not contain an explicit statement of the three-fifths rule. Edmund Randolph likewise opposed the Morris report. He feared that legislative control of representation would result in a small political faction in Congress postponing readjustments as the population increased or shifted, leaving power in the hands of the Atlantic states while the people moved westward. Madison, too, objected to the late introduction of the principle that the legislature should represent "wealth" after the committee of the

[44] Farrand, ed., *Records*, I, 536.
[45] *Ibid.*, 540-542.
[46] *Ibid.*, 559-560.

whole had accepted the idea that it should reflect population.[47] Representation based on wealth, even though the latter included slaves, would create a legislature under the domination of the existing states, with no provision for automatic adjustments in the future.

Confronted with these numerous objections, the delegates returned Morris's report to another committee composed of one member from each state. On July 10 the new chairman, Rufus King, submitted a second report which created more problems than it solved. King's committee proposed to increase representation in the lower house of the first Congress from fifty-six, as was suggested in the Morris report, to sixty-five. In this increase the New England states gained more representatives than the southern states, and the report stimulated sectional suspicions. King stirred more when he foolishly defended the increased representation for New England by claiming that it was a fair price for counting the slaves. Arguing that the real conflict was "between the Southern and Eastern [states]," he warned that New Englanders would demand concessions and offered to agree to count the slaves if it did not create a southern majority in the first Congress and if the South yielded certain commercial rights to New England.[48] By connecting the slave issue to sectional interests, however, King changed its significance in the Convention's debates, and by using it to justify concessions for New England, he inadvertently set the stage for the defeat of the proposal to leave control of representation to the national legislature. Although he talked of sectional compromise, neither he nor Morris endorsed an explicit rule which would

[47] Ibid., 561-562.
[48] Ibid., 566-567. It is significant, because it reveals the motives and values of King, that on the day Madison opposed the Morris report King defended it. King willingly defended the principle of counting slaves when the rule was not explicit, when representation ratios would be controlled by the national Congress, and when he believed that the South would grant major sectional concessions because of it. It is incorrect, however, on the basis of King's ideas, to suggest that the North agreed to the clause in order "to obtain a government that would protect its commercial, financial, and industrial interests." Simpson, "Slave Representation," *Journal Southern Hist.*, VII (1941), 319. As late as August 8, King tried to connect the principle of counting slaves with commercial concessions. After the committee on detail restricted national power over commerce he insisted that "either slaves should not be represented, or exports should be taxable." As a measure of northern sentiment, however, it is noteworthy that the majority refused to support him. The last vote on the three-fifths clause came on August 8 when King tried to establish a sectional compromise between the counting of slaves and national control of commerce. Only New Jersey joined him. Farrand, ed., *Records*, II, 220-223.

guarantee that slaves would be used in the future to determine representation. Both wanted to protect the interests of Atlantic states by having future legislatures determine representation,[49] and both also wanted concessions from the South in exchange for including slaves in determining representation. But the first objective conflicted with the second, as they soon discovered when South Carolina, while supporting Morris's position against the West, reacted to King's attitude toward the South. Since his report gave no assurance of how the national legislature might view the question of representation for the South in the future, King undermined South Carolina's support for the idea of legislative control over representation when he suggested that enumeration of slaves was a matter for negotiation even in the Convention.

King's behavior garnered additional southern votes for the republican position that the sovereignty of the people demanded a periodic census to determine representation and prevent the development of rotten boroughs under the domination of entrenched faction. Subsequently, Edmund Randolph and Hugh Williamson proposed "that in order to ascertain the alterations that may happen in the population and wealth of the several States a census shall be taken of the free inhabitants of each State, and three fifths of . . . [those] of other description" and that "the representation [be regulated] accordingly."[50] The South Carolinians, however, did not like the resolution. Previously they had supported the three-fifths rule, but after listening to Rufus King, demanded that "blacks be included in the rule of Representation, *equally* with the Whites." They were also disturbed by the particular wording of Randolph's and Williamson's motion. In James Wilson's proposal slaves had been classified as persons, but Randolph and Williamson appeared to regard them as property when they retained Morris's phrase "population and wealth." If that was to be the case, the South Carolinians wanted all the slaves counted. Pierce

[49] While King may have harbored antislavery sentiments, his biographer correctly points out that King was not a moralist. There is no evidence to suggest that King's opposition to slavery shaped his attitude toward representation or western expansion in 1787. He feared the political power of the West more than he feared slavery because he was willing to accept the principle of counting slaves as long as the counting was done by the national legislature. Robert Ernst, *Rufus King, American Federalist* (Chapel Hill, N. C., 1968), 107n. See also Joseph L. Arbena, "Politics or Principle? Rufus King and the Opposition to Slavery, 1785-1825," *Essex Institute Historical Collections,* CI (1965), 65.

[50] Farrand, ed., *Records,* I, 575-580.

Butler argued that economically the "labour of a slave in South Carolina was as productive and valuable as that of a freeman in Massachusetts, that as wealth was the great means of defence and utility to the Nation they were equally valuable to it with freemen; and that consequently an equal representation ought to be allowed for them in a Government which was instituted principally for the protection of property."[51] By no means was the South united behind South Carolina on this matter, however. George Mason, a planter-aristocrat from Virginia who owned about three hundred slaves, was for counting the slaves in some way, but he could not philosophically "regard them as equal to freemen and could not vote for them as such."[52]

But the major attack upon Randolph's and Williamson's census came from Gouverneur Morris. He admitted that his primary "objection was that the number of inhabitants was not a proper standard of wealth," and to prevent northern support for the census opened an attack on the three-fifths clause. Ironically, Paterson had used the same tactic earlier against Morris's report. Morris did not object to counting slaves for purposes of representation, but he was against basing representation on population calculated by a constitutional census. He cleverly exploited poor verbal construction in Randolph's and Williamson's proposal, which was phrased so that the word "population" paralleled "free inhabitants" and the word "wealth," the phrase "three-fifths of those of other descriptions." Morris wanted to know whether Randolph and Williamson intended slaves to be considered as wealth and, if they did, "Why... no other wealth but slaves [was] included." Moreover, he warned that the North would reject the Constitution if the idea of counting slaves was made explicit in a census. Rufus King agreed that the proposed census "would excite great discontents among the States having no slaves."[53] Although he claimed that he opposed the census because of the three-fifths clause, King like Morris would clearly have opposed it anyway. The confused phraseology of Randolph's and Williamson's statement, plus the sectional attack on it by Morris and King, resulted in a temporary defeat of the three-fifths principle as it was set forth in the census proposal. Delegates who had already accepted the general principle of counting slaves agreed that it might cause difficulties during

[51] Ibid., 580-582.
[52] Ibid., 581; McDonald, We the People, 72.
[53] Farrand, ed., Records, I, 582-586.

ratification. James Wilson himself was convinced that the proposal was impolitic, because northerners would find it difficult to accept a census that explicitly combined "blacks with whites."

Thus, the Convention's third vote on the three-fifths principle, a vote on *how* the principle would appear in the Constitution, resulted in its rejection. At the same time Morris achieved his primary objective with the unanimous defeat of Randolph's and Williamson's plan for a census. The significance of this vote has not always been seen because the sectional rhetoric of the debate obscured the fact that the actual clash was over the census and not the three-fifths clause.[54]

The rejection of the census forced the delegates to return to consideration of Morris's report which granted "the Legislature . . . authority to regulate the number of Representatives . . . upon the principles of their wealth and number of inhabitants."[55] Just as had King, Morris promised that under the plan the legislature would take slaves into account in its calculations. The principle of including them in determining representation was not in dispute in spite of Morris's and King's denunciation of the three-fifths clause. The difference between the plans was that in Morris's the principle would be *implicit* whereas in Randolph's and Williamson's it was *explicit*.

Morris's victory was short-lived, however. He had warned that an explicit statement of a three-fifths rule would encourage the importation of slaves, and South Carolinians, who opposed any federal interference with the slave trade, worried about his ultimate intentions. The day after his defeat of the census, some delegates became paranoic. William R. Davie of North Carolina saw a northern conspiracy existing "to deprive the Southern States of any share of Representation for their blacks" and threatened that his state would not join a union without a three-fifths clause and a census. Others demanded that the system of representation be fixed "and the execution of it enforced by the Constitution." Morris had not expected this development and pleaded with southerners not to force the northern states to consider "a representation of Negroes" during ratification. "What can be desired by these [southern] States more," he begged, "than has been already proposed; that the Legislature shall from time to time regulate Representation according to population and

[54] *Ibid.*, 586-588.
[55] *Ibid.*, 559, 591.

wealth."⁵⁶ Ratification of the Constitution would be easier in the North if northerners did not know that they were approving the principle of counting slaves in a rule of representation controlled by Congress.

Southern representatives, however, demanded that the three-fifths principle be made explicit in the Constitution. The more Morris tried to defend his position the more chimeras he raised. South Carolinians began to transform the whole issue into a defense of the institution of slavery. Charles C. Pinckney, the cousin of Charles Pinckney and a planter who had lost nearly two hundred slaves during the Revolution,⁵⁷ called for a census so that "property in slaves should not be exposed to danger under a Government instituted for the protection of property." Edmund Randolph catered to the growing southern apprehension by demanding "that *express* security ought to be provided for including slaves in the ratio of Representation."⁵⁸

In order to calm fears, Morris offered a minor concession that ultimately destroyed his whole plan. He suggested that the rule of representation be adjusted to the rule of direct taxation. Without specifying *which* tax, Morris moved "that direct taxation ought to be proportioned to representation."⁵⁹ He refused, however, to alter the major aspect of his plan. The power to apportion both direct taxes and representation would reside in the legislature. Morris's concession merely limited congressional power in an indirect manner; the assumption was that congressmen would not indiscriminately increase the representation of their states if the same action resulted in an increase of their direct taxes. Direct taxation and representation would always be in the same ratio; the exact formula for each would be determined by Congress, not the Constitution.

This was not a substantive concession to southerners or those who wanted the legislature to reflect the population of an expanding republic automatically. For them the problem was how to provide for a census which contained an explicit rule of representation without raising the hackles of scrupulous northerners during ratification. James Wilson solved the problem by building on Morris's idea while destroying its most important part. He suggested that the rule of direct taxation be ex-

⁵⁶ *Ibid.*, 592-593.
⁵⁷ McDonald, *We the People*, 80.
⁵⁸ Farrand, ed., *Records*, I, 593-594. Italics added.
⁵⁹ *Ibid.*, 592-593.

plicit and recommended that it be the 1783 rule containing the three-fifths clause. The rule of representation would then be the same as the rule of direct taxation.[60] Wilson had neatly turned the tables to destroy congressional control over the rule of representation. What appeared to be a quid pro quo in the final draft of the Constitution obscured the real dispute in the Convention, where the struggle over the three-fifths clause had not been a sectional quarrel over the representation and taxation of slaves. The principle of counting slaves in some manner for the purposes of representation had long been generally acceded to, and while Wilson's specific solution helped still northern criticism during ratification by permitting Federalists to point out the tax concession, the latter was no concession at all because the delegates had not envisioned direct taxes as a major source of revenue. When Rufus King later asked the delegates, "what was the precise meaning of *direct* taxation?," no one was able to answer him.[61] Wilson's motion was a device for basing the rule of representation on a census ordained by the Constitution[62] and was not opposed by southern delegates. The Convention approved Wilson's plan by a vote of six to two. Only New Jersey and Delaware opposed it, as they had Wilson's earlier motion in the committee of the whole. This time, however, Massachusetts and South Carolina each also divided its vote.[63] James Wilson had achieved a political marriage of the slave interest with the ideals of expansive and popular republicanism. Southern concerns about slavery helped to assure a more democratic procedure for determining representation. Sectionalism undeniably was an important factor in Convention politics, but the final form of the three-fifths clause was determined by more than a struggle between the North and the South. It was also propounded by delegates who preferred a fixed constitutional rule for the determination of representation rather than leaving it to the dictates of

[60] *Ibid.,* 595.
[61] *Ibid.,* II, 350.
[62] George Ticknor Curtis, *Constitutional History of the United States from Their Declaration of Independence to the Close of the Civil War,* I (New York, 1889), 416. My views owe a great deal to Curtis's interpretation of the three-fifths clause. Curtis's work has been ignored generally because he continued to write about the Constitution within the abolitionist frame of reference while other historians were beginning to ignore slavery as a central problem in American politics. See also Warren, *Making of the Constitution,* 291, 585n. In an otherwise perceptive analysis, Warren failed to see that the three-fifths clause was connected with the issue of a census instead of slavery.
[63] Farrand, ed., *Records,* I, 596-597.

the national legislature.[64] The price of popular republicanism for whites, however, was explicit recognition of slavery in the United States Constitution.

Exactly how much of a concession it was will always be debated.[65] It would have been impossible to establish a national government in the eighteenth century without recognizing slavery in some way, and it can be argued that recognition did not imply approval of the institution. On the other hand, southerners in the Convention and during ratification did refer to the clause as a concession to the South.[66] At the same time, it held out an inducement to southerners to free their slaves by promising to increase their representation in proportion.[67]

Opposition to the clause during ratification was for the most part not in terms of its effect on the institution of slavery. Many northern antifederalists objected to it, not because it sanctioned slavery, but because it violated Lockean principles of government. John Locke had not written with a slave society in mind, but a Massachusetts antifederalist could quote him to prove that men "being in the state of slavery, not capable of

[64] S. Sidney Ulmer has recently identified four voting blocs of states in the Constitutional Convention: Sub-group I (S. C., Ga., and N. C.); Sub-group II (N. Y., N. J., Conn., Del., and Md.); Sub-group III (Mass. and N. H.); and Sub-group IV (Pa. and Va.). While sectional forces in American politics were present in the Constitutional Convention, Ulmer's statistical work suggests that regionalism was more powerful than sectionalism in shaping voting blocs. He concluded "that the factors dividing and allying state delegations in the Convention were regional in nature." Moreover, as the cooperation between Madison and Wilson demonstrated, "on issues relating to population . . . Virginia and Pennsylvania frequently voted together." The fight for a census was led by Sub-group IV. S. Sidney Ulmer, "Sub-group Formation in the Constitutional Convention," *Midwest Journal of Political Science*, X (1966), 288-303.
[65] Howard A. Ohline, Politics and Slavery: The Issue of Slavery in National Politics, 1787-1815 (unpubl. Ph.D. diss., University of Missouri, 1969), 22-66.
[66] William Blount *et al.* to Richard Caswell, Philadelphia, Sept. 18, 1787, Walter Clark, ed., *The State Records of North Carolina*, XX (Goldsboro, N. C., 1902), 777-779; [Tench Coxe], "Address to the Honourable Members of the Convention of Virginia," *The American Museum, or Repository of Ancient and Modern Fugitive Pieces, Prose and Poetical*, III (Jan.-June 1788), 426-433.
[67] Henry Tazewell to Thomas Jefferson, July 12, 1798, Jefferson Papers, Library of Congress, microfilm. In this letter which was written when Congress was debating the passage of the first direct tax Tazewell recommended that the tax on slaves over 50 years old be kept very high so that owners would be encouraged to free them and the southern states would increase their representation.

any property, cannot, in the state, be considered as any part of civil society, the chief end whereof, is the preservation of property."[68] "Brutus," a New York antifederalist whose articles circulated in New England, cited Montesquieu to demonstrate that in a free society the legislative power resided in the representatives of men who were free agents. Slaves were not free agents, and "it has never been alleged that those who are not free agents can . . . have anything to do in government, either by themselves or others."[69] Other northerners opposed it because they thought that northern property as well should be included in the rule of representation.[70] Basically the debate over the clause during ratification continued within the frame of reference established in the Convention. Although Luther Martin of Maryland warned that it would encourage the slave trade because it increased representation for new slaves imported from Africa,[71] no antislavery activist of the eighteenth century condemned it publicly as a sanction of the institution of slavery.[72] Moral condemnation of the clause emerged largely among later generations and for different reasons. The evidence, while admittedly impressionistic, suggests that in 1787 the counting of slaves for purposes of representation was not viewed as specific endorsement of slavery. When the delegates discussed the three-fifths clause they were usually talking about representation, not the power of the national government over the institution of slavery. Although at some point in the debates southerners interpreted the issue as such and rose to a defense of slavery, the general acceptance of the need

[68] "A Republican Federalist," *Massachusetts Centinel* (Boston), Jan. 19, 1788.
[69] "Brutus," quoted in Morton Borden, ed., *The Antifederalist Papers* (East Lansing, Mich., 1965), 154-155; Jackson T. Main, *The Antifederalists: Critics of the Constitution, 1781-1788* (Chapel Hill, N. C., 1961), 287, identified "Brutus" as Robert Yates.
[70] Thomas B. Waite to George Thacher, Jan. 8, 1788, Silas Lee to Thacher, Jan. 23, 1788, Thacher Papers, Chamberlin Collections, Boston Public Library; Hugh Williamson to James Iredell, July 7, 1788, Griffith J. McRee, *Life and Correspondence of James Iredell, One of the Associate Justices of the Supreme Court of the United States*, II (New York, 1858), 227.
[71] Martin, *Genuine Information*, in Farrand, ed., *Records*, III, 211.
[72] Many antislavery organizers either supported the Constitution or objected to the failure of the delegates to end the importation of slaves immediately. William Rotch to Moses Brown, Nov. 8, 1787, James Pemberton to Brown, Nov. 16, 1787, quoted in Thomas E. Drake, *Quakers and Slavery in America* (New Haven, Conn., 1950), 102, 88; Samuel Hopkins to Levi Hart, Jan. 29, 1788, Edward A. Parks, ed., *The Works of Samuel Hopkins*, I (Boston, 1852), 158; Brown to [?], Nov. 13, 1787, Richard T. Cadbury Collection, Haverford College, Haverford, Pa.

to count slaves in computing representation was most often related to eighteenth-century ideas about the proper structure of a national republican legislature and the need for a periodic census.

The three-fifths clause in its final form was the major instrument in uniting slave and nonslave states in a national legislature that represented a significant advance over the static form of English constitutional structure. Slavery and the fears of slaveholders acted to assure a more democratic political system for white men. The regrettable paradox of American Revolutionary republicanism was that the new nation had to acknowledge the existence of slavery in its legislature in order to be republican and that the major dispute in the Convention was not whether this should or should not be, but *how* it would be done.

The Electoral College at Philadelphia: The Evolution of an Ad Hoc Congress for the Selection of a President

Shlomo Slonim

With the approach of the bicentennial of the adoption of the Constitution, attention is once again focused on the drafting of that remarkable instrument of government. Among the provisions of the Constitution assured of closer examination is the one dealing with the Electoral College, the system devised by the Founding Fathers for the election of a chief executive.[1] No other constitutional provision gave them so much difficulty in its formulation. The subject of the method of electing a president was brought up in the Constitutional Convention on twenty-one different days and occasioned over thirty distinct votes on various phases of the subject. Over the years no other provision has drawn so much criticism or provoked so many constitutional amendments as has the Electoral College clause. Close to seven hundred proposals to amend the Electoral College scheme have been introduced into Congress since the Constitution was inaugurated in 1789. The most recent effort to revise the system for electing a president was undertaken in 1979, when a constitutional amendment, moved by Sen. Birch E. Bayh, Jr., of Indiana and endorsed by President Jimmy Carter, to institute popular election of the president, was soundly defeated.[2]

Two main interpretations have been put forward to explain the adoption of the Electoral College provision. On the one hand, the Progressive school, represented by such writers as J. Allen Smith and Charles Beard, maintained that the complicated, indirect method instituted for selecting a chief executive was a reflection of the Founding Fathers' deep distrust of democracy. The Framers, according to that

Shlomo Slonim is chairman of the Department of American Studies at The Hebrew University, Jerusalem.

[1] Constitution of the United States, Article II, sec. 1.

[2] Max Farrand, ed., *The Records of the Federal Convention of 1787* (4 vols., New Haven, 1937), II, 501, III, 166, 329, 458, 459. According to Max Farrand, "Whatever difficulties might have been encountered in other directions, they paled into insignificance in comparison with the problem before the convention of determining a satisfactory method of electing the executive." Max Farrand, *The Framing of the Constitution of the United States* (New Haven, 1913), 160. See also Max Farrand, "Compromises of the Constitution," *American Historical Review*, 9 (April 1904), 486; Herman V. Ames, *The Proposed Amendments to the Constitution of the United States during the First Century of Its History* (Washington, 1897), 75–76; Sen. Doc. No. 93, 69 Cong., 1 sess. (1926); Sen. Doc. No. 163, 87 Cong., 2 sess. (1963); Sen. Doc. No. 38, 91 Cong., 1 sess. (1969); Richard A. David, Congressional Research Service of Library of Congress, Report No. 85-36 Gov.; *Congress and the Nation*. V, 1977–1980 (Washington, 1981), 941–43; U.S. Congress, Senate, Committee of the Judiciary, *Direct Popular Election of the President and Vice President of the United States*, 96 Cong., April 9, 1979; and *Public Papers of the Presidents of the United States, Jimmy Carter 1977*, bk. 1, March 22, 1977 (Washington, 1980), 481–85.

view, deliberately precluded popular choice of the president to ensure that the leveling force of the masses would not threaten the rights of the propertied minority. That economic-determinist thesis has, in turn, been vigorously challenged by John P. Roche, who asserts that the Electoral College was but a last-minute compromise designed to allow the Constitutional Convention to wind up its business. It was, he writes, merely a "jerry-rigged improvisation . . . subsequently . . . endowed with a high theoretical content. . . . No one seemed to think well of the College as an institution. . . . The future was left to cope with the problem of what to do with this Rube Goldberg mechanism."[3]

Roche's antideterminist interpretation clearly denies an overall design to the Electoral College; it was in the nature of a makeshift contraption. That is not, however, the way contemporaries viewed the Electoral College. According to Abraham Baldwin, delegate for Georgia (as reported by John Pickering), "late in their session the present complex mode of electing the President and Vice-President was proposed; that the mode was perfectly novel, and therefore occasioned a pause; but when explained and fully considered was universally admired, and viewed as the most pleasing feature in the Constitution." And Alexander Hamilton, in Federalist No. 68, wrote: "The mode of appointment of the Chief Magistrate of the United States is almost the only part of the system, of any consequence, which has escaped without severe censure, or which has received the slightest mark of approbation from its opponents. . . . I venture somewhat further, and hesitate not to affirm that if the manner of it be not perfect, it is at least excellent." Max Farrand, in his succinct work, *The Framing of the Constitution of the United States*, sums up the attitude of the Framers toward the Electoral College: "For of all things done in the convention the members seemed to have been prouder of that than of any other, and they seemed to regard it as having solved the problem for any country of how to choose a chief magistrate."[4]

The true rationale and purpose of the Electoral College scheme can best be unraveled by a close examination of the Constitutional Convention debates. By following the tortuous course the Framers took during the summer months of 1787, we can gain insight into the influences that led them to institute such a complex procedure for selecting a president. The records of the convention debates also shed light on the extent to which the Founding Fathers were consciously guided by such factors as prevailing political theories and past republican practices—ancient or modern. In particular, how prominently did the state constitutional precedents

[3] J. Allen Smith, *The Spirit of American Government: A Study of the Constitution: Its Origin, Influence and Relation to Democracy* (New York, 1907), 135–36, 165; Charles A. Beard, *An Economic Interpretation of the Constitution of the United States* (New York, 1913), 161–62; John P. Roche, "The Founding Fathers: A Reform Caucus in Action," *American Political Science Review*, 55 (Dec. 1961), 799–816, esp. 810–11. John P. Roche was not the first to highlight the compromise nature of the Electoral College. See Farrand, "Compromises of the Constitution," 479–89; Farrand, *Framing of the Constitution*, 166–67; and Charles Warren, *The Making of the Constitution* (Boston, 1937), 621–23. Neither of the latter writers have accepted the assertion that in the eyes of the Framers the Electoral College was "a jerry-rigged improvisation." See the comments of Gouverneur Morris and James Madison in Farrand, *Records*, III, 405, 458, 464.

[4] Farrand, *Records*, III, 132, 403; E. M. Earle, ed., *The Federalist* (New York, n.d.), 441; Farrand, *Framing of the Constitution*, 175.

figure in the deliberations at Philadelphia? Did the other well-known clashes at the convention—large states versus small states, federalists versus nationalists, slaveholders versus nonslaveholders—inform the Electoral College debates? A detailed analysis of the 1787 discussions should also help to explain why the Electoral College scheme encountered so little criticism in the state ratifying conventions.[5]

Both the Virginia Plan and the New Jersey Plan, the foundation documents of the Constitution, called for election of the executive by the legislature, as was the practice in all but three of the states. In two of the three states where the choice was by popular election, in the event that no candidate received a clear majority, the choice would fall on the legislature. During the debates the delegates frequently referred to this pattern of state practice.[6]

That both the Virginia and the New Jersey plans endorsed selection by the legislature did not mean that they were at one on the mode of election. The legislature, in each case, was a very different body. Whereas the Virginia Plan provided for a popularly elected legislature with the representation of each state proportional to the size of its population, the New Jersey Plan proposed that the legislature remain (as under the Articles of Confederation) the representative body of the states, with each state entitled to one vote. Thus while the Virginia Plan called for a "National Executive" to be chosen by the "National Legislature," the New Jersey Plan envisaged a "federal Executive" to be appointed by "the U. States in Congs." In effect, therefore, at the very outset of the convention, the large and small states were at loggerheads over the method of selecting an executive no less than they were over the composition of the legislature.[7]

When, on June 1, the convention moved to debate the scheme outlined in the Virginia Plan for selection of the executive (the New Jersey Plan was first submitted on June 15), three distinct, but interrelated, issues arose for discussion: (1) the mode of election; (2) the term of office; and (3) the question of reeligibility. The three

[5] See the statements of James Wilson and Rufus King in Farrand, *Records*, III, 166, 461. See also that of Madison at the Virginia ratifying convention in Jonathan Elliot, ed., *The Debates in the Several State Conventions, on the Adoption of the Federal Constitution* (5 vols., Philadelphia, 1881), III, 494. See also Cecelia M. Kenyon, "Men of Little Faith: The Anti-Federalists on the Nature of Representative Government," *William and Mary Quarterly*, 12 (Jan. 1955), 13.

[6] Farrand, *Records*, I, 20–22, 242–45. In both plans the term of office was left blank while reeligibility was ruled out. Election of the executive by the legislature was provided for under the constitutions of Delaware, Georgia, Maryland, North Carolina, New Jersey, Pennsylvania, South Carolina, and Virginia. (In every instance of a bicameral legislature the executive was chosen by joint ballot. Other officers of government, however, were chosen by regular legislative procedures, allowing each house to exercise a veto on the choice of the other. On occasion that procedure produced deadlock and crisis.) Popular election of the executive was provided for under the constitutions of Massachusetts, New Hampshire, and New York. Under the last a simple plurality was sufficient to be elected, and there was no provision for a contingency choice. But in the former two, in the absence of a popular majority for any one candidate, the lower house chose two out of the top four candidates, and the upper house made the final choice out of the two selected. Ben: Perley Poore, comp., *The Federal and State Constitutions, Colonial Charters, and Other Organic Laws of the United States* (2 vols., Washington, 1877). Contingency proposals surfaced frequently during the convention debates and, of course, the Electoral College scheme contains such an arrangement.

[7] During the course of the convention two further plans were presented: the Pinckney Plan (May 29) and the Hamilton Plan (June 18). Under the former the executive would be chosen annually by both houses of the legislature in joint session; under the latter the executive would be selected by electors chosen by the people and would serve during good behavior. Neither plan figured in the convention debates and neither was ever voted on. The Hamilton Plan was not even moved to committee. Farrand, *Records*, I, 292, II, 135, III, 606, 617.

issues formed a sort of tripod where an imbalance on one side disrupted the balance of the whole. Since the executive was to be elected by the legislature, it was deemed essential that he not be eligible for reelection, for reeligibility would compromise his independence; but if he was to serve only one term, then it ought to be a reasonably lengthy one. The relationship between reeligibility and term of office was stressed throughout the debate. James Wilson favored a three-year term "on the supposition that a reeligibility would be provided for." This was endorsed by Roger Sherman who was "agst. the doctrine of [compulsory] rotation as throwing out of office the men best qualified to execute its duties." George Mason, on the other hand, favored "seven years at least" and a prohibition on reeligibility "as the best expedient both for preventing the effect of a false complaisance on the side of the Legislature towards unfit characters; and a temptation on the side of the Executive to intrigue with the Legislature for a re-appointment." In short order the convention, by a vote of 8 to 2, endorsed Mason's viewpoint (moved by Charles Pinckney) and decided that the executive should be chosen by the legislature for a seven-year term without right of reelection.[8] This was but the first of many times that the convention would settle for this formula.

In the course of the debate, two diverse, even conflicting challenges were directed at the proposed scheme. Wilson, a delegate from Pennsylvania and "a nationalist of the nationalists," advocated popular election of the executive. That system of electing "the first magistrate," he declared, though "it might appear chimerical," was really "a convenient and successful mode" as the experience of New York and Massachusetts had proven. On the next day, June 2, Wilson submitted a motion to divide the states into districts, the voters in each district to choose electors who, in turn, would select the "executive Magistracy." (The intervention of electors did not, apparently, make it any less "an election by the people" in Wilson's eyes.) In supporting his proposal Wilson argued for "an election without the intervention of the States." His suggestion evoked interest but also considerable skepticism. Thus Mason said he favored the idea but thought it "impracticable." Similarly, Elbridge Gerry of Massachusetts said he "liked the principle" but feared "that it would alarm & give a handle to the State partizans, as tending to supersede altogether the State authorities."[9]

And, indeed, at that very sitting, one of the convention's foremost "State partizans," John Dickinson of Delaware, moved "that the Executive be made remove-

[8] *Ibid.*, I, 68–88, III, 132, 167; Roche, "Founding Fathers," 810; George Bancroft, *History of the Formation of the Constitution of the United States of America* (2 vols., New York, 1889), II, 166.

[9] Charles C. Thach, Jr., *The Creation of the Presidency, 1775–1789: A Study in Constitutional History* (Baltimore, 1923), 85; Farrand, *Records*, I, 68, 69, 77, 80. This was the first of many times in the debate that the use of electors was proposed. Ultimately, of course, the convention adopted a system of indirect election in the form of the Electoral College. One can speculate on the precedents for the introduction of an intermediate step in the selection of an executive. In the Massachusetts ratifying convention, former Gov. James Bowdoin declared, "This method of choosing was probably taken from the manner of choosing senators under the constitution of Maryland." Elliot, *Debates in the Several State Conventions*, II, 127–28. Under that constitution the people chose electors, who, in turn, selected the fifteen members of the state Senate for a five year term. In Federalist No. 63 Madison gave high praise to that feature of the Maryland constitution. See also Ames, *Proposed Amendments*, 75–76. For Elbridge Gerry's role in the convention, see George Athan Billias, *Elbridge Gerry, Founding Father and Republican Statesman* (New York, 1976), 153–205, 331–39.

able by the National Legislature on the request of a majority of the Legislatures of individual States." "He had no idea of abolishing the State Governments as some gentlemen seemed inclined to do. . . . He hoped that each State would retain an equal voice at least in one branch of the National Legislature." James Madison and Wilson both objected to Dickinson's motion on the ground (inter alia) "that it would leave an equality of agency in the small with the great States."[10]

Neither Wilson's nor Dickinson's motion was received with much sympathy. (The votes were 2 to 8 and 1 to 9, respectively.) But these divergent suggestions reflected a contrast of views on the measure of state control to be exercised in the selection of the executive. In the eyes of such a nationalist as Wilson, even election by the legislature detracted from the national independent stature of the executive, whereas for Dickinson the states were not accorded adequate control over the nation's chief executive officer. The two viewpoints, in one shape or another, arose repeatedly during the numerous discussions the convention was to hold on the mode of electing an executive. Dickinson's comment on the composition of the legislature foreshadowed, at this early stage of the discussions, the growing dissatisfaction of the smaller states, with their diminished role in the organs of government.[11]

On June 15 (some two weeks after Dickinson's address), William Paterson presented the New Jersey Plan to the convention, and the issue of the small states versus the large states was joined. The controversy was not settled until July 7, after three weeks of protracted discussions. The Connecticut Compromise, which emerged, resolved the issue of the composition of the legislature.[12] But had it equally settled the procedure for the election of the executive? At first glance it would appear that it had done so since the convention's earlier decision to provide for election of the executive by the legislature remained intact. Delegates could not but realize, however, that the new legislature was a creature very different from the body previously entrusted with the task of selecting an executive. For one thing, the upper house now represented the states. Furthermore, as a result of the principle of equality of representation in the upper house, the smaller states would exercise willy-nilly an inordinate influence on the selection of a chief executive. It is perhaps not surprising, therefore, that no sooner had the convention adopted the Connecticut Compromise than the issue of the mode of electing the chief executive arose once again.

On July 17 Gouverneur Morris, one of the "leading conservatives" of the convention (and probably its "most brilliant member"), criticized the earlier decision to leave the selection of the nation's chief magistrate in the hands of the legislature. He moved to insert, in place of "National Legislature," "citizens of U.S."

[10] Farrand, *Records*, I, 78, 85, 86, 87, 244.
[11] *Ibid.*, 77, 78, 81, 87. Delaware, John Dickinson's state, alone favored his proposal. There is evidence that even before a quorum had assembled at the Constitutional Convention, the smaller states were already evincing anxiety about the outcome. See the letter of George Read of Delaware to Dickinson on May 21 in *ibid.*, III, 25–26. Subsequently Dickinson endorsed election of the executive "by the people as the best and purest source." *Ibid.*, II, 114. Clearly, Dickinson's present move was designed to ensure a federal system of government in which the role of the states was not entirely eclipsed.
[12] *Ibid.*, I, 242–45, 549–51.

He ought to be elected by the people at large, by the freeholders of the Country. . . . If the people should elect, they will never fail to prefer some man of distinguished character, or services; some man . . . of continental reputation. If the Legislature elect, it will be the work of intrigue, of cabal, and of faction. . . . He will be the mere creature of the Legisl: if appointed and impeachable by that body.[13]

Wilson supported the Morris motion for popular election and dismissed the argument that a majority of the people might be unable to agree on any one candidate. In such event, he said, "the expedient used in Masts." could be employed with the legislature choosing between the leading candidates. "This would restrain the choice to a good nomination at least, and prevent in a great degree intrigue & cabal." In response, Pinckney of South Carolina highlighted the fears of the smaller states.

[He] did not expect this question would again have been brought forward; An Election by the people being liable to the most obvious & striking objections. They will be led by a few active & designing men. The most populous States by combining in favor of the same individual will be able to carry their points.

Sherman of Connecticut also gave voice to the concern of the small states.

The sense of the Nation would be better expressed by the Legislature than by the people at large. The latter will never be sufficiently informed of characters, and besides will never give a majority of votes to any one man. They will generally vote for some man in their own State, and the largest State will have the best chance for the appointment.[14]

The smaller states clearly were concerned that in a straight-out popular election the larger states would overwhelm them. The smaller states had not fought for equality in one branch of the legislature only to see control of the executive go by default.

Mason of Virginia (a large state) did not share the fears of the small states. Nonetheless, he was sharply critical of the suggestion for nationwide popular election of the executive. He graphically portrayed the inability of the people to select a national figure:

He conceived it would be as unnatural to refer the choice of a proper character for a Chief Magistrate to the people, as it would, to refer a trial of colours to a blind man. The extent of the Country renders it impossible that the people can have the requisite capacity to judge of the respective pretensions of the Candidates.[15]

This passage is frequently cited as evidence of the Framers' lack of faith in democracy. If the words are examined in their context, however, it is evident that Mason was not challenging the *right* of the people to choose but, rather, their *ability* to

[13] Thach, *Creation of the Presidency, 1775–1789*, 35; Farrand, *Framing of the Constitution*, 21; Farrand, *Records*, II, 22, 29.
[14] Farrand, *Records*, II, 29–30.
[15] *Ibid.*, 31.

do so given the size of the electoral district within which they would have to exercise that right. The vast expanse of the United States, the difficulty of communication, and the unfamiliarity of the general populace with national personalities—all militated against an informed choice. In fact, as noted above, Mason had earlier expressed himself in favor of popular election but considered it "impractical," for the reasons, no doubt, he now enumerated by reference to "the extent of the Country." As Cecelia M. Kenyon, in discussing the stand of the anti-Federalists, has written:

> This belief that larger electoral districts would inevitably be to the advantage of the well-to-do partially explains the almost complete lack of criticism of the indirect election of the Senate and the President. If the "middling" class could not be expected to compete successfully with the upper class in Congressional elections, still less could they do so in state-wide or nation-wide elections. It was a matter where size was of the essence. True representation . . . could be achieved only where electoral districts were small.

It was in this sense that Mason, for one, found fault with nationwide elections of the executive. Under the circumstances, popular election of the executive would have the trappings of representative democracy but not the essence.[16]

The final speaker on Gouverneur Morris's proposal for popular election of the executive was Hugh Williamson of North Carolina, who added a new slant to the discussions. He reiterated the point made by the earlier speakers that "the people will be sure to vote for some man in their own State, and the largest State will be sure to succede." He went on to say, "This will not be Virga. however. Her slaves will have no suffrage." Williamson was adverting to a key advantage that the slave states presently enjoyed in the projected lower house, where slaves counted three-fifths for purposes of representation. If a system for direct popular election of the executive were instituted, the slave states stood to lose that advantage because only the enfranchised white population could actually vote, and the increment derived from the slaves would be lost. In effect, adoption of the Connecticut Compromise had forged a natural alliance between the small states and the slave states in reserving decisions for the legislature as currently constituted. The slave states gained an advantage in the lower house, and the smaller states gained one in the Senate (small slave states, such as the Carolinas, had a double advantage). It is hardly surprising, therefore, that Morris's motion for popular election was rejected by a vote of 1 to 9 with only his own state, Pennsylvania, voting in favor. Luther Martin of Maryland then proposed that the executive be chosen by electors appointed by the state legislatures. The proposal was defeated by a vote of 2 to 8. Election of the executive by the legislature was thereupon unanimously reendorsed.[17]

---

[16] Kenyon, "Men of Little Faith," 13. This analysis is reflected in Wilson's argument in the Pennsylvania Ratifying Convention on the method of electing a president. Farrand, *Records*, III, 167. See also Billias, *Elbridge Gerry*, 160. George Mason's record, both before and during the convention, demonstrates that he was a foremost champion of democratic causes. Farrand, *Records*, I, 48, II, 201-203, 273-74, 370, 637; Alfred H. Kelly and Winfred A. Harbison, *The American Constitution: Its Origins and Development* (New York, 1970), 120.

[17] Farrand, *Records*, II, 22, 32.

At this point, however, the convention took a peculiar step. As matters stood on July 17, the executive was (1) to be elected by the legislature; (2) to serve for seven years; and (3) to be ineligible for a second term. The latter two provisions were designed to ensure the executive's independence of the legislature. But now William Houston of Georgia moved that the clause on ineligibility be struck out. Morris supported the motion because ineligibility, he argued, "tended to destroy the great motive to good behavior, the hope of being rewarded by a re-appointment. It was saying to him, make hay while the sun shines." The argument apparently impressed the other delegates, who proceeded by a vote of 6 to 4 to strike out the ineligibility clause. Such a move, however, meant that one leg of the tripod was out of balance, since the legislature was now in a position to exert undue influence on the executive, who was beholden to it for reelection. By the same token, because the executive could serve more than once, a term as long as seven years was no longer warranted. Various delegates thus suggested substitution of a shorter term. Others, however, maintained that the only way to ensure the executive's independence was to provide that he serve "during good behavior." The latter proposal was vigorously condemned by Mason, who "considered an Executive during good behavior as a softer name only for an Executive for life. . . . the next would be an easy step to hereditary monarchy." The motion for instituting "good behavior" was defeated by a vote of 6 to 4, and the seven-year term was retained by the same margin. Clearly, the delegates were much troubled by the difficulty of maintaining the harmony of the tripod arrangement. Endowing the legislature with authority to reelect the executive compromised the latter's independence and posed problems in fixing the term of office. All this prompted thoughts that only by removing the selection of the executive from the legislature could the tripod be secured firmly. This idea, among others, surfaced in the full-dress debate on the issue held on July 19.[18]

Martin of Maryland opened the discussion with a proposal that the clause barring a second term be reinserted. He was supported by Edmund Randolph of Virginia, who stressed the need to ensure the executive's independence. "If he ought to be independent, he should not be left under a temptation to court a re-appointment. If he should be re-appointable by the Legislature, he will be no check on it." He warned the smaller states that reeligibility would work to their disadvantage, in particular, since the executive would undoubtedly court the larger states to ensure his reelection.[19]

Gouverneur Morris vigorously challenged the Martin proposal. Once again he advocated popular election of the executive, coupled with a right of reeligibility. "If he is to be the Guardian of the people let him be appointed by the people." In a lengthy address he extolled the virtues of popular election: "The Executive Magistrate should be the guardian of the people, even of the lower classes, agst Legislative tyranny, against the Great & the wealthy who in the course of things will necessarily compose — the Legislative body. . . . The Executive therefore ought to be so con-

---

[18] *Ibid.*, 23, 33, 35, 36.
[19] *Ibid.*, 52, 54–55.

stituted as to be the great protector of the Mass of the people." He recommended biennial elections of the executive, and in conclusion noted that popular election would make the plan of the constitution "extremely palatable to the people." Both Rufus King of Massachusetts and Paterson of New Jersey also endorsed popular election but feared that the people might not be able to settle on any one man. To obviate the difficulty they suggested "an appointment by electors chosen by the people for this purpose." At this point Wilson remarked that he "perceived with pleasure that the idea was gaining ground, of an election mediately or immediately by the people." Only Gerry spoke out against popular election, regarding it as "the worst [mode] of all." "The people are uninformed," he declared, "and would be misled by a few designing men." But even Gerry endorsed the notion of electors, except that he would entrust their selection to the state executives rather than to the state legislatures.[20]

Madison inveighed strongly against any role by the legislature in the selection of the executive since such an arrangement would tend to "establish an improper connection between the departments." During the debate of two days earlier, he had argued against reelection by the legislature: "A dependence of the Executive on the Legislature would render it the Executive as well as the maker of laws; & then according to the observation of Montesquieu, tyrannical laws may be made that they may be executed in a tyrannical manner." In the current debate Madison expressed doubts whether "an appointment in the 1st. instance [even] with an ineligibility afterwards would not establish an improper connection between the two departments." Inevitably, it would produce "intrigues and contentions." He therefore favored lodging the appointment in some other source. "The people at large was in his opinion the fittest in itself." Madison acknowledged, however, "one difficulty . . . of a serious nature attending an immediate choice by the people":

> The right of suffrage was much more diffusive in the Northern than the Southern States; and the latter could have no influence in the election on the score of the Negroes. The substitution of electors obviated this difficulty and seemed on the whole to be liable to the fewest objections.[21]

Madison's reference to the disparity of eligible voters between the North and the South highlighted, of course, the advantage the latter enjoyed under the three-fifths rule. The use of electors on something less than a directly proportionate scale would help preserve the relative advantage of the South (and of the smaller states). In this spirit Oliver Ellsworth of Connecticut moved that in place of "apptment by the Natl. Legislature" there be inserted "to be chosen by electors appointed by the Legislatures of the States in the following ratio": each state with less than 100,000 population—one vote; between 100,000 and 300,000—two votes; and above 300,000—three votes. Since the ratio was 1:3, no southern or small state had cause to feel disadvantaged, and it is not surprising, therefore, that the convention sum-

[20] *Ibid.*, 52-54, 55-56, 57.
[21] *Ibid.*, 34, 56-57.

marily proceeded to endorse the system of electors by a vote of 6 to 4. For the first time in the course of the deliberations, the legislature had been excluded from the executive-selection process. And with the removal of the legislature, the convention felt free to restore the reeligibility clause. The term of office was fixed at six years, and members of the legislature were forbidden to serve as electors.[22] Now the provision for choosing an executive was, in certain key features, approaching the ultimate form that would emerge from the convention.

But barely three days later, on July 23, doubts were expressed with regard to the system of electors just adopted. Houston "urged the extreme inconveniency & the considerable expense, of drawing together men from all the States for the single purpose of electing the Chief Magistrate." Obviously, it was envisaged that the electors under the scheme adopted would assemble in some central location to cast their votes. On the next day, July 24, Houston moved that the system of electors be abandoned in favor of restoring to the legislature the choice of the executive. "He dwelt chiefly on the improbability, that capable men would undertake the service of Electors from the more distant States." Houston was supported by Williamson, who argued that "the proposed Electors would certainly not be men of the 1st. nor even of the 2d. grade in the States. These would all prefer a seat in the Legislature." Interestingly, Gerry dismissed Houston's fears and urged retention of the system of electors. "The best men," he declared, would be honored to be electors, since "the election of the Executive Magistrate will be considered as of vast importance and will excite great earnestness." Nonetheless, Houston's motion was carried by a vote of 7 to 4.[23]

Thereupon Martin and Gerry moved to reinstate the ineligibility clause. Involvement of the legislature in selection of the executive compromised his independence, they maintained. "The longer the duration of his appointment the more will his dependence be diminished," said Gerry. "It will be better then for him to continue 10, 15, or even 20—years and be ineligible afterwards." Others proposed an eight- or eleven-year term of office. King recommended a twenty-year term since "this is the medium life of princes." In a footnote Madison remarked, "This might possibly be meant as a caricature of the previous motions in order to defeat the object of them." Williamson favored a seven-year term without eligibility for reelection, but would not object to a ten- or twelve-year term. "It was pretty certain he thought that we should at some time or other have a King; but he wished no precaution to be omitted that might postpone the event as long as possible."[24]

Once again the convention was thrown into disarray in its efforts to settle on a system for electing the executive that would not leave him overdependent on the legislature. Balancing the tripod—mode of election, term of office, and reeligibility—was proving to be an extremely difficult task. Gerry summed up the frustration

[22] Ibid., 50, 57, 58, 59, 60, 61, 63–64, 69.
[23] Ibid., 95, 97, 99, 100, 101. A possible explanation for the sudden change of heart on the scheme of electors may lie in the fact that a move to accord New Hampshire and Georgia two electors each, instead of the one each had been allotted, failed. Ibid., 60–61, 63–64.
[24] Ibid., 98–99, 100–101, 102.

of the delegates when he said, "We seem to be entirely at a loss on this head." He recommended that the problem be referred to the Committee of Detail, which was to be set up. "Perhaps they will be able to hit on something that may unite the various opinions which have been thrown out." Wilson, acknowledging "the difficulties & perplexities into which the House is thrown," proposed a scheme whereby a small group, drawn by lot from the legislature, would retire to make the choice "and not separate until it be made." "By this mode intrigue would be avoided . . . and . . . dependence . . . diminished." Gouverneur Morris warned the convention against denying the executive a right of reelection. "He will be in possession of the sword, a civil war will ensue." Wilson's proposal, he said, was worth considering. "It would be better that chance sd. decide than intrigue." Regardless, the delegates were not inclined to accept Wilson's novel suggestion precisely because it left too much to chance.[25]

On the next day, July 25, Ellsworth moved that the executive be selected by the legislature except where the incumbent stood for reelection. In that case the choice would fall to electors appointed by the state legislatures. Thereupon Madison delivered a lengthy address on the subject: "There are objections agst. every mode that has been, or perhaps can be proposed. The election must be made either by some existing authority under the Natil. or State Constitutions—or by some special authority derived from the people—or by the people themselves." The legislature, he declared, was "liable to insuperable objections." Besides compromising the independence of the executive, conferring the choice on the legislature would (1) "agitate & divide the legislature"; (2) lead to intrigues between the executive and "the predominant faction" within the legislature; and (3) result in foreign meddling in the election. He was also opposed to entrusting the selection of the national executive to the states, whether the choice devolved on their legislatures or on their executives. In conclusion, said Madison, the choice lay between direct elections and the use of electors. In the latter case, "as the electors would be chosen for the occasion, would meet at once, & proceed immediately to an appointment, there would be very little opportunity for cabal, or corruption. As a further precaution, it might be required that they meet at some place, distinct from the seat of Govt." But since that mode had just been rejected, there was little purpose in proposing it anew. There remained "election by the people or rather by the [qualified part_of them] at large. With all its imperfections he liked this best." He recognized, however, that there were two serious difficulties with this method. "The first arose from the disposition

[25] *Ibid.*, 97, 103, 105, 106. On the difficulties encountered by the delegates at this point, compare the descriptions by Robert A. Dahl and George Bancroft. Dahl observed, "Almost to the end, it [the convention] would move toward a solution and then, on second thought, reverse itself in favor of some different alternative. . . . The Convention twisted and turned like a man tormented in his sleep by a bad dream as it tried to decide." Robert A. Dahl, *Pluralist Democracy in the United States: Conflict and Consent* (Chicago, 1967), 84. Bancroft wrote, "The convention was now like a pack of hounds in full chase, suddenly losing the trail. It fell into an anarchy of opinion and one crude scheme trod on the heels of another." Bancroft, *History of the Formation of the Constitution*, II, 170. Some writers have suggested that Wilson's notion of a choice by lot was drawn from the example of the Ephori elections in ancient Greece. See John Fiske, *The Critical Period of American History 1783–1789* (Boston, 1901), 281; and Richard M. Gummere, *The American Colonial Mind and the Classical Tradition* (Cambridge, Mass., 1963), 186.

in the people to prefer a Citizen of their own State, and the disadvantage this wd. throw on the smaller States." Madison expressed the hope "that some expedient might be hit upon that would obviate" that possibility. "The second difficulty arose from the disproportion of [qualified voters] in the N. & S. States, and the disadvantages which this mode would throw on the latter." The latter handicap, he surmised, would be overcome with the passage of time as the population of the South increased. In any case, "local considerations must give way to the general interest." Madison declared that as a southerner "he was willing to make the sacrifice."[26]

Madison's remarks served to highlight the underlying causes of the opposition to popular election of the executive — the disadvantage from which both the smaller and the southern states would suffer. The fact was confirmed when, immediately after Madison had concluded his remarks, Ellsworth (one of the authors of the Connecticut Compromise) declared, "The objection drawn from the different sizes of the States, is unanswerable. The Citizens of the largest States would invariably prefer the Candidate within the State; and the largest States wd. invariably have the man." The same theme was taken up by Williamson, who said "an election of the Executive by the Legislature . . . opened a door for foreign influence. The principal objection agst. an election by the people seemed to be, the disadvantage under which it would place the smaller States." He suggested that as a "cure" each person should vote for three candidates, two of which would presumably be from states other than his own "and as probably of a small as a large one."[27]

Both Gouverneur Morris and Madison liked the Williamson idea. Morris suggested that "each man should vote for *two* persons one of whom at least should not be of his own State." Madison endorsed the Morris amendment and said that the effect would be that "the second best man in this case would probably be the first, in fact." He expressed fears, however, that after having voted for his favorite candidate, each citizen would throw away his second vote on some obscure person "in order to ensure the object of his first choice. But it could hardly be supposed that the Citizens of many States would be so sanguine of having their favorite elected, as not to give their second vote with sincerity to the next object of their choice."[28]

Dickinson suggested a means to combine popular election and selection by the legislature. He himself, he declared, "had long leaned towards an election by the people which he regarded as the best and purest source." The difficulty arose "from the partiality of the States to their respective Citizens." But could this "partiality" not be put to use in the search for an executive magistrate? Let the citizens of each state select their favorite son, and from the thirteen candidates thus nominated let the legislature, or electors appointed by it, make the final choice.[29] Because Dickinson did not submit a formal proposal, his scheme never came to a vote. But it did raise the possibility of dividing the nominating and selection procedure so that the legislature would make the final choice from a list of candidates nominated in .

---

[26] Farrand, *Records*, II, 107–11.
[27] *Ibid.*, 111, 113.
[28] *Ibid.*, 113–14. [Emphasis added.]
[29] *Ibid.*, 114–15.

the states. The procedure was clearly patterned on the contingency arrangements under the Massachusetts and New Hampshire constitutions in the event that no gubernatorial candidate received a popular majority.

The complexity of the task involved in formulating a mode of election was never better demonstrated than at this stage of the debate, which extended over several davs. The convention voted down in seriatim various ideas that had been put forward in the course of the debate. Thus Ellsworth's suggestion that in cases where an incumbent stood for election, the choice be left to state-appointed electors rather than to the national legislature was turned down by a vote of 4 to 7. And Williamson's popular-election proposal (as amended), whereby each person would vote for two candidates, one of whom would not be a citizen of his own state, was defeated by the narrow margin of 5 to 6. A motion by Pinckney for a system of rotation, so that no person serve as executive for more than six years out of twelve, was defeated by the same close margin.[30] The convention adjourned on July 25 without having decided on either the term of office or the matter of reeligibility. The only element that now stood was the decision to have the legislature make the choice.

On the next day, July 26, Mason delivered a lengthy oration in support of restoring once again the seven-year term coupled with ineligibility. He emphasized "the difficulty of the subject and the diversity of the opinions concerning it [that] have appeared. Nor have any of the modes of constituting that department been satisfactory." Earlier in the debate Pierce Butler of South Carolina and Gerry of Massachusetts had both vigorously challenged the idea of popular election of the executive. "The Govt. should not be made so complex & unwieldy as to disgust the States. This would be the case, if the election shd. be referred to the people," declared Butler. According to Gerry the proposal for "popular election in this case" was "radically vicious. The ignorance of the people would put it in the power of some one set of men dispersed through the Union & acting in Concert to delude them into any appointment. He observed that such a Society of men existed in the Order of the Cincinnati." Mason, in challenging the various proposals that had surfaced, also repeated his earlier opposition to popular election. Such an election meant "that an act which ought to be performed by those who know most of Eminent characters, & qualifications, should be performed by those who know least." He was also unable to support Williamson's suggestion that each person vote for several candidates since he was convinced that it "would throw the appointment into the hands of the Cincinnati," as Gerry had observed. The suggestions that the choice be made by the state legislatures or by special electors had all been found wanting. Nor had the idea of a "lottery" produced "much demand" for its "tickets," said Mason. He concluded, therefore, that "an election by the Ntl. Legislature as originally proposed was the best" (that is, for a single term of seven years). In opposing reelection he declared:

> Having for his primary object, for the pole star of his political conduct, the preservation of the rights of the people, he held it as an essential point, as the very pal-

<hr>

[30] *Ibid.*, 107, 111–12, 115. A rotation requirement in the office of governor was present in eight state constitutions.

ladium of Civil liberty, that the great officers of State, and particularly the Executive should at fixed periods return to that mass from which they were at first taken, in order that they may feel & respect those rights & interests, which are again to be personally valuable to them.[31]

These remarks prompted a rare comment by Benjamin Franklin:

> It seems to have been imagined by some that the returning to the mass of the people was degrading the magistrate. This he thought was contrary to republican principles. In free Governments the rulers are the servants, and the people their superiors & sovereigns. For the former therefore to return among the latter was not to *degrade* but to *promote* them—and it would be imposing an unreasonable burden on them, to keep them always in a State of servitude, and not allow them to become again one of the Masters.

In response, Gouverneur Morris said:

> In answer to Docr. Franklin, that a return into the mass of the people would be a promotion. instead of a degradation, he had no doubt that our Executive like most others would have too much patriotism to shrink from the burden of his office, and too much modesty not to be willing to decline the promotion.

At the same time Morris pronounced himself opposed to the whole paragraph on the selection of the executive if reeligibility be denied. Despite that objection, the convention adopted Mason's proposal by a vote of 7–3–1 and reendorsed selection by the legislature, for a seven-year term, without right of reelection. This formula was taken up in late July by the five-member Committee of Detail for incorporation into the draft constitution that it was to prepare.[32]

Although the convention had resolved on election by the legislature, no one had broached the question whether it was to be by joint ballot of both houses (voting together) or by each house acting separately. In the eight states where the legislature chose the executive, the election was by both houses jointly. Other state officials, however, were chosen according to regular legislative procedure, with each house exercising a veto. The latter arrangement for the selection of a president would give the states, especially the smaller states, substantial leverage in the choice of the executive. One document of the Committee of Detail in the Farrand collection hints that the committee experienced considerable difficulty in settling the matter. Randolph, a member of the committee, had originally written that the executive shall be elected "by joint ballot." Subsequently, "joint" had been crossed out, and Randolph had added to an emendation of South Carolina's John Rutledge the words "& in each Ho. havg a Negative on the other." However, the final report of the Committee of Detail, issued on August 6, reverted to the simple form adopted by the convention plenum, namely, "He shall be elected by ballot by the Legislature." The relevant provision (X) on the election of an executive (for the first time labeled

[31] *Ibid.*, 112, 114, 118–20.
[32] *Ibid.*, 116, 117, 120–21, 128. [Emphasis in original.]

"The President of the United States") read as follows: "He shall be elected by ballot by the Legislature. He shall hold his office during the term of seven years; but shall not be elected a second time."[33]

When the convention on August 7 took up the committee's report, the issue of electing the president arose in discussion of the procedures of the legislature (for the first time called the "Congress"). According to Article III of the draft constitution, each house "shall, in all cases, have a negative on the other." Mason expressed doubts regarding "the propriety of giving each branch a negative on the other 'in all cases.'" He assumed that there were some cases in which no negative was intended, "as in the case of balloting for appointments." Morris moved to insert "legislative acts" in place of "all cases." Sherman objected that such wording would "exclude a mutual negative in the case of ballots." Nathaniel Gorham of Massachusetts supported election by joint ballot and cited the difficulties experienced in his own state in selecting officers because of separate balloting by each house of the state legislature. "If separate ballots should be made for the President, and the two branches should be each attached to a favorite, great delay, contention & confusion may ensue." Wilson also advocated a joint ballot, "particularly in the choice of the President. Disputes between the two Houses, during & concerning the vacancy of the Executive might have dangerous consequences," he declared. Nonetheless, Morris's motion failed to carry by a tie vote, 5 to 5. In the meantime, however, Madison argued that a provison spelling out a negative by one house on the other was in any case unnecessary since the same was implied by the very existence of a bicameral legislature. Madison's motion to strike out the reference to a mutual negative in the legislature carried by a vote of 7 to 3.[34] Since the powers of each house were left unchanged, the vote in effect postponed a decision on the matter of legislative balloting for the office of president.

When on August 24 the convention took up the provision on the election of the executive in the report of the Committee of Detail, the delegates were once again divided on the procedure of balloting by the legislature. The previous week, on August 17, a similar clash had arisen over appointment of the treasurer by the legislature (as envisaged under the report of the Committee of Detail). Gorham had moved to insert "joint" before "ballot." "Mr [Roger] Sherman opposed it as favoring the large States." Nonetheless, Gorham's amendment was upheld by a vote of 7 to 3. Now Rutledge moved to make election of the executive also by "joint" ballot "as the most convenient mode of electing." But, as on the previous occasion, Sherman objected to the motion "as depriving the *States* represented in the *Senate* of the negative intended them in that house." Gorham again responded that "it was wrong to be considering, at every turn whom the Senate would represent. The public good was the true object to be kept in view." His words, in turn, drew the following retort from Jonathan Dayton of New Jersey: "It might be well for those not to consider how the Senate was constituted, whose interest it Was to keep it out of sight. — If

[33] *Ibid.*, 145, 185.
[34] *Ibid.*, 177, 193, 196–97.

the amendment should be agreed to," he declared, "a *joint* ballot would in fact give the appointment to one House. He could never agree to the clause with such an amendment."[33] At this point Daniel Carroll of Maryland, with the support of Wilson, vainly tried to have "election by the people" inserted in place of "by the Legislature." The motion was quickly dismissed by a vote of 2 to 9.

Reverting to the proposal for a joint ballot, David Brearley of New Jersey, in opposing the proposal, reminded the delegates that "the argument that the small States should not put their hands into the pockets of the large ones did not apply in this case." This was a reference to the demand of the larger states that money bills originate in the House of Representatives and not be subject to amendment in the Senate. That arrangement had formed an essential part of the Connecticut Compromise. In effect, Brearley was arguing that, unlike money bills, which affected the larger and wealthier states more directly and which were, therefore, left to the determination of the lower house, the selection of an executive concerned all states, smaller no less than larger, and was therefore a legitimate subject for Senate control. In contrast, Wilson "urged the reasonableness of giving the larger States a larger share of the appointment and the danger of delay from a disagreement of the two houses." He also pointed out that the Senate had a privileged position in other spheres, "balancing the advantage given by a joint balot in this case to the other branch of the Legislature." Madison pointed out that even with a joint ballot, the larger states would still not exercise influence commensurate with their size. "The rule of voting will give to the largest State, compared with the smallest, an influence as 4 to 1 only, altho the population is as 10 to 1." This, declared Madison, "cannot be unreasonable as the President is to act for the *people* not for the *States*." But the most telling speech in favor of a joint ballot was delivered by John Langdon of New Hampshire. In his home state, he declared, "the mode of separate votes by the two Houses was productive of great difficulties. . . . He was for inserting 'joint' tho' unfavorable to N. Hampshire as a small State." The proposal for a joint ballot of both houses was accepted by a vote of 7 to 4, with two small states (New Hampshire and Delaware) breaking ranks and voting with the large states. The smaller states did not concede defeat, however. Immediately after the vote, Dayton of New Jersey, seconded by Brearley of the same state, moved to insert after "Legislature" the words "each State having one vote." The motion failed, by the close vote of 5 to 6.[36] (Delaware, in this instance, sided with its natural allies, the smaller states.)

It was now Gouverneur Morris's turn to express displeasure at the decision of the convention. The executive, he complained, can never be truly independent if he is chosen by the legislature. "Cabal & corruption are attached to that mode of election: so also is ineligibility a second time . . . rivals would be continually intriguing to oust the President from his place." He proposed that as a means of guarding against "all these evils," the president "be chosen by Electors to be chosen by the people

---

[33] *Ibid.*, 314–15, 401, 402. [Emphasis in original.]
[36] *Ibid.*, I, 524, 526, II, 397, 402–403. [Emphasis in original.] Although the executive in New Hampshire was elected by popular vote, other officers were selected by the legislature, with each house voting separately.

of the several States." His motion was defeated by the narrow margin of 5 to 6 in one vote and by a split vote, 4–4–2 (1 absent) on a second try.[37]

But the convention was apparently still not satisfied with the arrangements it had settled on for choosing the president. Although it had confirmed election by the legislature in joint ballot, it was not yet ready to determine with finality the term of office or the reeligibility issue. Those matters were postponed, at the suggestion of the New Jersey delegation, to the next day, August 25.[38] The matter was not broached then, however, and apparently the convention preferred to let the issue ride.

The convention's continuing vacillation and soul-searching on the whole subject was subsequently revealed when on August 31 the delegates took up for consideration Article XXIII of the draft constitution. That provision described the procedures for instituting the government, including a direction to Congress to "choose the President of the United States." Morris moved to strike those words out of the provision, "this point, of choosing the President not being yet finally determined." The clause was struck out by the rather surprising vote of 9–1–1 (one state divided). Clearly the convention had not yet pronounced the last word on the method of selecting a president. The delegates, even at this late stage, were still groping for a solution free of the serious shortcomings raised against every single method proposed to date. At the conclusion of the day's session, the issue of the election of a president, together with all other pieces of unfinished business, were referred to a committee composed of a representative from each state. Apparently the convention was hoping that the members of the committee, as Gerry had put it, would be able to come up with something that would "unite the various opinions which have been thrown out."[39]

The Brearley Committee on Unfinished Parts (named thus after its chairman) completed its work on procedures for electing an executive in four days and reported back to the Convention on September 4. The result was the Electoral College.[40] It was striking in its innovation and quite remarkable for having combined all the salient features of the numerous plans proposed during the debate while having overcome the deficiencies of each. First and foremost, it removed the choice of president from the Congress and conveyed it to an independent, ad hoc body whose sole function was the selection of a chief executive. The independence of the president was thus assured while cabal and foreign influence were safely excluded, and the president was free to run for reelection without fear that his independence would be compromised. Yet at the same time, and this was the really critical point, in terms of numbers the Electoral College was an exact replica of Congress, since each state was entitled to as many votes in the Electoral College as it had in Congress, with even the smallest state entitled to at least three votes; moreover, the southern states

[37] *Ibid.*, II, 397, 404.
[38] *Ibid.*, 397–98, 404.
[39] *Ibid.*, 103, 472, 473, 480, 481.
[40] According to Charles Warren, the reason for the success of the committee is that it consisted of "almost the ablest men from each State." Warren, *Making of the Constitution*, 621n1. See also Roche, "Founding Fathers," 810.

would enjoy the bonus of the three-fifths rule. The smaller and the southern states thus would continue to enjoy the relative advantage they possessed in Congress itself, either in the Senate or in the House of Representatives, or in both. In mathematical terms the advantage in the first Congress (with sixty-five members in the House of Representatives and twenty-six in the Senate) was as follows:

Delaware (smallest state)

$$\frac{1 + 2 = 3}{65 + 26 = 91}$$

Virginia (largest state)

$$\frac{10 + 2 = 12}{65 + 26 = 91}$$

Thus, as a result of the Electoral College, the ratio was 1:4 rather than 1:10 as it would have been had size of population been the sole criterion.[41]

In effect, the Electoral College was simply a special congress elected to choose a president, without the shortcomings of the real Congress. Since the electors would never assemble together at one national site but would meet to vote "in their respective States" and immediately thereafter disband, there was no danger of corruption, plotting, or cabal. As Gouverneur Morris indicated, "The principal advantage aimed at was that of taking away the opportunity for cabal." To prevent the larger states from dominating the selection process, each elector was to vote for two persons, one of whom, at least, was not to be a citizen of his own state. At the same time, since a majority was required for selection of the president, no elector would be prone to throw away his second vote. Thus the outcome would be, not simply the selection of thirteen favorite sons, but a genuine possibility that a national figure would be chosen at the first round. In the event that no candidate received an absolute majority in the Electoral College, the Senate would choose the president (from the five highest on the list). In effect, the smaller states were to get two bites of the cherry under the new plan. First, they retained their numerical advantage in the Electoral College. Second, if no candidate succeeded in obtaining an absolute majority, the choice would devolve on the Senate, where again the smaller states had a built-in advantage. As noted above, this contingency arrangement was derived from the constitutions of Massachusetts and New Hampshire.[42]

Presentation of the Electoral College scheme to the convention excited considerable surprise. "Mr. Randolph & Mr. Pinkney wished for a particular explanation &

[41] Constitution of the United States, Article I, secs. 2, 3. In the 1790 census Delaware had a population of 59,000 while that of Virginia was 692,000. In the 1792 elections Virginia elected nineteen members to the House of Representatives whereas Delaware continued to elect only one. Since the Electoral College total was 132, the resultant ratio was Delaware; 3:132; Virginia, 21:132. Thus the ratio was 1:7 rather than 1:12 as the population figures would warrant. (These figures allow 3 votes for 5 blacks under the census.) U.S. Bureau of the Census, *Historical Statistics of the United States, Colonial Times to 1970*, (Washington, 1975), pt. 1, pp. 24, 36; *ibid.*, pt. 2, pp. 1074, 1085. Representation in the House was apportioned on the basis of 30,000 population per seat. Constitution of the United States, Article I, sec. 2.

[42] Farrand, *Records*, II, 501.

discussion of the reasons for changing the mode of electing the Executive." Gouverneur Morris served as the committee's spokesman in explaining the "reasons" for the new proposal: (1) "The danger of intrigue & faction if the apptmt should be made by the Legislature." (2) "The inconveniency of an ineligibility" were the choice to remain with the legislature. (3) "The difficulty of establishing a Court of Impeachments, other than the Senate," which would be an improper body to judge the executive if he were to be chosen by the legislature. (4) "No body had appeared to be satisfied with an appointment by the Legislature." (5) "Many were anxious even for an immediate choice by the people." (6) "The indispensable necessity of making the Executive independent of the Legislature.—As the Electors would vote at the same time throughout the U.S. and at so great a distance from each other, the great evil of cabal was avoided."[43]

In response, Mason expressed his satisfaction that the plan "had removed some capital objections, particularly the danger of cabal and corruption." It was liable, however, "to this strong objection, that nineteen times in twenty the President would be chosen by the Senate, an improper body for the purpose." Randolph "dwelt on the tendency of such an influence in the Senate over the election of the President in addition to its other powers, to convert that body into a real & dangerous Aristocracy." Pinckney and Rutledge also argued that conferring the choice on the Senate, even in the ultimate resort, was likely to compromise the president's independence. Sherman apparently sensed that some delegates were objecting to the Senate because of the influence of small states there. He "reminded the opponents of the new mode . . . that if the Small States had the advantage in the Senate's deciding among the five highest candidates, the Large States would have in fact the nomination of these candidates." Nonetheless, when Mason moved that the choice be made from the top three rather than the top five, the smaller states objected. Sherman declared he "would sooner give up the plan." Apparently, the smaller states reasoned that a choice out of five rather than three allowed them some prospect to land a candidate of their own. Other delegates stressed that, in fact, the choice would most likely be made in the Electoral College, and there would be no need to resort to the Senate. "The increasing intercourse among the people of the States," declared Baldwin, "would render important characters less & less unknown; and the Senate would consequently be less & less likely to have the eventual appointment thrown into their hands." Wilson also stressed that "Continental Characters will multiply as we more & more coalesce, so as to enable the electors in every part of the Union to know & judge of them." Gouverneur Morris similarly felt that the matter would be settled by the electors and would never reach the Senate. Madison considered it "a primary object to render an eventual resort to any part of the Legislature improbable." He referred to two features of the plan that made such an eventuality unlikely. First, given the reluctance of the large states to see the choice fall to the Senate, their "concerted effort . . . would be to make the appointment in the first instance conclusive." Second, the fact that the vice-presi-

[43] *Ibid.*, 500.

dent, unlike the president, could be selected without a majority would deter electors from wasting their second votes and would heighten the chance that the choice would be made in the Electoral College.[44]

The delegates, it appears, were impressed with the Electoral College scheme, which so successfully blended all the necessary elements to ensure a safe and equitable process for electing a president and which reserved considerable influence for the states. They beat back, by large majorities, every attempt to upset the plan and to restore legislative selection of the executive. There was, however, considerable sentiment against leaving the ultimate choice in the hands of the Senate. Mason regarded it as "utterly inadmissable. He would prefer the Government of Prussia to one which will put all power into the hands of seven or eight men, and fix an Aristocracy worse than absolute monarchy." Mason was vigorously supported by Wilson, who complained that too much power was concentrated under the Constitution in the Senate. As a means of avoiding resort to the Senate, Mason proposed that the candidate receiving the highest number of ballots in the Electoral College be pronounced president whether or not the vote constituted a majority. Wilson proposed that the final choice be accorded the whole legislature rather than the Senate alone. The convention, however, rejected both proposals, just as it rejected numerous other proposals that tended to alter the finely tuned instrument that had evolved. The Electoral College constituted a package deal in which diverse interests and safeguards were neatly balanced. Even the slightest change was likely to undermine the entire structure and to make the machinery inoperable. The delegates were not prone to tamper with the delicate compromise. Only in the matter of the Senate as the venue of ultimate resort were the delegates ready to accept change. Sherman, alert to objections that the Senate represented a center of "aristocracy," proposed that the House of Representatives be substituted for the Senate in the ultimate resort, with voting by states, not per capita. Since this proposal, in contrast to the other suggestions, preserved state power, the amendment was readily accepted by a vote of 10 to 1. Another amendment readily accepted (this time unanimously) was a clause barring "a member of the Legislature of the United States or who holds any office of profit or trust under the United States" from serving as an elector. An incidental by-product of the new scheme was the emergence of the office of vice-president, designed to take care of the electors' second vote. Some delegates voiced opposition to creation of the office, and others protested that the vice-president's appointment as ex officio president of the Senate would violate the principle of the separation of powers. But once again the vast majority wished to preserve the Electoral College plan intact, and the office of vice-president and his role in the Senate were overwhelmingly confirmed.[45]

[44] Ibid., 500, 501, 507, 511, 512–13, 514, 523; Bancroft, History of the Formation of the Constitution, II, 177. The remarks by Abraham Baldwin, Wilson, Gouverneur Morris, and Madison demonstrate that a considerable body of opinion at the convention did not share Mason's view that "nineteen times in twenty" the selection would be made in the Senate (House). Roche's claim that "no one seriously disputed [Mason's] point" is thus unsupportable. Moreover, as Madison notes, certain features of the Electoral College scheme were specifically designed to heighten the prospects of a final choice in the College. On this point, see Warren, Making of the Constitution, 629. But cf. Farrand, Framing of the Constitution, 167; and Farrand, Records, III, 405.
[45] Farrand, Records, II, 507, 511, 512, 513, 514, 515, 517–21, 522–23, 525–29, 532, 536–38. Gouverneur Morris quipped that the vice president "will be the first heir apparent that ever loved his father." Ibid., 537.

The convention records demonstrate that the protracted discussion over the mode of electing an executive was but a continuation of the struggle that marked the debate on the composition of the legislature. The smaller states were no more prepared to concede to the large states domination of the process of selecting a chief executive than they were prepared to allow them to dominate the legislature. From a truly "nationalist" choice, as envisaged under the Virginia Plan, the United States executive was transformed, in the give-and-take of the debates at Philadelphia, into a "federal" institution in which the rights and interests of the states, particularly the smaller states, would also be safeguarded.[46] The compromise that marked the creation of the Electoral College is thus revealed as simply a second round of the Connecticut Compromise in settling large state–small state differences.

This second stage of the running battle between the large and the small states was distinguished from the first in several ways. The dispute over the mode of electing an executive never assumed the same dimensions of crisis that nearly disrupted the convention with respect to the issue of the composition of the legislature. Of that confrontation Gouverneur Morris said that "the fate of America was suspended by a hair."[47] After having backed down on the issue of the legislature, the large states were neither able nor willing to create a new impasse. Nevertheless, a major and prolonged struggle (down to the wire) ensued over the system to be instituted for choosing an executive.

Second, the small states were not the only ones to feel directly affected by the various schemes proposed. Once the Connecticut Compromise had accorded the smaller states a handsome increment in the Senate, they understandably refused to contemplate removal of the choice from the legislature. But the slave states were no less reluctant to agree to such a move since it would dissipate the advantage they had secured in the lower house through the three-fifths rule. As a result, a natural alliance existed between the two groups—the slave states and the smaller states—in reserving the decision to the national legislature. However, according the legislature such a role would inevitably have compromised the executive's independence, something that tended to violate the principle of the separation of powers, regarded as sacrosanct by the Founding Fathers. To overcome this deficiency, it was decided that the executive's term of office be relatively long (seven years) and that he be ineligible for reelection. Those conditions, however, were found wanting in other respects, so that the delegates kept probing and testing for an alternative to the triangular arrangement—choice by the legislature, long term, ineligibility.

Now it was the turn of the small states to make a valuable concession, which represents a third noteworthy aspect of the Electoral College compromise. Given the equality of both houses in the legislature, the Senate would be free to exercise a veto in the choice of the executive. In the interest of preventing deadlocks, however, several smaller states resolved to endorse a joint ballot of both houses in selecting

---

[46] See the subsequent comment of Jonathan Dayton, delegate from New Jersey: "The States, whatever was their relative magnitude, were equal under the old Confederation, and the small States gave up a part of their rights as a compromise for a better form of government and security; but they cautiously preserved their equal rights in the Senate and in the choice of a Chief Magistrate." *Ibid.*, III, 400–401. See also the remarks of Gouverneur Morris, *ibid.*, 405; and of Rufus King, *ibid.*, 462.

[47] *Ibid.* 391.

an executive. Unlike the Connecticut Compromise, in which the concession of the smaller states was limited to granting the lower house the right to initiate money bills, in this instance the concession was significant and meaningful. It paved the way for a transference of the responsibility of choosing the executive from the legislature to some outside body. The most logical outside body was the people, in direct popular elections. Such a step, however, would have canceled the advantages enjoyed by the smaller and the slave states in the legislature. In response, the Committee on Unfinished Parts invented the Electoral College—an ingenious means of preserving the built-in advantages of those states while removing the choice from the legislature. The Electoral College represented a congress away from home for the express and limited purpose of choosing the nation's chief magistrate. The institution of the Electoral College represented the first, indeed the primary, compromise in the arrangements for selecting an executive. National and federal elements were neatly balanced therein. But it was only part of the package. In the event that the Electoral College failed to come up with a sufficiently national choice, the Senate (ultimately the House of Representatives) as the constitutive body of the states, would choose. In effect, therefore, in the event that the Electoral College became a mere nominating body under the domination of the large states, the smaller and the slave states would be well placed to exercise a controlling voice over the final election in the Senate (House of Representatives).[48] (Although the three-fifths rule did not operate at this point, the slave states retained influence by virtue of the number of southern states present.)

The convention's records indicate that many delegates favored direct popular election of the executive but, for the reasons noted, were unable to institute such a system. The most prominent advocates of direct elections were those campaigning for a strong executive—Wilson, Gouverneur Morris, and Madison. Their motives possibly were mixed. They were opposed to lodging the choice in the legislature because the executive's independence would be compromised. They were also concerned about the disproportionate influence of the smaller states in that body. As Martin told the Maryland legislature, "Those who wished as far as possible to establish a *national* instead of a *federal* government, made repeated attempts to have the President chosen by the people at large." Democratic doctrine—the belief that the executive should represent the mass of the people—also seems to have been a factor. In the end the proponents of direct elections achieved partial success. Although the election of the president was not to be a direct act of the people, the state legislatures would be free, if they wished, to confer the choice of electors upon the people themselves. Indeed, that seems to have been the expectation of the

[48] At various times the contingency arrangement, with the House of Representatives voting by states, has been depicted as the key element of compromise in the Electoral College scheme. See, for instance, Farrand, "Compromises of the Constitution," 487–88; and Farrand, *Records*, III, 458, 461, 464. However, as noted, this is only part of the package. The first and fundamental element of compromise lay in the composition of the Electoral College. As summed up by Baldwin, "The Constitution in directing *Electors* to be appointed throughout the United States equal to the whole number of the Senators and Representatives in Congress . . . had provided for the existence of as respectable a body as Congress, and in whom the Constitution on this business has more confidence than in Congress." *Ibid.*, 382. See also the remarks of Gouverneur Morris, *ibid.*, 405; and of King, *ibid.*, 461.

Framers. For this reason Madison, in one of the last sessions of the convention, described the election of the president as one "by the people."[49]

Only a few delegates—most notably Mason, Gerry, and Butler—were opposed in principle to direct election of the executive. But such opposition reflected, as least in the case of Mason, not mistrust of representative democracy, but a conviction that the extent of the country and the difficulty of communication did not permit informed selection of a national candidate. True representation could work only over a small area where the people could be acquainted firsthand with the candidates. An attempt to apply representative democracy on a national scale was a distortion of the principle and would simply lead to the manipulation of elections by nefarious characters. The ultimate solution of state electors was, from that standpoint, a sound means of giving expression to the popular will, and it was viewed in that light by the antifederalists in the state ratifying conventions.

What clearly emerges from the foregoing is that, contrary to the claim of the Progressive historians, antimajoritarianism was by no means the primary motivation behind the creation of the Electoral College. Nor was it, as Roche would have it, simply the product of a last-minute accident of history. Design and purpose guided the creation of the Electoral College. At the same time, however, it would be wrong to suggest that the Electoral College was based on some grand concept of political theory. Also, there is no evidence that the convention was inspired in the matter by classical or medieval precedents. Not once did the delegates advert to the procedures that prevailed in ancient Rome or Greece or in republican Venice. (The Federalist Papers, equally, do not mention any such historical forerunners of the Electoral College.) The delegates were confronted with a practical problem arising from the constellation of clashing forces at Philadelphia, and they devised a practical solution—an ad hoc congress reflecting faithfully the pattern of weighted voting that was an integral part of the operation of the real Congress. The precedents guiding their deliberations were all drawn from state practice.[50]

Two alternatives presented themselves. The indirect method of selection by the legislature and the direct method of popular choice (qualified by a contingency procedure entailing a legislative role). The latter method represented too national a choice for some; the former, while it offered a satisfactory federal solution, clashed with accepted republican principles. Concepts that had come to be viewed by many as essential components of representative government—separation of powers, limited terms of office, reeligibility, rotation in office, and devices for minimizing electoral corruption—were analyzed and weighed in the search for an unassailable solution. Thus if political theory did not inform the creation of the Electoral College, it provided the essential backdrop to the evolution of this new instrument of government. The device of a congress away from home represented, in sum, an

[49] Ibid., 217, 330, 422–23, II, 587, I, 50. [Emphasis in original.] See also Federalist Papers Nos. 60 and 68.
[50] King commented, "The members of the Convention in settling the manner of electing the Executive of the U.S. seem to have been prejudiced in favor of the manner, to which they were accustomed, in the election of the Governor of their respective States." Ibid., III, 459. Also, as indicated earlier, the notion of establishing an electoral college may well have been drawn from the precedent of the Maryland senate. Elliot, Debates in the Several State Conventions, II, 127–28.

adaptation of state experience modified by the need to resolve the central dispute at Philadelphia, namely the large state–small state controversy. Concessions to the federal impulse were reflected in the manner in which the composition of the Electoral College was fixed; in the option accorded the state legislatures to appoint the electors; and in the ultimate choice being bestowed upon the House of Representatives, voting by states. These features stamped the compromise nature of the Electoral College and assured its acceptability both within the convention and without. For in the eyes of its admirers, the Electoral College represented a brilliant scheme for successfully blending national and federal elements in the selection of the nation's chief magistrate.

The Evolution of the Electoral College at the Constitutional Convention 1787.

Date	Source of Proposal	Proposal	Action Taken	Idea Reflected in EC Scheme	Citation in Farrar Records of Constitutional Convention
May 29	Virginia Plan	Election by national legislature without right of reeligibility. Term undefined.	See next entry		I, 20-22.
June 1	Pinckney (Mason)	Election by legislature for 7 year term without right of reelection.	Adopted June 1. Vote 8:2		I, 77, 78, 81, 5
May 29	Pinckney Plan	Annual election by both houses of legislature in joint ballot.	Never voted upon		II, 135; III, 6(
June 1	Wilson	People choose electors who select executive.	Rejected June 2. Vote 2:8	✓	I, 77, 81.
June 1	Dickinson	Removal of Executive by national legislature upon request of majority of state legislatures.	Rejected June 2. Vote 1:9		I, 78, 87.
June 15	New Jersey Plan	Plural executive to be elected by national legislature representing states without right of reeligibility. Term undefined. Removeable by Congress upon request of majority of state executives.	Never voted upon		I, 242-45.
June 18	Hamilton Plan	Election by electors chosen by people; to serve during good behavior.	Never taken up for consideration		I, 292; but cf. III, 617-18.
July 17	Gouverneur Morris	Election "by the Citizens of the United States."	Rejected July 17. Vote 1:9		II, 22, 32.
July 17	Luther Martin	Election by electors appointed by state legislatures.	Rejected July 17. Vote 2:8	✓	II, 22, 32.
July 17	Wm. Houston	To strike out ineligibility clause.	Adopted July 17. Vote 6:4	✓	II, 23, 33.

323

Date	Source of Proposal	Proposal	Action Taken	Idea Reflected in EC Scheme	Citation in Farrand Records of Constitutional Convention
July 19	Oliver Ellsworth	Executive to be chosen by electors appointed by state legislatures in ratio range of 1:3. Term of 6 years; unlimited right of reelection.	Adopted July 19-20. Vote 6:3:1; 8:2	✓	II, 50, 57-53.
July 24	Wm. Houston	Election by legislature.	Adopted July 24. Vote 7:4		II, 97, 101.
July 24	James Wilson	Election by group of electors to be drawn by lot from legislature.	Unanimously postponed		II, 97, 106.
July 24	Elbridge Gerry	State legislatures elect executive; if no candidate receives a majority lower house nominates 2 of 4 and upper house makes final choice.	Overwhelmingly rejected.		II, 98-99, 101.
July 25	Oliver Ellsworth	Election by legislature but where incumbent is standing selection be made by electors appointed by state legislatures.	Rejected July 25. Vote 4:7		II, 107, 111.
July 25	Pickney	No person serve in executive more than 6 years out of 12.	Rejected July 25. Vote 5:6		II, 107, 115.
July 25	Williamson	Each person votes for 2 candidates one of whom should not be of voter's state.	Rejected July 25. Vote 5:6	✓	II, 107, 115.
July 26	Mason	Election by legislature for 7 year term without right of reelection.	Adopted July 26. Vote 7:3:1		II, 117, 120.
Aug. 24	Rutledge	Election by legislature in joint ballot.	Adopted Aug. 24. Vote 7:4		II, 397, 402-3.
Aug. 24	Daniel Carroll	Election by the people.	Rejected Aug. 24. Vote 2:9		II, 397, 402.

Date	Source of Proposal	Proposal	Action Taken	Idea Reflected in EC Scheme	Citation in Farrand Records of Constitutional Convention
Aug. 24	Gouverneur Morris	Election by electors chosen by people.	Rejected Aug. 24. Votes 5:6, 4:4:2	↙	II, 397, 404.
Aug. 24	Dayton	Election by legislature with each state having one vote.	Rejected Aug. 24. Vote 5:6	✓	II, 397, 403.
Sept. 4	Brearley Committee on Unfinished Parts	Election by electors appointed by state legislatures. Number of electors for each state proportionate to representation in Congress. In absence of majority vote in Electoral College, Senate chooses out of top 5 candidates.	Adopted Sept. 6. Vote 9:2	✓	II, 517-21, 525-2
Sept. 5	Rutledge	Election by legislature in joint ballot. Term of 7 years without right of reeligibility.	Rejected Sept. 5. Vote 2:8:1		II, 507, 511.
Sept. 5	Wilson	Contingency selection by legislature rather than Senate.	Rejected Sept. 5. Vote 3:7:1		II, 507, 513.
Sept. 6	Sherman	Contingency selection by House of Representatives rather than Senate, with each State delegation in House having one vote.	Adopted Sept. 6. Vote 10:1	✓	II, 518-19, 527.

* This chart lists each of the proposals on the mode of electing the executive, as well as several crucial amendments; it does not record the action of the Convention on every single amendment proposed.

Perspectives in American History, New Series, I, 1984.

SOLVING A CONSTITUTIONAL PUZZLE: THE TREATYMAKING CLAUSE AS A CASE STUDY

Jack N. Rakove

A judge, like an executive adviser, may be surprised at the poverty of really useful and unambiguous authority applicable to concrete problems of executive power as they actually present themselves. Just what our forefathers did envision, or would have envisioned had they foreseen modern conditions, must be divined from materials almost as enigmatic as the dreams Joseph was called upon to interpret for Pharaoh. A century and a half of partisan debate and scholarly speculation yields no net result but only supplies more or less apt quotations from respected sources on each side of any question. They largely cancel each other.

JUSTICE ROBERT JACKSON
(Opinion in *Youngstown Sheet & Tube Company v. Sawyer*[1])

EVERY MODERN student of the Constitution has had occasion to ponder Justice Jackson's lament about the difficulty of recovering the original intentions of the framers. Even if the origins of many of their decisions are neither as obscure nor as enigmatic as the Justice implied, events in recent years have repeatedly illustrated how vital a role the interpretation of the Constitution can still play in the resolution of major disputes — and how difficult it is to reach intellectual consensus when the outcomes of contemporary political controversies can hinge on the exegesis of eighteenth-century words and concepts. The recovery of the elusive "original meaning" of key constitutional clauses has thus attracted renewed interest among scholars, with the striking result that

The author wishes to acknowledge the support of Project '87.
1. 343 U.S. 579, 634–635 (1952).

233

provisions long regarded as moribund or obsolete—the impeachment clause, for example—have been exposed to intensive review.

Among the various provisions of the Constitution that have thus come under consideration, those involving the extent of presidential authority in matters of national security and foreign relations have been the most important. Questions about the allocation of war-making powers have received greater attention than closely related issues involving the conduct of foreign policy. Yet from the perspective of the historian, the Constitutional Convention's decision to divide the treatymaking power between the President and Senate remains as puzzling as it was momentous. In the draft constitution which the Committee of Detail presented on August 6, 1787, the power to make treaties and appoint ambassadors was assigned exclusively to the Senate. The debates and revisions of succeeding weeks, however, seemingly produced a major shift in the allocation of responsibility. By September 8, when the final debate on the treaty clause took place, the President had been empowered both "to make Treaties" and to "nominate . . . and appoint Ambassadors." And while in both cases he was to act "by and with the Advice and Consent of the Senate," the placement of these provisions within the executive article implies that the Convention had consciously chosen to give the President an initiative in the making of foreign policy.[2]

Modern judicial interpretation has certainly favored the conclusion that the wording and placement of the treaty clause were meant to give the executive a substantial advantage in the conduct of foreign policy. An appellate opinion in the recent litigation arising from President Carter's abrogation of the mutual assistance treaty with the Republic of China summarizes the prevailing doctrine succinctly: "in contrast to the lawmaking power, the constitutional initiative in the treaty-making field is in the President, not Congress."[3] Notwithstanding the continued vitality of such views within the courts, constitutional scholars have grown increasingly skeptical about the broad interpretation of executive power to which Justice

2. Max Farrand, ed., *The Records of the Federal Convention of 1787*, rev. ed. (New Haven, 1937), II, 183, 495, 533–534, 544.

3. *Goldwater v. Carter*, 617 F. 2d 697, 704–705 (1979). The following passage is also relevant to the doctrine of inherent executive power that will be discussed below (pp. 257–267): "The Constitution specifically confers no power of treaty termination on either the Congress or the Executive. We note, however, that the powers conferred upon Congress in Article I of the Constitution are specific, detailed, and limited, while the powers conferred upon the President by Article II are generalized in a manner that bespeaks no such limitation upon foreign affairs power." The opinion further notes that "It is significant that the treaty power appears in Article II of the Constitution, relating to the executive branch, and not in Article I, setting forth the powers of the legislative branch."

Sutherland gave definitive endorsement in his famous opinion in *United States v. Curtiss-Wright Export Corporation.*[4] Several recent analyses have concluded that the Federal Convention intended and expected the Senate to participate in the framing as well as the ratification of treaties, and thus to have no less important a role than the President in determining the principal goals of American foreign policy.[5] But the Convention's purposes still remain elusive. Was the President meant to serve only as the most convenient agent for the conduct of diplomacy, or did the framers also recognize his capacity to represent some larger conception of the national interest? Did they expect the Senate to give its advice continually throughout the course of negotiations? Was its consent to be required for the termination of existing pacts as well as the approval of new agreements? On these and a number of other questions, our surviving sources are less than explicit.

Viewed historically, the evolution of the treaty clause in the Convention raises three major questions. First, why was the President brought into the process at all? Second, how did the framers intend to divide the authority to conduct foreign relations between the President and the Senate? Third, what significance, if any, can be ascribed to the placement of the treaty clause within Article II? Was it merely a quirk of constitutional draftsmanship, or did it imply that the management of foreign relations was inherently an executive function, save for the specific exceptions that were enumerated in this and other clauses?

The discovery of satisfactory answers to these questions requires close consideration of each of the principal sources that are ordinarily brought

4. A useful introduction to the defects in this leading decision can be found in Charles Lofgren, "*United States v. Curtiss-Wright Export Corporation:* An Historical Reassessment," *Yale Law Journal,* 83 (1973): 1–32.

5. The most careful analysis of the evolution of the treaty clause is Arthur Bestor, "Respective Roles of Senate and President in the Making and Abrogation of Treaties: The Original Intent of the Framers Historically Examined," *Washington Law Review,* 55 (1979): 1–135; and see his earlier article, "Separation of Powers in the Domain of Foreign Affairs: The Original Intent of the Constitution Historically Examined," *Seton Hall Law Review,* 5 (1974): 527–665. Other useful discussions include W. Taylor Reveley, III, *War Powers of the President and Congress: Who Holds the Arrows and Olive Branch?* (Charlottesville, Va., 1981), pp. 74–99; Charles Lofgren, "War Making under the Constitution: The Original Understanding," *Yale Law Journal,* 81 (1972): 672–702; and Charles C. Thach, Jr., *The Creation of the Presidency, 1775–1789: A Study in Constitutional History* (Baltimore, 1922), pp. 76–139. The treaty power is also examined in Raoul Berger, *Executive Privilege: A Constitutional Myth* (Cambridge, 1974), pp. 117–140. Despite its promising title, Abraham D. Sofaer, *War, Foreign Affairs and Constitutional Power: The Origins* (Cambridge, Mass., 1976) does not offer a close analysis of the debates at Philadelphia; it is, however, more valuable for detailing the evolution of practice after 1789.

to bear on problems of interpreting the original meaning of constitutional clauses: the surviving records of the Federal Convention, the debates and commentaries of the period of ratification, and the writings of the various British and European authorities whom eighteenth-century Americans presumably knew so well. Moreover, because questions of foreign policy had loomed so large in the mounting criticism of the Articles of Confederation, we are also warranted in asking what lessons the framers might have drawn from immediate experience. Among the numerous constitutional problems that scholars have recently considered, few afford a better opportunity to weigh the respective merits and shortcomings of these different sources than the treaty clause, the origins of which make it an exemplary constitutional puzzle.

AT THE CONVENTION

Given the central importance of foreign affairs in the calling of the Constitutional Convention, it seems surprising that its records reveal so little about the allocation of the treaty power between the President and Senate. But in 1787, one must recall, the conduct of foreign relations was regarded as a problem more of federalism than of the separation of powers. As one legal scholar has observed, the framers "found the supremacy of national treaties over state law far more troublesome than the manner in which the United States would itself make treaties."[6] The reason for this lay in the immediate history of the Confederation. During the four years that had passed since the end of the Revolutionary War, the states had violated provisions of the Treaty of Paris relating to the rights of loyalist refugees and British creditors, and these actions had given Britain a pretext for refusing to surrender its northwestern forts. Moreover, the fact that Congress lacked the power to regulate foreign commerce, and thus to retaliate against nations discriminating against American merchants, was widely regarded as the reason why European countries had avoided negotiating satisfactory treaties of commerce with the new republic. Both concerns led the framers to see problems of conducting foreign affairs largely in terms of permitting the national government to exercise powers commensurate with its responsibilities.[7]

6. W. Taylor Reveley, III, "Constitutional Allocation of the War Powers Between the President and Congress, 1787-1788," *Virginia Journal of International Law*, 15 (1974): 82.
7. Frederick W. Marks, III, *Independence on Trial: Foreign Affairs and the Making of the Constitution* (Baton Rouge, 1973).

There are other ways of explaining why the delegates had so little to say about how treaties would actually be made, however. One is that debate requires disagreement to sustain itself, particularly when the deliberations are secret and the debaters are growing impatient to adjourn. If the allocation of the treaty power evoked little controversy, that may well indicate that there was broad initial agreement about placing that power in the Senate, and little perception later that the revisions made after August 6 had sharply altered the way in which it would be exercised.

Such at least is the thesis of Arthur Bestor, who has recently provided not only the most careful reconstruction of the drafting of the treaty clause but also the broadest interpretation of the authority meant to be reserved to the Senate. In his view, the final revisions of the treaty clause resulted not from "the settlement of sharply controverted issues" but rather from an "unspectacular process" involving "the gradual refinement of clauses that had been ambiguously worded or that had failed to express with sufficient exactness a consensus that already existed." The delegates' decision to involve the President in treatymaking came, Bestor concludes, after they realized that permitting the Senate to appoint ambassadors would violate the principle of a unitary executive. Despite the withering dissent of George Mason, a majority of the framers had agreed that executive power had to be vested in one person if the affairs of government were to be responsibly administered. If the Senate retained the power to appoint and instruct ambassadors, that responsibility would be both embarrassed and compromised. But in allowing the President to "nominate" ambassadors and "make" treaties, Bestor argues, the framers meant only that he would act as the Senate's agent and partner in negotiations, not as the independent author of policies the Senate could later ratify or reject only when treaties were formally submitted.[8]

The evidence for this consensus rests initially on the debate of June 1, when the delegates took up the question of executive power for the first time. The seventh article of the Virginia Plan which Edmund Randolph had introduced only three days earlier had called for the creation of a "National Executive" which, "besides a general authority to execute the National laws . . . ought to enjoy the Executive rights vested in Congress by the Confederation." Charles Pinckney opened the debate by

---

8. Bestor, "Respective Roles of Senate and President," pp. 88, 108–109. Bestor's argument, it should be noted, is not confined to these points. He stresses some matters that are not examined here, such as the sectional compromise over the regulation of commerce, and ignores others which I believe were more important, particularly the final decisions on the Electoral College.

declaring that "he was for a vigorous Executive but was afraid the Executive powers of [the existing] Congress might extend to peace & war &c which would render the Executive a Monarchy, of the worst kind, to wit an elective one." Pinckney's reservations rested on a problematic equation between the British Crown and the Continental Congress. Since the prevailing interpretation of the British constitution, as codified by William Blackstone, treated matters of war and peace as royal prerogatives, it could be argued that the major powers of the Congress were essentially executive in nature because it had supplanted the Crown in their exercise.[9]

The delegates were not eager to rise to the challenge of defining executive power. As James Madison reported in his notes, the brief introductory remarks of Pinckney and James Wilson were followed by "a considerable pause" that led Nathaniel Gorham (chairing the committee of the whole) to ask whether the question should be put. Serious debate began only after Benjamin Franklin reminded his colleagues of the importance of the subject now before them and John Rutledge "animadverted on the shyness of gentlemen on this and other subjects." Rutledge then went on to second his colleague Pinckney's views by declaring that "he was for vesting the Executive power in a single person, tho' he was not for giving him the power of war and peace." The two South Carolina delegates could be interpreted as stating merely that powers over war and peace could not be safely conferred on a republican executive, but succeeding remarks by Wilson and Madison confronted the theoretical problem more directly. In Wilson's view, "the Prerogatives of the British Monarch" were not "a proper guide in defining the Executive Powers. Some of these prerogatives were of a Legislative nature. Among others [*i.e.*, among these] that of war & peace &c." After other delegates had spoken on the issue of whether the executive should be unitary or plural, Madison rose to second Wilson's opinion. According to the notes of Rufus King, Madison "agrees wth. Wilson in his definition of executive powers—executive powers ex vi termini, do not include the Rights of war & peace &c. but the powers should be confined and defined."

The opinion that the executive should not be given power over war and peace went unchallenged. A more sustained discussion might have re-

9. Farrand, *Records*, I, 21, 64–74. James Madison gave succinct expression to this view in his well-known letter to Caleb Wallace, August 23, 1785, discussing his ideas of a suitable constitution for Kentucky. In discussing the construction of the executive branch, Madison noted that "Though it claims the 2d place [it] is not in my estimation entitled to it by its importance all the great powers which are properly executive being transferred to the Foederal Government." *The Papers of James Madison*, ed. Robert A. Rutland, *et al.* (Chicago and Charlottesville, 1962 on), VIII, 352.

vealed disagreement as to whether the considerations of prudence voiced by Pinckney and Rutledge mattered more than the theoretical statements of Wilson and Madison. But despite their brevity, the remarks of June 1 demonstrate that the framers believed that questions of war and peace — that is, the most critical subjects of foreign policy — were appropriate subjects for legislative determination rather than an inherent prerogative of executive power. Even in this first discussion, however, the question of how the executive branch would be constituted and selected took precedence over the consideration of the scope of its power. Nothing of substance was said, moreover, about the mechanics of framing and implementing foreign policy.

Once this debate was concluded, the entire subject of executive power commanded little attention prior to the appointment of the Committee of Detail on July 26.[10] How could so vital a subject go so long neglected?

The evolution of specific clauses cannot be understood independently of the political dynamics of the Convention. From late May until mid-July, the stalemate over representation effectively deterred the delegates from making significant progress on other issues. Until this question was resolved with the Great Compromise of July 16 (inaptly named, since the proponents of proportional representation for both houses of Congress did not compromise — they simply lost), they had little reason to invest great energy in determining either the general authority of the federal government or the precise allocation of power among its branches. Once the small states had secured an equal voice in the Senate, however, questions about the executive branch quickly came to the fore. They preoccupied the Convention during the ten days that preceded the adjournment of July 26 and the appointment of the Committee of Detail to prepare a polished draft based upon the resolutions already adopted. Yet even now questions about the actual powers of the executive received far less consideration than provisions for his election and term of office. Nothing at all was said about a presidential role in the conduct of foreign relations.

10. Under the New Jersey Plan, the treaty power would presumably have been left with Congress, since the only enumerated powers it bestowed on the executive, "besides their general authority to execute the federal acts," were "to appoint all federal officers not otherwise provided for, & to direct all military operations." Alexander Hamilton's plan of government is potentially more revealing, since its proposed "Governor" was "to have with the advice and approbation of the Senate the power of making all treaties." The provisions of Hamilton's plan, however, were not discussed at the Convention; and it is also worth noting that in his article listing the powers of the Senate, Hamilton gave it "the sole power of declaring war" as well as "the power of advising and approving all Treaties." Farrand, *Records*, I, 244, 292.

If a consensus did exist by late July, it rested on tacit assumptions rather than well articulated opinions. Even so, the relevant action of the Committee of Detail is fully consistent with what little had been said during the previous two months. Its report of August 6 assigned the Senate the exclusive power to make treaties and send ambassadors. The President's role in foreign affairs was confined to the essentially ceremonial function of receiving ambassadors.[11]

The treatymaking clause was not taken up until August 23.[12] Madison opened the debate by observing "that the Senate represented the States alone, and that for this as well as other obvious reasons it was proper that the President should be an agent in Treaties." What was obvious in 1787 is no longer so today. Bestor rightly notes that Madison's remark—it was not a motion—hardly implied "a wholesale transfer" of responsibilities from Senate to President. Madison's real concern, he suggests, was to avoid violating the already accepted principle that called for the creation of a unitary executive.[13]

But this inference is not directly supported by the records of the ensuing debate. Madison's notes on his own speech suggest that he was most troubled by the *representative* character of the Senate, where the states would retain the equal weight they enjoyed under the Confederation. And this concern was shared by the next speaker, Gouverneur Morris, who was no less ardent a supporter of proportional representation in both houses, and who may still have hoped to reverse the decision of July 16. After questioning whether treaties should be referred to the Senate at all, Morris moved an amendment that would have left their negotiation to the Senate but also required that "no Treaty shall be binding on the U.S. which is not ratified by a law"—in other words, approved by both houses of the legislature and presumably the President as well.

11. *Ibid.*, II, 183, 185.

12. It should be noted that the treaty power was discussed incidentally on August 15, when the Convention was debating whether the House of Representatives should have the right of originating revenue bills. George Mason supported this proposal by asserting that "He was extremely earnest to take this power from the Senate, who he said could already sell the whole Country by means of Treaties." This remark elicited a potentially significant comment from John F. Mercer of Maryland, who argued "that the Senate ought not to have the power of treaties. This power belonged to the executive department." *Ibid.*, II, 297. Mercer's remark is cited in support of broad interpretations of presidential power over foreign affairs; indeed, it is the single unequivocal statement in favor of such an interpretation that has been recorded for the entire Convention. But as Bestor notes, Mercer is virtually the last delegate whose opinion can be credited as evidence of his colleagues' feelings. Bestor, "Respective Roles of Senate and President," pp. 103–106.

13. Farrand, *Records*, II, 392–395 (for quotations in this and the following three paragraphs); Bestor, "Respective Roles of Senate and President," pp. 108–109.

The debate on this amendment was not well focused, but it did reveal that the Convention was not happy with the treaty clause as drafted. Nathaniel Gorham and William Samuel Johnson opposed the amendment on the grounds that "there was something of solecism in saying that the acts of a Minister with plenipotentiary powers from one Body, should depend for ratification on another," while James Wilson and John Dickinson supported it with arguments alluding to the representative character of the Senate. In the last recorded comment on the motion, Edmund Randolph observed "that almost every Speaker had made objections to the clause as it now stood," and moved to postpone debate. This motion failed on a tie vote, whereupon the Convention immediately rejected Morris's amendment decisively.

Enough had been said, however, to convince the delegates that the treaty clause did merit further consideration, for they then voted to postpone debate on the entire section. Madison thereupon suggested distinguishing "between different sorts of Treaties—Allowing the President & Senate to make Treaties eventual and of Alliance for limited terms—and requiring the concurrence of the whole Legislature in other Treaties." In his mind, at least, the rejection of the Morris amendment did not vindicate the principle of exclusive Senate control over foreign relations. But this was merely an offhand remark, not a motion. By this time it was late afternoon, and, perhaps because they were tired, the delegates voted to recommit the whole clause.

Far from demonstrating that the consensus of early June remained intact, the proceedings of August 23 suggest that the allocation of the treaty power was only now receiving serious consideration. Madison's notes reveal that questions had been raised about exclusive senatorial control of foreign relations, that these probably reflected concern with both the representative character of the Senate and the absence of any check on its actions, and most important, that few delegates were happy with the clause as written. They do not, however, indicate any strong interest in presidential treatymaking. Madison's reference to a role for the President was merely a "hint," and one which would limit his involvement to special cases.[14]

14. Morris, Wilson, and Madison apparently would have preferred making the House, rather than the President, the other participant in the treaty process. Given their role as leading spokesmen for the large states in the debates of June and July, it seems likely that their opposition to an exclusive senatorial power over treaties reflected continued resentment of the Great Compromise. The great obstacle they now confronted, however, was the objection that the larger and more popular chamber of the legislature would not possess the requisite secrecy and efficiency to be an effective partner in negotiations, particularly on occasions where urgent matters of war and peace were on the tapis.

Nor did even Madison worry about violating the principle of the unitary executive. In fact, immediately after rejecting Morris' amendment, the Convention enlarged the appointive powers of the Senate to include not only ambassadors and justices but "other public Ministers" as well.

The Convention had originally sent the treaty clause back to the Committee of Detail. But on August 31 this charge was superseded by a new decision "to refer such parts of the Constitution as have been postponed, and such Reports as have not been acted upon, to a Committee of a member from each State." It was in the lengthy second report of this Committee on Postponed Parts, delivered on September 4, that the key alterations concerning the treaty power were made.[15]

While the Committee on Postponed Parts left no record of its internal deliberations, there is one source that makes it possible to reconstruct at least part of its debate on the treaty clause. On January 16, 1788, when the South Carolina assembly was considering whether to call a ratification convention, several legislators raised substantive questions about the treaty clause. In response, two former members of the state's delegation at Philadelphia rose to explain why the Convention had joined President and Senate in treatymaking. Pierce Butler (who spoke first) had represented the state on the Committee, and to judge from the ensuing remarks of General Charles C. Pinckney, Butler had given a detailed account of its proceedings to his colleagues in the delegation.

Both of their speeches clearly indicate that the Committee had conducted a wide-ranging debate about the allocation of the treaty power. Butler recounted each of the objections that had militated against assigning "the sole power of making peace or war" to any one branch of the government. To give it to the Senate would risk "destroying the necessary balance" essential to preserving "the genius of a republic." Some members, Butler continued, "were inclined to give this power to the President," but that smacked too much of monarchy. In the case of the House, size posed "an insurmountable objection." Pinckney began his speech by reiterating these points. He took particular care to note his disagreement with the few delegates who thought the power "might safely be lodged" in the President alone, on the assumption that that officer would be both "responsible for his conduct . . . and more interested in making a good treaty

---

Morris' amendment was designed to answer this problem by confining the role of the House to ratification alone; Madison would have dealt with it by distinguishing classes of treaties in which the House could or could not participate safely.

15. Farrand, *Records*, II, 473, 481, 496–499.

than any other man in the United States." A President, Pinckney noted, was not so easily trusted: his situation "would be very different from that of a king," whose attachment to his country's welfare generally exceeded that of any of his subjects. Pinckney then concluded his remarks with a partial explanation of the Committee's eventual recommendation. "The different propositions made on this subject," he observed, "occasioned much debate. At last it was agreed to give the President a power of proposing treaties, as he was the ostensible head of the Union, and to vest the Senate (where each state had an equal voice) with the power of agreeing or disagreeing to the terms proposed."[16]

These two speeches fill a major gap in the records of the proceedings at Philadelphia. They confirm the suspicion that the session of August 23 had left the Convention highly uncertain of its desires, and that the debates within the Committee on Postponed Parts had not been confined within the limits of earlier discussions of the treaty power. The Committee had considered the range of arguments that could be advanced in favor of making either the Senate or the House or the Congress or the President the appropriate repository of this authority. It had also entertained notions that went beyond the idea that the President should either act merely as a check on the Senate or as its most appropriate agent in the actual conduct of diplomacy. While Pinckney himself may have felt that the President was less trustworthy than a king, his skepticism suggests that other delegates had voiced a more expansive view of the President's ability to represent a national interest. And if that idea was canvassed in the Committee, its decision to transfer the treaty clause to the executive article may have been carefully considered.

The revised treaty clause was listed seventh among the nine items which the Committee on Postponed Parts reported on September 4, and it was not taken up until the 7th. In the interim the Convention gave final consideration to the issue which James Wilson aptly called "the most difficult of all on which we have had to decide": the election of the President.

16. Jonathan Elliot, ed., *The Debates in the Several State Conventions, on the Adoption of the Federal Constitution* . . . (Washington, 1854), IV, 263–265; other legislators offered further comments on the treaty power, but these centered more on the issue of the legal status of treaties than the allocation of authority to make treaties. While Pinckney's description of the Senate "agreeing or disagreeing to the terms proposed" comes strikingly close to equating advice and consent with mere ratification or rejection, the general's remarks, when taken in their entirety, do *not* seem to cast the Senate in so narrow a role. For in both this speech and further comments the next day, Pinckney emphasized the contrast between the Senate and House by noting that the latter had been excluded from the treaty power because it "would be a very unfit body for negotiation"; *ibid.*, pp. 280–281.

Madison's notes for September 4–6 disclose only passing references to the treaty power *per se;* yet the decisions taken during the debate over the Electoral College provide a critical link in explaining why the Convention accepted a major presidential role in treatymaking so readily.[17]

The controversial feature of the method proposed for choosing a President was not the central innovation of the Electoral College itself, but rather the provision giving the Senate the power of election whenever the College failed to muster a majority for any candidate. In all likelihood, the key obstacle that the Committee had had to overcome was the familiar one of balancing the claims of large and small states. Its proposal was a genuine compromise. The large states would have the advantage in promoting candidates during the first stage of a presidential election, but should the final choice devolve upon the Senate—as many expected it usually would—the small states would exert the greater influence.

As opposed to the alternative of legislative election, the great virtue of the Electoral College was that it would reduce presidential dependence on the legislature, thereby both lessening the dangers of "intrigue & faction" and making the President safely eligible for reelection.[18] But the Committee had probably not thought through the implications of *all* the changes it was proposing. It had attempted to allay the reservations raised about the Senate during the debate of August 23 by giving the President a major role in treatymaking and appointments; but it had immediately undercut the force of this revision by making the Senate the potential electors of the President. As Randolph, Mason, Wilson, Rutledge, and Charles Pinckney quickly made clear, the plan was objectionable because (in Randolph's words) it would create "such an influence in the Senate over the election of the President in addition to its other powers, [as] to convert that body into a real & dangerous Aristocracy." This point was made several times on the 4th and 5th, and if any of the delegates had originally overlooked the connection between substantive powers and the

17. The report of September 4 and the debates of September 4–6 are in Farrand, *Records*. II. 493–531.

18. As William H. Riker has recently noted, one benefit of this compromise was to encourage each party to believe it had gained the upper hand. Some large state delegates predicted that the Electoral College would actually work, in part because the large states, anxious to avoid a decision in the Senate, would have a powerful incentive to make it work. Others, such as Roger Sherman and George Mason, thought that it would be a miracle if a President could ever be elected in that fashion. "On balance," Riker concludes, "most people anticipated just what would benefit them, a systematic bias that rendered the plan almost universally appealing." William H. Riker, "The Heresthetics of Constitution-Making: The Presidency in 1787, with Comments on Determinism and Rational Choice." *American Political Science Review*, 78 (1984): 1–16, quotation at p. 13.

mode of election, the final exchanges prior to the critical votes of September 6 must have removed all uncertainty. In a particularly forceful speech, James Wilson argued that the Senate's control over the election of the President would make him "the Minion of the Senate." Gouverneur Morris sought to deflect this charge by arguing that the Senate had been far more threatening *before* the Committee had divided its formerly exclusive powers over appointments and treaties with the President. But Hugh Williamson quickly answered this argument by reminding Morris that "The aristocratic complexion proceeds from the change in the mode of appointing the President which makes him dependent on the Senate."[19]

Notwithstanding the arguments that were levied against senatorial election of the President during these three days of debate, the original proposal was easily approved on September 6. To make either the whole legislature or the House the contingent electors of the President would only doom the entire proposal by giving the large states the advantage in *both* stages of an election. But Williamson reopened the discussion almost immediately, and Roger Sherman, a dogged parliamentarian, modified a suggestion he had broached earlier. Should the Electoral College not produce a majority, Sherman proposed, let the House make the decision, with the delegations voting as states. This scheme had the advantage of preserving the tacit compromise between large and small states. But its critical appeal lay, as Mason observed, in "lessening the influence of the Senate." With hardly a word of debate — and only Delaware dissenting — the Convention approved Sherman's amendment.[20]

In so doing, it also significantly enhanced the constitutional position of the President. For with this vote, the executive had ceased to be *politically* dependent on the body with which — should the rest of the Committee's report be adopted — it would share the powers of making treaties and appointments. A President who disagreed with the Senate over matters of foreign policy would have to fear neither impeachment nor for his reelection — unless, that is, his actions were also condemned by the House or a future Electoral College. Equally notable about the debates of Sep-

19. Farrand, *Records*, II, 513, 523–524; Bestor emphasizes the exchange between Wilson and Morris simply for the two speakers' comments on the treaty power. It is possible that the seemingly sharp clash of opinions between these two members of the Pennsylvania delegation was contrived, since the thrust of Wilson's position was to make the President more independent, a goal that Morris shared. On the other hand, Morris may have feared that if the Senate were attacked too vigorously, the whole compromise on the Electoral College would unravel. *Cf.* Bestor, "Respective Roles of Senate and President," pp. 120–123.
20. Farrand, *Records*, II, 527.

tember 4–6 is what they revealed about changing attitudes toward the Senate. No one attempted to justify the idea of an eventual election by the Senate in any other than expedient terms. Its only electoral virtue was its ability to protect the influence of the small states.

Thus when the Convention took up the treaty clause on September 7, the delegates presumably understood that the President could now serve as something more than a mere agent of the Senate. One could plausibly argue that the Convention had accepted a new and more expansive view of the presidential role in treatymaking *prior* to the actual considera- tion of the pertinent clause. Yet if only because so little was said about the role of the President during the debates of September 7–8, so sweeping a conclusion must be reached with care. In rendering the President politi- cally independent of the Senate, the framers may have understood that he would also be able to exercise a substantial degree of initiative in the making of foreign policy; but it is also possible that they construed the executive role more narrowly, as a check upon improper action by the Senate.

While the final debates on the treaty clause fail to provide a wholly satisfactory solution to this problem, they do yield three principal conclu- sions. First, the placement of the treaty clause within the executive article passed entirely without comment. If the Committee on Postponed Parts had thereby meant to assert that the conduct of foreign relations was in- herently an executive function, this piece of constitutional editing elicited neither approval nor criticism. Yet if the location of the treaty clause es- caped notice, the involvement of the President in treatymaking *was* a matter of some controversy. A few delegates, most notably Wilson and Madison, would still have preferred bringing the House into the treaty process while limiting the role the President would play in the most sensitive treaties. Finally, the Convention's preoccupation with the two-thirds clause strongly indicates that the framers did not mean to reduce the Senate to the mere task of ratification.

When the revised clause was first read on the 7th, James Wilson moved an amendment giving the House the same rights as the Senate in the making of treaties. Since treaties were "to have the operation of laws," Wilson argued, "they ought to have the sanction of laws also." This prin- ciple "outweighed" whatever "objection" might be made about the im- portance of maintaining "secrecy in the business of treaties." After Roger Sherman had answered Wilson by insisting that secrecy did matter, this proposal was decisively rejected. The emphasis given to secrecy in this ex- change is nonetheless significant: it would not have been the critical point if the role Wilson contemplated for the House was understood to involve ratification alone. Conversely, if the House was to be given the same authority as the Senate, the latter was still perceived to be involved in the treaty process from start to finish.

With the participation of the House at last ruled out, the Convention then unanimously endorsed, without further debate, the first part of the treaty clause ("The President by and with the advice and Consent of the Senate, shall have power to make Treaties"). It then briefly debated and unanimously approved presidential power to nominate and appoint ambassadors, justices, and other officials.

The remaining debate centered on the provision requiring the approval of all treaties by two-thirds of the Senate. The first objections were raised by Wilson, who protested that it would allow "a minority to controul the will of a majority," and by Rufus King, who argued that it was unnecessary because the President would "check" the Senate. Madison then moved two amendments. The first, which would have excluded peace treaties from the two-thirds rule, was originally approved without either comment or dissent. The second would have allowed two-thirds of the Senate to conclude treaties of peace "without the concurrence of the President."

These comments and motions reveal that the debate within the Committee on Postponed Parts had not yielded complete consensus on at least this aspect of the treaty power. King and Madison had been members of the Committee, and so had Pierce Butler, who supported Madison's second amendment. Madison and Butler both argued that an ambitious President might be tempted to prolong a war in order to retain the power that its conduct would bestow on him. But two other members of the Committee, Gouverneur Morris and Williamson, argued that presidential concurrence should be retained. Morris put the point directly when he declared "that no peace ought to be made without the concurrence of the President, who was the Guardian of the National Interests." Madison's second amendment was accordingly rejected, eight states to three.

Reservations about his first amendment — excluding peace treaties from the two-thirds rule — were also being voiced even before the Convention adjourned that day. The North Carolina delegates and Rufus King both moved to restore the two-thirds requirement to peace treaties where the "rights" of particular states might be sacrificed. Madison must have sensed that his first motion was in danger, for it was probably that evening that he drafted yet another amendment to require the concurrence of the House of Representatives for any treaty "by which the territorial boundaries of the U.S. may be contracted, or by which the common rights of *navigation* or *fishery* . . . may be abridged."[21]

When discussion resumed on the 8th, King criticized the exclusion of treaties of peace from the two-thirds requirement, while Wilson, ever the majoritarian, argued that "the requisition of two thirds [ought] to be struck out altogether." The Convention then agreed to reconsider the entire two-thirds clause. Its first action was to repeal Madison's amendment exempting peace treaties from the two-thirds requirement. A motion by James Wilson to eliminate the entire two-thirds provision was then roundly rejected. Four additional amendments, all designed to increase the size of a senatorial quorum (thus making the "two thirds" required for ratification a larger number of Senators), were also defeated, though two of these came within one vote of approval. In its last action on the treaty clause, the Convention then restored the two-thirds provision as it had originally been proposed by the Committee on Postponed Parts. The debate on these amendments was perfunctory, and the President was mentioned only once.[22]

The most striking feature of the debates of September 7 is that it was the two-thirds provision, rather than the new role of the President, that the delegates found controversial. Reservations about the composition of the Senate apparently weighed far more heavily in their thinking than any appreciation of the inherent value of presidential involvement in foreign relations. Some members, notably Wilson, Morris, and Madison, were clearly still perturbed by the disproportionately large voice the small states would enjoy in the conduct of foreign relations. Ideally, they would have preferred to remedy this defect by involving the House in the treaty process. The standard objections that could be directed against involving the House in the delicate business of diplomacy ruled this alternative out; but they also worked to make virtually the entire membership of the Con-

21. The debates of September 7–8 are *ibid.,* pp. 538–550; Madison's motion can be found *ibid.,* IV, 58. A note in the handwriting of John C. Payne, Madison's brother-in-law, plausibly assigns the date of September 7, 1787 to this memorandum.

22. Nathaniel Gorham argued against requiring a two-thirds approval of treaties because, unlike the procedures under the Confederation, "the President's consent will also be necessary in the new Govt." Prior to the vote to strike Madison's amendment exempting peace treaties from the two-thirds requirement, Roger Sherman "moved to annex a 'proviso that no such rights [as established by the Treaty of Paris] sh[ou]ld be ceded without the sanction of the Legislature.[']" This amendment, which was seconded by Gouverneur Morris and supported by Madison, was essentially similar to the one that Madison had apparently prepared after the debate of the previous day; it may also have been designed to serve as a substitute for the motions which the North Carolina delegates and Rufus King had introduced at the close of the session of September 7. Neither Madison nor the journal of the Convention records any vote on Sherman's proposal, however. Farrand, *Records,* II, 548.

vention more concerned with the protection of state and sectional interests within the Senate. The maneuvering over the two-thirds provision was the consequence of that concern.

On any list of the architects of an independent executive, Wilson, Morris, and Madison would rank high; yet only Morris seemed prepared to speak of the advantages of a major presidential role in the making of foreign policy in a forthright manner. Indeed, only in Morris' description of the President as "the general Guardian of the National interests" do we encounter a recognizably modern conception of the *representative* capacity of the executive branch. Yet even Morris would have welcomed the inclusion of the House in the entire treatymaking process had it been politically feasible, while Wilson and Madison seem to have preferred the involvement of the House to the proposed participation of the President. Nor are other references to the presidential role in treatymaking notably expansive: the comments of King and Gorham portray the President serving principally as a "check" upon the Senate. On balance, the Convention appears to have been more aware of the defects of the Senate and the limitations of the House than of any of the inherent virtues of a vigorous presidency. The additional responsibilities the office had acquired by early September are most prudently attributed to a belief that the Senate should not be allowed to act alone, and that the size, mutability, and popular character of the House precluded its involvement in foreign affairs. Nothing in the recorded comments of the delegates suggests that they had consciously fashioned a special role for the President to play; he had simply been given a share in the treatymaking process.

The presumption that it was the Senate that most needed checking reinforces the conclusion that the Convention did not intend to reduce the role of the Senate merely to ratifying or rejecting treaties that the President would negotiate independently. Advice, as Bestor concludes, was to be given at every stage of diplomacy, from the framing of policy and instructions to the final bestowal of consent. Had the President been imagined to exercise a general independence in the conduct of negotiations, it hardly seems likely that delegates anxious to preserve state or sectional interests within the Senate would have refrained from asking probing questions about his role. "The absence of controversy on the matter," Bestor notes, "is almost conclusive proof that no radical change from previously established practices was contemplated or apprehended."[23]

"Almost conclusive proof"— but not quite. While the evidence that the

23. Bestor, "Respective Roles of Senate and President," pp. 110–120, 101.

framers did not intend to limit the authority of the Senate to the mere ratification of treaties is indeed strong, their expectations about the role of the President remain elusive. The relocation of the treaty clause within the executive article cannot safely be dismissed as an incidental quirk of draftsmanship. Nor can one ignore the significance of the debates of September 4–6, when final adoption of the Electoral College seemed to hinge on finding a way to render the President politically independent of the Senate. Given that the proposals for the Electoral College and for shared presidential–senatorial power over treaties and appointments were presented within the same report of the Committee on Postponed Parts, the framers could certainly have grasped the relation between them almost intuitively. Indeed, one can hardly explain why the provision for a contingent election of the President would have proved so controversial without presuming that the framers were anxious to strengthen the position of the President *vis-à-vis* the Senate precisely in those areas where they would have to act in concert.

On this basis, then, it is difficult to accept the conclusion that the President was brought into the treaty process simply to serve as the agent of the Senate or to avoid violating the principle of a unitary executive. One accordingly has to ask whether the framers could have foreseen — or desired — the growth of presidential power over foreign relations that began to take place as soon as the Constitution went into operation. Since the records of the Convention are simply silent on this question, it is necessary to ask whether other sources that are ordinarily consulted on elusive matters of constitutional interpretation can here usefully be brought to bear.

RATIFICATION DEBATES AND COMMENTARIES

In April 1796, when the House of Representatives debated whether it had a right to inquire into the making of the Jay Treaty, James Madison delivered a famous pronouncement on how the Constitution was to be "expounded." The Constitution, Madison asserted,

was nothing more than the draft of a plan, nothing but a dead letter, until life and validity were breathed into it by the voice of the people, speaking through the several State Conventions. If we were to look, therefore, for the meaning of the instrument beyond the face of the instrument, we must look for it, not in the General Convention, which proposed, but in the State Conventions, which accepted and ratified the Constitution.[24]

24. Madison, speech on the Jay Treaty, April 4, 1796, in *The Writings of James Madison*, ed. Gaillard Hunt (New York, 1900–1910), VI, 272. The obvious difficulty with Madison's position is

Madison claimed too much, of course: the existing difficulties of explaining the intentions of the framers would be compounded tenfold if equal weight were given to the political outpourings of 1787–1788. But the debates and commentaries of the ratification campaign can still be put to valuable uses. They reveal, in the first place, how the Constitution was perceived immediately upon its publication, when its provisions were subjected to careful scrutiny, and before disputes over policies and the accretion of precedent began to influence its interpretation. Occasionally, too, as we have already seen, the ratification records contain telling remarks made by members of the Federal Convention.

For the most part, these first reactions to the treaty clause support the view that the power was to be genuinely shared between President and Senate, with the latter retaining the more influential role. If one can generalize about something as vague as "the ratifiers' expectations," they did not expect the President to acquire the dominant role in foreign policy.

The prevailing criticism of the treaty clause was based instead on the fear that the Senate would quickly learn to dominate the executive. "Consider the connection of the Senate with the executive," James Monroe asked the Virginia convention. "Has it not an authority over all the acts of the executive?" The President's power of nominating officers carried little weight, Samuel Spencer of North Carolina reasoned, since the Senate could simply reject his nominees until he acquiesced in their choices. A President who sought "to do any business," or even wished "to keep himself out of hot water," would have "to form a connection with that powerful body, and be contented to put himself at the head of the leading members who compose it."[25]

Others criticized the exclusion of the House from the entire treaty process. For one thing, the treaties the President and Senate made were to become the law of the land without gaining the full sanction of the legislature. For another, a Senate and President who colluded in framing an improper treaty would escape punishment, since the Senate was also the court of impeachment. "[C]an you impeach the Senate before itself?" the Pennsylvania Antifederalist John Smilie asked. Even if the House did impeach the President alone for a treaty he had made, Samuel Spencer ar-

---

that it resolves the problem by ignoring it; that is, it would substitute the first efforts at *interpretation* in the place of any evidence of the framers' *intentions*. Given the difficulty of finding the common denominator of such interpretations, much less weighing sober and considered criticisms against the more fantastic and dire predictions of 1788, it is difficult to avoid the conclusion that Madison's position in 1796 had more to do with politics that anything else.

25. Elliot, *Debates,* III, 221 (Monroe); IV, 116 (Spencer).

gued, "the Senate will not pronounce sentence against him, because they advised him to make it."[26]

Critics of the treaty clause expressed no fear of the President exercising an independent, let alone a decisive role in the conduct of foreign relations. What worried them instead was the danger of *joint* senatorial-presidential misconduct so guilefully contrived that even the security of the two-thirds clause would prove unavailing. Suppose that the President, in collusion with senators from one section of the country, secretly negotiated a treaty and then called a sudden meeting of the Senate to consider its ratification. Seven states could make a quorum; two thirds of a quorum could ratify a treaty; *ergo*, ten Senators from five states could transmute a treacherous negotiation into a treaty binding as the supreme law of the land. Eternal vigilance would truly be the price of holding a seat in the Senate. "If the Senators of the Southern states be gone but one hour," William Grayson told the Virginia convention, "a treaty may be made by the rest." Other critics of the treaty clause ignored the opportunities for procedural shenanigans but still wondered whether the two-thirds clause could adequately protect local or regional interests.[27]

Against such objections, reasonable or fantastic, the defenders of the Constitution offered sensible responses. Madison, for one, "thought it astonishing that gentlemen should think that a treaty could be got up with surprise, or that foreign nations should be solicitous to get a treaty only ratified by the senators of a few states." General criticism of the two-thirds provision could be answered by noting that the Articles of Confederation required essentially the same ratio for the adoption of treaties, without offering the additional security the President would provide.[28]

The critical point remains, however, that the Antifederalist case did not presume that the President would exercise a dangerously independent role, or that the Senate would have to check an overpowerful President. It rested instead on a conviction that neither could effectively check the other, and that the two acting together—as they would have to do—

26. Merrill Jensen, John P. Kaminski, and Gaspare Saladino, eds., *The Documentary History of the Ratification of the Constitution* (Madison, 1976 on), II, 460 (Smilie); Elliot, *Debates*, IV, 124–125 (Spencer).

27. See especially the comments of George Mason and William Grayson in the Virginia ratifying convention, *ibid.*, III, 499–502; and see Elbridge Gerry's objections to the Constitution, October 18, 1787, and the objections of George Mason (October 7, 1787), in Kaminski and Saladino, *Documentary History of Ratification*, XIII, 548, 348–350.

28. Elliot, *Debates*, III, 500 (Madison), 302–303 (Edmund Pendleton), 357–359 (George Nicholas); and see James Iredell's criticism of the published objections of George Mason, in *Pamphlets on the Constitution of the United States*, ed. Paul Leicester Ford (Brooklyn, 1888), pp. 342, 355.

could jeopardize a wide range of rights and interests. The actual objections that the Antifederalists raised are fully consistent with the framers' apparent expectation that the Senate would play at least an equal role in the making of foreign policy. Disagree as they might about how safely the treaty power would be exercised, Federalists and Antifederalists seem to have concurred in their understanding of how the power had actually been allocated.

Contemporary published commentaries on the Constitution confirm this impression. None does so more forcefully than *The Federalist*, which addressed the treaty power in two separate essays: number 64, written by John Jay, who, while not a delegate to the Philadelphia convention, was then in his fourth year of service as secretary for foreign affairs; and number 75, by Alexander Hamilton. While there are slight differences of emphasis between these two essays, they concur on all major points.

Jay devoted the opening paragraphs of his essay to showing that the treaty power would "be exercised by men the best qualified for the purpose," placing particular stress on the mode of election and tenure which the Convention had chosen for President and Senators. He then considered the nature of negotiation itself—a subject which his own experience had allowed him to contemplate in great detail. Here he did distinguish, in a limited way, between the respective functions that the two offices might perform. The successful negotiation of treaties, Jay observed, often depended on "perfect *secrecy* and immediate *despatch*"—traits which the President would obviously enjoy, but not the Senate. What at first seems to be an endorsement of a superior presidential role, however, actually supports a more modest claim. The President's special talents, Jay argued, would be employed in certain carefully defined circumstances: when, for example, "the most useful intelligence may be obtained, if the persons possessing it can be relieved from apprehensions of discovery," or on those extraordinary "occasions when days, nay, even hours are precious." "Those matters which in negotiations usually require the most secrecy and the most despatch," he continued, "are those preparatory and auxiliary measures which are not otherwise important in a national view, than as they tend to facilitate the attainment of the objects of the negotiation." The President's ability to manage negotiations was thus quite distinct from the authority to define the larger "objects" that were to be pursued. The latter responsibility, in Jay's view, lay closer to the genius of the Senate than to that of the President. In "our negotiations for treaties," Jay concluded, the Constitution would thus draw upon the peculiar virtues of both branches of government: the "talents, information, integrity, and deliberate investigations" of the Senate, and the "secrecy and despatch" of the President.[29]

While Jay's long personal involvement in American diplomacy makes his essay particularly authoritative, the argument of Hamilton's 75th *Federalist* is noteworthy for a different reason. For it was Hamilton who, in the Pacificus letters of 1793, subsequently offered the most expansive interpretation of presidential prerogative over foreign affairs. There he argued that *all* the executive power had been bestowed on the President, save for those exceptions which the Constitution specifically enumerated, and that the concept of executive power, as ordinarily understood, embraced the conduct of foreign relations.

This was not, however, the position he had taken as Publius in 1788. *Federalist* 75 opens with a brief rendition of the major objections that had been levied against the treaty clause. After endorsing the points that Jay had already made, Hamilton proceeded to consider "the trite topic of the intermixture of powers." Against the argument that the power to make treaties belonged "in the class of executive authorities"—and ought therefore to have been delegated solely to the President—Hamilton argued that "it will be found to partake more of the legislative than of the executive character, though it does not seem strictly to fall within the definition of either." Treatymaking was "a distinct department" of government, belonging to neither executive nor legislature, but properly divided between them. "The qualities" which Jay had "detailed as indispensable in the management of foreign negotiations" made the President "the most fit agent in those transactions," Hamilton concluded, "while the vast importance of the trust, and the operation of treaties as laws, plead strongly for the participation of the whole or a portion of the legislative body in the office of making them." The choice of language in this sentence is significant. The President is regarded as an "agent," and the Senate is depicted not as sharing an inherently *executive* power but rather as acting in a *legislative* capacity.[30]

In fact, the most striking feature of Hamilton's essay is that he seems almost to strain to justify *any* presidential involvement. Hamilton conceded that it would have been unwise to entrust the treaty power to the President alone: ambition and avarice might easily tempt "a man raised

29. [Alexander Hamilton, James Madison, and John Jay], *The Federalist*, ed. Benjamin F. Wright (Cambridge, 1961), pp. 420–425.
30. *Ibid.*, pp. 475–480.

from the station of a private citizen to the rank of chief magistrate" to betray his trust. The objections against an exclusive senatorial power were less weighty. The Senate could conceivably have been allowed to appoint its own ambassadors. But, Hamilton argued, such appointments would command less "respect" from foreign diplomats than the President would enjoy by virtue of his constitutional stature. At the same time, "the people would lose the additional security which would result from the cooperation of the executive." The President could not be trusted to act alone, but if linked to the Senate, "his participation would materially add to the safety of the society."

One wonders whether Hamilton was entirely sincere in *Federalist* 75. His other essays on the presidency, though similarly framed to rebut the ideas that the office was nothing less than "the full-grown progeny, of that detested parent," monarchy, candidly addressed the advantages of a vigorous executive.[31] It would be tempting to argue that the notion of executive power he later advanced as Pacificus represented views that were both authentic and longstanding. Yet private opinions and preferences matter less than his original understanding of how the Convention had actually allocated the treatymaking power. Nothing that Hamilton wrote in *Federalist* 75 contradicted the prevailing impressions of 1788. Just as the logic of debate led Antifederalists to argue that the treaty power had been improperly divided, the defenders of the Constitution had to stress the prudence of that division. On this issue, at least, both parties to the dispute read the language of the treaty clause in the same way.

None of the comments considered thus far supports the idea that contemporaries expected the President to acquire the initiative in the conduct of foreign relations; none can even be read to suggest that the President would be more in need of checking than the Senate. But on at least two other occasions, former members of the Convention discussed the treaty clause in ways which departed from the usual terms of debate, and which (like the South Carolina assembly debate examined earlier) may indicate how the framers had originally viewed the relation between President and Senate.

On December 4, 1787, James Wilson delivered a lengthy speech answering objections that had been made against the Constitution during the two weeks the Pennsylvania ratifying convention had already been in session. Much of his speech was devoted to defending the Senate, which had been attacked both for its "aristocratic" character and for its failure

31. In *Federalist* 67, *ibid.*, p. 436.

to represent the states according to population. In response to the charge that the Senate would control the making of treaties, Wilson pointed out that, by itself, "The Senate can make no treaties; they can approve of none unless the President . . . lay it before them." Wilson put the point even more sharply later in his speech. "With regard to their power in forming treaties," he noted, "they can make none; they are only auxiliaries to the President."[32]

Wilson's concern in making this argument was not to defend the inherent merits of presidential power; it was simply to show that the Senate would not act unchecked, and would indeed be subject to greater restraints than were currently imposed on the Continental Congress. His admission is nonetheless striking. Without presidential action, the Senate would be literally powerless in the conduct of foreign relations. If one assessed the balance of power between the two branches on this circumstance alone, the advantage would lie clearly with the executive. Was Wilson admitting this for the first time, or might he and his colleagues have grasped this point in early September?

One other exchange from the ratification debates supports a broad interpretation of the role that some delegates may have conceived for the President. In the first North Carolina convention, William Davie, a framer, declared that treatymaking was properly considered an executive responsibility, not only because negotiations required "secrecy, design, and despatch," but also because that department was not subject to "the violence, animosity, and heat of parties, which too often infect numerous bodies." In principle, Davie continued, "it would seem that the whole power of making treaties ought to be left to the President, who, being elected by the people of the United States at large, will have their general interest at heart." But principle alone had not prevailed. Instead, "that jealousy of executive power which has shown itself so strongly in all the American governments" had been reinforced by the fears of the small states, which had insisted on retaining "an equality of suffrage [in] the Senate," and with it "an absolute equality in making treaties." Thus it had been found "indispensable to give to the senators, as representatives of the states, the power of making, or rather ratifying treaties."[33]

Davie's preference for "ratifying" over "making" may, of course, be sig-

32. Jensen, *Documentary History of Ratification*, II, 480, 491.
33. Elliot, *Debates*, IV, 119–120. Davie had in fact left the Convention on August 13, and was accordingly not present for the key debates; however, he could still have received accounts from Richard Dobbs Spaight, who was also a framer-ratifier; Farrand, *Records*, III, 587.

nificant in its own right. But again, it is his image of the President which is the critical point. Davie envisions the President acting not merely as an agent of or check upon the Senate, but as an official broadly representative of the people, and peculiarly qualified to speak for "their general interest." The advantages he accordingly brings to the realm of foreign relations thus transcend the proverbial virtues of "secrecy" and "despatch." They include, as well, a capacity to frame more enlightened policy than the Senate, reflecting the jealousies of the states, would likely adopt.

Were it not for the comments of Wilson and Davie (as well as the recollections of Pierce Butler and General Charles C. Pinckney, discussed earlier), the records of the ratification period would favor the defenders of senatorial right rather than the advocates of presidential power. With these remarks, however, the evidence from the period of ratification preserves something of the uncertainty of the surviving records of the Convention. The ratifiers of the Constitution, like the framers, seemed to interpret "advice and consent" broadly: they expected the Senate to play a major and active role in the formation of treaties, even if, as Wilson realized, that body would be unable to act independently of the President. What remains elusive, however, is the degree of independence they intended or expected the President actually to exercise. John Jay could plausibly argue that presidential discretion would be confined to those "preparatory and auxiliary measures which . . . tend to facilitate the attainment of the objects of the negotiation," but he certainly knew from his own experience just how much leeway a diplomat could enjoy once negotiations were launched. In 1782, after all, Jay had taken the initiative in convincing his fellow peace commissioners to ignore their instructions from Congress and not inform their French allies of the terms of their bilateral negotiations with Britain. Moreover, none of the recorded comments on the treaty power deals directly with the consideration that would prove so important to its later exposition, its location within the executive article. Unless one assumes that its positioning was an oversight, a satisfactory interpretation of the text has to move beyond the debates of 1787–1788, and consider the wider context within which the treaty clause was written.

OTHER AUTHORITIES

Despite their best efforts to discover all the dangers inherent in the language of the Constitution, the Antifederalists overlooked the one provision which has most bedeviled interpretations of the scope of executive power. While the opening sentence of Article I stated that "All legislative powers herein granted shall be vested in a Congress of the United States," the comparable wording of Article II was left to read, "The executive power shall be vested in a President of the United States of America." From this simple omission of the words "herein granted," supporters of an energetic presidency have spun a far-reaching argument. While Congress could exercise only those powers which Article I expressly delegated, the authority of the President was derived, at least in part, from sources external to the Constitution, that is, from existing notions of the inherent scope of executive power. Thus, for example, when the issue of the removal of subordinate officials came before Congress in June 1789, some members argued that the silence of the Constitution in this area did not limit presidential authority because the power of removal stemmed directly from the general grant of executive power.

A comparable argument has been made in the realm of foreign affairs. If Congress possessed only the powers specifically enumerated in Article I, and if the framers assumed that the conduct of foreign relations was more properly classed among the executive powers, the authority of the Senate would be restricted to treaties alone. While "advice and consent" could still be construed broadly to enable the Senate to participate in every stage of treatymaking, the President could plausibly claim greater authority in every other aspect of the conduct of foreign relations. The location of the treaty clause within Article II could accordingly be read as evidence that the Convention meant to give the executive a decisive advantage in the jockeying for power that the brevity of the Constitution and the course of history would both foreseeably require.

From what source could such a conception have arisen? The framers could have been influenced by the example of the British constitution, which treated the conduct of foreign relations as an executive prerogative. Moreover, a generation "raised on Locke, Montesquieu, and Blackstone" would have defined executive power in the same terms that these major theorists of the separation of powers had already made familiar, and their writings may be interpreted as tending to treat the conduct of foreign relations as more closely connected to executive than to legislative power.[34]

34. Louis Henkin, *Foreign Affairs and the Constitution* (New York, 1972), p. 43. Henkin himself, however, stops well short of endorsing this assumption. Less cautious is Robert Scigliano, who argues that "Rather than look to 'British commentators' in general for the source of Hamilton's ideas on the powers of government, we should direct our attention to those two writers, Locke and his French counterpart Montesquieu, who above all others seem to have influenced his thinking on the

This interpretation deserves serious consideration because variations of these arguments were offered in the two most important constitutional debates of Washington's administration. Definitions of the inherent nature of executive power and references to the wording of the vesting clauses figured prominently in the 1789 debate over the President's removal power. The outbreak of war between Britain and France in 1793 provoked renewed discussion of this theory. In a famous exchange of newspaper essays, Hamilton (writing as Pacificus) and Madison (as Helvidius) debated whether President Washington had acted improperly by unilaterally issuing a proclamation declaring that the United States would act impartially toward the belligerents, without requesting the advice of the Senate to determine what obligations the United States had toward France under the treaty of alliance of 1778. Hamilton's opening defense of the proclamation placed particular stress on the vesting clause. "The general doctrine then of our constitution," he argued, "is, that the Executive Power of the Nation is vested in the President; subject only to the *exceptions* and *qualifications* which are expressed in the instrument." Madison responded with a powerful blast repudiating the idea that British precedent or the prior writings of European authorities could be used to guide interpretations of the federal Constitution — even though, four years earlier, he had himself relied on a simple definition of executive power in order to support the presidential right to remove lesser officials.[35]

Whether Madison or Hamilton had the better of this debate has been a subject of controversy ever since. What matters here is that in both 1789 and 1793 ready use was made of an argument from the inherent nature of executive power; and if such notions were available then, they obviously could have influenced the framers as well. We are thus warranted in asking whether thorny questions of constitutional interpretation can be resolved by examining the larger intellectual context in which the framers deliberated. Does recourse to the example of the British constitution or such external authorities as the theorists of the Enlightenment illuminate the general assumptions under which the framers and their contemporaries acted? Can relevant passages from Locke, Montesquieu, Blackstone, and other theorists be inserted into the silences of the Constitution and the

---

subject." Scigliano, "The War Powers Resolution and the War Powers," in *The Presidency in the Constitutional Order*, ed. Joseph Bessette and Jeffrey Tulis (Baton Rouge, La., 1981), p. 131.

35. The first Pacificus letter is reprinted in *The Papers of Alexander Hamilton*, ed. Harold C. Syrett and Jacob Cooke (New York, 1960–1978), X, 33–43, quotations at pp. 38–39; the first Helvidius letter can be found in *Writings of Madison*, VI, 138–151.

debates of 1787–1788? A substantial amount of constitutional commentary has rested on the plausible claim that the ideas of the framers cannot be understood without reference to the standard sources on which they relied. Yet at a time when historians have been at pains both to determine which European writers eighteenth-century Americans were reading — and how closely — and to stress how self-conscious they were about the novelty of their entire enterprise of founding, it is a claim that merits critical scrutiny.[36]

There is no mystery about how Madison would have dealt with this issue. The first Helvidius essay flatly rejects the notion that the doctrines of European writers can be used to explain American actions. Indeed, Madison's attitude toward such authorities is both disparaging and condescending. "[A] just analysis and discrimination of the powers of government" could not be expected even from the "jurists" who had written most extensively on international relations and law, because they did so "with eyes too much on monarchical governments, where all powers are confounded in the sovereignty of the prince." Locke and Montesquieu had admittedly paid greater attention to "the structure of government," but they, too, lay "under the same disadvantage, of having written before these subjects were illuminated by the events and discussions which distinguish a very recent period"— that is, the American Revolution. Moreover, both had been "warped" by an excessive regard to the government of England.[37]

Madison's assertions can be taken as evidence of his own attitudes, but

36. In a recent quantitative analysis of all references to European authorities found in 916 political pieces published in America between 1760 and 1805, Donald S. Lutz discovered that while "Montesquieu is cited heavily in pieces dealing with constitutional design," the principal use of Locke "lies in justifying the revolution and the right of Americans to write their own constitutions rather than in the *design* of any constitution, state or national. Locke's influence has been exaggerated in the latter regard," Lutz continues, "and finding him hidden in passages of the U.S. Constitution is an exercise that requires more evidence than has hitherto ever been provided." Donald S. Lutz, "The Relative Influence of European Writers on Late Eighteenth-Century American Political Thought," *American Political Science Review*, 78 (1984): 192–193. Notwithstanding its title, this essay does not deal with the problem of influence in any substantive sense. Far more informative on this point is John Dunn, "The Politics of Locke in England and America in the Eighteenth Century," in *John Locke: Problems and Perspectives*, ed. John W. Yolton (Cambridge, Eng., 1969), pp. 45–80. Dunn's argument is, however, consistent with Lutz's inference. As Dunn notes in his penultimate paragraph, "The readiness with which many scholars have detected the influence of the *Two Treatises* is at least in part a product of the fact that they have read so little else of the English political writing contemporary with it." But *cf.* Isaac Kramnick, "Republican Revisionism Revisited," *American Historical Review*, 87 (1982): 629–664.

37. That Madison should have felt this is not at all surprising—notwithstanding even his now famous application of the ideas of David Hume to the formulation of his theory of the extended republic. Madison had read many things; his contribution was to grasp their relevance to the American situation, and then to act on the basis of that perception.

did he also speak for his colleagues at Philadelphia and his contemporaries in general? The answer to this question requires asking three others: first, did external sources provide a coherent doctrine on which Americans could draw? Second, what evidence do we have of how Americans understood what they might have read? And, third, did they then act on the basis of that understanding? A brief consideration of each of these problems indicates why, in the specific case of the treaty power, this effort encounters awkward obstacles.

To begin with, recourse to the standard authorities does not reveal a clearly articulated or accepted doctrine of executive power that the framers could have readily applied. The control of foreign relations was a problem that neither Locke nor Montesquieu had considered carefully. Locke's brief discussion of relations among states is noteworthy in several respects, however. In the first place, Locke was careful to distinguish executive power, which involved "the execution of the municipal laws of the society within itself," from what he called "federative" power, that is, the "Power of War and Peace, Leagues and Alliances, and all the Transactions, with all Persons and Communities without the Commonwealth." These two powers, Locke noted, were "really distinct in themselves," but in practice "they are always almost united" in the same hands. Because the actions of "foreigners" could not be easily anticipated "by [the] antecedent, standing, positive Laws" which the executive ordinarily carried out, prudence rendered it "impracticable"—or dangerous—to place these two powers "in Persons that might act separately, whereby the Force of the Publick would be under different Commands: which would be apt sometime or other to cause disorder and ruine."[38] The critical feature of this argument is that Locke rested his case for vesting the federative power in executive hands on considerations of prudence, convenience, and efficiency, not right. Moreover, Locke also took care to note that the federative power, like the executive, was subordinate to the legislative will. Thus after declaring that the legislative power always retained the right to "resume" its own exercise of executive power "when they find cause, and to punish for any mall-administration against the Laws," Locke added a telling observation. "The same holds also in regard of the *Federative* Power, that and the Executive being both *Ministerial and subordinate to the Legislative*, which . . . in a Constituted Commonwealth, is the Supream."[39]

With Montesquieu, however, the distinction between federative and

38. Peter Laslett, ed., *John Locke's Two Treatises of Government: A Critical Edition with an Introduction and Apparatus Criticus* (Cambridge, Eng., 1960), pp. 383–384.
39. *Ibid.*, p. 387.

executive power *was* blurred, though it did not entirely disappear. The great contribution Montesquieu made to the theory of separation of powers was to treat the *puissance de juger* not merely as an aspect of executive power, but as a fundamentally distinct power of government. In attempting to define legislative, executive, and judicial power, however, Montesquieu betrayed some confusion. The opening sentence of his chapter on the English constitution declared that "In every government, there are three sorts of power: the legislative, the executive in respect to things dependent on the law of nations; and the executive, in regard to things that depend on the civil law." Under the first form of executive power the prince "makes peace or war, sends or receives embassies, establishes the public security, and provides against invasions"—activities that obviously correspond to Locke's federative functions. By the second form, the prince "punishes criminals, or determines the disputes that arise before individuals. The latter we shall call the judiciary power, and the other simply the executive power of the state." Read literally, this definition suggests that executive functions would be confined to external affairs alone, while the internal administration of the civil law would devolve entirely on the judiciary. After this "faltering start," however, Montesquieu went on to identify the essential powers of government as "that of enacting laws, that of executing the public resolutions, and that of judging the crimes or differences of individuals." A liberal reading of this famous passage could conclude that Montesquieu had eliminated Locke's distinction between federative and executive power, with the concerns of the executive now understood to embrace *both* internal and external affairs. If, however, one treats the negotiation of treaties as an aspect of "executing the public resolutions," Montesquieu would seem to follow Locke in recognizing the supremacy of the legislative will even in foreign relations.[40]

Montesquieu's efforts may thus have marked an advance over Locke, but they hardly provided a cogent or complete exposition of the problem. Together, as M.J.C. Vile has noted, Locke and Montesquieu had actually identified four types of power, but in *The Spirit of the Laws* that distinction had virtually collapsed.[41] On balance it would require a strained reading

40. [Charles] de Secondat, Baron de Montesquieu, *The Spirit of Laws*, trans. [Thomas] Nugent, 2nd ed. (London, 1752), pp. 215–216.

41. I have relied on the analyses in M. J. C. Vile, *Constitutionalism and the Separation of Powers* (Oxford, 1967), pp. 60–61, 86–87; and W. B. Gwyn, *The Meaning of the Separation of Powers: An Analysis of the Doctrine from Its Origin to the Adoption of the United States Constitution*, Tulane Studies in Political Science, IX (New Orleans, 1965), p. 78, n.1; pp. 100–103. It is a telling comment that neither of these excellent studies of the theory of separation of powers finds it necessary to devote

of Locke, and a generous overlooking of Montesquieu's brevity and confusion, to conclude that they regarded treatymaking as an inherently executive power.

Still, if the framers of the Constitution were not troubled by Montesquieu's confusion, his authority might have justified the placement of the treaty clause within Article II. But if they truly were inclined to regard foreign relations as an inherently executive power, a reliance on Montesquieu was unnecessary. Ample precedent for doing so could easily be found in the British constitution. It was the Crown that made treaties and declared war, and while those actions often invited or required parliamentary action of one kind or another, no commentator on the actual working of the constitution would have thought to suggest that the treaty power was inherently legislative in nature. The testimony of William Blackstone alone was conclusive on this point, and his authority would have easily outweighed the terse and imperfectly expressed ideas of Locke and Montesquieu.[42]

Can one accordingly conclude that the framers were guided by the authority of Blackstone (and perhaps Montesquieu) when they agreed to locate the treaty clause within Article II, and that they thereby affirmed that the control of foreign relations was essentially an executive function? A number of objections militate against such a conclusion. In the first place, the entire record of the Federal Convention demonstrates, as Madison observed, that the construction of the executive branch was a "peculiarly embarrassing" subject, resolved only after "tedious and reiterated discussions took place."[43] It was also, arguably, the problem which demanded

---

more than an occasional paragraph to considering the question of the management of foreign relations. Vile's discussion is particularly pertinent here: "between them, Locke and Montesquieu state at least *four* functions of government, not three: the legislative, the executive, the 'prerogative,' and the judicial. To bring the two middle ones together as 'executive' obscures the fact that in large areas of government activity those responsible for day-to-day government decisions will not be 'executing the law,' but exercising a very wide discretion. However," Vile adds, with Montesquieu "the idea that there are *three*, and only three, functions of government, was now established, except perhaps in the minds of those English lawyers who had actively to define the prerogative powers of the Crown." Vile, *Constitutionalism*, p. 87. One could argue that Hamilton's description of the treaty clause in *Federalist* 75 does resemble Locke's definition of federative power in Chapter XII of the *Second Treatise*, but this would not support the conclusion that Hamilton regarded foreign relations as an aspect of executive power.

42. See Bestor, "Separation of Powers in the Domain of Foreign Affairs," pp. 529–534; and Vile, *Constitutionalism*, pp. 101–105; William Blackstone, *Commentaries on the Laws of England*, 11th ed. (London, 1791), book 1, chap. 7, pp. 252–261.

43. The quotation is from Madison's famous letter to Jefferson of October 24, 1787, in *Papers of Madison*, X, 208.

the greatest measure of originality. Under such circumstances, it is difficult to see why the framers would have felt compelled to defer to the authority of Blackstone or to the example of the British Crown. A few members
of the Convention certainly felt that the British model deserved serious
consideration: Hamilton's famous speech of June 18 offers sufficient
testimony alone for this possibility.[44] But Hamilton was clearly the exception. After a decade of constitutional innovation undertaken in an atmosphere that had constantly reminded the Revolutionaries of the novelty
of their "experiment in republicanism," mimetic impulses no longer beat
deeply within American breasts. Given the evidence that a doctrine of
inherent executive power over war and peace was not influential at the
outset of the Convention—as the proceedings of June 1 conclusively
prove—it hardly seems likely that it would have become more attractive
as the debates wore on. Nothing in the records of the Convention suggests that the construction of the treaty clause was influenced in any way
by a desire to reconcile the intentions of the framers with the writings
of earlier authorities, however prestigious.

There is another, perhaps more powerful reason why the framers were
not inclined to regard foreign relations as an executive function. Whatever
uncertainty might have persisted about the precise allocation of the authority to make treaties, the framers were virtually of one mind when it
came to giving treaties the status of law. Compelling arguments for the
supremacy of national treaties over state law were being developed from
1783 on, perhaps receiving their most celebrated expression in the New
York case of *Rutgers* v. *Waddington*. The mounting "imbecility" of the
Confederation made it difficult to translate this principle into binding
practice, but that only clarified the task of the Convention. The imperative need to make treaties legally binding on both the states and their
citizens was widely recognized by 1787. The major consequence of this
perception was the ready adoption of the supremacy clause, which gave
treaties the status of law and made them judicially enforceable through
the federal courts. But the underlying recognition that treaties must be
legally binding would also alone have prohibited the Convention from
empowering the President to make them on his own authority.

All of these considerations tend to preclude the possibility that a reliance on external authorities and precedents influenced the evolution of
the treaty clause at *any* stage of the Convention's proceedings. Yet one

44. Farrand, *Records*, I, 282–311; on the basis of references cited earlier (see nn. 12, 33), one
would also have to add William Davie and John F. Mercer to this list.

final caveat must be noted. Once the Constitution was promulgated and its interpretation became a necessary aspect of American politics—first during the ratification campaign of 1787–1788, and then after the new government was actually organized—contemporary commentators did invoke these sources to make sense of what the Convention had actually done. It was the very novelty of the treaty clause in its final hybrid form that spurred contemporary observers to measure the framers' innovation against their own notions of the separation of powers.

The result was an array of opinions that seems to suggest that Madison was right to dismiss the whole business of canvassing earlier authorities as "a field of research which is more likely to perplex than to decide."[45] Attempts to apply the "hackneyed" doctrine of separation of powers to the question of foreign relations produced confusing results. It was no easy matter to determine precisely how the Constitution had violated the separation of powers. Had it done so by making the Senate "a part of the executive, having a negative in the making of all treaties," as the Federal Farmer complained, or rather, as Richard Henry Lee observed, by giving the President and Senate, "in some weighty instances (as making all kinds of treaties which are to be the laws of the land) . . . the whole legislative and executive powers"?[46] Other comments made after the Constitution took effect betray similar uncertainty. A notable example can be found in William Maclay's gloss on the treaty clause, recorded with characteristic asperity in his diary for June 14, 1789:

My mind revolts, in many instances, against the Constitution of the United States. Indeed, I am afraid it will turn out the vilest of all traps that ever was set to ensnare the freedom of an unsuspecting people. Treaties formed by the Executive of the United States are to be the law of the land. To cloak the Executive with legislative authority is setting

---

45. *Writings of Madison*, VI, 145.
46. *Observations Leading to a Fair Examination of the System of Government Proposed by the Late Convention . . . In a Number of Letters from the Federal Farmer* (n.p., 1787); Richard Henry Lee to Governor Edmund Randolph, October 16, 1787; both in Kaminski and Saladino, *Documentary History of Ratification*, XIV, 32–33, 367. The difference between the two objections just cited here might be taken as evidence that Richard Henry Lee was not the Federal Farmer. In a postscript to his letter, Lee included in his list of proposed amendments to the Constitution one to provide for the appointment of a privy council of eleven "to advise and assist in the arduous business assigned to the executive power." When he came to specify its duties, he argued that "In order to prevent the dangerous blending of the legislative and executive powers, and to secure responsibility, the privy, and not the senate shall be joined with the president in the appointment of all officers, civil and military, under the new constitution." No alteration in the exercise of the treaty function was proposed, however, implying that Lee did not regard its allocation between President and Senate as an improper distribution of a power that was exclusively executive in nature. *Ibid.*, p. 371.

aside our modern and much-boasted distribution of power into legislative, judicial, and executive—discoveries unknown to Locke and Montesquieu, and all the ancient writers. It certainly contradicts all the modern theory of government, and in practice must be tyranny.[47]

But when Alexander Hamilton advised President Washington on points of protocol, he suggested that while members of the House had no claim of access to the President, Senators did, since they were joined with him "in certain executive functions; treaties and appointments."[48] And in another oft-quoted gloss on the management of foreign relations, the first secretary of state asserted that "The transaction of business with foreign nations is *Executive altogether*. It belongs, then, to the head of that department except as to such portions of it as are specially submitted to the Senate. *Exceptions are to be construed strictly.*" On this issue, at least, Jefferson and Hamilton would seem to have been of one mind. Yet had Jefferson believed that such business involved anything more than routine matters, would he have been so anxious in 1793 to recruit Madison to answer the "striking heresies" about executive power that Hamilton had advanced as Pacificus?[49]

47. *The Journal of William Maclay, United States Senator from Pennsylvania, 1789–1791,* ed. Charles Beard ([1927]; New York, 1965), p. 73. The interpretation of Maclay's remarks, which pass over the "advise and consent" clause entirely, may be clouded by the fact that the first treaties laid before the Senate were those concluded with various Indian nations at Fort Harmar in January 1789. Under the Articles of Confederation, and during the pre-Revolutionary era as well, Indian "treaties" had been regarded as conclusive when the commissioners duly authorized to negotiate them affixed their signatures to the text; they were not subjected to the formal requirements of ratification by the Continental Congress or other higher authority. See Linda G. DePauw, ed., *Documentary History of the First Federal Congress* (Baltimore, 1972 on), II, *Senate Executive Journal and Related Documents,* 37–43; and Ralston Hayden, *The Senate and Treaties, 1789–1817* (New York, 1920), pp. 11–16.

48. Hamilton to Washington [May 5, 1789], in *Papers of Hamilton,* V, 337; but *cf.* the notes for Hamilton's argument in *Rutgers v. Waddington,* which include the statement that "The power of Congress in making Treaties is of a Legislative kind"; Julius Goebel, Jr., ed., *The Law Practice of Alexander Hamilton: Documents and Commentary* (New York, 1964), I, 377.

49. Jefferson, Opinion on the Powers of the Senate [April 24, 1790], in *The Writings of Thomas Jefferson,* ed. Paul Leicester Ford (New York, 1892–1899), V, 161–162. It is important to note that in this opinion Jefferson was dealing not with the treaty power but with the right of the Senate to designate the rank of diplomatic appointments. By stressing that the Constitution gave the presiden^r the prior right to "nominate" ambassadors, his argument can be invoked to call attention to a fundamental difference between the treaty and appointment provisions. Had the framers wished to give the president the explicit power of making treaties without prior senatorial advice, they could easily have found comparable wording to suit that purpose. Jefferson made the same point about presidential control of diplomacy again in 1793, when he told the French minister Genêt that the President was "the only channel of communication between this country and foreign nations" (letter of November 22, 1793, *ibid.,* VI, 451), and so did John Marshall in 1798 when he described the President as the

One conclusion at least can be drawn from this seemingly muddled set of references. Without denying that Americans possessed a general commitment to the doctrine of separation of powers, it is impossible to prove that some broad notion of inherent executive power was surreptitiously incorporated in the Constitution merely by the force of the venerable authority of Locke, Montesquieu, Blackstone, or other writers. Their real legacy was not enlightenment but confusion. Ideas so briefly and obliquely expressed could hardly serve as authoritative expressions of doctrine in 1787. Before the framers could have applied these sources to their debates, they would first have had to convince themselves not only that they understood what they had read, but also that it was pertinent to the task before them. There is no evidence that they attempted to do so, and good reason to believe that they were exercising independent judgment. There may well be other constitutional provisions whose interpretation can be aided by a careful reading of earlier theorists of separation of powers, but the case for their influence on the fashioning of the treaty clause or its location within the executive article remains weak.

EXPERIENCE AND INTENTION: A CIRCUMSTANTIAL HYPOTHESIS

Did the framers of the Constitution perceive advantages in giving the President a major role in the making of treaties? The sources examined so far do not provide a satisfactory answer to this question. But one area has not yet been explored: the lessons that the framers might have drawn from their own experience of conducting foreign policy under the Articles of Confederation. Is it possible that such lessons could have been applied not only to the supremacy clause—where their relevance is obvious—but also to the allocation of power between President and Senate? Beyond routine considerations of the advantages of executive "despatch," could recent events have given the framers good reason to favor a substantial presidential role in the making of policy?

"sole organ of the nation in its external relations, and its sole representative with foreign nations." See the discussion in Henkin, *Foreign Affairs and the Constitution*, pp. 45–50, 297–299, n. 10; 300, n. 18. It remains entirely possible, however, that the framers and their contemporaries were consciously distinguishing between routine communications and the framing of policy. Jefferson was certainly opposed to the claims for executive power that Hamilton made not only as Pacificus, but in prior deliberations within the cabinet. See Jefferson to Madison, June 29–30, 1793, in *Writings of Jefferson*, VI, 327–328, and his subsequent letters of July 18 and 22, 1793, in *Writings of Madison*, VI, 135–138.

The notion that useful inferences about the framers' intentions may be drawn from a careful reconstruction of their experience seems at once unobjectionable in theory but problematic in practice. No one would deny that the general experience of self-government since independence was the most important of all the causes leading to the making of the Constitution. Nor is it particularly difficult to trace such specific provisions as congressional control of the Indian trade or judicial cognizance of treaties to overt events occurring within a short span of years or even months preceding the Convention. Yet when it comes to considering the great political questions upon which the larger design of the Constitution seems to hinge, efforts to draw lessons from the framers' recent experience or from considerations of policy seem to falter.

American experience of diplomacy prior to independence was, of course, virtually nil: as Charles Thomson later recalled, British rule had kept the colonists "secluded . . . almost from all intercourse with foreign nations."[50] But this inexperience ended with the final imperial crisis of 1774-1776. Over the next decade, foreign relations became a subject of active debate and increasing political controversy. Nothing contributed more directly to the calling of the Constitutional Convention than the conviction that Congress was no longer capable of managing external affairs in a satisfactory manner.[51] Against this background, the framers' notions of how foreign relations ought to be conducted may well have been shaped by the course of events since independence. And this experience involved more than the formal weakness of Congress under the Articles of Confederation; it also illustrated the difficulty of deciding which interests any national government, strong or weak, ought to pursue.

Both the emerging national interest and the way in which it was to be determined had been easiest to define at the opening of the Revolution. The effective control over the conduct of American resistance which the Continental Congress quickly acquired and scrupulously sought to maintain grew directly from the political logic of a revolutionary situation. In 1774 this logic dictated that Congress would determine what demands the colonists would make of Britain if the crisis precipitated by

50. Thomson to Benjamin Franklin, August 13, 1784 (Bache Collection, American Philosophical Society). A decade earlier, Thomson had reminded his Boston correspondents that the colonies had no knowledge of diplomacy, and that they ought therefore to encourage "young men of fortune . . . to enter into foreign service, to visit foreign courts, and to establish acquaintances and connexions abroad." Charles Thomson to Samuel Adams and John Hancock, December 19, 1773, Letters of the Boston Committee of Correspondence (Bancroft Collection, New York Public Library).
51. See especially Marks, *Independence on Trial*, pp. 3-95.

the Coercive Acts was to be resolved by negotiation rather than force. From late 1775 on, the political situation also enabled Congress to hold an effective monopoly over contacts with foreign powers who could be expected to support America after independence seemed imminent. Although within Congress there were sharp debates about the wisdom of independence and the timing of specific measures (including the opening of relations with foreign nations), the delegates felt constrained to present the same united front to the British adversary, potential foreign allies, and their own constituents. The Ministry would not offer the concessions Congress demanded as the basis for reconciliation if the Revolutionary leadership revealed itself to be deeply divided; France would not risk war with Britain to support a country that might quickly revert to its earlier allegiance; and the American people would not make the sacrifices resistance required if they suspected that a body hailed as "the collected wisdom" of the continent was in reality a quarrelsome assembly unable to agree upon fundamental goals.[52]

In a revolutionary situation which placed a premium on securing a high degree of consensus, objections against congressional control over foreign relations were heard only from Loyalists. Moreover, continued British miscues enabled Congress to maintain not only the image but also much of the substance of unanimity. Neither the Howe Commission of 1776 nor the Carlisle Commission of 1778 succeeded in convincing Americans of the sincerity of the British government's interest in accommodation. Both missions seemed contrived to open fissures within the general population, particularly since they refused to acknowledge either the formal existence of Congress or its ability to exercise the major functions of external sovereignty.

Through the summer of 1778, then, issues of foreign relations worked to maintain both the authority of Congress and the general cohesion of the Revolutionary leadership and its supporters. One could almost say that June 1778 marked a final high point of Revolutionary unity. From then on, however, the imperatives of foreign affairs ceased to exert a unifying influence on Revolutionary politics, and became instead what they were long to remain: a source both of contention within Congress and of increasing mistrust without. The completion of the French alliance and the preservation of the popular commitment to independence hitherto had been the lodestars of congressional policy. Once these objects were secure,

52. This paragraph draws heavily on the argument presented in Jack N. Rakove, *The Beginnings of National Politics: An Interpretive History of the Continental Congress* (New York, 1979), chaps. 1-6.

the delegates were disillusioned to learn that future subjects of foreign policy would be far more disruptive of national unity.

This lesson was first revealed during the protracted struggle over diplomatic appointments and American peace terms that preoccupied Congress from the fall of 1778 until the late summer of 1779. At the request of Conrad Gérard, the French minister, Congress attempted to define the terms it would demand in the event that Britain accepted a Spanish offer of mediation and negotiations commenced. Delegates from the southern states were anxious to accommodate the French, especially after it became clear that the locus of combat was shifting to their region. But New England members insisted that a guarantee of American access to the Newfoundland fisheries had to be made an "ultimatum" of peace, and they had enough support scattered in other delegations to keep Congress deadlocked for months. While the New England delegates ultimately failed to make "Cod and Haddoc" the linchpin of American aims, they were reasonably content to have secured the appointment of John Adams as sole minister for negotiating peace. John Jay, his principal rival, was shunted off to Spain, and Benjamin Franklin was left in charge of the American mission in France, ending the bickering that had prevailed there since 1777, when Franklin, the paranoiac Arthur Lee, and the Yankee trader Silas Deane had been joined in an unhappy triumvirate.[53]

Many delegates realized that this protracted debate had served Congress poorly, and in the early 1780s efforts were made to prevent such passions from boiling over again. These met with only partial success. Key New England delegates resented the support their opponents had received from Minister Gérard, and even after Gérard was replaced by the more adroit Luzerne, they found good reason to suspect French influence. At Luzerne's prodding, a majority of Congress agreed to enlarge the American peace commission—thereby limiting the damage an obstreperous John Adams might do to French interests—and to require its members to accept French direction whenever negotiations finally occurred. Both measures seemed designed to subordinate New England's interest in the fisheries to the southern states' eager desire for peace.

In the end, of course, Adams, Jay, and a reluctant Franklin acted with a laudable opportunism, ignoring the instructions of Congress when the British negotiators offered to treat separately. Once Congress realized that its agents had done well to defy their orders, many delegates may have

53. A detailed account of these debates is *ibid.*, pp. 243–274.

seen in the generous terms which the American commissioners had secured an occasion for the nation as a whole to regain something of the general political harmony which had prevailed at the opening of the Revolution. True, the Treaty of Paris did contain two controversial provisions regarding the rights of Loyalists and British creditors. But while the refusal of certain states to enforce these articles became an issue *between* Congress and the states, such criticism as there was of the treaty did not threaten to revive divisions *within* Congress.

The irony of this situation was that the patriotic constraints that had carried Americans through the war quickly dissolved with independence secured. As in 1778, the attainment of an overarching national objective had the effect of legitimating the parochial claims of regions and individual states. By the summer of 1784 new issues were emerging to demonstrate that a broadly recognized national interest could itself no longer be said to exist. The closure of the British West Indies to American shipping posed a serious threat to northern merchants but not to southern planters whose commodities went elsewhere and who seemingly preferred to have their commerce under the control of Britain rather than New England. So, too, the dumping of British goods on American markets long deprived of the finer things may have punctured many a northern merchant's or artisan's dreams of postwar prosperity, but it hardly troubled southern planters anxious to return to prewar patterns of consumption. When Spain closed the Mississippi River to American navigation, however, the situation was reversed. The new settlements west of the Appalachians and along the Ohio River were regarded as outposts of the southern states. It was far from clear how the interests of the northern states would be hurt if Spain forced these settlers to look to New Orleans for protection.

Each of these problems is customarily regarded as one more count in the general indictment of the Articles of Confederation that was being prepared as the high hopes of peace gave way to the sobering realities of the mid-1780s. Each pointed to an area where an impotent Congress could not protect vital interests, and where a solution to some specific ill seemed to require the amendment of the Articles. If Congress could be given the authority to regulate foreign trade, for example, it could close American ports to British shippers until West Indian harbors were opened to American merchants. If Congress had revenues and resources adequate to its responsibilities, it would be in a better position to project enough force to maintain the loyalty of western settlers. And if the Articles could somehow be amended to assure that foreign treaties could be made binding on the states, the treaty violations cited by Britain as a pretext for retaining the northwestern posts would lose effect.

Yet to say that these problems pointed inexorably toward the creation of a stronger union reveals only half of their contribution to the movement that ultimately led to Philadelphia in 1787. For the dilemmas they posed were as much *political* as *constitutional*. The ability of Congress to exercise greater power required not only its possession of formal authority and sufficient resources, but also a capacity to agree on measures and policies, to define, that is, where the national interest actually lay. And this is precisely what the foreign policy developments of the mid-1780s had called into question.

The extent of this problem was not fully apparent during the first year of peace, but it quickly became so thereafter. In early 1785, a congressional committee led by James Monroe drafted an amendment to the Articles asking the states to grant Congress a general power to regulate commerce. This proposal foundered within Congress, where it encountered two sets of objections, one rooted in interest, the other based on ideology. A number of southern delegates feared that such a measure would enable northern merchants to control southern commerce; a group of New England members viewed any attempt to strengthen the Confederation as a potentially dangerous assault on the liberty of the states — even though their own constituents were thought to be the measure's intended beneficiaries.[54]

Far more alarming than the opposition to this amendment was the dispute over the navigation of the Mississippi that troubled Congress in the summer of 1786; it produced the sharpest and most explicitly sectional divisions that body had experienced since 1779. After months of tedious negotiations with a Spanish emissary, John Jay, secretary for foreign affairs, asked Congress to revise his instructions. Rather than insist that Spain immediately open the Mississippi to American navigation, Jay recommended that the United States abjure its claim to passage for a period

---

54. The most informative letters on this issue were those written by James Monroe, who played the leading role within Congress in bringing these proposals forward. See Monroe to Jefferson, December 14, 1784, and April 12, June 16, and August 15, 1785, in *The Papers of Thomas Jefferson*, ed. Julian P. Boyd (Princeton, 1950 on), VII, 573, and VIII, 76–80, 215–217, 382–383; Monroe to Madison, December 18, 1784, and July 26, 1785, in *Papers of Madison*, VIII, 188–190, 329–330; on the fears of the New England delegates, see especially the letters from the Massachusetts delegates to Governor James Bowdoin, August 18, 25 and September 3, 1785, in *Letters of Members of the Continental Congress*, ed. Edmund C. Burnett (Washington, 1921–1936), VIII, 188–190, 196–197, 206–210.

of years, in exchange for which Spain might at last agree to conclude a treaty of commerce. Southern delegates saw this proposal as an attempt to sacrifice their region's interests in western expansion for the benefit of northern merchants. In a series of roll calls conducted on strictly sectional lines, the seven states from Pennsylvania to New Hampshire pushed through the revision Jay had sought, even though a treaty negotiated along those lines could hardly be expected to secure the nine states required for ratification. It was the stark sectional alignments manifested in this dispute that encouraged speculation over whether the union might dissolve into two or three confederacies if the Articles were not soon amended.

These were the events that had provided the framers with their principal experiences in the making of foreign policy. From such episodes they could easily have drawn lessons about the sorts of political problems which the new government would have to resolve whenever it sought to exercise the enhanced authority the Constitution would bestow. Might such "lessons" also have influenced the evolution of the treaty clause? In particular, can they be used to explain why the framers finally acted to bring the President into the treatymaking process? An attempt to bridge gaps in the documentary record by inferring what the framers ought to have been thinking runs the risk of having to rely on not one but two circumstantial arguments. The first of these requires assuming that the historian can identify the lessons that the framers themselves could have drawn—and in all likelihood did draw—from recent events. And, in the second place, such an attempt must also provide a plausible basis for demonstrating how these concerns could actually have become operative within the framework of the Convention.

There can be no doubt that lessons of the past were invoked during the final debate of September 7-8, when the Convention seemed preoccupied with the provision requiring treaties to be approved by a two-thirds vote of the Senate. Surviving references are explicit. Gouverneur Morris described "the Fisheries [and] the Mississippi" as "the two great objects of the Union," and Elbridge Gerry—a key participant in the events of 1779—opposed James Madison's attempts to make peace treaties easier to approve because in such negotiations "the dearest interests will be at stake, as the fisheries, territories &c." Hugh Williamson of North Carolina evinced a similar concern when, late on the 7th, he proposed restoring the two-thirds requirement for peace treaties "affecting Territorial rights." The additional motion that Madison probably prepared the evening of the 7th had attempted to respond to this concern by requiring the concurrence of the House of Representatives for any treaty in which the United States had to make concessions involving territorial, commercial, or fishing rights. All but one of the motions considered on the 8th were designed to protect the rights of individual states or regions, and the strongest support for these proposals came from the southern states—and particularly from Georgia and the two Carolinas—reflecting their concern over the future of American expansion into the southwest.[55]

Some months later, Williamson reminded Madison that when James Wilson had objected to the two-thirds proviso, "it was replyed that the Navigation of the Mississippi after what had already happened in Congress was not to be risqued in the Hands of a meer Majority."[56] As Williamson's comment makes clear, the final jockeying over the two-thirds requirement reflected at least one obvious lesson that the framers could have drawn from recent history. The disputes of 1779 and 1786 had demonstrated that sectional rivalries involved something more than parochial attachments or even a growing tendency to translate disagreements over the apportionment of representatives and taxes into morally charged arguments about the legitimacy of slavery. Many of the framers had good reason to wonder whether vital state or regional interests would be adequately protected in a Senate where the states would retain the equal voice they enjoyed under the Articles. New England members who recalled the struggle over the fisheries would certainly have been justified in fearing that an expanding union would not be strongly committed to the protection of this particular maritime interest. By the same token, the Mississippi debate had taught southern delegates that many northern leaders were not firmly convinced of the benefits of settling new territories on either side of the Ohio River. Both regions had thus found themselves in the position of a threatened minority with vital interests at stake. Such interests would not be secure if treaties required the approval of a mere majority of the Senate.

The members of the Convention also knew that memories of these disputes would be revived when the Constitution was submitted to the states. This consideration, too, would have prevented the framers from contem-

55. Farrand, *Records*, II, 540–543, 547–550; IV, 58 (for Madison's amendment). It is important to note that Madison was well aware that the Mississippi issue would figure prominently in the ratification debates in Virginia, where Antifederalists led by Patrick Henry could be expected to argue that southern expansionist interests would not be adequately secured by any constitution which gave a national government greater power. And in fact the Mississippi issue was actively debated at the Virginia ratification convention; see especially the debates of June 13, 1788, in Elliot, *Debates*, III, 332–365.

56. Williamson to Madison, June 2, 1788, in *Letters of Members*, VIII, 746–747.

plating vesting the treaty power in the executive alone. State and regional interests were of such critical importance that they deserved, indeed required, expression through a representative institution. For this purpose the Senate offered an ideal forum: each state could be assured that its interests would be asserted with an equal voice and protected by an equal vote. The vivid force of this concern adds further support to the idea that the framers could not have equated "advice and consent" with mere ratification. There would be no point in advising the President of the particular interests of the states only after his diplomatic tasks were completed.

Both the two-thirds provision and the requirement of senatorial "advice and consent" can thus be seen as manifest results of the need to protect the interests of particular states, a need that recent events had vividly legitimated. But if lessons of recent history were applied for this purpose, is it conceivable that they also worked in the opposite direction, to endow the President with the capacity to pursue a larger national interest which could predictably take precedence over such parochial claims? Would this not have required the framers to draw contradictory inferences from the same set of experiences, and to incorporate conflicting lessons within the same clause of the Constitution?

Certainly earlier episodes could have been used to illustrate the dangers of allowing foreign policy to be made exclusively by a Senate that would bear an unfortunate resemblance to the existing Congress. In 1779, Congress had needed seven months to set its peace terms, even though Conrad Gérard had continually pressed for prompt action. For those members of Congress who believed that the premier object of American foreign policy was the preservation of a warm alliance with France, this deadlock had loomed as a threat to the nation's security as well as an embarrassing example of habitual congressional indecision. The stakes in 1786 had been less ominous. But even then, the contending advocates could still have found time to reflect that a process of policymaking that subjected urgent regional concerns to the vagaries of parliamentary maneuver would not always operate in the national interest. On both occasions, the exposure of vital matters to prolonged debate had produced a sense of frustration and resentment that tended to widen the dispute rather than promote compromise. Equally damaging was the fact that such a situation encouraged delegates to attempt to break the impasse within Congress by reaching out to their constituents or even the general public for support. Once the vital interests of their states were jeopardized, members of Congress had little choice but to act as representatives from their particular states, rather than as members of a national government responsible for pursuing some common good.

If the framers of the Constitution were thinking about these episodes, they could also have foreseen the advantages of an enhanced presidential role in both the making of foreign policy and the conduct of negotiations. They could have readily understood why the national interest would be well served by a constructive ambiguity that would enable successive Presidents to discover how much autonomy they could exercise. The great advantage of such a development would be to reduce the amount of political conflict that issues of foreign policy would generate. A President who enjoyed some leeway to control the process of diplomacy could also restrict the range of controversy that any negotiation might evoke. Rather than dwell on all the speculative contingencies that might ensue from this policy or that tactic, the Senate might be more inclined to defer judgment until the actual results of a negotiation became known. Given that the framers had good reason to worry about how the union would be preserved even after the Constitution was approved, such considerations can hardly be dismissed as improbable or fanciful. In fact, the experience of the first quarter century of national politics would demonstrate not only how valid such concerns were, but also how difficult it still remained to insulate the making of foreign policy from regional interests and political strife. The key point, however, is that the essential lessons could have been learned well before the controversy over the Jay Treaty precipitated the formation of the first party system.

A similar argument could have been made in favor of transferring the power to appoint ambassadors from the exclusive control of the Senate to presidential nomination and senatorial consent. Had the debate over peace terms in 1779 not become fused with the prior quarrels of the American commission in Paris, the factional divisions within Congress could possibly have been restrained within more manageable limits. But the outpouring of accusations between the partisans of Arthur Lee and Silas Deane flowed through and deepened these lines of division; indeed, their reverberations were still being felt as late as 1783–1784, when Lee and his allies were hounding Deane's partner and supporter, Robert Morris (then serving as congressional superintendent of finance). Moreover, Congress in 1779 had also had to consider the appointment of a peace commissioner and a minister to Spain, as well as a possible replacement for Franklin in Paris, and both within Congress and without, the suspicion arose that delegates seeking these positions for themselves were willing to endanger the reputation of Congress merely to satisfy their own ambitions.[57] Anyone wishing to illustrate the dangers of allowing a deliberative body to make sensitive appointments would have had only to consult the history of Congress in 1779 to produce a catalogue of evils.

That key framers of the Constitution were fully qualified to draw such lessons about policymaking and appointments alike is hardly open to doubt. Those who had attended Congress during the tumultuous debates of 1779 included three members of the Committee on Postponed Parts—Roger Sherman, Gouverneur Morris, and John Dickinson—as well as Daniel of St. Thomas Jenifer, Elbridge Gerry, William C. Houstoun, and Edmund Randolph.[58] Five other members had similarly served as delegates while the struggle over the Mississippi question was at its height: William Samuel Johnson, Rufus King (also on the Committee on Postponed Parts), Nathaniel Gorham, William Few, and Charles Pinckney. But in actuality none of the framers needed to have attended Congress to understand just how dangerous and disruptive these disputes had been. Concern about foreign relations may not have penetrated very deeply within the American population as a whole, but the framers traveled in circles where these issues mattered a great deal.

The history of American foreign policy since independence thus establishes at least a circumstantial case for suggesting why the Convention could have consciously agreed to frame the treaty clause in a way that would enable the President to act, in Gouverneur Morris' words, as "the general Guardian of the National interests." How many delegates endorsed this view is impossible to say. Madison obviously did not: his second amendment of September 7—which would have enabled the Senate alone to conclude treaties of peace—rested on the premise that the President could not be trusted in this role. Pierce Butler expressed this fear more pungently when, seconding Madison, he declared that he "was strenuous for the motion, as a necessary security against corrupt & ambitious Presidents." But the fact that their view did not prevail matters less than the candor with which it was expressed. By casting the *dangers* of presidential involvement in so harsh a light, and particularly by noting that the President could obstruct treaties for whatever reasons he chose, Madison and Butler drew their colleagues' attention to the extensive discretionary au-

57. See the published report (signed T.) in the *Pennsylvania Packet*, May 8, 1779; Rakove, *Beginnings of National Politics*, pp. 262-274.
58. Oliver Ellsworth had also been actively involved in the disputes of 1779, but he left the Convention before the major decisions on the treaty clause.

thority the revised clause would give the executive. And this in turn indicates that the framers understood the choice they were making, and that
Morris' positive image of the President now lay closer to the prevailing
views than the doubts of Madison and Butler. A grasp of the advantages
of giving the President an active role in treatymaking can thus be said
to follow logically from the considered rejection of Madison's amendment.

This seems all the more probable when one recalls that the decision
to accept a presidential role in the making of all treaties occurred in the
immediate wake of the final debate on presidential election. It was neither the novelty of the Electoral College nor the new powers proposed
for the President that troubled the imposing group of delegates who criticized the report of the Committee on Postponed Parts during the
proceedings of September 4–6. Their objections centered instead on the
Committee's failure to give the President what he would need to be able
to exercise those powers effectively: political independence from the Senate.
By the same token, the defenders of the report did not argue that the President needed to be tied more closely to the Senate. Their responses reflected
instead an inability to imagine how the compromise between large and
small states could be preserved if the second stage of the electoral process
was taken away from the Senate. Once Roger Sherman hit upon the idea
of having the House vote by states, the Convention fairly rushed to adopt
his suggestion.

What the debates of the entire week of September 4–8 establish, then,
is that the critical decisions on the presidency did involve something more
than the refinement of positions accepted earlier but expressed imperfectly. The fact that the framers failed to discuss these revisions does not
prove, as Arthur Bestor has argued, that no essential change in the role
of the President was intended or perceived; one can as readily argue that
silence indicated simple acceptance of the new proposal. However belatedly the proper scope of executive power came to be considered, the final
debates on this difficult matter were structured in a way that forced the
framers to recognize the link between the mechanism of election and the
new and substantive powers the President would exercise. Indeed, once
the debate over the Electoral College had left the President less dependent on the Senate, further discussion of the changes in the treaty clause
may have seemed unnecessary and even anticlimactic. The decision on
presidential election can thus be interpreted as a preliminary vote endorsing
a major presidential role in treatymaking.

The connection between these two subjects in turn supports the conclusion that the placement of the treaty clause within Article II was an act with interpretive significance, not an editorial quirk. Just how much initiative the framers expected or desired the President to exercise must remain truly speculative. At the minimum, the placement of the treaty clause may have established only a claim of presidential *equality* with the Senate—though even that would have major implications when set against the theory that the President was to serve merely as a check upon the Senate. Read more expansively, the relocation of the clause could have warranted the insight implicit in James Wilson's speech to the Pennsylvania ratifying convention: the President could conceivably negotiate a treaty without the Senate, but the Senate could do nothing at all without the President. The idea that the framers already accepted what might be called a maturely Hamiltonian idea of a *preeminent* presidential role is not supported by the explicit comments recorded in the debates of 1787–1788. But it is certainly possible that they understood the advantages of giving the presidency a basis for acquiring increasing influence over time. The regional concerns that had dominated American foreign policy since 1779 would not endure forever, and the establishment of a vigorous national government could itself help restore something of the overriding sense of national interest that had carried the Americans through the critical first phases of the Revolution. In such a case, the ability of the President to represent the national interest would naturally be enhanced.

What would remain elusive—were one to rely on the records of the Convention alone—are the concerns that enabled the framers to perceive the advantages of enlarging even the potential authority of the President. It is on this point that a consideration of their experience becomes pertinent. Lessons of the past clearly dictated retaining the two-thirds requirement for all treaties as a means of protecting the minority interests of states and regions. Indeed, one suspects that even had the Convention begun with the assumption that the treaty power properly resided in the executive alone, the outcome would have been little different. The same political considerations and historical lessons would then have worked in favor of senatorial involvement. But in a seemingly paradoxical way, these lessons could also have been applied to warrant a radically different conclusion. Would a Senate in which each state's concerns received full expresssion also prove capable of articulating the relatively broad conception of a national interest that had been so conspicuously absent from the deliberations of 1779 and 1786? It is significant that, having accepted the two-thirds provision as a legitimate defense for minority interests, the framers rejected further efforts to increase the size of a senatorial quorum, which would have made ratification of treaties even more difficult. The states deserved protection, but only within limits. Precisely because the framers knew that the states had to be given their due in the Senate, the image of the President as "general Guardian of the National interests" may have grown all the more compelling.

Recent critics of the most expansive interpretations of executive power are still correct to argue that the framers of the Constitution would not have construed "advice and consent" in the narrow terms of ratification. The belief that the Senate could of right express its views at every stage of the treatymaking process is well grounded in the surviving records of both the deliberations in Philadelphia and the debates and commentaries of the ratification campaign, and it gains added credibility when one reconstructs the larger political context within which the framers acted. Yet the claims for intended presidential discretion and even initiative in the making of foreign policy are more convincing than Arthur Bestor and Raoul Berger, among others, have allowed. The framers were in a position to recognize both the limits below which the authority of the Senate could not be reduced, and the benefits which might be gained by enabling successive Presidents to develop a capacity to speak in behalf of national interest.

The ambiguities of the treaty clause need not be seen, then, as the result either of unresolved contradictions or even of a compromise between two contending theories; rather, they marked a response to conflicting pressures and an attempt to reconcile several distinct goals. A constitution that failed to establish the supremacy of national treaties would simply affirm the most signal weakness of the Articles. A constitution that failed to promise protection to essential state and regional interests would be unlikely to secure ratification. And a constitution that failed to provide a mechanism for averting or reducing the divisive forces which recent events had released could not be expected to survive for any length of time. The first of these concerns pointed to the principle of the supremacy clause; the second led to the advisory role of the Senate and the security of the two-thirds requirement for treaty ratification; but the third was consistent with an emerging conception of a republican magistrate capable not only of faithfully executing the laws but also of serving in a representative capacity and articulating national interests. These conflicting pressures led the framers to create a national government vested with broad claims of supremacy yet saddled with a separation of powers that has often made a coherent notion of the national interest more, not less, difficult to pursue. It is the tension between this recognition of the need for greater national power and residual doubts about how such power would be used that best explains the apparent inconsistencies in the Constitution.

Such ambiguities and inconsistencies are more troubling to jurists whose duties require their resolution than to historians who simply have to explain why they are there. Historians can speak of the intentions of the framers and recognize that behind the brevity of a given clause there once lay a spectrum of complex views and different shadings of opinion. Some of these were the result of the interplay of issues within the Convention itself; others arose from the diverse interests and experiences upon which the framers individually acted. Still others reflected the larger world of ideas in which they were rooted: the world of Locke and Montesquieu, Hutcheson and Hume, Real Whigs and plain whigs, common lawyers and Continental jurists. Each of these sources is relevant to the solution of specific constitutional puzzles, but each must also be sifted and weighed. One understands why Justice Jackson may have yearned for the inspiration of Joseph, but the historian interested in these issues finds something to be said for the patience of Job.

The "Great National Discussion": The Discourse of Politics in 1787

Isaac Kramnick

A MERICANS, Alexander Hamilton wrote on October 27, 1787, in the New York *Independent Journal,* were "called upon to deliberate on a new Constitution." His essay, *The Federalist* No. 1, pointed out that in doing this Americans were proving that men could create their own governments "from reflection and choice," instead of forever having to depend on "accident and force." These deliberations on the Constitution would by no means be decorous and genteel. Much too much was at stake, and, as Hamilton predicted, "a torrent of angry and malignant passions" was let loose in the "great national discussion." His *Federalist* essays, Hamilton promised, would provide a different voice in the national debate; they would rise above "the loudness of [the opposition's] declamations, and the . . . bitterness of [its] invectives."

How does one read that "great national discussion" two centuries later? Most present-day scholars would follow the methodological guidelines offered by J.G.A. Pocock in this respect. The historian of political thought, Pocock suggests, is engaged in a quest for the "languages," "idioms," and "modes of discourse" that characterize an age. Certain "languages" are accredited at various moments in time "to take part" in the public speech of a country. These "distinguishable idioms" are paradigms that selectively encompass all information about politics and delimit appropriate usage. Pocock writes of the "continuum of discourse," which persists over time in terms of paradigms that both constrain and provide opportunities for authors with a language available for their use. To understand texts and "great national discussions," then, is to penetrate the "modes of discourse" and the meanings available to authors and speakers at particular moments in time. The scholar must know what the normal

Mr. Kramnick is the Richard J. Schwartz Professor of Government and associate dean of the College of Arts and Sciences at Cornell University. A version of part of this article appears in the author's introduction to *The Federalist Papers* (Harmondsworth, Eng., 1987); quotations from *The Federalist* in the article are from this edition. A shortened version of the article was delivered in March 1987 at a conference in Washington, D.C., sponsored by the United States Capitol Historical Society and the United States Congress, and organized by Professor Ronald Hoffman of the University of Maryland. An expanded version will appear in *To Form a More Perfect Union: The Critical Ideas of the Constitution,* edited by Ronald Hoffman and Peter J. Albert and published by the University Press of Virginia.

possibilities of language, the capacities for discourse, were. Paradigms change, to be sure, ever so slowly, and we recognize this subtle process through anomalies and innovations. But much more significant is the static and exclusive aspect of "modes of discourse." Pocock cautions that one "cannot get out of a language that which was never in it." People only think "about what they have the means of verbalizing." Anyone studying political texts, then, must use "the languages in which the inhabitants . . . did in fact present their society and cosmos to themselves and to each other."[1]

Problematic in this approach is the assumption that there is but one language—one exclusive or even hegemonic paradigm—that characterizes the political discourse of a particular place or moment in time. This was not the case in 1787. In the "great national discussion" of the Constitution Federalists and Antifederalists, in fact, tapped several languages of politics, the terms of which they could easily verbalize. This article examines four such "distinguishable idioms," which coexisted in the discourse of politics in 1787-1788. None dominated the field, and the use of one was compatible with the use of another by the very same writer or speaker. There was a profusion and confusion of political tongues among the founders. They lived easily with that clatter; it is we two hundred years later who chafe at their inconsistency. Reading the framers and the critics of the Constitution, one discerns the languages of republicanism, of Lockean liberalism, of work-ethic Protestantism, and of state-centered theories of power and sovereignty.[2]

I: CIVIC HUMANISM AND LIBERALISM IN THE CONSTITUTION AND ITS CRITICS

Contemporary scholarship seems obsessed with forever ridding the college curriculum of the baleful influence of Louis Hartz. In place of the "Liberal Tradition in America," it posits the omnipresence of neoclassical civic humanism. Dominating eighteenth-century political thought in Britain and America, it is insisted, was the language of republican virtue. Man was a political being who realized his telos only when living in a *vivere civile* with other propertied, arms-bearing citizens, in a republic where they ruled and were ruled in turn. Behind this republican discourse is a tradition of political philosophy with roots in Aristotle's *Politics,* Cicero's *Res Publica,* Machiavelli, Harrington, Bolingbroke, and the nostalgic country's virtuous opposition to Walpole and the commercialization of English life. The pursuit of public good is privileged over private interests,

[1] Pocock, *Virtue, Commerce, and History: Essays on Political Thought and History, Chiefly in the Eighteenth Century* (Cambridge, 1985), 7-8, 12-13, 58, 290.
[2] Even this list is not exhaustive. I leave to colleagues the explication of several other less discernible idioms of politics in the discourse of 1787, for example, the "language of jurisprudence," "scientific whiggism," and the "moral sentiment" schools of the Scottish Enlightenment.

and freedom means participation in civic life rather than the protection of individual rights from interference. Central to the scholarly enterprise of republicanism has been the self-proclaimed "dethronement of the paradigm of liberalism and of the Lockean paradigm associated with it."[3]

In response to these republican imperial claims, a group whom Gordon S. Wood has labeled "neo-Lockeans" has insisted that Locke and liberalism were alive and well in Anglo-American thought in the period of the founding.[4] Individualism, the moral legitimacy of private interest, and market society are privileged in this reading over community, public good, and the virtuous pursuit of civic fulfillment. For these "neo-Lockeans" it is not Machiavelli and Montesquieu who set the textual codes that dominated the "great national discussion," but Hobbes and Locke and the assumptions of possessive individualism.

Can we have it both ways? We certainly can if we take Federalist and Antifederalist views as representing a single text of political discourse at the founding. A persuasive case can be made for the Federalists as liberal modernists and the Antifederalists as nostalgic republican communitarians seeking desperately to hold on to a virtuous moral order threatened by commerce and market society. The Federalist tendency was to depict America in amoral terms as an enlarged nation that transcended local community and moral conviction as the focus of politics. The Federalists seemed to glory in an individualistic and competitive America, which was preoccupied with private rights and personal autonomy. This reading of America is associated with James Madison more than with anyone else, and with his writings in the *Federalist.*

Madison's adulation of heterogeneous factions and interests in an enlarged America, which he introduced into so many of his contributions to the *Federalist,* assumed that the only way to protect the rights of minorities was to enlarge the political sphere and thereby divide the community into so great a number of interests and parties, that

in the 1st. place a majority will not be likely at the same moment to have a common interest separate from that of the whole or of the

[3] J.G.A. Pocock, "An Appeal from the New to the Old Whigs? A Note on Joyce Appleby's Ideology and the History of Political Thought," Intellectual History Group, *Newsletter* (Spring, 1981), 47. Republican revisionism, often read as a critique from the right of hegemonic liberal scholarship, has been taken up by an unlikely ally, Critical Legal Studies, which from the left has embraced its communitarian focus and potential as an alternative to liberal possessive individualism. See, for example, Andrew Fraser, "Legal Amnesia: Modernism vs. the Republican Tradition in American Legal Theory," *Telos,* No. 60 (1984), 18, and Mark Tushnet, "The Constitution of Religion," *Connecticut Law Review,* XVIII (1986), 701.

[4] Wood, "Hellfire Politics," *New York Review of Books,* XXXII, No. 3 (1985), 30. Wood's magisterial *The Creation of the American Republic, 1776-1787* (Chapel Hill, N.C., 1969), remains the most brilliant guide to the American founding. The pages that follow should make apparent the debt I (and all who write on this era) owe Wood.

minority; and in the 2d. place, that in case they shd. have such an interest, they may not be apt to unite in the pursuit of it. It was incumbent on us then to try this remedy, and with that view to frame a republican system on such a scale & in such a form as will controul all the evils wch. have been experienced.[5]

In *Federalist* No. 10 Madison described the multiplication of regional, religious, and economic interests, factions, and parties as the guarantor of American freedom and justice. He put his case somewhat differently in a letter to Thomas Jefferson: "Divide et impera, the reprobated axiom of tyranny, is under certain conditions, the only policy, by which a republic can be administered on just principles."[6] Pride of place among "these clashing interests," so essential for a just order, went to the economic interests inevitable in a complex market society. They were described in the often-quoted passage from *Federalist* No. 10:

The most common and durable source of factions has been the various and unequal distribution of property. Those who hold and those who are without property have ever formed distinct interests in society . . . . creditors . . . debtors. . . . A landed interest, a manufacturing interest, a mercantile interest, a moneyed interest. . . . The regulation of these various and interfering interests forms the principal task of modern legislation.

Government for Madison, much as for Locke, was a neutral arbiter among competing interests. Indeed, in *Federalist* No. 43 Madison described the legislative task as providing "umpires"; and in a letter to George Washington he described government's role as a "disinterested & dispassionate umpire in disputes."[7] Sounding much like Locke in chapter 5, "Of Property," of the *Second Treatise*, Madison, in No. 10, attributed the differential possession of property to the "diversity in the faculties of man," to their "different and unequal faculties of acquiring property." It was "the protection of these faculties" that constituted "the first object of government." As it was for Locke—who wrote that "*justice* gives every Man a Title to the product of his honest Industry"—so, too, for Madison and the Federalists: justice effectively meant respecting private rights, especially property rights.[8]

Justice for the Federalists was less a matter of civic virtue, of public participation in politics, as emphasized by recent American historical

[5] Max Farrand, ed., *The Records of the Federal Convention of 1787* (New Haven, Conn., 1911), I, 136.
[6] Madison to Jefferson, Oct. 24, 1787, in Gaillard Hunt, ed., *The Writings of James Madison* . . . (New York, 1900-1910), V, 31.
[7] Madison to Washington, Apr. 16, 1787, *ibid.*, II, 346.
[8] John Locke, "First Treatise of Civil Government," in *Two Treatises of Government* . . . (1689), ed. Peter Laslett (Cambridge, 1960), chap. 4, sect. 42.

scholarship, or of a neoplatonic ideal of a transcendent moral order, as argued by scholars such as Walter Berns, than it was a reflection of the Lockean liberal world of personal rights, and most dramatically of property rights. It was a substantive, not procedural or civic, ideal of justice that preoccupied the framers in 1787. It was much more often their content, not their violation of due process, that condemned state legislative actions as wicked. With striking frequency, the condemnation of state laws that interfered with private contracts or established paper money schemes was cast in the language of "unjust laws." In South Carolina such laws were called "open and outrageous . . . violations of every principle of Justice." In New Jersey debtor relief legislation was criticized as "founded not upon the principles of Justice, but upon the Right of the Sword." The Boston *Independent Chronicle* complained in May 1787 that the Massachusetts legislature lacked "a decided tone . . . in favor of the general principles of justice." A "virtuous legislature," wrote a New Jersey critic in 1786, "cannot listen to any proposition, however popular, that came within the description of being unjust, impolitic or unnecessary." In Massachusetts the legislation sought by the Shaysites was seen to be acts of "injustice," establishing "iniquity by Law" and violating "the most simple ties of common honesty." The linkage between the procedural and substantive objections to the state legislatures was made clearly by Noah Webster. They were, he wrote, guilty of "so many legal infractions of sacred right—so many public invasions of private property—so many wanton abuses of legislative powers!"[9]

Madison, too, read justice as the substantive protection of rights. In his argument before the convention on behalf of a council of revision he pleaded that the president and judges should have the power to veto "unwise & unjust measures" of the state legislatures "which constituted so great a portion of our calamities."[10] This is equally evident in the pages of the *Federalist*. In No. 10, state actions reflecting "a rage for paper money, for an abolition of debts, for an equal division of property" were "schemes of injustice" and "improper or wicked project[s]." The fruit of unjust and wicked laws was the "alarm for private rights" that is "echoed from one end of the continent to the other." In No. 44 Madison equated the "love of justice" with hatred of paper money. Such pestilential laws required, in turn, sacrifices on "the altar of justice." The end of government itself was justice, Madison wrote in No. 51, and in No. 54 he refined this further by noting that "government is instituted no less for protection of the property than of the persons of individuals." It was the same for Hamilton, who

⁹ Berns, *Freedom, Virtue, and the First Amendment* (Baton Rouge, La., 1957). *State Gazette of South-Carolina* (Charleston), Mar. 5, 1787; quotation for New Jersey is in Wood, *Creation of the American Republic*, 406; *Independent Chronicle: and the Universal Advertiser* (Boston), May 31, 1787; *Political Intelligencer* (Elizabeth Town, N.J.), Jan. 4, 1786; quotation for Massachusetts is in Wood, *Creation of the American Republic*, 465; Webster quoted *ibid.*, 411.
¹⁰ Farrand, ed., *Records of the Federal Convention*, II, 73-74.

wrote in *Federalist* No. 70 of "the protection of property" constituting "the ordinary course of justice." In No. 78 Hamilton also described the "private rights of particular classes of citizens" injured "by unjust and partial laws."

The commitment in the preamble to the Constitution to "establish justice" meant for the framers that it would protect private rights, which would help it achieve the next objective—to "insure domestic tranquility." Should there be doubts about this, we have Madison as our guide to what "establish justice" meant. On June 6 he had risen at the convention to answer Roger Sherman's suggestion that the only objects of union were better relations with foreign powers and the prevention of conflicts and disputes among the states. What about justice? was the thrust of Madison's intervention. To Sherman's list of the Constitution's objectives Madison insisted that there be added "the necessity of providing more effectually for the security of private rights, and the steady dispensation of Justice. Interferences with these were evils which had more perhaps than any thing else produced this convention."[11]

The acceptance of modern liberal society in the Federalist camp went beyond a legitimization of the politics of interest and a conviction that government's purpose was to protect the fruits of honest industry. There was also an unabashed appreciation of modern commercial society. Secretary of Education William Bennett is quite right in his recent reminder that "commerce had a central place in the ideas of the Founders."[12] Hamilton, for example, in *Federalist* No. 12, insisted that

the prosperity of commerce is now perceived and acknowledged by all enlightened statesmen to be the most useful as well as the most productive source of national wealth, and has accordingly become a primary object of their political cares. By multiplying the means of gratification, by promoting the introduction and circulation of the precious metals, those darling objects of human avarice and enterprise, it serves to vivify and invigorate the channels of industry and to make them flow with greater activity and copiousness.

Hamilton was perfectly aware that his praise of private gratification, avarice, and gain flew in the face of older ideals of civic virtue and public duty that emphasized the subordination of private interest to the public good. He turned this very rejection of the republican moral ideal into an argument for the need of a federal standing army. This was a further blow to the ideals of civic virtue, which had always seen professional armies as evil incarnate, undermining the citizen's self-sacrificial participation in the defense of the public realm, which was the premise of the militia. America as a market society could not rely on the militia, according to Hamilton. "The militia," he wrote in *Federalist* No. 24, "would not long, if at all,

[11] *Ibid.*, I, 134.
[12] Bennett, "How Should Americans Celebrate the Bicentennial of the Constitution?" *National Forum*, LXIV (1984), 60.

submit to be dragged from their occupations and families." He was writing of manning garrisons involved in protecting the frontiers: "And if they could be prevailed upon or compelled to do it, the increased expense of a frequent rotation of service, and the loss of labor and disconcertation of the industrious pursuits of individuals, would form conclusive objections to the scheme. It would be as burdensome and injurious to the public as ruinous to private citizens."

In *Federalist* No. 8, another defense of standing armies, Hamilton acknowledged the eclipse of older civic ideals of self-sacrifice and participatory citizenship in commercial America: "The industrious habits of the people of the present day, absorbed in the pursuit of gain and devoted to the improvements of agriculture and commerce, are incompatible with the condition of a nation of soldiers, which was the true condition of the people of those [ancient Greek] republics."

Many of the Antifederalists, on the other hand, were still wedded to a republican civic ideal, to the making of America into what Samuel Adams called "a Christian Sparta." The very feature of pluralist diversity in the new constitutional order that Madison saw as its great virtue, the Antifederalists saw as its major defect. For the Antifederalist "Brutus" it was absurd that the legislature "would be composed of such heterogeneous and discordant principles, as would constantly be contending with each other." A chorus of Antifederalists insisted that virtuous republican government required a small area and a homogeneous population. Patrick Henry noted that a republican form of government extending across the continent "contradicts all the experience of the world." Richard Henry Lee argued that "a free elective government cannot be extended over large territories." Robert Yates of New York saw liberty "swallowed up" because the new republic was too large.[13]

Montesquieu and others had taught Antifederalists "that so extensive a territory as that of the United States, including such a variety of climates, productions, interests, and so great differences of manners, habits, and customs" could never constitute a moral republic. This was the crucial issue for the minority members of the Pennsylvania ratifying convention: "We dissent, first, because it is the opinion of the most celebrated writers on government, and confirmed by uniform experience, that a very extensive territory cannot be governed on the principles of freedom, otherwise than by a confederation of republics."[14]

Antifederalists' fears over the absence of homogeneity in the enlarged republic were as important as the issue of size. In the course of arguing

[13] Adams to John Scollay, Dec. 30, 1780, in Harry Alonzo Cushing, ed., *The Writings of Samuel Adams* (New York, 1904-1908), IV, 238; "Brutus," quoted in Herbert J. Storing, *What the Anti-Federalists Were For* (Chicago, 1981), 47; Henry, Lee, and Yates quoted in Leonard W. Levy, ed., *Essays on the Making of the Constitution* (New York, 1969), ix.

[14] Montesquieu quoted in Wood, *Creation of the American Republic*, 499; quotation for Pennsylvania is in Levy, ed., *Essays on the Constitution*, x.

that a national government could not be trusted if it were to allow open immigration, "Agrippa," the popular Antifederalist pamphleteer assumed to be James Winthrop, contrasted the much more desirable situation in "the eastern states" with the sad plight of Pennsylvania, which for years had allowed open immigration and in which religious toleration and diversity flourished:

> Pennsylvania has chosen to receive all that would come there. Let any indifferent person judge whether that state in point of morals, education, energy is equal to any of the eastern states . . . [which,] by keeping separate from the foreign mixtures, [have] acquired their present greatness in the course of a century and a half, and have preserved their religion and morals. . . . Reasons of equal weight may induce other states . . . to keep their blood pure.[15]

Most Antifederalists held that a republican system required similarity of religion, manners, sentiments, and interests. They were convinced that no such sense of community could exist in an enlarged republic, that no one set of laws could work within such diversity. "We see plainly that men who come from New England are different from us," wrote Joseph Taylor, a southern Antifederalist. "Agrippa," on the other hand, declared that "the inhabitants of warmer climates are more dissolute in their manners, and less industrious, than in colder countries. A degree of severity is, therefore, necessary with one which would cramp the spirit of the other. . . . It is impossible for one code of laws to suit Georgia and Massachusetts."[16]

A just society, for many Antifederalists, involved more than simply protecting property rights. Government had more responsibilities than merely to regulate "various and interfering interests." It was expected to promote morality, virtue, and religion. Many Antifederalists, for example, were shocked at the Constitution's totally secular tone and its general disregard of religion and morality. Equally upsetting was the lack of any religious content in Federalist arguments for the Constitution.

Some Antifederalists were angered that the Constitution, in Article VI, Section 3, prohibited religious tests for officeholders while giving no public support for religious institutions. Amos Singletary of Massachusetts was disturbed that it did not require men in power to be religious: "though he hoped to see Christians, yet, by the Constitution, a Papist, or an Infidel, was as eligible as they." Henry Abbot, an Antifederalist in North Carolina, wrote that "the exclusion of religious tests is by many thought dangerous and impolitic. They suppose . . . pagans, deists, and Mahometans might obtain offices among us." For David Caldwell of North Carolina, this

[15] "Letters of Agrippa," Dec. 28, 1787, in Herbert J. Storing, ed., *The Complete Anti-Federalist* (Chicago, 1981), IV, 86.
[16] Jonathan Elliot, ed., *The Debates of the Several State Conventions, on the Adoption of the Federal Constitution* . . . , 2d ed. (Philadelphia, 1863), IV, 24; "Letters of Agrippa," Dec. 3, 1787, in Storing, ed., *Complete Anti-Federalist*, IV, 76.

prohibition of religious tests constituted "an invitation for Jews and pagans of every kind to come among us." Since Christianity was the best religion for producing "good members of society, . . . those gentlemen who formed this Constitution should not have given this invitation to Jews and heathens."[17] Antifederalists held that religion was a crucial support of government. For Richard Henry Lee, "refiners may weave as fine a web of reason as they please, but the experience of all times shews Religion to be the guardian of morals." The state, according to some Antifederalists, had to be concerned with civic and religious education. Several made specific proposals for state-sponsored "seminaries of useful learning" to instill "the principles of free government" and "the science of morality." The state, they urged, should encourage "the people in favour of virtue by affording publick protection to religion."[18] Going a long step further, Charles Turner of Massachusetts insisted that "without the prevalence of *Christian piety and morals*, the best republican Constitution can never save us from slavery and ruin." He urged that the government institute some means of education "as shall be *adequate* to the *divine, patriotick purpose* of training up the children and youth at large, in that solid learning, and in those pious and moral principles, which are the *support*, the *life* and the SOUL of republican government and liberty, of which a free Constitution is the body."[19]

There was, not surprisingly, also a tendency in some Antifederalist circles to see the exchange principles of commercial society, so praised by the Federalists, as threats to civic and moral virtue. Would not the self-seeking activities "of a commercial society beget luxury, the parent of inequality, the foe to virtue, and the enemy to restraint"? The spread of commerce would undermine republican simplicity, for the more a people succumbed to luxury, the more incapable they became of governing themselves. As one Antifederalist put it, speaking critically of the silence of the Constitution on questions of morality, "whatever the refinement of modern politics may inculcate, it still is certain that some degree of virtue must exist, or freedom cannot live." Honest folk like himself, he went on, objected to "Mandevill[e]'s position . . . 'that private vices are public benefits'." This was not an unfamiliar theme to the men who would oppose the Constitution. Richard Henry Lee singled out the same source of evil, "Mandevilles . . . who laugh at virtue, and with vain ostentatious display of words will deduce from vice, public good!"[20]

The problem with the Federalist position for many Antifederalists was the inadequacy of its vision of community based on mere interests and their protection. The Antifederalists suspected that such a community

[17] Elliot, ed., *Debates*, II, 44, IV, 192, 199.

[18] Lee to Madison, Nov. 26, 1784, in James Curtis Ballagh, ed., *Letters of Richard Henry Lee* (New York, 1911-1914), II, 304; Storing, *Anti-Federalists*, 21.

[19] Storing, *Anti-Federalists*, 23.

[20] *Ibid.*, 73; Ballagh, ed., *Letters of R. H. Lee*, II, 62-63.

could not persist through what Madison called in *Federalist* No. 51 "the policy of supplying, by opposite and rival interests, the defect of better motives." A proper republican community, for these Antifederalists, required a moral consensus, which, in turn, required similarity, familiarity, and fraternity. How, they asked, could one govern oneself and prefer the common good over private interests outside a shared community small enough and homogeneous enough to allow one to know and sympathize with one's neighbors? The republican spirit of Rousseau hovered over these Antifederalists as they identified with small, simple, face-to-face, uniform societies.

Madison and Hamilton understood full well that this communitarian sentiment lay at the core of much of the Antifederalist critique of the new constitutional order. In *Federalist* No. 35 Hamilton ridiculed the face-to-face politics of those "whose observation does not travel beyond the circle of his neighbors and his acquaintances." Madison in No. 10 described two alternative ways of eliminating the causes of factions and thus the politics of interest: one by "destroying the liberty which is essential to its existence; the other by giving to every citizen the same opinions, the same passions, and the same interests." These were both unacceptable. To do either would cut out the very heart of the liberal polity he championed.[21]

Can one go too far in making the case for the Antifederalists as antiliberal communitarians or Rousseauean republicans? Some were, without doubt, but others responded to the enlargement of the federal government and the enhancement of executive power with a call for the protection of private and individual rights through a bill of rights. Even this, however, may be explained by their communitarian bias. If, after all, government was to be run from some city hundreds of miles away, by people superior, more learned, and more deliberative than they, by people with whom they had little in common, then individual rights needed specific protection. The basis for trust present in the small moral community where men shared what Madison disparagingly described as "the same opinions, the same passions, and the same interests" was extinguished.

An equally strong case can be made for the Federalists as republican theorists, and here we see full-blown the confusion of idioms, the overlapping of political languages, in 1787. There is, of course, Madison's redefinition of and identification with a republicanism that involved "the delegation of the government . . . to a small number of citizens elected by the rest" as opposed to a democracy "consisting of a small number of citizens who assemble and administer the government in person." But the crucial move in No. 10 that sets Madison firmly within the republican paradigm is his assumption that the representative function in an enlarged republic would produce officeholders who would sacrifice personal,

---

[21] Cf. Walter Berns, "Does the Constitution Secure These Rights?" in Robert A. Goldwin and William A. Schambra, eds., *How Democratic Is the Constitution?* (Washington, D.C., 1980), 73.

private, and parochial interest to the public good and the public interest. What made the layers of filtration prescribed by the new constitutional order so welcome was their ultimate purpose—producing enlightened public-spirited men who found fulfillment in the quest for public good. It is this feature of Madison's No. 10 that Garry Wills has drawn attention to as the crowning inspiration of Madison's moral republicanism. Republican government over a large country would, according to Madison,

> refine and enlarge the public views by passing them through the medium of a chosen body of citizens whose wisdom may best discern the true interest of their country, and whose patriotism and love of justice will be least likely to sacrifice it to temporary or partial considerations. Under such a regulation it may well happen that the public voice pronounced by the representatives of the people will be more consonant to the public good than if pronounced by the people themselves, convened for the purpose.

The greater number of citizens choosing representatives in a larger republic would reject "unworthy candidates" and select "men who possess the most attractive merit." A large republic and a national government would lead to "the substitution of representatives whose enlightened views and virtuous sentiments render them superior to local prejudices and to schemes of injustice." We know, given Madison's candor, what this meant.[22]

Working out the mechanisms by which this filtration process would "refine" and "enlarge" public views and enhance the quality of the men chosen to express them preoccupied the delegates at Philadelphia. This explains their lengthy deliberations over how governing officials such as the president and senators should be selected. Indirect processes of selection would, Madison wrote in his notes, "extract from the mass of the Society the purest and noblest characters which it contains."[23] The people involved in choosing the president or senators would be, according to Jay in *Federalist* No. 64, "the most enlightened and respectable." The Senate, Madison wrote in *Federalist* No. 63, would then be made up of "temperate and respectable" men standing for "reason, justice and truth" in the face of the people's "errors and delusions."

Madison privileged public over private elsewhere in the *Federalist* as well. In No. 49 he envisioned public "reason" and "the true merits of the question" controlling and regulating government, not particular and private "passions." Similarly, in No. 55 he saw "the public interests" at risk in large legislative assemblies where "passion" always triumphed over "reason." The smaller House of Representatives constructed by the

[22] See Garry Wills, *Explaining America: The Federalist* (Garden City, N.Y., 1981).

[23] Madison, "Vices of the Political System of the United States," in William T. Hutchinson *et al.*, eds., *The Papers of James Madison* (Chicago, 1962-   ), IV, 357.

Federalists would better ensure the victory of public good over self-interest.

The class focus of the Federalists' republicanism is self-evident. Their vision was of an elite corps of men in whom civic spirit and love of the general good overcame particular and narrow interest. Such men were men of substance, independence, and fame who had the leisure to devote their time to public life and the wisdom to seek the true interests of the country as opposed to the wicked projects of local and particular interests. This republicanism of Madison and the Federalists was, of course, quite consistent with the general aristocratic orientation of classical republicanism, which was, after all, the ideal of the independent, propertied, and therefore leisured citizen with time and reason to find fulfillment as *homo civicus.*

Filtering out mediocrity for Madison went hand in hand with disinterested pursuit of the public good. Many Antifederalists, for their part, saw legislatures as most representative when their membership mirrored the complexity and diversity of society—when, in fact, each geographical unit and social rank was represented. In offering the mirror, not the filter, as the model for representation, Antifederalists seemed to be calling for the representation of every particular interest and thus appear to resemble interest-centered liberals. It was they, as well as Madison in his nonrepublican passages, who, it can be claimed, articulated the politics of interest, to be sure in a language much more democratic and participatory. The classic expression of this Antifederalist interest theory of representation came from Melancton Smith, the great antagonist of Hamilton at the New York ratification convention. He told the delegates that "the idea that naturally suggests itself to our minds, when we speak of representatives, is, that they resemble those they represent. They should be a true picture of the people, possess a knowledge of their circumstances and their wants, sympathize in all their distresses, and be disposed to seek their true interests." Directly refuting the filtration model, Smith insisted that a representative system ought not to seek "brilliant talents," but "a sameness, as to residence and interests, between the representative and his constituents."[24]

Hamilton repudiated the Antifederalist interest theory in *Federalist* No. 35. "The idea of an actual representation of all classes of the people, by persons of each class," so that the feelings and interests of all would be expressed, "is altogether visionary," he wrote. The national legislature, Hamilton recommended, should be composed only of "landholders, merchants, and men of the learned professions." Ordinary people, however much confidence "they may justly feel in their own good sense,"

[24] Elliot, ed., *Debates,* II, 245; *Letters from the Federal Farmer,* in Storing, ed., *Complete Anti-Federalist,* II, 298. For Smith as author of the *Federal Farmer* see Robert H. Webking, "Melancton Smith and the *Letters from the Federal Farmer,*" *William and Mary Quarterly,* 3d Ser., XLIV (1987), 510-528.

should realize that "their interests can be more effectually promoted" by men from these three stations in life.

The confusion of paradigms is further evident when one analyzes in more detail these Federalist and Antifederalist theories of representation. The interest- and particularistic-oriented Antifederalists tended to espouse the traditional republican conviction, dominant in most states under the Articles of Confederation, that representatives should be directly responsible to their constituents and easily removable. This, of course, tapped a rich eighteenth-century republican tradition of demanding frequent elections. Implicit in the Federalist notion of filtration, however, was a denial of the representative as mere delegate or servant of his constituents. In Madison's republicanism the representative was chosen for his superior ability to discern the public good, not as a mere spokesman for his town or region, or for the farmers or mechanics who elected him. It followed, then, that Federalists rejected the traditional republican ideal of annual or frequent elections, which was so bound to the more democratic ideal of the legislator as delegate. It is no surprise to find Madison, in *Federalist* Nos. 37, 52, and 53, critical of frequent elections and offering several arguments against them. The proposed federal government, he insisted, was less powerful than the British government had been; its servants, therefore, were less to be feared. State affairs, he contended, could be mastered in less than a year, but the complexity of national politics was such that more time was needed to grasp its details. More important than these arguments, however, was the basic ideological gulf that here separated Madison's republicanism from the Antifederalist republican proponents of annual elections. Madison's legislators of "refined and enlarged public views," seeking "the true interest of their country," ought not to be subject to yearly review by local farmers and small-town tradesmen.

II: The Language of Virtuous Republicanism

The meaning of virtue in the language of civic humanism is clear. It is the privileging of the public over the private. Samuel Adams persistently evoked the idioms of Aristotle and Cicero. "A Citizen," he wrote, "owes everything to the Commonwealth." He worried that Americans would so "forget their own generous Feelings for the Publick and for each other, as to set private Interest in Competition with that of the great Community." Benjamin Rush went so far in 1786 as to reject the very core belief of what in a later day would come to be called possessive individualism. Every young man in a true republic, he noted, must "be taught that he does not belong to himself, but that he is public property." All his time and effort throughout "his youth—his manhood—his old age—nay more, life, all belong to his country." For John Adams, "public Virtue is the only Foundation of Republics." Republican government required "a positive

Passion for the public good, the public Interest .... Superiour to all private Passions."[25]

This is not all that virtue meant. Subtle changes were taking place during the founding of the American republic in the notion of virtue, and at their core was a transvaluation of public and private. Dramatic witness is given to these changes by Madison's *Federalist* No. 44 where he depicted paper money as a threat to the republican character and spirit of the American people. That spirit, however, was neither civic nor public in nature. The values at risk were apolitical and personal. Madison feared for the sobriety, the prudence, and the industry of Americans. His concern was "the industry and morals of the people." A similar concern appeared in William Livingston's worrying that his countrymen "do not exhibit the virtue that is necessary to support a republican government." John Jay agreed. "Too much," he wrote, "has been expected from the Virtue and good Sense of the People." But like Madison, when Americans became specific about exactly what the decline of virtue meant, their language was often noncivic and instead self-referential. Writing to Jefferson in 1787, friends told of "symptoms . . . truly alarming, which have tainted the faith of the most orthodox republicans." Americans lacked "industry, economy, temperance, and other republican virtues." Their fall from virtue was marked not by turning from public life (was there not, indeed, too much of that very republican value in the overheated state legislatures?) but by their becoming "a Luxurious Voluptuous indolent expensive people without Economy or Industry." Virtuous republican people could, in fact, be described in noncivic, personal terms by the very same men who used the language of civic humanism. John Adams could see the foundation of virtuous government in men who are "sober, industrious and frugal."[26]

One of the most striking aspects of political discourse in this era is the formulaic frequency with which this different sense of virtue is heard. For Joel Barlow in a 1787 Fourth of July oration at Hartford, the "noble republican virtues which constitute the chief excellency" of government were "industry, frugality, and economy." Richard Henry Lee described the virtuous as a "wise, attentive, sober, diligent & frugal" people who had established "the independence of America." A Virginian wondering whether America could sustain republican government asked, "Have we

[25] Adams to Caleb Davis, Apr. 3, 1781, in Cushing, ed., *Writings of Samuel Adams*, IV, 255, Adams to Scollay, Mar. 20, 1777, *ibid.*, III, 365; Rush quoted in Wood, *Creation of the American Republic*, 427, and Dagobert D. Runes, ed., *Selected Writings of Benjamin Rush* (New York, 1947), 31; J. Adams, in [Worthington Chauncey Ford, ed.], *Warren-Adams Letters* (Massachusetts Historical Society, *Collections*, LXXII-LXXIII [Boston, 1917-1925]), I, 201-202, 222.

[26] Theodore Sedgwick, *A Memoir of the Life of William Livingston* . . . (New York, 1833), 403; Jay to Jefferson, Feb. 9, 1787, in Julian P. Boyd *et al.*, eds., *The Papers of Thomas Jefferson* (Princeton, N.J., 1950-   ), XI, 129; letters to Jefferson are quoted in Wood, *Creation of the American Republic*, 424; J. Adams, "Thoughts on Government," in Charles Francis Adams, *The Works of John Adams* . . . , IV (Boston, 1851), 199.

that Industry, Frugality, Economy, that Virtue which is necessary to constitute it?"[27] The constitutions of Pennsylvania and Vermont actually enlisted the Machiavellian republican notion of the return to original principles for their noncivic definition of a virtuous people. They specified that "a frequent recurrence to fundamental principles, and a firm adherence to justice, moderation, temperance, industry, and frugality are absolutely necessary to preserve the blessings of liberty and keep a government free."[28]

The Antifederalists, ostensible communitarian and public-oriented foils to Madisonian interest-based liberalism, could also use this more personal idiomatic notion of virtue. The Articles were not at fault, according to John Williams of New York. The great problem was the decline of virtue in the middle 1780s, "banishing all that economy, frugality, and industry, which had been exhibited during the war." For the Antifederalist pamphleteer "Candidus," it was not a new constitution that America needed but a return to the virtues of "industry and frugality."[29]

The republican tradition had, to be sure, always privileged economy over luxury. From Aristotle and Cicero through Harrington and the eighteenth-century opposition to Walpole, republican rhetoric linked a virtuous republican order to the frugal abstention from extravagance and luxury. But there is more than the all-pervasive paradigm of republicanism at work here. The inclusion of industry in the litany of virtue directs us to another inheritance, to another language in which Americans in the late eighteenth century conceptualized their personal and political universe. Americans also spoke the language of work-ethic Protestantism derived from Richard Baxter, John Bunyan, and the literature of the calling and of "industry." In the later decades of the eighteenth century this was the discourse that monopolized the texts of the English Dissenters, James Burgh, Richard Price, and Joseph Priestley, whose writings were so influential in the founding generation.[30]

Central in work-ethic Protestantism was the vision of a cosmic struggle between the forces of industry and idleness. Its texts vibrated less with the dialectic of civic virtue and self-centered commerce than with the dialectic of productive hardworking energy, on the one hand, and idle unproductive sloth, on the other. Its idiom was more personal and individualistic

[27] Barlow quoted in Wood, *Creation of the American Republic*, 418; Lee to Arthur Lee, Feb. 11, 1779, in Ballagh, ed., *Letters of R. H. Lee*, II, 33; quotation for Virginian is in Wood, *Creation of the American Republic*, 95.

[28] Cited in O. G. Hatch, "Civic Virtue: Wellspring of Liberty," *National Forum*, LXIV (1984), 35.

[29] Elliot, ed., *Debates*, II, 240; "Essays by Candidus," in Storing, ed., *Complete Anti-Federalist*, IV, 129.

[30] See my "Republican Revisionism Revisited," *American Historical Review*, LXXXVII (1982), 629-654, and "Children's Literature and Bourgeois Ideology: Observations on Culture and Industrial Capitalism in the Later Eighteenth Century," in Harry C. Payne, ed., *Studies in Eighteenth-Century Culture*, XII (Madison, Wis., 1983), 11-44. Burgh is cited in *Federalist* No. 56.

than public and communal. Work was a test of self-sufficiency and self-reliance, a battleground for personal salvation. All men were "called" to serve God by busying themselves in useful productive work that served both society and the individual. Daily labor was sanctified and thus was both a specific obligation and a positive moral value. The doctrine of the calling gave each man a sense of his unique self; work appropriate to each individual was imposed by God. After being called to a particular occupation, it was a man's duty to labor diligently and to avoid idleness and sloth.

The fruits of his labor were justly man's. There was for Baxter an "honest increase and provision which is the end of our labour." It was, therefore, "no sin, but a duty to choose a gainful calling rather than another, that we may be able to do good." Not only was working hard and seeking to prosper the mark of a just and virtuous man and idleness a sign of spiritual corruption, but work was also the anodyne for physical corruption. Hard work disciplined the wayward and sinful impulses that lay like Satan's traces within all men. Baxter wrote that "for want of *bodily* labour a multitude of the idle Gentry, and rich people, and young people that are slothful, do heap up in the secret receptacles of the body a dunghill of unconcocted excrementitious filth . . . and dye by thousands of untimely deaths[.] . . . [I]t is their own doing, and by their sloth they kill themselves."³¹

The Protestant language of work and the calling is, of course, complementary to the liberal language of Locke with its similar voluntaristic and individualistic emphasis. Locke's *Second Treatise* and its chapter "Of Property," with its very Protestant God enjoining industrious man to subdue the earth through work and thus to realize himself, is, as Quentin Skinner insists, "the classical text of radical Calvinist politics."³² The kinship of work-ethic Protestant discourse to Locke has less to do with the juristic discourse of rights than with the Protestant theme of work. In the Protestant vocabulary there is much mention of virtue and corruption, but these have primarily nonclassical referents. Virtuous man is solitary and private man on his own, realizing himself and his talents through labor and achievement; corrupt man is unproductive, indolent, and in the devil's camp. He fails the test of individual responsibility. Few have captured the compatibility of the liberal and work-ethic Protestant paradigms as well as Tocqueville, albeit unintentionally. In *Democracy in America* he wrote of the American character in noncivic, individualistic terms that are at bottom central to both liberal and Protestant discourse. Americans, Tocqueville wrote, "owe nothing to any man, they expect nothing from any man; they acquire the habit of always considering themselves as

³¹ Baxter quoted in J. E. Crowley, *This Sheba, Self: The Conceptualization of Economic Life in Eighteenth-Century America* (Baltimore, 1974), 51, 17-18.
³² Skinner, *The Foundations of Modern Political Thought* (Cambridge, 1978), II, 239.

standing alone, and they are apt to imagine that their whole destiny is in their own hands."[33]

Contemporary scholars such as Edmund S. Morgan, J. E. Crowley, Joyce Appleby, and John Patrick Diggins have described this alternative paradigm of Protestantism and the Protestant ethic in eighteenth-century America and with it a language quite congenial to individualistic liberalism and the capitalist spirit.[34] Next to the Bible, the texts of Protestant moralists like Baxter were the most likely to be found in the libraries of eighteenth-century Americans.[35] From them Americans came to know the virtuous man as productive, thrifty, and diligent. Morgan and Crowley, especially, have documented how the American response to English taxation centered on a dual policy of self-denial and commitment to industry. Richard Henry Lee, as early as 1764, when hearing of the Sugar Act, assumed it would "introduce a virtuous industry." The subsequent nonconsumption and nonimportation policy of colonial protestors led many a moralist, in fact, to applaud parliamentary taxation as a blessing in disguise, recalling America to simplicity and frugality. As Morgan notes, the boycott movements were seen by many as not simply negative and reactive. "They were also a positive end in themselves, a way of reaffirming and rehabilitating the virtues of the Puritan Ethic."[36]

In this vocabulary, industry, simplicity, and frugality were the signs not only of a virtuous people but also of a free people. As one Rhode Island writer put it, "the industrious and the frugal only will be free."[37] The Boston *Evening-Post* of November 16, 1767, noted that "by consuming *less* of what we are not really in want of, and by industriously cultivating and improving the natural advantages of our own country, we might save our *substance, even our lands,* from becoming the property of others, and we might effectually preserve our *virtue* and our *liberty,* to the latest posterity." Three weeks later the *Pennsylvania Journal* proclaimed: "SAVE YOUR MONEY AND YOU WILL SAVE YOUR COUNTRY." In one of her famous letters to her husband, John, away at the Continental Congress, Abigail Adams revealed how salient the Protestant virtues were in the political context of her day. Would, she wrote, that Americans "return a little more to their primitive Simplicity of Manners, and not sink into inglorious

---

[33] Alexis de Tocqueville, *Democracy in America* (1835), ed. Richard D. Heffner (New York, 1956), 194.

[34] Morgan, "The Puritan Ethic and the American Revolution," *William and Mary Quarterly,* 3d Ser., XXIV (1967), 3-43; Crowley, *This Sheba, Self;* Appleby, "Liberalism and the American Revolution," *New England Quarterly,* XLIX (1976), 3-26, and *Capitalism and a New Social Order: The Republican Vision of the 1790s* (New York, 1984); Diggins, *The Lost Soul of American Politics: Virtue, Self-Interest, and the Foundations of Liberalism* (New York, 1984).

[35] Crowley, *This Sheba, Self,* 50.

[36] Lee to ———, May 31, 1764, in Ballagh, ed., *Letters of R. H. Lee,* I, 7; Morgan, "Puritan Ethic," *WMQ,* 3d Ser., XXIV (1967), 8.

[37] *Newport Mercury,* Feb. 28, 1774.

ease." They must "retrench their expenses. . . . Indeed their [*sic*] is occasion for all our industry and economy."[38]

From pulpit and pamphlet Americans had long heard praises of industry and denunciations of idleness. For Benjamin Colman, minister of Boston's Brattle Street Church, "*all Nature is Industrious and every Creature about us diligent in their proper Work.*" Constant activity was the human telos for Ebenezer Pemberton, an end even after death. He complained of those who thought that "the happiness of Heaven consisted only in Enjoyment, and a stupid Indolence." This Protestant paradigm of restless and disciplined human activity also spoke in the idiomatic terms of life as a race. The life of the virtuous Christian was "compared to a *Race*, a *Warfare; Watching, Running, Fighting;* all which imply Activity, Earnestness, Speed, etc." The race, according to Nathaniel Henchman, called "for the utmost striving of the whole Man, unfainting Resolute perseverance."[39]

Idleness, on the other hand, was a denial of the human essence. To be idle was to neglect "Duty and lawful Employment . . . for Man is by Nature such an active Creature, that he cannot be wholly Idle." Idleness for Americans had specific class referents. It was the sinful mark of the poor or the great, those below and those above the virtuous man of the middle. Cotton Mather made it clear that the idle poor had no claims on society. "*We should let them Starve,*" he wrote. As for the idle rich, Nathaniel Clap expelled them from the very fold of Christendom. "If Persons Live upon the Labours of others," he wrote, "and spend their Time in Idleness, without any Imployment, for the Benefit of others, they cannot be numb[e]red among Christians. YEA, If Persons Labour, to get great Estates, with this design, chiefly, that they and theirs may live in Idleness, They cannot be Acknowledged for Christians."[40]

America in the 1780s, Drew R. McCoy tells us, may well have had one of the highest rates of population growth in her history. For many, this conjured up fears of vast increases in the numbers of the poor and idle. Only a cultivation of domestic manufacturers would keep these idle hordes from the devil's hands. Once again the marriage of necessity and virtue led Americans to turn from foreign imports to local manufacture and domestic hard work. As Morgan noted of the pre-war boycott of the British, so McCoy characterizes similar promotion of native production in the 1780s "as the necessary means of making Americans into an active, industrious, republican people."[41] Indeed, in February 1787 one observer noted how absurd it was for Americans to support manufactures "at

[38] *Pennsylvania Journal* (Philadelphia), Dec. 10, 1767; Abigail Adams to John Adams, Oct. 16, 1774, in L. H. Butterfield *et al.*, eds., *Adams Family Correspondence* (Cambridge, Mass., 1963), I, 173.

[39] Colman, Pemberton, and Henchman quoted in Crowley, *This Sheba, Self*, 56, 57.

[40] Mather quoted *ibid.*, 59; Clap, *The Duty of All Christians* . . . (New London, Conn., 1720), 8.

[41] McCoy, *The Elusive Republic: Political Economy in Jeffersonian America* (Chapel Hill, N.C., 1980), 116.

several thousand miles distance, while a great part of our own people are idle." American manufactures would "deliver them from the curse of idleness. We shall hold out . . . a new stimulus and encouragement to industry and every useful art."[42]

Communitarian critics of an individualistic interest-based politics could also speak the Protestant language of sobriety, frugality, and industry and also locate these virtues in the particularly virtuous middle ranks of life. The Antifederalists were in good company, then, when they enlisted that language to condemn what they saw as the aristocratic character of the new constitutional order. The Federal Farmer saw the new Constitution resulting from the conflict between leveling debtors "who want a share of the property of others" and men "called aristocrats" who "grasp at all power and property." Uninvolved and victimized were the larger number of "men of middling property" who worked hard and made up the "solid, free, and independent part of the community." It was Melancton Smith, the bearer of a proud Protestant name, who best made the Protestant case for the virtuous middle against Hamilton's aristocratic Constitution at the New York ratifying convention. It was an evil Constitution, Smith claimed, because it restricted representation to the idle few, excluding those who were morally superior. What is crucial to note is that virtue here is apolitical and noncivic:

Those in middling circumstances, have less temptation—they are inclined by habit and the company with whom they associate, to set bounds to their passions and appetites—if this is not sufficient, the want of means to gratify them will be a restraint—they are obliged to employ their time in their respective callings—hence the substantial yeomanry of the country are more temperate, of better morals and less ambitious than the great.[43]

In his most recent collection of essays J.G.A. Pocock has suggested that in the eighteenth century "virtue was redefined," but he is wide of the mark in suggesting that "there are signs of an inclination to abandon the word" and in claiming that it was simply redefined "as the practice and refinement of manners." Virtue had for some time been part of the Protestant discourse with its nonrepublican image of virtuous man as productive, thrifty, and frugal. By the second half of the century this noncivic personal reading of virtue would be secularized, as in Adam Smith's negative assessment of the aristocrat who "shudders with horror at the thought of any situation which demands the continual and long exertion of patience, industry, fortitude, and application of thought. These

---

[42] *American Museum*, I (1787), 116, 119.
[43] *Letters from the Federal Farmer*, in Storing, ed., *Complete Anti-Federalist*, II, 253; Smith, *ibid.*, VI, 158.

virtues are hardly ever to be met with in men who are born to those high stations."[44]

Virtue was becoming privatized in the latter part of the eighteenth century. It was being moved from the realm of public activity to the sphere of personal character. The virtuous man partook less and less of that republican ideal that held sway from Aristotle to Harrington—the man whose landed property gave him the leisure necessary for civic commitment in the public arena, be its manifestations political or martial. Property was still important in the Protestant paradigm—not, however, as grantor of leisure but as the rightful fruit of industrious work.

Gordon Wood has noted that Carter Braxton more than any other in the founding generation of Americans sensed the tension between a republicanism based on public virtue—the "disinterested attachment to the public good, exclusive and independent of all private and selfish interest"—and an American polity where in reality most practiced a private virtue in which each man "acts for himself, and with a view of promoting his own particular welfare." Republican privileging of public over private had never been, according to Braxton, the politics of "the mass of the people in any state." In this observation lay Braxton's real insight. Republican virtue was historically the ideal of a circumscribed, privileged citizenry with an independent propertied base that provided the leisure and time for fulfillment in public life through the moral pursuit of public things, res publica. Americans, on the other hand, Braxton wrote, "who inhabit a country to which providence has been more bountiful," live lives of hard work and private virtue, and their industry, frugality, and economy produce the fruits of honest labor.[45] From our perspective, we can credit Braxton with perceiving the decline of republican hegemony in the face of the alternative worlds of Lockean liberalism and the Protestant ethic. What we now know is that one hears more and more in the course of the late eighteenth century a different language of virtue, one that rejects the assumptions of civic humanism. Citizenship and the public quest for the common good were for some replaced by economic productivity and industrious work as the criteria of virtue. It is a mistake, however, to see this simply as a withdrawal from public activity to a private, self-centered realm. The transformation also involved a changed emphasis on the nature of public behavior. The moral and virtuous man was no longer defined by his civic activity but by his economic activity. One's duty was still to contribute to the public good, but this was best done through economic activity, which actually aimed at private gain. Self-centered economic productivity, not public citizenship, would become a badge of the virtuous man. At the heart of this shift from republican to Protestant notions of

[44] Pocock, Virtue, Commerce, and History, 48, 50; Smith, The Theory of Moral Sentiments (1759), ed. D. D. Raphael and A. L. Macfie (Oxford, 1976), I, iii, 24.
[45] [Braxton], An Address to the Convention of ... Virginia, on the Subject of Government ... (Philadelphia, 1776), 15, 17. For Wood's discussion of this text see Creation of the American Republic, 96-97.

virtue was also a transvaluation of work and leisure. Many Americans in 1787 would have dissented vigorously from the centuries-old republican paradigm set forth in Aristotle's *Politics:* "In the state with the finest constitution, which possesses just men who are just absolutely and not relatively to the assumed situation, the citizens must not live a mechanical or commercial life. Such a life is not noble, and it militates against virtue. Nor must those who are to be citizens be agricultural workers, for they must have leisure to develop their virtue, and for the activities of a citizen."[46]

III: The Language of Power and the State

Lost today in the legitimate characterization of the Constitution as bent on setting limits to the power exercised by less than angelic men is the extent to which the Constitution is a grant of power to a centralized nation-state. This loss reflects a persistent privileging of Madison over Hamilton in reading the text. While posterity emphasizes the Constitution's complex web of checks and balances and the many institutionalized separations of powers, the participants in the "great national discussion," on whichever side they stood, agreed with Hamilton that the Constitution intended a victory for power, for the "principle of *strength* and *stability* in the organization of our government, and *vigor* in its operations."[47]

A pro-Constitution newspaper, the *Pennsylvania Packet*, declared in September 1787: "The year 1776 is celebrated . . . for a revolution in favor of liberty. The year 1787, it is expected, will be celebrated with equal joy, for a revolution in favor of Government." The theme was repeated by Benjamin Rush, also a defender of the Constitution. Rush wrote in June 1787 to his English friend Richard Price that "the same enthusiasm *now* pervades all classes in favor of *government* that actuated us in favor of *liberty* in the years 1774 and 1775."[48]

Critics of the Constitution saw the same forces at work. For Patrick Henry, "the tyranny of Philadelphia" was little different from "the tyranny of George III." An Antifederalist told the Virginia ratification convention that "had the Constitution been presented to our view ten years ago, . . . it would have been considered as containing principles incompatible with republican liberty, and, therefore, doomed to infamy." But the real foil to Hamilton, using the very same whig language, was Richard Henry Lee, who wrote in 1788: "It will be considered, I believe, as a most extraordinary epoch in the history of mankind, that in a few years there should be so essential a change in the minds of men. 'Tis really astonishing that the same people, who have just emerged from a long and cruel war in defense

---

[46] Aristotle, *The Politics*, bk. VII, chap. 9.
[47] Elliot, ed., *Debates*, II, 301.
[48] *Pennsylvania Packet, and Daily Advertiser* (Philadelphia), Sept. 6, 1787; Rush to Price, June 2, 1787, in L. H. Butterfield, ed., *Letters of Benjamin Rush* (Princeton, N.J., 1951), I, 418-419.

of liberty, should now agree to fix an elective despotism upon themselves and their posterity."[49]

But always there were other and louder voices using this same language in defense of the Constitution. Benjamin Franklin wrote that "we have been guarding against an evil that old States are most liable to, *excess of power* in the rulers; but our present danger seems to be *defect of obedience* in the subjects." For the *Connecticut Courant* it was all quite simple. The principles of 1776 had produced a glaring problem, "a want of energy in the administration of government."[50]

In the political discourse of 1787 there was thus a fourth paradigm at work, the state-centered language of power. It, too, reached back into the classical world, to the great lawgivers and founders Solon and Lycurgus, and to the imperial ideal of Alexander and Julius Caesar. Not republican city states but empire and, much later, the nation-state were its institutional units. Its doctrines and commitments were captured less by *zöon politicon, vivere civilere, res publica*, and *virtú* than by *imperium, potestas, gubernaculum*, prerogative, and sovereignty. Its prophets were Dante, Marsilio, Bodin, Richelieu, Hobbes, Machiavelli (of *The Prince*, not the *Discourses*), and James I. This language of politics was focused on the moral, heroic, and self-realizing dimensions of the exercise and use of power.

For Charles Howard McIlwain the recurring answer to this power-centered language of politics was the discourse of "jurisdictio"; for contemporary scholars it would be the law-centered paradigm or the language of jurisprudence and rights.[51] For our purposes, it is important to recognize how the discourse of power and sovereignty renders problematic the reading of the "great national discussion" as simply a dialogue between republicanism and liberalism. To be sure, as the language of Protestantism was complementary to and supportive of liberalism, so the state-centered language of power was closer to and more easily compatible with the discourse of republicanism. Hamilton was fascinated by the nation-state builders in early modern Europe, but his power-centered politics still touched base with much of the older republican ideal. It shared the reading of man as a political animal, as a community-building creature. It, too, privileged public life and public pursuits over a reading of politics that stressed the private context of self-regarding lives of individuals. It did not, however, share the participatory ideals of moral

---

[49] Elliot, ed., *Debates*, III, 436, 607; Lee to John Lamb, June 27, 1788, in Ballagh, ed., *Letters of R. H. Lee*, II, 475.

[50] Franklin to Charles Carroll, May 25, 1789, in Albert Henry Smyth, ed., *The Writings of Benjamin Franklin* (New York, 1907), X, 7; *Connecticut Courant*, quoted in Wood, *Creation of the American Republic*, 432.

[51] McIlwain, *Constitutionalism: Ancient and Modern* (Ithaca, N.Y., 1947). For a discussion of these other paradigms and languages see the essays in Istvan Hont and Michael Ignatieff, eds., *Wealth and Virtue: The Shaping of Political Economy in the Scottish Enlightenment* (Cambridge, 1983), and Pocock, *Virtue, Commerce, and History*.

citizenship, basic to much of the republican tradition, and this difference dramatically sets it off as a separate discourse.

In *Federalist* No. 1 Hamilton proclaimed his "enlightened zeal" for "the energy" and "vigor of government." His achievement, and that of the other young men at Philadelphia, was the creation of the American state. Some decades later, Hegel could find nothing in America that he recognized as the "state."[52] But that was in comparison with established European states, and in that sense he was quite right. What little there was of an American state, however, was crafted by Hamilton, Madison, and the framers of the Constitution, who began their work *de nouveau*, from nothing. There was no royal household whose offices would become state bureaus, no royal army from a feudal past to be transformed into an expression of the state's reality.

It was the experience of war that shaped the vision of America's state-builders. The war against Britain provided them with a continental and national experience that replaced the states-centered focus of the pre-1776 generation. A remarkable number of framers of the Constitution either served in the Continental army or were diplomats or administrative officials for the Confederation or members of the Continental Congress. Indeed, thirty-nine of the fifty-five delegates to the Constitutional Convention had sat in the Congress. This is where the generational issue, so brilliantly described by Stanley Elkins and Eric McKitrick, was so crucial.[53] Most of the principal Federalists had forged their identity in service to the war and the national cause and in dealing with the individual states' reluctance to assist that continental effort. Washington, Knox, and Hamilton were key figures in military affairs. Robert Morris was superintendent of finance, whose unhappy task it was to try to finance the war. John Jay had been president of the Confederation Congress for a short while and a central actor in trying to implement a common foreign policy for the thirteen states. While most of the Antifederalists were states-centered politicians whose heroics took place before 1776, most of the Federalists were shaped by the need to realize the national interest in an international war. Their common bond was an experience that transcended and dissolved state boundaries.

Madison and Hamilton had sat on the same committee of the Continental Congress in 1782-1783, working on the funding of the war and the maintenance of the French alliance. From experiences like this they and their state-building colleagues came to view the thirteen states collectively as a "country," a country among countries. If their country were going to live in a world of nation-states, it needed to become, like the others, a centralized nation-state with sovereign power to tax, regulate trade, coin

[52] Georg Wilhelm Friedrich Hegel, *The Philosophy of History*, trans. J. Sibree (New York, 1956), 84-87.
[53] Elkins and McKitrick, "The Founding Fathers: Young Men of the Revolution," *Political Science Quarterly*, LXXVI (1961), 181-216.

money, fund a debt, conduct a foreign policy, and organize a standing army.

The lack of such an American state was profoundly dispiriting to Hamilton. In *Federalist* No. 85 he declared that "a nation without a national government is, in my view, a sad spectacle." In No. 15 he was even more distraught: "We have neither troops, nor treasury, nor government for the Union . . . our ambassadors abroad are the mere pageants of mimic sovereignty." One can, in fact, construct a theory of the origin and development of the state in *The Federalist*, all from Hamilton's contributions. The state is defined in No. 15 as a coercive agent having the power to make laws. To perform this function, a state requires a stable and predictable system of taxation (Nos. 30, 36) and agencies of force, that is, armies and police (Nos. 6, 34). Especially important for Hamilton's theory of state development are Nos. 16 and 17. In the former he insisted that "the majesty of the national authority" cannot work if impeded by intermediate bodies: "It must carry its agency to the persons of the citizens." Independent and sovereign nations do not govern or coerce states; they rule over individuals.

Hamilton's preoccupation with money and arms as essential for state-building, and his zeal to push aside any intermediate bodies between the state and individuals, while directly relevant for the case he was making on behalf of the Constitution, were also heavily influenced by his perceptive reading of the pattern of state-building in Europe. This is revealed in the all-important *Federalist* No. 17, where Hamilton compares America under the Articles of Confederation to the "feudal anarchy" of medieval Europe. Clearly, for Hamilton, the separate American states were intermediate "political bodies" like "principal vassals" and "feudal baronies," each "a kind of sovereign within . . . particular demesnes." Equally evident is his sense that the pattern of European development, with the triumph of coercive centralized nation-states, should be reproduced in America under the Constitution. On both sides of the Atlantic, then, the state will have "subdued" the "fierce and ungovernable spirit and reduced it within those rules of subordination" that characterize "a more rational and more energetic system of civil polity." Nor is this state-building scenario unrelated to liberal ideological concerns. Hamilton in *Federalist* No. 26 sounds very much like the liberal theorists of state, Hobbes and Locke, when he writes of the role that the "energy of government" plays in ensuring "the security of private rights." However, Hamilton was interested less in the limited liberal state than in the heroic state; heroic state-builders like him cannot fear power, for power is the essence of the state. That power is so often abused does not rule out its creative and useful role. This was the message of a Hamilton speech to the New York legislature in early 1787:

> We are told it is dangerous to trust power any where; that *power* is liable to *abuse* with a variety of trite maxims of the same kind. General propositions of this nature are easily framed, the truth of which

cannot be denied, but they rarely convey any precise idea. To these we might oppose other propositions equally true and equally indefinite. It might be said that too little power is as dangerous as too much, that it leads to anarchy, and from anarchy to despotism. . . . Powers must be granted, or civil Society cannot exist; the possibility of abuse is no argument against the *thing*.[54]

All of the power-centered paradigm's euphemisms for power—"strength," "vigor," "energy"—come together in Hamilton's conception of the presidential office. The presidency was the heart of the new American state for Hamilton, just as the monarch or chief magistrate was for older European nation-states. In Hamilton's president could be heard the echoes of *potestas* and *gubernaculum*. Had he not argued at Philadelphia for a life term for presidents? Short of that, in *Federalist* No. 72 he supported the president's eligibility for indefinite reelection. How else, he asked, would a president be able to "plan and undertake extensive and arduous enterprises for the public benefit?" The president was the energetic builder of an energetic state. In *Federalist* No. 70 Hamilton argued: "Energy in the executive is a leading character in the definition of good government. . . . A feeble executive implies a feeble execution of the government. A feeble execution is but another phrase for a bad execution; and a government ill executed, whatever it may be in theory, must be in practice, a bad government."

Hamilton saw a close relationship between a state with energy and power at home and a powerful state in the world of states. At the Constitutional Convention he angrily replied to Charles Pinckney's suggestion that republican governments should be uninterested in being respected abroad and concerned only with achieving domestic happiness: "It had been said that respectability in the eyes of foreign Nations was not the object at which we aimed; that the proper object of republican government was domestic tranquillity & happiness. This was an ideal distinction. No governmt. could give us tranquillity & happiness at home, which did not possess sufficient stability and strength to make us respectable abroad."[55]

Hamilton was preoccupied with the interrelationship between commerce, state power, and international politics. A powerful state in his vision was a commercial state. In the competitive international system, nation-states sought to improve or protect their commercial strength, which led inevitably to wars. Powerful states therefore needed standing armies and strong navies. In *Federalist* No. 24 Hamilton insisted that "if we mean to be a commercial people, it must form a part of our policy, to be able to defend that commerce." In contrast to Paine and many isolationist Antifederalists, he rejected the notion that wars were fought only "by

[54] Harold C. Syrett *et al.*, eds., *The Papers of Alexander Hamilton* (New York, 1961-1979), IV, 11.
[55] Farrand, ed., *Records of the Federal Convention*, I, 466-467.

ambitious princes" or that republican government necessarily led to peace. Hamilton, the realist, ridiculed in *Federalist* No. 6 "visionary or designing men," who thought republics or trading nations immune from the natural conflicts of nation-states, who talked "of perpetual peace between the states," or who claimed that "the genius of republics is pacific."

> Have republics in practice been less addicted to war than monarchies? Are not the former administered by men as well as the latter? Are there not aversions, predilections, rivalships and desires of unjust acquisitions that affect nations as well as kings? Are not popular assemblies frequently subject to the impulses of rage, resentment, jealousy, avarice and of other irregular and violent propensities?

But Hamilton did not want to build an American state with all that statehood required—a financial and commercial infrastructure, energetic leadership, and powerful military forces—merely to allow America to hold its own in a world system characterized by conflict, competition, and clashing power. He had a grander vision for the American state, a call to greatness. In *Federalist* No. 11 Hamilton wrote of "what this country is capable of becoming," of a future glory for America of "a striking and animating kind." Under a properly "vigorous national government, the natural strength and resources of the country, directed to a common interest, would baffle all the combinations of European jealousy to restrain our growth." If Americans would only "concur in erecting one great American system," the American state would be "superior to the control of all transatlantic force or influence, and able to dictate the terms of the connection between the old and the new world." In the face of a vigorous American state Europe would cease to be "mistress of the world." America would become ascendant in the Western Hemisphere.

Hamilton's horizons were dazzling. His internationalism transcended the cosmopolitan vision of his fellow Federalists as it transcended the localism of the Antifederalists. The victory of the state center over the American periphery would in Hamilton's fertile imagination catapult America from the periphery of nations to the center of the world system.

It would be a heroic achievement for Hamilton and his colleagues in Philadelphia to create such a powerful American state. It would bring them everlasting fame, and, as Douglass Adair has told us, that may well have been the ultimate motive that prompted their state-building. In *Federalist* No. 72 Hamilton suggested that political leaders who undertake "extensive and arduous enterprises for the public benefit" are activated by "the love of fame, the ruling passion of the noblest minds." He was describing his ideal of an energetic president, the subject of the paper, and the heroic enterprise of constitutional state-building embarked on by him and his fellow Federalists. It would bring them the fame and immortality of a Lycurgus as described by Madison in *Federalist* No. 38. The classical and Renaissance discourse of power was replete with praise for creative wielders of *potestas.* Literate men in the eighteenth century, like Hamilton and Madison, knew that Plutarch in his *Lives of the Noble Greeks and Romans* reserved the greatest historical glory for the "law giver" and the "founder of commonwealth." In a text equally well known in this period, Francis Bacon's *Essays*, the top of a fivefold scale of "fame and honour" was occupied by "Conditores Imperium, Founders of States and Common-wealths." David Hume, who was well read by both Hamilton and Madison, echoed this theme. He wrote that "of all men that distinguish themselves by memorable achievements, the first place of honour seems due to legislators and founders of states who transmit a system of laws and institutions to secure the peace, happiness and liberty of future genera-tions." Hamilton must have seen himself and his fellow state-builders as achieving such everlasting fame. Ten years earlier, in a pamphlet attacking congressmen for not better realizing the potential of their position, he had written of true greatness and fame. He signed the pamphlet with the pseudonym "Publius," a fabled figure in Plutarch's *Lives* and the name later used by the authors of the *Federalist*. Hamilton's vision transcended the walls of Congress in the infant nation and spoke to the historic discourse of power.

The station of a member of C——ss, is the most illustrious and important of any I am able to conceive. He is to be regarded not only as a legislator, but as the founder of an empire. A man of virtue and ability, dignified with so precious a trust, would rejoice that fortune had given him birth at a time, and placed him in circumstances so favourable for promoting human happiness. He would esteem it not more the duty, than the privilege and ornament of his office, to do good to mankind.[56]

We must not lose sight of the other side in the "great national discussion," however. Hamilton's discourse of power with its vision of an imperial American state attracted the fire of Antifederalists like one of Franklin's lightning rods. It was Patrick Henry who most angrily and most movingly repudiated the Federalist state. Henry's American spirit was Tom Paine's. With the Federalist state America would lose its innocence, and "splendid government" would become its badge, its dress. On the ruins of paradise would be built, if not the palaces of kings, then armies and navies and mighty empires. At the Virginia ratifying convention Henry evoked a different language of politics.

The American spirit has fled from hence; it has gone to regions where it has never been expected; it has gone to the people of France, in search of a splendid government, a strong, energetic government.

[56] *Plutarch's Lives in Six Volumes* (London, 1758), I, 96; Bacon, "Of Honour and Reputation," in Richard Whatley, ed., *Bacon's Essays: With Annotations* (London, 1886); Hume, "Of Parties in General," in *The Philosophical Works of David Hume* (Edinburgh, 1826), III, 57; "Publius Letter, III," in Syrett *et al.*, eds., *Hamilton Papers*, I, 580-581.

Shall we imitate the example of those nations who have gone from a simple to a splendid government? Are those nations more worthy of our imitation? What can make an adequate satisfaction to them for the loss they have suffered in attaining such a government, for the loss of their liberty? If we admit this consolidated government, it will be because we like a great, splendid one. Some way or other we must be a great and mighty empire; we must have an army, and a navy, and a number of things. When the American spirit was in its youth, the language of America was different; liberty, sir, was then the primary object.[57]

What was Madison's relationship to the discourse of power and the Hamiltonian state? Madison was a state-builder, too, but his state was quite different from Hamilton's, and upon these differences a good deal of American politics in the next two decades, as well as to this day, would turn. Madison and Hamilton were in agreement on many things. They agreed on the need to establish an effective unified national government. They agreed on the serious threats to personal property rights posed by the state legislatures and on the role that a central government would play in protecting these rights. They agreed on the need to have the central government run by worthy, enlightened, and deliberative men. They agreed on the Constitution as necessary to provide the essential framework for commercial development through the creation of a national market, public credit, uniform currency, and the protection of contract. To be sure, Madison's vision tilted toward agrarian capitalism and Hamilton's toward manufactures and commerce. Where they markedly disagreed, however, was in giving positive, assertive power, "energy," and "vigor" to the state.

Hamilton held the new American state valuable for its own sake as assertive power. He saw the nation-state with its historic and heroic goals, seeking power in a competitive international system of other power-hungry states. Madison saw the nation-state as necessary only to protect private rights and thus ensure justice. Like Locke he saw the need for a grant of power to the state, but a grant of limited power. Madison saw the central government providing an arena for competitive power, where the private bargaining of free men, groups, and interests would take place, and the state would define no goals of its own other than ensuring the framework for orderly economic life. All the state would do was regulate "the various and interfering interests" or, as Madison put it to Washington in straightforward Lockean terms, be an impartial umpire in disputes. Energy in politics for Madison would come from individuals and groups seeking their own immediate goals, not from an energetic state seeking its own heroic ends.

What about Madison's governing elite of "enlightened views and virtuous sentiments," "whose wisdom may best discern the true interest of

[57] Elliot, ed., *Debates*, III, 53.

their country," of which he wrote in *Federalist* No. 10? Madison's "true interest" was not the "national interest" of Hamilton's realism. Nor was it some ideal transcending purpose or goal to which wise leadership would lead the state and those still in the shadows. Madison's enlightened leaders would demonstrate their wisdom and virtue more by what they did not do than by what they did. Being men of cool and deliberate judgment, they would not pass unjust laws that interfered with private rights. They would respect liberty, justice, and property, and run a limited government that did little else than preside over and adjudicate conflicts in a basically self-regulating social order. Did not Madison criticize in *Federalist* No. 62 the "excess of law-making" and the voluminousness of laws as the twin "diseases to which our governments are most liable"?

If the state legislators of the Confederation period had acted with self-restraint, there would have been no need for the institutions of the central state, but among generally fallen men they were an even more inferior lot, fired by local prejudices and warm passions. Should the unexpected happen and cooler men of enlightened views seek to do too much, that is, undertake what is described in *Federalist* No. 10 as "improper or wicked projects," then Madison's new constitutional government would rapidly cut them down as its multiplicity of built-in checks and balances preserved the Lockean limited state.

Madison's limited Federalist state might well appear meek and tame set next to Hamilton's energetic and vigorous state, but it was a matter of perspective. To the Antifederalists, even Madison's state, limited as it was by checks and balances and its cool men resisting the temptations of lawmaking, seemed a monstrous betrayal of the Revolution and its spirit. The Constitution could be seen, then, as the last, albeit Thermidorean, act of the American Revolution. Like most revolutions, the American began as a repudiation of the state, of power, and of authority in the name of liberty. Like most revolutions, it ended with a stronger state, the revival of authority, and the taming of liberty's excesses.

The American state would never be quite as bad, however, as the Antifederalists' worst fears. They had assumed, for example, that "Congress will be vested with more extensive powers than ever Great Britain exercised over us." They worried that "after we have given them all our money, established them in a federal town, given them the power of coining money and raising a standing *army* . . . what resources have the people left?"[58] The reason the results would not be quite that bad is that the new American state created by that "triple headed monster" of a Constitution was much closer to Madison's state than to Hamilton's—at least, that is, for the rest of the eighteenth century and through most of the nineteenth. The twentieth century would be another matter and another story.

[58] *Ibid.*, II, 159, 62.

CONCLUSION

The Federalists triumphed in the "great national discussion" that was the debate over the ratification of the Constitution. But posterity has not remembered simply the victorious advocates of the Constitution in 1787 and 1788. The Antifederalists have lived on in the American imagination as well. Their worst fears were never realized, which proves the glaring exception in a comparison of the American Revolution with other revolutions. The Antifederalists, while losers in 1788, were neither liquidated nor forced to flee. Nor, more significantly, were their ideas extinguished. Their values lived on in America, as they themselves did, and have been absorbed into the larger pattern of American political culture. The states have endured as vital parts of the American political scene and in the unique configuration that is American federalism have retained tremendous power in numerous areas of public policy. In celebrating the bicentennial of its Constitution America celebrates both the Federalists and the Antifederalists, for the living American Constitution is by now a blend of the positions both sides took during the "great national discussion," however untidy that may seem to constitutional purists.

Just as there ultimately was no decisive victor in the political and pamphlet battle, so, too, there was none in the paradigm battle. No one paradigm cleared the field in 1788 and obtained exclusive dominance in the American political discourse. There was no watershed victory of liberalism over republicanism. These languages were heard on both sides during the "great national discussion." So, too, were the two other paradigms available to the framers' generation, the Protestant ethic and the ideals of sovereignty and power. So it has remained. American political discourse to this day tends to be articulated in one or another of these distinguishable idioms, however untidy that may seem to professors of history or political philosophy.

The generations of Americans who lived through the founding and the framing have left us proof positive of their paradigmatic pluralism. They imprinted on the landscape of their experience place names by which future generations would know them and their frames of reference. They took the physical world as their text and wrote on it with the conceptual structures of their political language. My corner of the American text, Upstate New York, was settled by Revolutionary War veterans in the last decades of the eighteenth century. When they named their parcels of American landscape, they knew in what tongues to speak.

There is a Rome, New York, and an Ithaca and a Syracuse. There is a Locke, New York, a mere ten miles from Ithaca. There is a Geneva, New York, at the top of Cayuga Lake. And for the state builders fascinated with founders of states, there is even a Romulus, New York. Such is the archaeology of paradigms far above Cayuga's waters.

Liberalism, Republicanism & the Constitution

Richard C. Sinopoli
New York University

The ideas of the founders have been a subject of ceaseless interest to students of American politics. This article explores the founders' conception of citizenship as expressed in the debates over ratification of the 1787 Constitution. The author argues that the "republican revisionist" interpretation of the founding does not explain satisfactorily the founders' views of civic obligation and civic virtue. A theory is presented to explain both the founders' deep commitment to liberalism and their concern with fostering civic virtue, which the author contends were integrated by the founders by drawing upon eighteenth century moral sense thought as best expressed by David Hume.

Richard C. Sinopoli is Adjunct Assistant Professor of Political Science at New York University, from which he received his Ph.D. in 1986.

Over the past twenty years, interpretation of the political thought of both the framers of the 1787 Constitution and their opponents has undergone a major revision, the result of a growing literature that questions the ideological commitments of the founders.[1] The orthodoxy claiming that

---

1. The main revisionist works for this essay include the following: Bernard Bailyn, *The Ideological Origins of the American Revolution* (Cambridge, Mass.: Harvard University Press, Belknap Press, 1967); Bernard Bailyn, *The Origins of American Politics* (New York: Vintage Books, 1968); J. G. A. Pocock, *The Machiavellian Moment* (Princeton: Princeton University Press, 1975); J. G. A. Pocock, *"The Machiavellian Moment* Revisited: A Study in History and Ideology," *Journal of Modern History* 53 (March 1981): 49–72; Gerald Stourzh, *Alexander Hamilton and the Idea of Republican Government* (Stanford: Stanford University Press, 1970); Gordon S. Wood, *The Creation of the American Republic 1776–1789* (Chapel Hill: University of North Carolina Press, 1969). For a more comprehensive review of this literature see Isaac Kramnick, "Republican Revisionism Revisited," *The American Historical Review,* 87 (June 1982): 629–664; Robert E. Shalhope, "Toward a Republican Synthesis: The Emergence of an Understanding of Republicanism in American

American political thought is and always has been Lockean liberalism, with its emphasis on the protection of rights to life, liberty, and property, has been challenged by political theorists and historians who stress the importance of classical republican or civic humanist thought in shaping the political consciousness of the founding generation.[2]

Civic humanism is, above all, a theory of *citizenship*, but in a specifically Aristotelian sense of the term. It holds that the moral and rational faculties of individuals are developed fully only if they act as citizens. Only by actively taking part in the political life of one's community, by performing one's civic duties, can an individual become a virtuous, well-rounded person. Pocock summarizes this civic ideal as follows:

> Civic humanism denotes a style of thought . . . in which it is contended that the development of the individual toward self-fulfillment is possible only when the individual acts as a citizen, that is as a conscious and autonomous participant in an autonomous decision-taking political community, the polis or republic.[3]

The autonomy of citizens is founded in property, ownership of which enables freeholders to participate in politics independent of the will of others. Threats to autonomy, described as "corruption," are a central concern in the civic humanist tradition, because they undermine the moral character of the citizen by removing his capacity to act "virtuously," or in light of the common good as opposed to particular private interests.

This core idea, it is contended, survived transformations of republicanism from its Aristotelian origins through its incorporation into eighteenth century Anglo-American political controversies including the debates over the ratification of the 1787 Constitution. The revisionists differ over the degree to which the Federalists break with the civic humanist tradition, but they agree generally that Anti-Federalist criticisms of the Constitution emerged largely out of this tradition. These

---

Historiography," *William and Mary Quarterly*, 29 (Jan. 1972): 49–80; Jean Yarborough, "Representation and Republicanism: Two Views," *Publius*, 9 (Spring 1979): 77–98; Jean Yarborough, "Republicanism Reconsidered: Some Thoughts on the Foundation and Preservation of the American Republic," *Review of Politics*, 41 (Jan. 1979): 61–95.

2. The term founders and its cognates as used in this essay refers to both Federalists and Anti-Federalists. There can be little question that the Anti-Federalists contributed both to the Constitution itself, primarily by encouraging the inclusion of the Bill of Rights, and to the development of enduring themes in American political thought, many of which are discussed in this essay.

3. Pocock, "Civic Humanism and Its Role in Anglo-American Thought," *Politics, Language and Time* (New York: Atheneum, 1971), p. 85.

historians point especially to language in the ratification debates used by pamphleteers calling themselves Brutus, Cato, Republicus, etc., which stresses classical republican themes such as civic virtue and corruption, civic education and the merits of small republics.

It is surprising that the spread of republican revisionism has not been met by a more careful theoretical response than it has.[4] Since both practicing politicians and citizens rely on the "framers' intents" as a yardstick to measure present political practices, assessments of the founders' ideology is of current as well as historical interest. When divergent interpretations of this ideology are offered, some conceptual housecleaning is in order. It is especially so in this case, because the revisionist argument in its strongest form—the commitment to civic humanism—does not merely supplement Lockean liberal assumptions, but is in fact incompatible with them.

To see this, it is useful to start with a recent reconstruction of classical liberalism by Michael Sandel. In his discussion, "deontological" or rights-based liberalism is a mode of political argument culminating in Kant but essentially anticipated by Hobbes and Locke. Its core thesis may be stated as follows:

[S]ociety being composed of a plurality of persons, each with his own aims, interests, and conceptions of the good, is best arranged when it is governed by principles which do not themselves presuppose any particular conception of the good; what justifies these regulative principles above all is not that they maximize the social welfare or otherwise promote the good, but rather that they conform to the conception of right, a moral category prior to the good and independent of it.[5]

In the liberal social contract tradition, the sole justification of persons voluntarily surrendering their natural liberty in the state of nature is that only through some plan of cooperation can they be assured the security and independence to pursue aims of their own choosing. Yet it is hard to see where the classical republican idea of self-fulfillment *only* through acts of civic participation, guided by a commitment to the common

---

4. The historian Joyce Appleby has provided cogent responses to the revisionist thesis. This remark is in no way intended as a slight of her fine work. See, for example, *Capitalism and a New Social Order: The Republican Revision of the 1790s* (New York: New York University Press, 1984), and "Republicanism in Old and New Contexts," *William and Mary Quarterly*, 3rd ser., 43 (January 1986): 20–34.

5. Michael J. Sandel, *Liberalism and the Limits of Justice* (New York: Cambridge University Press, 1982), p. 1.

good, fits into this liberal worldview. The "virtue" of the Lockean liberal state is that it maintains neutrality among the competing conceptions of the good, i.e., of self-fulfillment, held by each individual and treats the pursuit of them as compatible with equal freedom for all.

I will argue that both the defenders and opponents of the 1787 Constitution were liberals. My analysis will focus on the letters of Publius and of Brutus of New York, which are commonly regarded as the best arguments for and against the proposed Constitution. This argument rejects a civic humanist reading of the founding of the American republic and contends that, to the extent that Brutus and Publius use terms drawn from the civic humanist tradition, this language is stripped of more of its original meaning than the revisionists recognize.

To be sure, the founders were concerned with the problem of citizenship. They understood that a liberal polity, like any other, requires a "virtuous citizenry" if it is to endure. It requires that a substantial proportion of its members undertake civic duties and bear costs in doing so, including the possible loss of their own lives to defend the commonwealth. Moreover, they knew that a liberalism stressing personal freedom over the common good was hard-pressed to provide rational grounds for undertaking civic obligations which were *convincing* and *effective* in practice. There was ample reason for Publius and Brutus to believe that individuals would be as inclined to be free riders as citizens and to be tyrants as legitimate rulers.

The question then becomes, how were problems of citizenship and civic virtue conceived by Publius and Brutus? Neither sought to promote civic virtue in the civic humanist sense. They were, however, concerned with the problem of fostering a *sentiment* of allegiance out of which would emerge a disposition to undertake civic duties. In fact, they debate vigorously the social and psychological conditions which foster this sentiment. This approach owes much to eighteenth century moral sense theories best expressed in the ethical and political writings of David Hume. The founders, like Hume, were aware of inadequacies in the liberal theory of political obligation, and both relied on sentiment to overcome them. If men could not be *convinced* to be good citizens, they may at least *feel* disposed to be so.

I. A Shared Liberalism

The letters of Publius and Brutus are a melange of historical references, theoretical statements and observations on the politics of their time. They are clearly not great works of political philosophy to rival the European masters, nor were they intended as such. Still, the practicing politicians who wrote them were not mere political technicians. The ratification debates called forth an explicit expression of political first principles and an application of these principles in establishing criteria for evaluating the existing governments of the Confederacy and the proposed Constitution. And at the core of these principles is a commitment to the liberal social contract tradition.

In Federalist 15, Hamilton likens the Constitution to a social contract and develops his argument on classical liberal, Hobbesian lines. The state governments under the Confederacy play a role in Hamilton's theory identical to that of individuals in Hobbes's state of nature. The states are entities pursuing their own ends unconstrained by laws backed by *sufficient force*. The law-making and enforcement powers of the national government lack adequate sanctions and thus amount to "nothing more than advice or recommendation" and are not the "resolutions or commands" they appear to be.⁶ This distinction parallels Hobbes's definition of positive law in *Leviathan* as "not counsel, but command" and his distinction between laws of nature which are no more than "qualities that dispose men to peace and obedience" from laws proper which are backed by the sword.⁷

Further, the inconveniences of the state of nature are essentially the same for each. Hamilton writes that, in an association such as that under the Articles of Confederation "where the general authority is confined to the collective bodies of the communities that compose it, every breach of law must involve a state of war and military execution must become the only instrument of civil obedience."⁸ Thus, if state X fails to contribute to the collective security of the confederacy, it is as much a threat to state Y's security as is the external enemy they are jointly sworn to resist. In such a situation, they are in a state of war with each other and the risks of actual war are correspondingly high.

For Hamilton, a rational plan of escape from this condition is for the states to contract with each other to establish a sovereign with sufficient power to ensure both the independence of each state from the use of force by the others and the contribution of each to the collective goods required by the union as a whole. This contract requires the states to surrender some liberty to direct their own affairs as they yield to the national government a share of sovereignty over their citizens. In return,

6. Alexander Hamilton, James Madison and John Jay, *The Federalist Papers*, ed. Clinton Rossiter (New York: The New American Library, 1961), No. 15, p. 110.

7. Thomas Hobbes, *Leviathan*, ed. Michael Oakeshott (New York: Macmillan Publishing Co. Inc., Collier Books, 1962), pp. 198, 200.

8. Hamilton, et al., *The Federalist*, No. 15, p. 110.

they gain the security and independence (if not as broad in scope, at least more assured) that they could not adequately provide for themselves individually or jointly under the Confederacy. Such a contract must form a government "equally energetic," if not identical in all details to that of the proposed Constitution of 1787.

This plan is the only solution for the problem of a weak form of cooperation which has become untenable. After a brief description of the inadequacies of the Confederacy, Hamilton writes that such an arrangement does "not deserve the name of government nor would any prudent man choose to commit his happiness to it."[9] Not consenting to the proposed Constitution indicates an inability to recognize where one's long-term interests lie. In classic liberal fashion, Hamilton does not define the nature of the happiness the prudent man ought to pursue. He does suggest, however, that wherever this happiness may lie, prospects of gaining and maintaining it over time are incompatible with the state of war which existed under the Articles.

Madison in Federalist 10 also follows the logic of classical liberalism, though not as explicitly as Hamilton. The thread of his argument shows much about both the moral foundations and the practical functions of the liberal state. Madison describes government's purpose as protecting the "faculties of man" from which "rights of property originate" as do economic inequalities.

The protection of these faculties is the first object of government. From the protection of different and unequal faculties of acquiring property, the possession of different degrees and kind of property immediately results; and from the influence of these on the sentiments and views of respective proprietors ensues a division of society into different interests and parties.[10]

This passage raises a number of questions. It is not self-evident, for example, that diversity in faculties gives rise to property rights, much less the right of unlimited acquisition that Madison seems to have in mind. Nor is it clear that faculties, insofar as they consist in "natural endowments," can establish entitlements of any sort.[11] It is less important, however, to criticize Madison on these grounds than to see why he presented his position in these somewhat obscure terms.

9. Ibid.
10. Ibid., No. 10, p. 78.
11. I have in mind here Rawls's conception of natural endowments as arbitrary from the moral point of view and, more importantly, the widely-held and long-standing intuition Rawls articulates. See John Rawls, *A Theory of Justice* (Cambridge: The Belknap Press of Harvard University Press, 1971), esp. chap. 1.

When Madison speaks of government protecting faculties, he is making an argument for political obligation to the liberal state that he is proposing. At the same time, he is using a yardstick provided by the liberal social contract tradition to measure the defects of American government under the Articles. The moral core of this tradition is that only through voluntary agreement to rules of justice, on condition of like agreement by others, can one exercise one's will with minimal external constraints. More pointedly, the strongest case the liberal state can make for the obedience of its subjects is that, without it, they are unable to exercise faculties freely and act as autonomous agents.

This argument can readily be applied to the choice situation of the ratification process. In Federalist 45, Madison contends that the purpose of the Revolution was to secure for Americans those goods which could not be secured under the arbitrary rule of the British. These goods are the "peace, liberty and safety" of the American people defined generally as their "happiness." Any government which similarly threatens these goods is not deserving of support for all the reasons noted above. This is as true of state governments under the Confederacy as it is of the British. If the national union is essential to the American people's happiness, Madison argues, it is "preposterous to urge as an objection to it . . . that such a government may derogate from the importance of the individual states."[12]

The obligation owed state governments is clearly a function of their ability to secure individual liberties. Their legitimacy decreases proportionately if they are unable to perform this task or if a diminution of their powers is required for its performance. It may be that supporters of the Confederacy have praiseworthy reasons for defending state sovereignty. Among these could be a sense of affection for the locality or, theoretically, a classical republican-inspired idea of the small state as the locus of active citizenship. Nonetheless, the moral weight of these reasons would be slight if states were not adequately "protecting faculties." That they were not doing so is, of course, precisely Madison's contention.

That Madison equates faculties with skills in acquiring property indicates a bourgeois or "possessive individualist" component to his liberalism, but this does not suggest that he is unconcerned with the "common good." His whole public life belies this contention. Rather, Madison sees the common good as problematic in a particular, ideologically constrained way. Since there are inevitable scarcities of goods in market

---

12. Hamilton, et al., *The Federalist*, No. 45, pp. 288-289.

economies and since exercising faculties is equated with acquisition, society is necessarily ridden with conflicts over scarce resources. Moreover, men naturally feel a passionate attachment to their own property, as well as to their opinions, religious beliefs, and so forth and by implication, a natural aversion to what they see as impeding their pursuit of the goods they desire. These passions are easily inflamed and manifest self-love in the narrowest sense. They "dispose men to vex and oppress each other [rather] than to co-operate for the common good."[13] This notion of the passions justifies Madison's observations that factions are sown in the nature of man, which in turn makes it necessary for the liberal state to regulate competing interests or, more starkly, to break and control the "violence of faction."

In Brutus's letters, there is less emphasis on conflicts over resources among the people. There is a stronger tendency to view the people within the individual states as unified by similar mores and habits that are more fundamental than are the divisions created by competing interests. The conflict of central concern to Brutus is between the people and the government. This more unitary view of civil society has encouraged at least one critic to suggest that Anti-Federalist references to liberal individualist themes were merely covers for deeper civic humanist commitments derived from an "older science of politics" based on a natural, organic notion of community and government.[14] A close reading of Brutus's texts, however, suggest a much stronger liberal commitment than this interpretation allows.

Brutus's criticisms of the Constitution can be divided into two classes, one general and one specific. The general argument is grounded, though not all that rigorously, in a political theory from first principles showing that "consolidated government" on a national scale is incompatible with "free government." Specific criticisms deal with the institutional inadequacies of the proposed national government in this regard, but the general argument is of more interest and its premises deserve to be quoted at some length. After noting that the "mutual wants of men" dictate the formation of societies, Brutus considers the origins of government:

> In a state of nature every individual pursues his own interest; in this pursuit it frequently happened that the possessions and enjoyments

13. Ibid., No. 10, p. 79.
14. Wilson Carey McWilliams, "Democracy and the Citizen: Community, Dignity, and the Crisis of Contemporary Politics in America," in *How Democratic is the Constitution?*, eds. Robert A. Goldwin and William A. Schambra (Washington, D.C.: American Enterprise Institute, 1980), p. 92.

of one were sacrificed to the views and designs of another; thus the weak were prey to the strong . . . [and] every individual was insecure; common interest therefore directed that government should be established, in which the force of the whole community should be collected, and under such directions as to protect and defend everyone who compose it. The common good, therefore is the end of civil government, and common consent the foundation on which it is established.[15]

In this exposition, there is no difference between Brutus and Publius on the purpose of government. To paraphrase Brutus, it is to protect, through legitimate use of force, the pursuit of possessions and enjoyments by each from the designs of others. Brutus sees government as conventional, not natural in the civic humanist sense, and citizens are required to surrender only their natural right of self-protection so that other rights which also exist prior to the establishment of government can be secured.

To effect this end [of establishing government] it was necessary that a certain portion of natural liberty should be surrendered, in order, that what remained should be preserved. . . . But it is not necessary for this purpose, that individuals should relinquish all individual rights. Some are of such a nature that they cannot be surrendered. Of these are the rights of conscience, the right of enjoying and defending life, etc.[16]

Brutus's argument is neither lucid nor complete in its account of the distinction between the origins of society and the founding of government, the full content of natural rights and other philosophical issues. It is clear, however, that the following liberal social contract assumptions are at the heart of his presentation. First, prior to any plans for social cooperation individuals are seen as fully-developed persons with their own conceptions of enjoyment, their own possessions, opinions, etc. Second, the threat each poses to the possessions and enjoyment of others justifies the establishment of government. Finally, the legitimacy of government diminishes if it usurps any natural rights beyond those necessary to maintain public order.

These theoretical considerations are at the core of Brutus's main contention that consolidated government makes free government impos-

15. Herbert J. Storing, ed., *The Complete Anti-Federalist,* 7 vols. (Chicago: University of Chicago Press, 1981), 2: 373.

16. Ibid.

sible. They introduce his claim that the proposed Constitution insufficiently checks the power-expanding tendencies of public officials. "Rulers," he argues, "have the same propensities as other men" and thus are as likely to use their power for "private purposes, and to the injury and oppression of those over whom they are placed, as individuals . . . in the state of nature are to injure and oppress one another."[17]

Both Publius and Brutus take the utility-maximizing motivations of rulers as a given. This being so, it is as critical as government's being able to control the people that it in turn be controlled. The adequacy of the Constitution's precautions for preventing abuses of power is much contested in the ratification debates. Disagreements abound not only over the electoral arrangements and the "auxilliary precautions" found in the Constitution itself but over the social and psychological conditions which promote a sense of legitimacy in government, and hence the fidelity of rulers and the allegiance of citizens. Not in question, however, are liberal understandings of the self, society, and government.

II. From Obligation to Allegiance: The Question of Civic Virtue

A liberal democratic polity, like any other which allows mass political participation, requires a "virtuous" citizenry. A substantial portion of the population must accept the legitimacy of governmental decisions concerning the arbitration of rights and the distribution of costs of collective goods. At minimum, citizens must be law-abiding. Beyond that, a significant number must also be willing to contribute actively to the public order by the disinterested performance of the duties of public office and even to sacrifice their lives in defense of the commonwealth. The notion that a polity could sustain itself if all citizens were disposed to be free riders and all rulers disposed to be tyrants was as alien to the founders' understanding of durable and legitimate government as it is to our own.[18] There are differences between Publius and Brutus over the conditions which best promote a sense of legitimacy in government and the corresponding willingness of citizens to undertake civic duties. There

17. Ibid.
18. Madison expressed this understanding on the floor of the Virginia Ratifying Convention when he said: "Is there no virtue among us? If there be not, we are in a wretched situation. No theoretical checks—no form of government can render us secure. To suppose that any form of government will secure liberty or happiness without any virtue in the people is a chimerical idea." Quoted in Saul Padover, ed., *The Complete Madison* (New York: Harper and Row, 1953), pp. 48–49.

are, however, fundamental similarities in the form and content of their arguments over these conditions which call into question the idea that any substantial civic humanist commitment informs their understanding of "civic virtue."

One similarity is that neither Publius nor Brutus provides a rational argument about the political obligation of citizens undertaking civic duties. Rather, they see the problem as the need to foster an *affective* bond between citizen and the state out of which the disposition to be civic-minded will emerge. Second, as Alasdair MacIntyre has noted, morality in the seventeenth and eighteenth centuries came generally to be understood as offering a solution to the problem of egoism equated with altruism.[19] Both Publius and Brutus fall into this pattern, as they treat the moral qualities which dispose citizens to support government as weaker, secondary sentiments that *check* primary instincts which are narrowly self-regarding.

Liberal contract theory provides an argument for undertaking civic duties which emerges from its understanding of the reasons for entering into a plan of social cooperation. Two aspects of this plan bear directly on the issue of obligation. The first is that the contract is mutually accepted, the product of an agreement freely made. Consent by each individual to the terms of the contract is the only legitimate grounds for being bound by those terms as this alone is compatible with the fundamental equality of all in the state of nature. Having consented, one is obliged to abide by the terms of the contract simply because one ought to keep one's word. The second aspect is that the plan be mutually beneficial. Each individual, insofar as he is rational, would consent to a cooperative plan only if he were better off with it than without it. The assumption of liberal contract theory is that all will be better off by cooperating, because only through a publicly-enforced legal framework can they gain the security and independence all rational agents desire. Thus, one ought to contribute to the maintenance of the public order if one has *voluntarily agreed* to receive the *benefits* provided by it.

This theory of obligation, however, is problematic. Classical liberals from Hobbes through the founders had reason to believe that even the "just" societies and governments they advocated would be composed largely of free riders or even criminals. They saw several difficulties in

19. This conception of morality differs sharply, as MacIntyre notes, from the Aristotelian one in which morality is perceived less as a restraint on egoism than as a realization of one's nature. MacIntyre's work, *After Virtue,* offers the best contemporary analysis of the virtues, including civic virtue, as understood in the Aristotelian framework. See *After Virtue* (Notre Dame, Ind.: University of Notre Dame Press, 1981), esp. p. 212.

establishing a *practice* of obligation. First, although the good of each individual is inextricably linked to the maintenance of the public order, it is rarely evident to any individual that his defection from support of that order poses an imminent threat to it. It is likely to appear to each, therefore, that he can take advantage of the benefits of cooperation while not paying the costs without jeopardizing the plan which provides those benefits.[20] The problem of defection is compounded if the society or polity is composed to any significant extent by "possessive individuals" who are involved in zero-sum conflicts with each other over the distribution of scarce resources. However the plan of cooperation is designed, it will inevitably be the case that some individuals can improve their relative position by disregarding the constraints on individual maximization of values that the plan imposes.[21] There are ample incentives, in other words, for rulers to become tyrants and for citizens to become free riders or criminals.

The founders conceived of political obligation in these terms, but they were equally aware of the practical limits of this conception. This awareness is best expressed by Publius but is shared by Brutus as well. In "The Vices of the Political System of the United States," which foreshadows Federalist 10, Madison considers the dangers of majority faction and the possible motives for a majority to restrain itself from abusing the "rights and interests of the minority, or of individuals." The first motive he considers is that of "a prudent regard to their own good as involved in the general and permanent good of the community."[22] This motive derives from what is thought best for one's own long-term interests. A prudent regard for my own good is a reason to respect others' rights because the common good (defined as the stability of government and the generality of laws) is the condition for each individual acquiring and maintaining

20. For discussion of problems in the liberal theory of political obligation see: C. B. Macpherson, *The Political Theory of Possessive Individualism* (New York: Oxford University Press, 1962); Carole Pateman, *The Problem of Political Obligation—A Critical Analysis of Liberal Theory* (New York: John Wiley and Sons, 1979).

21. For a sound analytical treatment of the problem of stability in plans of cooperation and its relation to liberal ideology see David Gauthier, "The Social Contract as Ideology," *Philosophy and Public Affairs,* 6 (Winter 1977): 130–164. It should be stressed that stability and free rider problems are endemic to any plan of cooperation which holds that individuals have their own ends and ought to be allowed to pursue them. Our conception of the nature of the ends they are likely to pursue can lead us to consider these problems more or less acute but cannot eliminate them. Thus, accepting the structure of my argument on the obligation problem and its application to the founders does not depend on attributing to them a "possessive individualist" conception of "human nature."

22. Marvin Meyers, ed., *The Mind of the Founder—Sources of the Political Thought of James Madison,* rev. ed. (Boston: Trustees of Brandeis University, 1981), p. 63.

whatever he desires. If today I can best satisfy my desires by violating another's rights, I may be restrained by the knowledge that tomorrow the shoe may be on the other foot. But Madison suggests that, though this motive ought to be "of decisive weight in itself, [it] is found by experience to be too often unheeded. It is too often forgotten, by nations as well as by individuals, that honesty is the best policy."[23]

Madison's empirical generalization is reinforced in axiomatic form by Hamilton in Federalist 15. "Power controlled or abridged," he writes, is "almost always the rival and enemy of the power by which it is controlled or abridged." Hamilton then applies this axiom to an analysis of the Confederacy's defects by arguing that it teaches us not to expect that "the persons entrusted with the administration of the particular members of the Confederacy will at all times be ready with . . . an unbiased regard to the public weal to execute the resolutions or decrees of the general authority."[24] The obligation of state leaders to support the central government as a result of their agreeing to the compact which established it and benefitting from its existence is of little practical consequence. The power-enhancing motivations of state leaders lead them to act on their short-term advantage against the public weal and, in so doing, against their long-term interests as well.

Brutus holds equally to an appropriative, individualist concept of man which tends to undermine the performance of civic duties. He is especially concerned about the tendency of rulers to violate public trusts and infringe on private rights, and his argument for the inclusion of a bill of rights in the Constitution is developed in these terms. The unwillingness of men in the state of nature to "conform themselves to the rule of immutable righteousness" and their tendency to exercise "fraud, oppression and violence" on one another required that "certain rules should be formed to regulate the conduct of all."[25] But the establishment of rules of justice and the obligations arising from them do not remake human character. The same propensities which led to the establishment of government persist in settled polities. Therefore rulers, given their power to do harm, ought to be restrained by a wide variety of checks including a bill of rights. Despite the moral weight of the proposition that each is under an obligation to sustain just institutions through civic actions, the individuals the founders describe are as likely to be free riders as citizens, as likely to be tyrants as legitimate rulers.

23. Ibid.
24. Hamilton, et al., *The Federalist*, No. 15, p. 111.
25. Storing, ed., *The Complete Anti-Federalist*, 2: 373.

The limits of liberal obligation were clearly taken into account in the debates over the proposed Constitution. That government must have sufficient coercive powers to compel citizens to perform such minimal state-supporting acts as the payment of taxes was not in dispute although the proper locus of this power was contested. Neither was there debate over the need for institutional restraints on rulers in the form of electoral accountability and other "auxilliary precautions." However, these conditions were considered necessary but not sufficient to sustain a policy able to protect rights and promote prosperity. That a sense of civic virtue had to exist among the citizenry if a republican cure for the diseases incident to republics was to be found was recognized by both sets of founders.

Civic virtue can be defined formally as a disposition among citizens to engage in activities which support and maintain a just political order. This definition is neutral with regard to the particular plan of justice the citizen supports, whether liberal democratic, Platonic, or other. Much of the ratification debate focused on the social, psychological, and institutional conditions which foster this disposition. Yet, a fundamental similarity exists in how Publius and Brutus approach these conditions and in their understanding of the concept of civic virtue itself. For both, civic virtue was understood as the product of a moral sentiment, or of an affective bond between citizen and ruler. This conception served a key purpose for the founders, because it filled the gaps left by the practical inadequacies of the liberal theory of obligation. If liberalism could not provide grounds for obligation which were both internally consistent and practically effective, a theory of sentiment could lead one to believe that most citizens would be virtuous most of the time. It could do so, that is, if a convincing argument could be made that the political system itself would foster this sentiment.

This understanding of virtue as sentiment and the focus on the empirical, socio-psychological conditions which promote it bear strong resemblances to the issues raised in the ethical and political writings of David Hume. Hume is less concerned with providing *reasons* for members of political communities to be good citizens than in explaining why, by and large, they are so. In this, the founders, whether wittingly or not, are his heirs.[26] For Hume, the practical effect of any moral idea depends on the

---

26. Introducing Hume into an essay concerned largely with problems of obligation in the liberal contract tradition may seem out of place unless two points are kept in mind. First, a strong case can be made that Hume is more a contract theorist than he is often taken to be. See David Gauthier, "David Hume—Contractarian," *The Philosophical Review* 88 (January 1982): 3–38, for an elaboration of this argument. Second, Hume's political use of

sense of approbation or disapproval associated with it. Reason can identify duties we ought to undertake, but without the existence of "warm
feelings and prepossessions in favor of virtue, and all disgust and aversion to vice," it is unlikely that we would actually do so.[27] This is as true
of political obligations as of other duties. The sense of approbation felt
for those who display public virtues derives from the perception of the
utility of these qualities and of government itself in promoting the
interests each has in public order and justice.[28]

The moral sense that motivates us to undertake civic duties is not to be
confused with an instinct. There are *natural* moral sentiments such as
love and benevolence, but they differ from those derived from the recognition of obligations. The former are instinctual feelings of affection
prior to any consideration of personal advantage. The latter are *acquired*
and restrain "primary instincts" which are narrowly self-regarding. The
political duty of allegiance is an example of the latter type of moral sentiment. It functions as a check on primary instincts which, as Hume notes,
"lead us either to indulge ourselves in unlimited freedom, or to seek
dominion over others." It does so as reason "engages us to sacrifice such
strong passions to the interest of peace and public order."[29] On reflection, we come to recognize that, though we may benefit in the short run
by violating rules of justice (a term Hume uses synonymously with property rights), we lose more in the long term than we gain by so doing. Prudence thus produces in us a sense of approbation for government and
dutiful public officials.

But Hume recognizes that a prudentially-based sense of approbation is
too weak a restraint to curb the inclinations of those possessive individuals he describes as sensible knaves.

> [T]hough . . . without a regard to property, no society could sub-
> sist; yet . . . a sensible knave, in particular incidents, may think,
> that an act of iniquity or infidelity will make a considerable addi-
> tion to his fortune, without causing any considerable breach in the

---

his theory of moral sentiments is to provide motives for adhering to norms required to sustain plans of social cooperation, not to provide the norms themselves. Whether the norms
are derived from contractual or utilitarian premises is therefore not relevant to the concerns
of this essay.

27. David Hume, *An Enquiry Concerning the Principles of Morals* (Indianapolis:
Hackett Publishing Co., 1983), p. 15.

28. Ibid., pp. 32, 34.

29. David Hume, "Of the Original Contract," in *David Hume's Political Essays,* ed.
Charles W. Hendel (New York: The Bobbs-Merrill Co., Inc., 1953), p. 55.

social union and confederacy. That *honesty is the best policy,* may be a good general rule; but it is liable to many exceptions; And he, it may . . . be thought, conducts himself with most wisdom, who observes the general rule, and takes advantage of all the exceptions.[30]

The knave is not likely to find convincing any argument for abiding by rules of justice. No prudentially-grounded argument is going to influence him as he has already quite sensibly calculated that defection from the rules is more advantageous to his interest than would be compliance with them.

In his response to the knave, Hume reintroduces considerations of moral sense. If members of the political community are to be disposed, by and large, to undertake civic duties, this disposition must come from a moral sentiment, not from reflection on interests. If the knave's "heart rebels not against such pernicious maxims, . . . he has indeed lost a considerable motive to virtue; and we may expect that his practice be answerable to his speculation."[31] Fortunately, Hume contends, there are reasons to believe that most hearts do rebel against the notion of such narrow self-seeking.

Experience teaches us that citizens do feel a sense of affection for their government if it provides the goods of security and justice. More important, however, this prudentially-based sense of approbation is converted over time into a habit of obedience to and support of government. "Antiquity," Hume argues, "always begets the opinion of right" (i.e., the right to rule); and "whatever disadvantageous sentiments we may entertain of mankind, they are always found to be prodigal of blood and treasure in the maintenance of public justice."[32] Hume suggests that the virtue of allegiance only fully takes hold of the public when it ceases to be based on reflection of any sort. But given a sound administration over time, this virtue will naturally, i.e., unconsciously, develop. When this habit appears, it becomes pointless to discuss civic virtue in any other than emotive terms. It consists in the bond of sentiment the citizen feels for community, government, and political leaders.

This eighteenth century notion of civic virtue, which Hume shares with the founders, bears only a superficial resemblance to the notion as it is employed in classical republican theory. As Pocock recognizes, civic virtue in the civic humanist framework is internally related to a notion of

---

30. Hume, *Enquiry,* p. 81.
31. Ibid., pp. 81–82.
32. See "Of the First Principles of Government," in *David Hume's Political Essays,* ed. Hendel, p. 24.

the self as fulfilled only through active citizenship. Such a notion necessarily entails the relationship between the good citizen and the good person, the political institutions and practices required for these ideals to
coincide, and the distinction of different orders in society based on their
contribution to the good of the whole. These are not, however, the kinds
of problems addressed by the founders in their discussions of civic virtue.

Indeed, the riddle of the relation between liberalism and the civic
humanist language in the founding debates is almost solved. The modern
notion of civic virtue is a necessary concommitant of core liberal
premises. Liberal polities require virtuous citizens but prudential deliberation can go only so far in creating them. If, however, civic virtue is
conceived as a sentiment restraining narrowly self-regarding inclinations
and, if this sentiment can be fostered, it may reasonably be argued that
citizens will be sufficiently virtuous to uphold a liberal democratic polity.
It remains only to show that Publius and Brutus conceived the problem
of a virtuous citizenry in these terms.

Brutus's account of allegiance and related public virtues fits well
within the theory developed above. His defense of a system of confederated small republics is suffused with the idea that only small states can
foster the "civic virtue" required to sustain "free government." This
defense is notable for its omissions, for absent is an argument that small
states are preferable because they alone can provide the political good
associated with civic humanism, the development of faculties through
civic participation. Present instead is an empirically-based argument
aimed at demonstrating the utility of small polities in fostering the sentiments of allegiance which dispose citizens to act virtuously.

Brutus's criticism of consolidated government begins with a distinction between authoritative government and rule by force. Any government which cannot count on citizen recognition of its authority must rely
on force if its edicts are to be obeyed. Men are motivated to obey laws
from "affection for the government or from fear."[33] Brutus argues convincingly that, in the absence of affection, governments become "nerve-
less and inefficient" and this increases the need for compulsion. He is
less persuasive, however, when he tries to show that state governments
can garner popular support while the proposed national federation could
not. This is so, he contends, because state governments benefit from sentiments of approbation which are based both in interest and in nature. As
to the former, Brutus claims that only in small states with small electoral
districts can the citizen be confident that representatives are actively pro-

33. Storing, ed., *The Complete Anti-Federalist*, 2: 370.

moting his group or occupational interest. With regard to the latter, he suggests that "intimate acquaintance" with legislators is a necessary condition for the public's disposition to comply with the laws they pass.

For Brutus, the antithesis of the confidence people have in government is suspicion or jealousy. Suspicion is a function of distance, both social and geographic, between representative and represented. He argues that the small number of representatives in the proposed national congress will increase the distance in both respects. Hence, representatives "will not be viewed by the people as part of themselves, but as a body distinct from them, and having separate interests to pursue" with the result of a "perpetual jealousy" between ruler and ruled.[34] Jealousy is the natural result when one must rely on a stranger to act as trustee for one's interests.

> If the person confided in, be a neighbor with whom his employer is intimately acquainted . . . his honesty and fidelity [are] unsuspected, and his friendship and zeal for the service of the principal unquestionable, he will commit his affairs into his hands with unreserved confidence. . . . But, if the person employed be a stranger, whom he has never seen, and whose character for ability and fidelity he cannot fully learn, . . . he will trust him with caution and be suspicious of all his conduct.[35]

The main thrust of Brutus's position is that friends make better representatives than strangers, because friends can be trusted not to set up shop for themselves upon taking power. Intimate acquaintance with representatives fosters a willingness to comply with laws both because we have a natural affection for those who write them and because we can be reasonably confident that representatives are promoting our interests. Further, to assure the latter grounds for confidence, it is required that legislators be "like the people" they represent. Brutus means by this that members of the legislature should be virtually a statistical sample of the various occupational interests in society. In this way, representatives will not only be acquainted with the interests of each group but will also "feel a proper sense and becoming zeal to promote their prosperity."[36] This

34. Ibid., p. 385.
35. Ibid.
36. Ibid., p. 380. This emphasis on group representation leads Yarborough to the somewhat surprising observation that "the intellectual heirs of the Anti-Federalists are the proponents of interest group representation, who stress the reflection of group interests as a means of securing individual rights." It is more common to associate the Federalists, especially Madison, with interest group representation. This reminds us again that debates between the two sets of founders were indeed what Storing has described as quarrels within a family. See Yarborough, "Republicanism Reconsidered," p. 88.

zeal will be matched by the affection we feel for things which advance our interests, and this affection will take the form of a sentiment of allegiance to the government and a corresponding willingness to be a good citizen.

Brutus, like Hume, tends to treat the allegiance/civic virtue problem more as a branch of a general psychological theory of motivation than as an essentially political problem. There is little political theory in the argument brought to bear either to show that small republics ought to be considered goods in themselves or to explain why citizens ought to consider themselves obliged to perform civic duties within them. The defense of small republics that Brutus makes is wholly empirical in character and rests on assumptions concerning the sources of sentiment and the institutional requirements for channeling it into a feeling of allegiance. Further, it is not clear what political theory objections Brutus could have made to a consolidated republic. For him, as much as for Publius, the most powerful justification for any government is that it enables individuals to pursue possessions and enjoyments freely within a legal framework, and a consolidated government could arguably provide this framework as effectively as could a confederation.

Publius's concern that citizens be virtuous, and his confidence that most will be, also closely parallels Hume's account of allegiance. For Publius, there are two foundations of allegiance that are intermingled: *sound administration* and *habit*. The utility of efficient government will result in a sense of approbation for the state, which will grow over time until it becomes habitual and citizens will be disposed to support the state without reflecting on the reasons for doing so.

Publius develops this argument with two purposes in mind. The first is to show that the bond of sentiment both he and Brutus see as a prerequisite of free government is not a function of the size of the polity but of its government's capacity to perform its essential tasks. These tasks are the neutral arbitration of rights and the provision of collective goods. The second purpose is more subtle. Publius agrees with the Anti-Federalists that state governments can make claims on the sentiments of their citizens that the national government cannot and sees this as a protection for the states under the proposed federal system.

Publius meets the second purpose by arguing first that, in Hamilton's words, the states will retain powers extending "to all objects which, in the ordinary course of affairs, concern the lives, liberties, and properties of the people, and internal order . . . and prosperity of the State."[37] And

---

37. Hamilton, et al., *The Federalist*, No. 45, pp. 292–293.

"being the immediate and visible guardian of life and property, . . . regulating all those personal interests and familiar concerns to which the sensibility of individuals is most immediately awake," states have a great advantage over the national government in "impressing upon the minds of the people affection, esteem, and reverence toward government."³⁸ State governments are the principal protector of rights through their justice systems and the main provider of collective goods. The utility of state government is, therefore, more evident to citizens than are the benefits they will receive from a strong national government. The states are the main beneficiary of that sense of approbation that derives from prudence. The only historical exception to this tendency was the "transient enthusiasms" felt for the national congress during and immediately after the Revolution, but even then the "attention and attachment" of the people soon returned to state affairs and state government."³⁹

Publius also takes note of nonprudential or natural sentiments which accrue more to state governments than to the national one. He mentions, for example, the ties of "personal acquaintance and friendship" between office holders and voters which reinforce state loyalties. He argues, however, that natural loyalties to the locality are not in themselves an argument against the legitimacy of the proposed federal government. Hamilton notes in Federalist 15 that the natural "predilection" felt for "local objects . . . can hardly fail to mislead the decision" to sufficiently empower a national sovereign.⁴⁰ If local affections blind one to the recognition of principles of cooperation which must be instituted nationally to be effective, there is no virtue in them.

Publius's next purpose is to refute Brutus's contention that only state governments can be legitimized by prudentially-based sentiments. In Federalist 27, Hamilton does this by stating "as a general rule that [the people's] confidence in and obedience to a government will commonly be proportional to the goodness or badness of administration."⁴¹ He then argues that there is no reason to suppose that the national government will be more poorly administered than state ones. Indeed, it is argued throughout *The Federalist* that a national government will be better-administered and better able to protect rights and promote prosperity. There is therefore every reason to suppose that, given an effective national government, the virtuous citizens of Virginia, Rhode Island, and other states will become the virtuous citizens of the United States.

38. Ibid., No. 17, p. 120.
39. Ibid., No. 46, p. 295.
40. Ibid., No. 15, p. 112.
41. Ibid., No. 27, p. 174.

The means of making this transfer of allegiance possible is to let time do its work on their affection.

> [T]he more the operations of the national authority are intertwined in the ordinary exercise of government, . . . the further it enters into those objects which touch the most sensible chords and put in motion the most active springs of the human heart, the greater will be the probability that it will conciliate the respect and attachment of the community. Man is very much a creature of habit. A thing that rarely strikes his senses will have but a transient influence upon his mind. A government continually at a distance and out of sight can hardly be expected to interest the sensations of the people.[42]

For Publius, the model citizen is not the active citizen we associate with civic humanist ideals. Rather, he is essentially a passive character whose disposition to support the state amounts to little more than a habit of obedience. It is best, therefore, that questions concerning rational grounds for obedience do not arise too often. If they do, the sentimental tie citizens feel for government will be weakened and, as a result, so will be the government's stability. This idea is behind Madison's reply in Federalist 49 to Jefferson's call for periodic constitutional conventions. Each call would "carry the implication of some defect in the government" and frequent ones would "deprive the government of the veneration which time bestows on all things and without which perhaps the wisest and freest governments would not possess the requisite stability."[43] This veneration seems to be an offshoot of the psychological law that time breeds familiarity which breeds affection. Love of the republic and a corresponding willingness to be a good citizen is not attributed, except very indirectly, to any moral qualities of the state but simply to the fact that it will grow old.

III. Conclusion

Republican revisionism has made several important contributions to our understanding of the founding of the American republic. It has raised questions about citizenship and civic virtue which orthodox scholars have tended to ignore. Thus, for example, rereading *The Federalist* in light of revisionist concerns, it becomes impossible to accept Dahl's argument in *A Preface To Democratic Theory* that Madison thought institu-

42. Ibid., p. 176.
43. Ibid., No. 49, p. 314.

tional checks and balances a sufficient condition for maintaining a stable political order. To the contrary, Madison was acutely aware of the need for popular support for government and sought to identify conditions which promoted it. The revisionist emphasis on the founders as heirs of European traditions of political discourse is also an important antidote to the non-ideological reading of the founding offered by writers such as Boorstin and Roche.[44] However the founders' ideologies are interpreted, it is clearly inappropriate to analyze them simply as pragmatic men solving practical problems.

The revisionists fall short, however, in equating the founders' understanding of citizenship and civic virtue with that of the classical republican tradition. It can be taken as axiomatic that any political system, if it is to be sustained, must be perceived as legitimate by a substantial proportion of its members. There are limits to the state's capacity to rely on coercion to assure compliance with its laws. Democratic forms of government require something beyond a minimal sense of legitimacy. The disposition of citizens to engage in activities which uphold the political order, i.e., civic virtue, becomes a necessity because of the wider range of civic duties the citizen can and is expected to undertake. It has been argued above that Publius and Brutus vigorously debate the conditions which foster civic virtue. Where I contest the revisionists is in their suggestion that this debate owes any substantial debt to civic humanism. Pocock, et al., are essentially correct in their understanding of classical virtue as internally related to the development of human faculties through civic participation. But, as has been shown above, both analytical and empirical evidence may be brought to bear to challenge the contention that this same understanding can be attributed to the American founders.

---

44. The classic statements of this non-ideological reading are Daniel J. Boorstin, *The Genius of American Politics* (Chicago: University of Chicago Press, 1953); and John P. Roche, "The Founding Fathers: A Reform Caucus in Action," *American Political Science Review*, 55 (Fall 1961): 799–816.

DEMOCRACY AND *THE FEDERALIST:*
A RECONSIDERATION OF THE FRAMERS' INTENT*

MARTIN DIAMOND

Claremont Men's College

It has been a common teaching among modern historians of the guiding ideas in the foundation of our government that the Constitution of the United States embodied a reaction against the democratic principles espoused in the Declaration of Independence. This view has largely been accepted by political scientists and has therefore had important consequences for the way American political development has been studied. I shall present here a contrary view of the political theory of the Framers and examine some of its consequences.

What is the relevance of the political thought of the Founding Fathers to an understanding of contemporary problems of liberty and justice? Four possible ways of looking at the Founding Fathers immediately suggest themselves. First, it may be that they possessed wisdom, a set of political principles still inherently adequate, and needing only to be supplemented by skill in their proper contemporary application. Second, it may be that, while the Founding Fathers' principles are still sound, they are applicable only to a part of our problems, but not to that part which is peculiarly modern; and thus new principles are needed to be joined together with the old ones. Third, it may be that the Founding Fathers have simply become; they dealt with bygone problems and their principles were relevant only to those old problems. Fourth, they may have been wrong or radically inadequate even for their own time.

Each of these four possible conclusions requires the same foundation: an understanding of the political thought of the Founding Fathers. To decide whether to apply their wisdom, or to add to their wisdom, or to reject it as irrelevant or as unwise, it is absolutely necessary to understand what they said, why they said it, and what they meant by it. At the same time, however, to understand their claim to wisdom is to evaluate it: to know wherein they were wise and wherein they were not, or wherein (and why) their wisdom is unavailing for our problems. Moreover, even if it turns out that our modern problems require wholly new principles for their solution, an excellent way to discover those new principles would be to see what it is about modernity that has outmoded the principles of the Founding Fathers. For example, it is possible that modern developments are themselves partly the outcome of the particular attempt to solve the problem of freedom and justice upon which this country was founded. That is, our modern difficulties may testify to fundamental errors in the thought of the Founding Fathers; and, in the process of discerning those errors, we may discover what better principles would be.

The solution of our contemporary problems requires very great wisdom indeed. And in that fact lies the greatest justification for studying anew the

* An earlier version of this was written at the request of the Fund for the Republic; the Fund's generous assistance is here gratefully acknowledged.

52

political thought of the Founding Fathers. For that thought remains the finest American thought on political matters. In studying them we may raise ourselves to their level. In achieving their level we may free ourselves from limitations that, ironically, they tend to impose upon us, *i.e.*, insofar as we tend to be creatures of the society they founded. And in so freeing ourselves we may be enabled, if it is necessary, to go beyond their wisdom. The Founding Fathers still loom so large in our life that the contemporary political problem of liberty and justice for Americans could be stated as the need to choose whether to apply their wisdom, amend their wisdom, or reject it. Only an understanding of them will tell us how to choose.

For the reflections on the Fathers which follow, I employ chiefly *The Federalist* as the clue to the political theory upon which rested the founding of the American Republic. That this would be inadequate for a systematic study of the Founding Fathers goes without saying. But it is the one book, "to which," as Jefferson wrote in 1825, "appeal is habitually made by all, and rarely declined or denied by any as evidence of the general opinion of those who framed and of those who accepted the Constitution of the United States, on questions as to its genuine meaning." As such it is the indispensable starting point for systematic study.

I

Our major political problems today are problems of democracy; and, as much as anything else, the *Federalist* papers are a teaching about democracy. The conclusion of one of the most important of these papers states what is also the most important theme in the entire work: the necessity for "a republican remedy for the diseases most incident to republican government."[1] The theme is clearly repeated in a passage where Thomas Jefferson is praised for displaying equally "a fervent attachment to republican government and an enlightened view of the dangerous propensities against which it ought to be guarded."[2] *The Federalist*, thus, stresses its commitment to republican or popular government, but, of course, insists that this must be an enlightened commitment.

But *The Federalist* and the Founding Fathers generally have not been taken at their word. Predominantly, they are understood as being only quasi- or even anti-democrats. Modern American historical writing, at least until very recently, has generally seen the Constitution as some sort of apostasy from, or reaction to, the radically democratic implications of the Declaration of Independence—a reaction that was undone by the great "democratic breakthroughs" of Jeffersonianism, Jacksonianism, etc. This view, I believe, involves a false understanding of the crucial political issues involved in the founding of the American Republic. Further, it is based implicitly upon a questionable modern approach to democracy and has tended to have the effect, moreover, of relegating the political teaching of the Founding Fathers to the pre-democratic past and thus of making it of no vital concern to moderns. The Founding

---

[1] *Federalist*, No. 10, p. 62. All references are to the Modern Library edition, ed. E. M. Earle.
[2] *Federalist*, No. 49, p. 327.

Fathers themselves repeatedly stressed that their Constitution was wholly consistent with the true principles of republican or popular government. The prevailing modern opinion, in varying degrees and in different ways, rejects that claim. It thus becomes important to understand what was the relation of the Founding Fathers to popular government or democracy.

I have deliberately used interchangeably their terms, "popular government" and "democracy." The Founding Fathers, of course, did not use the terms entirely synonymously and the idea that they were less than "democrats" has been fortified by the fact that they sometimes defined "democracy" invidiously in comparison with "republic." But this fact does not really justify the opinion. For their basic view was that *popular government was the genus, and democracy and republic were two species* of that genus of government. What distinguished popular government from other genera of government was that in it, political authority is "derived from the great body of the society, not from . . . [any] favoured class of it."[3] With respect to this decisive question, of where political authority is lodged, democracy and republic—as *The Federalist* uses the terms—differ not in the least. Republics, equally with democracies, may claim to be wholly a form of popular government. This is neither to deny the difference between the two, nor to depreciate the importance *The Federalist* attached to the difference; but in *The Federalist's* view, the difference does not relate to the essential principle of popular government. Democracy means in *The Federalist* that form of popular government where the citizens "assemble and administer the government in person."[4] Republics differ in that the people rule through representatives and, of course, in the consequences of that difference. The crucial point is that republics and democracies are equally forms of popular government, but that the one form is vastly preferable to the other because of the substantive consequences of the difference in form. Those historians who consider the Founding Fathers as less than "democrats," miss or reject the Founders' central contention that, while being perfectly faithful to the *principle* of popular government, they had solved the *problem* of popular government.

In what way is the Constitution ordinarily thought to be less democratic than the Declaration? The argument is usually that the former is characterized by

---

[3] *Federalist*, No. 39, p. 244. Here Madison speaks explicitly of the republican form of government. But see on the same page how Madison compares the republican form with "every *other* popular government." Regarding the crucial question of the lodgement of political authority, Madison speaks of republic, democracy and popular government interchangeably. Consider that, in the very paper where he distinguishes so precisely between democracies and republics regarding direct versus representative rule, Madison defines his general aim both as a search for "a republican remedy" for republican diseases *and* a remedy that will "preserve the spirit and the form of *popular* government." (p. 58.) Interestingly, on June 6 at the Federal Convention, Madison's phrasing for a similar problem was the search for "the only defense against the inconveniences of democracy consistent with the *democratic* form of government." Madison, *Writings,* ed. G. Hunt, Vol. 3 (G. P. Putnam's Sons, New York, 1902), p. 103. Italics supplied throughout.

[4] *Federalist*, No. 10, p. 58.

fear of the people, by preoccupation with minority interests and rights, and by measures therefore taken against the power of majorities. The Declaration, it is true, does not display these features, but this is no proof of a fundamental difference of principle between the two. Is it not obviously possible that the difference is due only to a difference in the tasks to which the two documents were addressed? And is it not further possible that the democratic principles of the Declaration are not only compatible with the prophylactic measures of the Constitution, but actually imply them?

The Declaration of Independence formulates two criteria for judging whether any government is good, or indeed legitimate. Good government must rest, procedurally, upon the consent of the governed. Good government, substantively, must do only certain things, e.g., secure certain rights. This may be stated another way by borrowing a phrase from Locke, appropriate enough when discussing the Declaration. That "the people shall be judge" is of the essence of democracy, is its peculiar form or method of proceeding. That the people shall judge rightly is the substantive problem of democracy. But whether the procedure will bring about the substance is problematic. Between the Declaration's two criteria, then, a tension exists: consent can be given or obtained for governmental actions which are not right—at least as the men of 1776 saw the right. (To give an obvious example from their point of view: the people may freely but wrongly vote away the protection due to property.) Thus the Declaration clearly contained, although it did not resolve, a fundamental problem. Solving the problem was not its task; that was the task for the framers of the Constitution. But the man who wrote the Declaration of Independence and the leading men who supported it were perfectly aware of the difficulty, and of the necessity for a "republican remedy."

What the text of the Declaration, taken alone, tells of its meaning may easily be substantiated by the testimony of its author and supporters. Consider only that Jefferson, with no known change of heart at all, said of *The Federalist* that it was "the best commentary on the principles of government which was ever written."[5] Jefferson, it must be remembered, came firmly to recommend the adoption of the Constitution, his criticisms of it having come down only to a proposal for rotation in the Presidency and for the subsequent adoption of a bill of rights. I do not, of course, deny the peculiar character of "Jeffersonianism" nor the importance to many things of its proper understanding. I only state here that it is certain that Jefferson, unlike later historians, did not view the Constitution as a retrogression from democracy. Or further, consider that John Adams, now celebrated as America's great conservative, was so enthusiastic about Jefferson's draft of the Declaration as to wish on his own account that hardly a word be changed. And this same Adams, also without any change of heart and without complaint, accepted the Constitution as embodying many of his own views on government.

The idea that the Constitution was a falling back from the fuller democracy

<hr/>

[5] *The Works of Thomas Jefferson*, ed. Paul L. Ford (The Federal Edition), Vol. 5 (G. P. Putnam's Sons, New York, 1904), p. 434.

of the Declaration thus rests in part upon a false reading of the Declaration as free from the concerns regarding democracy that the framers of the Constitution felt. Perhaps only those would so read it who take for granted a perfect, self-subsisting harmony between consent (equality) and the proper aim of government (justice), or between consent and individual rights (liberty). This assumption was utterly foreign to the leading men of the Declaration.

II

The Declaration has wrongly been converted into, as it were, a super-democratic document; has the Constitution wrongly been converted in the modern view into an insufficiently democratic document? The only basis for depreciating the democratic character of the Constitution lies in its framers' apprehensive diagnosis of the "diseases," "defects" or "evil propensities" of democracy, and in their remedies. But if what the Founders considered to be defects *are* genuine defects, and if the remedies, without violating the principles of popular government, *are* genuine remedies, then it would be unreasonable to call the Founders anti- or quasi-democrats. Rather, they would be the wise partisans of democracy; a man is not a better democrat but only a foolish democrat if he ignores real defects inherent in popular government. Thus, the question becomes: are there natural defects to democracy and, if there are, what are the best remedies?

In part, the Founding Fathers answered this question by employing a traditional mode of political analysis. They believed there were several basic possible regimes, each having several possible forms. Of these possible regimes they believed the best, or at least the best for America, to be popular government, but only if purged of its defects. At any rate, an unpurged popular government they believed to be indefensible. They believed there were several forms of popular government, crucial among these direct democracy and republican—or representative—government (the latter perhaps divisible into two distinct forms, large and small republics). Their constitution and their defense of it constitute an argument for that form of popular government (large republic) in which the "evil propensities" would be weakest or most susceptible of remedy.

The whole of the thought of the Founding Fathers is intelligible and, especially, the evaluation of their claim to be wise partisans of popular government is possible, only if the words *"disease," "defect,"* and *"evil propensity"* are allowed their full force. Unlike modern "value-free" social scientists, the Founding Fathers believed that true knowledge of the good and bad in human conduct was possible, and that they themselves possessed sufficient knowledge to discern the really grave defects of popular government and their proper remedies. The modern relativistic or positivistic theories, implicitly employed by most commentators on the Founding Fathers, deny the possibility of such true knowledge and therefore deny that the Founding Fathers *could* have been actuated by knowledge of the good rather than by passion or interest. (I deliberately employ the language of *Federalist* No. 10. Madison defined faction, in part, as a group "united and actuated by . . . passion, or . . . interest." That is, factions are groups *not*—as presumably the authors of *The Federalist* were—actuated by reason.) How this modern view of the value problem supports the conception of the Constitution as less democratic than the Declaration is clear. The Founding Fathers did in fact seek to prejudice the outcome of democracy; they sought to alter, by certain restraints, the likelihood that the majority would decide certain political issues in bad ways. These restraints the Founders justified as mitigating the natural defects of democracy. But, say the moderns, there are no "bad" political decisions, wrong-in-themselves, from reaching which the majority ought to be restrained. Therefore, ultimately, nothing other than the specific interests of the Founders can explain their zeal in restraining democracy. And inasmuch as the restraints were typically placed on the many in the interest of the propertied, the departure of the Constitution is "anti-democratic" or "thermidorean." In short, according to this view, there cannot be what the Founders claimed to possess, "an *enlightened* view of the dangerous propensities against which [popular government] . . . ought to be guarded," the substantive goodness or badness of such propensities being a matter of opinion or taste on which reason can shed no light.

What are some of the arrangements which have been considered signs of "undemocratic" features of the Constitution? The process by which the Constitution may be amended is often cited in evidence. Everyone is familiar with the arithmetic which shows that a remarkably small minority could prevent passage of a constitutional amendment supported by an overwhelming majority of the people. That is, bare majorities in the thirteen least populous states could prevent passage of an amendment desired by overwhelming majorities in the thirty-six most populous states. But let us, for a reason to be made clear in a moment, turn that arithmetic around. Bare majorities in the thirty-seven least populous states can pass amendments against the opposition of overwhelming majorities in the twelve most populous states. And this would mean in actual votes today (and would have meant for the thirteen original states) constitutional amendment by a minority against the opposition of a majority of citizens. My point is simply that, while the amending procedure does involve qualified majorities, the qualification is not of the kind that requires an especially large numerical majority for action.

I suggest that the real aim and practical effect of the complicated amending procedure was not at all to give power to minorities, but to ensure that passage of an amendment would require a *nationally* distributed majority, though one that legally could consist of a bare numerical majority. It was only adventitious that the procedure has the theoretical possibility of a minority blocking (or passing) an amendment. The aim of requiring nationally distributed majorities was, I think, to ensure that no amendment could be passed simply with the support of the few states or sections sufficiently numerous to provide a bare majority. No doubt it was also believed that it would be difficult for such a national majority to form or become effective save for the decent purposes that could command national agreement, and this difficulty was surely deemed a great virtue of the amending process. This is what I think *The Federalist* really means when it praises the amending process and says that "it guards equally against that extreme facility, which would render the Constitution too mutable;

and that extreme difficulty, which might perpetuate its discovered faults."[5] All I wish to emphasize here is that the actual method adopted, with respect to the numerical size of majorities, is meant to leave all legal power in the hands of ordinary majorities so long as they are national majorities. The departure from simple majoritarianism is, at least, not in an oligarchic or aristocratic direction. In this crucial respect, the amending procedure does conform strictly to the principles of republican (popular) government.

Consider next the suffrage question. It has long been assumed as proof of an anti-democratic element in the Constitution that the Founding Fathers depended for the working of their Constitution upon a substantially limited franchise. Just as the Constitution allegedly was ratified by a highly qualified electorate, so too, it is held, was the new government to be based upon a suffrage subject to substantial property qualifications. This view has only recently been seriously challenged, especially by Robert E. Brown, whose detailed researches convince him that the property qualifications in nearly all the original states were probably so small as to exclude never more than twenty-five per cent, and in most cases as little as only five to ten per cent, of the adult white male population.[6a] That is, the property qualifications were not designed to exclude the mass of the poor but only the small proportion which lacked a concrete—however small—stake in society, i.e., primarily the transients or "idlers."

The Constitution, of course, left the suffrage question to the decision of the individual states. What is the implication of that fact for deciding what sort of suffrage the Framers had in mind? The immediately popular branch of the national legislature was to be elected by voters who "shall have the qualifications requisite for electors of the most numerous branch of the State Legislature." The mode of election to the electoral college for the Presidency and to the Senate is also left to "be prescribed in each State by the legislature thereof." At a minimum, it may be stated that the Framers did not themselves attempt to reduce, or prevent the expansion of, the suffrage; that question was left wholly to the states—and these were, ironically, the very hotbeds of post-revolutionary democracy from the rule of which it is familiarly alleged that the Founders sought to escape.[7]

In general, the conclusion seems inescapable that the states had a far broader suffrage than is ordinarily thought, and nothing in the actions of the Framers suggests any expectation or prospect of the reduction of the suffrage. Again, as in the question of the amending process, I suggest that the Constitution represented no departure whatsoever from the democratic standards of the Revolu-

---

[5] *Federalist*, No. 43, p. 286.

[6a] *Middle Class Democracy and the Revolution in Massachusetts, 1691–1780.* (Cornell University Press, Ithaca, 1955).

[7] Madison must have thought that he had established this point beyond misinterpretation in *The Federalist*, No. 57. "Who are to be the electors of the federal representatives? Not the rich, more than the poor; not the learned, more than the ignorant; not the haughty heirs of distinguished names, more than the humble sons of obscurity and unpropitious fortune. The electors are to be the great body of the people of the United States. They are to be the same who exercise the right in every State of electing the corresponding branch of the legislature of the State." (p. 371.)

tionary period, or from any democratic standards then generally recognized.[8]

What of the Senate? The organization of the Senate, its term of office and its staggered mode of replacement, its election by state legislatures rather than directly by the people, among other things, have been used to demonstrate the undemocratic character of the Senate as intended by the Framers. Was this not a device to represent property and not people, and was it not intended therefore to be a non-popular element in the government? I suggest, on the contrary, that the really important thing is that the Framers thought they had found a way to protect property *without* representing it. That the Founders intended the Senate to be one of the crucial devices for remedying the defects of democracy is certainly true. But *The Federalist* argues that the Senate, as actually proposed in the Constitution, was calculated to be such a device as would operate only in a way that "will consist . . . with the genuine principles of republican government."[9] I believe that the claim is just.

Rather than viewing the Senate from the perspective of modern experience and opinions, consider how radically democratic the Senate appears when viewed from a pre-modern perspective. The model of a divided legislature that the Founders had most in mind was probably the English Parliament. There the House of Lords was thought to provide some of the beneficial checks upon the popular Commons which it was hoped the Senate would supply in the American Constitution. But the American Senate was to possess none of the qualities which permitted the House of Lords to fulfill its role; *i.e.*, its hereditary basis, or membership upon election by the Crown, or any of its other aristocratic characteristics.[10] Yet the Founding Fathers knew that the advantages of having both a Senate and a House would "be in proportion to the dissimilarity in the genius of the two bodies."[11] What is remarkable is that, in seeking to secure this dissimilarity, they did not in any respect go beyond the limits permitted by the "genuine principles of republican government."

Not only is this dramatically demonstrated in comparison with the English House of Lords, but also in comparison with all earlier theory regarding the division of the legislative power. The aim of such a division in earlier thought is to secure a balance between the aristocratic and democratic elements of a polity. This is connected with the pre-modern preference for a *mixed* republic, which was rejected by the Founders in favor of a *democratic* republic. And the tradi-

---

[8] This is not to deny the importance of the existing property qualifications for the understanding of the Founders' political theory. The legal exclusion from the franchise of even a very small portion of the adult population may have enormous significance for the politics and life of a country. This is obvious in the case of a racial, ethnic or religious minority. And the exclusion of otherwise eligible adult males on the grounds of poverty may be equally important. The property qualification clearly praises and rewards certain virtues, implies that the voter must possess certain qualities to warrant his exercise of the franchise, and aims at excluding a "rabble" from the operations of political parties. But important, therefore, as the property qualification was, it does not demonstrate that the Founding Fathers departed radically from the most important aspects of the principle of majority rule.

[9] *Federalist*, No. 62, p. 403.
[10] *Federalist*, No. 63, p. 415.
[11] *Federalist*, No. 62, p. 403.

tional way to secure this balance or mixture was to give one house or office to the suffrages of the few and one to the suffrages of the many. Nothing of the kind is involved in the American Senate. Indeed, on this issue, so often cited as evidence of the Founders' undemocratic predilections, the very opposite is the case. The Senate is a constitutional device which *par excellence* reveals the strategy of the Founders. They wanted something like the advantages earlier thinkers had seen in a mixed legislative power, but they thought this was possible (and perhaps preferable) without any introduction whatsoever of aristocratic power into their system. What pre-modern thought had seen in an aristocratic senate—wisdom, nobility, manners, religion, etc.—the Founding Fathers converted into stability, enlightened self-interest, a "temperate and respectable body of citizens." The qualities of a senate having thus been altered (involving perhaps comparable changes in the notion of the ends of government), it became possible to secure these advantages through a Senate based wholly upon popular principles. Or so I would characterize a Senate whose membership required no property qualification and which was appointed (or elected in the manner prescribed) by State legislatures which, in their own turn, were elected annually or biennially by a nearly universal manhood suffrage.

The great claim of *The Federalist* is that the Constitution represents the fulfillment of a truly novel experiment, of "a revolution which has no parallel in the annals of society," and which is decisive for the happiness of "the whole human race."[12] And the novelty, I argue, consisted in solving the problems of popular government by means which yet maintain the government "wholly popular."[13] In defending that claim against the idea of the Constitution as a retreat from democracy I have dealt thus far only with the easier task: the demonstration that the constitutional devices and arrangements do not derogate from the legal power of majorities to rule. What remains is to examine the claim that the Constitution did in fact remedy the natural defects of democracy. Before any effort is made in this direction, it may be useful to summarize some of the implications and possible utility of the analysis thus far.

Above all, the merit of the suggestions I have made, if they are accurate in describing the intention and action of the Founders, is that it makes the Founders available to us for the study of modern problems. I have tried to restore to them their *bona fides* as partisans of democracy. This done, we may take seriously the question whether they were, as they claimed to be, wise partisans of democracy or popular government. If they were partisans of democracy and if the regime they created was decisively democratic, then they speak to us not merely about bygone problems, not from a viewpoint—in this regard—radically different from our own, but as men addressing themselves to problems identical in principle with our own. They are a source from within our own heritage which teaches us the way to put the question to democracy, a way which is rejected by certain prevailing modern ideas. But we cannot avail ourselves of their assistance if we consider American history to be a succession of democratizations which overcame the Founding Fathers' intentions. On that view it is easy

[12] *Federalist*, No. 14, p. 85.
[13] *Ibid.*, p. 81.

to regard them as simply outmoded. If I am right regarding the extent of democracy in their thought and regime, then they are not outmoded by modern events but rather are tested by them. American history, on this view, is not primarily the replacement of a pre-democratic regime by a democratic regime, but is rather a continuing testimony to how the Founding Fathers' democratic regime has worked out in modern circumstances. The whole of our national experience thus becomes a way of judging the Founders' principles, of judging democracy itself, or of pondering the flaws of democracy and the means to its improvement.

III

What was the Founding Fathers' view of the good life? Upon what fundamental theoretical premises did that view of the good life depend? How comprehensive was their understanding of the dangers against which popular government was to be guarded? How efficacious were their remedies and what may have been the unanticipated costs of those remedies? These questions are clearly too vast to answer here and now. What follows is only a series of notes which bear upon the problems raised, and which I think may serve as general guides to what it is important to seek in studying the Founding Fathers.

The Federalist does not discuss systematically, as would a theoretical treatise, the question of the ends or purposes of government. That is, it does not deal systematically with philosophical issues. This is not to say that its authors did not have a view in such matters. But what that view was, and what are its implications for the understanding of the Constitution, is a subject on which I find it difficult to speak with confidence. I must still regard as open the question whether the authors of The Federalist, or the other leading founders, had themselves fully reflected on these matters, or whether they treated them as settled by thinkers like Locke and Montesquieu, or whether crucial premises in their thought were unreflectively taken for granted. But men cannot act on a political scale so vast as they did without having and employing a view of the politically fundamental; and it is this view which provides the crucial perspective for the understanding of their particular actions and thoughts.

Perhaps the most explicit fundamental utterance of The Federalist is the statement regarding

the great principle of self-preservation . . . the transcendent law of nature and of nature's God, which declares that the safety and happiness of society are the objects at which all political institutions aim, and to which all such institutions must be sacrificed.[14]

But self-preservation, it is made clear, includes more than mere preservation. This passage, which interestingly echoes the Declaration of Independence on the "laws of nature and of nature's God," emphasizes that preservation includes "happiness" as well as "safety." That is, The Federalist is aware of and explicitly rejects the kind of regime that would follow from a narrower view of self-preservation. For example, The Federalist seems explicitly to be rejecting Hobbes when, in another context, it rejects the view that "nothing less than the chains of despotism can restrain [men] from destroying and devouring one an-

[14] Federalist, No. 43, p. 287.

other."[15] But while it rejects the "chains of despotism," *i.e.*, the Hobbesean solution to the problem of self-preservation, it nonetheless seems to accept the Hobbesean statement of the problem. As it were, the primary fears of *The Federalist* are Hobbesean, that is, fears of "foreign war and domestic convulsion." Rejecting a despotic solution, the great aim of *The Federalist* is to supply a liberal and republican solution to the same problem. But while there is a great difference, never to be underestimated, between a liberal and a repressive, a republican and a monarchical solution, it may be that in making the same dangers and their solution *the* desideratum for the structure and functions of government much of the Hobbesean view is preserved.

The main object of *The Federalist* was to urge the necessity of a firm and energetic Union. The utility of such a Union, and therefore the chief ends it will serve, is that it will strengthen the American people against the dangers of "foreign war" and secure them from the dangers of "domestic convulsion." These functions of government are the most frequently discussed and the most vehemently emphasized in the whole work. To a very great extent, then, *The Federalist* determines the role of government with reference only, or primarily, to the extremes of external and internal danger. It is to avoid the pre-civil forms of these dangers that men form government and it is the civil solution of these dangers which, almost exclusively, determines the legitimate objects of government. But again, *The Federalist* repeatedly emphasizes that a "novel" solution is at hand. The means now exist—and America is uniquely in a position to employ them—for a republican solution which avoids the extremes of tyranny and anarchy. But notice that, on this view, liberalism and republicanism are not the means by which men may ascend to a nobler life; rather they are simply instrumentalities which solve Hobbesean problems in a more moderate manner. It is tempting to suggest that if America is a "Lockean" nation, as is so often asserted, it is true in the very precise sense that Locke's "comfortable preservation" displaces the harshness of the Hobbesean view, while not repudiating that view in general.

To be sure, *The Federalist* does make other explicit statements regarding the ends of government. For example: "Justice is the end of government. It is the end of civil society."[16] But this statement, to the best of my knowledge, is made only once in the entire work; and the context suggests that "justice" means simply "civil rights" which in turn seems to refer primarily to the protection of economic interests. That justice has here this relatively narrow meaning, as compared with traditional philosophical and theological usage, is made more probable when we take account of the crucial statement in *Federalist* No. 10. There the "first object of government" is the protection of the diverse human faculties from which arise the "rights of property" and the unequal distribution of property. The importance of this statement of the function of government is underscored when it is recalled how large a proportion of *The Federalist* deals with the improvements in "commerce" made possible by the new Constitution.

[15] *Federalist*, No. 55, p. 365.
[16] *Federalist*, No. 51, p. 340.

For example, in a list of the four "principal objects of federal legislation,"[17] three (foreign trade, interstate trade, and taxes) deal explicitly with commerce. The fourth, the militia, also deals with commerce insofar as it largely has to do with the prevention of "domestic convulsion" brought on by economic matters.

The very great emphasis of *The Federalist* on commerce, and on the role of government in nurturing it, may not be at all incompatible with the theme of "happiness" which is the most frequently occurring definition of the "object of government." The most definite statement is the following:

A good government implies two things: first, fidelity to the object of government, which is the happiness of the people, secondly, a knowledge of the means by which that object can be best obtained.[18]

The Federalist is not very explicit in defining happiness. But there are firm indications that what it had in mind has little in common with traditional philosophical or theological understandings of the term. At one place, *The Federalist* indicates that happiness requires that government "provide for the security, advance the prosperity, [and] support the reputation of the commonwealth."[19] In another, happiness seems to require "our safety, our tranquility, our dignity, our reputation."[20] Part of what these words mean is made clear by the fact that they summarize a lengthy indictment of the Articles of Confederation, the particulars of which deal in nearly every case with commercial shortcomings. Happiness, "a knowledge of the means" to which *The Federalist* openly claims to possess, seems to consist primarily in physical preservation from external and internal danger *and* in the comforts afforded by a commercial society; which comforts are at once the dividends of security and the means to a republican rather than repressive security.

What is striking is the apparent exclusion from the functions of government of a wide range of non-economic tasks traditionally considered the decisive business of government. It is tempting to speculate that this reduction in the tasks of government has something to do with *The Federalist's* defense of popular government. The traditional criticism of popular government was that it gave over the art of government into the hands of the many, which is to say the unwise. It would be a formidable reply to reduce the complexity of the governmental art to dimensions more commensurate with the capacity of the many. I use two statements by Madison, years apart, to illustrate the possibility that he may have had something like this in mind. "There can be no doubt that there are subjects to which the capacities of the bulk of mankind are unequal."[21] But on the other hand, "the confidence of the [Republican party] in the capacity of mankind for self-government"[22] is what distinguished it from the Fed-

[17] *Federalist*, No. 53, p. 350–51.
[18] *Federalist*, No. 62, p. 404.
[19] *Federalist*, No. 30, p. 186.
[20] *Federalist*, No. 15, p. 88.
[21] Letter to Edmund Randolph, January 10, 1788.
[22] Letter to William Eustis, May 22, 1823. The letters to Randolph and Eustis were brought to my attention by Ralph Ketcham's article, "Notes on James Madison's Sources for the Tenth Federalist Paper," *Midwest Journal of Political Science*, Vol. 1 (May, 1957).

eralist party which distrusted that capacity. The confidence in mankind's capacities would seem to require having removed from government the subjects to which those capacities are unequal.

IV

So far as concerns those ends of government on which *The Federalist* is almost wholly silent, it is reasonable to infer that what the Founders made no provision for they did not rank highly among the legitimate objects of government. Other political theories had ranked highly, as objects of government, the nurturing of a particular religion, education, military courage, civic-spiritedness, moderation, individual excellence in the virtues, etc. On all of these *The Federalist* is either silent, or has in mind only pallid versions of the originals, or even seems to speak with contempt. The Founders apparently did not consider it necessary to make special provision for excellence. Did they assume these virtues would flourish without governmental or other explicit provision? Did they consciously sacrifice some of them to other necessities of a stable popular regime—as it were, as the price of their solution to the problem of democracy? Or were these virtues less necessary to a country when it had been properly founded on the basis of the new "science of politics"? In what follows I suggest some possible answers to these questions.

The Founding Fathers are often criticized for an excessive attention to, and reliance upon, mechanical institutional arrangements and for an insufficient attention to "sociological" factors. While a moderate version of this criticism may finally be just, it is nonetheless clear that *The Federalist* pays considerable and shrewd attention to such factors. For example, in *Federalist* No. 51, equal attention is given to the institutional and non-institutional strengths of the new Constitution. One of these latter is the solution to the "problems of faction." It will be convenient to examine *Federalist* No. 10 where the argument about faction is more fully developed than in No. 51. A close examination of that solution reveals something about *The Federalist's* view of the virtues necessary to the good life.

The problem dealt with in the tenth essay is how "to break and control the violence of faction." "The friend of popular governments never finds himself so much alarmed for their character and fate, as when he contemplates their propensity to this dangerous vice." Faction is, thus, *the* problem of popular government. Now it must be made clear that Madison, the author of this essay, was not here really concerned with the problem of faction generally. He devotes only two sentences in the whole essay to the dangers of *minority* factions. The real problem in a popular government, then, is *majority* faction, or, more precisely, *the* majority faction, *i.e.*, the great mass of the little propertied and unpropertied. This is the only faction that can "execute and mask its violence under the forms of the Constitution." That is, in the American republic the many have the legal power to rule and thus from them can come the greatest harm. Madison interprets that harm fairly narrowly; at least, his overwhelming emphasis is on the classic economic struggle between the rich and the poor which made of ancient democracies "spectacles of turbulence and contention." *The* problem for the friend of popular government is how to avoid the "domestic convulsion" which results when the rich and the poor, the few and the many, as is their wont, are at each others' throats. Always before in popular governments the many, armed with political power, invariably precipitated such convulsions. But the friend of popular government must find only "a republican remedy" for this disease which is "most incident to republican government." "To secure the public good and private rights against the danger of . . . [majority] faction, and at the same time to preserve the spirit and the form of popular government, is then the great object to which our inquiries are directed."

Without wrenching Madison's meaning too greatly, the problem may be put crudely this way: Madison gave a beforehand answer to Marx. The whole of the Marxian scheme depends upon the many—having been proletarianized—causing precisely such domestic convulsion and usurpation of property as Madison wished to avoid. Madison believed that in America the many could be diverted from that probable course. How will the many, *the* majority, be prevented from using for the evil purpose of usurping property the legal power which is theirs in a popular regime? "Evidently by one of two [means] only. Either the existence of the same passion or interest in a majority at the same time must be prevented, or the majority, having such co-existent passion or interest, must be rendered, by their number and local situation, unable to concert and carry into effect schemes of oppression." But "we well know that neither moral nor religious motives can be relied on" to do these things. The "circumstance principally" which will solve the problem is the "greater number of citizens and extent of territory which may be brought within the compass" of large republican governments rather than of small direct democracies.

Rather than mutilate Madison, let me complete his thought by quoting the rest of his argument before commenting on it:

The smaller the society, the fewer probably will be the distinct parties and interests, the more frequently will a majority be found of the same party; and the smaller the number of individuals composing a majority, and the smaller the compass within which they are placed, the more easily will they concert and execute their plans of oppression. Extend the sphere and you take in a greater variety of parties and interests; you make it less probable that a majority of the whole will have a common motive to invade the rights of other citizens; or if such a common motive exists, it will be more difficult for all who feel it to discover their own strength, and to act in unison with each other.

I want to deal only with what is implied or required by the first of the two means, *i.e.*, preventing the majority from having the same "passion or interest" at the same time. I would argue that this is the more important of the two remedial means afforded by a large republic. If the majority comes to have the same passion or interest and holds to it intensely for a period of only four to six years, it seems certain that it would triumph over the "extent of territory," over the barriers of federalism, and separation of powers, and all the checks and balances of the Constitution. I do not wish to depreciate the importance of those barriers; I believe they have enormous efficacy in stemming the tide Madison feared. But I would argue that their efficacy depends upon a prior weakening of the force applied against them, upon the majority having been fragmented or deflected from its "schemes of oppression." An inflamed Marxian proletariat would not indefinitely be deterred by institutional checks or extent of territory. The crucial point then, as I see it, is the means by which a majority bent upon oppression is prevented from ever forming or becoming firm.

Madison's whole scheme essentially comes down to this. The struggle of classes is to be replaced by a struggle of interests. The class struggle is domestic convulsion; the struggle of interests is a safe, even energizing, struggle which is compatible with, or even promotes, the safety and stability of society. But how can this be accomplished? What will prevent the many from thinking of their interest as that of the Many opposed to the Few? Madison, as I see it, implies that nothing can prevent it in a small democratic society where the many are divided into only a few trades and callings: these divisions are insufficient to prevent them from conceiving their lot in common and uniting for oppression. But in a large republic, numerous and powerful divisions will arise among the many to prevent that happening. A host of interests grows up "of necessity in civilized nations, and divide[s] them into different classes, actuated by different sentiments and views." "Civilized nations" clearly means here large, commercial societies. In a large commercial society the interest of the many can be fragmented into many narrower, more limited interests. The mass will not unite as a mass to make extreme demands upon the few, the struggle over which will destroy society; the mass will fragment into relatively small groups, seeking small immediate advantages for their narrow and particular interests.

If the Madisonian solution is essentially as I have described it, it becomes clear that certain things are required for the solution to operate. I only mention several of them. First, the country in which this is to take place will have to be profoundly democratic. That is, all men must be free—and even encouraged—to seek their immediate profit and to associate with others in the process. There must be no rigid class barriers which bar men from the pursuit of immediate interest. Indeed, it is especially the lowly, from whom the most is to be feared, who must feel most sanguine about the prospects of achieving limited and immediate benefits. Second, the gains must be real; that is, the fragmented interests must from time to time achieve real gains, else the scheme would cease to beguile or mollify. But I do not want to develop these themes here. Rather, I want to emphasize only one crucial aspect of Madison's design: that is, the question of the apparently narrow ends of society envisaged by the Founding Fathers. Madison's plan, as I have described it, most assuredly does not rest on the "moral and religious motives" whose efficacy he deprecated. Indeed there is not even the suggestion that the pursuit of interest should be an especially enlightened pursuit. Rather, the problem posed by the dangerous passions and interests of the many is solved primarily by a reliance upon passion and interest themselves. As Tocqueville pointed out, Americans employ the principle of "self-interest rightly understood."

The principle of self-interest rightly understood is not a lofty one, but it is clear and sure. It does not aim at mighty objects, but it attains . . . all those at which it aims. By its admirable conformity to human weaknesses it easily obtains great dominion; nor is that dominion precarious, since the principle checks one personal interest by another, and uses, to direct the passions, the very same instrument that excites them.[23]

Madison's solution to his problem worked astonishingly well. The danger he wished to avert has been averted and largely for the reasons he gave. But it is possible to question now whether he did not take too narrow a view of what the dangers were. Living today as beneficiaries of his system, we may yet wonder whether he failed to contemplate other equally grave problems of democracy, or whether his remedy for the one disease has not had some unfortunate collateral consequences. The Madisonian solution involved a fundamental reliance on ceaseless striving after immediate interest (perhaps now immediate gratification). Tocqueville appreciated that this "permanent agitation . . . is characteristic of a peaceful democracy,"[24] one might even say, the price of its peace. And Tocqueville was aware of how great might be the price. "In the midst of this universal tumult, this incessant conflict of jarring interests, this continual striving of men after fortune, where is that calm to be found which is necessary for the deeper combinations of the intellect?"[25]

V

There is, I think, in *The Federalist* a profound distinction made between the qualities necessary for Founders and the qualities necessary for the men who come after. It is a distinction that bears on the question of the Founding Fathers' view of what is required for the good life and on their defense of popular government. Founding requires "an exemption from the pestilential influence of party animosities";[26] but the subsequent governing of America will depend on precisely those party animosities, moderated in the way I have described. Or again, founding requires that "reason" and not the "passions," "sit in judgment."[27] But, as I have argued, the society once founded will subsequently depend precisely upon the passions, only moderated in their consequences by having been guided into proper channels. The reason of the Founders constructs the system within which the passions of the men who come after may be relied upon.

Founders need a knowledge of the newly improved "science of politics" and a knowledge of the great political alternatives in order to construct a durable regime; while the men who come after need be only legislators who are but interested "advocates and parties to the causes they determine."[28] *The Federalist* speaks, as has often been observed, with harsh realism about the shortcomings of human nature, but, as has not so often been observed, none of its strictures can characterize the Founders; they must be free of these shortcomings in order to have had disinterested and true knowledge of political things. While

---

[23] *Democracy in America*, ed. Phillips Bradley (Knopf, New York, 1951) Vol. 2, pp. 122–23.
[24] *Ibid.*, p. 42.
[25] *Idem.*
[26] *Federalist*, No. 37, p. 232.
[27] *Federalist*, No. 49, p. 331.
[28] *Federalist*, No. 10, p. 56.

"a nation of philosophers is as little to be expected as the philosophical race of kings wished for by Plato,"[29] it is tempting to speculate that *The Federalist* contemplates a kind of philosopher-founder the posthumous duration of whose rule depends upon "that veneration which time bestows on everything,"[30] and in particular on a regime well-founded. But once founded, it is a system that has no necessary place and makes no provision for men of the founding kind.

It is clear that not all now regarded as Founding Fathers were thought by the authors of *The Federalist* to belong in that august company. Noting that "it is not a little remarkable" that all previous foundings of regimes were "performed by some individual citizen of pre-eminent wisdom and approved integrity,"[31] *The Federalist* comments on the difficulty that must have been experienced when it was attempted to found a regime by the action of an assembly of men. I think it can be shown that *The Federalist* views that assembly, the Federal Convention, as having been subject to all the weaknesses of multitudes of men. The real founders, then, were very few in number, men learned in the new science of politics who seized upon a uniquely propitious moment when their plans were consented to first by a body of respectable men and subsequently, by equally great good fortune, by the body of citizens. As it were, America provided a rare moment when "the prejudices of the community"[32] were on the side of wisdom. Not unnaturally, then, *The Federalist* is extremely reluctant to countenance any re-opening of fundamental questions or delay in ratifying the Constitution.

This circumstance—wisdom meeting with consent—is so rare that "it is impossible for the man of pious reflection not to perceive in it a finger of that Almighty hand."[33] But once consent has been given to the new wisdom, when the government has been properly founded, it will be a durable regime whose perpetuation requires nothing like the wisdom and virtue necessary for its creation. The Founding Fathers' belief that they had created a system of institutions and an arrangement of the passions and interests, that would be durable and self-perpetuating, helps explain their failure to make provision for men of their own kind to come after them. Apparently, it was thought that such men would not be needed.

But does not the intensity and kind of our modern problems seem to require of us a greater degree of reflection and public-spiritedness than the Founders thought sufficient for the men who came after them? One good way to begin that reflection would be to return to their level of thoughtfulness about fundamental political alternatives, so that we may judge for ourselves wisely regarding the profound issues that face us. I know of no better beginning for that thoughtfulness than a full and serious contemplation of the political theory that informed the origin of the Republic, of the thought and intention of those few men who fully grasped what the "assembly of demi-gods" was doing.

[29] *Federalist*, No. 49, p. 329.
[30] *Ibid.*, p. 328.
[31] *Federalist*, No. 38, p. 233.
[32] *Federalist*, No. 49, p. 329.
[33] *Federalist*, No. 38, p. 231.

Madison's
Theory of Representation
in the
Tenth Federalist

ROBERT J. MORGAN

For DECADES SCHOLARS have overlooked the full significance of James Madison's direct statement in the Tenth *Federalist*: "a scheme of representation . . . promises the cure for [faction] which we are seeking."[1] It is surprising that they have ignored, also, his related prescription of a constitutional equilibrium to be achieved by allocating representation between the major sections as the primary means of controlling this source of faction. The first step to be taken in founding the new American republic, he asserted, was "a change in the principle of representation."[2] Even when the Convention rejected his recommendation of equilibrium, the other change in representation was sufficiently novel and significant, Madison believed, to prove wrong the European theorists who opposed republicanism except in small trading cities. Europe had discovered representation, he conceded, but Americans could claim the merit of transforming that discovery by making "representation . . . the basis of unmixed and extensive republics."[3]

[1] Alexander Hamilton, John Jay, James Madison, *The Federalist*, introduction by Edward Meade Earle (New York: Modern Library, 1937), 59. Subsequent citation will show I do not mean to say that the subject of representation in the eighteenth century has been ignored. My point is that Madison's contribution to the theory of representation has been obscured by ideological interpretations of *The Federalist*, No. 10.

[2] James Madison, *The Writings of James Madison*, ed. Gaillard Hunt (9 vols.; New York: G. P. Putnam's Sons, 1900-10), II, 338; cited hereafter as *Writings*.

[3] *The Federalist*, II, 81 (No. 14).

From this preliminary understanding of Madison's purpose in writing the Tenth essay, I intend to develop five major points. First, in technical language, that essay contains a probabilistic causal theory of representation. It is not an explanatory theory to the effect that an increase in territory and population will multiply and diversify groups to the point where all will be so weak that none will permanently dominate opposing minorities.

Second, his essay does not support the theory that political stability depends solely, or even chiefly, on an underlying consensus of values beyond politics. Political stability is not maintained by competing groups of political elites.

Third, Madison intended to demonstrate that the durability of the American republic would depend *primarily* on a constitutional superstructure of representation flexible enough to control the struggle of opposing interests. He called representation the "pivot" of American republicanism.[4] The stability of constitutional government was seen to rest upon legislative stability achieved by combining the ideas of heterogeneity and equilibrium with representation. The ideal of this construct is the representative who is an independent man of republican virtue, tied to his constituents by duty, gratitude, and ambition and serving them with the affection of friends and the impartiality of judges.[5] His concept of equilibrium, however, was rooted in the harsher realities of sectional divisions.

Fourth, Madison's political theory was a conscious contribution to republicanism, the major revolutionary ideology of the seventeenth and eighteenth centuries. The American Revolution was made in the name of republicanism, although the ideological sources were English, not French. More was involved than a sentimental admiration of the ideals embodied in the literature of classical Greece and Rome.[6] Madison drew his allusions from schoolboy texts but got

[4] *Ibid.*, II, 411 (No. 63).
[5] *Ibid.*, II, 373 (No. 57); 285 (No. 43).
[6] Charles F. Mullett, "Classical Influences on the American Revolution," *Classical Journal*, 35 (November 1939), 92-104; Gilbert Chinard, "Polybius and the American Constitution," *Journal of the History of Ideas*, 1 (January 1940), 38-58; Richard M. Gummere, *The American Colonial Mind and the Classical Tradition* (Cambridge, Mass.: Harvard University Press, 1963), 173-190. The distinction between the sources of classical literary allusions and political ideologies becomes clear in Bernard Bailyn, *The Ideological Origins of the American Revolution* (Cambridge, Mass.: Harvard University Press, Belknap Press, 1967), 160-229.

his understanding of republicanism from Harrington and Sidney, the heroes of the "good old cause." The fact that elements of republican ideology were absorbed into Whiggery by 1689, obliging even Tories "to talk in the republican stile [sic]," as Hume remarked, complicated Madison's task and undoubtedly has confused our understanding of it. Nevertheless, Madison was explicit in saying that Americans would have to devise a new theory and practice that would avoid the "reproaches & evils which have resulted from the vicious representation in G. B."[7] This necessity would require all who took pride in the name "republican" to support the "spirit" of Federalists.[8]

Finally, this essay may contribute to a clearer understanding of the development of American political thought and institutions by showing that the prevailing pluralist theory of the American system is not rooted in an unbroken connection with the most theoretically sophisticated of the Founding Fathers.

I

Before I elaborate my theses, it may be helpful to point out summarily some other interpretations. The Progressive intellectuals discovered the Tenth *Federalist* and transformed it into a partisan tract which distorted Madison's meaning so effectively that it remains buried in polemical interpretations to this day. Smith was the first to contend that the essay was proof that the Constitution was to favor "the possessing as against the non-possessing classes."[9] Beard called it a theory of restraints on the propertyless urban masses.[10] Parrington knew better and let the matter go by calling the Tenth essay nothing more than the Federalists' statement of opposition to party government.[11] A generation later, Hartz put

[7] *Writings*, III, 316; Hume's remark about the absorption of republican ideology into Tory political discourse is found in David Hume, *Essays: Moral, Political and Literary*, ed. T. H. Green and T. H. Grose (2 vols.; London: Longmans, Green and Co., 1882), I, 140.

[8] *The Federalist*, 62 (No. 10).

[9] J. Allen Smith, *The Spirit of American Government* (Cambridge, Mass.: Harvard University Press, Belknap Press, 1965), 11, 205-206.

[10] Charles A. Beard, *The Economic Basis of Politics* (New York: Alfred A. Knopf, 1947), 16-19. This book was originally published in 1922, although Beard first expressed these views in a series of lectures in 1916. See "Preface to the 1945 Edition."

[11] Vernon L. Parrington, *Main Currents in American Thought* (3 vols.; New

down the Progressives as neo-Marxists trying to fob off the Constitution as a reactionary document in a nation lacking a genuine revolutionary tradition. The Tenth essay, on which they relied primarily Hartz concluded, was much too abstract and did no more than state a problem without solving it. The real restraint on civil commotion in America, he contended, has been a Lockean consensus to which Madison was as blind as Hamilton.[12]

This conclusion contrasts sharply with Dahl's; he greatly admires the essay and has used it to state the most comprehensive and influential theory of pluralism today. Dahl's interpretation is widely accepted as a "territorial-sociological principle" which serves as the ultimate guarantee against the evils of particularism and faction.[13] The explanation found in a British textbook is that Madison relied not solely on checks and balances but on the "sheer size and diversity of the American electorate" as well. The number and diversity of interests would render domination by any majority, sectional or otherwise, unlikely. The few relatively permanent divisions over issues would be moderated by others which constantly shifted. Consequently, no permanent "homogeneous and decisive pressure group" would control the system. It was Madison, therefore, who foresaw the operation of government in a "plural society." This

---

York: Harcourt Brace & Co., 1927), II, 284-288. He contended that No. 10 was an adaptation of "Milton and other seventeenth century republicans" for whom the "London rabble" provided a prophetic vision of the excesses of liberty. Parrington sharply distinguished Madison's "Federalist" vision of politics from the "Jeffersonian" which he so ardently admired. This interpretation still has considerable vitality among political scientists, despite sound historical scholarship to the contrary. For example, see James M. Burns, *Deadlock of Democracy* (New York: McGraw-Hill Book Co., 1971); Mason Drukman, *Community and Purpose in America* (New York: McGraw-Hill Book Co., 1971), 25-104; Jay A. Sigler, ed., *The Conservative Tradition in American Thought* (New York: Capricorn Books, 1970), 57-71; Walter E. Volkomer, *The Liberal Tradition in American Thought* (New York: Capricorn Books, 1970), 84-123. For a balanced view, see Adrienne Koch, *Jefferson and Madison: The Great Collaboration* (New York: Oxford University Press, 1950). The two men were "joined in an intimate and congenial partnership for a period of almost fifty years" in working out "a comprehensive ideology of democracy. . . ." Preface, n. p. See, also, Ralph Ketcham, *James Madison: A Biography* (New York: Macmillan Company, 1971).

[12] Louis Hartz, *The Liberal Tradition in America* (New York: Harcourt, Brace and World, Inc., 1955), 3-32, 66, 76-86.

[13] A. J. Beitzinger, *A History of American Political Thought* (New York: Dodd Mead & Company, 1972), 181.

understanding explains what we have been and what we are: how
the system functions and why it is stable, rooted in the founding
myths.[14] It refracts our perceptions of the present so much that
without it our vision would be very different.[15]

In Dahl's judgment, nowhere in American thought "is there a
more compactly logical, almost mathematical, piece of theory than
in Madison's *The Federalist*, No. 10. It is both convenient and intellectually rewarding to turn to Madison to discover a basic rationale for the American political system."[16] First, however, it must
be shown that his argument defending constitutional checks and
balances in No. 51 is mere ideology unsuitable for a scientific knowledge of politics. Social checks and balances arising out of social
pluralism are both more effective and more satisfying to scientific
students of society today. It is to this modern view that No. 10
contributes the basic premise, a *paraphrase* of Madison's words,
stated by Dahl as follows: "*Hypothesis 10*: To the extent that the
electorate is numerous, extended and diverse in interests, a majority
faction is less likely to exist, and if it does exist, it is less likely to
act as a unity."[17] Dahl derived this paraphrase from the passage
in which Madison laid down an "exceptionally important" proposition: "Extend the sphere and you take in a greater variety of parties
and interests . . ." (and so on to the end of this passage familiar to
all students of American politics and thought). I intend to show
that this paraphrase alters fundamentally the meaning of the text
which occasioned it.

In the course of developing this paraphrase, Dahl remarked that
Madison reached this hypothesis by a series of "exceedingly doubtful statements" and followed it with "an extremely dubious and
probably false set of propositions purporting to show that representation in a large republic will provide 'better' politicians and reduce the probability of the success of 'the vicious arts by which

[14] S. I. Benn and R. S. Peters, *The Principles of Political Thought* (New
York: The Free Press, 1965), 412.

[15] See, for example, C. Wright Mills, *The Power Elite* (New York: Oxford
University Press, 1956); Grant McConnell, *Private Power and American Democracy* (New York: Alfred A. Knopf, 1966); Theodore Lowi, *The End of Liberalism* (New York: W. W. Norton & Company, 1969); Paul Eidelberg, *The
Philosophy of the American Constitution* (New York: The Free Press, 1968).

[16] Robert A. Dahl, *A Preface to Democratic Theory* (Chicago: University of
Chicago Press, 1956), 5.

[17] *Ibid.*, 17, 21-22, 31.

elections are too often carried'."[18] Dahl did not elaborate his unfavorable judgment of the otherwise "lucid and compact" propositions in the essay. He said he would follow Madison only where
he was "most logical, consistent and explicit . . ." but without a
"perfect reproduction of his words. . . ."[19] Perhaps for this reason,
he said, he was puzzled at "a central theme of Madison's:"—the
threat of faction is from the "legislature, supposedly the stronghold
of the majority."[20] He might have been less puzzled had he explored the implications of his own observation that a constitution
"helps" to determine the relative strengths and weaknesses of groups
in the political struggle.[21]

II

Unlike Dahl, Madison defended the efficacy of constitutional restraints on power because he did not believe that social restraints
could be effectuated by the sort of group equilibrium which Dahl
has called the principle of political pluralism traced to the Tenth
essay. A month before he published this essay, Madison explained
to Jefferson why he believed as he did. A modern society is socially
heterogeneous; in a republic, governmental decisions are made on
the principle of majority rule. Because not all interests are affected
equally by such decisions, there must be an awareness of the need
for moderation which will insure government by consent rather
than force because the latter would be a denial of the republican
principle. In the abstract we could hope that three kinds of social
restraints would stay the hand of a majority: respect for the supremacy of the "general good;" a respect for "character;" and religious and moral instruction.

Experience, however, has demonstrated that a regard for the common good has never restrained a majority with "the public authority
in their hands." As for the second restraint, public opinion controls
the governing majority in a republic. The "standard is fixed by
those whose conduct is to be measured by it." Consequently, *no
increase in the numerical size of the majority* will alter the situation:
"two thousand individuals [will be] no less apt to oppress one thou-

18 *Ibid.*, 16.
19 *Ibid.*, 5.
20 *Ibid.*, 9.
21 *Ibid.*, 137.

sand, or two hundred thousand one hundred thousand." Finally, religious and moral tuition have failed utterly to restrain men acting in a *public* capacity because the standards of moral judgment applied to private conduct have no binding effect in political life. Men who had professed the strongest religious convictions had acted on occasion without remorse in ways at which their "consciences would revolt, if proposed to them separately in their closets." Religion, "kindled into enthusiasm . . . has been much oftener a motive for oppression than a restraint from it."

Because the art of the politician is likely to be used to mobilize majorities to act on any pretense, no matter how cynical, the lawgiver must use his art to contrive constitutional restraints upon unscrupulous majorities:

Divide et impera, the reprobated maxim of tyranny, is under certain qualifications the only policy on which a republic can be administered on just principles. It must be observed however that this doctrine can only hold within a sphere of mean extent. As in too small a sphere oppressive combinations may be too easily formed against the weaker party; so in too extensive a one, a defensive concert may be rendered too difficult against the oppression of those entrusted with the administration.[22]

This letter provides a major clue to Madison's meaning in the Tenth essay.

The subject of the essay is representative government. The discourse falls roughly into two parts: first, there is a discussion of the failure of the existing American constitutions to control the violence of faction. Despite their improvement over other forms of popular government, they do not provide a well-constructed union capable of controlling the effects of faction, among which the mutability of legislation is the most alarming. Next, there is a familiar definition of faction, the latent causes of which are shown in the nature of man and inflamed by the liberty of free governments. The danger of factional victories is real because the first object of such governments is to protect the fallible reason and diverse faculties of men out of which rights of property originate. The performance of this function has two significant consequences. Men who differ from each other in reason and faculties acquire different amounts and kinds of property. The influence of these differences upon the "sentiments and views of the proprietors" results in a division of

---

[22] *Writings*, V, 27-28 (to Thomas Jefferson, Oct. 24, 1787). Essay No. 10 was published Nov. 22, 1787.

society into various parties and interests.[23] Means consistent with republican liberty must be devised for controlling the effects of political conflict among those who pursue their interest through legislation, if a stable and just republic is to be maintained. A fundamental dilemma must be resolved, therefore, because legislation is enacted by representatives who normally are no more than "advocates and parties to the causes which they determine." Neither religious instruction nor indoctrination into the principles of republican civic rectitude will restrain the common disposition of humans to "vex and oppress each other [rather] than to cooperate for their common good."[24] Other means must be used to control the form of factional struggle to be most dreaded in America; that is, conflict among those who already fully enjoy their natural right to property in its various forms and also possess political rights of suffrage and representation.

The dilemma may be stated more generally. Our object is to secure the public good and private rights against a factional majority without perverting the "spirit and form of popular government."[25] In its most abstract, general form the solution seems to lie in finding means whereby either an interested majority is prevented from forming or, if it already exists, it is rendered ineffectual by its "*number* and *local* situation. . . ."[26] From this proposition it is evident that a pure democracy on the Classical model will not serve this end because the legislative majority in government is also the unrefined social majority.

A republic, however, is by definition characterized by "a *scheme of representation*" and it is this feature which "opens a different prospect, and *promises the cure* for which we are seeking."[27] Indeed, representation is the distinguishing mark of republican government and differentiates it from a democracy, the other type within the *genus* "popular government." The second distinguishing characteristic of a republic is that it embraces a "greater number of citizens, and greater sphere of country" than a democracy. Madison deduced two effects from these premises.

Representation provides the potential means of refining public

23 *The Federalist*, 55 (No. 10).
24 *Ibid.*, 56.
25 *Ibid.*, 58.
26 *Ibid.*
27 *Ibid.*, 59 (emphasis added).

opinion through the agency of elected representatives before it is transformed into legislation. Without a carefully designed electoral system, however, voting can result in the choice of either men of republican virtue or others moved by selfish ambition and a narrowly parochial vision of the public good. Therefore, the decisive question is "whether small or extensive republics are more favorable to the election of proper guardians of the public weal. . . ." The clear answer is decidedly in favor of a large republic because of "two obvious considerations."[28]

At this point the argument becomes more complex. The extension of a republic provides four *necessary* conditions, all likely to result in one desired effect: "the substitution of representatives whose enlightened views and virtuous sentiments render them superior to local prejudices and to schemes of injustice." Madison stated no sufficient cause in his theory. Therefore, it is a probabilistic causal theory. The first condition is that in any republic the number of representatives must be large enough to guard against the cabals of the few, but not so large as to fall prey to the confusion of the many. Next, the number of representatives in a large republic does not have to be proportionally as large as in a small republic to satisfy this condition. It, in turn, produces an effect: the proportion of "fit characters" for election will be greater in a large republic than in a small one (that is, given a larger population and fewer offices to fill). This complex condition results in "a greater probability of a fit choice."[29] A third condition (one treated as an effect of a republic's extension) is that each representative is chosen by a greater number of citizens in the large than in the small republic. Again, this condition has a likely effect: the *probability* that the choice of the representative will be affected by the "vicious arts" of election is reduced.

The other consideration which Madison notes is the fourth condition likely to produce the desired effect. The *federal* division of an extended republic differentiates the functions of representatives. Some are chosen deliberately and knowingly to serve the "aggregate interests" of the nation. Others will be chosen with an equal awareness to serve local, even parochial, interests. Both general and particular interests will be served simultaneously by this scheme of double representation. In short, a large republic can be federal

28 *Ibid.*
29 *Ibid.*, 60.

in structure. Within it the relatively greater number and diversity of interests will seek their ends at both levels of government. At the state level, where local interests are served, occasions will arise on which "factious leaders may kindle a flame within their particular States," but they will not spread it through the other states.[30] The old "rage for paper money" and similar kinds of familiar legislation may succeed in particular states, but it will be less apt to pervade the entire Union because the "representation of the Union will be most likely to possess these requisite endowments" of "enlightened views and virtuous sentiments."[31]

Among the other essays in *The Federalist*, No. 57 supports this understanding. There, Madison set out to refute the charge that members of the House of Representatives would be chosen from an elite insensitive to public opinion, because the House was too small to provide a "numerous representation" as the Antifederalists demanded. Madison replied that the only difference in respect of numbers between the state legislatures and the House would be that each member of the latter would be elected by "five or six thousand citizens. . . ." In the states, each representative would be elected by "about as many hundreds." If this difference is the basis for the charge, Madison continued, one should ask whether it is supported by "reason. . . ." And it cannot be "without mantaining that five or six thousand citizens are less capable of choosing a fit representative, or more liable to be corrupted by an unfit one, than five or six hundred."[32]

Madison's novel reversal of the theory that a republic must be small in size led to two general conclusions. The first, to repeat, was that representatives chosen from large, heterogeneous districts are likely to be independent of any single interest. The second was that Congress would more probably be insulated from localized factional struggles normally occurring in some districts. He hypothesized that at any one time an "ambitious" candidate would be able to mobilize voters in support of some measures, but it would "rarely happen to many districts at the same time."[33] In the state legislatures interests would vary according to their "number and local situation. . . ." The familiar struggles involving religious sects,

---

[30] *Ibid.*, 61.
[31] *Ibid.*
[32] *Ibid.*, 374 (No. 57).
[33] *Writings*, IV, 126.

creditors, and debtors, could be expected to appear in "particular states, but will be unable to spread to general conflagration through the other states."[34] This was Jefferson's understanding of his friend's theory. A republic must be "so extensive as that local egoisms may never reach its greater part. . . ."[35]

Madison's argument in *The Federalist* was based on reason, but, like Harrington and Hume, he did not separate it rigidly from experience, which he called "an instructive monitor."[36] Reason gave him knowledge of experience in logical form and thereby rendered it useful for the practice of the lawgiver. Consequently, it adds depth to our understanding of his theory to know what particular events led him to believe that political conflict should be moderated through representation.

III

Through intensive political study prior to the Convention, Madison concluded that the tendency toward faction would have to be curbed with what he called an "intermingled agency." Means had to be found for republican governments to provide "some disinterested and dispassionate umpire in disputes between different passions and interests in the state."[37] The new government would need the means of curbing the "variety of pernicious measures" enacted by the states.[38] Resort to force would be contrary to republican ideology. Representatives were needed, therefore, not as "mere

34 *The Federalist*, 58, 61 (No. 10). A careful comparison of the text of No. 10 with Madison's long speech on June 6, 1787, demonstrates clearly that the latter provided much of the text of the former, almost literally so, but not the whole of it because Madison did not explain there what he meant by insisting on the need to "enlarge the sphere. . . ." *Writings*, III, 102-103

35 Thomas Jefferson, *The Writings of Thomas Jefferson*, ed. Albert Ellery Bergh (20 vols.; Washington, D.C.: The Thomas Jefferson Memorial Association, 1907), IX, 299-300. This idea was subtly transformed by Lord Bryce into the premise of contemporary pluralists that a fragmented public opinion prevents the "tyranny of the majority." In America public opinion shows, "in the teeth of the old doctrine that republicanism was fit only for small communities, that evils peculiar to a particular district, which might be ruinous in that district if it stood alone, become less dangerous when it forms part of a vast country." James Bryce, *The American Commonwealth*, new and rev. ed. (2 vols.; New York: Macmillan Company, 1920).

36 *Writings*, III, 306.

37 *Ibid.*, II, 346-347.

38 *Ibid.*, III, 364.

advocates of state interests & views," but as "impartial umpires and guardians of justice and the general Good."[39] They could serve as umpires, if they were given adequate, new authority and were chosen in large districts directly by the voters. If Congress were given a negative on all the legislative acts of the states, it would have a defensive power to guard national interests, control rivalries among the states and secure minorities within them from "unrighteous measures."[40]

He formulated this theory of the moderating function of representatives chosen from large, heterogeneous districts by 1785 if not earlier. When Jefferson asked him to comment on his draft of a new constitution for Virginia, Madison recommended electing senators either state-wide or in large districts. Either practice would secure the "fittest characters . . . in proportion to the [size of the] districts."[41] Elections so regulated would provide the "most effectual remedy for the local biass [sic]" by insuring that representatives would attend to "the interests of the whole."[42] If "you extend the sphere" a greater number and variety of interests will elect representatives.[43]

English experience with parliamentary corruption had been decisive for Madison. He was convinced of the need for a representative to be impartial toward factions within his district and, especially, independent of effective intervention from the outside. If patronage and other "vicious arts" were used in elections, one group might be served at the expense of others. In that event, no dispassionate umpire would be available to moderate group struggles. "The greatest degree of treachery in representatives is to be appre-

---

[39] *Ibid.*, III, 293.

[40] *Ibid.*, II, 326-327.

[41] *Ibid.*, II, 339.

[42] Thomas Jefferson, *The Papers of Thomas Jefferson*, ed. Julian Boyd (18 vols.; Princeton, N.J.: Princeton University Press, 1950 to date), VI, 308-309. The exact date of these comments is unknown, although Jefferson sent the draft to Madison on June 17, 1783. See Editor's Notes, 305. In offering suggestions for a constitution for Kentucky, Madison urged that there be a senate and another branch not "too numerous"—perhaps 100 members elected from districts arranged by "geographical description. . . ." *Writings*, II, 167, 173 (to Caleb Wallace, Aug. 23, 1785). He objected, however, at the Convention to the original size of the House of Representatives, saying that the number was too small to "represent the whole inhabitants of the U. States." *Ibid.*, III, 390.

[43] *Writings*, III, 102.

hended where they are chosen by the least number of electors; because there is a greater facility of using undue influence, and the electors must be less independent." The inevitability of corruption in this sense could be "verified in the most unanswerable manner" in Britain. "Who are the most corrupt members of Parliament? Are they not the inhabitants of small towns and districts? The supporters of liberty are from the great counties." Most of the "ministerial majority [are] drawn from small circumscribed districts."[44] It was there that bribery had most prevailed and the influence of the Crown in elections was most dangerously exerted. The executive power of patronage can be expected to be used as "an engine of improper influence and favoritism."[45]

To this understanding he added an axiom drawn chiefly from experience in the Roman republic. "The people can never err more than in supposing that by multiplying their representatives beyond a certain limit, they strengthen the barrier against the government of a few."[46] The Roman Senate had too many members. Excessive size had tended to duplicate the divisions among the people. Madison drew two inferences from this experience: the more representatives are multiplied, the more they reflect the particular, diverse, and numerous interests of their constituents; hence, the more liable they became to be divided among themselves into factions. In respect to numbers, therefore, a legislature's "weight would be in inverse ratio" to its size. For this reason he opposed a large legislature which would tend to mirror exactly every interest in the community. A well-proportioned assembly will secure the benefits of "free consultation and discussion" and assure the supremacy of reason over passion. "Had every Athenian citizen been a Socrates, every Athenian assembly would still have been a mob."[47]

Additional evidence shows that Madison offered a causal theory which would give each region a defensive voting power. Obviously, if he had believed that an increase in the size and social diversity of the electorate restrains majority rule, there would have been no need to advocate a constitutional equilibrium between North and South. He had become increasingly concerned over sectional differences by the end of the Revolution. In 1781 he asked Jefferson: "What is to protect the Southern States, and for many

44 *Ibid.*, V, 158-159.
45 *Papers of Jefferson*, VI, 312.
46 *The Federalist*, 382 (No. 58, Madison).
47 *Writings*, III, 114; *The Federalist*, 361 (No. 55, Madison).

years to come, against the insults and aggressions of their northern
brethren?"[48] Certainly, in Madison's judgment, the group struggle
familiar to him resulted in no safe fragmentation of the majority, no
natural harmony nor social equilibrium acceptable to the weaker
party. By 1787 he had found a solution to the problem. The "first
step to be taken is, I think, a change in the principle of representation . . . [to] operate without the intervention of the States. . . ."[49]
Representation by direct popular election of the House and its allocation among the states on the basis of population would produce
the two major political effects he desired. It would appeal to the
"Eastern States by the actual superiority of their populousness, and
to the Southern by their expected superiority. . . ."[50]

Properly distributed, representation would protect republican
liberty, which can be secured only by giving "every peculiar interest a Constitutional power of defense."[51] Experience in Congress
had taught Madison that on no occasion had the large states co-
alesced to vote against the small ones. The circumstances of equality of size had not served as the basis for a common interest.[52] Nor
was there any basis for believing that it would do so in the future.
Instead, the cleavages were always a material conflict of interests
arising from differences of climate and slavery. "These two causes
concurred in forming the great division of interests in the United
States. It did not lie between the large & small States: It lay between the Northern and Southern. And if any defensive power
were necessary, it ought to be mutually given to these two interests."[53]

Madison was "so strongly impressed with this important truth
that he had been casting about in his mind for some expedient that
would answer the purpose." Representation was the most likely
one, if it were allocated "in one branch according to the number of
free inhabitants only; and in the other according to the whole
number counting the slaves as free. By this arrangement the
Southern scale would be advanced in one House, and the Northern

[48] *Ibid.*, I, 132. *The Papers of James Madison*, ed. William T. Hutchison
and William M. E. Rachal (7 vols.; Chicago: University of Chicago Press, 1962
to date), III, 124; also, 168-169, 262, 293.
[49] *Writings*, II, 338.
[50] *Ibid.*, II, 345.
[51] *Ibid.*, III, 332.
[52] *Ibid.*, III, 305.
[53] *Ibid.*, III, 333.

in the other."[54] Two considerations had restrained him from suggesting this solution at the outset of the Convention. First, he was unwilling to identify this diversity of interests on an occasion where it was but too apt to be raised. Second, different powers would have to be vested in the two houses to achieve a functional constitution. He warned emphatically, however, against the scheme of representation which gave each state an equal vote in the Senate. If the "proper foundation of government was destroyed by substituting an equality [of state voting power] in place of a proportional Representation, no proper superstructure would be raised."[55]

Ironically, no proposal to base representation on population was acceptable to delegates responding to northern mercantile interests. They believed that such a proposal would produce ultimately a southern majority and not an equilibrium. Rufus King conceded that some compromise was needed to form a union of such strongly conflicting interests. He said he "always expected that as the Southern States are the richest, they would not league themselves with the North unless some respect were paid to their superior wealth," but they could not subject the latter to the "gross inequality" implicit in their demands. He was willing to "yield something in the proportion of representatives for the security of the Southern. . . . No principle would justify giving them a majority."[56] Gouverneur Morris took the same position and warned the Southerners against seeking

a majority in the public councils. The consequence of such a transfer of power from the maritime to the interior and landed interest will he foresees be such an oppression of commerce, that we shall be obliged to vote for ye vicious principle of equality in the second branch in order to provide some defense for the Northern States against it. . . . [Should the South] get the power into their hands, and be joined as they will with the interior Country, they will bring on a war with Spain over the Mississippi.

This prospect would ally the middle states with the northeast against the South and new West.[57]

Madison was disturbed by the prospect that, if the states were represented equally in the Senate, a strategically located minority could often nullify the will of the majority. He believed that this

54 *Ibid.*
55 *Ibid.*, III, 432.
56 *Ibid.*, III, 387.
57 *Ibid.*, III, 421-422.

evil would increase as each new state was admitted. There would
be a dynamic growth of population and wealth in the future. Commerce was "easy and free . . . the people are constantly swarming
from the more to the less populous places—from Europe to America
—from the Northern and Middle parts of the United States to the
Southern and Western. They go where land is cheaper because
there labor is dearer." For the purposes of representation, therefore, the "number of inhabitants were an accurate measure of
wealth . . . and ability to support taxes."[58] Consequently, population, not states *per se*, ought to be the basis of representation.
Equality of the states in the Senate would give "*perpetuity* . . . to
the preponderance of the Northern against the Southern States. . . .
There were five states on the Southern, eight on the Northern side.
. . ." On the other hand, if Madison's proposal were accepted and
"a proportional representation [should] take place . . . the Northern
side would still outnumber the other; but not in the same degree,
at this time; and every day would tend towards an equilibrium."[59]

Madison's fundamental conviction emerges clearly from these observations. Social pluralism, unchecked by a constitutional superstructure of representation contrived to overcome the imbalance of
natural, "social" majorities, will ultimately fail to control the violence of faction in a "free" government. He reached this conclusion by combining his knowledge of British political development
and the unique condition of the American republic. To justify this
conclusion Madison had to revise some of the most influential, prevailing theories of politics. It is this context of eighteenth century
political theory and development, as well as Madison's vision of the
deepest cleavages to be overcome in America's future, that explains
why he and his most sophisticated peers linked the ideas of faction
and corruption with a theory of representation and the doctrine of
the separation of powers.

IV

Three days before *The Federalist* No. 1 was published, Madison
wrote a very long letter to Jefferson saying that he was confronted

[58] *Ibid.*, III, 404-405.

[59] *Ibid.*, III, 434. The proposal to continue equality of representation among
the states, Madison asserted, "must infuse *mortality* into a Constitution which
we wished to last forever." *Ibid.*, III, 316, 331-332 (emphasis added). The
Senate provided by the Convention "is only another edition of Cong[ress]. . . ."
Ibid., III, 338.

with the challenge of reformulating the "true Principles of Republican Government." He intended to "prove in contradiction to the concurrent opinions of the theoretical writers, that this form of government must operate not within a small but an extensive sphere."[60] James Wilson had stated the problem neatly at the Convention. In fashioning new political institutions it was necessary to consider both the "extent and manners" of the country and its people. The American people were "republican" in manners, but the country was so extended as to require a monarchy, according to Montesquieu, unless his recommendation of a confederated republic were adopted. That was acceptable, Wilson believed, if means were adapted to insure vigorous execution of the laws without destroying liberty. The great difficulty, however, was that the American people opposed "the corrupt multitude of Parliament" in the Revolution without renouncing the "unity represented by the King."[61]

More was involved here than mere rustic, puritanical fastidiousness which some scholars have thought prompted the Antifederalists to predict a similar development under the new Constitution.[62] This rejection of parliamentary corruption was virtually universal among republicans, both English and American, who attached the most fundamental political significance to it. They understood it to be the means by which the executive was manipulating the development of factions, insulated from a minuscule electorate, and unbalancing the Constitution by redistributing power, wealth, and status in society. It was endlessly condemned by the neo-classical republicans of the Country Party in Britain and the Americans who both used and transformed their ideas a half-century later in preparation for the Revolution.[63] To curb corruption and the consequent development of faction, the republicans prescribed basic changes in representation that would effect a purifying reduction in the executive prerogative which they distrusted as inherently manipulative.

Even if these views are accepted, a modern reader might rightly

[60] Writings, V, 128.

[61] Max Farrand, ed., Records of the Federal Convention (3 vols.; New Haven, Conn.: Yale University Press, 1913), I, 71-72.

[62] Cecelia Kenyon, The Antifederalists (Indianapolis: Bobbs-Merrill Company, 1966), lviii.

[63] Bailyn, Ideological Origins; J. G. A. Pocock, "Machiavelli, Harrington and English Political Ideologies in the Eighteenth Century," William and Mary Quarterly, 3rd ser., 22 (October 1965), 549-583.

ask why Madison thought that he had developed a radically new theory of the function of representation over an extended territory as a key element of the solution to the problem which Wilson had stated: how could the republicanism of American manners be matched with a republican form of government in a nation so extensive that monarchy was the only workable form of strong government according to Europe's most learned theorists? Even a summary answer requires note that republicanism was a revolutionary ideology which had, supposedly, little effect in Britain, but claims the American Constitution as its enduring monument.[64] It was attractive enough to stimulate some intellectually powerful critics, including Hobbes, Hume, and Montesquieu.[65] Madison blamed the latter two in particular for their "artifices" which eulogized monarchy by discrediting republicanism.[66] The fact is, however, that English republicans had left a fundamental contradiction to be resolved. With some of the oversimplifications necessary in an essay I will show how Madison fulfilled his promise to Jefferson by contradicting Hume and Montesquieu, who argued that only small states can be republics, whereas large states must be monarchies, especially those which are agricultural societies undergoing the early stages of modernization. Next, I will summarize Madison's explicit analysis of the likely consequences of the inevitable rise of the commercial and manufacturing classes and the eclipse of the American agrarian majority as part of the process of modernization which was evident to knowledgeable observers of British development. Finally, I will sketch the ways in which American republicans reformed representation as a remedy to protect their interests.

[64] Caroline Robbins, *The Eighteenth Century Commonwealthman* (Cambridge, Mass.: Harvard University Press, 1959), 4.

[65] Thomas Hobbes, *Leviathan*, ed. Michael Oakeshott (Oxford: Basil Blackwell, n. d.). He called the republicans "mad dogs" bitten with "tyrannophobia," 214. Too many of them had become addicted to the false doctrines of the Greeks and Romans, "supposing there needed no more to grow rich, than to change, as they had done, the form of their government" in "imitation of the Low Countries. . . ." *Ibid.*, 213. See generally Z. S. Fink, *The Classical Republicans* (Evanston, Ill.: Northwestern University Press, 1945, 1962), chap. 29; T. A. W. Gunn, *Politics and the Public Interest in the Seventeenth Century* (London: Routledge & Kegan Paul, 1969); Perez Zagorin, *A History of Political Thought in the English Revolution* (London: Routledge & Kegan Paul, 1954), 132-163.

[66] *The Federalist*, 81 (No. 14).

The major theorists agreed that the fundamental issue to be resolved was whether a republic or a monarchy was the form of regime necessary to control the struggle of factions in countries where a dynamic change was affecting the relative power of the landed and commercial interests, as they were commonly called. It was assumed that the form of a constitution must be consistent with the dominant form of property. Harrington, the most sophisticated English republican, laid down the axiom that the distribution of property determines the distribution of power. By this he meant that whoever controls the dominant form of property—and he favored land over money—would also control the army and the legislature. Hobbes had been seriously in error on this point, he contended. An agrarian republic, supported by a law to insure the permanent division of the land among numerous freeholders together with a militia under their command, could cover a nation as large as England. In addition, it could expand into an empire overseas where God's work could be done.[67] The classical republicans of the seventeenth century shared many of his views, but they took Venice as their model of a republic. By implication, at least, this choice supported the view expressed by Harrington that republics dominated by commerce had to be small. He cited the Dutch example.[68] Montesquieu repeated this point of view a century later without essential modification except to suggest that a confederation of republics might have the military strength equivalent to a royal army without sacrificing liberty, which is the "spirit" of a republic.[69] Without such liberty, the citizens of a republic could not expect to engage in the peaceful pursuit of profitable commerce on a plane of equality. It was the prevalence of Montesquieu's teaching in America which strengthened the Antifederalists' strong objections to the scheme of representation in Congress along with the scope of its power and the absence of a restriction against a standing army in time of peace.

David Hume concurrently added an entirely new and more challenging set of theoretical propositions. First, he laid down one

[67] Charles Blitzer, An Immortal Commonwealth (New Haven, Conn.: Yale University Press, 1960), 127-135, 169-172. Zagorin, History of Political Thought, 132-145.

[68] Fink, Classical Republicans, 52-89.

[69] Charles Louis de Secondat, Baron de Montesquieu, The Spirit of the Laws, trans. Thomas Nugent with an introduction by Franz Neumann (2 vols.; Hafner Library of Classics, 1949), I, 51, 68, 126-130, 378.

"universal axiom" of political science. Republics always ruin their provinces, although they do extend liberty to the commercial class. The latter dominate the legislature and contrive restrictions on trade and lay taxes which enable them to "draw some private as well as public advantage" from their public offices. Further, they lay the seeds of rebellion by contracting a public debt and mortgaging the public revenues to repay it. Thus, republican public officers become both public creditors and tax collectors. Even in the British monarchy these policies had been followed to the extent that an effort had been made to divide the *"landed* and *trading* part of the nation," but without success. These two interests would not fatally oppose each other, he predicted, until "our public debts do encrease [sic] to such a degree as to become altogether oppressive and intolerable."[70]

This part of Hume's analysis challenged Madison because Hume repeated the familiar argument that the dominant form of property in a republic is money and the interest is commercial. Secondly, he raised the specter of domination of the agrarian majority in America by the rising financial and commercial interests if the constitution adopted were republican.

[70] Hume, *Essays*, 130, 127-141 *et passim*. It is well established that Madison was influenced by Hume's philosophy and his discussion of factions. See Douglas Adair, "That Politics may be Reduced to a Science: David Hume, James Madison and the Tenth Federalist," *Huntington Library Quarterly*, 20 (August 1957), 343-360; Ketcham, *James Madison*, 32-50, 187-188. I believe Hume's influence was much greater and Locke's much less than Ketcham has concluded. Through Hume Madison must have known Harrington's theory of republican constitutionalism on which all three men agreed. See Hume, *Essays*, on the rule of law, 105-106. Harrington's *Oceana* was the "only valuable model of a commonwealth" available. Hume, *Essays*, 481. Ketcham ignores the significance of Madison's attachment to experimentation rooted in experience in which he follows Hume as closely as an American *making* a constitution could. See Robert McRae, "Hume as a Political Philosopher," *Journal of the History of Ideas*, 12 (April 1951), 285-290; and G. B. Mathur, "Hume, Kant and Pragmatism," *Journal of the History of Ideas*, 16 (April 1955), 198-208. Madison's discussion of the problem of creating the presidency at the Convention of 1787 is clear proof that he had studied Hume's analysis of the role of royal corruption by dividing and ruling the antagonistic landed and mercantile interests in Parliament. See his speech in *Writings*, III, 108-109. Harrington was so well known in America by the time of the Revolution that Madison could not have been ignorant of *Oceana*. H. F. Russell Smith, *Harrington and His Oceana* (Cambridge, England: At the University Press, 1914; New York: Octagon Books, 1971), 152-200.

Hume complicated the argument even further by modifying Harrington's dictum that political power depends upon property. British political development demonstrated that the struggle of these two great interests could be prevented from becoming civil war only by the artful use of royal corruption. British monarchy, he found, was no longer devoted to the exclusive support of "birth, titles and place," but, instead, valued "industry and riches" equally. From this observation he inferred that the British system had evolved to the point where it had become an empire of laws by combining the essential natures of "both species of civil polity," republic and monarchy. The consequence was that in Britain the two interests received almost the same treatment which the commercial interest enjoyed in republics and the landed interest secured in monarchies. Hume believed that this transformation had been effected by the shrewd use of parliamentary corruption which rested first upon the royal prerogative and next on the practices associated with the theory of virtual representation. The great personal wealth of the monarch and his prestige, as well as the prerogative, made his power to intervene in every dimension of parliamentary affairs one vital factor in maintaining the system. Virtual representation insured that the members of Commons would not be "obliged like Dutch deputies to receive instructions" from their constituents. If this were not the practice, "no skill, popularity or revenue" could support the monarchy in a test of strength with elected representatives so that the system would be quickly reduced to a "pure republic of no inconvenient form. . . ."[71] Once that transition was complete, the result would be either a "Cromwell" or a "supreme legislature. . . ." In the latter event, every election of the popular assembly would deteriorate into a civil war.[72]

In reaching his general conclusion that executive manipulation of

[71] Hume, Essays, 112-113; see, also, 120, 122-126, 490-491. Hume specifically rejected the doctrine of the Country Party that Parliament should be free of royal influence. Ibid., 121. In his invaluable study, Pole makes the reason clear: "Had merchants been unable to get into Parliament, the Constitution would have cracked. But here, it was the perverse merit of the rotten boroughs and burage tenures that they came to the rescue . . . as glittering prizes on the road to the House of Commons." T. R. Pole, Political Representation in England and the Origins of the American Republic (New York: Macmillan Company, 1966), 452.

[72] Ibid., 126.

the legislature was essential to avoid ultimate political violence, Hume embraced that side of Machiavelli's teachings—the Florentine element—which the English republicans had rejected as emphatically as they had admired his *Discourses*.[73] Hume's recognition of the importance of political art as an element of power modified Harrington's principle. Further, his analysis corresponded with the understanding which Madison and his most sophisticated peers shared. "Corruption" was a political code word in the eighteenth century. Pocock has shown that spokesmen for the English Country Party, who were neo-classical republicans, opposed corruption because they understood it was unbalancing the ancient constitution and enriching a minority of the population. Their criticisms showed their "awareness of the changing role of government," and not merely the market economy, "as historical determinants" of social transformation.[74] Bailyn has demonstrated, further, that this ideology was well known and copied in detail in the American colonies by 1740.[75]

When Madison turned from European theories of political stability to the social structure of republican America, he found both striking similarities and significant differences, not the least of which was the opportunity to submit to "practice an experiment which seems to be founded on the best theoretic principles" despite their novelty.[76] Hartz has ridiculed Madison and his contemporaries for being so overwhelmed by European thought and experience that they engaged in a "shadow war" of social conflict.[77] On neither count is this assessment correct. Madison said that he was "not

---

[73] Fink, *Classical Republicans*, 11-16; Zagorin, *History of Political Thought*, 133-135, 139.

[74] Pocock, "Machiavelli," 578.

[75] Bailyn, *Ideological Origins*, 34-47. It is Bailyn's thesis that the American Revolution was "above all else" ideological, political, and constitutional and not a struggle to transform society. *Ibid.*, vi.

[76] *Writings*, V, 197.

[77] Hartz, *Liberal Tradition*, 81. Hartz's analysis of American thought rests heavily on his restricted definition of great revolutionary thought. Its essence, "elsewhere in the world has been the effort to build a new society on the ruins of the old one . . . an experience America has never had." *Ibid.*, 66. Contrast with Locke's view: "He that will with any clearness speak of the dissolution of government ought, in the first place, to distinguish between the dissolution of the society and the dissolution of the government. . . ." John Locke, *The Second Treatise of Civil Government*, ed. T. W. Gough (Oxford: Basil Blackwell, 1946), 103; chap. 19, par. 211.

unaware of circumstances which distinguish the American from other popular governments . . . and . . . render extreme circumspection necessary in reasoning from one to the other. But . . . it still may be maintained that there are many points of similitude which render these examples not unworthy of our attention."[78]

Madison remarked at the Convention that, in "framing a system which we wish to last for ages, we shd. not lose sight of the changes ages will produce."[79] In 1787 most of America was still like Virginia as Parrington characterized it—"*Oceana* seated by the James."[80] But every decade would bring changes resulting in dangerous stresses on the stability of the system, including the deep differences of political culture between the two sections. Madison thought the universal hope of acquiring property and its widespread distribution due to the effects of free institutions would provide part of the consensual basis of the system. He understood that devotion to this Lockean principle was not enough, however. He agreed with the European writers, republican and monarchist alike, who unswervingly rejected the argument that belief in a natural right to unequal amounts of property is a guarantee of the stability of civil society. Had this value consensus been a sufficient cause, as Hartz contends it has been in America, there would have been no reason to fear republicanism or to support royal corruption.

Madison believed that consensus upon the value of private property was not a sufficient condition of civic harmony because of the relationships among the "three principal classes into which our citizens were divisible . . . the landed, the commercial, & manufacturing." Of these, the latter two were increasing daily in proportion to the first which would eventually become a minority. So far, Harrington's fear that capital would be invested in land so as to concentrate its ownership in a few hands had not materialized in America. Very "few of the mercantile, & scarcely any of the manufacturing class chusing whilst they continue in business to turn any part of their Stock into landed property." For this reason men of each group "understand less of each others [sic] interests & affairs,

---

[78] *The Federalist*, 411 (No. 63).

[79] *Writings*, III, 286.

[80] Parrington, *Main Currents*, II, 5. Despite his thesis that the basic cleavage in America until the Civil War was between industrial capitalists and agrarians, he persisted upon following Smith (to whom he fondly dedicated *Main Currents*) in treating Madison as a polemicist of class warfare.

than men of the same class inhabiting different districts." This tendency to particularize and isolate one interest from another because of the *kinds* of property involved was exacerbated by the fact that general legislation would not affect all of them equally. The various and unequal effects of legislation and of political loyalty imposed upon men representing these differences of interest made it "particularly requisite therefore that the interests of one or two of them should not be left entirely to the care, or impartiality of the third."[81]

The validity of this rule was demonstrated by the way in which the "landed interest had borne hard on the mercantile interest" in some states.[82] It was instructive that the strongest proponents of the agrarian laws were men who possessed large holdings of land—more so than any other class. They had acquired large amounts of land on credit and then secured their own election to the legislatures "with a view to promoting an unjust protection against their creditors." Madison predicted that similar behavior could be expected from the election to office of public creditors, just as Hume had called such behavior the one universal axiom in the politics of republics.[83] Furthermore, experience had taught Madison that among "individuals of superior eminence & weight in Society, rivalships were much more frequent than coalitions."[84] He believed these observations justified his conviction that he could "see in the populous Countries of Europe now, what we shall be hereafter,"[85] despite our lack of either the "hereditary distinctions of rank" or the "extremes of wealth and poverty" found there.[86]

Madison and his colleagues did not look to Europe exclusively for political instruction, but drew, also, on the revolutionary beliefs and

81 *Writings*, IV, 76.
82 *Ibid.*, III, 102.
83 *Ibid.*, IV, 73, 75-76.
84 *Ibid.*, III, 305.
85 *Ibid.*, IV, 76.
86 *Ibid.*, III, 286. He conceded that the growth of population eventually would exacerbate the tendencies toward class cleavages growing out of inequality of wealth and the rest of life's "blessings." Because he believed that there are rights of persons to be protected, he advocated constitutional guarantees for their security, as well as that of the major, distinctive property "interests" involved. *Ibid.* See, for example, *Writings*, IV, 124-127. Beard chose to ignore Madison's complex analysis of the sources of faction, although Beard concluded that differences of "political psychology" arise out of "different degrees and *kinds* of property." Beard, *Economic Basis*, 27 (emphasis added).

practices of the republicans of 1776. On the other hand, Madison rejected some of their teaching, but not because his aim was simply to curb the "factious multitude" as the Progressives and some others have claimed.[87] The republicans of 1776 widely condemned faction and the corruption practiced by Crown agents in the colonies. They promised that republicanism would restore the primacy of the common good and secure the moral regeneration of American society which was forsaking its rustic simplicity and frugality for the ostentatious opulence and profligacy appropriate to a royal court.[88] One of the first and most important changes in government which they made to curb the twin evils of faction and corruption was to fix in their state constitutions the formulae for distributing representation according to fixed ratios or categories. Many attempts had been made to do this during British rule to guarantee representation where the colonists thought it was deserved, but they were unsuccessful.[89] Many Americans agreed with Locke that wealth and population provided the most equitable bases of representation, but they rejected his belief that it would be achieved by an exercise of the royal prerogative.[90] We take this practice for granted today, but it was intended to be a radical reform at that time. It supposedly insured that representation would be continuously redistributed on a known and rational basis to accommodate the rapid

[87] Parrington, *Main Currents*; Eidelberg, *Philosophy of the Constitution*; Gordon S. Wood, *Representation in the American Revolution* (Charlottesville: The University Press of Virginia, 1969), concludes that the Framers sundered government from society so as to make the modern politics of competing parties possible, 64. For a similar argument see David G. Smith, *The Convention and the Constitution* (New York: St. Martin's Press, 1965), 62-63. This pluralist argument ignores Madison's concern that *legislation* (like Supreme Court decisions) rests on a formal rule: namely, that a numerical majority makes all official decisions, regardless of the degree to which public opinion may be fragmented over their substance.

[88] Gordon S. Wood, *The Creation of the American Republic* (New York: W. W. Norton & Company, 1972), 65-70, 91-124.

[89] *Ibid.*, 83-90, 162-196; Pole, *Political Representation*, 169-204, 250-280, 284-296. Pole points to the importance attached to the independence of both electors and representatives as a republican ideal. Reform of corrupt representation was a major issue in Britain and America during this time. "One word united all reformers in anger: 'corruption.'" *Ibid.*, 458. Pole points to the radical character of the American reform of basing representation on population and wealth, the standards bitterly resisted in Britain by Burke who "richly manured" the interests of the oligarchs, 342-344, 353-382, 462.

[90] Locke, *Second Treatise*, 79.

changes anticipated in population. In this important respect England provided no satisfactory model.

The revolutionary republicans rejected, also, the theory of virtual representation prevailing in Britain and praised by Hume and Burke. Instead of it, they advanced the agency theory and the various means, including instructions, by which representatives could be held strictly accountable to the voters of their districts. Because it was almost universally agreed that the colonies had a diversity and multiplicity of interests, it was argued that a "numerous" representation was required to secure a direct voice for every worthy interest.[91] This theory was so important to the American revolutionaries that it had attained the status of conventional wisdom by 1787. Antifederalists used it widely to denounce what they called insufficient representation provided by the new Constitution. It violated "the leading principle of the revolution." One legislature could not "represent so many different interests" without reducing the diverse American people to a uniform standard of "morals, habits and laws. . . ."[92]

Without any doubt, Madison intended to reverse the assumption underlying this belief. The Tenth essay was intended to replace it with the new theory that the assumed diversity and multiplicity of interests required representation apportioned on the mean. Fewer members would require larger districts. Extend the sphere and you take in a greater variety of interests. In addition, as he told Jefferson, the legislature then is not so large as to fall into numerous cliques which easily fall prey to the manipulative skills of an artful executive.[93] This argument, placed in this context, might seem to be no more than clever advocacy were it not for the overwhelming

[91] Bailyn, *Ideological Origins*, 162-164; Alfred de Grazia, *Public and Republic* (New York: Alfred A. Knopf, 1951), esp. 74-79. Even Burke believed that a reduction of Crown influence in Parliament was needed reform, but he violently disagreed with the radicals' demand for representation based upon individuals as the essential means of eliminating corruption. *Ibid.*, 36-49. Madison's frequent references to the situation in Britain renders the meaning of his notes of speeches clear.

[92] Paul Leicester Ford, ed., *Essays on the Constitution of the United States* (Brooklyn: Historical Printing Club, 1892), 65. Kenyon, *Antifederalists*, cvi-cxiv; Jackson T. Main, *The Antifederalist: Critics of the Constitution* (Chapel Hill: University of North Carolina Press, 1961). Main's over-arching conclusion is that the struggle over ratification was "primarily a contest between the commercial and non-commercial elements of the population," 280.

[93] See notes 20 and 76 above.

evidence in Madison's writings that he attached the most fundamental significance to it as a basic reformation of political theory
and a major contribution to the republican cause. Perhaps the
most useful key to his meaning was his contention that the "spirit"
of faction necessarily pervades all the operations of government.
Few assertions, standing alone, were more repugnant to republicans
whose basic aim for a century and a half had been to banish faction
from government. But Madison did not intend his revision to be a
betrayal of republican government. "From the first moment that
my mind was capable of contemplating political subjects, I never
. . . ceased wishing success to a well regulated republican government." Its establishment in America is "my most ardent desire."[94]

V

Madison's analysis of European and American political theory and
practice, together with his perception of social structure and cleavages in America, reveal why he believed that a new theory of representation would lay the foundation for the effective implementation of the doctrine of the separation of powers. The American
revolutionary tradition required, so to speak, that he discover the
theoretical foundation for a new political system which would curb
the worst excesses of faction without reintroducing any institution
capable of restoring "corruption" on the British model. At the same
time, he understood that Britain's experience with modernization
inevitably would be replicated more or less in American society despite the differences arising from the lack of a feudal tradition and
the depth of the sectional division. The social change which the
British monarchy was supporting through parliamentary corruption
would come here, too, but the prevailing *republican* ideology favored
a less active role by the executive than was the practice in Britain.
This situation spurred Madison to show that the only solution to the
problem of faction consistent with the principle of majority rule was
the admission of the spirit of faction into government. Factions
were the necessary consequence of believing it both "politic and
just that the interests and rights of every class should be duly represented and understood in the public Councils." Representatives
were elected in districts to "equally understand and sympathize
with the rights of the people in every part of the Community."[95]

[94] *Writings*, V, 197.
[95] *Writings*, IV, 76. In 1792 Madison published a brief essay introducing a

Once every interest is represented in the legislature, the spirit of faction is also admitted, because the assembly is "sufficiently numerous to feel all the passions" of the people.[96] At this point the problem is whether legislative stability can be achieved under such circumstances. If executive corruption is to be avoided in conformity with republican belief, legislative "sovereignty" must be rendered "sufficiently neutral between the different parts of Society to controul [sic] one part from invading the rights of others" without simultaneously creating a public authority so independent of the community as to be "an interest adverse to that of the entire Society."[97] Having rejected Hobbes, an avowed enemy of republicanism, Madison tried to meet head-on Hume's predictions that either (1) the commercial and mercantile majority would prevail at the cost of the landed interest, or (2) the struggle of the two groups for control of a "supreme" legislature would deteriorate into a civil war. Hume's conclusion confirmed the unshaken republican belief that the active mobilization of voters in the face of such social divisions was certain to produce the alternate violence of faction.[98] The periodic alternation in power of one group could be achieved only at the expense of its defeated opponent. In any society marked by a few sharply differentiated interests, factional control would be the probable outcome of electoral contests for control of the government.

The fundamental conclusion which Madison reached, therefore, was that a representative republic in which the legislative power naturally would predominate as the immediate agent of the people must incorporate all interests so as to permit them to participate continuously in governance. Government by party, or faction, through the periodic alternation of disparate interests, and its consequent instability of laws, was unacceptable in eighteenth century America. Here is the root of the distinctive American conception of constitutional government. This understanding illuminates Mad-

---

republican theory of occupations to achieve liberty and security. "A perfect theory on this subject would be useful . . . because it would be a *monition against empirical experiments of power*, and a model to which the *free choice* of occupations by the people might gradually approximate the order of society." *Ibid.*, VI, 96 (emphasis added).

[96] *The Federalist*, 322-323 (No. 48).

[97] *Writings*, V, 32.

[98] Fink, *Classical Republicans*, 32; Zagorin, *History of Political Thought*, 139, 153-155.

ison's reliance on the choice of representatives from large districts to be upright and independent.[99] They will provide a necessary "intermingled agency."[100] The sectional equilibrium of representation, which he proposed unsuccessfully, would have contributed to the same over-arching goal: legislative stability coupled with public responsibility and responsiveness. His theory was not rooted, as one of his most persistent contemporary critics claims, in "a pervading distrust of the people when organized in a bloc. . . ."[101] Madison, always the political realist, denied that they are ever so mystically united as to constitute a bloc. At a time when both the New England commercial interests and the great planters of the South distrusted a powerful central government, no responsible politician and analyst who joined theory with practice could defend any constitutional system leaving an intense and active minority without hope of immediate and effective participation in the political system.[102]

Most scholars who believe that social pluralism guarantees the protection of rights better than constitutional checks have claimed that the Tenth and Fifty-first essays are separable. Moreover, they treat the former as the rationale of the American system and reject the latter as either illogical or a political encumbrance.[103] The fact is that they were inseparable in Madison's theory as the structure

[99] *Writings*, V, 159.

[100] *Ibid.*, IV, 125.

[101] Burns, *Deadlock*, 334.

[102] For example, the New England Antifederalist, "Agrippa," complained that the new Constitution would subject "the sober and active people of the North" to the "idle and dissolute inhabitants of the South. . . ." Ford, *Essays on the Constitution*, 91. This probably was political code language, stressing the importance of savings and capital accumulation in a growing commercial society. See further, Kenyon, *Antifederalists*, xciii-xciv.

[103] Dahl, *Preface to Democratic Theory*, chap. 1. See Franz Neumann's essay advocating a union of "pluralistic social structure" with increased "administrative power" as the antidote to the "deadweight of the separation of powers doctrine" so that administration might become "the major instrument of social change." Montesquieu, *Spirit of Laws*, lxiv. Burns, *Deadlock*, 204 ff. Very influential in establishing this conception of the executive-group axis as the new form of democracy in America was Pendleton Herring, *The Politics of Democracy* (New York: W. W. Norton & Company, 1940), 300-304, 309, 325-329, 379-390. David B. Truman, "The American System in Crisis," *Political Science Quarterly*, 74 (December 1959), 481-497, offers a description of leadership that is more pluralistic than the monistic, national ideal found in Herring, de Grazia and Burns.

of the argument in No. 51 will show. The functional theory of the separation of powers evolved out of the English Civil War to counter the theory of the balanced constitution.[104] It was essential to the republicans' efforts to destroy traditional society. They opposed rigid social stratification based upon ranks ordained by government as an "artificial" aristocracy. For this reason *all restraints upon governmental power had to be built into the constitutional order* and not on the neo-feudal residue of corporations, churches, guilds, great titled families, and the like. This was the basic point of their difference with Hobbes who prescribed a restraining power external to what Madison called society or the community.[105] His model of the upright and independent legislator strategically situated to moderate the conflicts of interests in society depended wholly upon the theory that powers must be functionally separated. This doctrine was prominent among the theories held by American revolutionaries in 1776. Here it was expected to have a major effect very different from what its eighteenth century proponents expected in England. There it linked the rising middle class with the executive while permitting an evolutionary alteration of the theory of the balanced constitution.[106] In America it would permit the rising commercial and manufacturing interests to participate continuously in legislation while cutting them off from the assistance of "corruption" as it was practiced in Britain through the exercise of the royal prerogative. The American president would depend for "political exaltation" on "personal merit alone." He would "stand in need, therefore, of being controuled [sic], as well as supported."[107] The agrarian majority would be assured for decades to come that legislation would be enacted without an analog to the corruption of Parliament.

The thrust of Madison's theory is that the stability of the political system depends chiefly upon the stability of the legislature. In a republic the executive is limited in so far as he cannot intervene decisively in the redistribution of legislative power among interests in order to give preference to one over others. This theory was a manifestation of the general republican preference for society con-

[104] M. J. C. Vile, *Constitutionalism and the Separation of Powers* (Oxford, England: At the Clarendon Press, 1967), 53-75.

[105] *The Federalist*, 339 (No. 51).

[106] Vile, *Constitutionalism*, 99.

[107] *Writings*, III, 108.

sisting of a competitive meritocracy. The future expansion of the population would be rapid, and notably towards the South and West in Madison's judgment, but its basic composition would not change immediately.[108] The constitutional provisions for apportionment would insure that, as rapidly as they appeared, new interests would gain entry into the legislature and participate in the fundamental republican function—legislation. This provision would institute an empire of laws, not of men, even in the face of the contingencies of change. His complementary theory of legislative equilibrium rooted in the realities of sectionalism was not generic to republican theory but unique to American conditions. Its rejection almost certainly doomed Madison's theory of legislative stability to failure and thrust the burden of adjusting the conflict more upon the president than I believe Madison originally intended.

Madison's theory that the stability of the American republic would depend upon a constitutional superstructure of representation to modify the social power of conflicting interests bears little resemblance to the pluralists' political universe. This is so because, above all, Madison understood the widespread American objection to the political consequences of Hume's correction of Harrington's doctrine that power follows property. Here was a clear recognition that a constitution cannot permanently curb the dynamics of social change as long as public power is the instrument for simultaneously creating new forces in a society and waging political warfare between old and new. Our early republicans had grave reservations about the capacity of a republic to survive a "gifted political entrepreneur,"[109] manipulating the support of an uninformed electorate and mediating the struggle of groups standing between the individual and the state. Indeed, Madison's republican ideology was an explicit repudiation of the unarticulated Burkean premise underlying the pluralist theory of social restraints. Republicans sought to free the individual from the constricting embrace of traditional social structures which the modern pluralists have revived in slightly revised form. They seek to insulate the individual from a political world which, it is alleged, he neither understands nor controls. This protection is a reaction against the ideal of personal independence which was the very foundation of American repub-

108 *Ibid.*, III, 404-405.
109 Dahl, *Who Governs?* (New Haven, Conn.: Yale University Press, 1960), 7.

licanism.[110] The extension of this ideal into the constitutional order was the bedrock of Madison's theory of factional control.

Madison differed from today's pluralists in at least one other fundamental respect. He believed public power and private influence are distinctly different. Like Hobbes, he believed that there "never was a government without force."[111] Furthermore, within "all governments there is a power which is capable of oppressive exercise. . . . Make the number as great as you please, the impartiality [of those who rule] will not be increased."[112] Madison and his fellow republicans differed from Hobbes, however, because he insisted on treating the consent of the governed and the unity of the state as necessary fictions while ascribing to the state a real unity of arms to enforce the law. Madison agreed with the republicans that, in an ultimate test of power, it is neither constitutional restraints nor public opinion, but a popular militia which is the "solution to the first problem of politics."[113] He certainly did not believe that the superstructure of representation, the embodiment of public opinion in a democracy, eliminates force from public authority.

Madisonian republicans and modern pluralists, alike, turned away from Hobbes, but their rejection of this common philosophical protagonist yields a false identification of the two and blinds us to the real meaning of the Tenth *Federalist*. American pluralists owe their principal intellectual debt, I believe, to Arthur F. Bentley and John Dewey. Bentley reduced the essential characteristic of gov-

---

[110] Yehoshua Arieli, *Individualism and Nationalism in American Ideology* (Baltimore: Penguin Books, 1966), 179-206. Contrast with the widely shared view that plural social groups provide a sounder basis of representation: "Distinctions of race, class, economic groupings, and other *fixed social determinants,* are politicized." de Grazia, *Public and Republic,* 204 (emphasis added). The anti-individualist (and democratic) manifestations of pluralist representation are explicit. *Ibid.,* 240 ff. See also, Robert G. Dixon, *Democratic Representation* (Oxford, England: Oxford University Press, 1968), who understands Dahl and de Grazia to be supporters of new "institutions of representation to better serve the needs of pluralist reality that has replaced the direct democracy excesses of past decades. . . ," 52; see his erroneous assertion that Madison opposed large legislative districts, 40-42.

[111] *Writings,* III, 108.

[112] *Ibid.,* IV, 122.

[113] Robert A. Dahl and Charles E. Lindblom, *Politics, Economics and Welfare* (New York: Harper & Row, 1953, 1963), 273. For Madison's view read *The Federalist,* Nos. 43 and 46; also, *Writings,* III, 238, 278-284, 454; V, 193-196. Madison accepted the republican doctrine that a democratized militia is the only safe form to be given the ultimate coercive power of government.

ernment from force to pressure and converted interests into groups
known positively only by their activity. Government is "stated" as
the "functioning of groups."[114] Dewey, although he explicitly rejected European pluralism, also denied the distinctively coercive
power of government and substituted the group for the individual
as the bearer of rights.[115] The work of the "state," Dewey asserted,
is "integration and consolidation," serving merely as "an instrumentality for promoting and protecting other and more voluntary forms
of association." Therefore, its "supremacy" approximates the activity of those who "in producing [music] are doing what is intrinsically worthwhile."[116] Government merely harmonizes the socially
fundamental activities of private groups in a community integrated
by shared values.

It is precisely this reduction of force into pressure, the subordination of the individual to the group, and the transformation of government into the harmonizer rather than the creator of social conflict that renders the pluralists' interpretation of the Tenth *Federalist* unintelligible to its author. Bentley, Dewey, Dahl, and Truman
have drained from Madison's understanding of political life any
reason for believing that a constitutional superstructure is an essential restraint upon the art and will of political entrepreneurs. The
pluralists' conception of power is critical to this development. It is
a pretense which renders philosophy suspect and defenseless as
mere ideology.

It may be more suggestive than definitive to say that the origins
of contemporary pluralism are to be found in Bentley and Dewey,
but it is clear that they are not supplied by Madison.[117] To say this

114 *The Process of Government* (Chicago: University of Chicago Press, 1908;
Cambridge, Mass.: Harvard University Press, Belknap Press, 1967), 181-222,
258, 434-446, 456.

115 *The Public and Its Problems* (New York: Henry Holt & Co., 1927), 73,
87. He defined law as no more coercive than the banks which "confine the
flow of a stream." *Ibid.*, 54.

116 *Reconstruction in Philosophy* (New York: Henry Holt & Co., 1920;
Boston: Beacon Press, 1957), 202-203. See also Dewey, *Democracy and Education* (New York: Macmillan Company, 1916; The Free Press, 1966), 81-89.
Because "a democratic society repudiates the principle of external authority, it
must find a substitute in voluntary disposition and interests. . . ." *Ibid.*, 87.

117 I venture to say that even Calhoun provides little foundation for modern
pluralism, despite a suggestion that it is he, rather than Madison, who understands the modern view of group politics. Ralph Lerner, "Calhoun's New
Science of Politics," *American Political Science Review*, 57 (December 1963),

is to point to some basic discontinuities in the history of American political thought.

918-932. Calhoun's concurrent majority enjoyed a brief vogue as the foundation of pluralism until Dahl turned Madison into its chief theorist. See Peter Drucker, "A Key to American Politics; Calhoun's Pluralism," *Review of Politics*, 10 (October 1948), 412-426; Margaret L. Coit, "Calhoun and the Downfall of States Rights," *Virginia Quarterly Review*, 28 (Spring 1952), 191-208; and Charles M. Wiltsie, *John C. Calhoun, Sectionalist, 1840-1850* (Indianapolis: Bobbs-Merrill Company, 1951), 426. The fact is that Calhoun, like Madison, was a constitutionalist whose fundamental premises Dahl has denied. See Vile, *Constitutionalism*, 303-314. Calhoun, in truth, denied Dahl's conclusion by asserting that modernization in a democracy accelerates social diversity and inequality to the point where intolerable tensions erupt in civil war. John C. Calhoun, *Works*, ed. Richard K. Cralle (6 vols.; New York: D. Appleton, 1853-56), I, 40-43.

The Political Psychology of
The Federalist

Daniel W. Howe

HE *Federalist Papers* are often treated as a kind of secular scripture,
an authoritative statement of how American political institutions
work or should work. Even assuming that the authors—Alexander
Hamilton, James Madison, and John Jay—shared the passion for fame
they understood so well, they must have succeeded ·here beyond their
wildest dreams. Today, lawyers cite *The Federalist* in their briefs. Conservatives have treated it as the embodiment of traditional wisdom; liberals
have found in it the origins of broker-state pluralism. Most of the
scholarship dealing with *The Federalist* has been written by political
scientists, theorists, or commentators whose concerns lead them to
inquire into the enduring validity of the papers. Sometimes their judgments are critical but, even then, are based on the assumption that the
papers should be evaluated by the standard of their present relevance.[1]
This article is written from the standpoint of intellectual history. It does
not seek an accurate description of the American polity, or a normative
statement of values we should try to live up to, but an understanding of a
document in the context of its age. To extend the metaphor of secular
scripture, I propose to locate *The Federalist* in what biblical scholars call its
Sitz im Leben, its original setting in life. As Rudolph Bultmann showed in
his great works on the New Testament, scriptures need to be related to

Mr. Howe is chair of the Department of History at the University of California,
Los Angeles. He wishes to thank the John Simon Guggenheim Memorial
Foundation and the University of California for their support during the preparation of this article, and the following scholars for their helpful comments and
criticisms: Joyce Appleby, Richard Beeman, Ruth Bloch, Norman Fiering, J. R.
Pole, Robert A. Rutland, and Gordon S. Wood.
[1] Canonization of *The Federalist* began early; Thomas Jefferson prescribed it as a
required text at the newly founded University of Virginia. What I call the
"scriptural" approach to *The Federalist* has produced some superb scholarship—for
example, Martin Diamond, "The Federalist, 1787-1788," in Leo Strauss and
Joseph Cropsey, eds., *The History of Political Philosophy* (Chicago, 1972), 631-651,
and Gottfried Dietze, *The Federalist: A Classic on Federalism and Free Government*
(Baltimore, 1960). Those who criticize *The Federalist* in terms of its present
validity include Robert A. Dahl in *A Preface to Democratic Theory* (Chicago, 1956);
James MacGregor Burns in *The Deadlock of Democracy: Four-Party Politics in
America* (Englewood Cliffs, N.J., 1963); and Morton White in *The Philosophy of the
American Revolution* (New York, 1978).

their own world view before we can accurately assess what timeless truths they may convey to us.

Recent scholarship has demonstrated the importance of the intellectual conventions of an age in defining an author's intentions. This essay addresses what J.G.A. Pocock terms "the politics of language"—that is, the study of how the vocabulary and assumptions of an intellectual paradigm can be put to political use.[2] Only by examining the theory of eighteenth-century faculty psychology can we discover the original meaning and context of such crucial terms as "interest," "balance," "reason," "passion," and "virtue" in *The Federalist*.

The authors of *The Federalist* were practical men, writing under intense pressures, with a strong sense of the campaign strategy they were pursuing. They submerged their individual differences in the collective *persona* of Publius, who for our purposes may be treated as a single author.[3] Since faculty psychology was a widely shared set of assumptions, it was natural for Publius to employ it. We may infer that Publius advocated adoption of the Constitution in the terms he did not only because he believed in a certain model of human nature but also because he expected that model would make for an effective presentation. The particular version of faculty psychology that Publius employed influenced both his substantive arguments (his political science) and his techniques of persuasion (his rhetoric).[4]

FACULTY PSYCHOLOGY

Probably every reader of *The Federalist* has noticed that its arguments are based on ideas about universal human nature. These ideas form a coherent model. But no one has identified the sources of this model or analyzed how Publius used it in defining his audience and constructing his case. Most interpreters of Publius have presented only a partial picture of his model of human nature. Some have considered him a pessimist in the tradition of Thomas Hobbes and John Calvin, emphasizing the need to

[2] J.G.A. Pocock, *Politics, Language and Time: Essays on Political Thought and History* (New York, 1971), 19; cf. Quentin Skinner, "Some Problems in the Analysis of Political Thought and Action," *Political Theory*, II (1974), 277-303.

[3] Even those who have thought they detected differences between Madison's Publius and Hamilton's have not claimed that these extended to his psychology. See Alpheus Thomas Mason, "The Federalist—A Split Personality," *American Historical Review*, LVII (1952), 625-643.

[4] For more on the rhetoric of Publius see Albert Furtwangler, *The Authority of Publius: A Reading of the Federalist Papers* (Ithaca, N.Y., 1984); Forrest McDonald, "The Rhetoric of Alexander Hamilton," *Modern Age*, XXV (1981), 114-124; Robert Lee Silvey, "Language, Politics and *The Federalist*: A Linguistic Approach to Interpretation" (Ph.D. diss., City University of New York, 1982); and Donald Rolland Wagner, "The Extended Republic of *The Federalist*: An Examination of Publius' Rhetoric" (Ph.D. diss., University of Georgia, 1979).

impose control on the evil passions of man.[5] More often, Publius has been treated as a proto-liberal, concerned with men pursuing their own interests, sometimes rationally calculated, in a system more amoral than immoral.[6] Most recently, scholars have sometimes treated Publius as a classical republican who believed in the possibility of virtue in human affairs.[7] All these interpretations can be synthesized within the paradigm of the faculty psychology Publius employed, which found places in human nature for passion, interest, and virtue.

The word "faculty," like the word "facility," is derived from the Latin for "power." "What is a power but the ability or faculty of doing a thing?" asks Publius, rhetorically (33:3).[8] Faculty psychology, in ancient, medieval, or modern times, is the study of the human powers. From Pythagoras, Plato, Aristotle, and the Stoics onward, human nature has been sorted out into different powers, some shared with plants, some with animals, and some— the rational and moral powers—with God. The medieval scholastics elaborated the system and the Protestant reformers retained it. John Locke and other philosophers of the Enlightenment modified the tradition but carried it on. In the form Publius inherited, faculty psychology was hierarchical. It treated human nature as including all the components of "the great chain of being" from mere existence to animation, sensation, and rationality. Mankind lived in a "middle state," part of nature yet above

---

[5] For example, Benjamin F. Wright, "*The Federalist* on the Nature of Political Man," *Ethics*, LIX (1949), 1-31, and Richard Hofstadter, *The American Political Tradition and the Men Who Made It* (New York, 1948), 3-17. For recent arguments that Publius is in the tradition of Hobbes see George Mace, *Locke, Hobbes, and the Federalist Papers* (Carbondale, Ill., 1979); or of Calvin see John Patrick Diggins, *The Lost Soul of American Politics: Virtue, Self-Interest, and the Foundations of Liberalism* (New York, 1984).

[6] The scholarly literature (stemming from Charles Beard and Harold Laski) treating Publius as a proto-liberal pluralist is so large that it has a historiography of its own; see Paul F. Bourke, "The Pluralist Reading of James Madison's Tenth *Federalist*," *Perspectives in American History*, IX (1975), 271-295.

[7] Gordon S. Wood argues that Publius retained a concern with virtue in government even while transcending classical political theory in other ways (*The Creation of the American Republic, 1776-1787* [Chapel Hill, N.C., 1969], 505, 606-615). Garry Wills emphasizes Publius's concern for virtue even more (*Explaining America: The Federalist* [Garden City, N.Y., 1981]). See also two articles by Jean Yarbrough: "Representation and Republicanism: Two Views," *Publius*, IX (1979), 77-98, and "Republicanism Reconsidered: Some Thoughts on the Foundation and Preservation of the American Republic," *Review of Politics*, XLI (1979), 61-95.

[8] There are so many editions of *The Federalist* in circulation that I have chosen to cite it by number and paragraph, separated by a colon. I use the edition by Jacob E. Cooke (Middletown, Conn., 1961), which has the most complete scholarly apparatus, along with Thomas S. Engeman *et al.*, eds., *The Federalist Concordance* (Middletown, Conn., 1980), which is keyed to it. I have modernized spelling and punctuation.

it—both body and spirit, animal and divine, neither all good nor all evil.[9]

All systems of faculty psychology are essentially teleological, since the faculties are defined in terms of their purpose. As the moral philosopher Francis Hutcheson explained it, divine providence so designed the human faculties that "they form a machine, most accurately subservient to the necessities, convenience, and happiness of a rational system."[10] When a person allowed certain faculties to get out of control, he was perverting the divinely intended harmony of the system. Earlier generations had synthesized faculty psychology with Christianity, identifying the perverse misuse of God-given faculties with sin. Human passions (or affections, as they were also termed) were legitimate faculties in their place, but there was a standing danger that they might be indulged or followed inordinately. Archbishop Thomas Cranmer had expressed it in his Litany: "From all inordinate and sinful affections, . . . Good Lord, deliver us." The conventional theological formulation held that the proper supremacy of reason among the faculties had been jeopardized by the corruption of human nature in the Fall. As John Milton wrote in *Paradise Lost,*

> Reason in man obscured, or not obeyed,
> Immediately inordinate desires
> And upstart passions catch the government
> From reason, and to servitude reduce
> Man till then free . . .[11]

In his studies at Princeton, Madison had been exposed to the same Calvinist tradition as Milton, in which both freedom and virtue were equated with the supremacy of rationality.

The influence of psychology on political theory and rhetoric was facilitated in the eighteenth century because all three subjects were often

[9] See H. M. Gardiner *et al., Feeling and Emotion: A History of Theories* (New York, 1937), 89-118; Perry Miller, *The New England Mind: The Seventeenth Century* (Cambridge, Mass., 1939), 239-279; William T. Costello, *The Scholastic Curriculum at Early Seventeenth-Century Cambridge* (Cambridge, Mass., 1958), 94-97; and Norman Fiering, *Moral Philosophy at Seventeenth-Century Harvard: A Discipline in Transition* (Chapel Hill, N.C., 1981), chaps. 3 and 4. For the application of faculty psychology to literature and philosophy see Arthur O. Lovejoy, *The Great Chain of Being: A Study of the History of an Idea* (Cambridge, Mass., 1936), and E.M.W. Tillyard, *The Elizabethan World Picture* (New York, 1944). The concept of psychological "faculties" does not lack defenders even today: see Jerry A. Fodor, *The Modularity of Mind: An Essay on Faculty Psychology* (Cambridge, Mass., 1983).

[10] Francis Hutcheson, *An Essay on the Nature and Conduct of the Passions and Affections . . .* (1742), ed. Paul McReynolds (Gainesville, Fla., 1969), 183 (emphasis deleted and capitalization modernized).

[11] *The Book of Common Prayer* (1549), "Litany and Suffrages"; *Paradise Lost,* Bk. 12, lines 86-90. See J. Rodney Fulcher, "Puritans and the Passions: The Faculty Psychology in American Puritanism," *Journal of the Behavioral Sciences,* IX (1973), 123-139.

treated at the time in connection with the enormous intellectual structure called moral philosophy, the ancestor of all the modern social sciences as well as of ethical theory and epistemology as we know them.[12] This philosophical connection gave to eighteenth-century psychology and political economy their strongly normative coloration. The interlocking relationships among various disciplines within moral philosophy made it all the easier for Publius to base on his concepts of applied psychology both his ideas about good government and his techniques for persuading men to adopt it.

Eighteenth-century science was taxonomic in its preoccupations, and the faculty psychologists of the time struggled toward greater precision and debated definitions. The powers of man were arranged in a kind of natural history of the mind by a series of Enlightenment moral philosophers beginning with the earl of Shaftesbury. In the elaborate system developed by Thomas Reid, the human faculties were classified as "mechanical," "animal" (called "sensitive" by Aristotelians), and "rational." The mechanical powers were involuntary reflexes. The animal or sensitive powers were physical appetites (hunger and sex), instinctive desires (like gregariousness), and—most important for Publius—the "passions" or "affections," which we would call the emotions. The rational powers included both conscience (called the "moral sense" by many writers) and prudence, or self-interest.[13]

Reid's system was followed by a large and distinguished school, including the Scottish evangelical cleric and moral philosopher John Witherspoon, who emigrated to America to become president of Princeton, a signer of the Declaration of Independence, and the teacher of James Madison. Not that the influence of this form of faculty psychology has to be traced through personal connections: it was common intellectual property in the eighteenth century, and both Madison and Hamilton (who had been educated at Anglican King's College) employed it in *The Federalist*.[14] Madison and Hamilton did not need to confer about whether

[12] Rhetoric had a history of its own going back to the medieval *trivium*, but in the 18th century a "new rhetoric" appeared, associated with moral philosophy, particularly in Scotland. Adam Smith lectured on rhetoric while holding the chair of moral philosophy at Glasgow; Hugh Blair, the age's most widely read writer on rhetoric, was strongly influenced by Scottish moral philosophy. Other writers bridging the two disciplines included George Campbell and Lord Kames. See Gladys Bryson, *Man and Society: The Scottish Inquiry of the Eighteenth Century* (Princeton, N.J., 1945); Daniel Walker Howe, *The Unitarian Conscience: Harvard Moral Philosophy, 1805-1861* (Cambridge, Mass., 1970); Wilbur Samuel Howell, *Eighteenth-Century British Logic and Rhetoric* (Princeton, N.J., 1971); and Drew R. McCoy, *The Elusive Republic: Political Economy in Jeffersonian America* (Chapel Hill, N.C., 1980).

[13] Thomas Reid, "Essays on the Active Powers of Man" (1788), in William Hamilton, ed., *The Works of Thomas Reid*, 6th ed. (Edinburgh, 1863), II, 543, 551, 572, 579.

[14] At the time Madison and Hamilton were writing *The Federalist*, the last

to accept the conventions of faculty psychology; these were presuppositions of their argument. But it is a mark of their successful collaboration that they both resorted to faculty psychology with such eloquence and power in the construction of their case.

The version of faculty psychology formulated by Reid and adapted by Publius to his own purposes had two distinctive characteristics. The first of these was the degree of rationality accorded to self-interest. This contrasted sharply with the faculty psychology of the medieval scholastics and Protestant reformers, who had treated motives of self-regard (or self-love) as "passions." The second distinguishing mark of this school was that the moral sense was considered a rational faculty, in contrast with the opinion of eminent critics such as Hutcheson, David Hume, and Adam Smith (all of them Scots like Reid and Witherspoon), who held that the moral sense was an affection, that is, an emotion.[15] We know that Publius took several of his arguments—notably the one showing the advantages of large republics over small ones—from Hume. But when it came to the fundamentals of human nature, Publius stood by the more conventional outlook typified by Reid. Hume's view of human motivation as entirely passionate, exemplified in his dictum that "reason is, and ought only to be the slave of the passions," challenged traditional faculty psychology and did not lend itself to Publius's purposes.[16]

Of central importance to Publius's strategy was his treatment of the motives of self-interest. "Interest" for Publius, and for eighteenth-century writers in general, was not yet simply equated with economic interest but meant self-regarding motivation broadly understood. At the same time,

---

volume of the definitive redaction of Reid's lectures (cited above) was just being published. I have not determined whether either of them had access to it, but the faculty psychology they drew on was a pattern of thought with which they and their readers were well familiar, not a paraphrase or transcription of any single book.

[15] Scholars have rightly emphasized Publius's debt to Scottish writers; see esp. Douglass Adair, "That Politics May Be Reduced to a Science: David Hume, James Madison, and the Tenth *Federalist,*" *Huntington Library Quarterly,* XX (1957), 343-360; Roy Branson, "James Madison and the Scottish Enlightenment," *Journal of the History of Ideas,* XL (1979), 235-250; and Wills, *Explaining America.* In doing so, however, they have sometimes created the misleading impression that all Scottish philosophers thought alike. For a corrective see Daniel Walker Howe, "European Sources of Political Ideas in Jeffersonian America," *Reviews in American History,* X (Dec. 1982), 28-44.

[16] David Hume, "A Treatise of Human Nature: Being an Attempt to Introduce the Experimental Method of Reasoning into Moral Subjects," in *The Philosophical Works* (London, 1886), II, 195. On Madison's use of Hume see Adair, "Politics Reduced to a Science," *Huntington Lib. Qtly.,* XX (1957), 343-360; Geoffrey Marshall, "David Hume and Political Skepticism," *Philosophical Quarterly,* IV (1954), 247-257; and Theodore Draper, "Hume and Madison: The Secrets of Federalist Paper No. 10," *Encounter,* LVIII (Feb. 1982), 34-47. Unlike Madison's Publius, Hamilton's Publius openly acknowledged his use of Hume (*Federalist,* 85:14).

Publius fully recognized that "it is a general principle of human nature that a man will be interested in whatever he possesses" (71:1), especially his material possessions. Albert O. Hirschman has shown how, in the course of the eighteenth century, certain self-regarding motives such as avarice and ambition, which had previously been classified as "passions," came to be grouped into a new category called "interests" and ranked as rational rather than sensitive powers, even though they still retained some of the characteristics associated with passions.[17] Eighteenth-century faculty psychology was a discipline in flux, Publius knew (37:6). He took remarkable advantage of this transitional moment in the history of ideas. He treated self-interest as an intermediate motive, sometimes partial, short-term, and passionate (in the derogatory sense of "selfish passions" [20:21]), but capable of being collective, long-range, and rational. Short-term self-interest he identified with the Articles of Confederation and with his adversaries; long-term self-interest he allied with reason, virtue, and the Constitution.

By his use of faculty psychology Publius placed his arguments in the context of Enlightenment behavioral science. Throughout *The Federalist* appeal is made to immutable scientific laws of human behavior illustrated by historical examples and confirmed by the Americans' own experiment in free government (16:1, 22:13, and *passim*).[18] But the strategy also connected Publius with an even larger context. This was the classical, medieval, and modern tradition identifying liberty with order. Faculty psychology had always taught that the liberty of the individual's will required preventing any faculty from disturbing the harmony of the mind (especially any passion from usurping the authority of reason). Publius made use of the paradigm to present his case for guarding political liberty with social order. In both systems, parts were subordinated to the welfare of the whole, balances were struck between conflicting motives, and order was based on a rational hierarchy.

THE HIERARCHY OF MOTIVES

The faculty psychology employed by Publius posited a definite sequence of rightful precedence among conscious motives: first reason, then prudence (or self-interest), then passion.[19] The tragedy inherent in the

[17] Albert O. Hirschman, *The Passions and the Interests: Political Arguments for Capitalism before Its Triumph* (Princeton, N.J., 1977).

[18] On this context see Merle Curti, *Human Nature in American Thought: A History* (Madison, Wis., 1980), esp. 5-7, 88-91, 107-112, as well as H. Trevor Colbourn, *The Lamp of Experience: Whig History and the Intellectual Origins of the American Revolution* (Chapel Hill, N.C., 1965). All in all, *The Federalist* is one of the masterpieces of what Henry F. May has called "The Moderate Enlightenment" in *The Enlightenment in America* (New York, 1976).

[19] James P. Scanlan first sorted out Publius's treatment of human motives into

human condition was such, however, that these motives varied inversely in power: passion was the strongest and reason the weakest. Alexander Pope, who summed up so much of the conventional wisdom of the age, declared, "The ruling passion conquers reason still."[20] Upon this model of human nature Publius based his political philosophy. "Why has government been instituted at all?" asked Hamilton's Publius. "Because the passions of men will not conform to the dictates of reason and justice without constraint" (15:12). Madison's Publius agreed: "What is government itself but the greatest of all reflections on human nature? If men were angels, no government would be necessary" (51:4).

The juxtaposition of "reason and justice" was typical of Publius; sometimes he spoke similarly of wisdom and virtue (for example, 2:10). The rational faculty, for Publius as for Reid, was the one that apprehended objective truth, both descriptive and normative (or, as they would have said, "speculative" and "practical"). Yet reason-cum-conscience was but a feeble monarch over the other faculties. If it had might, as it has right, it would rule the world, the great eighteenth-century moralist Joseph Butler had affirmed.[21] Publius put it this way: "There are men who could neither be distressed nor won into a sacrifice of their duty; but this stern virtue is the growth of few soils" (73:1).

Within the category of self-interest, "immediate interests," as Publius called them, "have a more active and imperious control over human conduct than general or remote considerations" (6:9). Consequently, the interests that most resembled passions were stronger than those partaking of the nature of prudential reason. These rules of individual motivation were also applicable to political entities. "The mild voice of reason, pleading the cause of an enlarged and permanent interest, is but too often drowned before public bodies as well as individuals, by the clamors of an impatient avidity for immediate and immoderate gain" (42:9). Distinctions could also be made among the social affections (or passions) in terms of their power. People show less and less emotional attachment to groups as these get progressively larger: "a man is more attached to his family than to his neighborhood, to his neighborhood than to the community," et cetera (17:4). More tragically, "to judge from the history of mankind, we shall be compelled to conclude that the fiery and destructive passions of war reign in the human breast with much more powerful sway than the mild and beneficent sentiments of peace" (34:4).

This psychology gave Publius his basis for discrediting the Articles of Confederation: the Articles relied too much on "the weaker springs of the human character" (34:4). "It was presumed that a sense of their true

---

these three groupings, though he did not connect them with faculty psychology or 18th-century rhetorical theory ("*The Federalist* and Human Nature," *Rev. Politics.* XXI [1959], 657-677).

[20] *Moral Essays*, Epistle III, line 153.

[21] Joseph Butler, *Five Sermons Preached at the Rolls Chapel and a Dissertation upon the Nature of Virtue* . . . (1726), ed. Stephen Darwall (Indianapolis, Ind., 1983), 40.

interests, and a regard to the dictates of good faith, would be found sufficient pledges for the punctual performance of the duty of the members to the federal head. The experiment has, however, demonstrated that this expectation was ill-founded and illusory" (23:7-8). As usual, history confirmed the precepts of moral philosophy.

Yet the same psychology that taught the statesman that political institutions must take account of the perversity of human nature posed a great problem for the political advocate. How could one persuade the public to adopt the institutions it so sorely needed? Some eighteenth-century rhetorical theorists, such as the highly regarded Scot Hugh Blair, openly advised the judicious invocation of the passions in persuasive expression.[22] Yet Publius does not invoke them; indeed, he deplores them. "It is the reason of the public alone that ought to control and regulate the government," writes Madison-Publius. "The passions ought to be controlled and regulated by the government" (49:10). His own rhetoric is coldly and carefully rationalistic, as in the famous Number 10, where he argues on the basis of a sequence of dual alternatives to create an impression of impeccable deductive logic. Sometimes Publius reasons from "axioms," as in Number 23; elsewhere he prefers an inductive approach citing the "lessons of history," as in Number 20. Throughout, the reader Publius addresses is "an impartial and judicious examiner," one who is "dispassionate and discerning" (61:1).

Norman Fiering has described the eighteenth century as the time of an intellectual revolution in which reason was displaced from supremacy by "the lowly and dangerous passions."[23] The sentimentalist school of moral philosophy already mentioned challenged the rational nature of the moral sense; rhetoricians like Blair legitimated the passions; religious pietists and evangelicals demanded an awakening of holy affections; the subversive psychology of Hume, like that of Hobbes earlier, attributed all human motivation to passion, denying even the possibility of rational control. This growing acceptance of the affections or passions was alien to Publius; if it was a revolution, he was a counterrevolutionary. To him, the passions were dangerous. Like the Old Lights who opposed the Great Awakening, Publius distrusted "enthusiasm" (1:5, 46:3, 83:18). He judged policy questions by whether they conduce to the supremacy of reason, rejecting a proposal to call frequent constitutional conventions because "the *passions*, therefore, not the *reason*, of the public would sit in judgment" (49:10). He deplored the formation of political parties because they appealed to passion rather than reason (50:6).

If Publius was rather old-fashioned in his distrust of passion, he was quite up to date in his techniques for controlling it. While Christian philosophers of earlier times had typically striven to repress undesirable

---

[22] Hugh Blair, *Lectures on Rhetoric and Belles Lettres* (Philadelphia, 1866), 234-264. First published in 1783, this textbook was reprinted many times in America, beginning in Philadelphia in 1784.

[23] Fiering, *Moral Philosophy*, 148.

feelings, the Enlightenment hit upon the technique of balancing them off against each other, "like the antagonist[ic] muscles of the body," in Hutcheson's simile. Even antisocial motives could have their uses in a system making proper use of the principle of countervailing passions.[24] Madison-Publius heartily endorsed "this policy of supplying, by opposite and rival interests, the defect of better motives" (51:5). He summed up the advantages of the separation of political powers in terms of countervailing psychological passions: "Ambition must be made to counteract ambition" (51:4). Hamilton-Publius applied the same psychology when urging the wisdom of making the president eligible for re-election: the temptation to abuse power would be counterbalanced by the desire to stay in office, so that "his avarice might be a guard upon his avarice" (72:5). In *The Federalist*, the Constitution is presented as a marvel of social engineering, based on a sound psychology, that will use human nature to control human nature, among both governors and governed, without requiring recourse to tyrannical coercion.[25]

Publius's rhetoric, like his political science, sought to turn selfishness to advantage. He enlisted prudential motives on the side of reason and virtue, to add "the incitements of self-preservation to the too feeble impulses of duty and sympathy" (29:13). His argument was designed to show that "the safety of the whole is the interest of the whole" (4:11). The crisis of the Revolutionary war had temporarily "repressed the passions most unfriendly to order and concord" (49:7); what was needed now was a new sense of crisis, which would once again ally an enlightened prudence with reason and virtue to overcome passion and petty self-seeking.

While recognizing that it is not easy to know the good, Publius has no doubt that the good does objectively exist (71:2). And for all his disparagement of the strength of rational and virtuous motives, he still assumes they too exist and have a fighting chance to prevail. "As there is a degree of depravity in mankind which requires a certain degree of circumspection and distrust, so there are other qualities in human nature which justify a certain portion of esteem and confidence. Republican government presupposes the existence of these qualities in a higher degree than any other form" (55:9). Publius never goes so far as to embrace utilitarianism; he never actually defines the moral good in terms of collective benefits. But he does argue that a collective prudence can assist and foster virtue. The Constitution, Publius is confident, will provide a setting designed to promote the worthy qualities over the unworthy ones—and, as we shall see, the worthy people over the unworthy ones as well.

[24] Hutcheson, *Essay*, ed. McReynolds, 183. There is a perceptive discussion of this in Hirschman, *Passions and Interests*, 20-31.

[25] See Maynard Smith, "Reason, Passion and Political Freedom in *The Federalist*," *Journal of Politics*, XXII (1960), 525-544.

FACULTY PSYCHOLOGY AND THE POLITICAL ORDER

The analogy between the human mind and the political commonwealth, "in which there are various powers, some that ought to govern and others that ought to be subordinate," is one of the oldest staples of philosophical discourse.[26] It remained as popular with the eighteenth-century "moderns" as it had been with the "ancients"; indeed, the grouping of both psychology and "civil polity" (political theory) under the umbrella of moral philosophy encouraged it. Publius was convinced that groups had dynamics analogous to those of individuals, with the same tragically inverse relation between the legitimacy of motives and their power. "In all very numerous assemblies, of whatever characters composed, passion never fails to wrest the scepter from reason" (55:3), and the more numerous the assembly, "the greater is known to be the ascendancy of passion over reason" (58:14). Once dominated by passion, an assembly became a "mob" (55:3). It was a misfortune that the debate over the Constitution "touches the springs of so many passions and interests" (37:1); so it was all the more essential to keep the discourse on a high level and out of the hands of demagogues.

Publius wanted a system of government that would provide scope for the exercise of the faculties, which he called "liberty," and offer security to retain their fruits, which he called "justice" (for example, 10:6, 8). The faculties of different people were not equally developed; some were more wise and virtuous than others, just as some were more adept at making money. A well-designed system of government should allow men the exercise of their political faculties and favor those whose "fit characters" (10:17) were most politically desirable. "The aim of every political constitution is or ought to be," Publius wrote, "to obtain for rulers, men who possess [the] most wisdom to discern, and [the] most virtue to pursue, the common good of the society"—though he was cautious enough to add, "and in the next place to take the most effectual precautions for keeping them virtuous" (57:3). Publius did not envision a free-for-all like that of the later social Darwinians; he wanted a teleological—that is, purposeful—system designed to favor wisdom and virtue. Of course there would always be struggles, just as there are within the breast of even the upright citizen, but a good constitution would moderate them and influence their outcome.[27]

[26] Quotation from Reid, "Essays," in Hamilton, ed., *Works,* 573, discussing Pythagoras. This analogy had also been prominent in Aristotelian, Thomistic, Renaissance, and Reformation thought. For examples of reasoning by analogy in 18th-century America see Robert H. Wiebe, *The Opening of American Society: From the Adoption of the Constitution to the Eve of Disunion* (New York, 1984), 9.

[27] By no means would all commentators on *The Federalist* agree with this paragraph, but see David F. Epstein, *The Political Theory of the Federalist* (Chicago, 1984); Yarbrough, "Representation and Republicanism," *Publius,* IX (1979), 77-98; and Paul Carson Peterson, "The Political Science of *The Federalist*" (Ph.D. diss., Claremont Graduate School, 1980), 96-99. Wills is inclined to admire

The best example Publius could offer his readers of a wise and virtuous elite was the Constitutional Convention itself. "Without having been awed by power, or influenced by any passions except love for their country, they presented and recommended to the people the plan produced by their joint and very unanimous counsels" (2:10). This is a highly idealized picture of the convention, crafted for rhetorical purposes to illustrate a perfect rationality. ("Love of country" as a good passion will be considered below.) The delegates rose above party and faction to achieve "unanimity," Publius claimed (37:9). That the delegates were actually far from unanimous in endorsing the outcome of their deliberations was irrelevant. The Fathers of the convention occupied a place in Publius's scheme analogous to the semimythic lawgivers of antiquity—Solon, Lycurgus, Romulus (38:1-4)—and required some veneration even before their work was implemented. "Let our gratitude mingle an ejaculation to heaven for the propitious concord which has distinguished the consultations for our political happiness" (20:21), he wrote in a rare expression of religious devotion. As a benevolent Providence had designed the faculties of (unfallen) man for the welfare of the individual, the wise lawgiver contrived a complex machinery in harmony with (fallen) human nature for the welfare of the community.

Throughout *The Federalist* there runs an implicit analogy between the human mind and the body politic. Just as the mind has faculties of reason (knowing wisdom and virtue), prudence (knowing self-interest), and the passions, so there are in society a small natural aristocracy of wisdom and virtue, a larger group of prudent men capable of understanding their enlightened self-interest, and the turbulent masses, who are typically motivated by passion and immediate advantage. Publius recognized a certain correlation between the development of the faculties and social class. A man whose station in life "leads to extensive inquiry and information" would be able to rise above "the momentary humors or dispositions which may happen to prevail in particular parts of the society" and make a good political leader (35:10). Artisans, on the other hand, "are sensible that their habits in life have not been such as to give them those acquired endowments, without which in a deliberative assembly the greatest natural abilities are for the most part useless," and would tend to elect better-educated merchants and professional men as their political representatives (35:6). This elitism will come as no surprise in the light of what we have learned about patterns of deference in eighteenth-century American political culture.[28] Although Publius was probably not writing

---

Publius's dedication to virtuous leadership (*Explaining America,* 268-270), while Wood detects an element of class hypocrisy in it, even while stressing that the Constitution and the theory of popular sovereignty invented to justify it were later put to democratic use (*Creation of the Republic,* 471-508).

[28] See J. R. Pole, "Historians and the Problem of Early American Democracy," *AHR,* LXVII (1962), 626-646. Locke, too, believed in the "differential rationality"

for an audience of artisans, he claimed that artisans would agree with him and credited them with sense. He noted that "there are strong minds in every walk of life that will rise superior to the disadvantages of situation" but felt that "occasional instances of this sort" did not invalidate the general rule (36:1).

"The idea of an actual representation of all classes of the people by persons of each class is altogether visionary," Publius insisted. Most political representatives in the new government would and should be large landholders, merchants, or professional men (35:6-11). If a single social group could be identified as impartial, it was the professionals, who were not tied to any particular property interest as the landowners and merchants were (35:7). The short-sighted masses were not likely to look after the general interests of society as well as these elite groups. To be sure, "the people commonly *intend* the PUBLIC GOOD," Hamilton-Publius granted. "But their good sense would despise the adulator, who should pretend that they always *reason right* about the *means* of promoting it" (71:2). Madison-Publius, enumerating examples of "wicked" legislation in Number 10, cited only instances that, in their eighteenth-century context, favored the have-nots against the haves: paper money, an abolition of debt, an equal division of property (10:22). It was all to the good that only a few farsighted "speculative" men would pay attention to the affairs of the new national government, while the "feelings" of the average citizens were occupied with the mundane affairs of their particular states (17:8). Federal tax policy was a subject Publius considered particularly well entrusted to a small group of "inquisitive and enlightened statesmen" that did not attempt to mirror the diverse composition of society (36:5; cf. 35:5, 10).

Publius defined his audience as consisting of "the candid and judicious part of the community" (36:17). Yet he was not engaged in an academic inquiry; he was an advocate, a campaigner. He had to combine rationality with motivation in order to persuade effectively. He found the key to his rhetorical problem in eighteenth-century faculty psychology, in the concept of enlightened self-interest. Bishop Butler had taught that the conscience could enlist the aid of prudence to help it control the passions. By the latter part of the century this had become a standard technique for strengthening the motive to rationality in human behavior.[29] Publius, for all his pessimism about the weakness of unaided reason, was convinced that a well-designed constitution could make rational and moral use of self-interested motives. Before this constitution could be implemented, however, the public would have to be persuaded that it was not only just but also in their own true interest.

Publius credits his audience with being members of the wise and virtuous elite. But he does not appeal only to disinterested motives. He is

---

of the social classes, according to C. B. Macpherson, *The Political Theory of Possessive Individualism: Hobbes to Locke* (Oxford, 1962), 230-238.

[29] W. E. Gladstone, ed., *The Works of Joseph Butler* (Oxford, 1896), I, 97-98; Hirschman, *Passions and Interests*, 43.

eager to demonstrate how the proposed Constitution can be of tangible benefit to various economic interests (see especially Numbers 4, 11, 12, and 13) as well as to "the prosperity of commerce" in general (12:2) and, in the largest sense, to all who have an interest in "the effects of good government" (37:5). There are, then, two audiences implied for his presentation: the direct audience of dispassionate inquirers and the larger, indirect audience capable of enlightened self-interest. Even if most members of the direct audience already supported the Constitution, *The Federalist* serves a campaign function. The indirect audience will be enlisted in the cause (presumably by the readers) in order to help control the passionate multitude. Although Publius does not make it explicit, there is an analogy with the cooperation he foresees in Congress between the disinterested professional men and the representatives of the great landed and mercantile interests (36:1). This interpretation, derived from internal analysis of *The Federalist,* is supported by what we know from other sources about the conduct of eighteenth-century electioneering. Robert H. Wiebe describes it thus: "The gentry addressed their speeches and pamphlets, rich with learned allusions and first principles, to one another, not to the people, who would have to receive their instruction from others closer to them in the hierarchy. The art of persuasion centered around the conversion of a secondary tier of gentlemen."[30]

Against the rationalistic and elitist appeal of *The Federalist,* the Antifederalists seem to have employed a rhetorical strategy of their own. They concurred in the faculty psychology's estimate of the weakness of human nature, perhaps even more consistently than Publius did: they refused to believe in the ability of even an elite few to follow the guidance of wisdom and virtue. If there was any hope of overcoming evil, it lay in the common sense and feeling of the common man, which they addressed.[31] Publius complained that the Antifederalists' rhetoric suggested "an intention to mislead the people by alarming their passions, rather than to convince them by arguments addressed to their understandings" (24:8). To their distrust of any officeholders Publius replied that "the supposition of universal venality in human nature is little less an error in political reasoning that the supposition of universal rectitude" (76:10). If supporters of the Constitution were willing to trust the rulers, its opponents (according to Publius) placed too much faith in the masses who were

[30] Wiebe, *Opening of American Society,* 40. Clinton Rossiter comments that *The Federalist* served as "a kind of debater's handbook in Virginia and New York" during the ratification campaign; see his "Introduction" to *The Federalist Papers* (New York, 1961), xi.

[31] See Cecelia M. Kenyon, "Men of Little Faith: The Anti-Federalists on the Nature of Representative Government," *William and Mary Quarterly,* 3d Ser., XII (1955), 3-43; Lois J. Einhorn, "Basic Assumptions in the Virginia Ratification Debates: Patrick Henry vs. James Madison on the Nature of Man and Reason," *Southern Speech Communication Journal,* XLVI (1981), 237-340; and Curti, *Human Nature,* 112-116.

ruled—"but a nation of philosophers is as little to be expected as the philosophical race of kings wished for by Plato" (49:6).

FACULTY PSYCHOLOGY AND MIXED GOVERNMENT

The Constitution, most recent scholarship agrees, broke with the venerable tradition of "mixed government" that balanced monarchy, aristocracy, and democracy, by rejecting the European practice of representing different orders of society in the legislative body.[32] Publius boasted that Americans had discovered the secret of "unmixed" republican government (14:4). Yet Madison, Hamilton, and the other framers of the Constitution also respected many of the values of mixed government as these had been passed down from ancient, medieval, and early modern political writers—such values as stability, balance, and the supremacy of common over partial interests (63:9-12).[33] Could these be salvaged in the new polity? Publius's creative response to this problem was to argue that the proposed Constitution conferred the procedural benefits of mixed government without its social inequities. The elements it mixed were no longer monarchy, aristocracy, and democracy, but executive, legislative, and judicial. Checks and balances among these branches were "powerful means by which the excellencies of republican government may be retained and its imperfections lessened or avoided" (9:3). Publius provided a kind of mixed government with a psychological rather than a social justification. Through faculty psychology, he described what he saw as the advantages of mixed government that the Constitution would preserve, even for a country without a European social structure.

For Publius, the art of governing was a decision-making process analogous to that of an individual; the institutions of government were analogous to the individual's faculties of mind. In both cases, reaching a right decision required a careful act of balancing. Precipitate, ill-advised

[32] For example, Diamond, "Federalist," in Strauss and Cropsey, eds., *History of Political Philosophy*, 642-643; Wood, *Creation of the Republic*, 553-652, 602-615; Wills, *Explaining America*, 104-107; and George W. Carey, "Separation of Powers and the Madisonian Model: A Reply to the Critics," *American Political Science Review*, LXXII (1978), 151-164. The European theorists of mixed government who were most relevant to the Americans are described in Z. S. Fink, *The Classical Republicans: An Essay in the Recovery of a Pattern of Thought in Seventeenth-Century England* (Evanston, Ill., 1945); Caroline Robbins, *The Eighteenth-Century Commonwealthman* ... (Cambridge, Mass., 1959); and J.G.A. Pocock, *The Machiavellian Moment: Florentine Political Thought and the Atlantic Republican Tradition* (Princeton, N.J., 1975).

[33] See Gilbert Chinard, "Polybius and the American Constitution," *Jour. Hist. Ideas*, I (1940), 38-58; Paul Eidelberg, *The Philosophy of the American Constitution: A Reinterpretation of the Intentions of the Founding Fathers* (New York, 1968); and Paul Peterson, "The Meaning of Republicanism in *The Federalist*," *Publius*, IX (1979), 43-75.

action was to be avoided; long-term prudence and morally right actions were desired. An individual did well to act from more than one motive, since reason was weak and the passions were unreliable. In politics, then, a measure of institutional complexity was advantageous, since "the oftener a measure is brought under examination, the greater the diversity in the situations of those who are to examine it, the less must be the danger of those errors which flow from want of due deliberation, or of those missteps which proceed from the contagion of some common passion or interest" (73:8). The intention was not so much to frustrate particular social groups as to provide the right mix of motives. A well-structured government would resemble the balanced mind of a wise person, while a poorly constructed government, like a weak mind, was prone to fall under the tyranny of some capricious passion (63:7).

In Publius's argument there is a marked, if implicit, tendency for the different branches of government to mirror particular faculties of mind. As we have seen, Publius's rhetoric sorted his potential audience into three horizontally defined, hierarchically ordered groups—rational men, self-interested men, and passionate men—and addressed only the first two. But these groupings would not do for the structure of government, since all the functions of government should be rational. Therefore Publius invoked a different set of faculties in explaining the structure of government, a grouping equally legitimated by psychological tradition but "vertical" rather than "horizontal" in conception. The psychological faculties to which the branches of government correspond were all aspects of reason: "understanding," "will," and "conscience." These conventional terms of faculty psychology provide keys to Publius's exposition of the powers of the legislative, executive, and judicial branches of government, respectively. In an individual, the understanding received and processed information, the will took action, and the conscience or moral sense judged right from wrong. In the system of faculty psychology Publius was following, all were supposed to operate rationally and resist the "impulse of passion."[34]

The judiciary, in Publius's scheme, was the conscience of the body politic, interpreting its common moral standards (84:4). Not only did Publius invest this branch with the power of judicial review of legislation (78:10-12), he even asserted that judges had a power to correct the operation of "unjust and partial laws," whether or not these were unconstitutional (78:19). For one who doubted the virtue of mankind in general, Publius reposed astonishing confidence in that of judges—but this was because of the faculty they exercised, which was at once the most reliable and the weakest. "The judiciary, from the nature of its functions, will always be the least dangerous" branch of government, he explained; it has "neither force nor will, but merely judgment" (78:7). The executive branch partook of the qualities of the "will," which explains why "energy"

[34] Reid, "Essays," in Hamilton, ed., *Works*, II, 533-536 (reason v. passion), 537-541 (understanding and will), 589-592 (conscience).

and "unity" were so essential to it, even in a republican system (70:1, 7). As the will ought to implement fixed principles and the conclusions of the understanding in Reid's psychology, so the executive ought to enforce only the laws enacted by the legislature. In identifying the executive with the will, Publius was not making the presidency supreme but emphasizing its rationality and subordination to the law.

The understanding was the faculty through which the individual acquired knowledge of the world, and Publius conceived of the legislative branch as the one through which the government acquired "a due knowledge of the interests of its constituents" (56:1). "Interests," as we know, could be either rational or passionate. The faculty of the understanding included both "rational" and "sensitive" aspects, among the latter being dangerous motives of passion. The legislature likewise had both rational and emotional aspects; indeed, it possessed a weakness for "all the passions which actuate a multitude" (48:5). In traditional faculty psychology the will "had the special task, among others, of controlling the passions lodged in the sensitive appetite."[35] Fortunately, the president, embodiment of the faculty of the will, had a veto over congressional legislation that could prevent "unqualified complaisance to every sudden breeze of passion, or to every transient impulse" (71:2). Within the legislature itself, Publius looked to the Senate to impart more of the rational quality he feared might be deficient in the House of Representatives (62:9). Due to their longer terms, larger constituencies, and indirect method of election, senators would be "more out of the reach of those occasional ill humors or temporary prejudices" to which democratic assemblies are prone (27:2).

Discussions of the ratification of the Constitution usually point out that its proponents wanted a stronger, more energetic government. Yet analyses of *The Federalist* often emphasize the limitations on governmental power it endorses. An understanding of Publius's faculty psychology helps resolve this seeming paradox. The branches of government he wanted to strengthen were ones he associated with the most rationality: the judiciary, the executive, and the Senate; the elements he wanted to limit he associated with narrow self-interest and the passions: the state governments and all popular assemblies, including the House of Representatives. While the national government would express the general welfare, Publius identified the states with partial views (15:14); and when the states became subject to "violences" and "passions," he expected that the federal government "will be more temperate and cool" (3:14, 16).

More important even than one-to-one correspondences between governmental institutions and psychological faculties is Publius's pervasive argument that just as a healthy human mind balances short-, intermediate-, and long-term goals, so should a healthy polity. As the individual possesses powers responding to each of these objectives, so should a commonwealth. This carryover of attitudes derived from faculty psychology into

[35] Fiering, *Moral Philosophy*, 147.

the realm of politics helps explain Publius's misgivings about majority rule. Hamilton-Publius and Madison-Publius agreed that only the "deliberate sense of the community," not every numerical majority, was entitled to prevail (71:2; 63:7). *The Federalist* quoted Jefferson with approval: "An *elective despotism* was not the government we fought for" (48:8). As Publius presented the matter, it was not so much the people themselves who were being limited as their passions, nor any aristocracy that was being empowered, but the qualities of virtue and wisdom. From our point of view, of course, there resulted a compromise of majority rule. "The people," Publius warned, "stimulated by some irregular passion, or some illicit advantage, or misled by the artful misrepresentations of interested men, may call for measures which they themselves will afterwards be the most ready to lament and condemn." Enforced delay was the appropriate remedy, "until reason, justice, and truth can regain their authority over the public mind" (63:7). Publius wanted calm and thorough deliberation; if this should occasionally prevent a good law from passing—a possibility he admitted (62:6)—so be it. "Every institution calculated to restrain the excess of law-making, and to keep things in the same state, in which they may happen to be at any given period, [is] much more likely to do good than harm" (73:9).

FACULTIES AND FACTIONS

Publius's analogy between psychology and political science extends to his treatment of factions, which has been the most interesting aspect of *The Federalist* to twentieth-century commentators. Madison's Publius defines faction as the collective expression of "some common impulse of passion, or of interest, adverse to the rights of other citizens, or to the permanent and aggregate interests of the community" (10:2). (Hamilton's Publius uses the word in the same sense.) "The latent causes of faction are thus sown in the nature of man" (10:7). "Faction" was not a value-free concept for Publius; a faction was by definition evil. The idea of inevitable evil in human nature did not surprise men who were well acquainted with the Christian doctrine of original sin and its secularized versions in eighteenth-century faculty psychology.

Although Publius mentions only "passion" and "interest" in his initial definition of faction, his discussion also refers to "opinion" as a source of faction. It would appear that even the faculty of reason, being "fallible" and prone to corruption by "self-love," can give rise to factions of a theological or ideological nature (10:6-7).[36] More often, however, factions stem from passions—writ large and inflamed by ambitious demagogues. In

[36] Hume, whom Madison-Publius was following here, made it clearer that factions could derive from "principle," that is, reason, as well as from "interest" and "affection." See Adair, "Politics Reduced to a Science," *Huntington Lib. Qtly.,* XX (1957), 343-360.

this collective form, passions become more dangerous than ever: "a spirit of faction" can lead men "into improprieties and excesses for which they would blush in a private capacity," pointed out Hamilton's Publius (15:12). "But the most common and durable source of factions," continues Number 10, derives from motives of self-interest, specifically, "the various and unequal distribution of property" (10:7)—an inequality that has already been traced to "the diversity in the faculties of men" (10:6).

Most of the modern analyses of what Publius says about faction have focused on property interests rather than on psychological faculties. One consequence of this has been that little attention has been devoted to the important connection between faction and passion.[37] All factions, even those that do not originally derive from passion, have the effect of unduly strengthening passion over reason. Partisanship comes to substitute for independent judgment (49:10, 50:6). Publius has a horror of "the arts of men who flatter [the people's] prejudices to betray their interests" (71:2). The demagogue is a sinister figure in *The Federalist*. He lurks ready to exploit the passions and create a faction. He is the natural enemy of the statesman, who has virtue and the common interest at heart.[38] The Constitution, Publius argues, will provide a context within which the statesman can defeat the demagogue. Fittingly, he both begins and ends his series of letters with warnings against demagogues (1:5, 85:15).

Most factions arise from the class of motives called interests, intermediate between passion and reason. There is a legitimate scope for the rational pursuit of one's interest but only in a broad context. Eighteenth-century moral philosophy invariably drew a distinction between benevolent and malevolent passions; implicit in *The Federalist* is an analogous distinction between benevolent and malevolent interests.[39] The Constitution will be in the true common interest. By definition, the interests that produce faction are adverse to the common interest; therefore they are narrow and evil. Publius also condemns motives of short-term interest that are closely akin to passion (for example, 3:15, 42:11). Narrow or short-sighted interests are not ennobled in Publius's presentation; a good government will "break and control" their violence (10:1), not be the vehicle for their expression and rule.[40] Such interests pose a particular problem in the legislative branch. One of the reasons why that branch is so prone to the evils of factionalism, Publius argues, is that legislators are constantly cast in the dual role of advocates and judges in the causes

[37] Epstein corrects this in *Political Theory of the Federalist*, 68-72.

[38] Madison may well have intended the figure of the demagogue to correspond to his rival Patrick Henry, providing another instance of how Publius used the conventions and vocabulary of the age to his political purposes.

[39] Cf. Scanlan's distinctions between "true" and "immediate" interests and between "common" and "personal" interests ("*Federalist* and Human Nature," *Rev. Politics*, XXI [1959], 663, 664).

[40] Wills, for all that his work has been justly criticized, is absolutely right to stress this point (*Explaining America*, 201-207).

WILLIAM AND MARY QUARTERLY

before them (10:8). Their self-interest corrupts what should ideally be a disinterested pursuit of the common good.

Publius maintains that the Constitution will be able to limit "the violence of faction" (10:1) in three different ways. The first is suppression by military force. This is discussed by Hamilton's Publius in Number 9 and Madison's Publius in Number 43; it shows how seriously they took the threat that factions posed to legitimate government. However, there were two alternatives to force in dealing with factions. Both alternatives derived from models developed in faculty psychology; they are described primarily in Madison's Number 10. One of these methods was to enlighten the quality of the self-interest involved, in this case by refining it through the medium of representatives who would take broader views than their constituents and hence be less susceptible to demagogy and factionalism. Representatives of "enlightened views and virtuous sentiments" would be "superior to local prejudices and to schemes of injustice" (10:21). The other method was to pit factions against each other so that they cancel each other out, just like countervailing passions. Both methods work better in a large republic than a small one, Madison points out, since the larger constituency provides a more effective filter for the talents of representatives and also a larger number of "parties and interests," reducing the chance that any one of them will be able to oppress the rest (10:20). "In the extent and proper structure of the Union, therefore, we behold a republican remedy for the diseases most incident to republican government," concludes Number 10. The Constitution will be beneficial not only because of its carefully designed structure of checks and balances but also because it creates a large, and therefore stable, republic.

Madison-Publius placed less faith in enlightened representatives to mitigate the evils of faction than in the countervailing effect of other factions (10:20). Hamilton-Publius, though he had much less to say about the principle of countervailing factions, also endorsed it (for example, 26:10). This does not mean that Publius considered factions good, but only that he accepted their inevitability and sought to mitigate their effects. The "policy of supplying, by opposite and rival interests, the defect of better motives, might be traced through the whole system of human affairs, private as well as public," he pointed out, placing his political science in the context of psychology (51:5). Just as passions like ambition could be made to counteract the ambition of others, so could factions neutralize each other's evil—especially if there are enough of them that "you make it less probable that a majority of the whole will have a common motive to invade the rights of other citizens" (10:20). "In the extended republic of the United States, and among the great variety of interests, parties, and sects which it embraces, a coalition of a majority of the whole society could seldom take place on any other principles than those of justice and the general good" (51:10). Justice and the general good were the goals. What looks to twentieth-century eyes like broker-state pluralism was, to Publius's contemporaries, subsumed within a familiar scheme of eighteenth-century moral philosophy, the principle of countervailing passions.[41]

Of course, factions could be majorities as well as minorities (10:2). Indeed, the factions Publius was chiefly worried about were the ones that commanded a majority; minority factions were easily limited. But "when a majority is included in a faction, the form of popular government . . . enables it to sacrifice to its ruling passion or interest both the public good and the rights of other citizens" (10:11). Thus Publius's desire to limit faction was related to his desire to limit majority rule, as well as to his desire to control passion and affirm the supremacy of reason and virtue— qualities that Publius assumed were "comprehensible only by a natural elite," as Gordon S. Wood has observed.[42]

POLITICAL REPRESENTATION AND VIRTUE

Having seen how Publius constructed his political science on the model of his faculty psychology, it becomes apparent why political representation should identify an elite of wisdom and virtue. The governors of a polity should be analogous to the higher faculties of an individual. A "republic," which Publius defined as a representative democracy (39:4), was preferable to a direct democracy because of the superior quality of the representatives as compared with the people as a whole. A system of representation could "refine and enlarge the public views by passing them through the medium of a chosen body of citizens whose wisdom may best discern the true interest of their country and whose patriotism and love of justice will be least likely to sacrifice it to temporary or partial considerations" (10:16).

As means of achieving the proper ends of representation, Publius considered large constituencies superior to small ones. They provided a larger pool of talent from which to recruit "fit characters" (10:17), and those who represented large constituencies "will be less apt to be tainted by the spirit of faction" (27:2), since they would have more varied interests to serve. Publius accordingly argued that the national government would successfully recruit "the best men in the country" for its elective offices (3:8). It has been observed that Publius was adapting what had been considered the traditional advantages of "virtual" representation (the wisdom of the representative) to a political situation where only "actual"

[41] Thanks to Adair and Wills, Publius's indebtedness to David Hume is well recognized. However, the principle of countervailing passions was widely accepted by 18th-century moral philosophers, nor was its application to factions peculiar to Hume; Adam Ferguson, for example, endorsed it in *An Essay on the History of Civil Society* (Edinburgh, 1767). See also Arthur O. Lovejoy, *Reflections on Human Nature* (Baltimore, 1961), 37-66.

[42] Wood, *Creation of the Republic,* 610.

representation was practiced.[43] This may be compared with his adaptation of the advantages of "mixed government" to a situation where no legally recognized estates of the realm existed.

Representation, according to Publius, was a refining process in which higher faculties (that is, motives and abilities) were sorted out, concentrated, and strengthened. Indirect elections performed this function better than direct ones. This is why he reposed special confidence in senators and presidents, who would be elected indirectly (64:4, 68:8). Repeatedly, we have seen how Publius put his faith in complexity as a means of inhibiting passion, both in individuals and in groups. Government is divided into state and federal authorities along one axis, and into legislative, executive, and judicial branches along another. Society itself is beneficially complex, being composed of many interests, as is human nature with its varied faculties. By the same token, complex elections are safer and more effective than simple ones. Publius also believed long terms better than short ones, since experience is so valuable (53:9), and—within limits—fewer representatives better than more, since smaller bodies are more selective and partake less of the "infirmities incident to collective meetings of the people." The danger in large assemblies is that "ignorance will be the dupe of cunning and passion the slave of sophistry" (58:14).

Can one go so far as to argue that Publius believed it was the responsibility of government to promote virtue in general, or that the Constitution would make Americans a more virtuous people than they already were? Some commentators have thought so, though they have had to draw on evidence outside *The Federalist* to make their case.[44] It is clear that Publius tried to enlighten self-interest and enlist it on the side of reason rather than on the side of passion. It is also clear that he wished to reward the qualities of *public* virtue and wisdom with political power. However, he has little to say about the highest faculties of *private* morality and speculative reason because the specific task before him did not require discussing them. No one then felt that ratification of the Constitution touched upon the educational or religious institutions of the country, for example. Publius's letters are single-minded in their focus on the campaign for ratification. They are masterpieces of special pleading. Accordingly, it is a mistake to try to extract from them a complete political theory or a comprehensive statement of the relation between government and virtue such as one finds in Aristotle.

In spite of the knowledge and admiration of the ancients that Publius and his generation possessed, the classical conception of civic virtue was

[43] See Yarbrough, "Representation and Republicanism," *Publius*, IX (1979), 77-98.

[44] For example, Ralph Ketcham, "Party and Leadership in Madison's Conception of the Presidency," *Quarterly Journal of the Library of Congress*, XXXVII (1980), 258. Martin Diamond addressed this elusive question in a series of articles reaching slightly varying conclusions; see esp. "Ethics and Politics: The American Way," In Robert H. Horwitz, ed., *The Moral Foundations of the American Republic* (Charlottesville, Va., 1977), 39-72.

alien to *The Federalist*. The ancient philosophers, particularly Aristotle, held that human nature could only be properly fulfilled through political participation; the truly good man had to be politically active.[45] Publius acknowledged no such imperative. In Number 10 he defended representation, which the ancient world never developed, as superior to participatory self-government. Life under the Articles of Confederation had left him disillusioned with widespread political participation and American public virtue; that is why American political institutions needed to be restructured to strengthen the hand of virtue. The experience of public service would no doubt benefit the representatives themselves, by broadening their views, so one could argue that Aristotelian virtue was still relevant to them. And, after all, Aristotle never expected his standards of civic virtue to apply to any but a small elite. But it would not have served Publius's purposes to pursue this subject explicitly, and he did not. He was more interested in proving the utility of the representatives to the government than the utility of the government to the representatives.

The neoclassical school of Machiavelli, Harrington, and Montesquieu developed its own elaborate tradition of civic virtue as a precondition for free government.[46] The Antifederalists drew heavily upon these writers, especially Montesquieu, to argue that republican virtue would be corrupted in a large and centralized polity.[47] Publius's relationship to the neoclassical tradition was more ambiguous. What this tradition had to say about balanced government as a safeguard against faction and demagogy was still relevant to him, but its conception of the sentiment of patriotism played only a very small role in *The Federalist*. "Virtue," as Publius used the word, was not simply equivalent to love of country, as it was for Montesquieu; it was a moral quality that included a sense of honor and justice. Still less did it resemble Machiavelli's *virtù*, the dynamic force of character that can reshape a polity. Publius's "virtue" was a quality of rational insight, not a sentiment or feeling.[48] When Publius had occasion to mention patriotism or love of country, he clearly labeled it a "passion" (2:10; cf. p. 496 above), and he treated it as something quite different from virtue. He assumed that such sentiments of loyalty would attach themselves more firmly to the states than to the new national government (17:4). To the extent that national institutional traditions could be cultivated, adding the sentiments of habit to other motives for obedience to government, that would of course be all to the good (27:4; 49:6).

[45] *Politics*, Bk. I, chap. 2.
[46] Besides Pocock, *Machiavellian Moment*, see also Yarbrough, "Republicanism Reconsidered," *Rev. Politics*, XLI (1979), esp. 70-75.
[47] See Herbert J. Storing, "Introduction," in *The Complete Anti-Federalist* (Chicago, 1981), I, 15-23, 46-47, 73.
[48] Wills treats Publius as an ethical sentimentalist but presents scarcely any evidence to justify this (*Explaining America*, 185-192). His argument that Thomas Jefferson was an ethical sentimentalist, presented in *Inventing America: Jefferson's Declaration of Independence* (Garden City, N.Y., 1978), remains highly controversial.

Both the classical and the neoclassical schools had based republican institutions on civic virtue. Publius retained the connection between republicanism and virtue, but he considered civic virtue a rarity and used the paradigm of faculty psychology to prove it. He went on to justify the Constitution as a system that could enhance the power of public virtue, drawing on principles developed by moral philosophers for enhancing the power of virtue in the individual.

At the end, Publius recurs to his rhetorical strategy and points with modest pride to his success. "I have addressed myself purely to your judgments and have studiously avoided those asperities which are too apt to disgrace political disputants" (85:4). He has proved at least some parts of his case with the conclusiveness "of mathematical demonstration" (85:14). The tone has been in keeping with Publius's objectives. He writes on behalf of a small group of lawgivers to a minority audience, through whom he hopes to reach a decisive segment of the political community. He writes to demonstrate that the Constitution will approve itself to the enlightened self-interest of practical men. He writes of society through psychological metaphors, showing that the Constitution will control the disorders and instabilities he terms "passion."

The argument itself is at one with the rhetoric in which it is couched. An elite of wise and virtuous lawgivers have constructed a system to pool and maximize society's small store of reason and morality. The system depends on mingling these scarce resources with baser but more plentiful ones to achieve a serviceable alloy of mixed motives. Not even the most complex, carefully devised electoral system can guarantee the best rulers, so "enlightened statesmen will not always be at the helm" (10:9). But if a virtuous person is unavailable, a selfish one may do, provided his self-interest coincides with social utility. Hence the emphasis on broadening and enlightening self-interest. Even some of the passions can be put to work: "the love of fame," for example, "the ruling passion of the noblest minds" (72:4), can motivate a statesman to deeds of public service.[49] Like Jonathan Edwards, Publius considered true virtue a rare and precious metal; unlike Edwards, he would accept counterfeit tender if it could purchase social advantage.

Publius was actually more typical of eighteenth-century writers on moral philosophy than was Edwards. Publius was writing in a tradition stemming from Bernard Mandeville's once-startling dictum: "Private vices by the dextrous management of a skillful politician may be turned into public benefits."[50] A far greater moral philosopher, Adam Smith, had

[49] See Lovejoy, *Reflections on Human Nature*, 153-193, and Gerald Stourzh, *Alexander Hamilton and the Idea of Republican Government* (Stanford, Calif., 1970), 95-106.

[50] Bernard Mandeville, *The Fable of the Bees; or, Private Vices, Public Benefits*, ed. Douglas Garman (London, 1934), 230; see Nathan Rosenberg, "Mandeville and Laissez-Faire," *Jour. Hist. Ideas*, XXIV (1963), 183-196.

applied this principle to the economic realm. A well-designed economic system, Smith taught, would take advantage of the psychological fact that individuals pursue wealth for themselves under the (mistaken) impression that it will bring them happiness. It was a providence of God that men's very selfishness and foolishness could serve society. Like Publius, Smith never confused socially useful behavior with genuine virtue.[51] Another contemporary of Publius, Benjamin Franklin, also sought to enlist selfishness in the public cause by teaching that honesty was the best policy.

Given the task of advocating the Constitution in the America of 1787-1788, the way Publius made use of faculty psychology was brilliant. It provided a much more effective vocabulary than the old-fashioned one of "mixed government" that John Adams persisted in using.[52] It put Publius in the mainstream of eighteenth-century educated opinion and spoke directly to the cultural values of the gentry class who constituted his primary audience, while avoiding any direct challenge to more democratic values that would have been tactically unwise. But while working within the intellectual and social conventions of his age, Publius adapted faculty psychology to an original and distinctive message. Despite its pessimism about human nature, his message is ultimately optimistic. Reason can, if aided by wisely contrived institutions, reassert its rightful supremacy. Chaos and coercion are not the only alternatives. *E pluribus unum* was the paradoxical motto of the Union: "out of many, one." Publius had argued just such a set of paradoxes: out of passion, reason; out of complex procedures, a just result; out of selfishness, the common good.

Publius's use of faculty psychology, originally designed for the circumstances of 1787-1788, also helps account for the lasting popularity of *The Federalist* and its conversion into secular scripture. Membership in Publius's audience is not restricted by time and place; it can be achieved by anyone who wants it. Conceptualizing his readers in terms of their faculties, Publius addresses the better nature within each complex person. He wins us over by insisting that he will not (*sic!*) flatter us, that he trusts our judgment because we too understand the weakness of human nature (63:7). Whatever selfishness may characterize most people, "no partial motive, no particular interest, no pride of opinion, no temporary passion or prejudice" must influence us. Each of us can act "according to the best of his conscience and understanding" (85:5). "What more could be desired by an enlightened and reasonable people?" (77:11).

[51] See A. L. Macfie, *The Individual in Society: Papers on Adam Smith* (London, 1967), 53-54, 75-81, and Joseph Cropsey, "Adam Smith and Political Philosophy," in Andrew S. Skinner and Thomas Wilson, eds., *Essays on Adam Smith* (Oxford, 1975), 132-153.

[52] See Wood, *Creation of the Republic*, 567-587; John R. Howe, Jr., *The Changing Political Thought of John Adams* (Princeton, N.J., 1966); and Joyce Appleby, "The New Republican Synthesis and the Changing Political Ideas of John Adams," *American Quarterly*, XXV (1973), 578-595.

The Madisonian Moment

Jack N. Rakove†

No period in the evolution of American political culture exerts a more potent hold over our historical imagination than the era of independence and constitution-writing that is sometimes portentously described as "The Founding." Two explanations immediately suggest why this is the case. The first (and more obvious) emphasizes the partly symbolic yet highly functional role that the Revolutionary era has always played in providing Americans with both a political vocabulary and shared notions of national identity. The deliberations of that era provide the one set of consensually accepted reference points to whose authority we can appeal even as we mangle the nuances and complexities of what the Founders thought and did or criticize the consequences of the decisions they imposed on posterity. The various ways in which later generations have recalled The Founding have thus themselves become so essential an element of American political culture that one can legitimately ask why a society not known for its deference to patriarchal authority feels a continuing need to invoke the wisdom of the constitutional Fathers.[1] But at another level, the appeal of the Founders must rest, more subtly, on some authentic and substantive quality of their thought and experience. To the historian, perhaps the most engaging aspect of that experience is the extraordinary self-consciousness with which the Revolutionaries—in 1776 and in 1787—grasped the novelty of the opportunity that independence had forced upon them. As Hannah Arendt once observed, it was the participants' "ever-repeated insistence that nothing comparable in grandeur and significance had ever happened in the whole recorded history of mankind" that accounts for "the enormous pathos which we find in both the American and the French revolutions." One finds it in the note of exultation with which John Adams concluded his 1776 pamphlet, *Thoughts on*

---

† A.B. 1968, Haverford College; Ph.D. 1975, Harvard University; Associate Professor of History, Stanford University.
[1] On the general subject of the cultural history of the Constitution, see Michael G. Kammen, A Machine That Would Go of Itself: The Constitution in American Culture (1986).

473

Government—"You and I, my dear friend, have been sent into life at a time when the greatest lawgivers of antiquity would have wished to live"—and again a decade later in the oft-quoted introductory paragraph of the first *Federalist* essay, when Alexander Hamilton observed that "It has been frequently remarked that it seems to have been reserved to the people of this country . . . to decide the truly important question, whether societies of men are really capable of establishing good government from reflection and choice, or whether they are forever destined to depend for their political constitutions on accident and force."[2]

None of the Founders better illustrates the dual dimensions of this appeal—the symbolic and the experiential—than James Madison. Although his reputation long languished in the shadow of his friend, Thomas Jefferson, Madison is now regarded "as the most profound, original, and far-seeing among all his peers."[3] His essays in *The Federalist* mark the principal point of entry for all scholarly inquiries into the general theory of the Constitution, overshadowing not only Alexander Hamilton's influential but more pointed discussions of executive and judicial power in the later numbers of Publius, but also the debates at the Federal Convention itself. The famous 10th and 51st essays, in particular, enjoy the status of proof-texts. At the same time, the symbolic importance and real influence his writings have attained in the contemporary interpretation of the Constitution accurately reflect Madison's own conviction that his ideas clearly marked a radical break with the received wisdom of his age. No one better exemplified his own boast in *Federalist* 14 that it was the "glory of the people of America" not to have allowed "a blind veneration for antiquity, for custom, or for names, to overrule the suggestions of their own good sense, the knowledge of their own situation, and the lessons of their own experience."[4]

Two considerations help to justify the enormous critical attention that Madison's writings as Publius have commanded. First, as public texts available to the American political nation of 1787-88, the essays may plausibly be said to have reflected either some gen-

---

[2] Hannah Arendt, On Revolution 27 (1963); John Adams, Thoughts on Government (1776), in Robert J. Taylor, ed., 4 Papers of John Adams 92 (1979); Federalist 1 (Hamilton), in Benjamin F. Wright, ed., The Federalist 89 (1961).

[3] Michael Kammen, A Season of Youth: The American Revolution and the Historical Imagination 72 (1976).

[4] Robert A. Rutland, Charles F. Hobson, William E. Rachal, and Frederika Teute, eds., 10 The Papers of James Madison 288 (1977). For facility of citation, all references to Madison's contributions to The Federalist will be made to this work.

eral understanding of the Constitution prevailing at the moment of its adoption—or at least the understanding that one of its major framers hoped its adoption would inculcate among the American political nation. Second, because many of the objections against the Constitution that *The Federalist* set out to answer were drawn from the received authorities of the day, its arguments can be located within the great tradition of liberal political theory to which it made the new republic's most significant contributions. That tradition defines the proper context within which the essays are to be read.[5]

These dual considerations certainly serve the needs of students of political theory, who can read sources selectively; and they may even satisfy that criterion of "originalism"—itself Madisonian—which holds that the only extrinsic sources that can be legitimately applied to fix the original meaning of the Constitution must be public documents available to those whose acts of ratification gave the Constitution its force as supreme law. If our principal interest in The Founding is merely to extract from its voluminous records certain seminal statements to serve as fictive symbols of a pristine original meaning, then endless exegeses of such sacred texts as *The Federalist* and the Declaration of Independence may still be in order. But if our purpose is to understand how Madisonian thought arose in the first place, we cannot presume that a text is authoritative merely because it is public, but must ask instead how well particular expressions of that thought reflected the purposes of its author. From the perspective of the historian, the common tendency to reduce Madison's ongoing efforts to resolve problems of republicanism to his writings as Publius is to rob the experience of "the founding" of much of its meaning. A more serious error still is to treat as writ arguments that Madison himself regarded as problematic. The quest for the historical Madison thus requires relating the familiar arguments of *The Federalist* to the more complex body of ideas and concerns from which they emerged and of which they were only a partial expression.

Arguably it is all the more important to do so at a time when glib calls to return to a "jurisprudence of original intention" have

---

* Under this heading, I would include especially the various essays of the late Martin Diamond, who deserves equal credit with Adair (his colleague at Claremont) for the modern interpretative interest in the arguments of Publius. See especially his essays, The Federalist, 1787-1788, in Leo Strauss and Joseph Cropsey, eds., The History of Political Philosophy 631 (1972); and Democracy and *The Federalist*: A Reconsideration of the Framers' Intent, 53 Am.Pol.Sci.Rev. 52 (1959).

again been heard in the land. Whenever such calls are allowed to rest on crude and fragmentary caricatures of a complex historical reality, we should recognize that it is our own political culture, more than that of "The Founders," which is being exposed.

The classic statements of Madisonian theory are found, of course, in his best known contributions to *The Federalist*: the discussion of the advantages of an extended republic in *Federalist* 10, and the sustained analysis of the theory of separation of powers in essays 47-51. The central arguments of these essays are familiar and can be restated succinctly. In *Federalist* 10, Madison sought to explain why an extended national republic would better secure both "the public good and private rights" against the dangers of majority misrule than could the existing states of the American union. Madison offered two solutions—or rather, hypotheses—to justify the superiority of large over small republics. First, "extend[ing] the sphere" of the polity and thereby multiplying "the distinct parties and interests" which it contains will reduce the risk that factious majorities will be able to unite among the population and act on their impulses. Second, the mechanisms of election and representation will somehow work to bring into the national legislature men "whose enlightened views and virtuous sentiments render them superior to local prejudices and to schemes of injustice." Through these two means—one, in effect, negative, the other positive—Madison professed to find "a republican remedy for the diseases most incident to republican government."[6]

In his discussion of the separation of powers in *Federalist* 47-51, Madison further sought to defend the Constitution against the charge that it had improperly distributed legislative, executive, and judicial powers. The mere constitutional declaration of "the boundaries of these departments" erected only "parchment barriers" against the abuse of power—especially abuse emanating from the legislature, which experience demonstrated was "everywhere extending the sphere of its activity, and drawing all power into its impetuous vortex." Madison dismissed the idea that periodic reviews of the Constitution or appeals to the people could provide adequate correctives. Instead, in the brilliantly drawn defense of the Constitution's checks and balances in essay 51, he concluded that the "auxiliary precautions" of a divided legislature elected by different constituencies for different terms, reinforced by an executive wielding a veto and also enjoying a special relation with the

---

[6] 10 Papers of Madison at 263-270 (cited in note 4).

Senate, would best preserve the constitutional allocation of power by encouraging "ambition . . . to counteract ambition." Further security against usurpation could be found in the division of public power "between two distinct governments," state and national. Notably, however, Madison concluded the entire discussion by evoking the argument of *Federalist* 10, reminding his readers that the most effective cure for the danger of legislative aggrandizement lay in extending the sphere of the republic in order to prevent the "reiterated oppressions of factious majorities."[7]

These brief summaries of Madison's argument barely hint at the nuances of his thought, which have in fact been elaborately studied, criticized, and sometimes simply regurgitated in a host of scholarly commentaries of greater and lesser degrees of originality.[8] Earlier interpretations used *Federalist* 10 either to attest to the self-interested motives of the propertied class for whom Madison presumably spoke, or else to identify Madison as a founding father of pluralism in his "essentially modern grasp of the group character of politics and of the play of organized groups on political institutions."[9] Much recent Madisonian scholarship has instead been dedicated to relating the hypotheses that Madison was proposing to the issues of his own age. One leading theme in the current canon of interpretation stresses the ingenuity with which Madison developed and deployed the insights of David Hume—especially in the essay on "The Idea of a Perfect Commonwealth"—to counter the axioms about republican government that contemporaries associated with "the celebrated Montesquieu." What Madison clearly sought to refute was the conviction that stable republics could endure only in small, relatively homogeneous societies whose citizens possessed similar interests and the self-denying civic virtue required to preserve their form of government against its inherent

---

[7] Id. at 448-454, 456-464, 470-472, 476-480. It is rarely noticed that the argument that "The interest of the man must be connected with the constitutional rights of the place" works best for the federal judiciary, whose life tenure presumably fosters the deepest personal attachment to upholding the authority of their office against the competing claims of the other branches.

[8] The bicentennial has contributed to the resurgence of interest in *The Federalist*. Among the best works on this subject recently published, see especially David F. Epstein, The Political Theory of *The Federalist* (1984); Morton White, Philosophy, *The Federalist*, and the Constitution (1987); the essays collected in Charles R. Kesler, ed., Saving the Revolution: *The Federalist Papers* and The American Founding (1987); and a particularly innovative essay by Daniel W. Howe, The Political Psychology of *The Federalist*, 44 Wm. & Mary Q. 485-509 (1987).

[9] Paul F. Bourke, The Pluralist Reading of James Madison's Tenth *Federalist*, 9 Persp.in Am.Hist. 271-273 (1975).

tendency to decay toward strife and anarchy. By locating "the latent causes of faction" not merely in the diversity of economic interests within any modern society but also in the fallible reason, passions, and opinions of the species, Madison was insisting that a candid recognition of popular vice—as opposed to a naive faith in enduring popular virtue—could be converted into a persuasive defense of the enduring stability of an extended republican regime. In all of this, a far from modest Madison was consciously challenging the errors of the recognized authorities of his age.[10]

As soon as the quest for the historical Madison moves beyond the philosopher-advocate of *The Federalist*, two complementary sets of problems define the major issues in Madisonian scholarship. The first is to trace the evolution of the concerns and ideas that guided Madison during the three-year period (1786-89) in which he led the political movement that brought about the adoption of the Constitution and its first ten amendments. Here the central problem is to reconcile divergences between his public and private positions—or to put the point another way, to set the public defense of the Constitution in *The Federalist* in the context of Madison's prior and private analyses of what he called the "vices of the political system of the United States" and the specific remedies he sought, and often failed, to convince the Federal Convention to adopt.[11] The second set of problems looks beyond the constitutional politics of the late 1780s to the intense partisan conflicts of

---

[10] The great pioneer of this interpretation was the late Douglass Adair. See his two seminal essays, The Tenth Federalist Revisited, and "That Politics May Be Reduced to a Science": David Hume, James Madison, and the Tenth Federalist, reprinted in Trevor Colbourn, ed., Fame and the Founding Fathers: Essays by Douglass Adair 75-106 (1974). Garry Wills, Explaining America: The Federalist (1981) develops Adair's insights in excessive detail. The extent of Madison's reliance on Hume has recently been challenged in Edmund S. Morgan, Safety in Numbers: Madison, Hume, and the Tenth *Federalist*, 49 Huntington Library Q. 95 (1986).

[11] This essay summarizes views I have developed at greater length elsewhere, notably in The Great Compromise: Ideas, Interests, and the Politics of Constitution Making, 44 Wm. & Mary Q. 424-457 (1987); The Structure of Politics at the Accession of George Washington, in Richard Beeman, Stephen Botein, and Edward C. Carter II, eds., Beyond Confederation: Origins of the Constitution and American National Identity 261 (1987); Mr. Meese, Meet Mr. Madison, 258 Atlantic Monthly 77 (Dec. 1986); and with Susan Zlomke, James Madison and the Independent Executive, 17 Presidential Stud.Q. 293-300 (1987). A somewhat different view of Madison is offered in three essays by Lance Banning: James Madison and the Nationalists, 1780-1783, 40 Wm. & Mary Q. 227 (1983); The Hamiltonian Madison: A Reconsideration, 92 Va.Mag.of Hist. & Biog. 3 (1984); and The Practicable Sphere of a Republic: James Madison, the Constitutional Convention, and the Emergence of Revolutionary Federalism, in Beeman et al., eds., Beyond Confederation at 162. Also valuable is Charles F. Hobson, The Negative on State Laws: James Madison, the Constitution, and the Crisis of Republican Government, 36 Wm. & Mary Q. 215-235 (1979).

the 1790s, when the Madison who had written of "curing the mischiefs of faction" in *Federalist* 10 and who had hoped to vest the national government with an absolute veto over all state laws organized the nation's first opposition party and wrote the Virginia Resolutions of 1798.[11]

Madison's arguments about the superiority of large over small republics are perhaps best characterized as predictions or hypotheses remaining to be verified. But his analysis of the problem of faction *within the states* was decidedly empirical and experiential, in the dual sense of lessons drawn from both the evidence of recorded history and the experience of republican government in America since 1776. In his preparations for the Convention, Madison had read widely in the history of ancient and modern confederacies,[12] but the conclusions he drew from that research tended to reinforce lessons derived more directly from his service in the Continental Congress (1780-83) and the Virginia legislature (1784-86). His analysis was predicated on the inability of either the citizens or the legislators of the states to pursue measures that would respect the general interests of the union, the true public good of their own communities, or the rights of minorities and individuals. In the political context of the mid-1780s, when the amendment of the Articles of Confederation and the reform of the state constitutions written at the time of independence were regarded as two separate projects, his great achievement was to explain the failings at both levels of government in terms of the shortcomings of state legislators and their constituents. On the one hand, their parochial attitudes and interests demonstrated that "a unanimous and punctual obedience of 13 independent bodies, to the acts of the federal government, ought not to be calculated on." But equally important was Madison's indictment of the character of lawmaking within the states. The "multiplicity," "mutability," and "injustice" of the "vicious legislation" the states had enacted since independence, he concluded, called "into question the fundamental principle of republican Government, that the majority who rule in such Governments are the safest Guardians both of public Good and of private rights." Part of the evil he attributed to the character (or lack of it) of the lawmakers themselves, who typically

---

[11] On this point, which is discussed only peripherally in this essay, see John Zvesper, The Madisonian Systems, 37 West.Pol.Q. 236 (1984).

[12] His notes on his readings are reprinted in Robert A. Rutland, William M.E. Rachal, et. al., eds., 9 Papers of Madison 3-24 (1975); additional notes can be found in 10 Papers of Madison at 273-281 (cited in note 4).

sought office from motives of "ambition" and "personal interest," and only rarely from genuine considerations of "public good." But in Madison's view, "a still more fatal if not more frequent cause" of unjust legislation "lies among the people themselves." Madison's theory of faction sought to explain why this was the case by demonstrating that neither considerations of "public good" nor "respect for character" nor even "religion" could restrain an interested or impassioned majority from improper acts.[14]

This acute diagnosis of the parochial allegiances of state legislators and citizens formed the foundation for the program that Madison hoped to persuade the Federal Convention to adopt. His first and perhaps most important conclusion was that the national government could no longer rely on the voluntary compliance of the states, but had to be empowered to enact, execute, and adjudicate its own laws. In the Convention, this simple yet momentous conclusion was seriously challenged, if at all, only during the brief debate over the New Jersey Plan. But the heart of the Madisonian program lay not in this discovery per se, but in the way in which his observations about the "vices" of state politics influenced his thinking on four major issues: the nature of representation in the extended republic; the demand, closely related to the representation issue, for the apportionment of seats in both houses of a bicameral Congress; the need to enhance the authority of the weaker branches of government, the executive and judiciary, against an overreaching legislature; and most difficult of all, the basis and extent of the supremacy that he clearly hoped the union would henceforth enjoy over the states in the "compound republic" of a federal system. It is under this last heading that Madison's notion of the protection of individual and minority rights is best considered.

Madison's positions on each of these general issues merit separate examination. While a short summary cannot do justice to the many nuances of his thinking, it can at least identify those aspects of his program that appear most problematic not from the perspective of modern theory but rather within the historical context of The Founding itself.

1. *Representation.* The Madisonian image of society was rec-

---

[14] His conclusions were summarized in a memorandum on "The Vices of the Political System of the United States," (from which the quotations in this paragraph are taken) and in three letters written respectively in March-April 1787 to Thomas Jefferson, Edmund Randolph, and George Washington. 9 Papers of Madison at 345-357, 317-322, 368-371, 382-387.

ognizably modern in its acceptance of the multiple and mutable sources of faction; but in his theory of representation, Madison clung to traditional ideals of legislative responsibility that seemingly echo the classic statements of Edmund Burke. While abandoning the insistence that popular virtue was the mortar from which the republic had to be built, Madison still hoped that national legislators would transcend the parochial interests and passions of their electors in order to frame laws and policies embodying a public good representing more than the aggregated preferences of the general population. Madison's aspirations for congressmen thus marked the opposite side of his animus against state legislators, and in this respect, his position can be used—to follow the influential formulation of Gordon S. Wood—to illustrate the social character of the Federalist movement that supported adoption of the Constitution. Out of their aversion to the petty demagogues who controlled the state assemblies, Wood argues, the Federalists of 1787-1788 hoped "to restore a proper share of political influence to those who through their social attributes commanded the respect of the people and who through their enlightenment and education knew the true policy of government." Madison's ideal Congress thus resembled the legislature Burke had envisioned when, in his famous speech to the Bristol electors, he declared that Parliament was not "a congress of ambassadors from different and hostile interests" but described it instead as "a deliberative assembly of one nation, with one interest, that of the whole."[15]

In Georgian Britain, the theory of virtual representation was closely tied to the defense of the malapportionment and limited suffrage that the colonists and their sympathizers in the mother country had denounced before the Revolution. Far from relying on the "corrupt" practices that Americans regarded as the great rot of eighteenth-century British parliamentary politics, Madison's optimal hopes for the inculcation of virtuous representation presupposed the existence of large and equitably apportioned electoral units. He hoped to institute electoral procedures for both houses of

---

[15] Gordon S. Wood, The Creation of the American Republic, 1776-1787, 506-518 (quotation at 508) (1969); the famous passage from Burke's 1774 Speech to the Electors of Bristol is quoted in id. at 175; and see Wood's recent restatement of this theme in Interests and Disinterestedness in the Making of the Constitution, in Beeman et al., eds., Beyond Confederation at 69-109 (cited in note 11). A particularly valuable treatment of Madison's ideas can be found in Robert J. Morgan, Madison's Theory of Representation in the Tenth Federalist, 36 J.Pol. 852-885 (1974), which, title notwithstanding, is not confined to that single essay alone.

Congress that would work to bring men of "enlightened views and virtuous sentiments" into office.[16] In the case of the House of Representatives, Madison and his allies at the Federal Convention argued that the establishment of large constituencies would effectively nullify the improper electoral tactics that localist politicians could exploit. Local demagogues would somehow neutralize each other, while candidates of established reputation and merit would alone be able to fashion district-wide majorities. The larger the electoral unit, the better. Madison was not committed to the idea that representatives should be chosen by electors residing only within individual districts, but was instead willing to experiment with statewide election of delegations or statewide voting for members from particular districts.[17]

It was, however, to the Senate that Madison looked most ardently for the recruitment of a suitably broad-minded and disinterested corps of legislators capable of discerning the true public good. At least as early as 1785, he had seen in the proper composition of the upper house the first and most potent line of defense against the excesses of majoritarian misrule and "vicious legislation."[18] His ideal Senate was to be elected either indirectly or by constituencies so large as to erase any substantive degree of electoral accountability; his ideal senator would serve an extended term of nine years and hopefully not take up office until he reached so mature an age that completion of a single term would exhaust his ambition.[19] Madison's notion of senatorial independence was so radical that it risked ceasing to be a scheme of representation in any meaningful sense of the term.

This image of the Senate thus presupposes serious doubts about how well popularly elected congressmen would withstand the factious popular pressures to which he had found state legislators vulnerable. In a notable speech on June 26, Madison spoke as if he

---

[16] Federalist 10, in 10 Papers of Madison at 269 (cited in note 4).

[17] Rakove, Structure of Politics 269-270 (cited in note 11); on the advantages of large electoral districts, see especially the remarks of James Wilson, George Mason and Madison during the debate of June 6, in Max Farrand, ed., 1 The Records of the Federal Convention of 1787 132-136, 143 (2d rev.ed. 1987).

[18] The clearest statement of this is found in a letter to Caleb Wallace of August 23, 1785, in Robert A. Rutland, William M.E. Rachal, et. al., eds., 8 Papers of Madison 350-351 (1973) (discussing the potential form of a constitution for Kentucky, should it separate from Virginia). In addition, see his interesting comments of October 1788 on the same subject in his Observations on "Draught of a Constitution for Virginia," in Robert A. Rutland, Charles F. Hobson, et. al., eds., 11 Papers of Madison 285-286 (1977).

[19] Speech of June 26 at the Federal Convention, in 10 Papers of Madison at 76-78 (cited in note 4).

did expect the House to succumb, even going so far as to identify
the conditions under which a factious majority might eventually
coalesce made up of "those who will labour under all the hardships
of life, & secretly sigh for a more equal distribution of its blessings"—i.e., property.[20] At some future point in the nation's development, a majority of the enfranchised population might no longer
find themselves "placed above the feelings of indigence." Then a
well constructed Senate would prove especially important to halt-
ing redistributive attacks on existing rights of property—such as
the landed estates of the great planter class to which Madison's
own family belonged. Here as on other occasions in 1787 and 1788,
there can be no doubt that concern with the protection of property
lay at the very center of Madison's anxieties about republican government. At the same time, Madison's image of the House of Representatives often seems to leave it resembling the state legislatures he so much despised. In *The Federalist*, it is true, the need
to counter Antifederalist accusations that an exalted Congress
would be effectively insulated from the concerns of the population
naturally led Madison to emphasize the genuinely representative
qualities of the lower house. Yet when he depicted the likely character of the House as "an assembly of men called for the most part
from pursuits of a private nature, continued in appointment for a
short time, and led by no permanent motive to devote the intervals
of public occupation to a study of the laws, the affairs, and the
comprehensive interests of their country," he explicitly conceded
that at least one chamber might prove vulnerable to the same mutability of policy he had condemned in the states.[21]

To reconstruct Madison's original thinking about the problem
of representation in this way thus suggests that he recognized from
the start that his hopes and expectations were not easily reconciled. There can be no doubt, on the one hand, of his strong attrac-
tion to a Burkean ideal of representative responsibility—to the vision of a legislature composed of disinterested men who could
speak intelligently for the needs and views of their constitutents
but then vote on the basis of some larger notion of public good.
But to make this ideal the core of the Madisonian system—as sev-

---

[20] Id.
[21] From Federalist 62, in id. at 538-539. The authorship of this particular essay has in
the past been a subject of dispute, but the consensus of recent *Federalist* scholarship has
supported the conclusion that authorship is properly assigned to Madison. See, e.g., 10 Papers of Madison at 540. Without ignoring the risk of circularity, one might add that this
essay's discussion of the danger of "mutability in the public councils" has a strongly Madisonian ring.

eral recent commentators have been inclined to do—requires ignoring the extent to which it was compromised by the more realistic and pessimistic view of politics that had driven Madison to espouse it in the first place.[22] For beyond the arithmetical assumptions that supported the prediction that more cosmopolitan legislators could emerge triumphant from large electoral districts, Madison's scheme of popular elections remained little more than a statement of faith. His own ideas as to which electoral procedures were most likely to produce the desired results remained indefinite, and he did not develop an adequate theory of ambition to explain what types of candidates would actually compete for office: virtuous patriots, or lawyers tired of debt chasing. In fact, Madison himself appears to have sensed that his optimistic hopes for securing a virtuous representation had been pegged too high. While waiting for the First Federal Congress to muster a quorum, he reflected that the Antifederalists' "predictions of an anti-democratic operation [in the new government] will be confronted with at least a sufficient number of the features which have marked the state governments."[23]

Equally problematic were his expectations for the Senate. In Madison's original view, the great imperative was to prevent the state legislatures from having any direct share in its election. The logic of his analysis of the problems of the state constitutions suggested that the assemblies could rarely be relied upon to appoint senators who would possess either the nationalist orientation he desired or the will to use the proposed national veto on state laws to any useful extent. "If an election by the people, or thro' any other channel than State Legislatures promised as uncorrupt & impartial a preference of merit," he told the delegates, "there could surely be no necessity for an appointment by those Legislatures."[24] But his hopes for the Senate were undermined by the difficulty of providing a credible or practical alternative to the idea of legislative election, which had the further advantage of maintaining the practice for the Continental Congress, and by his colleagues' apparent conviction that both the adoption of the Constitution and the later avoidance of conflict between national and state govern-

---

[22] For an extreme statement, see Garry Wills, Explaining America: The Federalist (1980).

[23] James Madison to Thomas Jefferson (March 29, 1789), in 12 Papers of Madison at 38. For the potential sources of Madison's discouragement, see Rakove, Structure of Politics at 286-294.

[24] Speech of June 7, 1787 in 10 Papers of Madison at 40 (cited in note 4).

ments required giving the latter some share in the election of the former.

   2. Proportionality. This brief sketch of Madison's ideas of representation should suggest why any attempt to describe his scheme of government as "Madisonian democracy" begs more questions than it answers.[25] The actual basis on which Madison expected legislative majorities to form in Congress remains less than clear. But rather than suggest that majorities would result from a process of bargaining among representatives speaking for the plurality of interests within the larger society, it seems more likely that Madison hoped that the diversity of interests would discourage any majorities from forming until a compelling conception of public good could somehow emerge to transcend the interplay of parochial interests.

   If there was any democratic element in Madison's scheme, it was his conviction that principles of proportional representation should be followed for both houses of Congress. Before the Convention, he decided that this was the "ground-work" upon which all else depended. It was, in fact, his insistence upon this point that best explains why the conflict between large and small states over voting in the Senate preoccupied the delegates for the first seven weeks of debate.[26]

   This commitment to proportional representation in both houses poses two problems. The first involves, again, the elevated function of the Senate. Why was proportional representation in the upper house so crucial if Madison's basic purpose was to convert the Senate into a truly independent chamber of nationally-minded statesmen? If local and state concerns would find their adequate voice in the House, there was no compelling theoretical reason to insist upon proportional voting in the Senate, especially if Madison hoped senators would be chosen by indirect election or through super-districts. Pragmatic calculations were thus probably more important. Madison simply assumed that the large states would approve "the necessary concessions of power" to the union only if proportional voting were instituted in the two houses the new Congress would require because—unlike the existing Continental Con-

---

   [25] For a noteworthy caricature of something called "Madisonian democracy," see Robert H. Bork, Neutral Principles and Some First Amendment Problems, 47 Ind.L.J. 2-3 (1971).
   [26] 9 Papers of Madison at 369, 383 (cited in note 13). See the discussion in Rakove, 44 Wm. & Mary Q. at 429-436 (cited in note 11).

gress—it would have full legislative authority.[27]

The second problem that Madison's commitment to proportionality raises is theoretically more significant because it identifies a fundamental difficulty with his theory of faction. To counter the predictable objection of the small states that any departure from the principle of an equal state vote would leave their constituents at the mercy of the large states, Madison and his allies had to fashion arguments to prove why the small states neither needed nor deserved the privilege of the equal state vote even in one house of Congress. That is exactly what Madison's theory enabled them to do, in two ways. First, by promising to cure the mischiefs of faction, it held out the prospect that all interests would be equally well secured by the virtuous legislators who would henceforth occupy Congress. The small states would admittedly lose influence in the new Congress, but the theory of faction purported to explain why their rights and interests would still be adequately protected. Second, and more important, his analysis of the sources of faction explained why states, as such, did not deserve representation. Implicit in its logic lay the recognition that the states, as political entities, embodied only the fictitious legal personality of all corporations. All states possessed interests (or congeries of interests), but by locating the roots of faction in the attributes of individuals—in their interests, occupations, opinions, passions, and their disparate "faculties"—Madison in effect was arguing that the real constituent elements of the society were people, not corporate entities or territorital units. Moreover, the motives that would lead the small states to cooperate within the Convention would cease to operate once the new government took effect, for their representatives would never vote on the basis of the size of their state but rather to pursue the interests of their constituents. Similarly, one of the most potent arguments that Madison and his allies deployed during the Convention was to defy the spokesmen for the small states to identify a single occasion on which the disparate interests of the three most populous states (Virginia, Pennsylvania, and Massachusetts) could ever lead them to fashion a federal condominium. The small states never effectively countered this argument; the best they could do was to suggest that, after all, the Senate should represent not so much the states as communities but rather the state governments—and all state governments were

---

[27] Madison simply assumed, in short, that "the smaller states must ultimately yield to the predominant will." 9 Papers of Madison at 371, 383.

equal.[28]

Madison's approach worked well so long as the choice lay between representing states as aggregates of population or as corporate units. But the concurrent need to define the exact basis for apportionment (even in one house) threatened the entire theory of faction. Here the critical issue was slavery. From Madison's perspective, the Southern demand to count slaves for purposes of representation had one theoretical advantage: by identifying a deeper conflict that was destined to outlast the ephemeral struggle between small and large states, it demonstrated why the claim for an equal state vote was meretricious. As Madison reminded his colleagues on June 30:

> the states were divided into different interests not by their difference of size, but by other circumstances; the most material of which resulted partly from climate, but principally from the effects of their having or not having slaves. These two causes concurred in forming the great division of interest in the U. States. It did not lie between the large & small States: it lay between the Northern & Southern, and if any defensive power were necessary, it ought to be mutually given to these two interests.

The logical solution, he continued, was to base representation in one house on free population alone, and in the other on total population, slaves included. But given his conviction that the Senate should be given greater powers than the House, a "disequilibrium of interests" would result from any effort to impose a solution along these lines, since one section would be particularly advantaged in the upper house.[29]

Madison's reluctance to convert this suggestion into an actual proposal illustrates the deeper predicament the framers felt when it came to the issue of slavery. Perhaps the best that can be said for Madison's positions on these issues is that they illustrate the difficulty or impossibility of balancing moral embarrassment over the very existence of slavery against the candid recognition that the social systems (and thus arguably the political cultures) of at least five states demanded its preservation. There can be no doubt that Madison abhorred slavery on moral grounds. Early in the Convention, before any question explicitly implicating slavery had

---

[28] These points are discussed far more extensively in Rakove, 44 Wm. & Mary Q. at 424-457 (cited in note 11).

[29] 10 Papers of Madison at 90 (cited in note 4).

yet been broached, he observed that "the mere distinction of color [had been] made . . . a ground of the most oppressive dominion ever exercised by man over man"; near the close of debate, and again in *Federalist* 42, he opposed the continuation of the slave trade until 1808 as "dishonorable to the national character."[30] But moral embarrassment did not prevent Madison from attempting to weave specific protections for sectional interests into the political fabric of the Constitution. He concluded his final speech opposing the Great Compromise by reminding the Convention that "the real difference of interests lay, not between the large & small but between the N. and Southn. States. The institution of slavery & its consequences formed the line of discrimination."[31] Similarly, while agreeing with James Wilson that an election by the "people at large" would provide the "fittest" mode for the appointment of the executive, the fact "that the right of suffrage was much more diffusive in the Northern than the Southern States" led him instead to support the scheme of an electoral college presumably because it would enhance the prospects for the election of Southern candidates.[32] And again, on July 21 he opposed an exclusive Senatorial power over the selection of the judiciary in part because it would "throw the appointments entirely into the hands of the Northern States," thus creating "a perpetual ground of jealousy & discontent" among the Southern states.[33] Finally, Madison explicitly understood that the "republican guarantee" clause would enable the union to assist individual states in the suppression of slave rebellions.[34]

As it happened, of course, the three-fifths rule the Convention adopted to protect Southern interests in the lower house proved less important than the Great Compromise giving each state an equal vote in the Senate, which provided a handier mechanism for preserving the sectional "equilibrium." But in his candid avowal of the gross reality of sectional differences, Madison identified a critical—not to say fatal—flaw in his general theory of faction. Perhaps states did not constitute objective interests deserving representation. But the stark recognition that regional social systems based

---

[30] Id. at 33, 157, 405.

[31] Id. at 102.

[32] Id. at 107-108.

[33] Id. at 111.

[34] See the respective references to this point in the memorandum on the vices of the political system, 9 Papers of Madison at 350-351 (cited in note 13); his speech to the Convention of June 19, in 10 Papers of Madison at 58; and Federalist 43, in 10 Papers of Madison at 415 (cited in note 4).

on slave and free labor had already established great, permanent, and dichotomous sources of conflicting interests in the extended republic could not be readily reconciled with the pluralist imagery of the theory of faction. For what did one see when the United States was described in these terms: a society embracing a "multiplicity of interests," or a nation divided into two great and potentially antagonistic regions whose cultures rested on fundamentally opposed values? And what notion of legislation was more compatible with this image: one that promised protection to all interests, defined principally in terms of the attributes of individuals, yet that would also allow duly constituted majorities to govern? Or one that implied, as the small states had long insisted, that the first task in constructing the new government was to erect specific constitutional defenses for certain broad groupings of states? And what Southern state could possibly allow the national government to exercise a veto "in all cases whatsoever" over its laws, if doing so might yield control over the vital institution of slavery to a potentially hostile majority?

For Madison, then, the institution of slavery served as both an extreme example of the extent to which interested majorities could be driven to deprive fellow men (though not citizens) of their rights,[35] and as a vital minority interest and right that the new Constitution would have to protect not only for it to have any chance of adoption, but also to preserve the union it was meant to embody. In this sense, the theory of faction worked quite well when it came to identifying the specific sources of the distinctive interests, opinions, and passions of the South; by implication, it also explained why the protection of minority rights (of slaveholders) against a potential factious majority (of non-slaveholders) was essential to the aggregate public good (the survival of the union) he hoped the reconstituted government would pursue. Where the theory of faction broke down was in failing to anticipate—or perhaps in anticipating all too well—how the mischiefs of faction could be cured should the question of slavery eventually lead to the coalescence of factious majorities within each of the nation's two gross regional divisions.

3. *Separation of powers.* Nothing better illustrates the pragmatic cast of Madison's mind than his efforts to modify the strict theory of the separation of powers that so many Americans had seemingly imbibed from their reading of "the celebrated Montes-

---

[35] This is the immediate point of the reference to "the mere distinction of colour" in the speech of June 6, in 10 Papers of Madison at 33.

quieu." Privately Madison may have wondered whether there was much to learn from this great French sage; in 1793, he dismissed appeals to both Montesquieu and Locke as "a field of research which is more likely to perplex than to decide."[36] But in 1788, with Antifederalists insisting that the Constitution violated "the political maxim, that the legislative, executive and judiciary departments ought to be separate and distinct," it was impossible to avoid confronting the axiom head on. This Madison first sought to do (in *Federalist* 47) by using the evidence of practices under the British constitution and the American state constitutions to demonstrate both that Montesquieu could not have meant what his popular interpreters claimed he meant, and also that the Americans had already departed from a strict separation of powers, even while espousing a ritualized allegiance to the principle.[37]

Once one moves past Madison's ingenious effort to undermine the Antifederalist appeal, three points deserve mention in any survey of his substantive ideas about the separation of powers. First, those ideas were generated primarily within the context of his critique of state politics, and as such cannot be divorced from his concern with popular faction, even if certain familiar passages in *The Federalist* imply that the central purpose of the separation of powers is to "oblige [the government] to control itself."[38] Second, Madison's own preferred solutions to the problem of protecting the executive and judicial branches from legislative encroachments involved more radical departures from the idea of strict separation than the Constitution itself proposed. Third, while Madison be-

---

[36] Robert A. Rutland, Thomas A. Mason, Jeanne K. Sisson, eds., 15 Papers of Madison 68 (1985).

[37] Federalist 47, in 10 Papers of Madison at 448-454.

[38] Federalist 51, in 10 Papers of Madison at 477. The argument that Madison's theory of separation of powers was rooted in the counter-majoritarian component of his thought is an important part of the modern liberal critique of Madison associated notably with the political scientists Robert Dahl and James MacGregor Burns. Without going as far as they do in stressing the anti-democratic animus of Madison's thought, I agree (as the analysis below suggests) that for Madison the greatest dangers to which the wholesale violation of the separation of powers would lead were to be found not in legislative tyranny per se but in legislative instrumentality in factious majoritarian violations of private rights. The modern liberal critique can be traced in many ways to Charles Beard, who made *Federalist* 10 a central source for his great work, An Economic Interpretation of the Constitution (1913). On Beard's use of Madison, see Shlomo Slonim, Beard's Historiography and the Constitutional Convention, 3 Persp.in Am.Hist. 173 (1986), which, however, presents a view of the separation of powers issue at variance with that offered here. An important criticism of the liberal critique of Madison is George W. Carey, Separation of Powers and the Madisonian Model: A Reply to the Critics, 72 Am.Pol.Sci.Rev. 151 (1978), which is, however, marred by its apparent reliance on *The Federalist* to the exclusion of other sources.

lieved that there were core functions of government that could be denominated as legislative, executive, and judicial in nature, he doubted the practicability of erecting landmarks that could distinguish these functions in a clear and noncontrovertible manner.

Much of the novelty of Madison's analysis lies in his efforts to suggest that, in a republic, "legislative usurpations" are in reality more dangerous than the "executive usurpations" that good republicans traditionally feared. Looking backward to colonial grievances under the *ancien regime*, the constitution-writers of 1776 had eviscerated the executive branch while ignoring the potential risks of legislative supremacy. Annual elections, they assumed, would enable the electorate to control the legislature should it overstep its constitutional bounds to interfere with the legitimate operations of the other branches. But the experience of state politics since independence demonstrated that electoral remedies alone were not enough: the "interested views" of legislators could often lead them to "join in a perfidious sacrifice" of the "interest, and views, of their Constituents," and then to contrive to have their "base and selfish measures, masked by pretexts of public good and apparent expediency."[39]

It was this incapacity of the electorate to check its own representatives that first led Madison (in his pre-Convention analysis of the "Vices of the Political System of the United States") to question the fundamental republican principle that popular majorities were "the safest Guardians both of public Good and of private Rights."[40] But in explaining *why* this was the case, Madison pushed republican theory even further. For as the concluding section of his memorandum makes clear, the greater danger to republican principles and the protection of liberty would come from the population itself. Electoral mechanisms of protection were certainly imperfect and subject to manipulation, but Madison doubted whether a supine people would acquiesce in their own enslavement. He was thus far less concerned with the prospect that a legislative oligarchy would subvert the independence of the weaker branches in order to pursue its own evil purposes than with the dangers that would arise from representatives acting as instru-

---

[39] Federalist 48, in 10 Papers of Madison at 456-457. The disparaging comments on state legislators appear in the pre-Convention memorandum on the "Vices of the Political System," in 9 Papers of Madison at 354. Madison had twice evoked the image of the legislative "vortex" in the Convention; see his speeches of July 17 and 21, in 10 Papers of Madison at 104, 109. On the weakening of executive power under the first state constitutions, see Wood, Creation of the American Republic at 127-161 (cited in note 15).

[40] 9 Papers of Madison at 354 (cited in note 13).

ments of their electors. Ambitious and demagogic rulers would always remain a problem, but the crucial factor was the relation between the people and their representatives. "In our Governments the real power lies in the majority of the Community," Madison reminded Jefferson after the Constitution was ratified, "and the invasion of private rights is chiefly to be apprehended, not from acts of Government contrary to the sense of its constituents, but from acts in which the Government is the mere instrument of the major number of the constituents."[41] For Madison, then, the idea of separated powers could never be sharply distinguished from the general problem of majority misrule. At the Convention, his defense of the Senate, the executive veto, and his proposed executive-judicial Council of Revision all presumed a "twofold" purpose for establishing checks on the lawmaking authority of Congress (and again, especially, the lower house): to defend the rights of the weaker branches, and "to prevent popular or factious injustice."[42] The two functions were intimately linked because the worst consequences of legislative manipulation of the weaker branches would be the facilitation of the violations of private rights that legislators responsive to factious majoritarian interests would be intent on pursuing. For in Madison's analysis, since most wrongful legislation could be traced not to legislative irresponsibility but, on the contrary, to the very fidelity with which lawmakers were obeying the wishes of interested majorities, it was naive to expect the community to mobilize itself against the excesses of its duly elected representatives. Further, in any contest between the legislature and the weaker branches, the opinions and passions that also gave rise to partisan behavior would generally tend to work in favor of the representatives. They would command a popular confidence that the executive and judiciary could rarely if ever hope to attain, even when legislative "usurpations" were "so flagrant and so sudden, as to admit of no specious coloring." The public could thus never be counted upon to decide a dispute on "the true merits of the question," because public opinion would "inevitably be connected with the spirit of preexisting parties, or of parties springing out of the question itself."[43]

From this presumption of the inherent and persistent political

---

[41] James Madison to Thomas Jefferson (Oct. 17, 1788), in 11 Papers of Madison at 298 (cited in note 18).

[42] Speeches of June 4, June 26, July 21, Sept. 12, in 10 Papers of Madison at 25, 76-77, 109, 166 (cited in note 4).

[43] Federalist 49, in 10 Papers of Madison at 462-463.

weakness of the executive and judiciary, Madison struggled to modify the theory of separation of powers in a particularly ingenious if impractical way. When in the mid-1780s he had first considered the evils of "fluctuating & indigested laws," he had sought relief, first, in the traditional idea of a well constituted senate as an immediate check on an impetuous lower house, and second, in the appointment of "a standing committee composed of a few select and skilful individuals" who would have the responsibility of drafting all bills in a technically competent manner.[44] By 1787 his dual concerns with improving the quality of lawmaking and protecting the executive and judiciary against legislative interference had fused to produce a more radical proposal: to combine the executive and judiciary into a Council of Revision armed with a limited veto over national laws and empowered to serve, in effect, as an advisory council to Congress.[45]

Madison's rationale for this proposal and his disappointment over its rejection are noteworthy in several respects. They again reveal his doubts whether even a refined system of elections would produce the ideal corps of legislators his more optimistic pronouncements envisioned. Instead, Madison consciously preferred to bring the judiciary directly into the lawmaking process itself, and in doing so "to restrain the legislature from encroaching on the other co-ordinate departments, or on the rights of the people at large; or from passing laws unwise in their principle, or incorrect in their form." He thus hoped to improve the quality of law at its source, giving American law codes "the perspicuity, the conciseness, and the systematic character" they otherwise lacked. More important, the proposal for uniting the executive and judiciary rested on the fear of the popular majorities lurking behind the legislature. Alone, neither the executive nor the judiciary could resist the legislature, speaking as it would for the political will of the community; united in the Council of Revision, they might gain sufficient stature to provide an effective check against legislative excess. The presence of the judges on the Council would have the added advantage of bracing the political will of an otherwise timorous executive while assuring that the veto would be exercised on appropriate rather than arbitrary grounds.[46]

---

[44] 8 Papers of Madison at 351-352 (cited in note 18).

[45] See point 8 of the Virginia Plan, in 10 Papers of Madison at 16.

[46] Speeches of June 4, June 6, July 21, in 10 Papers of Madison at 25, 35-36, 109-110. After the rejection of the Council of Revision, Madison subsequently moved (August 15) to have acts of Congress submitted separately to the executive and judiciary. 2 Records of the

Indeed, at times Madison seemed to expect more from the judiciary than the executive. In 1785, he had suggested that the executive was actually the least important branch of government, and while in 1787, he consistently worked to enhance presidential independence from Congress, his notions of executive power were the least developed facet of his thought.[47] By contrast, the idea of giving the judiciary political powers illuminated, by its very novelty, the crucial considerations that led him to contemplate so deep an inroad on the theory of strict separation of powers. The proposal is explicable only in terms of his fundamental concern with the protection of the private rights of individuals and minorities against majority misrule. If an active advisory role for the judiciary would deter the adoption of laws that would adversely affect such rights, any damage done to the axiomatic interpretation of separation of powers would be a trivial price to pay.

Madison was thus prepared to sacrifice the theoretical purity and symmetry of the strict theory of separation of powers to attain the practical benefits he believed would ensue. But at a more abstract level, his criticisms of republican lawmaking worked to undermine the supposed distinctions upon which the theory of separation of powers ultimately rested. While Madison recognized that the framing, execution, and adjudication of laws were to some extent distinguishable activities, his image of the plasticity and reach of legislative authority led him to doubt whether any logically rigorous division of powers would ever prove efficacious. "If it were possible it would be well to define the extent of legislative power," he observed in 1785, "but the nature of it seems in many respects to be indefinite."[48] He returned to this basic problem repeatedly in 1787-88: within the Convention, in his correspondence with Jefferson, and finally in *The Federalist*. In *Federalist* 10, for example, it appeared in his reflection on the way in which "the regulation of these various and interfering [economic] interests forms the principal task of modern legislation." But "what are many of the most important acts of legislation," he then asked, "but so many judicial determinations, not indeed concerning the rights of single persons,

---

Federal Convention at 298 (cited in note 17). His continued attachment to the idea of a revisionary power for the judiciary is also attested to in his October 1788 comments on Jefferson's draft of a constitution for Virginia. 11 Papers of Madison at 292-293.

[47] 8 Papers of Madison at 352-353 (cited in note 18); 9 Papers of Madison at 370, 385 (cited in note 13); and see his first remarks at the Convention on executive power, 10 Papers of Madison at 22-23 (cited in note 4).

[48] 8 Papers of Madison at 351.

but concerning the rights of large bodies of citizens"?[49] The thought recurred in essay 48, where Madison justified his emphasis on legislative usurpations by noting that the legislature can "mask under complicated and indirect measures, the encroachments which it makes, on the co-ordinate departments. It is not unfrequently a question of real nicety in legislative bodies, whether the operation of a particular measure, will, or will not extend beyond the legislative sphere."[50] Presumably, the very act of lawmaking allows the legislature to determine many of the rules by which the weaker branches will enforce its will. And in the brilliant meditation of *Federalist* 37, where Madison sought to explain why reasoning about politics was more difficult than reasoning about the natural world, he generalized the point in this way:

> Experience has instructed us that no skill in the science of government has yet been able to discriminate and define, with sufficient certainty, its three great provinces, the legislative, executive, and judiciary; or even the privileges and powers of the different legislative branches. Questions daily occur in the course of practice, which prove the obscurity which reigns in these subjects, and which puzzles the greatest adepts in political science.[51]

Lest one think that this skeptical view of either the theoretical or practical basis for separating powers was dictated by an expedient need to justify the Constitution's violation of a "sacred maxim," it is notable that Madison made the same point in his private writings. "Even the boundaries between the Executive, Legislative & Judiciary Powers," he wrote Jefferson some months earlier, "though in general so strongly marked in themselves, consist in many instances of mere shades of difference."[52]

What thus seems most significant about Madison's approach to issues of separation of powers was his refusal to offer dogmatic solutions for a complex reality. His pragmatic efforts to enhance the independence of the weaker branches must be set against his reasons for fearing that all such attempts must ever remain problematic: the flexible power of the dominant branch of government, which could always deploy "an infinitude of legislative expedients"

---

[49] 10 Papers of Madison at 265-266. The other aspects of the argument of *Federalist* 10 have commanded so much attention that this insight has often been neglected; but see Epstein, Political Theory of *The Federalist* at 82-86 (cited in note 8).

[50] Federalist 48, in 10 Papers of Madison at 457.

[51] Federalist 37, in 10 Papers of Madison at 362.

[52] James Madison to Thomas Jefferson (Oct. 24, 1787), in 10 Papers of Madison at 211.

to pursue its ends; the force of popular will within a republican polity; and the logical difficulties of defining and distinguishing the very powers the doctrine itself sought to protect.[53]

4. *Federalism and the Problem of Rights.* Of all the issues that engaged Madison in the great moment of the Founding, the one he regarded as "the most nice and difficult" was certainly the problem of establishing "the due partition of power, between the General & local Governments."[54] Conceding from the outset that his goal was to find some "middle ground, which may at once support a due supremacy of the national authority, and not exclude the local authorities wherever they can be subordinately useful," Madison and his colleagues faced the unenviable task of solving the same problem on which the British empire had foundered a decade earlier.[55] But for reasons both theoretical and practical, he doubted whether any line between state and national jurisdictions could ever be accurately drawn. The same strictures that weakened any rigid classification of the separated powers applied with even greater force to the task of delineating the separate spheres of state and national law. Drawing upon his ever unflattering portrait of state legislators, Madison assumed that state officials "will be continually sensible of the abridgment of their power [by the Constitution], and be stimulated by ambition to resume the surrendered portion of it." In this effort they would be aided, in part, by the political support they would draw from their immediate constituents, but also by the "impossibility of dividing powers of legislation, in such a manner, as to be free from different constructions by different interests, or even from ambiguity in the judgment of the impartial."[56]

Just as Madison assumed that the parochialism of state lawmakers would not magically disappear with the adoption of the Constitution, so he also believed that individual and minority rights within the states would remain vulnerable to repeated violations. Indeed, the arithmetical logic of his analysis of the sources and mechanics of faction could support no other conclusion. Factious majorities would continue to form within the smaller compass of the states, and they could be counted upon not only to resist national laws and policies whenever interest dictated, but also to enact those unjust laws that Madison found so offensive. The mere

---

[53] 10 Papers of Madison at 212.
[54] 10 Papers of Madison at 209.
[55] 9 Papers of Madison at 383 (cited in note 13).
[56] 10 Papers of Madison at 211.

enlargement of national authority would not cure the vices of the American political system unless the union could somehow be empowered to act to protect private rights against state legislation. Accordingly, his preferred solution to the dual problems of federalism and the protection of rights was to give the national government "a negative *in all cases whatsoever* on the legislative acts of the states, as heretofore exercised by the Kingly prerogative." Such a power would be vested in Congress (or possibly in the Senate alone) and would ideally be exercised with the advice of the proposed Council of Revision. Armed with this veto, the union could protect itself against the interfering laws that the states could be expected to enact, however messy the actual division of legislative power between the two spheres of government might remain. But more important, the negative would further enable the national government to act as a "dispassionate and disinterested umpire in disputes" arising within each of the states, and thus to curb "the aggressions of interested majorities on the rights of minorities and of individuals."[57]

This pet proposal was, of course, far too radical to secure the acceptance of the delegates at Philadelphia—much less the approval of the state ratification conventions. Although James Wilson and Charles Pinckney supported it vigorously, its defects were hard to ignore. How, for example, could Congress possibly survey the entire output of state legislation and still attend to its own business? Conversely, once Madison and Wilson failed to persuade the Convention of the dangers of allowing the state legislatures to elect the Senate, even they found it difficult to imagine how Congress would ever muster the political will to overturn state legislation.[58]

The significance of this proposal rests, however, on its logic rather than its obvious impracticality. Madison left Philadelphia convinced that the Constitution "will neither effectually answer its national object nor prevent the local mischiefs which every where excite disgusts against the state governments."[59] The principal ba-

---

[57] 9 Papers of Madison at 383-384. A comparison of this passage from the letter to Washington of April 16, 1787 with the somewhat murky language in the penultimate paragraph of the concurrently written memorandum on "Vices of the Political System" strongly suggests that Madison's image of the national government as umpire was designed to describe its role in mediating disputes within individual states, and not to characterize national legislation.

[58] See the debates of June 8 and July 17, 1 Records of the Federal Convention at 164-168; 2 Records of the Federal Convention at 25-36 (cited in note 17).

[59] James Madison to Thomas Jefferson (Sept. 6, 1787), in 10 Papers of Madison at 163-

sis for this pessimistic assessment was the rejection of the national negative on state laws, whose justification within the context of his general theory of faction Madison made the central subject of a lengthy letter he wrote to Jefferson five weeks after the Convention adjourned. The logic of this remarkable letter belies the optimism of *Federalist* 10, which was published a month later. Here, as in his ensuing exchanges with Jefferson on the question of a bill of rights, Madison revealed, by restating the dual purposes the absolute veto was meant to serve, how little the debates at Philadelphia had shaken his analysis of the vices of American republicanism. Madison recognized that these tasks had devolved instead on the judiciary, but he doubted whether judicial remedies would prove effective, in part because the political weakness of the judiciary would likely prove unavailing against a defiant state, and in part because the limited protection that the Constitution extended to particular rights fell "short of the mark. Injustice may be effected by such an infinitude of legislative expedients, that where the disposition exists it can only be controuled by some provision which reaches all cases whatsoever."[60]

Clearly, Madison erred in underestimating the authority of the judiciary and the import of the supremacy clause. In a brief but well known passage in *Federalist* 39, he did allude to the Supreme Court as "the tribunal which is ultimately to decide controversies relating to the boundary between the two jurisdictions" of national and state government.[61] But in his letter to Jefferson, he reaffirmed his doubts whether a politically weak judiciary, which could only respond to state actions that had already taken place, would serve as an effective line of defense against a recalcitrant state without requiring the "recurrence to force" that the framers hoped to avoid. Whatever its drawbacks, Madison still regarded the national veto as the best assurance against the great "evil of imperia in imperio." With it, the national government would possess a decisive means of asserting its supremacy, no matter how ragged or imprecise the boundaries between national and state authority would necessarily remain. Without it, Madison foresaw continued dangers of conflict between the union and the states, among states, and within states. Moreover, the limitation of national legislative authority to the powers enumerated in article I, § 8 would leave the states free to act precisely in those areas where they had already

---

164 (cited in note 4).

   [60] 10 Papers of Madison at 209-214.

   [61] Federalist 39, in 10 Papers of Madison at 381.

evinced their propensity for injustice. As Madison further observed
in *Federalist* 45: "The powers reserved to the several States will
extend to all the objects which, in the ordinary course of affairs,
concern the lives, liberties, and properties of the people."[62]

Thus when Madison set out to describe the compound republic of the United States in *The Federalist*, his efforts led to conclusions that were typically nuanced but also uncharacteristically
ironic. Take, for example, *Federalist* 39's familiar description of a
regime combining both "federal" and "national" features. Consistent with Madison's sensitivity to the epistemological difficulty of
fitting political phenomena into neat categories, *Federalist* 39 emphasized the novel and hybrid features of the proposed system,
substituting a detailed balancing of its national and federal aspects
for the axiomatic view that detected no middle ground between
state sovereignty or national consolidation. But at the same time,
Madison now converted arguments he had skewered at Philadelphia into reassurances proffered to the opponents of the Constitution. The image of a union "partly national, partly federal" had
originally been used by Oliver Ellsworth to defend the claim for an
equal state vote in the Senate.[63] In his final remarks before the so-
called Great Compromise, Madison had dismissed that formulation
out of hand on the simple grounds that the new government would
always "operate on the people individually" and never on "the
States as Political bodies."[64] But in *Federalist* 39, he revived Ellsworth's image to epitomize the mixed features of the new system.

Even more revealing, however, was the way in which he sought
to allay Antifederalist objections that the Constitution would reduce the states to impotence. At Philadelphia, Madison and other
nationally minded delegates had decried the centrifugal tendencies
inherent in treating the states as quasi-sovereign entities. In weighing the respective dangers that the union and the states posed to
each other, they had consistently argued, as Madison noted on
June 21, that "the examples of other confederacies" and "our own
experience" demonstrated "the greater tendency in such systems
to anarchy than to tyranny; to a disobedience of the members than
to usurpations of the federal head."[65] Now all the considerations
that had been adduced as threatening the possibility of effective
national government could at least be turned to the purpose of ex-

---

[62] Federalist 45, in 10 Papers of Madison at 431.

[63] 1 Records of the Federal Convention at 468-469 (cited in note 17).

[64] 10 Papers of Madison at 101.

[65] 10 Papers of Madison at 67-68.

plaining why fears of national tyranny were unfounded. As Madison observed in *Federalist* 45,

> The state governments will have the advantage of the federal government, whether we compare them in respect to the immediate dependence of the one on the other; to the weight of personal influence which each side will possess; to the powers respectively vested in them; to the predilection and probable support of the people; to the disposition and faculty of resisting and frustrating the measures of each other.[66]

When viewed within the comprehesive framework of Madison's thought, all of these factors—including, most strikingly, the prediction that "the members of the federal legislature will be likely to attach themselves too much to local objects"[67]—went to prove not only that the states had little to fear, but also that the new national government would likely turn out to be ineffective if not incompetent. Madison's argument was entirely sincere but less than candid. The solutions he described would prove effective enough, but the problems they were proposed to meet were unlikely to occur.

So, at least, Madison still thought in 1788, but within a decade, he understood that these points had more merit than he had realized at the time. For there is a second irony in Madison's use of arguments whose validity he had to accept because he had struggled to overcome the consequences to which he thought they ineluctably led. To the opposition leader of the 1790s, the existence of independent state jurisdictions and an electoral system responsive to public opinion and constituent interests offered crucial political advantages. Once his quarrel with Federalist financial and foreign policies sapped the hopes and expectations for national governance that had moved the Constitutional Father of the 1780s—once events confirmed the prediction of *Federalist* 10 that indeed "enlightened statesmen will not always be at the helm"—the reassurances of *The Federalist* provided plausible justification for building a majority coalition based on interest and opinion to restore the national government to its proper course. Not all majorities, it turned out, were factious.[68] Public opinion, which Madison had

---

[66] *Federalist* 45, 10 Papers of Madison at 430.

[67] Federalist 46, in 10 Papers of Madison at 440-441.

[68] The literature on the development both of political parties and of the ideological adjustments necessary to legitimate their existence is extensive. Perhaps the best introduction to the subject remains Richard Hofstadter, The Idea of a Party System (1970).

once dismissed as an ineffective check against the abuse of public power, now appeared as a vital support of the complex "partitions and internal checks of power" that were the distinctive features of the American republic.[69]

In a similar vein, the developments of the 1790s encouraged Madison to reassess his earlier views on the utility of bills of rights, which in the 1780s he had also dismissed as so many "parchment barriers" against the real threat of majority tyranny. Political calculations, not a fundamental change of opinion, were what led him by late 1788 to accede to the idea that a bill of rights could be safely added to the Constitution so long as no door was thereby opened for more substantive or structural amendments. As the qualifications in both his letters to Jefferson and his June 1789 speech proposing the amendments make clear, Madison still believed that the political checks predicted by his theory of the extended republic afforded the strongest protections for individual and minority rights. The greater danger by far would arise from majorities acting through government and swayed by desires and opinions that the mere existence of a bill of rights could never counteract. Bills of rights were useful, he grudgingly conceded for two purposes only: first, if they gradually assumed "the character of fundamental maxims" that could serve an educative function for the general population and thus "counteract the impulses of interest and passion;" and second, if they provided a "good ground for an appeal to the sense of the community" against a government seeking to establish its own tyrannical rule over the rights of the citizenry. But when Madison wrote this in October 1788, he clearly thought that by far the greater and more immediate dangers to liberty would arise not from self-aggrandizing rulers but from among the mass of the population.[70] It would take the political ex-

---

[69] See Madison's brief newspaper essays on Public Opinion and the Government of the United States 170, in Robert A. Rutland, Thomas A. Mason, et. al., eds., 14 Papers of Madison 217-218 (1983).

[70] The key document (from which the quotations in this paragraph are taken) is Madison's letter to Jefferson of October 17, 1788; 11 Papers of Madison at 297-300 (cited in note 18). It reveals how little of his deeper analysis of the problem of rights had been shaken by a year's debate over the ratification of the Constitution, just as the letter he had written Jefferson almost exactly a year earlier defending the unlimited national veto indicates how little Madison had been persuaded by contrary arguments at the Convention. Nevertheless, in the difficult campaign election he waged against his friend James Monroe for election to the first House of Representatives, Madison let it be known that he would support amendments. See his letter to George Eve (Jan. 2, 1789), in 11 Papers of Madison at 404-405. Were it not for the depth of Madison's commitment to this promise, reinforced by his analysis of the political advantages of amendments, it is quite possible that the First Congress would have ignored the entire subject. Madison's speech in the House of Repre-

perience of the 1790s, and especially the Adams administration's use of the Sedition Act to punish the opposition Republican press, to convince Madison that these two potential functions of a bill of rights were not matters of idle speculation.

There are, of course, many good reasons why these and other nuances of Madison's thought can be safely ignored by everyone but historians. The very fact that, at the Convention, Madison lost so many of the points he regarded as most important suggests, after all, that his role in the making of the Constitution may be overrated. Or again, under his own canon of constitutional interpretation, only those of his statements that can be thought to have influenced the public campaign for ratification or to have reflected the public mind deserve privileged status. The great texts of *The Federalist* may plausibly be said to enjoy that character, but reflections recorded only in personal papers, or even speeches given at Philadelphia, do not.

Yet in at least one crucial respect, the problematic aspects of Madison's political thinking remain relevant to the constitutional discourse of a political culture—our own—which is still enjoined to defer to the orignal meanings, intentions, or understandings of the Constitution. The logic of originalism, when probed to its ultimate legalistic foundation, rests on the conviction that determinate meanings were attached to the provisions of the Constitution at the moment of its adoption, and that these meanings express the voice of popular sovereignty to a degree that later judicial exegeses cannot pretend to attain. It is not an idle question whether such assumptions can ever amount to anything more than the useful fictions that the conventions of constitutional adjudication seem to require. In truth, we have no verifiable way of knowing how the Constitution was understood by the nation at the time of its ratification; and the relevance to particular acts of interpretation of a ratification process that allowed the state conventions only to accept or reject the document *in toto* remains equally elusive. The simple existence of significant constitutional controversies that are coeval with the organization of the new government in 1789 demonstrates how artificial the search for some pristine moment of original understanding must become. Rather than search for one set of fixed meanings, it may make more sense to attempt simply to recover the terms of debate, and then, perhaps, it may prove possible to identify original meanings of greater and lesser degrees

---

sentatives of June 8, 1789, accurately restates his opinions on the subject. Robert A. Rutland, Charles F. Hobson, et. al., eds., 12 Papers of Madison 196-209 (1979).

of probability.[71]

Over time, it is true, Madison himself came to argue that the popular understanding of the Constitution prevailing at the time of ratification should limit the reach of interpretation, and that major changes should be effected by Article V amendments, not judicial fiat.[72] Ironically enough, however, this idea was apparently not part of his own original understanding of the Constitution, but rather a response to political developments of the 1790s. In 1787 and 1788, Madison's disparaging views of the sources and character of public opinion and debate could hardly have led him to conclude that the ratification campaign would erect clear standards for the later interpretation of the Constitution.[73] But by 1792, as the leader of a nascent opposition party, Madison was disposed to reassess the general place of public opinion; and explicitly political calculations soon led him to appreciate the value of converting the ratification debates into a standard of constitutionality. Against the latitudinarian definitions of "necessary and proper" or "executive power" that Hamilton used to legitimate his financial and foreign policies, this position had the obvious advantage of implying that the Constitution would never have been ratified had the American people understood that its meaning could be made so malleable. Other developments similarly led Madison to modify his original skepticism about the political weakness of the judiciary and to develop a more profound appreciation of and attachment to the view of the Supreme Court that he had sketched, however tersely, in *Federalist* 39.[74] In this there was a striking consistency to his thought. In 1787 he had believed that future population movements would bring Northern and Southern states into rough

---

[71] As Gordon S. Wood has recently observed: "It may be a necessary fiction for lawyers and jurists to believe in a 'correct' or 'true' interpretation of the Constitution in order to carry on their business," but historians, by contrast, have the obligation to explain why "contrasting meanings" have beeen attached to the Constitution throughout its history. Gordon S. Wood, Ideology and the Origins of Liberal America, 44 Wm. & Mary Q. 628, 632-633 (1987). For my own reflections on the role of history in the debate over original intent, see Rakove, Comment, 47 Md.L.Rev. 226 (1988).

[72] For various expressions of this idea, see Madison's speech in the House of Representatives (April 6, 1796), and at a much later date, his letters to Thomas Ritchie (Sept. 15, 1821), J. G. Jackson (Dec. 27, 1821), and Nicholas P. Trist (Dec. 1831); 3 Records of the Federal Convention at 374, 447-450, 516-518 (cited in note 17). For a good short discussion, see Ralph L. Ketcham, James Madison and Judicial Review, 8 Syracuse L.R. 158 (1956-57).

[73] If the ratifiers of the Constitution did not understand that their understanding of what they were adopting would guide later interpretations, does Madison's theory of interpretation fail on its own grounds?

[74] See, for example, his explicit reaffirmation of this principle in his letter to Jefferson (June 27, 1823), in Gaillard Hunt, ed., 9 Writings of James Madison 140-143 (1910).

parity; by the time of his retirement from the presidency thirty
years later, he understood that this would never be the case.[75] Accordingly, as he reminded Spencer Roane, the leading Virginia
apostle of states-rights theory, it was in the interest of the Southern states not to challenge the jurisdiction of the Court precisely
because the greater danger the South faced would come from the
political advantages the North would enjoy in Congress as its population growth outstripped that of the South.[76] He criticized Marshall's opinion in *McCulloch* not because it favored national powers over states' rights, but rather because he feared that its
reliance on the necessary and proper clause would henceforth
make it more difficult for the Court to limit the legislative reach of
Congress. The great danger remained, in other words, that of the
factious majority.[77]

It is a mark of the acuity and breadth of Madison's original
analysis of the vices of American republicanism that so much of
what he wrote and said at the great moment of the founding anticipated the developments to which he would respond, both politically and intellectually, over the next half century. Sometimes
these responses took the form of modest shifts of emphasis; sometimes they recognized that arguments once made for rhetorical
purposes had been more astute or prescient than he had realized at
the time; and occasionally, as in his acceptance of the idea of political party, responses to events led Madison to accept radically new
positions. Like any intellectual, he valued his consistency, and he
typically sought to emphasize the continuities in his thought. But
to the historian, it is the evidence of his continually thinking, more
than those continuities, that makes the appeal to a fixed original
meaning seem so artificial and false to the historical record. This
appeal asks us to freeze a special moment of history—let us call it,
with apologies to J. G. A. Pocock, the Madisonian moment—to
take, as it were, a snapshot of constitutional history and endow it
with a significance that was not recognized at the time. The Madis-

---

[75] On this point, see Drew McCoy, James Madison and the Visions of American Nationality in the Confederation Period: A Regional Perspective, in Beeman et al., eds., Beyond
Confederation at 226-258 (cited in note 11).

[76] "[W]hatever may be the latitude of Jurisdiction assumed by the Judicial Power of
the U.S.," Madison reminded Roane, "it is less formidable to the reserved sovereignty of the
States than the latitude of power which it has assigned to the National Legislature; & that
encroachments of the latter are more to be apprehended from impulses given to it by a
majority of the States seduced by expected advantages, than from the love of Power in the
Body itself." Letter (May 6, 1821), in 9 Writings of Madison at 57-59 (cited in note 74).

[77] James Madison to Spencer Roane (Sept. 2, 1819), in Gaillard Hunt, ed., 8 Writings of
Madison 448-453 (1908).

onian moment was special not because those participating in "The Founding" thought they had possessed perfect knowledge of what the new Constitution meant, but rather because they understood the remarkable opportunity they were enjoying. They did not think that they would understand the Constitution less well after it went into operation. Madison himself stated the crucial point in *Federalist* 37 when he observed that "All new laws, though penned with the greatest technical skill, and passed on the fullest and most mature deliberation, are considered as more or less obscure and equivocal, until their meaning be liquidated and ascertained by a series of particular discussions and adjudications." There is no reason to suppose that the Constitution could be exempted from this general rule.[78]

---

[78] 10 Papers of Madison at 362 (cited in note 4).

Metaphor and Imagination in James Wilson's Theory of Federal Union

Stephen A. Conrad

"Through metaphor, the past has the capacity to imagine us, and we it."
—Cynthia Ozick, in "The Moral Necessity of Metaphor"[1]

American federalism is nothing more—and nothing less—than a metaphor. This was how James Wilson, the most prominent lawyer at the Philadelphia Convention, came to approach the novel problem of understanding and conveying what federalism in a modern republic should mean. The Federal Republic created in 1787 was, for Wilson, more than a matter of ingenious political design, more than a matter of the "new science of politics," and more than a matter of constitutional law or constitutionalism itself—unless the Constitution were seen to "comprehend" the moral purpose and moral promise of the new nation.

To Wilson, this view of the importance of the moral content of republican federalism was entailed by the "knowledge" that he took to be the necessary foundation of the Republic. It was this knowledge of certain fundamental principles—of "moral science," human nature, and the nature of language, and, more generally, of "cultivation" as a political and social process that was also an end in itself—that ultimately justified "the People" as the "sublime" metaphor governing American constitutional theory.

Yet, for all Wilson's faith in figurative "comprehensiveness," his distinctive approach to securing the New Republic through a federal union of the American People seems to have proved less and less compelling to his contemporaries the more he tried to pursue it as far as his vision of a politics of cultivation directed.

I. INTRODUCTION AND OVERVIEW

"[T]he text of the Constitution provides the beginning rather than the final answer to every inquiry into questions of federalism."
—Justice Blackmun, for the Court, in *Garcia v. SAMTA* (1985)[2]

---

1. The Moral Necessity of Metaphor: Rooting History in a Figure of Speech, Harper's Mag., May 1986, at 62, 68.
2. Garcia v. San Antonio Metropolitan Transit Authority, 469 U.S. 528, 547 (1985).

3

The American Founding of the 1780s generated such novel formulations of federal theory that it should hardly be surprising that the language of those formulations is so ambiguous.[3] Ever since the 1780s this fund of ambiguity has helped to sustain disagreement—not least within our current Supreme Court—over what "conception" of federalism is "proper" to the Founding.[4] In the present essay I discuss the federal theory of James Wilson, a lawyer who was a leading founder,[5] in order to reconsider this problem of ambiguity by examining at some length how and why Wilson conceived his own theory of American federal union largely in terms of metaphor and other figurative language. Here I take this language to be not merely politic equivocation, incidental to the debates at the Founding, but a material part of Wilson's ambitiously "comprehensive" federal theory.

In other words, I try to take Wilson's figurative rhetoric as seriously as he

---

3. For a valuable perspective on the novelty of American federal theory, see the substantially unpublished dissertation by Patrick Riley, Historical Development of the Theory of Federalism, Sixteenth-Nineteenth Centuries (Harvard University, 1968), esp. ch. xvi, as read in light of the preceding chapters. For the Founders' own avowals—and protestations—of novelty, the evidence abounds: e.g., Madison's Federalist Papers No. 37 at 233 and No. 14 at 88 (J. Cooke ed., Cleveland: World Publishing Co., 1961). Cf. 1 Max Farrand, ed., The Records of the Federal Convention of 1787, at 338 (4 vols.; rev. ed. New Haven, Conn.: Yale University Press, 1937) ("Farrand, Records"): Madison's Notes of June 20, reporting remarks of the soon-to-be Anti-Federalist John Lansing on the Virginia Plan: "He had another objection. The system was too novel & complex."

In contemplating throughout this essay what I consider the *positive capability* of ambiguity, I have been especially influenced by William E. Connolly, Politics and Ambiguity (Madison: University of Wisconsin Press, 1987), e.g., at xi: "the competing ideals of individualism and communalism, liberalism and radicalism, negative freedom and positive freedom, tend to converge in obscuring the ambiguous character of standards, ideals, and ends most worthy of endorsement."

For a characterization (by the leading historian of American federalism as it is embodied in constitutional *law*) of Madison's federal theory as "ambiguous," see Harry N. Scheiber, Federalism and the Constitution: The Original Understanding, *in* Lawrence M. Friedman & Harry N. Scheiber, eds., American Law and the Constitutional Order: Historical Perspectives 85, 87 (Cambridge, Mass.: Harvard University Press, 1978).

4. Quoting Martha A. Field, Comment—*Garcia v. San Antonio Metropolitan Transit Authority*: The Demise of a Misguided Doctrine, 99 Harv. L. Rev. 84, 85 (1985). Cf. Laurence H. Tribe, American Constitutional Law 154 (Mineola, N.Y.: Foundation Press, 1978) (re: the *Younger* doctrine" and its aftermath in general, "it is clear from the Supreme Court's decisions that a concern for federalism is the chief underpinning of the *Younger* cases. The Court, however, has explained neither the exact content nor the precise status of that concern"). Cf. also Geoffrey R. Stone et al., eds., Constitutional Law 209 (Boston: Little, Brown & Co., 1986) (apparent consensus on the Court that "federalism serves important values"; "the real dispute" arises "over how the[se] values of federalism are to be protected"). See also the symposium in 19 Ga. L. Rev. 789 (1985), esp. the introduction by A.E. Dick Howard, at 789, *Garcia* and the Values of Federalism: On the Need for a Recurrence to Fundamental Principles.

5. The documentary record would seem to leave little room for doubt about Wilson's actual importance. See, e.g., Max Farrand's estimation of Wilson's standing at the Federal Convention itself; Farrand, The Framing of the Constitution of the United States 197 (New Haven, Conn.: Yale University Press, 1913) ("Farrand, Framing") (Wilson was "[s]econd to Madison and almost on a par with him. . . . In some respects he was Madison's intellectual superior"). Nevertheless, the durability of Wilson's renown has proved to be quite another matter. By the time of his early death in 1798, Wilson had already fallen into the obscurity in which his name still languishes. In a previous essay (cited *infra* note 12), I tried to begin to contribute both to earlier explanations for Wilson's fall and to earlier efforts to rehabilitate him. Professor Samuel H. Beer has kindly apprised me that his forthcoming synoptic study of American federalism will, in its treatment of the founding, focus largely on Wilson. I am also told that Professor Garry Wills will shortly be publishing a book on Wilson.

himself did.[6] At the Philadelphia Convention and afterward, Wilson adopted, adapted, or devised a number of figures of speech and figurative allusions with which to convey his vision of American federalism. And he marshaled this language prominently and consistently. But more to the point, he incorporated into his federal theory—if, indeed, he did not predicate it on—an elaborate moral epistemology that held figurative language and shared imagination to be at least as important as logical argument or reason itself. It would seem, then, that we cannot expect to understand this framer's theory of federalism in its own terms unless we understand something of his theory of metaphor.

The length of this article, not to mention its occasional and, I think, unavoidable allusiveness, calls for an overview of the general argument.

In *Section II*, I turn to what lay at the heart of Wilson's constitutional theory: his abiding concern with the "fundamental" authority of "moral science." Wilson approached practical moral theory as a true "science" precisely because he believed that the most important principles of practical morality are *empirically* verifiable.

Thus, while embracing the new American "science of politics," he resisted, in the name of "science," any notion of the autonomy of politics—or of any other endeavor of the mind. Instead, he insisted on deriving political science from the "just" principles of *moral* science. And here he was following

---

6. In trying to take Wilson's rhetoric seriously, I need not subscribe entirely to—but I must and do gratefully acknowledge the influence of—the approach to "law as rhetoric" exemplified in the work of James Boyd White, who "has been the foremost rhetorician of law in our academic culture" (quoting Richard H. Weisberg, Law and Rhetoric, 85 Mich. L. Rev. 920, 920 (1987)). See, e.g., White's Law as Rhetoric, Rhetoric as Law: The Arts of Cultural and Communal Life, 52 U. Chi. L. Rev. 684 (1985), esp. at 701: "Rhetoric, in the highly expanded sense in which I speak of it, might indeed become the central discipline for which we have been looking so long." White's article is a version of a chapter in his book Heracles' Bow: Essays on the Rhetoric and Poetics of the Law (Madison: University of Wisconsin Press, 1985). Cf. White's more recent exposition of his "literary-rhetorical view of intellectual and cultural life" in Thinking About Our Language, 96 Yale L.J. 1960, 1965 (1987).

For a useful dictionary of terminology—often figurative and/or rhetorical—associated with American federalism, see William H. Stewart, Concepts of Federalism (Lanham, Md.: University Press of America, 1984) (published as part of the Terminology of Federalism project of the Association of Centers for Federal Studies). And for recent examples of analysis *and critique* of the rhetoric of American federalism, see Peter Gabel, The Mass Psychology of the New Federalism: How the Burger Court's Political Imagery Legitimizes the Privatization of Everyday Life, 52 Geo. Wash. L. Rev. 263 (1984); Mark Tushnet, Deviant Science, 59 Tex. L. Rev. 815, esp. at 825 (1981) (on a Madisonian conception of "the social psychology of federalism" inhering in the "ties of affection and sentiment to the locality"). See also Milner S. Ball, Lying Down Together: Law, Metaphor, and Theology 72-76, 79–80, 90, 91, 113–14 (Madison: University of Wisconsin Press, 1985).

On the Founding itself, see John Zvesper's work treating the decade of the 1790s, Political Philosophy and Rhetoric: A Study of the Origins of American Party Politics (Cambridge: Cambridge University Press, 1977), e.g., at 15: "The major theme of this study is the tension between the practical aims and the rhetorical necessities of modern political philosophy."

The published work that is perhaps closest, in its approach and focus, to what I am attempting in the present essay is that of Albert Furtwangler, *viz.*, his American Silhouettes: Rhetorical Identities of the Founders (New Haven, Conn.: Yale University Press, 1987); and The Authority of Publius: A Reading of the Federalist Papers (Ithaca, N.Y.: Cornell University press, 1984). Cf. Daniel Walker Howe, The Political Psychology of *The Federalist*, 44 Wm. & Mary Q., 3d ser., at 483 (1987), esp. at 486, including the citations in n.4.

the lead not of David Hume but of Hume's most prominent contemporary critics, the Scottish Common Sense school of Thomas Reid and Reid's epigones. This moralistic approach to republican theory led Wilson to emphasize the moral capability of "the People" themselves as the "real" foundation of any republic.

In *Section III*, I examine Wilson's applications—and extensions—of this polite moral science in the context of the American Founding. I focus particularly on Wilson's Common Sense affirmations about the mimetic nature and moral capability of language. To Wilson, the moral significance of language was manifest, above all, in how the evidence of language testifies to the predominance of the "social operations" of the human mind. Faithful to Reidian Common Sense, but also appealing to the authority of American political experience, Wilson presumed to apply Reid's ideas by "extending" upon them. He took special pleasure in coining a new metaphor—"moral abstraction"— to convey to the citizens of the new American nation the "progressive" Common Sense argument that the human capacity to widen the ambit of social ties and affections is as strong, capable, and "susceptible of improvement" as is the human capacity to generalize from the particular to the general, through the mental process of "*intellectual* abstraction." By "moral abstraction," Wilson meant to invoke the mounting testimonials in the polite Atlantic culture of the day to the "powers of the imagination."

In *Section IV*, I explore how Wilson's linguistic turn in moral epistemology sustained his confidence in the epistemological authority of metaphor. I take as my point of departure a passage from Wilson's 1790-91 law lectures, which, when read in the context of his other writings, suggests how Wilson saw metaphor as a means not merely of conveying moral knowledge but also of acquiring and augmenting it.

Wilson had learned from Scottish Common Sense that metaphors are creations of the human imagination, but that imagination, as an act of human "reflection," is an operation as authentic to the mind as is any other. Thus reflection and imagination import the authority of that most compelling guide, *experience*. Still, Wilson's faith in the moral capability of the imagination—as epitomized for him in the moral capability of metaphor—was not entirely the result of his having imbibed so much Scottish philosophy. He was also inspired by his belief that for the first time a nation—America—had realized the politics of a true "civil society." This belief was crucial to Wilson's reconceptualizing the idea of "experience" itself so that it included the processes and products of the human imagination.

In *Section V*, I discuss the idea of figurative personality. It was chiefly through this idea that Wilson tried to comprehend how in a republic the People comprise both a single, general person and the aggregated respective personalities of the individual citizens. Convenient as this synthesizing ambiguity may have been for Wilson's politic purposes as an apologist for the "Federalist persuasion," the ambiguity was nonetheless also genuinely important to his guiding vision of American republicanism as an enterprise in moral reform.

In this enterprise, American society, and each citizen, was under the duty to cultivate all the resources of personality—not least "self-knowledge." Since Common Sense taught that it is not reason but the moral sense that enables individuals and societies to determine their ultimate ends, Wilson justified his vision of the ultimate ends of American republicanism by recurring to the moral sense theory that the Common Sense school had "scientifically" rehabilitated. But in expounding his moral sense doctrine, he attended less to the technical arguments of philosophers than to the vindication of those arguments to be found in the nature of human language itself. Wilson was interested especially in what could be learned from language at its most "morally estimable." So strong, in fact, was the high-cultural orientation of Wilson's thought and so keen his interest in cultivated language that, in his theory of the American federal republic, *taste* became an analog of the *state* itself, and cultural management became a key task of Federalist politics.

In *Section VI*, I argue that, because Wilson's underlying *theory* of metaphor has been so little noticed, the significance of his metaphorical approach to American federalism has been substantially overlooked. The metaphors and other figurative language that Wilson used to develop his federal theory were intrinsic to that theory even—indeed, especially—when his language was at its most conventional: For him it was, after all, the "connexions," not the discontinuities, between the individual and the "publick" mind that must be the principal bonds of association in any truly republican federal union.

Although Wilson early joined in the campaign for national union, his federal theory was never as "consolidationist" as that of some of his eventual Federalist allies. But he did perhaps develop the most inherently positive notion of a federal American nation as an ideal important in itself—because, for Wilson, strong national government was an ideal instinct with the most progressive civic psychology of republicanism.

I try to reinforce this point by recalling that Wilson was credited with having coined the very term "Federal Republic" as the name for the new form of government proposed by the Philadelphia Convention. I then consider this coinage, like Wilson's coinage "moral abstraction," as *a metaphor*. Drawing on widely endorsed general theories of metaphor, I argue that to Wilson these two coinages served as metaphors for one another. And I compare and contrast Wilson with Madison in order to highlight the antireductive, intentionally ambiguous, essentially metaphorical nature of Wilson's approach to formulating and solving the very same problems of modern republicanism that engaged Madison.

How Wilson meant to incorporate yet transcend a Madisonian political science is substantially encapsulated in Wilson's prescription for "enlarging the sphere"—where Wilson refers not to a mere expansion of the territorial sphere of politics but to enlarging the powers and the scope of the faculty of moral abstraction. For Wilson this prescription was the at once modern, "scientific," *and* authentically republican key to inculcating the "extended patriotism" a federal republic requires of its citizens.

In *Section VII*, I treat Wilson's "comprehensive" approach to understanding and explaining federal republicanism through his multiplication of metaphors for political representation. Through such metaphors Wilson developed a theory of representation that looked to the "sublimation" of the People themselves, over and above any process whereby the virtue of the People was to be "purified," or "refined," through representation as a means of *filtering* "the publick mind."

No less than Madison, Wilson exalted the importance of the electoral suffrage; but more than Madison he projected how the reciprocal effects of a general right of suffrage might improve "the People themselves." This was a matter that Wilson thought the new American political science had neglected. And it was a matter that he thought his metaphorical moral science was especially well suited to "elucidate."

Wilson's use of metaphors and other figurative language is sometimes interesting for the ambiguities it harnesses to Wilson's immediate purposes, for example, to justify the authority of an elected representative to lead rather than follow his constituency, while not exceeding his charge as *but a representative*. Wilson's metaphors and their ambiguities are more interesting, however, when Wilson addresses the problems and purposes of federal union. For it was only in discussing the politics of the "enlarged" territorial, psychic, and moral sphere that Wilson could move to the essential question about the *quiddity* of the American People, a question not about *who* but about *what* the federated American People represents. With this question Wilson intensified his focus on moral personality, and thus opened the way to a deeper appreciation of the moral capability of the federal design: By affording Americans *dual, concurrent* citizenship—in one of the several states *and* in the nation—federal union offered a historic opportunity for inculcating the sense of power combined with subordination that is essential to enlarging the moral capability of any citizen. But to Wilson even more important were the "expanded patriotism" and "expansion of mind" that federal union would afford as the basis of a true nation embodied in a great national government.

Yet Wilson expected from the American Federal Republic so much more of the true patriotism of moral imagination than had ever before been achieved that the only historical precedent for the American federal union he could countenance was the unrealized plan of Henry IV and Elizabeth I for a federation of Europe, in their legendary Grand Design. Such was Wilson's unabashedly visionary ideal of the new American nation.

Finally, in *Section VIII*, I conclude by taking account of the chief points in my analysis of Wilson's visionary constitutionalism and by reconsidering how they bear on one another to yield, if not an exemplar or even a lesson, at least an example that should be of interest to constitutional historians and theorists today.

II. THE FUNDAMENTAL AUTHORITY OF "MORAL SCIENCE"

> "For a people wanting to themselves, there is indeed no remedy in the political dispensary."
>
> —Wilson, in his *Lectures on Law* [7]

Among his contemporaries Wilson was often said to be remarkably "erudite" and "profound."[8] Indeed, in what survives of his speeches, lectures, and judicial opinions, his erudition is still rather hard to overlook. But Wilson's contemporary reputation as one of the most profound, most "philosophical" of the framers at Philadelphia now begs explanation. In a sense, it did even at the time. In the series of lectures he prepared for delivery to law students in Philadelphia in the early 1790s, Wilson went to great lengths to explain why he believed it necessary to base the founding of the new nation, in turn, on the "solid foundation"[9] of contemporary philosophy. And, while it was no more unorthodox in the late 18th century[10] than it is in the late 20th[11] to view

---

7. See text *infra* at note 31.

8. See, e.g., the characterizations of Wilson by contemporary witnesses in 3 Farrand, Records 91–92 (William Pierce) & 236–37 (a French diplomat); George W. Corner, ed., The Autobiography of Benjamin Rush: His "Travels Through Life" together with his *Commonplace Book* for 1789-1813, at 150 (Princeton, N.J.: Princeton University Press, 1948) ("Corner, ed., Autobiography of Rush"); John Bach McMaster & Frederick D. Stone, Pennsylvania and the Federal Constitution, 1787–1788, at 183 (Lancaster: Historical Society of Pennsylvania, 1888) ("McMaster & Stone"): Wilson was said, by an Anti-Federalist critic, to be "a man of sense, learning and extensive information"; Burton A. Konkle, The Life and Times of Thomas Smith, 1745–1809, A Pennsylvania Member of the Continental Congress 193–94 (Philadelphia, 1904) (Jasper Yates, commenting on Wilson's Nov. 24, 1787 speech at the Pennsylvania ratifying convention) (repub. on microfiche frame 242 in the microfiche supplement to The Documentary History of the Ratification of the Constitution, vol. 2—Ratification of the Constitution by the States: Pennsylvania, ed. Merrill Jensen (Madison: State Historical Society of Wisconsin, 1976) ("Jensen, ed.").

For testimonials to Wilson's erudition and/or profundity by some later authorities, see 1 Robert Green McCloskey, ed., The Works of James Wilson 2 (Cambridge, Mass.: Harvard University, Belknap Press, 1967) (2 vols. consecutively paginated) ("McCloskey, Works"); McCloskey's short article, James Wilson, in 1 Leon Friedman & Fred L. Israel, eds., The Justices of the United States Supreme Court, 1789–1969: Their Lives and Major Opinions 79, 79 (New York: R.R. Bowker Co., 1969) ("McCloskey, James Wilson"); McMaster & Stone at 758; Randolph G. Adams, ed., Selected Political Essays of James Wilson 41–42 (New York: Alfred A. Knopf, 1930) ("Adams, Selected Essays"). See also Adams, The Legal Theories of James Wilson, 68 U. Pa. L. Rev. & Am. L. Reg. 337, esp. at 337–38 (1920) (reprinted as ch. 7 in Adams, Political Ideas of the American Revolution: Britannic-American Contributions to the Problem of Imperial Organization, 1765–1775 (3d ed. New York: Barnes & Noble, Inc., 1958) ("Adams, Legal Theories"), ("Adams, Political Ideas").

9. 1 McCloskey, Works 222–23 and *passim*.

10. See, e.g., Morton White, Philosophy, *The Federalist*, and the Constitution (New York: Oxford University Press, 1987). Cf. Paul Eidelberg, The Philosophy of the American Constitution (New York: Free Press, 1968). But for a brief critique of Morton White's "static . . . account of philosophy" in The Federalist, see the review by G. Edward White in 74 J. Am. Hist. 499–500

American constitutionalism as inextricable from underlying philosophical principles, Wilson was especially emphatic and assiduous in elaborating this view.

The philosophical principles that Wilson expounded were not original to him; nor did he claim to have organized, much less to have invented, an integral "system" of thought. His philosophy was, instead, a congeries of "polite"[12] principles of the day that were, he thought, nonetheless harmonious, even mutually authorizing—and not merely useful and pleasing to contemplate but also, and above all, true. Knowing, not merely thinking or learning, was for Wilson the ultimate aim of any inquiry aptly called philosophical; and thus all philosophy should aspire to "science," in the strictest cognate meaning of that nearly universal term of the era.

To understand Wilson's reputation in his own day as perhaps the most philosophical of the framers it is important to appreciate how he could and did, while impressing without surprising his contemporary audiences, orient all his ideas on law, politics, and society toward practical philosophy and, at the same time derive all practical philosophy from an elemental moral epistemology so "true," so certain that it constituted for him an authentic "moral science." Here, as in other aspects of Wilson's approach at its most philosophical, the apparent contrast with Madisonian theory is instructive.

For example, in a noted[13] passage in *Federalist* No. 37, Madison seeks in part to justify the imperfection and inconclusiveness of Federalist "political science" by alleging the limited capacity of other sciences—even the most advanced or important sciences, like those that address the physical world or the

---

(1987). And for an interesting critique of Eidelberg's application of "Aristotelian criteria," see Paul Peterson, The Meaning of Republicanism in The Federalist, in Daniel J. Elazar, ed., Republicanism, Representation, and Consent: Views of the Founding Era 43–76 (New Brunswick, N.J.: Transaction Books, 1979) (reprinted from 9 Publius, The Journal of Federalism (1979)).

   11. A convenient and broad (even if slightly dated) attempt at a survey of current proponents of this view is to be found in Laurence E. Wiseman, The New Supreme Court Commentators: The Principled, the Political, and the Philosophical, 10 Hast. Const. L.Q. 315 (1983). For criticism of the "philosophical" approach to American constitutional theory, see, e.g., Michael Walzer, Philosophy and Democracy, 9 Pol. Theory 379 (1981); and John Hart Ely, Democracy and Distrust: A Theory of Judicial Review 56-60 (Cambridge, Mass.: Harvard University Press, 1980).

   12. See Stephen A. Conrad, Polite Foundation: Citizenship and Common Sense in James Wilson's Republican Theory, 1984 Sup. Ct. Rev. 359 ("Conrad, Polite Foundation"). Cf. the work of Lawrence Eliot Klein, refining and extending arguments in Klein's dissertation, The Rise of "Politeness" in England, 1660-1715 (Johns Hopkins University, 1983); e.g., Lawrence Klein, The Third Earl of Shaftesbury and the Progress of Politeness, 18 Eighteenth-Century Stud. 186 (1984–85); and Lawrence E. Klein, Berkeley, Shaftesbury, and the Meaning of Politeness, 16 Stud. in Eighteenth-Century Culture 57 (1986). And cf. comments on the ideal of "politeness" in J.G.A. Pocock, Virtue, Commerce, and History: Essays on Political Thought and History, Chiefly in the Eighteenth Century, e.g., 114–15, 236–37, and *passim* (Cambridge: Cambridge University Press, 1985) ("Pocock, Virtue"). Indeed, a prominent review of this collection of essays by Professor Pocock focuses on precisely the theme in question: Mark Goldie, The Rise of Politeness, Times Literary Supp., June 27, 1986, at 715; cf. the review by Conrad, 5 Law & Hist. Rev. 286 (1987).

   13. E.g., David F. Epstein, The Political Theory of The Federalist 114-18 (Chicago: University of Chicago Press, 1984) ("Epstein, Political Theory"); Aviam Soifer, Truisms That Never Will Be True: The Tenth Amendment and the Spending Power, 57 U. Colo. L. Rev. 793, 812 n.77 (1986).

human mind itself. Owing to the very procedures in which the meaning of "science" inheres, no science, says Madison, can pretend to determinate knowledge: Science, strictly speaking, is an endeavor "to contemplate and discriminate objects, extensive and complicated in their nature," in order to make "distinctions," to "trace boundaries," to classify, and thus ultimately to "define" with such "precision" the nature of and relationships among the objects of study that they no longer occasion "ingenious disquisition and controversy." Science is, then, something more than informed opinion and contingent consensus only to the extent—albeit the considerable extent—of the virtues of scientific procedure.[14]

Wilson, on the other hand, conceived of science somewhat differently, not only as to its established capacity and its ultimate aims, but even as to its characteristic procedures. He tended to discount analysis and to disparage definitions. During one of his early law lectures, in what he acknowledged might seem an "excursion"[15] from his task at hand (conveying to his students a "conception" of "law in general"), and in a contrasting parallel to Madison's "skeptical digression"[16] in Federalist No. 37, Wilson seems to have eschewed as unscientific exactly what Madison had portrayed as necessary (if not also sufficient) to the practice of science, namely, definition and analysis: "I am not insensible [said Wilson] of the use, but, at the same time, I am not insensible of the abuse of definitions. In their very nature, they are not calculated to extend the acquisition of knowledge, though they may be well fitted to ascertain and guard the limits of that knowledge, which is already acquired."[17]

Moreover, he added, any method of inquiry that posits definitions, with an eye to building extensive "systems"[18] upon them, threatens to conceal much knowledge that might otherwise lie within our reach. Definitions and the systems of classification built upon them, "unless they are marked by the purest precision, the fullest comprehension, and the most chastised justness of thought [rigorous empiricism] . . . will perplex instead of unfolding . . . will darken instead of illustrating."[19]

Although it is clear from the writings of Wilson and Madison generally

---

14. The Federalist No. 37, at 234–37 (J. Cooke ed. 1961). But notice the apparent contrast between the way Madison here speaks of the sciences, including political science, and the way Hamilton, in Federalist No. 9, at 51, speaks on the same subject: "The science of politics, however, like most other sciences has received great improvement [of late]. The efficacy of various principles is now well understood, which were either not known at all, or imperfectly known to the ancients." The tension in evidence here is nicely captured in Morton White's discussion of the "principles" of the American Revolution itself, in The Philosophy of the American Revolution 230–39 (New York: Oxford University Press, 1978).

15. 1 McCloskey, Works 101 (cited in note 8).

16. The phrase is Epstein's (cited in note 13); see at 117; cf. at 114, where Epstein characterizes the passage in question as "a short essay concerning the human understanding."

17. 1 McCloskey, Works 98.

18. Id. at 371 (Wilson against Cartesian "love of system"); cf. at 200.

19. Id. at 99. In his law lectures Wilson recalls these earlier passages when he later turns to the importance of the "social operations" of the human mind, at 229ff. See my discussion of these "social operations," infra text at note 82ff.

that their respective conceptions of science were not as divergent as these isolated passages might suggest—or were, indeed, not basically at odds at all—
these passages do point to a difference in emphasis that discloses an important
difference (though not necessarily a disagreement) in outlook. Madison, the
prudent, complex skeptic, here sounds resigned to a species of scientific
"truth" that is tentative, contingent, and "unavoidably" incomplete; whereas
Wilson affirms a conception of science *as knowledge* in which, together with
"precision," "the fullest comprehension", or comprehensiveness, is of the
essence.[20]

In all their theoretical ruminations, both these founders, unsurprisingly,
tended to invoke the authority of modern "science" and to embrace empiricism as the touchstone of any scientific method.[21] And Madison, as well as
many another American Federalist, consistently voiced a concern for precision
and comprehensiveness in his political thought. But Wilson's distinctive concern for, at the same time, both "the purest precision" and "the fullest comprehension" led him at times to a distinctive approach in his attempt to
appropriate the authority of "science" to Federalist apologetics.

Still, it was not so much science in general as it was one fundamental
science that Wilson sought to enlist in the Federalist cause. This was "the
science of morals." And it is here that the apparent contrast between Wilson
and Madison may seem especially striking. On the one hand, Wilson's moralistic emphasis might seem to root his ideas firmly in a now distant early modern period. On the other hand, nothing in Madison's genius can still seem
more accessibly modern than Madison's concern to formulate a constitutionalism which, while it might "economize on virtue"[22] and even encourage moral
growth,[23] would not need to draw routinely on the resources of civic morality
in order to give effect to the Federalists' new design for the nation.[24]

Although Wilson at times subscribed to what have come to be called

---

20. See 1 McCloskey, Works 200, for an example of Wilson's vehemently shunning
reductionism.
21. For Wilson's earnestly—even if problematically—empirical conception of political science, see *id.* at 390. Cf. Madison in Federalist No. 14 at 83–89, 87 & *passim* (J. Cooke ed. 1961),
on the importance in political science of "good sense" and of knowledge of one's own particular
situation and experience. For analysis of The Federalist that posits an interplay there between
"Lockean rationalism" and "Humean empiricism," see Morton White, Philosophy, *The Federalist*,
and the Constitution *passim* (New York: Oxford University Press, 1987).
22. I take this phrase from Bruce A. Ackerman, The Storrs Lectures: Discovering the Constitution, 93 Yale L.J. 1013, 1031 & *passim* (1984).
23. Cf. James Madison's Autobiography, ed. Douglass Adair, 2 Wm. & Mary Q., 3d ser.,
191 (1945), esp. at 197, where Madison contemplates the polite theme of the contemporary "taste
for the improvement of the mind and manners."
24. Cf. Epstein, Political Theory (cited in note 13), esp. at 62 & 64. Still, it has become
common for scholars to notice, and even emphasize, something not unlike an apparent moralism
in Madison's occasional remarks—thus Meyer Reinhold, in his Classica Americana: The Greek
and Roman Heritage in the United States 145 (Detroit: Wayne State University Press, 1984)
(citing Paul Merrill Spurlin, Montesquieu in America, 1760–1801, at 261–62 (University: Louisiana State University Press, 1940)): "The primacy of virtue in a republic had the support also of
Madison, who said in the debate on the Constitution at the Virginia ratifying convention: 'No
theoretical checks, no form of government can render us secure. To suppose that any form of

Madisonian claims about the importance of the structure and operations of political institutions,[25] nevertheless, his distinctive and doctrinaire emphasis on "the people" as the most important, even if impalpable, institution of republican government led him to a corresponding emphasis on civic morality that is notable for so prominent a Federalist. Wilson could and did agree that the superstructure of any republican government must be "formed . . . proportioned, and organized in such a manner" that "wisdom and strength" would stand as the twin "pillars" supporting the institutional "fabrick." It is nevertheless, he insisted, "on the basis of goodness" alone that these pillars must rest; and this basis of goodness must consist in "the people at large."[26] Madison, for his part, similarly acknowledged that, "A dependence on the people is, no doubt, the primary controul"[27] on a republican government. But, characteristically, Madisonian theory thereupon proceeds to emphasize "the necessity of auxiliary precautions"[28] and to contemplate the best mechanisms for "correcting the infirmities of popular Government."[29]

---

government will secure liberty or happiness without any virtue in the people, is a chimerical idea.' "

As these remarks might be taken to indicate, it is unlikely that Madison believed, and it is inconceivable that he would have professed at the Virginia ratifying convention, that the American republic could entirely dispense with "virtue" or "moral foundations." Again, my point of contrast between Madison and Wilson is a matter of relative emphasis and of differing conceptions of the American moral economy—not a matter of a wholesale difference in operative constitutional theory. Cf. Lance Banning, Some Second Thoughts on "Virtue" and the Course of Revolutionary Thinking, in J.G.A. Pocock & Terence Ball, eds., Conceptual Change and the Constitution (Lawrence: University of Kansas Press, forthcoming 1988) (manuscript kindly supplied by Professor Banning) ("Pocock & Ball. eds.").

Moreover Hamilton, in Federalist No. 31, at 194–95 (J. Cooke ed. 1961), tends to pair in a single phrase "the sciences of morals and politics" to affirm the "principles of moral and political *knowledge*" (emphasis added) and the "degree of certainty" that attends them, even if it is a lesser degree than is sometimes found in "mathematics," e.g., in the "maxims," or axioms, or "geometry."

25. E.g., 1 McCloskey, Works 289-90. Cf. Lance Banning, The Practicable Sphere of a Republic: James Madison, the Constitutional Convention, and the Emergence of Revolutionary Federalism, in Richard Beeman et al., eds., Beyond Confederation: Origins of the Constitution and American National Identity 162, 182 (Chapel Hill: University of North Carolina Press, 1987) ("Beeman et al., Beyond Confederation").

26. 1 McCloskey, Works 303; 2 McCloskey, Works 778; cf. vol. 1 at 174, 290, & 315. Contrast Hannah Arendt, On Revolution (rev. ed. Harmondsworth, Eng.: Penguin Books, 1965) ("Arendt, On Revolution"), esp. at 203: "What counted was neither wisdom nor virtue, but solely the act [of Foundation] itself, which was indisputable." Cf. my text *infra* at note 44.

27. Federalist No. 51, at 349 (J. Cooke ed. 1961). Cf. Washington, in-a letter of Feb. 7, 1787, to Marquis de Lafayette, as excerpted in Michael Kammen, ed., The Origins of the American Constitution: A Documentary History, 101, 102 (New York: Viking Penguin, 1986) (under the proposed Constitution "the general government is arranged [such] that it can never be in danger of degenerating into a monarchy, an Oligarchy, an Aristocracy, or any other despotic or oppressive form, so long as there shall remain any virtue in the body of the People.").

28. Federalist No. 51, at 349 (J. Cooke ed. 1961).

29. In Madison's 1788 Remarks on Mr. Jefferson's Draft of a Constitution, in Marvin Meyers, ed., The Mind of the Founder: Sources of the Political Thought of James Madison 56 (1st ed. Indianapolis: Bobbs-Merrill Co., 1973) ("Meyers, Mind of the Founder, 1st ed.").

The shifts in point of view within this paragraph are intentional. Through them I mean to allude to an important problem to which I try to remain sensitive throughout this essay: the ambiguous relationship between, on the one hand, Madison's actual statements and restatements of his constitutional theory at particular times, and, on the other hand, reified "Madisonian the-

Without ever contradicting Madisonian theory, Wilson typically advocated structures and procedures of government more thoroughly and more
directly popular than those Madison preferred. And Wilsonian theory consistently proves loath to turn its focus away from its dearest first principle:[30]
"For a people wanting to themselves, there is indeed no remedy in the political dispensary. From their power there is no appeal: to their errour their is
no superiour principle of correction."[31]

Thus given over, at least by the late 1780s,[32] to a "democratic faith"[33]
about which Madison and most other Federalists had grown more doubtful,
Wilson might seem to us to have been harking back nostalgically to an inexpe-
rienced, early Revolutionary republicanism—if not, indeed, to the seminal republican theory of Montesquieu himself.[34] But, in any case, this was not the
way Wilson saw the matter. Rather, in muting what is now sometimes taken
to be a prototypically modern and recognizably Humean strain in Federalist
theory[35]—that is, by resisting the notion that the principles of republican government may constitute an autonomous science and may, indeed, be "reduced" to such a science[36]—Wilson was convinced he spoke for the

ory" as it has been variously synthesized so as to take on a significance of its own quite distinct if
not necessarily different from anything or even everything Madison actually said.

30. See, e.g., Wilson's speech of Nov. 24, 1787, in the Pennsylvania ratifying convention, in
Jensen, ed., at 349 (cited in note 8); cf. at 362.

31. 1 McCloskey Works 296 (remarking, in his law lectures, on the significance of the "next
election" as a "remedy" for "mischief" in government); cf. 2 McCloskey, Works 724, in a celebrated pamphlet of 1774: "If, then, the inhabitants of Britain possess a sufficient restraint upon
any of these branches of the legislature, their liberty is secure, provided they be not wanting to
themselves." And cf. the very similar formulation of this thought in Jensen, ed., at 349; cf. at 362.

32. Cf. George M. Dennison, The "Revolution Principle": Ideology and Constitutionalism
in the Thought of James Wilson, 39 Rev. Pol. 157 (1977), esp. at 164ff.

33. Andrew C. McLaughlin, James Wilson in the Philadelphia Convention, 12 Pol. Sci. Q. 1,
15 (1897).

34. See, e.g., Montesquieu's fable of "the Troglodytes" in The Persian Letters (1721), ed. &
trans. J. Robert Loy, at 59–66 & 284–85 (New York: World Publishing Co., 1961).

35. On the distinct but related issue of interpreting the political theory of Hume himself as
"modernizing" or not, and, indeed, "republican" or not, see Duncan Forbes, Hume's Science of
Politics, in G.P. Morice, ed., David Hume: Bicentenary Papers 39 (Edinburgh: Edinburgh Uni-
versity Press, 1977) ("Morice on Hume"). Cf. Forbes, Hume's Philosophical Politics (Cambridge:
University Press, 1975); Frederick G. Whelan, Order and Artifice in Hume's Political Philosophy
(Princeton, N.J.: Princeton University Press, 1985); David Miller, Philosophy and Ideology in
Hume's Political Thought (Oxford: Clarendon Press, 1981).

From Whelan's "perspective" on this matter, "it is ironic than an uncharacteristic speculation of Hume's [in the essay Idea of a Perfect Commonwealth] was apparently influential in shaping the thought of James Madison. . . . The irony is that Hume offers this highly untypical essay as
a speculative exercise, almost a jeu d'esprit, and he begins it with the disclaimer that to 'try experiments merely upon the credit of supposed argument and philosophy, can never be the part of a
wise magistrate. . . .' Hume's empiricism of course permits and indeed encourages cautious experimentation . . . within limits that are difficult to specify. The confidence that the Federalist authors
and other American revolutionaries expressed in philosophy or science as a guide to fashioning
new governments, however, often seems to have exceeded these limits." Whelan, supra, at 342-43.
But see James Moore, Hume's Political Science and the Classical Republican Tradition, 10 Can. J.
Pol. Sci. 809 (1977), esp. at 833–39.

36. I allude here to themes prominent in a sequence of scholarly literature commonly traced
to several articles by Douglass Adair, beginning with "That Politics May Be Reduced to a Science": David Hume, James Madison, and the Tenth Federalist, 20 Huntington Lib. Q. 343 (1957).
Those articles, and later scholarship in the same vein, are conveniently reviewed, and pointedly

progressive and scientific van of contemporary republicanism.

It was, then, expressly to "science," understood as knowledge, and, more specifically, to recent progress in science, that Wilson appealed in order to justify his unexceeded optimism about a foundation for the Constitution in the "goodness" of "the people."[37] And in espousing his optimism, Wilson made it clear that, for justification, he did *not* look chiefly to political science, which he considered a science yet in its "infancy,"[38] and, at best, a science still insufficiently "unbiassed," even by 1790, to import the full authority of science at all.[39]

By turning, instead, to authoritative new discoveries in "moral science," Wilson meant to address the problems of ambivalence and pessimism that colored the republican theory of even the most admired progressive champions of "enlightenment" in Europe: Despite the authority of the mordant scenarios of Montesquieu's *histoire raisonnée*,[40] and in the face of the discouraging catalog of violence and despotism in Beccaria's universal history of nation building,[41] Wilson invoked the authority of new knowledge about the moral capability of human nature. Thus, at once "comprehending" but superseding the earlier best wisdom of European republican theorists, Wilson envisioned that Americans were in a position to hope more for popular government than Montesquieu or Beccaria had ever imagined. And Wilson believed this hope was thoroughly justified by the new knowledge that now for the first time promised an authentically popular redemption of the republican ideal.

---

disputed, by James Conniff in The Enlightenment and American Political Thought: A Study of the Origins of Madison's *Federalist Number 10*, 8 Pol. Theory 381 (1980). For an account of Madisonian theory as Humean in ways that Adair's articles, and work derived from them, do not tend to emphasize, see Roy Branson, James Madison and the Scottish Enlightenment, 40 J. Hist. Ideas 235 (1979).

37. Cf. one of Wilson's most characteristic and most quoted public remarks, e.g., as one reporter recorded it from Wilson's Nov. 24, 1787 speech: "After a period of six thousand years has elapsed since the Creation, the United States exhibit to the world, the first instance, as far as we can learn, of a nation, unattacked by external force, unconvulsed by domestic insurrections, assembling voluntarily, deliberating fully, and deciding calmly, concerning that system of government, under which they would wish that they and their posterity should live." Jensen, ed., at 353; cf. at 342 (cited in note 8). In this or a similar formulation Wilson's remark has been quoted by, e.g., Donald H. Meyer, The Democratic Enlightenment 154 (New York: G.P. Putnam's Sons, Capricorn Books, 1976); and by Farrand, Framing, at 62 (cited in note 5). Cf. Hamilton's seemingly less reassured and less reassuring view of the same historic moment as a "crisis," in which Americans had yet to resolve "the important question, whether societies of men are capable or not, of establishing good government from reflection and choice, or whether they are forever destined to depend, for their political constitutions, on accident and force." Federalist No. 1, at 1 (J. Cooke ed. 1961).

38. Jensen, ed., at 353; cf. at 342. See also 1 McCloskey, Works at 80. And cf. 2 McCloskey, Works at 785, and my discussion in sec. VII *infra* at note 213.

39. 1 McCloskey, Works 80. Cf. Madison in Federalist No. 37, e.g., at 235 (J. Cooke ed. 1961): "Questions daily occur in the course of practice, which prove the obscurity which reigns in these subjects, and which puzzle the greatest adepts in political science."

40. See, e.g., Montesquieu's Considerations on the Causes of the Greatness of the Romans and Their Decline (1734, 1748), trans. David Lowenthal (Ithaca, N.Y.: Cornell University Press, 1968); cf. Montesquieu's fable of "the Troglodytes" (cited in note 34).

41. 1 McCloskey, Works 263 (citing Beccaria's famous Essay on Crimes and Punishments, ch. 26).

Wilson averred that one great source of this new knowledge, about the feasibility and necessity of thoroughly popular republicanism, lay in the experience of the American Revolution itself.[42] But to rest content with the knowledge, however momentous, that had been realized in the American revolutionary experience would be tantamount to reducing a progressive "revolutionary principle" to a hidebound "revolutionary precedent." It was just such a reductive tendency that Wilson saw and deplored in the conventional British constitutional theory codified, as it were, by Blackstone, which diminished the Glorious Revolution of the 1680s by making too much of the event itself and too little of its essential, even if inchoate, principle: that political obligation must be grounded on consent.[43]

Wilson's distinction between "revolutionary principle" and "revolutionary precedent"—and his anxious concern that even in America the latter might eclipse the former—are only the most telling of many indications that he thought it not simply wrong but dangerous to exalt political experience as self-justifying. It is, then, only by ignoring much of what is most characteristic of Wilson's mature constitutional theory that we could, following Hannah Arendt's "interpretation of the success of the American Revolution in terms of the Roman spirit," impute generally to the American founders the notion that the Americans' very "act of foundation" authorized itself.[44]

In the late 1780s and 1790s, Wilson's anxious appeal for authority beyond the Revolutionary experience, beyond the subsequent and "augmenting" act of foundation itself,[45] and even beyond the new "science of politics" that became both talisman and legacy of the Federalist campaign,[46] is most evident in Wilson's appeal to the authority of "moral science." And so far from looking for guidance to David Hume, or to any Humean orientation of the day, for a philosophical authorization of American Federalist theory, Wilson couched his appeal to moral science in the terms of an elaborate refutation of the speculative skeptical philosophy Hume personified.

On at least one occasion Wilson referred to Hume, although only in passing and apparently not by name, as "a very sensible writer on political sub-

---

42. Jensen, ed., at 362; cf. at 348.

43. 1 McCloskey, Works 77–79. Cf. Jensen, ed., at 343: "even at the Revolution [of 1688], when the government was essentially improved, no other principle was recognized, but that of an original contract between the sovereign and the people—a contract which rather excludes than implies the doctrine of representation." Cf. at 354. And see generally Stanley N. Katz, The American Constitution: A Revolutionary Interpretation, in Beeman et al., Beyond Confederation, at 23–37, esp. 32–33 (cited in note 25); David S. Lovejoy, The Glorious Revolution in America (New York: Harper & Row, 1972), e.g., at 182 (reference to assertion of a principle of "consent to laws and taxes"); H.T. Dickenson, The Eighteenth-Century Debate on the "Glorious Revolution," 61 History 28 (1976).

44. Arendt, On Revolution ch. 5, at 199, 203, and passim (cited in note 26). Cf. Richard S. Kay, Preconstitutional Rules, 42 Ohio St. L.J. 187 (1981); Kay, The Illegality of the Constitution, 4 Const. Commentary 57 (1987); Kent Greenawalt, The Rule of Recognition and the Constitution, 85 Mich. L. Rev. 621 (1987); Ackerman, 93 Yale L.J. at 101ff. (cited in note 22).

45. Arendt at 201–3.

46. Cf. Gordon S. Wood, The Creation of the American Republic, 1776–1787, esp. ch. XV (New York: W.W. Norton, 1969) ("Wood, Creation").

jects."[47] But usually Wilson spoke as ill of Hume as of Blackstone. Indeed, Wilson considered Hume an even more pernicious thinker than Blackstone: for if Blackstone was, as Wilson said, a covert apologist for despotism, Hume was a subtle enemy of human knowledge itself, who thus would disarm mankind of its chief weapon not only against despotism but also against every other threat to human happiness.[48]

The animus against Hume that pervades Wilson's mature constitutional theory was really, then, something of a fixated reaction to only one part of the product of Hume's versatile pen. Wilson does not seem to have troubled with, or been troubled by, Hume's Tory histories or Hume's elegant essays on social, political, and moral theory. It was, rather, Hume's promotion of the "profound . . . abstract philosophy . . . commonly called *metaphysics*"[49]—in other words, Hume's speculative claims about certain fundamental matters of epistemology and human nature—that so provoked Wilson. Hypersensitive to the doctrine of "universal scepticism" that Hume seemed to teach,[50] and unwilling to contemplate the detachment of "speculative philosophy" from "practical philosophy" and social life,[51] Wilson came to believe there was nothing more important to securing the American republic than the reconstruction of the "polite" unity of truth, virtue, and happiness as a premise for republican civic culture.[52]

Whether Hume is fairly judged to have stood among or against the advocates of "politeness,"[53] especially as it might inform republican civic culture,[54]

---

47. 1 McCloskey, Works 297.
48. *Id.* 79, 103–5, 214, 216, 221–22. Cf. Conrad, Polite Foundation, esp. at 375–76 (cited in note 12). And cf. Donald W. Livingston, Hume's Philosophy of Common Life 25 (Chicago: University of Chicago Press, 1984): "Until well into the twentieth century, Hume's philosophical writings were viewed as skeptical in an especially vicious way."
49. Here I am quoting from Hume's Section I, Of the Different Species of Philosophy, *in* An Enquiry Concerning Human Understanding (1777 ed.), at paras. 5 & 9, in Enquiries Concerning Human Understanding and Concerning the Principles of Morals, ed. L.A. Selby-Bigge; 3d ed., ed. P.H. Nidditch, at 9 & 11 (Oxford: Clarendon Press 1975) ("Nidditch, ed.").
50. Cf. the following passage, as quoted from Hume—in order to illustrate his epistemology at its most Pyrrhonist extreme—in Henry Laurie, Scottish Philosophy in Its National Development 62 (Glasgow: James Maclehose & Sons, 1902): "The most perfect philosophy of a natural kind only staves off our ignorance a little longer; as perhaps the most perfect philosophy of the moral or metaphysical kind serves only to discover larger portions of it." Contrast, however, the analysis of Hume's speculative philosophy by John P. Wright, The Sceptical Realism of David Hume (Minneapolis: University of Minnesota Press, 1983); see esp. Wright's last chapter, on Descartes and Malebranche as important sources for Hume's "sceptical realism" in his conception of human nature.
51. Cf. Hume in sec. IX, pt. II, para. 228 of An Enquiry Concerning the Principles of Morals, *in* Nidditch, ed., at 279 (cited in note 49): "Truths which are *pernicious* to society, if any such there be, will yield to errors which are salutary and *advantageous*." For an interpretation of Hume's practical philosophy that is particularly attentive to the Common Sense context and content of Hume's writings generally, see David Fate Norton, David Hume: Common-Sense Moralist, Sceptical Metaphysician (Princeton, N.J.: Princeton University Press, 1982) ("Norton on Hume").
52. Cf. 1 McCloskey, Works 147 & *passim* (cited in note 8).
53. On Hume as a partisan of "politeness," see John Christian Laursen, From Court to Commerce: David Hume and the French Vocabulary of "Politeness" in the Scottish Enlightenment (essay presented at a conference on "The Political Thought of the Scottish Enlightenment in Its European Context," Edinburgh, Aug. 1986, and distributed by the Conference for the Study

Wilson endorsed the adversarial school of contemporary philosophy that consolidated under the leadership of Hume's leading critic Thomas Reid and that took its identity from its aversion to Hume's "insideous" and "illiberal" skepticism. This was the self-proclaimed Common Sense school, whose name signified their championship of the "sovereign" moral and epistemological authority of the mental faculty of "Common Sense," and whose mission eventually extended to a defense of all polite culture against the Humean threat.[55] Because the burden of argumentation by the Common Sense philosophers lay chiefly, however, with the crucial question of the "truth" of men's "moral beliefs,"[56] the term "moral science" came to epitomize what they were most determined to establish.

James Beattie, the leading contemporary popularizer of Reidian Common Sense, chose for his most accessible compendium of Common Sense doctrine the title *Elements of Moral Science*. This two-volume work comprised Beattie's "abridgment" of the course of lectures he regularly gave at his own Scottish university, in Aberdeen.[57] But the Aberdonian Dr. Beattie was lionized as a didact much more in England and in America than at home in Scotland, and the *Elements of Moral Science*, together with Beattie's other works and those of Reid and other members of their school, became a staple of belletristic literature in the new American republic, especially in the "wholly and *highly* federal"[58] capital Philadelphia.[59]

of Political Thought). Cf. Laursen, Sceptical Politics in Hume and Kant: Letters, Philosophy, and the Language of Politics chs. 2 & 4 (Ph.D. diss., Johns Hopkins University, 1985). And see Ralph S. Pomeroy, Hume's Proposed League of the Learned and Conversible Worlds, 19 Eighteenth-Century Stud. 373 (1986); Nancy S. Struever, The Conversable [sic] World: Eighteenth-Century Transformations of the Relation of Rhetoric and Truth, in Rhetoric and the Pursuit of Truth: Language Change in the Seventeenth and Eighteenth Centuries 77, esp. 79–94 (Los Angeles: Clark Memorial Library, University of California, 1985).

54. Forbes, in Hume's Science of Politics, at 42 (cited in note 35), reminds us that "Rousseau wrote in his *Confessions* of Hume's *'ame republicaine'* "; and Forbes himself refers to "Hume's republicanism," albeit a republicanism "purely academic." Cf. Moore, 10 Can. J. Pol. Sci. (cited in note 35).

55. Stephen A. Conrad, Citizenship and Common Sense: The Problem of Authority in the Social Background and Social Philosophy of the Wise Club of Aberdeen, esp. chs. 4-8 (New York: Garland Publishing Co., 1987) ("Conrad, Citizenship").

56. The most forceful recent exposition of this point is, I believe, David Fate Norton, Hume and His Scottish Critics, in McGill Hume Studies, ed. Norton et al., 309 (San Diego, Cal.: Austin Hill Press, 1976). For a contrasting interpretation of Reid's truth claims, see Paul Vernier, Thomas Reid on the Foundations of Knowledge and His Answer to Skepticism, in Stephen F. Barker & Tom L. Beauchamp, eds., Thomas Reid: Critical Interpretations 14 (Philadelphia: Philosophical Monographs, 1976) ("Barker & Beauchamp on Thomas Reid").

57. See Beattie's own advertisement to the 1790 edition, published in Edinburgh, at p. iii of the facsimile reproduction, intro. James R. Irvine (Delmar, N.Y.: Scholars' Facsimiles & Reprints, 1976).

58. Benjamin Rush, in a letter of March 19, 1789, in 1 L.H. Butterfield, ed., Letters of Benjamin Rush 507 (2 vols.; Princeton, N.J.: Princeton University Press, 1951) ("Butterfield, Rush Letters"). Nevertheless, it would seem that Rush's characterization was grounded, at most and at best, on a "sublimation of politics," for which Professor George Dargo provides the most compelling concise explanation of which I am aware; Dargo, Parties and the Transformation of the Constitutional Idea in Revolutionary Pennsylvania, in Patricia U. Bonomi, ed., Party and Political Opposition in Revolutionary America 98, esp. at 111 (Tarrytown, N.Y.: Sleepy Hollow Press, 1980). On Wilson's "sublimation" of politics, see my text *infra* at sec. VII.

Such American appropriation of Scottish ideas and exemplars, from the mid-18th century onward, is a feature of early American republican culture that is now familiar—indeed, sometimes overemphasized.[60] But even *if* so historically astute a philosopher as Alasdair MacIntyre may be claiming too much for the glory of Enlightened Scotland in surmising that there remain unanswered some important general questions of "causation" about this Scottish "influence" on early American "social, moral, and political change,"[61] nevertheless, James Wilson's overt and elaborate appropriation of the authority of Reidian moral science to early American Federalism was a project so important to Wilson himself and so emblematic of Wilson's political culture that students of the Founding cannot afford to overlook it. Neither our historical understanding of the Founding[62] nor our historically informed constitutional theory[63] is so comprehensive or authoritative as to permit us to neglect the example of an important framer like Wilson, who, in his appeals to "moral science," reached for the fullest comprehensiveness and addressed questions about authority that he thought were even more fundamental than the Founding itself.

III. "MORAL ABSTRACTION" AS A PATENT METAPHOR

". . . a principle of good will as well as of knowledge."

59. See, e.g., Andrew Hook, Scotland and America: A Study of Cultural Relations, 1750-1835, ch. 6, esp. at 79 (Glasgow: Blackie, 1975). Cf. Henry F. May, The Enlightenment in America at, e.g., 209, 343ff. (New York: Oxford University Press, 1976). And see Rush's Aug. 1, 1786 letter to Beattie, informing him that Rush had just procured Beattie's admission to the American Philosophical Society, and assuring Beattie that, "The American Revolution, which divided the British Empire, made no breach in the republic of letters." 1 Butterfield, Rush Letters 394 (cited in note 58).

60. In addition to the works by Hook and May cited in note 59, and to Donald H. Meyer, The Democratic Enlightenment (New York: G.P. Putnam's Sons, Capricorn Books, 1976), see D.H. Meyer, The Instructed Conscience: The Shaping of the American National Ethic (Philadelphia: University of Pennsylvania Press, 1972); Garry Wills, Inventing America: Jefferson's Declaration of Independence (Garden City, N.Y.: Doubleday & Co., 1978); Wills, Explaining America: The Federalist (Garden City, N.Y.: Doubleday & Co., 1981). For what I believe remains the most cogently argued warning against overemphasizing this Scottish influence on the American Founding, see Ronald Hamowy, Jefferson and the Scottish Enlightenment: A Critique of Garry Wills's Inventing America: Jefferson's Declaration of Independence, 36 Wm. & Mary Q., 3d ser., 503 (1979).

61. Alasdair MacIntyre, After Virtue: A Study in Moral Theory 272 (2d ed. Notre Dame, Ind.: University of Notre Dame Press, 1984) (in "Postscript to the Second Edition").

62. See, e.g., James H. Hutson, The Creation of the Constitution: Scholarship at a Standstill, 12 Revs. Am. His. 463 (1984); cf. Hutson, Riddles of the Federal Constitutional Convention, 44 Wm. & Mary Q., 3d ser., 411 (1987).

63. See, e.g., Frank I. Michelman, The Supreme Court, 1985 Term—Forward: Traces of Self Government, 100 Harv. L. Rev. 4 (1986); cf. Michelman, The Place of Republicanism in American Constitutional Law (paper presented at Annual Meeting, Association of American Law Schools, Los Angeles, Jan. 1987; manuscript kindly supplied by the author). See also William E. Nelson, Reason and Compromise in the Establishment of the Federal Constitution, 1787-1801, 44 Wm. & Mary Q., 3d ser., 458, esp. 483-84 (1987).

—Wilson, in his *Lectures on Law*[64]

In terms of Wilson's own approach, and in light of prevalent interests among intellectual historians and constitutional theorists today,[65] the most conspicuous feature of Wilson's attempt to ground Federalist arguments in moral science is his appeal to the epistemological authority of language. According to the "philosophy of mind" taught by Reid, whom Wilson thought no less a paragon in that field than Francis Bacon had proved to be in the "philosophy of matter,"[66] language can serve as more than the pleasing and necessary medium of human knowledge.[67] Sometimes language can serve as evidence of, and even a way to, knowledge. Indeed, language by itself is sometimes capable of serving us as an authentic *proxy* for knowledge.

The Common Sense case for ascribing such capability to language rested primarily on arguments derived from a conception of language as unmediated mental experience. Or, as Wilson politely reformulated this tenet of the Common Sense philosophers, "language is the picture of human thoughts; and, from this faithful picture, we may draw certain conclusions concerning the original."[68] Implicating without confronting the question how even the most accurate pictures of our thoughts can ever establish anything "conclusive" about them, Wilson's affirmation here about the *fidelity* of human language to the human mind was, in and of itself, a point of the greatest importance to him. Moreover, Wilson's affirmation departed from some of Madison's and Hume's statements on this matter.

For example, Madison, in his skeptical digression in *Federalist* No. 37, suggests he is resigned not only that the "objects" men seek to understand are often intractably indistinct, and that the imperfect human faculties often prove too weak to penetrate "obscurity." He is also resigned that language, as the medium necessary for men's expressing their ideas to one another, is "unavoidably inaccurate" and often "inadequate."[69] Still, here, even in Madison's scrupulous prudence and his ostensible tendency to resignation, there is nothing that necessarily contradicts Wilson's own Common Sense

---

64. 1 McCloskey, Works 162.
65. See, e.g., David A. Hollinger's observations on the current "linguistic imperialism" in his field, in American Intellectual History: Some Issues for the 1980s, in the collection of Hollinger's essays In the America Province: Studies in the History and Historiography of Ideas 176 (Bloomington: Indiana University Press, 1985). On the "linguistic turn" in intellectual history more generally, see Donald R. Kelley, Horizons of Intellectual History: Retrospect, Circumspect, Prospect, 48 J. Hist. Ideas 143 (1987). For samples of the linguistic turn in contemporary American constitutional theory, see the relevant articles in symposia like 58 So. Cal. L. Rev. 277 (1985) and 60 Tex. L. Rev. 373 (1982).
66. See Wilson's opinion in the case of Chisholm v. Georgia, 2 Dallas 419, 453–54 (1793). Cf. 1 McCloskey, Works 216–17, 193–94 (cited in note 8).
67. See, e.g., 1 McCloskey, Works 231, 237–38.
68. *Id.* at 135. Cf. I.A. Richards on the representative 18th-century Common Sense literary criticism of Kames, in Richards, The Philosophy of Rhetoric 16 ff. & 98 ff. (New York: Oxford University Press, 1936). On the important connection between Kames and Reidian Common Sense, see Conrad, Citizenship chs. 5–6 & *passim* (cited in note 55).
69. Federalist No. 37, at 236–37 (J. Cooke ed. 1961).

views. With Hume's stated position, however, Wilson felt that he—and Common Sense—were at loggerheads.

What elicited from Wilson his strongest affirmations about the capability of language in discovering and enlarging men's knowledge of "true principles," especially knowledge of moral truth, was Hume's perceived challenge to what is now sometimes called the "constitutive function" of language. It is, so Wilson affirmed, "in consequence of language" that "we are united by political societies, government, and laws."[70] And it was just this power of language to discover and represent to us general reality, and even to create and augment human society, that Hume appeared to deny. Indeed, Hume's perceived attack on language occasionally took on the air of an attack against not just human knowledge but all of culture and society—or at least what was "best" in them, in the moral sense of "best."

When Hume apparently sought to discredit, even while disavowing any intention to "depreciate," "[a]ll polite letters" as "nothing but pictures of human life in various attitudes and situations," it was what Hume considered to be the necessary particularity of the "pictures," or images, of polite letters that bore the brunt of his critique.[71] As a modern student of Hume has phrased it, Hume took the position that "the meaning of no general term can be an image."[72] And if this was what Hume meant to argue, or was any part of what contemporary readers might have imputed to Hume's endeavors at the "profound" species of philosophy, then it should not be difficult to see how reading, much less misreading, Hume could have provoked a defensive campaign on behalf of the social, moral, and epistemological authority of language.[73]

For example, when the Common Sense philosophers read the *Treatise of Human Nature* they encountered Hume's charge that "by profession" poets are "liars" who "always endeavour to give an air of truth to their fictions."[74] How Hume justified this seeming affront to poetry, with "poetry" here taken to stand for any and all language for which claims of intrinsic truth are made, involved nothing less than the entire argument of the *Treatise*. And it was for the acknowledged purpose of refuting Hume's argument, comprising the historic consummation of the false "idealism" of deluded geniuses from Plato to

---

70. 1 McCloskey, Works 231.

71. An Enquiry Concerning Human Understanding, *in* Nidditch, ed., at 9, 10 (cited in note 49).

72. Páll S. Árdal, Convention and Value, *in* Morice on Hume 51, 56 (cited in note 35).

73. For an example of a similar reaction to Hume from a modern scholar particularly concerned with questions of language, culture, and epistemology, see the much praised albeit controversial work of Owen Barfield, e.g., his Poetic Diction: A Study in Meaning (London, 1928), esp. Preface to the Second Edition (2d ed. New York: McGraw-Hill Book Co., 1952, 1964). Nevertheless, contrast the readings of Hume by some leading modern scholars, e.g., Norman Kemp Smith, The Philosophy of David Hume: A Critical Study of Its Origins and Central Doctrines (1941; reprint ed. New York: Garland Publishing Co., 1983); and Norton on Hume (cited in note 51).

74. A Treatise of Human Nature, bk. I, pt. III, sec. X, ed. L.A. Selby-Bigge (1888); 2d ed., ed. P.H. Nidditch, at 121 (Oxford: Clarendon Press, 1978).

Locke and Berkeley,[75] that Thomas Reid launched his campaign to restore Common Sense to its rightful place of "sovereign authority" in philosophy.

Notwithstanding the current modest revival of interest in Reid's contributions to philosophy,[76] there is little prospect today of rehabilitating Reid to preeminence as the philosopher who has engaged the argument of Hume's *Treatise* most thoroughly and refuted it most irrefutably. But in the period of the autumnal, pre-Kantian Enlightenment, Reid was in fact often singled out as the philosopher who had discovered how best to "cut up" Hume's metaphysics "by the roots." So said George III of what Dr. Beattie had accomplished in the *Essay on Truth*, Beattie's best-selling polemic written to retail (albeit at an enormous intellectual discount) the gist of Reid's philosophy to the polite reading public. Now itself wholly dismissed for its empty pretense to philosophical argument, Beattie's *Essay* in his own day won him considerable renown, a pension from the King, and a sitting with Sir Joshua Reynolds that resulted in an allegorical portrait of Beattie, entitled "The Triumph Truth," which shows the good doctor clutching his *Essay* while an angel cows three dark, primitive figures who resemble Hume, Gibbon, and Voltaire.[77]

In the context of the Atlantic culture of the day, there was, then, nothing eccentric about Wilson's apprising his law students in 1790 that Thomas Reid's 1764 *Inquiry into the Human Mind* had marked the beginning of a new, constructive epoch of reaffirmation in philosophy. Reid's ideas had succeeded in clearing away "the rubbish, which, during the long course of two thousand years, had concealed the foundations of philosophy."[78] But Reid and his school had, by 1790, accomplished even more: In disposing of the "idealist" tradition in philosophy, which had for so long contended that knowledge of the human mind is beyond the reach of immediate human understanding,[79] the Common Sense school had reconceived the entire enterprise of philosophy, and had already met "with the most encouraging success" in accumulating discoveries about human nature that were as useful as they were conclusive.[80]

Wilson's reformulation of a Common Sense for America was, nevertheless, peculiarly his own in the degree of its exhilaration at the novelty and the promise of the Common Sense approach in moral science. When Wilson

---

75. 1 McCloskey, Works 213–14.

76. For an overview, see Keith Lehrer, Reid's Influence on Contemporary American and British Philosophy, *in* Barker & Beauchamp on Thomas Reid 1–7 (cited in noted 56). Cf. Louise Marcil-Lacoste, Claude Buffier and Thomas Reid: Two Common-Sense Philosophers (Kingston & Montreal: McGill-Queen's University Press, 1982) ("Marcil-Lacoste"). See also the fledgling journal *Reid Studies*, edited by Melvin T. Dalgarno and published by the University of Aberdeen; and the multivolume series of publications of Reid's hitherto unpublished manuscripts, under the general editorship of Charles Stewart-Robertson.

77. See James Beattie's London Diary, 1773, ed. Ralph S. Walker, at 42 and *passim* (Aberdeen: University of Aberdeen, 1946).

78. 1 McCloskey, Works 216 (cited in note 8).

79. E.g., *id.* at 213–15.

80. *Id.* at 217; cf. at 194 (Reid an "experienced judge of human nature").

compared Reid to Bacon,[81] the point was not simply to acknowledge Reid's greatness. Wilson meant to indicate specifically that Reid, like Bacon, had devised a plan of scientific inquiry so comprehensive within its sphere that its prosecution might happily realize a history of unlimited progress—even while the outlines of the plan and its clarion empiricism were continually rejustified by the success of each new discovery. Bacon's perfect genius for organizing all inquiry in the domain of the physical sciences had been vindicated in just this way; and Wilson envisioned a comparable glory for Reid's comprehensive restructuring of the scientific investigation of the human mind. In fact, by 1790 Wilson could point to an entire field of recent developments in the science of the mind that seemed to sustain this comparison with Bacon's achievement, but that promised for Reid a repute even higher than Bacon's, because these developments promised improvements not merely in man's material circumstances but in his moral life.

It was, above all, in the investigation into "the principles of society" that Reid and Common Sense had made revolutionary progress.[82] For Reid and his school had, in good Baconian fashion, established an entirely new field of inquiry in social philosophy, namely, the scientific inquiry into the "social," as distinguished from the "solitary," operations of the individual human mind.[83] To Wilson, the mere recognition of this field as a endeavor to examine an *irreducible*[84] constituent part of human nature was as momentous a revolution in philosophy as the American War for Independence had been in politics.[85]

This was not to say, however, that this "profounder" revolution, a revolution in men's knowledge of themselves, was unrelated to politics. To the contrary, "the spirit of patriotism" had done much, Wilson said, to foster this *new science* of the "social operations" of the mind.[86] And it was chiefly Wilson's view of the reciprocally fortifying relationship between the new social psychology and the new American politics of patriotism that led him, as a lawyer and a politician—even if not a true philosopher—to hazard a contribution to the fast developing "social science"[87] of the day. There might seem to have been reassurance, as well, in the fact that his contribution was, for the

---

81. Cf. my text at note 66 *supra*. On Reid's Baconianism in general, see Marcil-Lacoste at 131–40 (cited in note 76). On the avowed Baconianism of the rhetoric of Reid's moral science in particular, see Charles Stewart-Robertson, The Pneumatics and the Georgics of the Scottish Mind, 20 Eighteenth-Century Stud. 296 (1987).

82. 1 McCloskey, Works 229.

83. *Id.* at 230ff. At this point in his lectures, Wilson makes an interesting reference to his earlier express reservations about relying for knowledge on "definitions." Cf. my text *supra* at note 17.

84. 1 McCloskey, Works 230; cf. at 200, 228–29 (Wilson *contra* Hobbist reduction of the social passions into "selfishness" and "self-love"). Cf. *infra* note 112.

85. Cf. Wilson's remark that Reid's philosophy would open "the most enrapturing prospects." 1 McCloskey, Works 201.

86. *Id.* at 229.

87. See, e.g., Gladys Bryson, Man and Society: The Scottish Inquiry of the Eighteenth Century (Princeton, N.J.: Princeton University Press, 1945); Ronald L. Meek, Social Science and the Ignoble Savage (Cambridge: Cambridge University Press, 1976).

most part, only a matter of terminology. And yet Wilson thought terminology so important in itself that his contribution might nevertheless guide Americans as they were beginning to try to understand themselves as "a People" and appreciate what the Founding of the 1780s already meant and ultimately could mean.

Expressly relying on analogy, and pursuing what he called "a figurative extension" of language in order to arrive at a new metaphor, Wilson coined the term "moral abstraction" to distinguish a very important social operation of the mind he thought had gone unappreciated because it had never had a name.[88] That new advances in knowledge require new terms was, for Wilson, one of the most important lessons taught by Reid.[89] Thus, even in reaching for a new term, Wilson was not departing from Reid's Common Sense; he was putting it into practice. And in the familiar Common Sense idiom that Wilson used to explain to his law students what he meant by "moral abstraction" (for example, in characterizing moral abstraction as an "active" moral "power," Wilson was borrowing the signal terms from the titles of two of Reid's major works),[90] Wilson once again endorsed Common Sense moral science even as he opened the way to seeing something new about its political significance.

What tempted Wilson to his metaphor, and what justified it to him so completely, was the fecund analogy that he thought already securely established by the Common Sense school, between men's intellectual faculties and their moral faculties, and between both these classes of faculties and the faculties of sensory perception.[91] Moreover, among the Common Sense theorists the impetus toward synthesis and unity in the science of the mind was so strong[92] that Wilson was quite faithful to Common Sense in presuming that the greater imprudence lay not in extending such analogies too far but in failing to recognize how much the various faculties of the mind necessarily do partake of one another.[93] Wilson was thus drawing on the accrued authority of the Common Sense school when he introduced to his law students his coinage "moral abstraction" as a patent metaphor evincing the fundamental Common Sense analogy between men's intellectual powers and their moral powers.[94]

"Abstraction," said Wilson, is a general power of the mind that had thus far been associated exclusively with the operations of the intellect. Philoso-

---

88. 1 McCloskey, Works 161ff. (cited in note 8).

89. Cf. Chisholm v. Georgia, 2 Dallas 419, 454 (1793).

90. 1 McCloskey, Works 162. The titles of Reid's two last, and longest, works are Essays on the Intellectual Powers of Man (1785) and Essays on the Active Powers of the Human Mind (1788).

91. See 1 McCloskey, Works 202ff. (on the relationship between external and internal "sense").

92. E.g., id. at 201.

93. Cf. id. at 199 (general concurrence of the will and the understanding). Cf. discussion of this passage in Conrad, Polite Foundation 381ff. (cited in note 12).

94. 1 McCloskey, Works 161-62.

phers had long taught that our power of "intellectual abstraction" enables us to perceive similarities among the individual objects of nature and, by the "progress" of this same power, to classify these objects and "refer them to a higher genus, till we arrive at *being*, the highest genus of all."[95] Equally real and more important, but as yet quite unappreciated, however, was men's power of "moral abstraction."

This power of moral abstraction is, said Wilson, "a principle of good will as well as of *knowledge*."[96] And it is significant that Wilson in so saying drew no distinction, formal or otherwise, between "power" and "principle." It was his use of these terms interchangeably that (at least as a matter of language) justified his moving immediately to a conclusion that this power is "susceptible" of unlimited "generalization," or "extension," in the objects it "embraces," namely, other individuals and groups of persons.[97] But Wilson's underlying justification for moving directly to this conclusion lay in more than semantics; it lay in what Thomas Reid's Common Sense school had recently "proved" about the similarity of the operations of our intellectual and moral powers, and about the substantial mutual participation of both intellection and feeling in every act of the mind. This is the point of Wilson's insistence that moral abstraction is more than a merely affective inclination to "benevolence and sociability," more than the commonly recognized, indeed, universally experienced, but supposedly unthinking impulse of fellow feeling.[98]

In Wilson's own quotations from some earlier insightful authorities who had glimpsed what he claimed to be the first student of human nature not to discover but to name, it is evident that by coining the new term "moral abstraction" Wilson intended to advocate a higher regard for the capability of the human *imagination*. When the imagination is properly informed and constrained—and so the imagination is by its nature inclined to be when it is cultivated in the setting of civil society—then it is fully capable of *knowledge*. For, as the cultured French politician Jacques Necker had seen, imagination of this sort is in fact a "thinking faculty" of the mind.[99] But some earnest philosophers had "doubted or denied" this insight. Even the enlightened English natural lawyer Thomas Rutherforth had asserted that the morally engaged imagination is "merely notional," in that the "social union" the mind posits among men is a "connexion" that "is only made by the mind for its own convenience."[100] Thus, what Reidian Common Sense had accomplished was to complete and to vindicate earlier tentative and controverted insights (such as Cicero's and Necker's) about the "real" existence and the "power" of the

---

95. *Id.* at 162.
96. *Id.* (emphasis added).
97. E.g., *id.* at 163–64.
98. Cf. Norman S. Fiering, Irresistible Compassion: An Aspect of Eighteenth-Century Sympathy and Humanitarianism, 37 J. Hist. Ideas 195 (1976).
99. 1 McCloskey, Works 162. Cf. bibliographical glossary in 2 McCloskey at 854.
100. 1 McCloskey, Works 163; cf. 2 McCloskey 855. Also cf. Wilson on "moral perception" as an operation of "the understanding," e.g., at 1 McCloskey 233.

moral imagination as a thinking faculty. The most excellent moral acts of the imagination, acts of moral abstraction, should now be understood to import "knowledge": What we only imagine can be and sometimes is "the truth."

Such was the argument captured in Wilson's analogizing, synthesizing metaphor "moral abstraction." It was an argument that drew at every point on Common Sense polemics against a *perceived* attempt to degrade the human imagination by portraying it as a faculty incapable of ascertaining knowledge or truth.[101] To be sure, Wilson's argument reflected widespread aesthetic theories and assumptions in 18th-century Atlantic culture that had for some time been encouraging an increased interest in the "varieties" and the "powers" of the imagination.[102] Nevertheless, Wilson did not couch his argument strictly or even chiefly in the terms of yet another enlightened analysis of "the faculty of imagination." Instead, he relied on his metaphor to carry most of the burden of his argument. And in this reliance he considered that he was not taking recourse to mere rhetoric; rather, he was appealing more directly to the epistemological authority of the imagination than any reasoned argument ever could. What might have otherwise seemed the defect of circular argument in his reliance on one novel metaphor to establish the truth claims for metaphor in general was thus, in his view, amply justified on the strength of the most compelling and reassuring authority of all in moral, or any other, science: experience.

IV.   IMAGINATION AS "EXPERIENCE" IN CIVIL SOCIETY

" 'The good experienced man,' says Aristotle, 'is the last measure of all things.' "

—Wilson, in his *Lectures on Law*[103]

How it can be that a metaphor imports the authority of "experience" is

---

101. Cf. Robert Eberwein, James Beattie and David Hume on the Imagination and Truth, 12 Tex. Stud. Literature & Language 595 (1971). For an account of Hume's conception of the imagination that sets it in the broad context of 18th-century literary theory generally, see James Engell, The Creative Imagination: Enlightenment to Romanticism 52 & *passim* (Cambridge, Mass.: Harvard University Press, 1981). For an especially pertinent analysis by a leading historian of philosophy that focuses on "the imagination" in arguing that "[t]he whole of Hume's constructive philosophy of human nature was unperceived by Reid and Beattie—and so by the later critics who took their cue from Reid and Beattie," see D.D. Raphael, "The true old Humean philosophy" and Its Influence on Adam Smith, *in* Morice on Hume at 23, 25 (cited in note 35).

102. As Professor Pocock has recently suggested, this increased interest in the imagination is a matter to which historians of literature and of philosophy have attended so carefully for so long now that it is all the more remarkable that historians of political thought have thus far done so little to come to terms with its significance. Pocock, Virtue 66–67 & n.46 (cited in note 12).

103. 1 McCloskey, Works 139 (cited in note 8); Wilson here cites Francis Hutcheson, A System of Moral Philosophy (cf. bibliographical glossary in 2 McCloskey at 852). Cf. *infra* note 111.

only hinted at in the one key passage—and a notable passage it is—[104] in Wilson's law lectures where he pauses expressly to affirm the "necessity" and "advantage" of metaphor in moral science. Although in this isolated passage Wilson falls short of formulating anything that amounts to a general theory of metaphor, he does incorporate into the passage, if only elliptically, enough of his case for the *empirical* authority of metaphor that the passage merits quotation in full:

> In the philosophy of the human mind, it is impossible altogether to avoid metaphorical expressions. Our first and most familiar notions are suggested by material objects; and we cannot speak intelligibly of those that are immaterial, without continual allusions to matter and the qualities of matter.
>
> Besides, in teaching moral science, the use of metaphors is not only necessary, but, if prudent, and honest, and guarded, it is highly advantageous. Nature has endowed us with the faculty of imagination, that we may be enabled to throw warming as well as enlightening rays upon truth—to embellish, to recommend, and to enforce it. Truth may, indeed, by reasoning, be rendered evident to the understanding; but it cannot reach the heart, unless by means of the imagination. To the imagination metaphors are addressed.[105]

Elliptical as Wilson is in these remarks, nevertheless, he sounds quite clearly a number of his favorite Common Sense themes: for example, the importance of the relationship between the *physical* senses and all the other operations of the mind; and also the limited capacity of the faculty of reason to convey all that men, nevertheless, do *know*. What is missing here, or rather, what Wilson barely intimates, is his view of the necessity of metaphor and imagination not merely in our conveying *to others* but in our acquiring *for ourselves*, that is, our "conceiving" of, some kinds of knowledge. It is this primary service performed by metaphor and imagination in helping us not merely to share but, in the first instance, to *acquire* knowledge that, in Wilson's view, makes us so dependent on metaphor and imagination for progress in moral science. And yet this apparent distinction between *acquiring* and *sharing* moral knowledge was, paradoxically, of significance to Wilson mostly because he considered it a distinction that ultimately should not and could not be maintained. For this reason he was more interested in and reliant upon metaphor itself as an actual, social phenomenon of language than he was concerned with imagination as a "metaphysical," even though very real, faculty of the mind.

---

104. I venture this remark at the encouragement of Professor Aileen Ward, who has been kind enough to share with me her reaction to the passage in question: that it was quite unusual at that time (the early 1790s) for a writer, at least an Anglophone writer, to wax as expressly self-conscious as Wilson does here about the moral purpose of metaphor. For Ward's own wide-ranging study of the theory of metaphor, see her The Unfurling of Entity: Metaphor in Poetic Theory (New York: Garland Publishing Co., 1987).

105. 1 McCloskey, Works 101; cf. 2 McCloskey, Works 778, for another instance of Wilson's articulately self-conscious use of metaphor, in his 1788 July Fourth Oration.

Again following Reid, Wilson emphasized that knowledge is available to men not just through observation but also through reflection, because reflection is an "experience" as authentic to the human mind as is any other. Reid did not stint in crediting Descartes with the recovery of this principle to philosophy; although Reid did claim that, by effectively transcending Cartesian dualism,[106] he had accomplished something new in reconciling this Cartesian insight with the outward-looking perspective of the British empirical tradition.[107] In any event, Wilson thought himself on the firmest common ground, occupied both by Common Sense and every eminent skeptic including the Pyrrhonist Hume, in taking "experience" as the most authoritative guide in all aspects of philosophy and life.[108]

In Wilson's day, and especially in the context of the disputes in philosophy and politics that most engaged him, "experience" was a shibboleth, like— and problematically related to—"science," that admitted of variable meanings.[109] How did Wilson's own conception of scientifically authoritative experience come to include and even exalt the phenomena of figurative language? And why did he become especially concerned with metaphor as both a social manifestation and a reflexive inculcation of what he called "moral abstraction"?

Merely to pose such questions in these terms is to point to an answer, because these questions call attention once again to Wilson's abhorrence of phenomenalism and reductionism. To the threat of these chronic pathologies that jaundiced so much "profound" philosophical inquiry into human nature, Wilson responded by reaffirming the salutary authority of *immediate* experience, even while he also insisted that the directly ascertainable significance of any particular experience is more *general* than itself.

These professedly revisionist contentions, so typical of the Common Sense approach, led Wilson to a very absorptive and naive phenomenology. After all, a defensive resolve to apply phenomenological interpretations indiscriminately was, as the name of the Common Sense school indicates, much of what the school undertook in assuming the term "sense" for their cause: They appealed to the "felt," or "sensed," reality of "phenomena" of the mind in their explanation of the nature of "reflection" as well as "observation," "intuitive knowledge" as well as "discursive knowledge," and impalpable so-

---

106. Cf. 1 McCloskey, Works 201, 205, 223–25, 371–72; cf. at 213. Cf. Henry Guerlac, Newton's Changing Reputation in the Eighteenth Century, in Carl Becker's Heavenly City Revisited, ed. Raymond O. Rockwood, at 3 (Hamden, Conn.: Archon Books, 1968); Charles C. Gillispie, The Edge of Objectivity: An Essay in the History of Scientific Ideas (Princeton, N.J.: Princeton University Press, 1960).
107. Cf. Morton White, The Philosophy of the American Revolution 157-60 (New York: Oxford University Press, 1978).
108. E.g., 1 McCloskey, Works 183. Cf. Donald W. Livingston, Hume's Philosophy of Common Life 11–15 & passim (Hume on the authority of "experience") (cited in note 48).
109. An especially concise and balanced discussion of this familiar matter is Michael Lienesch, Interpreting Experience: History, Philosophy, and Science in the American Constitutional Debates, 11 Am. Pol. Q. 379 (1983).

cial institutions as well as the most palpable and simple episodes in the private mental experience of individuals in everyday life.

Indeed, there was no more frequent motif in Common Sense moral science than the reassertion of the absolute truthfulness and the practical necessity of the internal "sense" that "everyone" has of human society as a "real," external phenomenon. And, in Wilson's case, it was his assumptions and arguments about the "real" nature of American society[110] that provided him with a naively phenomenological justification for so reconceptualizing "experience" that this shibboleth of modern science could compass and establish the empirical authority of metaphor.

Just as Scottish Common Sense had revolutionized moral science by pioneering scientific inquiry into the social operations of the mind, so American political experience had, by the late 1780s, afforded a historic confirmation of what Common Sense had already disclosed, and what it promised, about these social operations. In Wilson's view, Americans had begun to realize, for the first time in history, the politics of a "civil society." And Wilson's controlling notion of civil society was largely what both inspired and required him to reconceive the meaning of "experience" in a way that put metaphor at the center of moral science: Wilson thought civil society to be an indispensable setting for, and object of, just the sorts of imaginative acts of moral abstraction that give metaphor much of its moral significance.

In trying to convey what he meant by "civil society" as a general phenomenon—and why it is an important source, means, and end of the republican culture he envisioned for America—Wilson occasionally took pains to specify what civil society is not.

In the first place, civil society is not, and must not be confounded with, "natural society." Wilson did not deny that the circumstances of social association we call "natural society" can exist and have existed among mankind; but, in all candor, he confessed that he thought natural society, at least as an object of inquiry in moral science, neither an attractive nor even an interesting phenomenon to contemplate. With Aristotle, he frankly preferred to predicate his moral science on human nature as it is found in an "improved" condition.[111] And although Wilson did not mean to detract at all from the certain knowledge attested by everyone (except for a few disingenuous or deluded Hobbists[112]) that sociability is intrinsic to human nature,[113] Wilson did deny, without the slightest trace of irony, that the "rude" circumstances commonly designated "natural society" are, or could ever have been, "natural" to

---

110. Cf. Dennison, 39 Rev. Pol. 157, esp. at 190–91 (cited in note 32).

111. Cf. 1 McCloskey, Works 139; cf. at 87, 164–65, 200.

112. See esp. id. at 228–29. Whether Wilson's reading of Hobbes was the correct reading or even a defensible reading is a question that I do not mean to address. For a recent interpretation that finds in the Leviathan something quite different from the "asocial individualism" often found there, by Wilson's contemporaries and ours, see Ron Replogle, Personality & Society in Hobbes's Leviathan, 19 Polity 570 (1987). Cf. supra note 84.

113. E.g., 1 McCloskey, Works, esp. at 227, 233–36.

man.[114] To Wilson this was a conclusion so abundantly indicated by a variety of "moral" and "physical" "causes" that to belabor the point would only lead him into the reductionism and absurdly false analytical logic of Hume and his ilk. Faithful to the methods of Common Sense phenomenology, Wilson chose to establish the affinity of human nature for "civil," rather than "natural," society by describing, not by trying to define, what he meant by the term "civil society."[115]

Nevertheless, if there was to Wilson any single distinctive feature of civil society that seemed to stand out as its hallmark, it was that in civil society the bonds among men are secured *by laws*.[116] For this apparently legalistic view of civil society Wilson cited Cicero as his principal authority.[117] And although in Wilson's day there was hardly anything exceptional in an American lawyer's calling upon the authority of this greatest lawyer of republican Rome,[118] Cicero served Wilson especially well as a symbol with which to mitigate the importance of legalism, even as Wilson dwelt on the importance in civil society of the principle of community through law.

In fact, Wilson's reservations about unmitigated legalism are implicit throughout the documentary record of his mature constitutional theory. Illustrations of this point range from countless particular remarks to the most salient general features of his approach, not the least of these general features being, as I have already noted, the premium Wilson placed on the authority of moral, as distinguished from political or legal, science.[119] As for his particular remarks bearing on this point, a striking example is Wilson's statement at the Philadelphia Convention that he did not want to require officers of the new national government to take oaths to support the government, because he thought that, "A good Govt. did not need [the security of legal oaths]. . . . and a bad one could not or ought not to be supported"—not even by its own elected officials![120]

But it is in emphasizing his pointedly ambiguous "Ciceronian" concep-

---

114. Cf. *id.*, esp. at 130.
115. Cf. *id.* at 161, 211, 231, 280.
116. E.g., *id.* at 238–39, 280; Jensen, ed., at 356, 358–59 (cited in note 8); cf. *id.* at 344–45, 346.
117. 1 McCloskey, Works 239.
118. Among the many relevant excellent studies, two are of special interest here: Stephen Botein, Cicero as Role Model for Early American Lawyers: A Case Study in Classical "Influence," 73 Classical J. 313 (1978); and even closer to my own emphasis, Robert A. Ferguson, Law and Letters in American Culture 74 (Cambridge, Mass.: Harvard University Press, 1984) (on the Ciceronian ideal as calling for "professional knowledge, where 'profession' meant 'the search after truth'. . . . moral duty . . . . an intrinsic love of learning and literature").
119. Cf. Wilson's resistance to "defining," or "conceiving" of, law as a rule at all. He favored, instead, a conception of "law" *as relation* rather than as "rule." See 1 McCloskey, Works 100–101 (but see at 63); see also at 123, for Wilson's appreciation of this idea of law as a "Roman" ideal. Cf. Arendt, On Revolution 187ff. (cited in note 26).
120. 2 Farrand, Records 87 (cited in note 3). For a biographical sidelight that may be important in understanding Wilson's position here, see Charles Page Smith, James Wilson: Founding Father, 1742–1798, at 114–15 (Chapel Hill: University of North Carolina Press, 1956) ("Smith on James Wilson").

tion of "civil society" that Wilson leaves the least doubt about his view of the importance of qualifying and moderating the nonetheless essential authority of law in a republic. And Wilson makes this point most clearly by specifying, again, what civil society is *not*.

For, as important as it was to Wilson to distinguish "civil society" from "natural society," he thought it even more important to emphasize that "civil society" must also be distinguished from "civil government." A disregard for this latter distinction is a fundamental error in constitutional theory that he thought had been all too common (even in America[121])—and always subversive of human "happiness" and "liberty." In Wilson's hierarchy of authority, as in Locke's, civil government ranked *below* civil society. Indeed, Wilson identified "the state" itself not with any institution of government at all, but thoroughly and exclusively with "civil society."[122] "Let government," he said, "—let even the constitution be, as they ought to be, the handmaids . . . of the state."[123] And in explaining why republicanism in principle permits no real distinction between "the state" and "civil society," or between either of these two institutions and a third, namely "the People" themselves, Wilson absorbed all three into a description that he applied to each.

What lends coherence to this description, which Wilson often repeated with little variation, is the predominance throughout of an idea of figurative personality: In a republic, it can and should be said that "the state," "civil society," and "the People" themselves are variant terms for precisely the same thing; each of these terms stands for the "artificial," "moral person" comprising "a complete body of free natural persons, united together for their common benefit" and properly considered "as having an understanding and a will . . . peculiar to itself . . ., as deliberating, and resolving, and acting."[124]

V. POLITICS AS CULTIVATION

> "Again he could not agree that property was the sole or primary object of Governt. & Society. The cultivation & improvement of the human mind was the most noble object."
>
> —Madison's *Notes* of Wilson's July 13 remarks at the Federal Convention[125]

The idea of figurative personality in Wilson's description, although far from unique to the Ciceronian conception of constitutional republicanism,

---

121. Jensen, ed., at 348 (cited in note 8); cf. at 361–62.
122. E.g., 1 McCloskey, *Works* 239, 270.
123. *Id.* at 239; cf., e.g., at 109.
124. *Id.* at 239, 270, 401; Chisholm v. Georgia, 2 Dallas 419, 455 (1793). Cf. George Armstrong Kelly, *Mortal Man, Immortal Society? Political Metaphors in Eighteenth-Century France*, 14 Pol. Theory 5 (1986).
125. 1 Farrand, *Records* 605 (cited in note 3).

could nevertheless, in Wilson's day, be quite effectively associated with Cicero—not least because of the proverbial eloquence of Cicero's occasional testimonials to the *real* existence of "the People" as the sole embodiment of the "state" in a republic.[126] And yet, as wholeheartedly as Wilson endorsed Cicero's own naive (or perhaps canny) realism in this matter, by the same token, the splendid figures of Cicero's rhetoric fully supported Wilson in emphasizing as well that, real though the people and civil society are as the embodiment of the state in a republic—indeed, they are its most important and only enduring reality—this reality is, by virtue of its *general* nature, ambiguous. For whenever we "contemplate" the general personality that *is* a republic, at the same time "we should never forget, that . . . those, who think and speak and act, are men."[127]

This synthesizing ambiguity was, after all, at the heart of Wilson's political metaphors, just as it had been at the heart of Cicero's. In Wilson's case, as I have argued elsewhere,[128] such ambiguity may have served, among other things, to palliate certain ideological tensions in Wilson's immediate political environment, for example, the tensions between what many scholars take to have been a "republican" orientation and an antithetical "liberal" orientation that were in contentious counterpoise in early American political thought.[129] But in Wilson's program and rhetoric of "comprehensiveness," the capability of metaphor was not limited to expedient political purposes. Or at least no such limitation could, I infer, prudently be acknowledged in so

---

126. See, e.g., George H. Sabine, Cicero and the Roman Lawyers, ch. 9 in Sabine's A History of Political Theory, esp. at 171–72 (New York: Henry Holt & Co., 1937).

127. Chisholm v. Georgia, 2 Dallas 419, 455–56 (1793). Cf. William Penn's remark in his preface to the Frame of Government: "Governments, like clocks, go from the motion men give them; and as governments are made and moved by men, so by them they are ruined too"; as quoted by Gerhard Casper, Constitutionalism, in 1 Leonard W. Levy et al., Encyclopedia of the American Constitution 473, 476 (4 vols.; New York: Macmillan Publishing Co., 1986).

Moreover, Professor John Christian Laursen tells me that he finds "a parallel" between Wilson's language as quoted here and Kant's formulation of his Sixth Proposition in the Idea for a Universal History with a Cosmopolitan Purpose; see Kant's Political Writings, ed. Hans Reiss, trans. H.B . Nisbet 46–47 (Cambridge: Cambridge University Press, 1970). Yet how different Kant's (and Penn's, and even Madison's) qualms sound from Wilson's optimism! E.g., in the Sixth Proposition, when addressing the challenge of obtaining "for public justice a supreme authority which would itself be just," in light of the "problem" that "*is both the most difficult and the last to be solved by the human race*"—namely "[t]he difficulty . . . [that] man is an animal who needs a master," Kant writes: "But this master will also be an animal who needs a master. Thus while man may try as he will, it is hard to see how he can obtain for public justice a supreme authority which would itself be just, whether he seeks this authority in a single person or in a group of persons selected for this purpose. For each of them will always misuse his freedom if he does not have anyone above him to apply force to him as the laws should require it. Yet the highest authority has to be just *in itself* and yet also be a *man*. This is therefore the most difficult of all tasks, and a perfect solution is impossible. Nothing straight can be constructed from such warped wood as that which man is made of."

128. Conrad, Polite Foundation 366–74 (cited in note 12).

129. See the following pair of companion essays on the current posture of scholarly debate on this topic: Lance Banning, Jeffersonian Ideology Revisited: Liberal and Classical Ideas in the New American Republic, 63 Wm. & Mary Q., 3d ser., at 3 (1986); Joyce Appleby, Republicanism in Old and New Contexts, 63 Wm. & Mary Q., 3d ser., at 20 (1986). Cf. J.G.A. Pocock, Between Gog and Magog: The Republican Thesis and the *Ideologia Americana*, 48 J. Hist. Ideas 325 (1987).

self consciously new a political culture where the language of politics—as typified by aphorisms like Wilson's that "[t]he present is gilded by the prospect of
the future"[130]—already betrayed an anticipation of the problem that Americans' liberal republicanism would prove to have "little but its moral promise
to sustain it."[131]

More than Madison or any of the other leading Federalists of the time,
Wilson projected how this moral promise might be redeemed. His project was
nothing less than to improve human nature by engaging it in the processes of
its own reform.[132] To other philosophically minded founders—John Adams
and Benjamin Rush, for example—these processes of "reformation" were, as
they were to Wilson, the "great object" of a truly republican "social science."[133] But with something of the audacity that is, perhaps, peculiar to the
novus homo,[134] Wilson, not unlike Cicero himself, went further than any of the
other leading political actors of his day in attempting to synthesize a "comprehensive," conventionally "philosophical" vision of republicanism as an enterprise in moral reform.

By identifying the engine of republicanism—civil society itself—with
moral personality, Wilson could even recur directly to what he took to be the
very first among "first principles" in moral philosophy in order to maintain
that, in a republic not only are the individual citizens, but civil society as a
collective entity is under the duty to cultivate "self-knowledge."[135] It followed
from this Delphic, if not strictly Socratic, first principle that it is also incumbent on civil society to cultivate the other attributes of personality, including
will, understanding, memory, and imagination—indeed, *every* mental faculty
that is "susceptible" of cultivation.

To Wilson what was most encouraging in the American revival of a republicanism of figurative personality was that the new "science" of social psy-

---

130. 1 McCloskey, Works 146 (cited in note 8). Cf. Wilson's rewriting of Pope's aphorism
"Man never *is*, but always *to be* blest" so as to render it both "more consolatory" and "more just":
"man ever *is; for* always to be blest." *Id.* (The emphasis is Wilson's.)

131. Judith N. Shklar, Ordinary Vices 70 (Cambridge, Mass.: Harvard University, Belknap
Press, 1984) ("Shklar, Ordinary Vices").

132. On Publius's aim not to *reform* and *improve* but merely to *harness* and *control* human
nature, see Maynard Smith, Reason, Passion and Political Freedom in *The Federalist*, 22 J. Pol. 525
(1960); cf. Howe, 44 Wm. & Mary Q. at 494 (cited in note 6).

133. E.g., John Adams in a letter of 1785: "The social science will never be much improved,
until the people unanimously know and consider themselves as the fountain of power"; 9 Charles
Francis Adams, ed., The Works of John Adams, Second President of the United States 538, 540
(10 vols.; Boston: Little, Brown & Co.; 1850–56, 1854). Cf. David Freeman Hawke, Benjamin
Rush: Revolutionary Gadfly 358-80 (Indianapolis: Bobbs-Merrill Co., 1971).

134. Cf. 1 McCloskey, Works 26ff. & 43–48 (editor's Introduction); McCloskey, James Wil-
son 85–86, 94–95 (cited in note 8); Smith on James Wilson at 159ff. & *passim* (cited in note 120).
For more recent scholarship that treats the facts and the political significance of social mobility in
the Philadelphia of Wilson's day, see Thomas M. Doerflinger, A Vigorous Spirit of Enterprise:
Merchants and Economic Development in Revolutionary Philadelphia ch. 6 (251–80) (Chapel
Hill: University of North Carolina Press, 1986), esp. at 255 (citing Steven James Broebeck,
Changes in the Composition and Structure of Philadelphia Elite Groups, 1756–1790 (Ph.D. diss.,
University of Pennsylvania, 1972)).

135. E.g., 1 McCloskey, Works 157.

chology had lately begun to uncover so much important knowledge about the real and direct "connexions" between the individual human mind and the public mind. And at the same historic moment that these connections had been scientifically vindicated against the mounting skeptical challenge that culminated in Hume, the American people had also proved, even to acutely skeptical political scientists like William Paley, that the cardinal moral virtue of the individual republican citizen, namely probity, could in fact be so general throughout civil society that probity would suffice as the ground and security of political obligation.[136]

Given the many disappointments that unsettled early American political experience[137]—not least those to which the records of debate at the Philadelphia Convention bear witness—it must be somewhat puzzling now to encounter the nearly uniform sense of *certainty* that typifies Wilson's "philosophical" approach to the problems addressed by Federalist theory. From the late 1780s onward, Wilson's claims to certain "knowledge" remained as frequent and insistent as his claims to comprehensiveness.

Yet it is important to notice that for Wilson knowledge was but another "species of judgment"—although none the less true and certain for that.[138] And though in collapsing the idea of knowledge into the idea of judgment, Wilson avowedly contradicted no less a philosophical authority than Locke in the *Essay Concerning Human Understanding*, Wilson was, however, squarely in accord with the best authority in the culture of his own times. More than any of the other fifty-five framers at Philadelphia, it appears, Wilson took an approach to republican theory that was, in our terms, even more "cultural" in its concerns than it was "philosophical," not to mention "political" or "legalistic." Still, such distinctions as these would have had little if any meaning to Wilson or most of his contemporaries. In Wilson's day the term "philosophical," as it was so often applied to Wilson's republican theory by himself and others, is likely to have meant something quite similar to what we today might mean by the term "cultural"—especially if we mean to connote not only breadth of vision but also a special concern for the importance of the enhancing interrelationships among the perceived elements of social life.

In trying to understand Wilson's distinctiveness it is helpful to notice his special concern for republican "culture" chiefly as that term allows for the ambiguities in what any social phenomenon signifies, at the same time that the term presupposes both some "goodness" in what it designates and—most important of all—a "susceptibility" of improvement. Thus understood, the real meaning of "culture" lies not so much in what it *is* but in the *processes* of

---

136. *Id.* at 240.
137. For an example of Wilson's own articulation of such disappointments, see his Nov. 24, 1787 speech in Jensen, ed., at 347–48 (cited in note 8); cf. at 360–61.
138. 1 McCloskey, Works 209, 394; cf. at 387–88: a universal opinion is entitled to "the character of a first principle of human knowledge."

cultivation.[139]

As recent scholarship on the American Founding has often noted, the cultivation of republicanism in America was the organizing focus for much of Wilson's founding vision. No single remark by him at the Philadelphia Convention or afterward is as often quoted by modern scholars[140] as Wilson's astonishing assertion at Philadelphia that, orthodox republican theory and the consensus of his fellow delegates notwithstanding, "he could not agree that property was the sole or the primary object of Governt. & Society. The cultivation & improvement of the human mind was the most noble object."[141]

As a noble object of cultivation, the American "publick mind" concerned Wilson no less than did the individual mind of each free and independent citizen. And nowhere did Wilson find better evidence for his belief in the reality and importance of the public mind than in language itself.

Especially in the American republic, where unfulfilled purposes, together with the processes of "improvement," were already "known" to be the vital sustenance of politics, Wilson thought it necessary to appreciate the fundamental limitations, as well as the capabilities, of the several mental faculties. From a Common Sense perspective, prudence required, above all, that the founders not overlook the limits of the capability of human *reason*. To Wilson, at least, it was as axiomatic in any "just" science of government as it was in the fundamental science of morals that, while reason may assist us in choosing the best means to our "ultimate ends," reason can do nothing to assist us

---

139. Cf. Frederick M. Kenner, The Chain of Becoming—The Philosophical Tale, the Novel, and a Neglected Realism of the Enlightenment: Swift, Montesquieu, Voltaire, Johnson, and Austin (New York: Columbia University Press, 1983), esp. pt. I, The Chain of Becoming, and ch. 2, The Chain of Being, the Chain of Events, and the Chain of Becoming.

140. See, e.g., Rogers M. Smith, Liberalism and American Constitutional Law 208-9 (Cambridge, Mass.: Harvard University Press, 1985); Epstein, Political Theory 210 n.60 (cited in note 13); Gordon S. Wood, Interests and Disinterestedness in the Making of the Constitution, in Beeman et al., Beyond Confederation 69, 83 (cited in note 25).

141. 1 Farrand, Records 605 (cited in note 3). Cf. 2 McCloskey, Works 776 (Fourth of July Oration, 1788) (cited in note 8). And see Thomas A. Horne, Bourgeois Virtue: Property and Moral Philosophy in America, 1750–1800, 4 Hist. Pol. Thought 317, esp. 337ff. (1983). Quite correctly, in my view, Horne at 339 places Wilson in a class of moralists about whom Horne says: "The most important characteristic of the property theory found in these moralists is that property rights are derived from moral duties in such a way as to make such rights subordinate to the public good. Property rights do not define the public good; they cannot stand against it."

The distinctiveness of Wilson's idea of the "most noble" end of government and society, as expressed here, is all the more evident if one accepts Martin Diamond's characterization of "the new political science" of the American founders in general: "the new political science gave a primacy to the efficacy of means rather than to the nobility of ends: The ends of political life were reduced to a commensurability with the human means readily and universally available. In place of the utopian end postulated by the ancients, the forced elevation of human character, the moderns substituted a lowered political end, namely human comfort and security. . . . This removal of the task of character formation from its previously preeminent place on the agenda of politics had an immense consequence for the relationship of ethics and politics in modern regimes." Diamond, Ethics and Politics: The American Way, in Robert H. Horwitz, ed., The Moral Foundations of the American Republic 75, 83 (3d ed. Charlottesville: University Press of Virginia, 1986). Cf. Arendt, On Revolution 90 (cited in note 26) ("Montesquieu's great insight that even virtue must have its limits"); J.G.A. Pocock, The Machiavellian Moment: Florentine Political Thought and the Atlantic Republican Tradition 491-92 (Princeton, N.J.: Princeton University Press, 1975) ("Pocock, The Machiavellian Moment").

in determining those ends.[142]

Common Sense taught that the ends of republican government, because they are ultimately moral ends, are traceable exclusively to "moral sense" rather than to reason. Indeed, by 1790 much of what the Common Sense school of philosophers had lately accomplished had been intended, and was indeed interpreted, as a scientific vindication of 18th-century British moral sense theory, from Shaftesbury and Butler onward.[143] Importing all the empirical authority that the Common Sense school had restored to the "senses" in general, the "moral sense" became no longer a mere sentiment but a "power of moral perception . . . both intellectual and active," and fully able to "judge as well as inform."[144]

Particularly with regard to Wilson's federal theory, what may today be most noteworthy in Wilson's exposition of the reconfirmed moral sense theory of the late 18th century is how it intensifies Wilson's own Common Sense preoccupation with the authority of language. And in Wilson's federal theory the authority of language becomes not so much the authority of "philosophy" but of culture at large: "Languages were not invented by philosophers . . .," says Wilson, "[t]hey were contrived by men in general, to express common sentiments and perceptions." The very "structure of languages," which testifies to the reality and truth of the moral distinctions perceived by the moral sense, compels the conclusion that the existence of the moral sense must be presumed in any "scientific" attempt to understand human affairs.[145]

Yet when Wilson proceeds from this initial question of the existence of the moral sense to questions about its capabilities in the practical matters of morals, politics, and law, he begins to turn his attention away from the structure of language viewed "universally" and toward the actual phenomena of the language of the Atlantic culture of his day at its most "morally estimable."[146] In other words, it is precisely to the language of "polite letters" that he turns. And "moral sense," when examined in this practical sphere, becomes for him very much a matter of what he calls "internal taste."[147]

As for guides in such matters, figures like Pope and Addison take on an

---

142. 1 McCloskey, Works 132–43, 206, 213—esp. at 137 & 141: "Reason judges either of relations or of matters of fact"; cf. at 136, on a secondary class of moral truths that are deduced by reasoning. Cf. also Smith, 22 J. Pol. (1960) (cited in note 132).

143. See, e.g., D. Daiches Raphael, The Moral Sense (London: Oxford University Press, 1947). Cf. the specific passages and cross-references in the anthology, 2 Raphael, British Moralists, 1650-1800, at 172–75, 267ff., 300–301 (2 vols.; Oxford: Clarendon Press, 1969). Cf. Howe, 44 Wm. & Mary Q. at 492, 497, & passim (cited in note 6).

144. 1 McCloskey, Works 133, 143, 203, 209, 225.

145. Id. at 135. Cf. Benjamin T. Spencer, The Quest for Nationality: An American Literary Campaign 56 (Syracuse, N.Y.: Syracuse University Press, 1957) (quoting Noah Webster's remark that language is "not framed by philosophers"). But for Webster, this notion was, of course, a premise not for universalism but nationalism, in the restrictive sense. Cf. Richard Bridgman, The Colloquial Style in America 6–8, 43 (New York: Oxford University Press, 1966).

146. 1 McCloskey, Works 135.

147. Id. at 142, 393. Cf. Madison as quoted by Adrienne Koch at xv in her Introduction to her edition of Notes of the Debates in the Federal Convention of 1787, Reported by James Madison (Athens: Ohio University Press, 1966) ("Koch, Notes").

importance equal to that of Plato and Aristotle. In fact, in Wilson's most extensive set of reflections on American federal theory, which came in his law lectures, poets and bellelettrists take on an importance even greater than the greatest philosophers. The rhetoric of "polite letters" and the "pure diction" (as Wilson appropriates it from among the many dictions) of Augustan poetry are the moral idiom deemed most effective for animating American federal union, through "the social operation" of "moral abstraction."[148] Indeed, in Wilson's vision of republican politics, as in some modern conservative—and elegantly contested—reconsiderations of the "ethics and imagery" of the "Augustan humanists," "[s]tyle and institutions are ultimately the same thing."[149] And "taste" becomes more than a literal anagram of the word "state;" taste becomes an important cultural analog of the state.[150] Thus, for Wilson, American republicanism becomes primarily a matter of "cultivation." And Federalist politics, in particular, must assume the tasks of cultural management.[151]

---

148. On "pure diction" in this sense and in this context, see Donald Davie, Purity of Diction in English Verse, esp. at 29–40 (London: Routledge & Kegan Paul, 1967).

I have been forcefully reminded by Professor Aubrey Williams that the uses Wilson made of Augustan verse (and prose) amount to a selective appropriation that cannot be and should not be our own—if only (but probably not only) because we have now come to know the Augustans better than Wilson and his polite contemporaries cared or dared to during the "Victorian Prelude" of the late 18th century. Cf. Maurice J. Quinlan, Victorian Prelude: A History of English Manners, 1700–1830, esp. ch. 8, Changing Taste and Temperament (rev. ed. London: Frank Cass & Co., 1965). For examples of authentically Augustan verse impolite to the point of the scatological, Professor Williams recommends Jonathan Swift's "Dick, a Maggot," "A Beautiful Young Nymph Going to Bed," and "Cassinus and Peter."

149. Quoting Paul Fussell, The Rhetorical World of Augustan Humanism: Ethics and Imagery from Swift to Burke (Oxford: Clarendon Press, 1965). See esp. ch. 9 (at 211–32), the title of which is taken from Burke: "The Wardrobe of a Moral Imagination." Fussell's concluding sentences at 232 capture a point central to his argument about why the Augustan humanists took rhetoric so seriously: "And as we have seen, just as 'drapery' is the dress of man, style is the dress of thought. The dress may vary from Poor Tom's rags to Johnson's 'laced or embroidered waistcoat', but in expression as well as in action external conventions are indispensable: the 'dresses' which clothe thought come from the same objective 'moral' wardrobe as the conventions and institutions which humanize and dignify man. Styles and institutions are ultimately the same thing, and in either to try to invent one's own is to renounce one's humanity."

Whether Fussell gives an *accurate* account of "Augustan humanism" in general, or any part of it, is not a question I mean to confront here—any more than I mean to try to resolve questions about the philosophical or ethical merit of Wilson's own "mimetic literalism." But for an authoritative critique of such naive literalism as purveyed in the polite literary theory of the ubiquitous Kames (who was Reid's patron and whose ideas are fairly taken as just the sort of 18th-century Atlantic orthodoxy Wilson meant to endorse), one need look no further, as I have said, than I.A. Richards' Philosophy of Rhetoric itself (New York: Oxford University Press, 1936). And for a more recent—and an authentically Johnsonian—critique of the mimetic confusion of "words" with "things" (where "things" include both "nature" and "morals"), see Jean H. Hagstrum, Samuel Johnson Among the Deconstructionists, 39 Ga. Rev. 537, esp. at 540 (1985), quoting René Wellek: " 'the relation of mind and world is more basic than language' "; and at 546, quoting Johnson against "the shameful act of 'imposing words' (the 'daughters of earth') for ideas (clear mental images) or for things (the 'sons of heaven')."

150. This is my reformulation of a provocative generalization couched in *very* similar terms by Daniel Cottom, in a book to which I am greatly indebted, The Civilized Imagination: A Study of Ann Radcliffe, Jane Austen, and Sir Walter Scott 24 (Cambridge: Cambridge University Press, 1985) ("Cottom, The Civilized Imagination").

151. Cf. Linda K. Kerber, Federalists in Dissent: Imagery and Ideology in Jeffersonian America, esp. ch. 6, Images of Social Order (Ithaca, N.Y.: Cornell University Press, 1970).

VI. "ENLARGING THE SPHERE": THE "FEDERAL REPUBLIC" AS METAPHOR

". . . this many headed monster . . . the favoured bantling must have passed through the short period of its existence without a name, had not Mr. *Wilson*, in the fertility of his genius suggested the happy epithet of a *Federal Republic*."

—An Anti-Federalist pamphleteer, writing as "A Columbian Patriot" in 1788[152]

In his law lectures of 1790–91, when Wilson arrived at the point of trying to explain and justify the federal union recently created under the new national Constitution, he was presented with but one more in a series of opportunities to hold forth on his own theory of American federalism. As a leading participant at the Philadelphia Convention, and as the acknowledged leader of the nationally influential ratification campaign in Pennsylvania, Wilson by this time had already had a number of occasions to pronounce on the subject. But unlike the circumstances at the Philadelphia Convention, or those during the ratification debates—to say nothing of the cases on which Wilson sat as an associate justice of the first national Supreme Court—the occasion of his law lectures afforded him license to indulge to the utmost his penchant for "comprehensiveness." In the lecture that comes down to us under the title "Of Man, As a Member of a Confederation,"[153] what is most likely to surprise a reader today is that, in making a case for the federal union he had done as much as anyone to establish, Wilson appeals for supporting authority at crucial points in his argument much more to the poetry of Alexander Pope and James Thomson than to the theories of any philosopher or to the practical wisdom of any statesman.

In fact, ever since Wilson's own days as a law student, he had shown a special interest in polite literature and had made a point of displaying that interest in what he himself wrote.[154] In 1777 he had even adopted the name "Addison" as his pseudonym in waging an early and unsuccessful campaign of published letters and addresses calling for the Pennsylvania Constitution to be replaced with one more to the liking of the Republican party in that state.[155] In any case, by the time Wilson began delivering his law lectures, in December of 1790, not only had he led the Republicans to victory in their long campaign to secure the sort of state constitution they wanted, he had also established quite a reputation for himself as a polished rhetorician—albeit one whose haughty demeanor and bespectacled squint may sometimes have diminished

---

152. See text at note 177 *infra*.
153. A passing remark by James Wilson's first editor, his son Bird, suggests that the elder Wilson himself was not the one who assigned the separate lectures their respective titles. 1 McCloskey, Works 64 (in Preface by Bird Wilson) (cited in note 8).
154. Cf. Conrad, Polite Foundation, esp. at 361ff. (cited in note 12).
155. Smith on James Wilson 114–15 (cited in note 120).

the full effect of his eloquence.[156]

Wilson's friend and sometime political ally Benjamin Rush once wrote that Wilson's "eloquence was of the most commanding kind," and that, when Wilson spoke on the floor of the Continental Congress, "Not a word ever fell from his lips out of time, or out of place, nor could a word be taken from or added to his speeches without injuring them."[157] By 1790 Wilson was known particularly for his evocative, figurative rhetoric, whose "occasional simplicities" and " 'brilliant conceits' " alike, while sometimes eliciting "sneers," seem nevertheless to have proved generally rather effective in swaying his audiences.[158] In his great speech of November 24, 1787 at the Pennsylvania ratifying convention, Wilson moved his adversaries to mock him for his "fertile imagination" in his displays of the same rhetorical style that prompted his allies to compare his "power" and "elegance" with those of Demosthenes and Cicero.[159]

Modern scholars, as well, have often remarked on Wilson's "masterful" rhetoric,[160] especially his prominent use of metaphors.[161] And yet even in calling attention to Wilson's penchant for metaphor, the most astute modern commentators have not paused to say much about it. Perhaps it is in the very nature of Wilson's metaphors that they do not or cannot arrest the attention of readers today. Even at their most original, these metaphors now tend to sound utterly conventional and hardly very imaginative. But, then, Wilson himself was much more interested in promoting a "reconciliation"[162] between convention and imagination than in exploring even the most fruitful contradictions between them. To him it was the importance of the connections not the discontinuities between the individual mind and the public mind that chiefly justified his conspicuous use of figures of speech.

Metaphor was, I am arguing, so prominent in Wilson's political rhetoric

---

156. See generally *id.*, e.g., at 3, 10, 25, 136, 202, 266, 294. Cf. McMaster & Stone at 183 & 187 (cited in note 8) (on Wilson's "lofty carriage"); 3 Farrand, Records 92 (cited in note 3): "No man is more clear, copious, and comprehensive than Mr. Wilson, yet he is no great orator. He draws the attention not by the charm of his eloquence, but by the force of his reasoning"; Sanderson's Biography of the Signers to the Declaration of Independence, rev. & ed. Robert T. Conrad 499, 520 (Philadelphia: Thomas, Cowperthwait & Co., 1848).

157. Corner, ed., Autobiography of Rush 150 (cited in note 8).

158. McMaster & Stone, at 758–59 (Sketches of the Members of the Pennsylvania Convention, quoting from Graydon's Memoirs).

159. See Jensen, ed., at 339 (cited in note 8), ed. note (quoting "Centinel" and Francis Hopkinson); cf. microfiche frame 242 (Jasper Yates: "one of the most sensible, learned and elegant speeches . . . on the new Constitution of the United States, that my ears were ever gratified with").

160. See, e.g., Richard E. Amacher, American Political Writers, 1588–1800, at 146 (Boston: Twayne Publishers, 1979).

161. E.g., Ralph A. Rossum, James Wilson and the Pyramid of Government: The Federal Republic, 6 Pol. Sci. Reviewer 113 (1976) (reprinted in Ralph A. Rossum & Gary L. McDowell, eds., The American Founding: Politics, Statesmanship, and the Constitution 62 (Port Washington, N.Y.: Kennikat Press, 1981)). Cf. Geoffrey Seed, James Wilson 95 (Millwood, N.Y.: KTO Press, 1978) ("Seed on Wilson").

162. 1 McCloskey, Works 185 (cited in note 8). Cf. Conrad, Polite Foundation 368 & *passim* (cited in note 12).

largely because his theory of metaphor was so important to his "comprehensive" approach to republican political culture. Given his vision of republicanism in America, where *popular* power, knowledge, virtue, and happiness were to nourish one another, it stood to reason that Wilson's Federalist rhetoric *and theory* would incorporate a salient poetics of federalism. Indeed, a poetics for American federal theory might seem to have been essential to prudent hopes for its success. After all, the America of the early national period was not very far removed, either in time or in political culture, from the Revolutionary era itself, during which Americans had "quoted Addison, Thomson, Pope, Milton, and Shakespeare as political authorities hardly less often than they [had] quoted Locke or Montesquieu."[163] If anything, by the 1790s Americans' enthusiasm for the cultural instruction they took from teachers like Hugh Blair and James Beattie further encouraged this tendency to cultivate a figurative and affective rhetoric of republicanism, which would speak directly to the heart as well as to the mind of the citizenry. Furthermore, the candid aspirations to high culture that were espoused by many partisans of the Federalist persuasion may have made a poetics of American federal union seem all the more indispensable for identifying such a union with American republicanism.[164]

But, as I have already suggested, it would be wrong, or at least insufficient, to try to account for Wilson's metaphorical approach entirely in terms of the *constraints* of the politics of his day. His poetics of American federalism, as they reflected his highly affective conception of federal union, were very much bound up both with his distinctively positive idea of an American "nation," and with his idea of what "knowledge" itself is and how it should be increased and put to use in a republic.

Even today there remains some room for debate over how thoroughly and seriously Americans pondered any idea of a truly national union prior to the successful movement that led the "nationalist assault"[165] during the early days of the Philadelphia Convention.[166] In any event, James Wilson's own

---

163. Kenneth Silverman, A Cultural History of the American Revolution: Painting, Music, Literature, and the Theatre in the Colonies and the United States from the Treaty of Paris to the Inauguration of George Washington, 1763–1789, at 83–84 (New York: Thomas Y. Crowell Co., 1976).

164. Consider, e.g., John Adams's famous remark, "The science of government is my duty to study, more than all other sciences. . . . I must study politics and war, that my sons may have liberty to study mathematics and philosophy, geography, natural history and naval architecture, navigation, commerce, and agriculture, in order to give their children a right to study painting, poetry, music, architecture, statuary, tapestry and porcelain"; quoted in Adrienne Koch, Power, Morals, and the Founding Fathers: Essays in the Interpretation of the American Enlightenment 101 (Ithaca, N.Y.: Cornell University Press, 1961). Cf. Linda K. Kerber, Federalists in Dissent, esp. chs. 1 & 4 (cited in note 151); Emory Elliott, Revolutionary Writers: Literature and Authority in the New Republic, 1725–1810 (New York: Oxford University Press, 1982).

165. Cf. Clinton Rossiter, 1787: The Grand Convention 159ff. (reprint ed. New York: W.W. Norton, 1987).

166. For a convenient overview of Americans' limited consideration *before* 1787 of the matter of national union, see Samuel H. Beer, Federalism, Nationalism, and Democracy in America (Presidential Address, American Political Science Association, 1977), 72 Am. Pol. Sci. Rev. 9,

view was that, although in 1776 the 13 American colonies had declared their independence *"Unitedly,"* as one nation, "not *Individually,"* as separate states[167]—and despite Wilson's own efforts in the Continental Congress as early as 1777 to forge an effective national government[168]—nevertheless, the union provided for in the Articles of Confederation remained an inadequate association largely because it had been born out of "necessity not of choice."[169] Nothing in the early years of the Revolutionary settlement did anything, however, to diminish Wilson's own commitment to a vision of a strong national union, not merely as an expedient recourse in coping with the immediate problems of government in the 1780s but as a guiding ideal instinct with the most progressive republic theory. By the time of the Philadelphia Convention, Wilson was also saying that he had become as convinced as anyone could be that the majority of American citizens, as well, wanted a national union embodied in an "energetic" national government—and, again, not as a mere expedient against the political "evils" and "complaints" of the day, but as a further step toward fulfilling a national ideal that was a desirable and justifiable end in itself.[170]

10–12 (1978). Cf. Merrill Jensen, The Ideal of a National Government During the American Revolution, 58 Pol. Sci. Q. 356 (1943). Two recent and important works that address this matter are Jack N. Rakove, The Beginnings of National Politics: An Interpretive History of the Continental Congress, esp. at 183–191 (New York: Alfred A. Knopf, 1979); and Peter S. Onuf, The Origins of the Federal Republic: Jurisdictional Controversies in the United States, 1775–1787 (Philadelphia: University of Pennsylvania Press, 1983).

167. 1 Farrand, Records 324 (June 19th) (cited in note 3); cf. at 329. Indeed, Wilson's remarks at the Philadelphia Convention remain today "[t]he authority perhaps most often cited" in support of this argument for the historic Revolutionary foundation of American nationalism. Raoul Berger, Federalism: The Founders' Design 22 (Norman: University of Oklahoma Press, 1987); cf. at 33, where Berger tries to portray Wilson as later "departing from his earlier remarks"; nevertheless Berger does so by quoting Wilson's later remarks out of context, and indeed, by going so far as to quote Wilson's dicta in an important Supreme Court case of 1796 without reference to the holding of the Court, in which Wilson joined.

168. See, e.g., Seed on Wilson 26 (cited in note 161), for Wilson's and John Adams's efforts in this regard. Cf. William Winslow Crosskey & William Jeffrey, Jr., Politics and the Constitution in the History of the United States: vol. 3, The Political Background of the Federal Convention 99–105 (Chicago: University of Chicago Press, 1980) (on John Dickinson's own 1776 plan for a strong plan of union and its influence on Dickinson's former pupil Wilson). Cf. James H. Hutson, John Dickinson at the Federal Constitutional Convention, 40 Wm. & Mary Q., 3d ser., at 256, esp. 262 (1983); Milton E. Flower, John Dickinson: Conservative Revolutionary 237 & passim (Charlottesville: University Press of Virginia, 1983).

169. Koch, Notes 162 (cited in note 147).

170. 1 Farrand, Records 253 (cited in note 3); Jensen, ed., at 348 (cited in note 8). Cf. 1 Farrand 49: "On examination it would be found that the opposition of the States to federal measures had proceded [sic] much more from the Officers of the States, than from the people at large"; cf. also at 133.

For an especially probing reconsideration of the "ends" of American federalism, see a classic article by Martin Diamond—which is interesting not least for its argument that the formulation of a complete theory of the ends of American federalism came not at the Founding but with Tocqueville: The Ends of Federalism, 3 Publius 129 (1973). See esp. 146–147, where Diamond discusses Tocqueville's hopes that "disinterested" and "instinctive" patriotism would develop in America as a result of *decentralization*: "Thus, free institutions, generated and sustained by administrative decentralization, draw men into interested cooperation and then, Tocqueville hopes, by habituation into an authentic sympathy with their fellow men. . . . Administrative decentralization is the leading artifice for the creation of that new kind of patriotism." See also 142–43,

In focusing on this vision of a strong national union for purposes more than instrumental, Wilson was indeed somewhat distinctive, perhaps unique, at least among the first rank of Federalists during the late 1780s and early 1790s. For example, as between a truly "federal" union of the 13 states and a thoroughgoing "consolidation" of them under one government, Wilson took pains at the Philadelphia Convention to distinguish his own genuinely "federalist" position from the "consolidationist" nationalism mooted there by Hamilton and others.[171] And Wilson was never one to dwell, as did Hamilton, writing later as Publius, on the improvement of administrative efficiency as the principal advantage of strong national government.[172] By the same token, even within the span of the Philadelphia Convention, to say nothing of the early 1790s, Wilson's nationalism proved less changeable than that of Madison himself.[173]

In the language of the day, one might say—even if too summarily—that, at the Founding of the late 1780s, Wilson was a more thoroughly republican Federalist than Hamilton, and a more "highly Federalist"[174] republican than Madison. And yet it was because these terms—"federalism" and "republicanism"—were so important as key[175] designations and points of reference in the debates of the time that they were not without their necessary ambiguities.[176]

---

where Diamond discusses Tocqueville's notion of federal "decentralization" as a check against despotism.

171. For but one example of Hamilton's avowedly consolidationist nationalism, see 1 Farrand, Records 286 ("a compleat sovereignty in the general Governmt."); cf. at 355 for remarks of William Samuel Johnson to the effect that "One Gentleman alone (Col. Hamilton) . . . boldly and decisively contended for an abolition of the State Govts." Cf. Wilson, in *id.* 137, 322–23, and 2 Farrand, Records 10. For evidence that such a distinction, between consolidationism and Wilson's own position, was perceived by contemporaries at the Convention, see 1 Farrand, Records 355 (Johnson). For other consolidationist remarks besides Hamilton's, see *id.* at 136-37, 424 (George Read).

172. Cf. Gerald Stourzh, Alexander Hamilton and the Idea of Republican Government (Stanford, Cal.: Stanford University Press, 1970) ("Stourzh, Alexander Hamilton"), at 82–83 and at corresponding endnote 23, esp. for Hamilton's quotation of Pope, in Federalist No. 68: "Though we cannot acquiesce in the political heresy of the poet who says—'For forms of government let fools contest— / That which is best administered is best.'—yet we may safely pronounce, that the true test of good government is its aptitude and tendency to produce good administration." Stourzh observes, at 83, that this is "a recurring theme of Hamilton's political writing."

173. Cf. Banning, *in* Beeman et al., Beyond Confederation (cited in note 25); Banning, The Hamiltonian Madison: A Reconsideration, 92 Va. Mag. Hist. & Biog. 3, 7, & *passim* (1984). But see *contra,* Charles F. Hobson, The Negative on State Laws: James Madison, the Constitution, and the Crisis of Republican Government, 36 Wm. & Mary Q., 3d ser., at 215 (1979).

174. Cf. 1 Butterfield, Rush Letters 507 (cited in note 58).

175. See Raymond Williams' notion of "keywords" as words, involving "ideas and values," that are of sufficient strategic importance in contests for power and authority such that those who care about victory are likely to be moved to invoke these words, and to try to appropriate them. Keywords are, then, keys to entire agonistic vocabularies and are evidence of contests deemed suitable for, and worthy of, articulate dispute. Williams, Keywords: A Vocabulary of Culture and Society 16-17 & *passim* (rev. ed. New York: Oxford University Press, 1983). Cf. a new work that was, unfortunately, published too late for me to profit from it in writing and revising the present article, Daniel T. Rodgers, Contested Truths: Keywords in American Politics Since Independence (New York: Basic Books, 1987).

176. On the ambiguous nature of the term "federalism" at the Founding, the best discussion remains, I believe, Martin Diamond, The *Federalist*'s View of Federalism, *in* George C.S. Benson, ed., Essays in Federalism 21, esp. at 24ff. (Claremont, Cal.: Institute for Studies in Federalism,

When Wilson's position is reconsidered now, in the context of the nature and range of the language of American politics at the Founding, it is especially interesting to recall that at least one engaged observer of the day pointed to Wilson as the Federalist who had first coined the term "Federal Republic." Writing as "a Columbian Patriot," Mercy Warren in early 1788 published a pamphlet condemning the proposed Constitution and characterizing the new form of government to which it would give birth as a "bantling" that might have gone "without a name, had not Mr. *Wilson*, in the fertility of his genius, suggested the happy epithet of a *Federal Republic*."[177] Whether Warren's ascription is accurate is a question difficult to settle and, in any case, beside my point here. Rather, it is the fact of Warren's ascription itself, accurate or not, that is significant for my argument, because the ascription reminds us that, in the debates of the time, some able disputants took the niceties of language quite seriously, and perceived (or presumed) that Wilson did more than most.

In this light, the term "Federal Republic," like Wilson's avowed coinage "moral abstraction," assumes the significance of a metaphor. Indeed, in his "comprehensive theory" of American federalism, Wilson treated the terms "federal republic" and "moral abstraction" as metaphors *for one another*. In so doing he was attempting to "reconcile" a number of "seeming contradictions"[178] in Federalist theory and to augment not only the *means* for achieving American federal union, but also the "real" *source* he thought most important to sustaining such a union and the *ends* that should guide and control American federalism.[179] It was precisely the capability of metaphor for synthesizing source, means, and ends[180] that tempted Wilson to a "comprehensive" vision of American federal union that was so self-consciously metaphorical.

In the 1780s the project of relating any conception of American federal union to any meaningful concept of American "nationality" would seem to have required some reference to abstraction, if only because it was so manifest

---

1961). Among the many important discussions of the ambiguities of "republicanism" at the Founding, I find especially helpful Linda K. Kerber, The Republican Ideology of the Revolutionary Generation, 37 Am. Q. 474 (1985).

177. For the authoritative modern edition of the pamphlet in question—Observations on the New Constitution, And on the Federal and State Conventions. By a Columbian Patriot (Boston, 1788)—see 4 Herbert J. Storing, ed., The Complete Anti-Federalist 270 (7 vols.; Chicago: University of Chicago Press, 1981). I quote here from p. 275. The editor, at 286, suggests that Warren's reference is to Wilson's Nov. 24, 1787 speech; see Jensen, ed., note 8, at 341–42 (cited in note 8). Cf. the same 1788 pamphlet, reprinted in Pamphlets on the Constitution of the United States, ed. Paul Leicester Ford 1 (Brooklyn, N.Y., 1888; reprint ed. New York: Da Capo Press, 1969). Ford attributed the pamphlet to Elbridge Gerry.

On the case for Warren's authorship, and on her Anti-Federalist views generally, see Lester H. Cohen, Explaining the Revolution: Ideology and Ethics in Mercy Otis Warren's Historical Theory, 37 Wm. & Mary Q., 3d ser., at 200, 202ff. (1980).

178. 1 McCloskey, Works 185. Cf. note 162 *supra*.

179. Cf. Diamond, 3 Publius 129 (1973) (cited in note 170). Also cf. Arendt, On Revolution 44ff., 136, & *passim* (cited in note 26), to the effect that the American Revolution augmented merely the means not the ends of government.

180. Cf. Wayne C. Booth, Metaphor as Rhetoric: The Problem of Evaluation, in Sheldon Sacks, ed., On Metaphor 47, 67 (Chicago: University of Chicago Press, 1979) ("Booth, Metaphor").

at the time that a concrete American nationality, in the form of a general American culture, did not yet exist.[181] But in this respect Wilson sought to make a virtue out of what might have been a vice in American Federalist theory, especially as Federalist theory law open to the disturbing criticism that it departed from the essential principles of neoclassical republicanism.

If, as Samuel Johnson tells us, it is in the nature of a metaphor that it "gives . . . two ideas for one," and if, as I.A. Richards adds, the tension or disparity between the two ideas given is likely to be at least as important as any suggested resemblance between them,[182] then during the American Founding of the 1780s the new term "Federal Republic"—and perhaps it was Wilson's coinage—might be said to have operated as a rich and problematic (if ultimately not quite the most important) metaphor in the American language of politics.

Familiarity with the neoclassical maxim that a republican form of government is practicable only in a polity of small territorial extent aroused anxiety among Federalists and Anti-Federalists alike over the question whether an American federal union would seem to, or would in fact, compromise American republican principles. And it was this general anxiety—over the problem that a "Federal Republic" posed a contradiction in terms—that Madison addressed in the stunning linguistic and theoretical turn consummated in his *Federalist* paper No. 10.[183] There Madison secured the American reconception of what republicanism *as government* meant: whereas classically, republicanism had meant *self government*, it became something quite different in the American identification of republicanism with *government by others*, namely, the citizens' representatives.[184]

Madison consolidated this identification of republicanism with representation largely by means of an argument culminating in his celebrated prescription that, in order to "provide for the safety, liberty, and happiness of the

---

181. For a compelling recent argument in support of this point, see John M. Murrin, A Roof without Walls: The Dilemma of American National Identity, in Beeman et al., Beyond Confederation at 333 (cited in note 25). Cf. J.R. Pole, Enlightenment and the Politics of American Nature, in Roy Porter & Mikuláš Teich, eds., The Enlightenment in National Context 192, 208–9 (Cambridge: Cambridge University Press, 1981) ("Pole, Enlightenment"). See also Joshua I. Miller, Local Ideas in Early American Politics: Decentralist Ideas and Practices, 1630-1789 (Ph.D. diss., Princeton University, 1984).

182. Richards, The Philosophy of Rhetoric 93, 96, 126–27 (New York: Oxford University press, 1936). Cf. Paul Ricoeur, The Rule of Metaphor: Multi-disciplinary Studies of the Creation of Meaning in Language, trans. Robert Czerny et al., at 76 (Toronto: University of Toronto, 1975) ("Ricoeur, Rule of Metaphor") ("The pioneering job done by I.A. Richards' *The Philosophy of Rhetoric* cannot be overestimated").

183. For Madison's own anticipation of this argument in Federalist No. 10, see 1 Farrand, Records 134–36 (cited in note 3).

184. Cf. Pocock, Virtue 16n. & 271 (cited in note 12); and Pocock, The Machiavellian Moment 522ff., 538, & *passim* (cited in note 141). On Hamilton's express appreciation—by 1777—of the conceptual novelty of the "representative democracy" of the American republics, see Stourzh, Alexander Hamilton 50ff. (cited in note 172).

584

Community,"[185] the territorial "sphere" of electoral politics in America not only could be but would have to be "extended."[186] And, as I have already indicated, Madison's argument in this vein, however much or little it may have owed to Hume, proved at least as ingenious, successful, and altogether important as any other Federalist contribution to the "new science of politics." It is probably not too much to say that this Madisonian prescription, for "extending the sphere" of politics in order to control and harness demiurgic factionalism, has also proved to be even more important to American federal theory since the Founding than it was to the eponymous Federalists in the years of their initial triumphs.

While both Madison's "original" Federalist theory and the "Madisonian theory" of federalism as it has been variously reconstituted ever since do include much of importance besides this insight about the need for "extending" the territorial "sphere" of politics in a modern republic, it is in no way inauthentic to view this insight as an operative principle absolutely central to Madison's vision of American federal union. Indeed, in reconsidering the American "Federal Republic" of the 1780s as a metaphor, it would seem that the principal function, if not the intention, of Madison's argument for "extending the sphere" was nothing less crucial than reducing into the concrete terms and practicable mechanics of the new political science the "apparent contradiction" a federal republic initially posed.

Emanations of this reductive approach can be found in much of Madison's own record of the development of his federal theory at the time of the Founding, perhaps most notably in his famous remark at the Philadelphia Convention on June 19 that "The great difficulty lies in the affair of Representation; and if this could be adjusted, all others would be surmountable."[187] In the terms of the analysis of metaphor that have become so widely used since I.A. Richards introduced them, the "Federal Republic" was, in the founders' political culture, a new metaphor, the tenor (or "principal subject") of the metaphor being "republicanism," the vehicle (or "what it is compared to") "federalism," and the ground (or basis for their comparison, interrelation, and interaction) the "affair of representation."[188] It is, then, chiefly Madison's focus on this third element, "representation," as the key to what a "federal republic" means, that gives that meaning something of a metaphorical quality.

At the same time, however, there is something too reductive to be called

---

185. 1 Farrand, Records 53 (cited in note 3). Cf. John Zvesper, The Madisonian Systems, 37 West. Pol. Q. 236, 252 (1984).

186. Federalist No. 10, at 64 (J. Cooke ed., 1961).

187. 1 Farrand, Records 321 (cited in note 3).

188. Richards, The Philosophy of Rhetoric, at Lecture V, "Metaphor," esp. at 96-97 (New York: Oxford University Press, 1936). Cf. Morse Peckham, Metaphor: A Little Plain Speaking on a Weary Subject, in Peckham, The Triumph of Romanticism 401, 406 (Columbia: University of South Carolina Press, 1970) ("Peckham, Metaphor"); Geoffrey N. Leech, A Linguistic Guide to English Poetry 151 (Harlow, Eng.: Longman, 1969); Ricoeur, Rule of Metaphor 24, 57, & passim (cited in note 182).

truly metaphorical about Madison's stroke of genius in defining the fundamental matter of representation as a matter of constitutional design, and
thereby addressing it as a problem to be handled according to a political science of mechanistic "adjustment." Geoffrey Leech, a modern student of metaphor who is generally sympathetic to I.A. Richards' approach to the topic,
suggests that it is only in a simile and not in a metaphor that the "ground" of
comparison is specified. According to this distinction, then, Madison's idea of
the federal republic, because expressly, specifically, *and definitively* predicated
on his operative prescription for extending the territorial sphere of politics,
would seem to be more a simple simile than a rich metaphor. "Metaphor,"
says Leech, "is inexplicit with regard to both the ground of comparison, and
the things compared. This is not only a matter of indefiniteness . . . but of
ambiguity."[189] Or, as Ricoeur puts the matter even more evocatively
(although he, no less than Leech, acknowledges his large debt to Richards):

> Reflective lucidity applied to metaphorical talent consists in good part in
> locating the "ground" of the metaphor in its underlying "rationale."
> Whether the metaphor concerned be dead (the leg of a chair) or living
> (an author's metaphor), our procedure is the same: we look for its
> ground in some shared characteristic. But this characteristic does not
> necessarily lie in a direct resemblance between tenor and vehicle; it can
> result from a common attitude taken to them both. And a vast range of
> intermediary cases fans out between these two extremes. . . . [I]f meta-
> phor consists in talking about one thing in terms of another, does it not
> consist also in perceiving, thinking, or sensing one thing in terms of
> another.[190]

While Madison's federal theory may have proved, from the early 1790s
onward, flexible enough to permit him to shift from his nationalist position
during the making and ratification of the Constitution to his advocacy of
states' rights thereafter,[191] the thoroughly modern social scientist's reductionism of Madison's seminal Federalist political science did not relish the ambiguities of *representation as metaphor* so much as it sought to obviate them. This is
a point, like so many others, that a comparison of Madison with Wilson does
much to highlight.

Wilson also thought that the creation and preservation of an American
federal union required, as he said, "enlarging the sphere." Yet in this respect
Wilson's primary focus was quite different from Madison's. When Wilson
spoke of "enlarging the sphere," it was not the territorial sphere of politics
that concerned him but rather, once again, the boundless sphere comprising

---

189. Leech at 157 (cited in note 188).
190. Ricoeur, Rule of Metaphor 81–82, 83 (author's notes omitted) (cited in note 182).
191. At least one leading senior scholar of Madisonian political thought, Professor Marvin
Meyers, considers that this shift of position "must" have left Madison "theoretically embarrassed." Meyers, Mind of the Founder at xlii (rev. ed. Hanover, N.H.: University Press of New
England, 1981) ("Meyers, Mind of the Founder," rev. ed.).

the "powers" of the human mind. So he told his law students. The sphere to be "enlarged" was, for him, the mental and moral sphere of everyday public and private life, including "the social and benevolent affections," all the "finer operations of the mind," and—not least—all "knowledge" itself that serves and improves the "community" at large.[192]

In sum, whereas for Madison the crux of American federal theory lay, as a matter of disengaged political science, in extending the sphere of electoral politics, for Wilson the vital principle of American federal theory lay in "enlarging the sphere" of "moral abstraction," both in the "publick mind" and in the individual minds of the citizens. And for Wilson, enlarging this sphere was at least as much a matter of moral science as of political science. A federal union of authentically republican personality would require no less than this, because, said Wilson, for a citizenry "[t]o embrace the whole, requires an expansion of mind, of talents, and of temper."[193]

None of these points of comparison and contrast between Wilson and Madison necessarily marks an irreconcilable disagreement between their respective theories of federalism. By and large, Wilson's founding vision of American federal union tended to supplement and complement Madison's rather than contradict it. Above all, Wilson and Madison agreed that an idea of representation was at the heart of American republicanism.[194] And Wilson, at least as forthrightly although not as exclusively as Madison, associated the idea of representation with "the act of election."[195] Moreover, Wilson was as emphatic as Madison in the view that enlarging the electoral districts in America would be quite necessary for the federal republic they both projected.[196] And Madison, for this part, as early as 1783, was already contemplating the theme that later came to predominate in Wilson's exposition of federal theory: the capability of a civic sociology wherein the "extended" patriotism of some citizens would gravitate toward "the disinterested object of aggrandizing [the] community."[197]

---

192. 1 McCloskey, Works 235 (cited in note 8).
193. Id. at 267.
194. Id. at 311–12, 301–3; 2 McCloskey, Works 785; cf. at 721–46. Indeed, to Wilson, the *extension* of the principle of political representation in America was an important part of what made American republicanism unique. Cf. Jensen, ed., at 343–44, 354–55 (cited in note 8).
195. Cf. 1 McCloskey, Works 364.
196. See, e.g., 1 Farrand, Records 133 (cited in note 3).
197. Meyers, Mind of the Founder, 1st ed., at 36 (cited in note 29): "let it be observed—that the same active and predominant passion of the human breast, which prompts mankind to arrogate superiority and to the acquirement of riches, honor and power, which restricted to the selfish purposes of an individual we term *ambition*, is when extended to the disinterested object of aggrandizing a community, what we dignify with the appelation of *patriotism*—that the exertion of this principle being as advantageous to a republic, as it is useful to a man,—whoever will make the interest of his country his own, and shew a blind devotion to its views and prejudices, will . . . be honoured with the flattering distinction of *patriot*." These are words ascribed to Madison writing in 1783. Cf. the implications, for any theory of disinterested patriotism in an extended sphere, that are evident in Madison's remarks written in what Meyers, at 502, indicates was "[a]bout 1821": "We must not shut our eyes to the nature of man, nor to the light of experience. Who would rely on a fair decision from three individuals if two had an interest in the case opposed to

Thus, in respect to the overall distinction I am suggesting between, on the one hand, Madison's Federalist plan, as conceptualized chiefly in terms of a structural and operational political science, and, on the other hand, Wilson's Federalist vision as conceptualized chiefly in terms of a figurative moral science of civic personality, the evidence abounds that each of these partners in the early Federalist campaign supported much the same program. Nevertheless, the typifying differences in focus and emphasis between Wilson and Madison do indicate a difference in orientation that is important, no matter how little it precluded partnership between them as politicians or as apologists.

This difference in orientation is nowhere clearer than on the underlying question whether a moral purpose in federal union was intrinsic to the "moral promise" of that union. Knowingly or not, Madison tended to agree with Hume that, as David Epstein has summarized a point made by both Madison and Hume, "men in groups are less moved by . . . 'moral . . . motives' . . . than [men] are individually."[198] "Respect for character," said Madison, "is always diminished in proportion to the number among whom the blame or praise is to be divided. Conscience . . . is known to be inadequate in individuals: In large numbers, little is to be expected from it."[199] Thus, in the political science of an American federal republic, Madison thought the connections between the respective individual minds of the citizens and the public mind should not be a central concern of theorists, because such connections were, in the practice of republican politics, of limited, even if more than negligible, importance.

Here, it would seem, Wilson very much disagreed. He looked upon federal union in the new Republic as an independent moral value in and of itself, precisely because such a union, by increasing the sphere of actual and imagined association among the citizens, would serve both to increase greatly the fund of civic virtue and to give this fund of virtue greater political and moral effect.[200] In Wilson's resolutely antireductive view of federal union, as of everything else, "the connexion of affection" was no less important or capa-

---

the rights of the third? Make the number as great as you please, the impartiality will not be increased, nor any further security against injustice be obtained, than what may result from the greater difficulty of uniting the wills of a greater number" (at 504). Contrast Wilson on "expanded patriotism," in 1 McCloskey, Works 268.

198. Epstein, Political Theory 90 (cited in note 13) (discussing Hume's essay Of the Independency of Parliament, and Madison's Federalist No. 10).

199. 1 Farrand, Records 135 (cited in note 3).

200. Here, again, I do not mean to assert that there was a *wholesale* difference between Wilson's and Madison's ideas in this respect. After all, the theme in question here is prominent in some of Madison's own 1791 and 1792 *National Gazette* essays, on the civic capability of political parties. See Edward C. Dreyer, Making Parties Respectable: James Madison's *National Gazette* Essays (paper presented to American Political Science Association and Center for the Study of the Constitution, Chicago, Sept. 5, 1987) (drawing heavily on earlier work by Lance Banning and John Zvesper). Thus, one should beware the temptation to hold Madison hostage to what may seem the puzzling inconsistencies with which he can be charged *if* one focuses exclusively on his contributions to The Federalist. Cf. Morton White, Philosophy, The Federalist, and the Constitution 159–68, esp. 166 (New York: Oxford University Press, 1987).

ble than "the connexion of interest"; and it was the equal importance of both these connections that supported his conception of an "expanded patriotism"—a "passion for the commonweal"—as a matter of "knowledge" as well as feeling.[201]

Wilson's "comprehensive" theory of the Federal Republic thus included—but also extended beyond—the "affair of representation," at least if one followed Madison in defining the affair of representation entirely as a matter of electoral politics. And because Wilson's federal theory was based on a moral science (rather than an avowed "political science") that relied so much on metaphors for its epistemological foundation, Wilson's federal theory took metaphors seriously—and no less so because they might be conventional, abstract, or ambiguous. To the contrary, it was only in terms of such metaphors that Wilson could reach another question that Madisonian political science tended to neglect. This question, although meaningless unless understood as a matter of metaphor, was also a question about representation: Not *who* but *what* does a "Federal Republic" represent? As a matter of course, Wilson answered the question in terms of another metaphor: "moral abstraction." And in addressing the question what "moral abstraction" represents, Wilson could not and did not escape *further* appeals to metaphor. Indeed, he sought them at every turn. In this way he meant to cast light on what a federal union in a republic means—by multiplying metaphors for representation itself, in order to conjure up a context of meaning for the Federal Republic as a new metaphor.

VII. METAPHORS FOR REPRESENTATION AS METAPHORS FOR AMERICAN FEDERALISM

"The dimensions of the human mind are apt to be regulated by the extent and objects of the government under which it is formed."
—Benjamin Rush to David Ramsay, in March or April 1788[202]

At the Philadelphia Convention there was no other Federalist to rival James Wilson as a principled and consistent advocate of direct popular elections. From his first general proposal (on May 31) for direct popular election of "both branches of the National Legislature"[203] to what may have been his last rueful allusion (on September 4) to his failure ever to muster much sup-

---

201. 1 McCloskey, Works 268. Yet, again, any assertion of a thoroughgoing difference between Wilson and Madison in this respect seems to me dubious—not to mention imprudent, in light of some of the most careful and subtle recent scholarship on Madison's "nationalism," e.g., Drew R. McCoy, James Madison and Visions of American Nationality in the Confederation Period: A Regional Perspective, *in* Beeman et al., Beyond Confederation 226, 244, & *passim* (cited in note 25).

202. See 1 Butterfield, Rush Letters 453, 454–55 (cited in note 58). Cf. text *infra* at note 246.

203. 1 Farrand, Records 52.

port among the other delegates for a provision for direct popular election of the President,[204] Wilson repeatedly indicated his distaste for the "interjection"[205] of any electors between the citizen voters and their elected officers.

Thus frustrated in his advocacy of direct election as a "first principle" that he had hoped would permeate the national Constitution, Wilson later recouped somewhat by securing a provision for the popular election of state senators in Pennsylvania, under the new Pennsylvania constitution adopted in 1790.[206] In his most famous speech at the Pennsylvania constitutional convention, Wilson heaped ridicule on the very idea of intermediary electors, based as this idea must be, he said, on the mistaken notion that such electors serve as "political alembicks" who by their own "purifying virtues" somehow "sublimate" and "refine" the representatives thus indirectly elected.[207]

Whether or not this notion of "sublimation" and "refinement," or "filtration," through indirect election had an important place in Madison's Federalist political science,[208] it had, then, virtually none in Wilson's more popular constitutionalism or in his more "comprehensive" theory of representation.[209] A quite different notion of "sublimation" and "refinement" *was*, however, of the greatest importance to Wilson in his vision of republican citizenship, emphasizing as it did not the occasional act of voting at the polls, but instead the everyday civic routine that Wilson thought the very right of suffrage should and would induce among the People.[210] Not the electoral mechanics of faction counterbalancing faction,[211] then, and, indeed, not merely the isolated act of voting, but rather *both* the actual exercise of the right

---

204. 2 Farrand, Records 501. For an interesting reconsideration of this matter from the vantage point of 1987, see Eric R.A.N. Smith & Peverill Squire, Direct Election of the President and the Power of the States, 40 West. Pol. Q. 29 (1987).

205. 2 McCloskey, Works 789 (cited in note 8).

206. Cf. Smith on James Wilson at 300–303 (cited in note 120).

207. 2 McCloskey, Works 792–93.

208. For a short restatement of the view that Madison, and Hamilton, in The Federalist, "set forth" a "republican" theory of "refined representation . . . through the election of the best men, to promote . . . responsiveness to constituents and care for the common good of society," see Jean Yarbrough, Representation and Republicanism: Two Views, in Daniel J. Elazar, ed., Republicanism, Representation, and Consent: Views of the Founding Era 77 (New Brunswick, N.J.: Transaction Books, 1979); reprinted from 9 Publius (1979). Yarbrough tends to contrast (e.g., at 97) this conception of "refined representation" with the contemporary British conception of "virtual representation."

For emphasis, to the point of overemphasis, on this same theme in both Madison's *and Wilson*'s ideas on representation, see Garry Wills, Explaining America: The Federalist 238–47 (Garden City, N.Y.: Doubleday & Co., 1981). The best corrective of Wills's misapprehension of Madison in this respect is Banning, 72 Va. Mag. Hist. & Biog. at 12–14 & passim (cited in note 173); cf. Epstein, Political Theory 99–107 (cited in note 13).

209. For a hint of Wilson's grudging resignation to the *fait accompli* with respect to the indirect election of senators in the national legislature, see 1 McCloskey, Works 414ff. Cf. Seed on Wilson 106 (cited in note 161).

210. For portrayals of this routine, see 2 McCloskey, Works 787–88 & 1 McCloskey, Works 404–5. Cf. Conrad, Polite Foundation 384 (cited in note 12); and Michelman, 100 Harv. L. Rev. at 54 (cited in note 63).

211. This is not to say that Wilson disagreed with Madison about the importance of "regulating" that "esprit de corp" the "ebullition" of which tends to factionalism. See 1 McCloskey, Works 266–67.

of suffrage *and* that abstract right itself serving to induce quotidian citizenship—for Wilson these together were the quintessential "sublimating" and "refining" agents in the politics of a republic. According to his vision, as he gave voice to it in his great speech of December 31, 1789 at the Pennsylvania constitutional convention, and as he reiterated it shortly thereafter in his law lectures,

> the right of suffrage, properly understood, properly valued, properly cultivated, and properly exercised, is a rich mine of intelligence and patriotism . . . an abundant source of the most rational, the most improving, and the most endearing connexion among the citizens . . . [; it is also] a most powerful, and, at the same time, a most pleasing bond of union between the citizens, and those whom they select for the different offices and departments of government.[212]

This conception of the right of suffrage as a "rich mine" and "abundant source," and a "powerful" and "pleasing" "bond," was something that Wilson thought the political science of his day had as yet done very little to elucidate and appreciate. Indeed, Wilson went out of his way to emphasize that, if it was fitting, as he thought, to characterize political science generally, "with regard to other subjects," as "still in its infancy," then it should be added that, particularly "with regard to" the right of suffrage, political science was even less advanced.[213]

To Wilson the inadequacy of political science in this particular "regard" was so egregious that his appeal to the alternative, complementary authority of his essentially metaphorical moral science became all the more important. The best way to a "proper understanding, valuation, cultivation, and exercise" of the right of suffrage lay open, as he saw it, not through the mechanics of the new science of politics but through the proliferation of enlightening and evocative metaphors for the suffrage, *and* for all the other contextual phenomena that were part of, or that could enhance, its significance.

Wilson's practice of adding to the general tissue of political metaphors of the day was, however, far from unique to him, for all that he appears to have excelled at it. Metaphors were so common in the public language of the time as now to seem hardly worthy of much notice. For example, when Madison in *Federalist* Paper No. 47 wanted to invoke the full force of the new American concept of political obligation based on "a consent that closely and actively

---

212. 2 McCloskey, Works 789; cf. 1 McCloskey, Works 405.
213. 2 McCloskey, Works 785. (Note what we today would consider the inversion in Wilson's use of the terms "infancy" and "childhood"; Wilson's meaning is nevertheless clear enough.) Cf. Hamilton's views on the political science of republican elections, e.g., in Federalist No. 35 and No. 36—esp. Hamilton's prescient insight about the importance of a "scientific" understanding of the "psychology" of voting behavior, an insight discussed in Judith N. Shklar, Alexander Hamilton and the Language of Political Science, in Anthony Pagden, ed., The Languages of Political Theory in Early-Modern Europe 339 (Cambridge: Cambridge University Press, 1987).

joined voter and representative,"[214] he referred to *"the chain of connection, that binds the whole fabric of the constitution in one indissoluable bond of unity and amity."*[215] And very much to the point of Madison's figure of speech was that he was not thereby artfully contributing a new metaphor but instead simply quoting from the New Hampshire constitution. James Wilson, then, was merely repeating a familiar phrase in the American public litany of the founding era when he often referred to consensual political representation in America as "the chain of communication between the people and those, to whom they have committed the exercise of the powers of government."[216]

It would be both tedious and not very revealing to catalog Wilson's numerous metaphors for, or bearing directly on, representation, consensual obligation, and the suffrage. For example, Wilson frequently spoke of "representation" in America as "at once . . . the basis and the cement of the superstructure" of government,[217] and as "the faithful echo of the voice of the people."[218] He called "free and equal elections" the "original fountain, from which all the streams of administration flow";[219] and he referred to direct elections "not only as the corner Stone, but as the foundation of the fabric" of government.[220]

Somewhat more interesting, perhaps, than Wilson's often unproblematic use of such conventional metaphors are those instances when Wilson may have been intentionally or unintentionally taking recourse to metaphors in order to avail himself of the irresolution their ambiguities bespoke. For example, sometimes Wilson drew on the undifferentiated Newtonianism so common in the speech of the day[221] in order to compare the phenomena of political representation with the phenomena of "opticks."

Once, in professing his deference, as a delegate at the Philadelphia Con-

---

214. Beer, 72 Am. Pol. Sci. Rev. at 10 (cited in note 166).

215. Federalist No. 47, at 327 (J. Cooke ed. 1961).

216. 1 McCloskey, Works 403; cf. *id.* at 312; 2 McCloskey, Works 764, 786. Cf. Jensen, ed., at 344 (cited in note 8); cf. at 355.

217. E.g., Jensen, ed., at 343–44.

218. 1 McCloskey, Works 313.

219. *Id.* at 402. Cf. "the People" as "noble source" and "abundant fountain," in Jensen, ed., at 349; cf. at 363. And cf. Madison's use, at the Philadelphia Convention, of this rather commonplace figure of speech for "the People"; 2 Farrand, Records 476 (cited in note 3). Raoul Berger, Federalism: The Founders' Design at 44 n.114 (Norman: University of Oklahoma Press, 1987) gives other instances of it.

220. 1 Farrand, 359.

221. See esp. William Powell Jones, The Rhetoric of Science: A Study of Scientific Ideas and Imagery in Eighteenth-Century English Poetry 9ff. & *passim* (Berkeley: University of California Press, 1966). Cf. Douglas Bush, Newtonianism, Rationalism, and Sentimentalism, ch. 3 *in* Science and English Poetry: A Historical Sketch, 1590–1950, at 51–78 (New York: Oxford University Press, 1950); J.H. Randall, Jr., The Newtonian World Machine, *in* Arnold B. Arons & Alfred M. Bork, eds., Science & Ideas: Selected Readings 138, 158ff. (Englewood Cliffs, N.J.: Prentice-Hall, 1964).

Of special interest for my purposes: L.L. Laudan, Thomas Reid and the Newtonian Turn of British Methodological Thought, *in* Robert E. Butts & John W. Davis, eds., The Methodological Heritage of Newton 103 (Toronto: University of Toronto Press, 1970); and Louise Marcil-Lacoste, Reid's Understanding of Newton's Methodological Rules, *in* Marcil-Lacoste at 124–31 (cited in note 76).

vention, to the constituency who had elected him, Wilson said, "I have no right to imagine that the reflected rays of delegated power can displease by a brightness that proves the superior splendor of the luminary from which they proceed."[222]   What lends special interest to this optical metaphor is the fact and the way that Wilson used it to attenuate an ambiguity in his own theory and practice of representation. For, despite his pointed language about the voice of representatives as but the "faithful echo of the voice of the people,"[223] and about the power and authority of representatives as but "the pale light of the moon" compared with the original popular sovereignty that is the "beaming splendour of the sun"[224] in a republican political system, Wilson nevertheless did exercise and defend considerable discretion for himself in his capacity as a delegate. This is, after all, the subtle point of his figurative deference in his optical metaphor: that his good judgment in the exercise of his discretion as a delegate so redounds to the credit of the constituency whom he reflects that he has no "right" to presume that such representation would "displease" them.[225]

It is, however, where the nature of federal union is concerned that Wilson's metaphorical approach to political representation becomes most interesting, because it is in his distinctive conception of representative democracy in the Federal Republic that Wilson accomplishes most in using the intrinsic ambiguity of metaphor to advance American republicanism as a matter of moral science. It is, in other words, in Wilson's federal theory that there is the most important relationship between, on the one hand, his theory of the moral significance of metaphor and, on the other hand, his concern to find the best way to "a proper understanding, valuation, cultivation, and exercise" of the right of suffrage.

So much did this right—properly understood, valued, cultivated, and exercised—epitomize American republicanism for Wilson that, unlike

---

222. Jensen, ed., at 341 (cited in note 8); cf. at 352. On "The Bonds of a Metaphor," see Richard Sennett, Authority 77–83 (New York: Alfred A. Knopf, 1980).

223. 1 McCloskey, Works 313 (cited in note 8).

224. Id. at 403.

225. Cf. 1 Farrand, Records 132–33 (cited in note 3), for a remark by Wilson, on June 6, that I think is especially revealing of the complexity of his theory of political representation: "The Govt. ought to possess not only 1st. the *force* but 2ndly. the *mind or sense* of the people at large. The Legislature ought to be the most exact transcript of the whole Society. Representation is made necessary only because it is impossible for the people to act collectively." Wilson thus urged that not just the *will* but the complete mind, or sense, of each citizen and of "the publick mind" be represented. And Wilson's emphasis on the importance of the Common Sense distinction between will and understanding, or will and knowledge, would then seem to suggest an important—perhaps a central—place in Wilson's republican theory of representation for the authority of what the People "know," not merely what they want. The implication is, I believe, that Wilson envisioned republican institutions that would, in thus representing the full self, effectively represent the People, both individually and collectively, at their best, as judged in light of what *they know* is best. Cf. Conrad, Polite Foundation, at 381ff. (cited in note 12).

That Wilson's is *not* a Burkean theory of virtual representation would seem to be clear, not just implicitly, from so much of what Wilson says elsewhere, but also expressly, in Wilson's unequivocal rejection of the unrepublican "creed" he clearly perceived in Burke's writings. See 2 McCloskey, Works 574ff.

Madison,[226] he tended to envision federal union not so much as a republican "corrective" for the previous vices of American republicanism but as a climactic "sublimation" of "the People" themselves.

As I have suggested, Wilson took very seriously this ubiquitous metaphor "the People" as an established reality in American politics. And for him, much of the reality of "the People" in America lay in the fact that the right of suffrage and the principle of representation had for the first time in history been sufficiently extended to vindicate this classical metaphor as more than mere cant. Even in Britain, by contrast, although the principle of representative government was known and had been partially instituted, it remained confined to but one "narrow corner of the British constitution."[227] Thus, said Wilson, the British government is, in truth, "a Government without a People." And this provocative assertion seemed to lead Wilson to a question that he chose to ask in apparently metaphysical terms: "*What*, then, or *where*, are the PEOPLE?"[228]

For Wilson, an authentically republican answer to this question had to "comprehend" the public personality of the citizens, considered both individually and collectively, with citizenship conceived of in terms of the right to vote and otherwise to be represented in their government.[229] And yet in continually addressing this question—in what does the quiddity of "the People" consist?—Wilson's answer at its most "comprehensive," while incorporating, nevertheless exceeded this formal, legalistic conception of citizenship.[230] Citizenship extended beyond its legal and political significance to encompass *moral* personality, especially moral imagination.

Indeed, because, in addition to the "original sovereignty" that the suffrage embodies, "obedience" is also, in Wilson's view, "a distinguishing feature in the countenance of a citizen," he took note of Aristotle's insight that "a citizen is one partaking equally of power *and* subordination."[231] But what was most distinctive to Wilson's own perspective on republican citizenship was that he reformulated Aristotle's classically republican insight in the terms of late 18th-century moral science. From this perspective, his theory of republican citizenship implicated Sir Joshua Reynolds as much as Aristotle, at least insofar as Reynolds taught that a "submission to others is a deference" altogether necessary if we are to attain "a true idea of what imagination is."[232]

If, as Wilson saw the matter, the cultivation of republican culture in

226. Banning, *in* Beeman et al., Beyond Confederation, esp. at 184ff. (cited in note 25).

227. Jensen, ed., at 354 (cited in note 8).

228. Chisholm v. Georgia, 2 Dallas 419, 462.

229. E.g., 1 McCloskey, Works 73, 406 (cited in note 8); 2 McCloskey, Works 573.

230. E.g., Chisholm v. Georgia, 2 Dallas 419, 463. Contrast Arendt, On Revolution, esp. at 107 (cited in note 26).

231. 2 McCloskey, Works 573–74 (emphasis added); cf. at 576.

232. Sir Joshua Reynolds, Discourses Delivered to the Students of the Royal Academy, ed. Roger Fry 206, 209 (London: Seeley & Co., 1905). I owe this reference to Cottom, The Civilized Imagination 17 (cited in note 150).

America depended foremostly on a process of improvement in the moral imagination of the People themselves, and if, as he had come to see more and more by the late 1780s, American republicanism, despite the improving capability of both an extensive suffrage and the civic education of civil society,[233] stood in need of further reform, then the creation of a federal union was as much a moral necessity as a political policy. Thus, whereas many of the founders, together with Madison, approached federal union chiefly as a matter of governmental structure, and therefore tended to conceive of it in terms of divided sovereignty and the respective apportionment of "national" and "state" agency, Wilson maintained such a consistent focus on the People themselves that he conceived of federal union primarily in terms of citizenship rather than government.

At the very center of his vision of federal union, then, was his projection that such a union would effectively "double" the civic personality of every citizen. As Wilson is reported by Rufus King to have said on June 25 at the Philadelphia Convention, in an American federal republic, "Every man will possess a double Character, that of a Citizen of the U.S. & yt. of a Citizen of an individl. State."[234] It was the context of debate over direct popular election of the Senate that occasioned this remark by Wilson. And it was Wilson's singular focus on popular sovereignty and his stubborn advocacy of popular political power that led him thus to formulate more clearly than any other delegate at the Convention a conception of federal union derived from this principle of dual citizenship.[235]

Madison's record of Wilson's contributions to the debates of June 25 conveys even more clearly Wilson's distinctive grasp of this conception of dual citizenship. And, as Madison reports, Wilson formulated his conception in terms that invite special attention to the process of "abstraction" in Wilson's own political science—and in his moral science, as well. According to Madison's notes, on the 25th when Wilson undertook to "explain" why direct popular election of the national Senate was so important, he returned to the general "portrait" of the Federal Republic he envisioned. This expressly "pictoral" approach afforded Wilson occasion

> to observe the twofold relation in which the people would stand. 1. as Citizens of the Gen'l Gov't. 2. as Citizens of a *particular* State. The Genl. Govt. was meant for them in the first capacity; the State Govts. in the second. Both Govts. were derived from the people—both meant for the people—both therefore ought to be regulated on the same principles. The same train of ideas which belonged to the relation of the Citizens to their State Govts. were applicable to their relations to the Genl. Govt. and in forming the latter, we ought to proceed, by *abstracting* as much as

233. Cf. Conrad, Polite Foundation (cited in note 12).
234. 1 Farrand, Records 416 (cited in note 3).
235. Cf. Wood, Creation 530 (cited in note 46); Smith on James Wilson, at 235–36 (cited in note 120).

possible from the idea of State Govts.[236]

Thereupon Wilson proceeded to reemphasize the Federalist principle that the general government was not to be "an assemblage of States, but of individuals for certain political purposes." Still, as important as this principle was to Federalist political science in general, and to Wilson's clarifying focus on dual citizenship as perhaps the fundamental conceptual innovation of that political science,[237] this passage is also significant as it evinces the *concept of abstraction* itself that directed both Wilson's moral science and his political science—and that led Wilson to derive the latter from the former.

It was this guiding concept of abstraction that led Wilson beyond an essentially classical (or neoclassical) conception of citizenship to a Federalist vision in which federal union was to be a political analog of the faculty of moral abstraction itself. As Wilson pointed out, even Cicero had thought it a mark of the surpassing excellence of classical republican theory that no citizen in a republic "should be obliged to belong to more than one society, since a dissimilitude of societies must produce a proportioned variety of laws."[238] Indeed, in 1776 Wilson himself had invoked this very principle of unitary and integral citizenship as an argument against Parliamentary authority over the American colonies.[239] But by the time of the Founding, Wilson had learned so much from the American political experience and from Common Sense moral science that he was among the first[240] to see the advantage, indeed, the necessity of superseding the orthodox republican principle of the indivisibility of citizenship.

By the late 1780s Wilson was as fully aware as Madison[241] of the widespread incidence of vicious disregard for and actual abuse of the right of suffrage in America. What Wilson had witnessed in his home state of Pennsylvania apparently prompted him to ask the delegates to the Pennsylvania constitutional convention in late 1789, "What is the right of suffrage, which we now display, to be viewed, admired, and enjoyed by our constituents? Is it to go to an obscure tavern in an obscure corner of an obscure district, and to vote, amidst the fumes of spiritous liquors, for a justice of the peace?"[242] And shortly thereafter Wilson lamented to his law students that in America the polls, as "the theatre of original sovereignty" in the republic, had all too often proved a scene of the "debauchery and deception" of rank

---

236. 1 Farrand, Records 405–6 (emphasis added).
237. Cf. McLaughlin, 12 Pol. Sci. Q. 13 (cited in note 33).
238. 1 McCloskey, Works 245 (quoting Cicero's Pro Balbo, ch. 13).
239. See Wilson's Address to the Inhabitants of the Colonies. . . . [1776], in Adams, Selected Essays 103, 106 (cited in note 8): "Now the same collective Body cannot delegate the same Powers to distinct representative Bodies."
240. Cf. Randolph Adams' judgment that Wilson in 1776 anticipated what eventually became the theory of the British Commonwealth; *id.* at 12.
241. See, e.g., Adair, 2 Wm. & Mary Q. 199–200 (cited in note 23).
242. 2 McCloskey, Works 786.

electioneering.[243]

To Wilson, then, the critical problem of American republicanism in the 1780s was the problem that the right of suffrage was not properly "understood" and "cultivated" by the new political science, and was not properly "valued" and "exercised" by the People themselves. In response to this problem, Wilson projected that the formation of a federal republic as a common national enterprise would "expand the sphere" of American politics in a way that would engage the social psychology of moral abstraction in a mutually enhancing relationship with the fulfillment of the ideal of an American nation. The creation of an effective and energetic national government itself would do much, Wilson thought, to strengthen the connection with the "commonwealth" that each citizen in a republic should "feel."

Virtually from the outset of the Philadelphia Convention, Wilson made it clear that he "supposed" the People would prove "more attached" to such a national government than they had been and would be to their state governments, because the People would view the national government "as being more important in itself, and more flattering to their pride." This was an insight about the psychology of citizenship that Wilson offered as a supplement and complement to the Madisonian principle he also fully understood and endorsed, that increasing the size of electoral districts would diminish the danger of "improper elections," because "[b]ad elections proceed from the smallness of districts which give an opportunity to bad men to intrigue themselves into office."[244]

Notwithstanding, however, the importance of extending the electoral sphere, it was the psychological aspect of citizenship that most concerned Wilson. He agreed wholeheartedly in this matter with Benjamin Rush, who had encountered in his own education in America and Scotland the same moral science to which Wilson looked for fundamental authority. In a letter to David Ramsay in March or April of 1788,[245] Rush wrote about the proposed national Constitution:

> The dimensions of the human mind are apt to be regulated by the extent and objects of the government under which it is formed. Think then, my friend, of the expansion and dignity the American mind will acquire by having its powers transferred from the contracted objects of a state to the more unbounded objects of a national government!—A citizen and a legislator of the free and united states of America will be one of the first characters in the world![246]

---

243. 1 McCloskey, Works 158.
244. 1 Farrand, Records 133 (cited in note 3).
245. An especially good treatment of Ramsay as a high Federalist will be found in Peter S. Onuf, State Sovereignty and the Making of the Constitution, in Pocock & Ball, eds. (manuscript kindly supplied by Professor Onuf) (cited in note 24).
246. 1 Butterfield, Rush Letters 453, 454–55 (cited in note 58).

In joining Rush in such assertions and aspirations,[247] Wilson, however, eventually went further than Rush, by setting out in elaborate detail in his law lectures the principles of the Common Sense moral science on which his and Rush's civic psychology was founded.[248] For, as Wilson chose to explain to his law students at great length, it was largely on the basis of this Common Sense moral science that he expected to see among the American citizenry "the social operations and emotions of the mind rise to a most respectable height."[249] Indeed, in Wilson's first recorded remarks at the Philadelphia Convention, he had augmented what was apparently his favorite metaphor for republican government, the pyramid, in his reference to "the federal pyramid" as a suasive metaphor for a federal union that would, if instituted, raise the American Republic to a higher level, in the structure and dignity of its government, at the same time that the "base" of this government, in "the people" themselves, would be "broadened" and strengthened.[250]

During his series of law lectures, by the time that Wilson arrived at his extensive discussion of American federalism, he had already introduced all the basic principles of his moral science as a foundation for his federal theory. He had thus prepared the way for conveying his Federalist vision in its quintessentially metaphorical terms. Moreover, in a preceding lecture he had already quoted prominently from the Fourth Epistle of Pope's *Essay on Man* to convey to his students, in the terms of Pope's metaphors and images, the capability of "social affection"[251] and "moral abstraction"[252] for attaining to the

247. But note Wilson's qualifications, e.g., in 1 McCloskey, Works 267 (cited in note 8).
248. Note, however, that Rush, unlike Wilson, went further in his nationalism, e.g., in that he, at the Pennsylvania ratifying convention, "insinuated that he saw and rejoiced at the eventual annihilation of the state sovereignties"; McMaster & Stone, at 300 (cited in note 8), quoted in part by Wood, Creation 529 (cited in note 46). Cf. "Harrington"—probably Rush—in a May 30, 1787 essay reprinted in John P. Kaminski & Gaspare J. Saladino, eds., The Documentary History of the Ratification of the Constitution, vol. 13—Commentaries on the Constitution, Public and Private 116, 118–19 (Madison: State Historical Society of Wisconsin, 1981): "Let the states . . . come forward, and first throw their sovereignty at the feet of the convention." I owe this reference to Onuf (cited in note 245).
249. 1 McCloskey, Works 236.
250. 1 Farrand, Records 49 (May 31).
251. 1 McCloskey, Works 227. In expounding on how man's "social affection acts . . . unmixed and uncontrolled," Wilson at id. quotes Ep. IV, vv. 39–46:
There's not a blessing individuals find,
But some way leans and harkens to the kind.
No bandit fierce, no tyrant mad with pride,
No caverned hermit rests self-satisfied.
Who most to shun or hate mankind pretend
Seek an admirer, or would fix a friend.
Abstract what others feel, what others think,
All pleasures sicken, and all glories sink.
Cf. at 241 (Wilson's quotation from Ep. II).
252. 1 McCloskey, Works 233–34. In picturing the process of "moral abstraction" as a mental faculty partaking of "our passions and affections . . . our moral perceptions, and the other operations of our understandings [sic]," Wilson quoted Ep. IV, vv. 365-372:
The centre mov'd, a circle straight succeeds,
Another still, and still another spreads.
Friend, parent, neighbor first it will embrace,
His country next, and next all the human race;

"[e]xpanded patriotism" that Wilson extolled as "a cardinal virtue" in the American federal republic.[253]

Even in the Federal Republic, Wilson acknowledged, there would, of course, be citizens who would, for one reason or another, not experience this "expansion of mind," and, indeed, citizens, who would even seduce or dupe others away from true patriotism.[254] But, in contrast to Madison, Wilson projected that, as a prudential matter, American federalism would adequately secure "patriotick emanations of the soul" among the People at large; and these "emanations"—this social psychology of republican federalism—must and would serve as the impalpable foundation for the Federal Constitution that the delegates in Philadelphia had devised. It was in large part this popular foundation to which Wilson alluded when, in his November 24, 1787 speech at the Pennsylvania ratifying convention, he spoke of a "comprehensive federal republic."[255]

In that speech Wilson also said that it had been the "great end" of the Federal Convention to "frame" a "federal and national constitution."[256] This compound term, so consonant with Madison's own theory as set out in *Federalist* No. 39, is significant in recalling the point that, unlike Hamilton and Rush, for example, Wilson sought, virtually from the outset of the Federalist campaign, to promote a nationalism that, for all its affective national patriotism, would also preserve the federal principle, as embodied in a necessary, though subordinate, role for the several state governments.

Wide and more wide, th' o'erflowings of the mind
Take ev'ry creature in, of ev'ry kind;
Earth smiles around, with boundless bounty blest,
And heav'n beholds its image in his breast.

But contrast Pope's scatological use of the same metaphor, concentric circles in water, in The Dunciad, bk. III, lines 403–10. I owe this reference to Aubrey Williams; cf. *supra* note 148.

In Hume's *Treatise of Human Nature* the image of concentric circles is invoked, although not precisely in those terms, for something very like what Wilson himself (1 McCloskey, Works 266; cf. at 162) acknowledges to be a principle of "concentricity" in our relations with others. See the *Treatise*, bk. III, pt. II, sec. II, Nidditch, ed., at 488 (cited in note 74): "Now it appears, that in the original frame of our mind, our strongest attention is confin'd to ourselves; our next is extended to our relations and acquaintance; and 'tis only the weakest which reaches to strangers and indifferent persons." Cf. sec. I (at 483–84): "A man naturally loves his children better than his nephews, his nephews better than his cousins, his cousins better than strangers, where every thing else is equal." Cf. also the discussion in sec. III (501–13), "Of the rules, which determine property," for Hume's notions of the progressive weakening of connections as the degree of succession becomes more distant. I owe these references to my good friend Professor Edward ("Ned") McClennen.

Cf. to Hume's ideas and language what a student of Adam Smith's Theory of Moral Sentiments calls Smith's "theory of the spheres of human intimacy": Russell Nieli, Spheres of Intimacy and the Adam Smith Problem, 47 J. Hist. Ideas 611, 620ff. (1986). And cf. Cicero, as quoted by Wilson, in 1 McCloskey, Works 162.

The difference here between Wilson, on the one hand, and Hume and Smith and Cicero, on the other, would seem to turn on Wilson's emphasis on overcoming, through the cultivation of moral abstraction and an expanded patriotism, what Wilson himself acknowledges to be the psychology of centripetal "concentricity" that all four thinkers find in human nature.

253. 1 McCloskey, Works 268 (cited in note 8).
254. *Id.* at 267.
255. Jensen, ed., at 345 (cited in note 8).
256. *Id.* at 361.

At the Philadelphia Convention on June 7, when John Dickinson compared national union in a federal system to the relationship between the sun and the planets in "the Solar System," Wilson immediately seized on the metaphor and amplified it, in order to disavow any aim at national "consolidation," and to emphasize the inherent ambiguity that must inform a constitution that is at once "national and federal." Wilson said,

> He did not see the danger of the States being devoured by the Nationl. Govt. On the contrary, he wished to keep them from devouring the national Govt. He was not however for extinguishing these planets as was supposed by Mr. D.—neither did he on the other hand, believe that they would warm or enlighten the Sun. Within their proper orbits they must still be suffered to act for subordinate purposes.[257]

To be sure, Wilson presumed that, should a "difference" ever arise between the "interest of a single state" and that of "the Union"—and he projected that such differences could be avoided[258]—then the "welfare of the whole should be preferred to the accommodation of the part."[259] Thus it was that Wilson concluded his law lecture on federal theory with a quotation from no less an authority than the poet James Thomson, in support of the principle of civic psychology that the mind of the citizen is, by its own natural capability for moral abstraction, ultimately drawn to the "*central* parent-publick" by the force, as it were, of "moral gravitation."[260]

Still, it was not primarily the resonant nationalism in the pure diction of Thomson's verses but rather the synthesis of knowledge and virtue they reaffirmed that, above all, made for the welcome congruence Wilson saw between

---

257. 1 Farrand, Records 153–54 (cited in note 3). Cf. Madison's "recurrence," on June 8, to "the illustrations borrowed from the planetary System"; *id.* at 165 ("This prerogative of the General Govt. is the great pervading principle that must controul the centrifugal tendency of the States; which, without it, will continually fly out of their proper orbits and destroy the order & harmony of the political system"). Cf., as well, Robert Davidson, An Oration on the Independence of the United States of America 15 (Carlisle, Pa.: Kline & Reynolds, 1787), as quoted by Lienesch, 11 Am. Pol. Q. at 397 (cited in note 109).

258. See, e.g., 1 McCloskey, Works 264 & 2 McCloskey, Works 764; Jensen, ed., at 344 (all cited in note 8). But most interesting of all, perhaps, is Wilson's faith that codification of the law could prevent such nation-state conflicts. See the long quotation from a letter Wilson wrote to Washington in 1791, in which Wilson offered to undertake the task of codifying the law of the United States (!), in Lucien Hugh Alexander, James Wilson, Patriot, and the Wilson Doctrine, 183 N. Am. Rev. 971, 976 (1906). Cf. Perry Miller, The Life of the Mind in America: From the Revolution to the Civil War (Books 1–3) 240–41 (New York: Harcourt, Brace & World, 1965); 1 McCloskey, Works 59–64 (Wilson's 1791 letter to the Pennsylvania Speaker of the House, proposing a similar codification of Pennsylvania law). Contrast Madison's views, at least later in life: e.g., see Meyers, Mind of the Founder, 1st ed., at 431 (cited in note 29).

Also cf. 1 Farrand, Records 166–67, 356 (cited in note 3).

Furthermore, unlike Madison, Wilson tended to see the human propensity to factionalism as generally amenable to regulation through the civic regimens of republicanism. Cf. McCloskey, Works 266–67.

259. *Id.* at 267–68; Jensen, ed., at 346; cf. at 351; 2 Farrand, Records 615.

260. 1 McCloskey, Works 268-69 (emphasis added). And, in fact, Wilson did pursue the logic of his theory of moral abstraction, from a conception of national citizenship to a conception of international citizenship. See, e.g., *id.* at 162–64. Cf. my text *infra* at note 301.

Thomson's polite poetics and the polite moral science that sustained Wilson's own federal theory. In Thomson Wilson found what Douglas Bush has helped 20th-century readers to appreciate: that Thomson's verses stood as a culmination of an 18th-century tradition of the "discursive mixture of description and reflection," especially as Thomson's poetry attested to a sense of "truth spontaneously felt."[261] Moreover Wilson saw a thoroughgoing correspondence between this conception of "truth" and Montesquieu's conception of republican "virtue." For, as Montesquieu had said, "Virtue in a republic is a most simple thing . . . it is a sensation that may be felt by the meanest as well as by the highest person in a state."[262]

From both Pope and Thomson, then, Wilson's "modern" republican theory could draw on the cultural authority of "philosophical poets" who were "much too clever to be philosophers"[263] of the "profound species" that Hume encouraged.[264] Through the use of conventional[265] metaphors, which recognized "the particular" but also moved by abstraction beyond it to a recognition of "general nature,"[266] a poet such as Thomson commanded an authority that was regarded as much as a matter of truth as of rhetoric, to any extent that the distinction might have been meaningful at the time.[267]

In Wilson's law lecture on federalism there is also a telling implicit endorsement of the Aristotelian principle that poetry is "more philosophical than history because it is more 'universal.' "[268] For Wilson ultimately makes it clear that, in his own avowedly "philosophical" approach to a theory of American federal union, the authority of history counts for little—and, at that, mostly as history can be invoked against its own authority.

Wilson intimated this point in his remarks of June 25 at the Federal Convention when he alluded to the well known model of European federal union envisioned in the Grand Design of Henry IVth of France.[269] But among all of

261. Bush, Science and English Poetry 64, 67 (cited in note 221). Granted, Bush's approach to Thomson must now seem a little too simple, in light of work like that of Ralph Cohen, The Unfolding of The Seasons (Baltimore: Johns Hopkins Press, 1970). But Cohen's reading of Thomson occasionally approximates Bush's views as quoted here; see, e.g., Cohen at 328-29.

262. 1 The Spirit of the Laws, bk. V, ch. 2; trans. Thomas Nugent, intro. Franz Neumann, at 40 (two vols. in one. New York: Hafner Publishing Co., 1949).

263. Bush, Science and English Poetry at 63 ("Pope was much too clever to be a philosopher").

264. Cf. J.M. Cameron, Doctrinal to an Age: Notes Towards a Revaluation of Pope's Essay on Man, in Maynard Mack, ed., Essential Articles for the Study of Alexander Pope 353, esp. at 358–59 (rev. ed. Hamden, Conn.: Archon Books, 1968). For an interesting and relevant aside from Wilson on Pope, see 2 McCloskey 596-97 (cited in note 8). And for what remains the seminal work of modern scholarship on Pope's Essay on Man, see Maynard Mack's Introduction to his edition of the poem, in the Twickenham series (London: Methuen, 1950).

265. Cf. Morse Peckham, Metaphor 420 (cited in note 188).

266. Walter Jackson Bate, From Classic to Romantic: Premises of Taste in Eighteenth-Century England (New York: Harper & Bros., 1946), esp. ch. 3 ("Johnson and Reynolds: The Premise of General Nature"). Cf. Donald Davie, Purity of Diction in English Verse 40–53 (London: Routledge & Kegan Paul, 1967); and Ricoeur, Rule of Metaphor 99 (cited in note 182).

267. Cf. Peckham, Metaphor, esp. at 401-2.

268. Cf. Booth, Metaphor, at 68 (cited in note 180).

269. E.g., 1 Farrand, Records 405 (cited in note 3). On the Grand Design itself, which is

Wilson's public remarks on American federalism that have come down to us, it is only in his law lecture on the topic that he elaborates his point fully: Although, as Wilson's own survey of history concluded, the American experiment with an extensive federal union had no precedent in *actual* historical experience,[270] the history of the human *imagination* did afford a precedent. And Wilson took this precedent as but another vindication of his idea that the civilized imagination is by far the most important source of experience in moral science, and therefore in political science, as well. Even though Henry and his minister Sully, together with Elizabeth of England, had failed to realize their shared vision of a new model of European federal union, this did not mean that their vision had been but a "presumptuous and extravagant . . . chimera."[271] To such a putative charge Wilson responded with "the poet's exclamation," in this instance a couplet taken, again, from Pope:

> Truths would you teach, or save a sinking land?
> All fear, none aid you, and few understand.[272]

Indeed, the visionary character of the Grand Design was, to Wilson, not a shortcoming of the project but the chief mark of its greatness. Thus, after having reviewed a number of historic examples of confederations, both ancient and modern, and having found all of them wanting as models worthy of emulation, Wilson turned to the unrealized Grand Design as a plan for a "sublime system" of federal union that he thought "must be interesting as well as instructive" to Americans.[273] And, although in earlier discussing those other, inadequate historic examples of experiments with federalism, Wilson had tended to concentrate on the details of their structure and operation, his lengthy discussion of the visionary Grand Design maintained one consistent and quite different focus: appreciating that what had inspired this hitherto unique plan of federal union, what would have animated it if it had been established, and what remained important about it, was its moral purpose and moral promise. Wilson said,

> One inference may be drawn from the nature of the design, which Henry had formed. It was not a design inspired by mean and despicable ambition: it was not a design, guided by base and partial interests: it was a design, in the first place, to render France happy, and permanently

now generally attributed to Sully rather than to Henry himself (cf. Madison's own revision of his *Notes*, *id.*), see Peace Projects of the Seventeenth Century. . . , ed. J.R. Jacob & M.C. Jacob (New York: Garland Publishing Co., 1972). Cf. Desmond Seward, *The First Bourbon: Henri IV, King of France and Navarre* 186-201 (London: Constable, 1971). Also of interest here—and most to the point perhaps—is Heinrich Mann's novel, trans. from the German by Eric Sutton, *Henry, King of France* (Woodstock, N.Y.: Overlook Press, 1985), esp. "Book Eight: The Great Plan."

270. For Wilson's survey, see 1 McCloskey, *Works* 247–54 (cited in note 8).
271. *Id.* at 259–60.
272. *Id.* at 260 (quoting from the Essay on Man, Ep. IV, vv. 265–66).
273. *Id.* at 261.

happy: but as he well knew that France could not enjoy permanent felicity, unless in conjunction with the other parts of Europe; and as he was well pleased that the other parts of Europe should participate in the felicity of France; it was the happiness of Europe in general which he laboured to procure; and to procure in a manner so solid and so durable, that nothing should afterwards be able to shake its foundations.[274]

Such was the allusive encomium Wilson incorporated into his law lecture as a way of preparing his audience for the culminating passage in this his most thorough exposition of the federal theory that he had advocated and defended on so many other occasions:

Let me add another remark, which has been made in Europe, and which, with pride and joy, may be transferred to America. "Henry The Great has always had the honour of being considered as the author of the most important invention for the benefit of mankind, that has yet appeared in the world; the execution of which may, perhaps, be reserved by Providence, for the greatest and most capable of his successors." This rich succession has been reaped in America. Here the sublime system of Henry the Great has been effectually realized, and completely carried into execution.[275]

It was, then, the "sublime" moral purpose of American federalism that was, to Wilson, its most important feature as a republican political project.

This is most generally evident, perhaps, in the way Wilson articulated his ideas about representation. As expounded through his continual appeals to metaphor, his conception of representation consistently bespoke the mode of thought of his Common Sense moral science. It was a mode of thought that, like the late 18th-century ideal of polite culture itself, tended to see nearly every politically significant duality as an opportunity for mutual enhancement through the ambiguities of reciprocal influence. It was, for just this reason, a mode of thought essentially and thoroughly metaphorical.[276] And so thoroughly did it infuse Wilson's popular constitutionalism of moral personality that Wilson came to project the sublimation, or "subliming," of popular authority itself through the ambiguities of metaphor.[277]

---

274. Id. at 260.
275. Id. at 261.
276. Cf. Ricoeur, Rule of Metaphor 99 (cited in note 182) (on the attenuated "polarity" between "singular identification" and "general predication"); and cf. the analogous distinctions (e.g., vehicle/tenor, focus/frame, modifier/principal subject) that Ricoeur draws from the work of I.A. Richards, Max Black, and others, at 99 and passim.
277. Cf. Dennison, 39 Rev. Pol. (cited in note 32).

VIII. CONCLUSION: THE MANDARIN DEMOCRACY OF "DEMOCRATIC NATIONALISM"

"Our pride is more offended by attacks on our tastes than on our opinions."

—La Rouchefoucauld, *Maxims* [278]

In this article I have called attention to a number of the salient dualities in the articulate political culture of America during the climactic years of James Wilson's public career, the late 1780s and early 1790s. Those dualities included, to name but a few: morals and science; virtue and politics; imagination and experience; judgment and knowledge; society and individual; general nature and particular nature; elected representative and enfranchised citizen; nation and state; and—of special interest to me, and to Wilson and many of his contemporaries during those years—Federalism and republicanism.

Some commentators of that time virtually *identified* the two elements in some of those dualities; and occasionally a commentator even tended to see analogies, or relationships of nearly identical correspondence, between and among such dualities. Other commentators saw, instead of virtual identities, virtual antinomies. The variety of views was great—greater, perhaps, than we yet appreciate in our historical treatments of the Founding. In any case, the complexity of the views of a few familiar leading figures—above all, Madison—is commonly, if not fully, appreciated.

Compared and contrasted with Madisonian theory as a bench mark, the complexity of Wilson's approach to the same problems of American constitutionalism that concerned Madison becomes most interesting where Wilson's endeavors at theorizing proceed in a way quite different from Madison's, yet lead Wilson to similar conclusions and prescriptions.

For this reason I have wanted to attend much more to *how* Wilson practiced theory than to the important but less interesting—because less neglected and, I believe, ultimately *less important*—matter of his substantive political positions and his practical politics in the unsettled early moments of the Federalist period.

From this perspective, it would be both difficult and wrong to continue to overlook the self-conscious metaphorizing in Wilson's method. Not only did he emphasize it, and his contemporaries remark on it, but—and here is my chief concern—Wilson went to great lengths to "justify" his metaphorizing. And in justifying his essentially metaphorical, figurative approach to American constitutionalism, he thought that he was also justifying a strongly nationalist, yet genuinely federal, conception of the Federal Republic.

---

278. As quoted in Pierre Bourdieu, *Distinction: A Social Critique of the Judgement of Taste* (1979), trans. Richard Nice, at 257 (Cambridge, Mass.: Harvard University Press, 1984).

Professor Robert McCloskey, the modern editor of Wilson's collected *Works*, characterized Wilson's federal theory as a theory of "democratic nationalism." And McCloskey added that the very idea of democratic nationalism was, in Wilson's day, "so unusual that it seemed incongruous."[279] The point is well taken.

From the outset the entire Federalist campaign was widely associated with "aristocratic" impulses in the American political culture of "revolutionary settlement." And Wilson's own personal demeanor and political alliances (to say nothing of his avid and clumsy chasing after public office and private wealth) evidently made it all the more difficult for many of his contemporaries to understand, much less to accept, his professedly democratic Federalism. Unsurprisingly, during the ratification debates, his cleverest political adversaries sometimes railed to best effect against Wilson and the proposed Constitution by scorning the very idea of democratic nationalism as dangerous "sophistry" and by mocking Wilson's exposition of the idea as patent "equivocation" and "evasion."[280]

So charged the author of a notable essay, first printed on November 6, 1787 in a Philadelphia newspaper, who sought to regain the ground the Anti-Federalists had recently lost in the aftermath of Wilson's widely circulated State House Speech of October 6. This essay was not the first major public reply to Wilson's speech,[281] but for the purposes of the argument I have tried to develop in the preceding pages, this November 6 essay is especially significant. Unlike most other Anti-Federalist rebuttals to Wilson, which rejected the idea itself of democratic nationalism as vicious political science inimical to the ideal of popular republican virtue,[282] the Anti-Federalist author of the essay in question seems to have appreciated that, for Wilson, democratic nationalism was as much a pretense to greater "knowledge" as to greater virtue, and as much a matter of "exalted imagination" as of political science.[283]

And yet, for all his insightfulness, this Anti-Federalist author could not or would not credit Wilson's rhetoric as argument, either sincere or coherent. In the view of this adversary, Wilson's "sublime" federal theory was, at worst, a disguise and, at best, a delusion.[284] In any case, it was incumbent on any true "patriot" to proclaim that Wilson's "high idea" of democratic national-

---

279. McCloskey, James Wilson 85 (cited in note 8); cf. 1 McCloskey, Works 25 (editor's Introduction).

280. Jensen, ed., at 210–16, 213 (cited in note 8).

281. See *id.* at 192–98, esp. 198 n.1.

282. The pamphlet by Mercy Warren that I have discussed briefly, in my text *supra* at note 177ff., is another exception in this respect, as its authoritative modern editor points out: see 4 Herbert J. Storing, ed., The Complete Anti-Federalist 271 (Chicago: University of Chicago Press, 1981).

283. Jensen, ed., at 213–14.

284. Cf. Rufus King's anticipation of this theme on June 19 at the Federal Convention, as King's words are recorded in Madison's Notes: 1 Farrand, Records 323 (cited in note 3): "He conceived that the import of the terms 'States' 'Sovereignty' 'national' 'federal,' had been often used & applied in the discussion inaccurately & delusively."

ism was, in fact, "tainted with the spirit of *high aristocracy*."[285]

During the ratification debates Wilson answered the charge of covert aristocracy made against him and his federal theory—for example, by citing the consistency of his preference for the democracy of direct popular elections.[286] But, paradoxically, his federal *theory* proved more difficult to defend than the actual positions he had taken in supporting and promoting the creation of the Federal Republic—so difficult, or complex, it seems, that he saved his most thoroughgoing statement of constitutional theory and self-justification for the classroom, or, more precisely, for his written law lectures, which he hoped would stand as his most lasting contribution to patristic commentary on the new Constitution.

It was the setting of the classroom, or rather, the format of his self-indulgent professorial lectures, that elicited from Wilson his most "comprehensive" exposition of American federalism, because his constitutional theory in general derived from a moral epistemology that Wilson himself apparently considered too "philosophical" for the political forum—except as he could routinely expound that philosophy in terms of its own shaping mentality of metaphor. In fact, more than one eminent historian has surmised that even in these lectures Wilson sadly overestimated the taste of his contemporaries for his manifestly "diffusive . . . scholarly and elegant" way of presenting his views on "general jurisprudence," "the Constitution," and the "Federal Government."[287] Perhaps, then, given the mandarin[288] character of his ideal of a politics of moral cultivation through "moral abstraction," Wilson's "democratic faith" was not as great as we have repeatedly been told by the handful of scholars who have tried to rehabilitate him.

But an alternative explanation for the eventual, or, rather, the quick decline of Wilson's distinctive federal theory is equally plausible. According to this explanation, the climax of Wilson's career as a theorist of American federalism came neither at the Philadelphia Convention, nor during the ratification debates, nor even in the classroom, but on the bench. It came in his judicial opinion in the 1793 case of *Chisholm v. Georgia*.[289] There he invoked "the People" as a metaphor of such "comprehensive" authority and significance that this metaphor rendered not only the "sovereignty" of a "state" a solecism but "popular sovereignty" itself a tautology.[290]

The political and legal reaction to the decision in *Chisholm* was an imme-

285. Jensen, ed., at 213. Cf. Smith on James Wilson at 266 (cited in note 120) (quoting the same Anti-Federalist writer).

286. E.g., Jensen, ed., at 169–70 (the State House Speech).

287. Charles Warren, A History of the American Bar 348 (Boston: Little, Brown & Co., 1911), at 348; cf. 346–47, 349. Cf. Perry Miller, The Life of the Mind in America: From the Revolution to the Civil War (Books 1–3) 141 (New York: Harcourt, Brace & World, 1965).

288. This term was suggested to me by Professor R. Kent Newmyer.

289. Cf. Seed on Wilson 141 (cited in note 161).

290. 2 Dallas 419, 454–56. For a convenient, and typically acute, exposition of how the logic of Wilson's republican theory was, by the time of his law lectures, pointing beyond the concept of

diate and widespread outcry of protest that soon became a campaign to "over-rule" the Court by amending the Constitution itself.[291] Acting first in their national legislature and then in their several state legislatures, "the People" thus reacted to the Chisholm decision in a way that has sometimes been taken to mark the only occasion "in its history [when] the federal judiciary [has] had its jurisdiction directly curtailed by constitutional amendment."[292] This apparently popular reaction against Chisholm's "symbolic affront to [state] sovereignty"[293] suggests, perhaps, that the tasteful formulas of synthesizing ambiguity that were at the heart of Wilson's theory of metaphor—and at the heart of his theory of American federalism—were, to the American "publick mind" of his day, more problematic and less engaging than Wilson "knew."[294]

In Wilson's written opinion in Chisholm, it seems to have been his *style* and his *way* of "reasoning," even more than his holding, that proved most provocative. A passage from a letter written by the framer William Davie to his (and Wilson's) friend Associate Justice James Iredell is so illustrative of the predominant reaction to Wilson's opinion—both in 1793 *and today*[295]—that it deserves to be quoted at length:

I confess I read some of these arguments [in Chisholm] and particularly

---

"sovereignty" altogether, see Adams, Political Ideas 185ff. (cited in note 8). But see Pole, Enlightenment 210 (cited in note 181).

And for two recent corroborations of Robert McCloskey's general claim that Wilson's ideas often anticipated those of later American constitutional theorists, especially where Wilson might seem to have been out of step with the development of republican theory in his own time, see Andrzej Rapaczynski, From Sovereignty to Process: The Jurisprudence of Federalism after Garcia, 1985 Sup. Ct. Rev. 341, esp. 346-59; and Akhil Reed Amar, Of Sovereignty and Federalism, 95 Yale L.J. 1425, esp. at 1520 (1987), where Amar selects as authority in support of his own conception of what American federalism should be precisely those passages from Wilson's Chisholm opinion that reveal Wilson at his most quintessentially Common-Sensical.

291. See, e.g., Doyle Mathis, Chisholm v. Georgia: Background and Settlement, 54 J. Am. Hist. 19, 25ff. (1967); Mathis, The Eleventh Amendment: Adoption and Interpretation, 2 Ga. L. Rev. 207, 224ff. (1968); and the citations collected in Wilfred J. Ritz, American Judicial Proceedings First Printed Before 1801, at 146-48 (Westport, Conn.: Greenwood Press, 1984).

292. Alfred H. Kelly et al., The American Constitution: Its Origin and Development 167 (6th ed. New York: W.W. Norton, 1983). But see generally William A. Fletcher, A Historical Interpretation of the Eleventh Amendment: A Narrow Construction of an Affirmative Grant of Jurisdiction Rather than a Prohibition Against Jurisdiction, 35 Stan. L. Rev. 1033 (1983).

293. Fletcher, 35 Stan. L. Rev. at 1058 (cited in note 292). That the Chisholm case had an effect on the People at, but *only* at, the symbolic level is reaffirmed in John Orth, The Judicial Power of the United States (New York: Oxford University Press, 1987) at 19: "Chisholm was part of the high drama of public affairs"; and at 28: "The search for the original understanding on state sovereign immunity. . . . The understanding of the electorate let alone of the populace as a whole upon a topic so esoteric was undoubtably nil."

294. Cf. the remark in Archibald Cox, The Role of the Supreme Court in American Government (New York: Oxford University Press, 1976), at 117: "The Court must know us better than we know ourselves. Its opinions may, as I have said, sometimes be the voice of the spirit, reminding us of our better selves."

295. Cf., e.g., the views collected in David P. Currie, The Constitution in the Supreme Court: The First Hundred Years, 1789-1888, at 15, nn.75 & 76 (Chicago: University of Chicago Press, 1985). See also Julius Goebel, Jr., The Common Law and the Constitution, in W. Melville Jones, ed., Chief Justice John Marshall: A Reappraisal 101 (Ithaca, N.Y.: Cornell University Press, 1956), at 112: "Even the professor on the Court, Mr. Justice Wilson, held in check the academic penchant for display, giving way to it only in Chisholm v. Georgia" (footnote omitted).

that by Mr. Wilson with astonishment: however, the scope and propriety of this elaborate production called an argument, were expressly reserved for the contemplation of "a *few*, a *very few* comprehensive minds;" and, perhaps, notwithstanding the tawdry ornament and poetical imagery with which it is loaded and bedizened, it may still be very "profound." On this I shall give no opinion: but as a law argument it has certainly the merit of being truly "*original*." His definition of the American States as sovereignties is more like an epic poem than a Judge's argument, and we look in vain for legal principles or logical conclusions. . . . [T]his whole argument of his seems to be the rhapsody of some visionary theorist.[296]

Nevertheless, if the "publicity" accorded to the written opinions of the justices of the Supreme Court in its early years was in fact as "scant" as some historians believe,[297] then it is possible, as Robert McCloskey suggested more than once, that Wilson did, after all, "know" the American People better than they knew themselves at the Founding, better than they later came to know themselves, and even better than they *yet* know themselves.[298]

To vindicate such a generous interpretation of Wilson's visionary constitutionalism would, however, require not only a "comprehensive" review of two centuries of constitutional history but also an insight into the future to which conventional historical scholarship seldom aspires. Still, any such vindication would have to begin by coming to terms not only with the question of what Wilson thought he knew but also with the questions of why and how he thought he knew it. Thus, even a modest contribution toward answering these latter questions about one of the most curiously obscure of our most important founders should have something to offer today, both to backward-looking constitutional historians and to forward-looking constitutional theorists.

At least I believe so; and here I have presented an argument sympathetic to (but, I trust, not uncritical of) Wilson in order to explain *why* I believe so.

As Professor Peter Onuf has observed, in the late 1780s, "[T]he Federalists succeeded in shifting debate forward in time . . . to project the inevitable transformation of the American states into hostile sovereignties."[299] As a leading Federalist, Wilson projected that far, and further still—in some respects, even more profoundly, perhaps, than Madison did. For Wilson's conception of federal union, while less liberal, or at least, less pluralistic—and also less contingent on the vagaries of politics—than Madison's, was, at the same

---

296. 2 Griffith J. McRee, Life and Correspondence of James Iredell, One of the Associate Justices of the Supreme Court of the United States 382 (2 vols. 1857. Reprint ed., 2 vols. in 1; New York: Peter Smith, 1949).

297. Fletcher, 35 Stan. L. Rev. at 1058 n.115 (cited in note 292) (citing Charles Warren).

298. 1 McCloskey, Works 1–6, 46–47 (editor's Introduction) (cited in note 8); McCloskey, James Wilson 79–80, 89–90, 95–96 (cited in note 8), esp. at 96: "Perhaps he has been unappreciated by the future, [sic] because America, though following in his footsteps, has never quite caught up with him."

299. Onuf, State Sovereignty and the Making of the Constitution, in Pocock & Ball, eds. (cited in note 24).

time, more intrinsically expansible. And this expansibility of Wilson's conception of federal republicanism, or republican federalism, was for the most part owing to the way Wilson thought, talked, and wrote about federal union. He relied on a language of metaphor and a "figurative realism" so ambiguous—not necessarily *vague*, but purposefully ambiguous—that, while plainly rooted in the social theology of the conservative, "polite" Atlantic culture of his day, his metaphors might at times seem to some progressive constitutional theorists today even more "modern"—and more politically and morally capable—than Madisonian liberalism at its historic best.[300]

Not only was Wilson's conception of federalism so expansible that it pointed beyond nationalism to internationalism,[301] his basic idea of constitutional authority was so inherently ambiguous that no other founder of the 1780s spoke or wrote so remarkably like the American political theorist who has lately explored the relationship between politics and ambiguity most thoroughly: Professor William E. Connolly argues in his recent book about this relationship that "the mode of authority appropriate to modernity involves an appreciation of its ambiguous character . . . [A]n appreciation of ambiguity must be installed in the institutional matrix of society if authority is to assume its appropriate place in modern life."[302]

Nevertheless, Professor Connolly ultimately qualifies and questions his point even while making it: "We need the word, though not it alone, to give definition to social life, but the word disciplines as it forms. Is politics, at its best, a medium through which to cultivate attentiveness to each side of the equation?"[303]

Here, from the modern political theorist, comes a warning not expressed or implied in any of Wilson's extant writings or in the words of Cynthia Ozick, the modern novelist and critic from whom I took my principal epigraph at the head of this article. Professor Connolly's warning is one about the political inadequacy of language alone. It is also a warning about the limited capability of *knowledge* itself in politics, regardless of whether the knowledge is "imagined" or otherwise.[304]

Restated so as to address the governing metaphor of Wilson's constitutional theory, this is a warning that "the People" is, strictly speaking, much more an "invented entity"[305] than an "imagined reality." And the *invention* at issue, while a matter of ambiguity, is not only a matter of metaphor, but of

---

300. Cf. Ira L. Strauber, The Rhetorical Structure of Freedom of Speech, 19 Polity 507 (1987), esp. at 528. Note that Strauber, in his approach, aligns himself with others, including James Boyd White (see works cited in note 6) and Lief H. Carter. See Carter, Contemporary Constitutional Lawmaking: The Supreme Court and the Art of Politics (New York: Pergamon Press, 1985).
301. See 1 McCloskey, Works 270–83, esp. 282–83. Cf. Adams, Selected Essays 38–42 (cited in note 8).
302. Connolly, Politics and Ambiguity 128 (Madison: University of Wisconsin Press, 1987).
303. Id. at 160–61.
304. Id. at xi–xii.
305. Shklar, Ordinary Vices 71–72 (cited in note 131).

historical *and* contemporary life and things—of "the sons of heaven": As an "invention," in both senses of that ambiguous term, *the American People*, is *in part* an entity that we now *find* already established in American constitutionalism; but it is also an entity that we continually must and do *contrive*, both as an end in itself and as a means to other ends that are also so difficult to articulate that they too continually require us to rely on Wilson's governing metaphor, *and* on much else that no metaphor could "comprehend."

The "powers of the imagination" have their practical limits—as Wilson found out. Benjamin Rush's diary contains a December 1796 entry that tells something about the personal price Wilson, as one of the great early speculators on the future of America, eventually paid for a visionary impulse that became a compulsion: "This month great [financial] distress pervaded our city [of Philadelphia] from failures, &c. . . . 150, it is said, occurred in 6 weeks, and 67 people went to jail . . . . Judge Wilson deeply distressed; his resource was reading novels constantly."[306]

This, however, is not to say Wilson was necessarily wrong in believing that, if the American Constitution fails, the cause will be a failure of imagination on the part of "the People themselves."

---

306. George W. Corner, ed., The Autobiography of Benjamin Rush: His "Travels Through Life" together with his *Commonplace Book* for 1789–1813, at 236–37 (Princeton, N.J.: Princeton University Press, 1948).